SECOND EDITION

Commercial Banking
THE MANAGEMENT OF RISK

DONALD R. FRASER
Hugh Roy Cullen Chair in Business Administration
Texas A&M University

BENTON E. GUP
Robert Hunt Cochrane/Alabama Bankers Chair of Finance
University of Alabama

JAMES W. KOLARI
Chase Professor of Finance
Texas A&M University

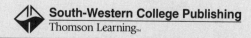
South-Western College Publishing
Thomson Learning

Australia • Canada • Denmark • Japan • Mexico • New Zealand • Philippines
Puerto Rico • Singapore • South Africa • Spain • United Kingdom • United States

Commercial Banking: The Management of Risk, 2/e by Fraser, Gup, and Kolari

Vice President/Publisher: Jack W. Calhoun
Acquisitions Editor: Michael B. Mercier
Developmental Editor: Dennis Hanseman
Marketing Manager: Julie Lindsay
Production Editor: Sandra Gangelhoff
Manufacturing Coordinator: Charlene Taylor
Media Technology Editor: Kurt Gerdenich
Media Production Editor: Kristen Meere
Internal Design: Sandy Kent, Kent and Co., Cincinnati
Cover Design: Ross Design, Cincinnati
Cover Photos: © Photodisc
Production House: Trejo Production
Printer: R. R. Donnelley & Sons Company, Crawfordsville Manufacturing Division

For more information contact South-Western College Publishing, 5101 Madison Road, Cincinnati, Ohio, 45227 or find us on the Internet at http://www.swcollege.com

For permission to use material from this text or product, contact us by
• telephone: 1-800-730-2214
• fax: 1-800-730-2215
• web: http://www.thomsonrights.com

Library of Congress Cataloging-in-Publication Data
Fraser, Donald R.
    Commercial banking : the management of risk / Donald R. Fraser, Benton E. Gup, James W. Kolari.—2nd ed.
        p. cm.
    Includes bibliographical references and index.
    ISBN 0-324-02718-4 (alk. paper)
        1. Bank management.   2. Risk management.   I. Gup, Benton E.   II. Kolari, James W.
    III. Title.
HG1615.F73 2000
332.1'2'068—dc21
                                                                    00-025868

This book is printed on acid-free paper.

DEDICATION

FRASER – *To Eleanor*

GUP – *To Jean, Lincoln, Andrew and Carol, and Jeremy*

KOLARI – *To Karie and Wes*

Brief Contents

Contents

PART ONE *Introduction*

CHAPTER 2

The Bank Regulatory Environment 29

CHAPTER 3

Evaluating Bank Performance 58

PART TWO *Asset/Liability Management:*
Controlling Interest Rate Risks

PART THREE *Balance Sheet Management: Risks and Returns*

CHAPTER 7

Commercial and Industrial Lending 201

APPENDIX 7A

Financial Analysis 239

APPENDIX 7B

The Cost of Capital 267

PART FOUR *Financial Analysis*

CHAPTER 12

Liabilities Management 428

PART FIVE   *Loan Portfolio Management*

Preface

A recent article in *The Economist* noted that banks have been at the heart of economic activity for eight centuries, and that they are still preeminent, even though other financial intermediaries are growing in importance (October 30, 1999, 89). But today, banking services are much different in scope. For example, the recent passage of the Financial Services Modernization Act of 1999 (Gramm-Leach-Bliley Act) allows banks, securities firms, and insurance companies to merge with one another and to offer customers one-stop shopping for financial services. Under this Act, the trend of increased bank involvement in securities and insurance will surely accelerate in the years to come.

The second edition of this book reflects the dramatic changes that have occurred in banking in recent years. Throughout our text, we emphasize the key forces that are changing the face of banking: consolidation, competition, deregulation, global banking, international crises, and technology.

A central theme of this book focuses on bank management as risk management. Bankers take risks in order to make a profit. Because of changes in the industry, both the risks and the opportunities for growth and profit are increasing. Therefore, we examine new ways to manage risk, such as credit scoring, credit derivatives, and interest rate swaps, to name a few.

Users of the first edition of our text will find important changes. First, we have reorganized the chapter sequence to make it more consistent with current bank management practices. We have also added new chapters dealing with electronic banking and financial services. And because the pace of change is so rapid, we have added numerous references to relevant Internet sites throughout the text to enable you to keep up with the latest developments in banking and the factors affecting financial services.

Text Organization

This book is divided into five parts. Part One explains what banks are and the functions they perform. It also delves into the major laws that shaped our financial structure in the past and that will reshape them in the future. Finally, it explains how to evaluate a bank's financial performance.

Part Two covers asset and liability management. In it we examine the factors that affect the value of a bank and techniques for managing that value, including the use of financial derivatives.

Part Three is concerned with the asset side of the balance sheet, which involves lending and investment portfolio management. Banks make most of their profit from lending, and therefore we carefully examine the principal activities of lending to businesses and individuals. Banks also invest some of their funds in securities, so we examine their investment decisions as well.

Part Four focuses on the right-hand side of the balance sheet, which measures bank capital and bank liabilities. These are particularly important chapters because bank regulators are changing the capital requirements to better reflect the risks that banks take. Also, banks' traditional deposit sources of funds face increased competition from other types of financial institutions.

Part Five deals with domestic and international financial services. We have added two new chapters, one dealing with electronic banking and the other with the wide range of financial services offered by banks. We have also included a chapter on the off-balance sheet activities that are becoming increasingly important. Finally, a chapter on global financial services covers some international aspects of banking.

Pedagogical Features

To make our text the most teachable on the market, we have included a number of important features. They are designed to reinforce the key ideas developed in the text, and to demonstrate how those ideas can be used in practice.

- Each chapter includes at least one *Managerial Issues* box. These boxes deal with issues that bank managers must consider in their day-to-day operations and in guiding the future of their banks.

- In addition, each chapter also includes at least one *Managing Risk* box. These boxes reinforce our theme that bank management is risk management.

- A *Case Study* appears at the end of each chapter. The cases provide students a feel for the kinds of issues that bank managers confront, and challenge them to put their newly acquired skills to work in solving management problems.

- An extended *Appendix on Financial Analysis* appears at the end of Chapter 7. It explains how to analyze financial statements. This type of analysis is a key element in the commercial loan process.

- Because constant practice is essential to mastery, we have provided a large number of end-of-chapter *Questions and Problems*. They were carefully designed to provide practice in solving managerial problems.

- Finally, as already mentioned, we have scattered a large number of *Internet Margin Notes* throughout the book. Each note provides a brief description of a relevant Web site and provides the URL for accessing that site.

Supplementary Package

To help both students and instructors, we provide a full package of supplementary items. These include:

- An *Instructor's Manual* (ISBN: 0-324-02719-2) that contains a description of each chapter, solutions to the end-of-chapter problems and cases, and additional problems and questions that may be used in testing.

- A dedicated *Web site* (http://fraser.swcollege.com). At this site, you will find a variety of useful tools, including:
  — *Internet Applications* that link directly to the Web sites mentioned in the text's Internet margin notes.
  — *Wall Street Analysts Reports* from Investext/Gale Group. You can download analysts' reports on all types of financial services firms.
  — *Learning Resources* that provide online student support. Students can access PowerPoint files, link to news sources, and do research at a variety of business and government sites.
  — *Teaching Resources* that instructors can download, once they have registered and been assigned a password.

- A discounted subscription to *American Banker.com* is available to professors who adopt *Commercial Banking*. Adopters should contact their local South-Western College Publishing sales representative for more information.

- *InfoTrac College Edition* is an online library of articles from hundreds of journals. It can be packaged with this text at no additional cost.

- Instructors who like to employ cases will find many possibilities available through *CaseNet*. A complete list of cases, and instructions on how to order them, are available at http://casenet.thomson.com.

- Comprehensive teaching packages are available to adopters.

- A subscription to Thomson Investors Network provides a wealth of information and tools useful in making informed investment decisions. At this Web site, you can access live stock quotes, a portfolio tracker, business news, a variety of company and industry reports, market analysis and commentary, and much more. Adopting professors can receive a complementary subscription. Students who purchase *Commercial Banking* can subscribe at a deeply discounted rate. Contact your local South-Western representative or visit http://www.thomsoninvest.net for details.

Acknowledgments

We want to express our gratitude to a number of individuals who, through their comments and suggestions, helped us continue to improve the quality of this book.

James Barth	Auburn University
M.E. Bond	University of Memphis
Ben Branch	University of Massachusetts, Amherst
Conrad Ciccotello	Georgia Institute of Technology
Steven Dennis	Ball State University
David Ely	San Diego State University
Anne Gleason	University of Central Oklahoma
Jack Griggs	Abilene Christian University
Alan Grunewald	Michigan State University
Donald Hunkins	Northwood University
William Jackson	University of North Carolina
James Kehr	Miami University
Kenneth Kopecky	Temple University
Gary Koppenhaver	University of Iowa
Donald Mullineaux	University of Kentucky
Manferd Peterson	University of Nebraska, Lincoln
Rose Prasad	Central Michigan University
James Ross	Radford University
Robert Schweitzer	University of Delaware
David Schauer	University of Texas, El Paso
Sherrill Shaffer	University of Wyoming
Suresh Srivastava	University of Alaska
Edward Waller	University of Houston, Clear Lake
Larry White	Mississippi State University
Bob Wood, Jr.	Tennessee Tech University

Special thanks are due to Sandy Gangelhoff, South-Western College Publishing, for her help in the editing and final preparation of this text.

CHAPTER I

Functions and Forms
of Banking

After reading this chapter you
will be able to:

■ Understand what a bank
is and how banks differ from
other financial service organizations such as savings and
loans and mutual funds.

■ Explain the types of services banks offer to their
deposit and loan customers.

■ Understand the motiva-
tion behind bank behavior
such as pricing deposits
and loan rates.

■ Understand how banks
get their funds and what
they do with them.

■ Describe the economic
and financial forces that
have changed how banks
operate and the basic management strategies of individual banking organizations.

For many centuries banks have played a vital role in the financial system. That vital role continues today, although the forms of banking have changed as the needs of the economy have changed. This chapter provides an overview of the role of commercial banks by concentrating on six questions.

1. What is a bank?

2. What do banks do?

3. Why do they perform those services?

4. How do banks compare with other financial service organizations?

5. What factors have affected the operations of commercial banks and other financial service organizations?

6. What are the principal sources and uses of funds for banks?

The discussion focuses on the manager of the bank; that is, the focus is from inside the banking institution looking outward at the environment within which banks operate. In examining each of the questions already listed, the basic aim is to acquaint the existing or potential manager of the bank with the information and/or techniques necessary to succeed in managing the organization. ■

1.1 ▐ WHAT IS A BANK?

The answer to the question "What is a bank?" might seem quite simple. In reality, however, it is complicated. One reason for the complexity is the distinction between the legal definitions of commercial banks and the functional definition of what banks do.[1] For example, some of the functions of banks are performed by nonbank competitors. Another reason why defining a bank is complicated is that the legal definition changes over time, and different countries may have different legal definitions. Likewise, the functions of a bank have changed over the years.

In the United States, a *bank* is defined by federal and state laws and by the bank regulators. Let's consider the definition of a bank in a historical context.

The National Currency Act of 1863, which was rewritten as the National Bank Act of 1864, created the Office of the Comptroller of Currency (OCC) and national banks, which are banks with a national charter issued by the OCC. This first federal law regulating national banks said that a national banking association shall have the power to carry out the "business of banking." It defined the business of banking as "discounting and negotiating promissory notes, drafts, bills of exchange, and other evidences of debt; by receiving deposits; by buying and selling exchange, coin, and bullion; by loaning money on personal security; and by obtaining, issuing, and circulating notes."[2]

The Bank Holding Company Act of 1956 changed the definition of a bank. Under this act, banks accepted deposits that could be withdrawn on demand, and they made commercial loans.[3] Commercial loans are loans made to a business customer for the purpose of providing funds for that business.[4] This definition contained a loophole for banks that accepted deposits and made loans to individuals in the form of consumer loans but that did not make commercial loans. These institutions were defined as a nonbank bank, and they were not subject to the same federal regulations as a bank. This loophole allowed nonbank banks to conduct operations that were not available to banks at that time.

The nonbank bank loophole was closed by the Competitive Equality Bank-

---

1. For further discussion of this point, see Jerry L. Jordan, "The Functions and Future of Retail Banking," Federal Reserve Bank of Cleveland, *Economic Commentary* (Sept. 15, 1996).
2. National Bank Act, 12 U.S.C.A. 24 (7).
3. A bank holding company is defined as a company that controls one or more banks. The term *control* means owning 25 percent or more of the voting shares, but in some cases control can occur at lower levels of ownership.
4. *Board of Governors v. Dimension Financial Corporation*, 474 U.S. 361 (1986).
5. Although the nonbank bank loophole was closed, about 160 enterprises were allowed to continue to operate as nonbank banks, subject to certain limitations.

ing Act of 1987 (CEBA) and no new nonbank banks were chartered.[5] The new definition of a bank became a financial institution that accepts deposits and makes loans. CEBA further modified the definition of a bank to include only those institutions that had their deposits insured by the Federal Deposit Insurance Corporation (FDIC).

At the turn of the century, the legal definition of a **bank** is an organization that makes loans, has FDIC-insured deposits, and has been granted banking powers either by the state or the federal government. This text uses the term *bank* and *commercial bank* interchangeably.

The legal definition of a bank is important because other types of financial institutions offer the same or similar services but are not subjected to the same regulations as banks. For example, credit unions accept deposits and make loans. Their deposits, however, are not insured by the FDIC, nor are they subject to the same regulations or taxes as banks. Similarly, finance companies make loans, and money market mutual funds are a substitute for deposit. Accordingly, GE Capital, Fidelity Funds, and Merrill Lynch provide "banking and financial services," even though they are not banks in the legal sense of the word. Bankers argue that this legal distinction gives the nonbank financial institutions an unfair competitive advantage because they are not regulated to the same degree. And, in fact, banks' share of total loans and deposits has declined over the years.

In addition to taking deposits and making loans, banks have been granted legal powers to provide other financial services. The financial services that they offer have changed over the years as new technologies emerge. The services listed in Table 1.1 provide an indication of the range of expanded services offered by banks. Before these services became available in the last half of the twentieth century, banks offered only a small number of basic services. Not surprisingly, managers of commercial banks continue to lobby Congress to change the laws and regulations in order to provide additional financial services. Managers of the nonbank competitors lobby just as hard to prevent bank competition in those areas. Much of the debate over bank regulation centers on the controversy between bankers and other financial service providers over the limits of bank power.

Types of Banks

It is common practice to classify banks by the markets they serve. The largest banks serve markets throughout the world and are referred to as *global, international banks,* or *money center banks,* such as Chase Manhattan Bank Corp.

Most medium and large banks are *full service banks* that provide a wide range of financial services, for example, AmSouth Bank, and BankAmerica. In Europe and other foreign markets, banks that can provide the complete range of banking services are called *universal banks.*

The majority of the banks in the United States are small and medium-size *retail* or *consumer banks* that serve the credit needs of their local communities.

TABLE 1.1	Banking Services

Expanded Services	Basic Services
Cash management services	Non-interest-bearing transaction accounts
Consumer loans	Commercial loans
Credit and debit cards	Savings accounts
Derivatives	
Electronic banking	
Fixed- and floating-rate certificates of deposit	
Foreign exchange	
Insurance, annuities	
Interest-bearing transaction accounts	
Leases	
Mutual funds	
Real estate loans	
Trust services	
Trade finance for international transactions	
Underwriting selected securities	

These banks also offer a wide range of financial services by using *correspondent banks*—larger banks that provide financial services—and by outsourcing. Outsourcing refers to acquiring services from specialized vendors such as insurance companies and mutual funds.

Finally, a few banks concentrate on dealing almost exclusively with medium and large businesses. These specialized banks are known as *wholesale banks*, such as LaSalle National Bank, and U.S. Trust Company of California.[6] They do not extend home mortgage credit, consumer loans to retail customers, or loans to small businesses or small farms. In addition, a few large banks that specialize in a narrow product line, such as credit cards or motor vehicle loans, are called *limited purpose banks*, or *monoline banks* because of their focus primarily on one line of business, for example, MBNA.

See http://www.occ. treas.gov/ *for a listing of wholesale and limited purpose banks at the web site for the Office of the Comptroller of the Currency.*

6. The definitions of banks reflect the general use of those terms, not the legal definitions, or those used by bank regulators. The OCC's *Comptroller's Corporate Manual—Charters*, which is available on their web page, provides their current definitions of various types of banks. Even here the terms are confusing. For example, a "CEBA Credit Card bank" is one type of a limited purpose bank.

1.2 WHAT DO BANKS DO?

Most of the functions performed by commercial banks for their customers can be divided into three broad areas:

1. Payments
2. Intermediation
3. Other financial services

Payments

Banks are the core of the **payments system**. The payment refers to the means by which financial transactions are settled. Banks also dispense of coin and currency. Many financial transactions in the United States involve checking accounts at commercial banks. Therefore, the means by which such payments are settled is an integral part of the payments system. The payments system also involves the settlement of credit card transactions, electronic banking, wire transfers, and other aspects in the movement of funds.

The role of banks in the payments system takes on an important social dimension because an efficient payments system is vital to economic stability and growth. At one time, commercial banks had a monopoly on transactions accounts, but no longer. Savings and loans, savings banks, and credit unions (known collectively along with commercial banks as depository institutions), as well as money market mutual funds and brokerage firms also offer transactions accounts.

Commercial banks, along with the Federal Reserve System, are the heart of the payment system. The payment system can be divided into two parts: the *retail payments system* used by individuals to pay their bills or receive funds, and the *large-dollar payments system* used by business concerns and governments to handle large-dollar domestic and international payments and receipts.

The retail payments system in the United States makes extensive use of paper checks. However, electronic payments and credit and debit cards are becoming increasingly important means of retail payments. Banks also provide coin and currency to businesses and individuals for cash transactions.

Large-dollar payments in the United States are electronic payments between commercial banks that are using the **Fedwire** (a wholesale wire transfer system operated by the Federal Reserve System), with more than 300,000 transfers per day amounting to about $1 trillion. In addition, the Clearing House Interbank Payments System, or CHIPS, is a private electronic transfer system operated by large banks in New York that transfers another $1 trillion per day, principally involving international movements of funds. Further, the Society for Worldwide Interbank Financial Telecommunication (SWIFT) is operated by banks throughout the world to facilitate international payments. (Refer to Chapter 13 for further discussion of the payments systems.)

Financial Intermediation

Through **financial intermediation,** banks act as economic units whose principal function is to obtain funds from depositors and others and then lend those funds to borrowers. They also provide other financial services. In financial terms, deposits represent bank liabilities, and loans are assets. A bank's profit is the difference between the rates at which they borrow and lend after taking into account their expenses.

Bank Balance Sheet	
Assets	**Liabilities and Equity**
Loans	Deposits
Other assets	Equity

DEPOSIT FUNCTION Commercial banks act as intermediaries between those who have money (savers or depositors) and those who need money (borrowers). As financial intermediaries, they enhance economic efficiency and economic growth by allocating capital to its best possible uses.[7] Banks obtain deposits from savers by offering deposit instruments the following benefits:

1. A wide variety of denominations, interest rates, and maturities

2. Risk-free (FDIC-insured) deposits

3. A high degree of liquidity

These characteristics meet the needs of most savers better than bonds and stocks, which may have high denominations, high risk, and less liquidity. Non-bank financial institutions may offer similar services, such as money market mutual funds, but mutual fund shares are not FDIC-insured.

LOAN FUNCTION Commercial banks use deposits to make loans to borrowers. Historically loans were concentrated in short-term commercial lending, hence the term *commercial* bank. Today, however, banks make every type of loan legally permissible. By doing so, they gain expertise in evaluating and monitoring the risks associated with lending.

Financial intermediation between depositors and borrowers is crucial to the growth and stability of the economy. Economic growth depends on a large volume of savings and the effective allocation of the savings to productive and profitable uses. By offering depositors financial instruments with desirable risk/return characteristics, commercial banks encourage savings and, by effectively screening credit requests, they channel funds into socially productive and profitable uses.

7. The role of financial intermediaries in economic development is explained in Zsolt, Becsi, and Ping Wang, "Financial Development and Growth," Federal Reserve Bank of Atlanta, *Economic Review* (Fourth Quarter 1997), pp. 46–62.

Other Financial Services

In addition to their traditional role of providing financial intermediation between depositors and borrowers, commercial banks provide a variety of other financial services that are discussed further in Chapters 5, 6, and 15. Some of these services are briefly described here.

OFF-BALANCE SHEET RISK TAKING Banks can generate fee income by dealing in financial derivatives such as futures, options, interest rate swaps, and financial futures.[8] For example, a bank may guarantee the payment of another party. These guarantees are contingent claims and do not appear on the bank's balance sheet. The standby letter of credit is perhaps the best known of those contingent claims and involves the agreement by a bank to pay an agreed-upon amount on presentation of evidence of default or nonperformance of the party whose obligation is guaranteed. Finally, banks make extensive use of interest rate swaps to hedge interest rate risk—the risk of adverse movements in market rates of interest.

INSURANCE-RELATED ACTIVITIES Commercial banks are able to offer insurance products. These products include but are not limited to annuities and credit life insurance.

SECURITIES-RELATED SERVICES Commercial banks provide a number of brokerage services as well as selling mutual funds. They also offer investment banking services such as underwriting municipal securities—securities issued by state and local governments. They also trade foreign currencies and U.S. government securities.

TRUST SERVICES Commercial banks may operate "trust" departments in which they receive a fee to manage the funds of others under the terms of a trust agreement. Because the bank does not "own" the assets held in trust, they do not show up on the bank's balance sheet. In their fiduciary role through the trusts, banks manage estates, employee pension and profit-sharing programs, and a variety of securities-related activities for corporate businesses.

8. For additional information, see Benton E. Gup and Robert Brooks, *Interest Rate Risk Management: The Banker's Guide to Using Futures, Options, Swaps and Other Derivatives* (New York: McGraw-Hill, 1993); *Interest Rate Risk: Comptroller's Handbook* (Washington, D.C.: Office of the Comptroller of the Currency, 1997).

1.3 BANKS AS PRIVATE FIRMS WITH A PUBLIC PURPOSE

Commercial banks in the United States are private corporations that provide payments services, financial intermediation, and other financial services in anticipation of earning profits from those activities. The payments system and intermediation are required for economic growth. Like any other for-profit corporation, a bank's principal goal is to maximize shareholder wealth. Thus, decisions on lending, investing, borrowing, pricing, adding or dropping services, and other activities depend on their impact on shareholder wealth.

Shareholder wealth is measured by the market value of a bank's stock and the amount of cash dividends paid. Market value depends on three factors: (1) the cash flows that accrue to bank shareholders, (2) the timing of the cash flows, and (3) the risk involved in cash flows. Management decisions, then, involve evaluating the impact of various strategies on the return (the amount and timing of the cash flows) and the risk of those cash flows (Figure 1.1).

Bank Risk Management

Banks accept risk in order to earn profits. Through **bank risk management**, they balance alternative strategies' risk/return characteristics with the goal of maximizing shareholder wealth. In doing so, banks recognize that, in light of different types of risk, the impact of a particular investment strategy on share-holders depends on the impact on the total risk of the organization. The Office

FIGURE 1.1   Bank Goals and Constraints

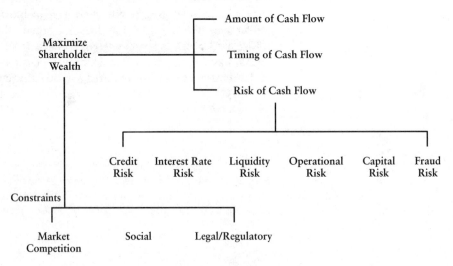

of the Comptroller of the Currency (OCC), which regulates national banks, lists nine risks for bank supervision purposes.[9]

1. **Credit risk** is the risk to earnings and capital that an obligor will fail to meet the terms of any contract with the bank, or otherwise fail to perform as agreed. It is usually associated with loans and investments, but it can also arise in connection with derivatives, foreign exchange, and other extensions of bank credit. Although banks fail for many reasons, the single most important reason is bad loans. At the time the loans are made the decisions seemed correct. However, unforeseen changes in economic conditions, and other factors such as interest rate shocks, changes in tax laws, and so on, result in credit problems. Credit risk is the primary cause of bank failures in recent years, and it is the most visible risk facing bank managers.

2. **Interest rate risk** is the risk to earnings and capital associated with changes in market rates of interest. This risk arises from differences in timing of rate changes and cash flows (repricing risk), from changes in the shape of the yield curve (yield curve risk), and from option values embedded in bank products (options risk). In essence, the market value of a bank's assets—loans and securities—will fall with increases in interest rates. In addition, earnings from assets, fees, and the cost of borrowed funds are affected by changes in interest rates. Banks can reduce their interest rate risk by hedging with derivative securities and by using other asset/liability management techniques described in other chapters of this book.

3. **Liquidity risk** is the risk to earnings or capital arising from a bank's ability to meet the needs of depositors and borrowers by turning assets into cash quickly with minimal loss, being unable to borrow funds when needed, or falling short of funds to execute profitable securities trading activities. Given the large amount of bank deposits that must be paid on demand or within a short period, liquidity risk is a crucial factor in banking.

4. **Price risk** is the risk to earnings or capital arising from market-making, dealing, or taking positions in securities, derivatives, foreign exchange, or other financial instruments. For example, as a result of the financial crises in Russia in 1998, several large banks (i.e., Bankers Trust, BankAmerica, Citicorp, and others) suffered losses in their foreign exchange and derivatives positions.

---

9. Office of the Comptroller of the Currency, News Release NR 96-2, "OCC Formerly Launches Supervision by Risk Program With Distribution of *Large Bank Supervision Handbook*" (January 4, 1996). The risks listed by the OCC may differ from those listed by other bank supervisory agencies. For example, the Basle Committee on Banking Supervision (*Report on International Developments in Banking Supervision*, Report number 9, Basle, Bank For International Settlements, September 1994) lists credit risk, market risk, liquidity risk, operations risk, and legal risks. Nevertheless, collectively they cover the same areas of concern as the OCC list.

5. **Foreign exchange risk** is the risk to earnings or capital due to changes in foreign exchange rates relative to the domestic currency.

6. **Operational risk** is the risk to earnings or capital arising from problems associated with the delivery or service of a product. The year 2000 (Y2K) problem associated with outdated computer software at the turn of the century is an example of an operational risk. Operational risks encompass the efficiency and effectiveness of operations including management information systems, personnel, and frauds. For example, large-scale frauds have resulted in a number of bank failures in the United States and abroad.[10] Most frauds are small scale, however, and do not result in bank failures.

7. **Compliance risk** is the risk to earnings or capital arising from violations of laws, rules, regulations, and so on. For example, banks failing to meet minimum capital requirements must raise new capital, or they may close, be forced to merge, or take some other corrective action.

8. **Strategic risk** is the risk to earnings or capital resulting from bad business decisions that adversely affect the value of the bank.

9. **Reputation risk** is the risk to earnings or capital that results from negative public opinion of the bank. Negative public opinion can arise from poor service and failure to serve the community's credit needs, among other reasons. A recent survey revealed that consumers rank telephone companies ahead of banks in terms of service.[11] Negative public opinion also contributes to loss of market share and may be a potential source of litigation.

Constraints

Bank management must carefully balance risk and return in seeking to maximize shareholder wealth. However, such decisions are constrained by a number of factors. These constraints may be classified into three specific though overlapping areas:

1. **Market constraints:** A bank's growth and profitability is limited by the growth rate of the economy that it serves. If the economy is growing and prosperous, a soundly managed bank should grow and be profitable. If the economy is faltering due to deflation, natural disasters, recessions, or for other reasons, banks will suffer too. Most bank failures occur as a result of economic distress.

   Second, competition from other providers of financial services and from the capital market influence a bank's operations. For example, if a

---

10. For additional discussion of the role of bank frauds in failures, see Benton E. Gup, *Bank Failures in the Major Trading Countries of the World* (Westport, CT: Quorum Books, 1998); Benton E. Gup, *Targeting Fraud* (New York, McGraw-Hill, 1995).
11. Beverly Foster, "Transitions: An Interview with Julie Williams," *Journal of Lending & Credit Risk Management* (February 1999), pp. 8–13.

bank's management believes that it must charge 8% on a loan in order to be fully compensated for credit risk, but other lenders will provide credit to the borrower at 7%, then this market constraint has a potentially serious impact on the bank.

2. **Social constraints**: Social constraints stem from the historical position of the commercial bank at the core of the financial system. Because the financial performance of a bank is inextricably linked with the economic health of the community it serves, banks perform numerous social functions (and they are expected to do so) through their participation in local Chambers of Commerce, charities, and other activities that promote the economic development and quality of life.

3. **Legal and regulatory constraints**: Perhaps more significant are the legal and regulatory constraints on the portfolio management (i.e., its risk/return position) of a commercial bank.

   Legal and regulatory constraints are discussed in considerable detail in other parts of the book. It is sufficient at this point to mention the following constraints on bank operations:

   Constraints on balance sheet composition, including the prohibition on holding equity securities and minimum capital requirements

   Constraints on powers, including limitations on owning common stock, and so on.

   Constraints on customer relationships, including a large number of consumer protection laws

Most legal and regulatory constraints on bank behavior are designed either to reduce the risk of failure or to affect the price and allocation of bank credit. The risk reduction constraints stem primarily from the banking collapse of the 1930s. In contrast, the constraints designed to restrict the relationship of banks with their customers stem from the consumerism movement of the 1960s and 1970s. These subjects are examined in Chapter 2.

1.4 SIZE AND MARKET SHARE OF COMMERCIAL BANKS AND OTHER FINANCIAL SERVICE FIRMS

Table 1.2 reveals that the total assets of the various participants in the financial sector of the U.S. economy in 1998 exceeded $17 trillion. As the dominant financial institution in the United States, banks have more than $4 trillion in assets or 24% of the total.

Federally related mortgage pools accounted for the second largest share of assets, with 11.5% of the total. Their assets represent the outstanding principal balances of mortgage-backed securities insured or guaranteed by U.S.

MANAGING RISK

Continental Bank, Too Big to Fail

Continental Illinois Corporation, the parent holding company for Continental Illinois National Bank and Trust Company, was known as an extremely aggressive wholesale (business) bank during the late 1970s and early 1980s. With only one office in downtown Chicago, Continental grew into one of the largest banks ($47 billion in assets) in the country by selling large-denomination certificates of deposits to investors and using the proceeds to make corporate loans. For a time the strategy worked, and Continental experienced a rapid growth in earnings.

Unfortunately, Continental had two fundamental problems in its risk management. First, its appraisal of credit risk was faulty, and second, it had almost no stable core deposits to tide itself over if it got into trouble. Disaster struck in July 1982 when Penn Square Bank (a small suburban bank in Oklahoma City from which Continental had bought large amounts of oil and gas loans) was closed.

Continental had acquired more than $1 billion in loans (mostly oil and gas, or energy loans), and most of these loans were in default. As the story unfolded, Continental experienced an erosion of its deposit base—an erosion that eventually became a stampede—and the bank's earnings plummeted. Depositors with large-denomination deposits withdrew their funds (a silent run on the bank). The credit-quality problems became a liquidity crisis.

After a series of attempts to prop up the ailing bank, the Federal Deposit Insurance Corporation finally took control of Continental in 1984 (an action that has been referred to as the "nationalization" of the bank). Because bank regulators feared that Continental's problems might spread to other large banks, the Comptroller of the Currency went before the U.S. Congress to declare that Continental and 10 other of the nation's largest banks were "too big to fail" (TBTF).

The **too-big-to-fail doctrine** is important today because of the growth of megabanks, global banking, and the integration of banks with nonbank financial institutions (investment banking and insurance companies). Perhaps the expectation of a government bailout for large organizations if they get into financial difficulty leads those organizations to take on high risk in hopes of earning high returns.

The TBTF policy has been applied by governments when they believe that some event will result in severe economic distress.[12] In the United States, the government has intervened on behalf of banks, railroads (Reconstruction Finance Corporation), troubled government-sponsored enterprises (the Farm Credit System), Chrysler Corporation, and labor strikes. The TBTF policy has been applied in other countries as well.

government agencies, including Government National Mortgage Association (GNMA), Federal Home Loan Mortgage Corporation, Federal National Mortgage Association (FNMA), and Farmers Home Administration (FHA). These agencies facilitate the flow of mortgage funds in the capital markets. The mortgages guaranteed or insured by government agencies are held by financial institutions, including banks, and by individual investors.

12. Benton E. Gup, "Too-Big-to-Fail," *Bank Failures of the Major Trading Countries*, Chapter 5.

TABLE 1.2	Credit Market Assets	
Financial Sector	**Credit Market Assets ($ billions)**	**Percentage of Total**
Monetary authority	$446.5	2.6%
Commercial banks	4,195.6	24.3
Savings institutions	937.8	5.4
Credit unions	320.7	1.9
Bank personal trusts and estates	241.4	1.4
Life insurance companies	1,823.3	10.6
Other insurance companies	518.3	3.0
Private pension funds	912.1	5.3
State and local government retirement funds	621.4	3.6
Money market mutual funds	869.9	5.1
Mutual funds	1,007.0	5.8
Closed-end funds	95.9	0.6
Government-sponsored enterprises	1,048.1	6.1
Federally related mortgage pools	1,975.6	11.5
Asset-back securities issuers	1,138.4	6.6
Finance companies	593.7	3.4
Mortgage companies	58.9	0.3
Real estate investment trusts (REITs)	14.0	0.1
Brokers and dealers	227.8	1.3
Funding corporations	192.7	1.1
Total	$17,239.0	100.0%

Source: *Federal Reserve Bulletin*, Flow of Funds Accounts, Table 1.60 (January 1999), A41. Data are for the third quarter of 1998. Data are listed as they appear in the *Federal Reserve Bulletin* to facilitate classroom discussions with current information from the *Bulletin*.

Much of the data presented in the tables in this and other chapters comes from the Federal Reserve and the FDIC. To obtain the latest data from the Federal Reserve, see http://www.bog.frb.fed.us/. To obtain the latest data from the FDIC, see http://www.fdic.gov.

Life insurance companies, with $1.8 trillion in assets, accounted for the third largest share (10.6%) of the market. All other sectors account for substantially smaller shares.

Despite the absolute dollar size of commercial banks, they have lost market share to nonbank financial institutions. The data shown in Table 1.3 reveal that commercial banks' share of financial assets declined from 34% in 1980 to 24% in 1997. The reasons for the decline will be explained shortly.

Table 1.4 lists the largest banks in the world. The Mizuho Financial Group was formed by three large Japanese banks that plan to meld operations by

TABLE 1.3	Market Share of Financial Sector Assets ($ billions)	
	1980	**1997**
Commercial banks	$1,482 (34%)	$4,196 (24%)
Nonbank finance	$2,884 (46%)	$13,043 (76%)
Totals	$4,366 (100%)	$17,239 (100%)

Source: *Federal Reserve Bulletin*, Flow of Funds Accounts, Table 1.60 (January 1999), A41; U.S. Department of Commerce, *Statistical Abstract of the United States 1997* (1998), Table 774.

2002.[13] Deutsche Bank (Germany) was the second largest, followed by Banque Nationale de Paris (France), Citigroup (United States), and UBS (Switzerland). These banks attained their size largely through megamergers—the combination of large financial institutions.

Large foreign global banking firms operate throughout the world in competition with each other, with investment banking firms, and with other providers of financial services. They have large corporate customers (often multinational corporations) that have special financing needs.

See http://www.ffiec.gov /nic/ *for the largest U.S. banks and bank holding companies.*

In the United States, perhaps a dozen megabanks qualify as global banking firms, but a number of large regional banks do international banking as well. For example, Regions Bank (Alabama) provides trade financing for exporters

TABLE 1.4	Five Largest Banks in the World, 1999	
Banks, Country		**Total assets**
1. Mizuho Financial Group, Japan Includes Fuji Bank, Dai-Ichi Kangyo Bank, and Industrial Bank of Japan		$1.3 trillion
2. Deutsche Bank, Germany		866 billion
3. Bank Nationale de Paris, France		755 billion
4. Citigroup, U.S.A.		690 billion
5. UBS, Switzerland		687 billion

Source: "Topping the Charts," *American Banker* (August 23, 1999), p. 5.

13. Peter Landers, "Japanese Banks to Form Colossus," *Wall Street Journal* (August 20, 1999), pp. A7.

and importers in the Southeast. It has correspondent banking relationships with banks throughout the world. That, however, does not qualify it as a global bank.

I.5 MAJOR FACTORS AFFECTING BANKING AND MARKET SHARES

Shifts in the market shares of commercial banks and for other financial service organizations reflect the confluence of a number of economic, technological, and regulatory factors. The principal factors at work, with emphasis on those that most directly affect commercial banks, are described in the following sections.

Inflation and Volatile Interest Rates

Interest rates were relatively low and stable throughout the 1950s and early 1960s, averaging about 4–6%. Beginning in 1966, however, the inflation rate began to rise, and interest rates soared, with some rates reaching higher than 20% in the early 1980s. The sharp increase and high level of interest rates placed intense pressure on the financial system and contributed to the failure of a large number of institutions. Many institutions had borrowed short-term funds and made long-term loans at fixed rates of interest. When interest rates soared, their cost of borrowing increased, and exceeded the low fixed returns on their assets. In addition, the market value of their assets declined. Equally important, large numbers of borrowers defaulted on their loans. Between 1980 and 1994, more than 1,600 FDIC banks failed or needed assistance. Stated another way, 9.14% of the total number of banks in the United States failed during this period.[14] Savings and loan associations were also affected adversely by the changes in economic conditions. The number of savings and loan associations declined from 4,613 in 1980 to 1,345 in 1990 due to failures and mergers.[15]

Securitization

Securitization has had a substantial impact on the structure of the financial services industry. **Securitization** is the issuance of a debt instrument in which the promised payments are derived from revenues generated by a defined pool of loans. The pools include mortgage loans, credit card loans, car loans, and loans to businesses. Prior to the development of securitization, such small loans were considered unmarketable, and they remained on the balance sheets

14. *History of the Eighties: Lessons for the Future*, vol. 1 (Washington, D.C.: Federal Deposit Insurance Corporation, 1997), Chapter 1.
15. *Statistical Abstract of the United States, 1992* (Washington, D.C.: U.S. Department of Commerce, 1992), Table 794.

of the banks. However, securitization allows banks to package and sell the loans, thereby improving the bank's liquidity and increasing their access to capital markets.

In addition, securitization has allowed the traditional lending process to be separated into various parts: originating loans, packaging them for the sale to others, servicing loans, and funding loans. This unbundling of the lending process has opened the door for nonbank firms to compete in bank loan markets.

Technological Advances

Advances in technology have affected the competitive position of financial service providers. Changes in computer and communications technology have lowered the costs for processing financial transactions. As a result, these changes have spurred the development of large institutions that specialize in credit cards, investment services, and servicing securitized loans and allowed them to take advantage of **economies of scale**—high volume, low costs. Other institutions have developed or expanded their activities to provide banking services over the Internet. The firms that have been most effective in implementing the new financial technology have achieved an edge through automation and lower personnel costs.

Perhaps more important, the advances in technology have made the production of diverse financial services within one firm more feasible through increasing the prospects for realizing **economies of scope**—when two different products can be produced more cheaply at one firm than at two separate firms. For example, banks can offer a variety of services to distant customers over the Internet that might be too costly to offer from traditional brick-and-mortar facilities.

Finally, communications technology has expanded geographical boundaries over which financial services can be produced, thereby substantially intensifying competition in the industry.

Consumers

More sophisticated consumers have played a major role in the changing structure of the financial services industry. Greater education in personal money management, as well as high returns on financial assets have made fund flows more volatile. In addition, access to the Internet and online banking and investment services gives consumers of financial services the means to move funds around at low costs.

Capital Markets

Increased competition from the capital market has played a role in the decline of banks' market share of financial assets. Large, high-quality corporations have found that they can access funds cheaper through direct borrowing in the capital market (through selling commercial paper or other securities) than by borrowing from banks. For example, the prime rate (the base rate on corporate loans) was 8.25%, while the rate for 60-day commercial paper was 5.98% in late 1999.[16]

Deregulation

Deregulation has affected the operations of commercial banks and other depository financial institutions. **Deregulation** of banks refers to the reduction or elimination of laws that placed geographic limits on banks, restricted the products and services they can offer, and limited the rates they can pay. In the past, banks located in one state could not have branches in other states. The elimination of geographic barriers to entry in the 1990s contributed to the large number of bank mergers and the increased consolidation in the industry. The number of banks declined from 14,400 banks in 1985 to about 8,500 banks at the turn of the century as a result of mergers and failures. Economic concentration has occurred as a result of the mergers. In 1984, 42 banks controlled 25% of total deposits. In 1999, six banks controlled 25% of total deposits.[17]

Despecialization and Competition

If you want to know what's happening in banking today, read the American Banker *online at* http://www.americanbanker.com.

The despecialization of financial institutions has been an important force in changing the structure of the financial service industry. The trend is for banks to become a one-stop shopping center for all financial services, offering broker/dealer investment services, insurance products, mutual funds, trust services, and other financial services. Equally important in the despecialization trend are the expanded financial service offerings by bank's competitors such as Merrill Lynch, Fidelity Funds, and General Electric's GE Capital. Because they are not limited by the same legal and regulatory constraints as banks, they have a significant competitive advantage. Despecialization has also contributed to the increasing overlap of financial services offered by banks and nonbanking firms.

Globalization

The term *globalization* refers to the integration of individual countries' economies and financial markets into a single world market.[18] Globalization differs

16. Money rates are published daily in the *Wall Street Journal*. Data are for October 13, 1999.
17. Scott Baranick, "Megamerger Flood Prompts FDIC to Prep Quietly for a Megafailure," *American Banker* (January 22, 1999), pp. 1, 3.
18. Masaaki Shirakawa, Kunio Okina, and Shigenori Shiratsuka, "Financial Market Globalization: Present and Future," Institute for Monetary and Economic Studies, Bank of Japan, Discussion Paper No. 97-E-11, 1997.

from internationalization, which only refers to an increase in certain international transactions increase.

Globalization of financial service organizations has affected the operations and structure of many financial service organizations as the amount of funds flowing across national borders increases for both long-run investment purposes and short-run liquidity management. Foreign financial service organizations have entered the U.S. market, and many U.S. financial service firms have expanded abroad. For example, GE Capital bought Japan Leasing Corp, and T. Rowe Price Associates (a Baltimore asset-management company) entered into a joint venture with Daiwa Securities Company and Sumitomo Bank.[19] Deutsche Bank (Germany) acquired Bankers Trust (United States). The result of this global integration of financial markets is growing competition among financial service firms.

The impact of entry by foreign banks into the U.S. market has been striking. In 1980, foreign banks accounted for 18% of the total bank loans made to businesses in the United States. By 1995, foreign banks' share of the loan market increased to 35%, and they held 22% of total bank assets.[20] By the time these numbers were in print they were outdated by the ongoing process of global consolidation of firms.

1.6 ASSETS AND LIABILITIES OF COMMERCIAL BANKS

Table 1.5 presents the major assets and liabilities of the commercial banking industry. This table, with attention to the various functions performed by commercial banks, serves as a vehicle for a discussion of the general sources and uses of bank funds. An analysis of individual bank balance sheets is contained in Chapter 3, Financial Performance.

Assets

LOANS The credit creation function of commercial banks is reflected in the asset side of their balance sheet. As shown in Table 1.5, total loans were $3.3 trillion, making them the banks' largest asset. The three major categories of loans are commercial and industrial loans (C&I loans), real estate loans, and consumer loans. The relative shares of these loans are shown in Table 1.6.

19. J. Sapsford, "U.S. Financial Firms Delve Deeper in Japan," *The Wall Street Journal* (January 26, 1999), p. A13.
20. U.S. Department of Commerce, *Statistical Abstract of the United States, 1997*, Table 789.

TABLE I.5	Assets and Liabilities of Commercial Banks, October 1998

Assets	Amount ($ billions)
Bank credit	$4,490.5
Investments	1,218.3
U.S. government securities	773.0
Other	445.3
Loans	3,272.2
Interbank loans	226.2
Cash assets	243.8
Other cash assets	310.5
Total Assets	**$5,213.4**
Liabilities	**$4,792.3**
Total deposits	3,274.1
Transaction	668.2
Nontransaction	2,605.9
Federal funds and other borrowings	939.6
Net due to related foreign offices	223.1
Other liabilities	355.5
Equity Capital	**421.1**

Source: *Federal Reserve Bulletin* (January 1999), A15. (Data are listed in the same order they appear in the *Federal Reserve Bulletin* to facilitate classroom discussions with current information from the *Bulletin*).

TABLE I.6	Composition of Bank Loans

Type of Loans	1980	1998
Real estate	27%	40%
Commercial and Industrial (C&I)	39%	29%
Consumer	19%	16%
Other	15%	15%
Total	100%	100%

Source: U.S. Department of Commerce, *Statistical Abstract of the United States 1997*, Table 786; *Federal Reserve Bulletin* (January 1999), p. A15.

MANAGERIAL ISSUES

Planning for the Future

The stockholders of a bank elect a board of directors to oversee the bank's affairs and to ensure competent management. Part of the board's duties involve making strategic decisions about the future of the bank. Making management decisions is a complex process. For example, today at time period 0, it is necessary to make a decision about expanding into a new market, adding a new product, or some similar issue. The outcome of that decision can be good or bad. When the outcome is reviewed in the next time period, additional decisions must be made. If the original decision resulted in a good outcome, the board must now decide whether to continue on the same course of action or to change it. If the original decision had a bad outcome, should the bank abandon the project or make changes to improve the outcome? In subsequent time periods, additional decisions must be made about the success or failure of past decisions.

This simple example illustrates how one decision made today inevitably leads to additional decisions in the future. But it does not reveal the true complexity of the decision-making process. Suppose that a director must make five decisions today and has only five choices from which to select.[21] Only one combination of choices is possible. However, if a board is considering 10 choices, 252 possible combinations exist. With 100 choices, more than 75 million combinations are possible! What are the chances of making the correct decisions all of the time?

In 1980, C&I loans accounted for the largest portion of bank credit. These loans were used by businesses for acquiring inventory, carrying accounts receivable, and purchasing new equipment and real estate. In addition, substantial amounts of credit are also extended by commercial banks to securities firms and finance companies. Indeed, most small finance companies obtain the bulk of their funds from commercial banks. The large ones borrow in the capital market. In 1998, C&I loans accounted for only 29% of bank credit, making them the second largest loan category.

Real estate loans are the largest component of bank loans, accounting for 40% of the total, up from 27% in 1980. Real estate loans are used for the purchase of homes, income-producing properties, such as apartments and office buildings, and commercial properties. Real estate loans also include home equity loans in which a borrower's home is used as collateral for a personal loan.

The expansion in real estate lending is attributable to the declining role of savings and loan associations in our economy and the ability of banks to acquire them. In addition, the growth in longer-term time deposits at commercial banks has made bankers more willing to make long-term loans (more than

21. The combination C of n decisions taken x at a time can be determined by:

$$C_{x}^{n} = \frac{n!}{x!(N-x)!}$$

five years) and to hold less liquid assets. However, as a result of securitization, some real estate loans are liquid. Nevertheless, history tells us that long-term real estate loans, especially those for commercial properties, are more risky than short-term C&I loans.[22]

The third major type of credit at commercial banks is loans to individuals, or consumer loans, for the purchase of consumer durable goods, consolidation of debts, vacations, and for other purposes. In recent years, consumer loans have expanded rapidly, particularly in the form of credit extensions under credit card arrangements. Credit card debt at commercial banks increased from $236 billion in 1990 to an estimated $783 billion in 2000.[23]

The allocation of loans varies widely among banks of different sizes, different strategies, and different locations. Small banks focus on the local needs of the communities they serve. Thus, agricultural, consumer, and real estate loans often account for a larger fraction of their total loan portfolio than at large and global banks that serve a broader group of borrowers. Some large banks offer a full range of loans, while others specialize in credit cards, investment banking, and so on.

INVESTMENTS Commercial banks hold substantial amounts of liquid assets. A portion of the investment portfolio of commercial banks is held in short-term securities, especially U.S. Treasury securities. They hold a certain amount of liquid assets to offset the risk of the large volume of volatile transactions deposits, the role played by commercial banks in administering the nation's payments system, and the demand for loans. In addition, commercial banks play an important role in assisting the U.S. government in financing its own activities. Banks serve as a depository of the U.S. government (tax and loan accounts) as well as for state and local government securities. Federal tax collections are deposited at commercial banks, which play an important role in the sale of U.S. savings bonds.

CASH Commercial banks are the core of the payments system through the currency and coins they provide to individuals and businesses. This function is reflected on the balance sheet of commercial banks as a $243.8 billion holding of cash assets. Although we tend to associate banks with cash, it accounts for less than 5% of total assets. Banks must maintain an adequate supply of cash on hand to meet withdrawals, but because cash is a non-earning asset, banks usually hold only the minimum amount needed to operate efficiently.

22. See "International Banking Crises: The Real Estate Connection," in *International Bank Crises: Large-Scale Failures, Massive Government Interventions*, Benton E. Gup, ed. (Westport, CT: Quorum Books 1999).
23. U.S. Department of Commerce, *Statistical Abstract of the United States, 1997*, Table 799.

OTHER ASSETS Other assets—buildings, equipment, and other odds and ends—account for about 6% of total assets, which is a relatively small amount of non-earning assets. To put this percentage in context, consider that 94% of bank assets are financial assets—loans, investments, and cash. Loans and investments are earning assets and account for about 85% of total assets.

Deposits

Two closely related functions of the commercial banking industry are transaction accounts offered to the public, and administration of the payments system. These basic functions have been reflected historically in the large amount of transactions deposits at commercial banks, which can be withdrawn on demand. To offer these services, individual banks must cooperate with other banks in clearing and processing checks. This cooperation generates a large volume of interbank deposits (deposits from one bank held at another bank).

According to the Federal Reserve, **transaction accounts** include all deposits against which the account holder is permitted to make withdrawals by negotiable or transferable instruments, payment orders of withdrawal, or telephone or preauthorized transfers for the purposes of making payments to third parties.[24] Checking accounts and money market accounts are examples of transaction accounts. Accounts that limit the number of withdrawals to six or less are considered savings accounts. The role of passbook savings accounts has diminished sharply in recent years as banks and consumers rely more on money market deposits and money market mutual funds.

Equity

For the 100 largest bank web sites, see Online Banking Report's *listing at* http://www.onlinebankingreport.com/.

Equity represents a small but vitally important part of the balance sheet of commercial banks. In a market-based economy in which banks seek to maximize shareholder wealth, equity is the tangible representation of this private ownership. It is the owner's capital investment. Note, however, that equity capital finances a small portion—only about 8%—of the assets of a bank. Fundamentally, banks are highly leveraged business organizations; depositors and other creditors provide 92% of the funds that banks need to operate. Because of leverage, bank earnings increase dramatically during periods of prosperity. In contrast, economic declines are magnified into dramatic reductions in bank earnings, erosion in the capital account, and the failure of a large number of banks.

24. *Federal Reserve Bulletin*, Table 1:15, Reserve Requirements for Depository Institutions (September 1998).

1.7 BANK PROFITABILITY

Banks were especially profitable in the late 1990s. This section examines the reasons for this trend, including strong economic growth and banks taking on increased risks, earning higher fee income, and operating more efficiently.

Economic Growth

The primary determinant of bank profitability is the state of the economy, including economic growth, the level of interest rates, and other factors. If the economy is doing well, banks prosper. If the economy falters, banks suffer. Recall that credit risk—the risk that borrowers will default on credit obligations—is the greatest risk facing banks. The ability of borrowers to repay their loans is directly related to economic activity at both national and regional levels.

Regional differences in economic activity are important because the economy does not grow or contract at the same rate in all geographic regions. Changes in the price of oil in the 1980s had a greater impact in the Southwest than in other parts of the country. Accordingly, more banks in the Southwest had problems associated with declining oil prices and production than elsewhere.

Following the 1990–1991 recession, the U.S. economy experienced its longest peacetime expansion. Therefore, it is not surprising that banks did well too. The return on assets (ROA) is a broad measure of profitabilty. As a rule of thumb, a 1% ROA is considered good. As shown in Table 1.7, the ROA for commercial banks increased from the recession low of 0.48% in 1990 to 1.28% in 1999.

Increased Risk

Bank loan portfolios have shifted from short-term C&I loans to longer-term real estate loans. The interest rate charged on loans reflects their risk, maturity, and collateral values. The higher the risk and longer the maturity, the higher the interest rate charged. Table 1.8 shows the interest rates on selected loans.

TABLE 1.7	Return on Assets of Commercial Banks
1990	0.48%
1995	1.17%
1998	1.22%
1999 (June)	1.28%

Source: *FDIC Quarterly Banking Profile* (Second Quarter 1999). Data are for all FDIC-insured banks.

TABLE 1.8	Interest Rates on Loans
Real Estate Loans	
Home mortgage loan (contract rate)	6.74%
Regional mall	11.15%
Industrial	11.13%
Office building	11.24%
Consumer loans	
48-month car loan	8.44%
24-month personal loan	13.38%
Credit card plans	15.08%
Prime rate on loans to businesses	**8.25%**

Source: Data are from the Federal Reserve Statistical Release G.13 and G19 (November 2 and 5, 1999); *Federal Reserve Bulletin* (July 1999), I-34. Data for the commercial real estate properties are from *Valuation Insights and Perspectives* (Third Quarter 1999), p. 52.

Although home mortgage loans have an original average maturity of about 29 years, the average life of such loans is 7–12 years. Moreover, houses are generally good collateral and the loan-to-value ratios are about 80%. Commercial real estate developments, on the other hand, have a much higher degree of risk and substantially higher interest rates than home mortgage loans.

Likewise, credit card loans are not backed by collateral and have an indefinite maturity and a higher interest rate than personal loans and car loans. The **prime rate** is the reference rate used by banks to price their loans. Thus, the loans to businesses can be higher or lower than the prime rate depending on risk, maturity, collateral, and other factors.

Fee Income

Fee income (noninterest income) has become an important consideration to banks as more liberal banking regulations allow a wider range of financial services. Currently, banks charge fees for a variety of services provided to consumers, such as the following for business accounts:

- Cash deposits per $100, $0.05
- Check paid or other debit posted, $0.14
- Deposit or other credit posted, $0.25
- Inactive checking account fee (no activity for one year), $3/month

- Insufficient funds, $24
- Night depository, $15 per bag, $20 per year
- Stop payment charge, $24
- Telephone transfers, $3

In addition, banks earn fees from other financial service activities including brokerage, derivatives, mutual funds, trade finance, trust accounts, and so on. Noninterest income increased from 24% of banks net operating revenue in 1985 to 40% in 1998.[25]

Efficiency

Banks operate more efficiently than in the past. One method they use to gauge their operating efficiency is *efficiency ratios*, which measure the proportion of net operating revenues absorbed by overhead expenses. It is calculated by dividing noninterest expense less amortization of intangibles by total revenues. A lower value indicates greater efficiency. The ratio declined from about 66% in 1980 to 59% in 1998. Personnel expenses account for the largest part of overhead expense. Therefore, the decline in the ratio tells us that banks lowered their personnel expenses by operating with fewer people.

SUMMARY

A basic law of structural design is that form follows function. That concept applies to banking as well. The functions of banking are constant, but the forms of banking are changing.

In general terms, a bank is an organization that engages in specific financial services; it accepts FDIC-insured deposits and makes loans. Banks perform three basic functions: (1) they provide a leading role in the payments system; (2) they intermediate between depositors and borrowers by offering deposit and loan products; and (3) they provide a variety of financial services, encompassing fiduciary services, investment banking, and off-balance sheet risk taking. The controversy over the scope of banking activities centers on the issue of how far to allow banks to enter into these financial service activities.

Commercial banks are private, profit-seeking enterprises, that balance risk and return in their portfolio management with the goal of maximizing shareholder wealth. Shareholder wealth depends on three factors: (1) the volume of cash flows resulting from portfolio decisions, (2) the timing of those cash flows, and (3) the risk or volatility of the cash flows. Risks include credit risk, interest rate risk, liquidity risk, price risk, foreign exchange risk, and transaction,

25. *FDIC Quarterly Banking Profile* (Second Quarter 1998).

compliance, strategic, and reputation risks. The maximization of shareholder wealth is constrained by certain social responsibilities of banks as well as extensive legal and regulatory restrictions, including balance sheet and consumer protection constraints.

The environment within which bank managers operate has changed dramatically. The principal regulatory and competitive changes are (1) inflation and volatile interest rates, (2) securitization, (3) technological advances, (4) more sophisticated consumers, (4) competition from capital markets, (5) deregulation, (6) despecialization and competition, and (7) globalization. The net result of these changes is to increase the risk involved in bank management and the complexity of bank decision making.

In the discussion of balance sheets and profitability of commercial banks, the data revealed that loans account for the largest share of bank assets followed by investments. These loans and investments are funded by deposits and other borrowed funds, and to a lesser extent, equity. Among loans, the greatest share is real estate loans. During the 1990s, bank profitability increased as a result of a strong economy, increased risk taking, higher fee incomes, and greater efficiency.

Key Terms and Concepts

Bank (definition, functions, types)
Bank risk management
Compliance risk
Credit risk
Deregulation
Globalization
Economies of scale
Economies of scope
Fedwire
Fee income
Financial intermediation
Foreign exchange risk

Interest rate risk
Liquidity risk
Operational risk
Payments system
Price risk
Prime rate
Reputation risk
Securitization
Strategic risk
Too-big-to-fail doctrine
Transaction account

Questions

1.1   It is sometimes argued that bank managers are fundamentally involved in risk management. In what sense are they risk managers? Is their risk management similar to or different from that of managers of manufacturing and other nonfinancial firms?

1.2   How do commercial banks differ from other types of depository institutions such as credit unions?

1.3   List three broad functions of commercial banks. What other financial institutions compete with banks in providing these services to the public?

1.4 What is the principal goal of a commercial bank? How does profitability of a bank and the risks it faces affect this goal?

1.5 What are the principal factors that have affected the operations of commercial banks in recent years? Which (if any) of these are under the control of bank management?

1.6 What risk historically accounts for most bank failures?

1.7 What constraints do banks face in achieving their goals?

1.8 Discuss market share trends over time among commercial banks. Why has the market share of banks fallen?

1.9 What is meant by *securitization*?

1.10 What are the principal assets and liabilities of commercial banks? How have they changed over time?

1.11 What are some of the major external and internal factors that affect bank profits?

CASE STUDY

The Policy Consultant (Part I)

Jack Anderson is a policy consultant for North Information Services (NIS), a firm that specializes in lobbying Congress for banks and financial institutions that want to protect their economic interests. Mr. North, president and CEO of NIS asked Jack to prepare a brief for one of their major clients, an international bank, on the major issues that Congress will address this next term. For the first part of his brief, Jack is going to begin his research by reviewing the following sources of information available on the Internet concerning banking issues:

■ Speeches and testimony by members of the Board of Governors of the Federal Reserve System: *http://www.federalreserve.gov/*

■ Current federal legislation in the Committee on Banking and Financial Services: *http://www. house/gov/banking*

■ The *American Banker* newspaper: *http://www. americanbanker.com*

■ The Bank for International Settlements deals with international issues: *http://www.bis.org*

With information on these and other sources, Jack wants to address the following questions:

1. What are the current major issues facing domestic banks and their regulators?
2. What are the current major issues facing international banks and their regulators?
3. How might these issues affect the client?

CHAPTER 2

The Bank Regulatory Environment

After reading this chapter you will be able to:

- Understand the rationale for bank regulation.
- Explain why banking regulations changed during the 1980s and early 1990s.
- Describe the principal legislative changes in banking and the effects of those changes on banking operations.
- Evaluate the principal issues facing banks and bank regulators today.

Alan Greenspan, chairman, Board of Governors of the Federal Reserve System, had the following to say about the purpose of bank regulation: "If risk taking is a precondition of a growing economy, and if banks themselves exist because they are willing to take on and manage risk, what should be the objectives of bank regulation? The answer clearly should begin with the goal of circumscribing the incentive of banks to take excessive risks owing to the moral hazard in the safety net designed to protect the financial system and individual depositors. But the full answer must involve some benefit-costs tradeoffs between, on the one hand, protecting the financial system, and on the other hand, allowing banks to perform their essential risk-taking function.

"Herein lies the basic problem with much of U.S. banking law and regulation. The legislative process, in my judgment, has never adequately wrestled with the question of just how much risk is optional."

Source: Remarks by Alan Greenspan, chairman, Board of Governors of the Federal Reserve System, before the 29th Conference on Bank Structure and Competition, Federal Reserve Bank of Chicago (May 6, 1993). ■

If banking were not regulated to any greater extent than, say, restaurants, our banking system would operate a great deal differently than it does. Banks could be formed and liquidated with minimal limitations on their entry and exit from the banking market. Inefficient banks would go out of business. Competition would determine the prices and availability of banking services. Banks would also operate anywhere in the world without geographic or portfolio restrictions. Capital structure would be the prerogative of management. The cost of a bank's funds would be determined by its business and financial risk profile. And, of course, the penalty for either excessive or inadequate expansion of risk taking would be failure.

But banks (and other depository institutions) are not allowed to operate with such freedom. Both entry and exit are controlled and limited, as are mergers with other institutions and nonbanking firms. The scope and nature of banking activities are regulated.

2.1 WHY ARE BANKS REGULATED?

Banks are regulated for three different reasons. The first two reasons involve **prudential regulation** of banks, dealing with their safety and soundness. The third reason concerns social goals.

Prevention of Economic Disruption

First, banks are regulated to reduce the risk of large-scale failures that would adversely affect the level of economic activity. Although an individual bank that is poorly run should not necessarily be saved from failure, government and bank regulators must balance that event against concern over the adverse effects that one or more large bank failures may have in financial markets and the economy.[1]

In this regard, the smooth functioning of the economy is dependent on the money supply, the payments system, and an uninterrupted flow of credit. Bank demand deposits, other fully checkable deposits, savings deposits, and time deposits in amounts less than $100,000 are components of the money supply.[2]

1. For a discussion of the market failure theory of regulation, see C. F. Philips, *The Economics of Regulation* (Homewood, IL: Richard D. Irwin, 1969).
2. The M1 money stock includes currency held by the public, travelers checks, demand deposits, and other fully checkable deposits. The M2 money stock includes M1, savings deposits including money market deposits, time deposits in amounts of less than $100,000, money market mutual funds balances (except those restricted to institutional investors), certain overnight repurchase agreements and overnight Eurodollars. The M3 measure includes M2, time deposits of $100,000 or more, term repurchase agreements of $100,000 or more, certain term Eurodollars, and balances in money market mutual funds restricted to institutions. Source: "U.S. Monetary Policy: An Introduction," *FRBSF Economic Letter*, No. 99-01, Federal Reserve Bank of San Francisco (January 1, 1999).

Such accounts offered by banks and other depository institutions provide the liquidity, mobility, and acceptability necessary for our economy's payments system to function with ease and efficiency. Further, banks are the primary source of liquidity for other financial institutions and are the "transmission belt" for the implementation of monetary policy. A safe, sound banking system is thus viewed as essential to a nation's monetary system and financial marketplace.

A further concern of is that of systemic risk. *Systemic risk* occurs when bank failures are potentially contagious, and only then if the losses in one bank would cascade into other banks or to other economies throughout the world. Because the world's major economies are linked together through the financial markets and other business relationships, a major shock in the U.S. economy would have worldwide repercussions. Likewise, the East Asian financial crisis that began when Thailand devalued their currency in July 1997 had a ripple effect that spread throughout Southeast Asia, Russia, and Latin America.[3] Some large banks in the United States had trading losses in foreign exchange, and the stock market tumbled in the fall of 1998.

Federal Reserve Governor Meyer argues that "the possibility of a systemic failure of the banking system, and the moral hazard incentives created by the safety net that is designed to contain systemic risk, require some government supervision of banks."[4] In this case, *moral hazard* means that banks may take on more risk than is desirable from the deposit insurers' (safety net) point of view. If banks taking on the higher degree of risk are profitable, then shareholders gain. If, on the other hand, the banks fail, the FDIC loses. Therefore, some regulation is needed.

Guard Against Deposit Insurance Losses

In any debtor-creditor relationship, the creditor limits debtors' actions and monitors their behavior to ensure repayment of the loan. In the case of banks, the largest number of creditors are small depositors, most of whom are not capable of evaluating the financial condition of banks or monitoring their actions. Therefore, it is in the public interest to protect small depositors by having their deposits insured by a government agency, the Federal Deposit Insurance Corporation (FDIC). Thus, the FDIC represents the depositors and the public's interests to ensure that banks operate in sound fashion. If bank failures are large enough to exhaust the deposit insurance fund, the taxpayers will be called on to repay depositors. In the 1980s, more than 550 savings and loan associations (S&Ls) failed, which exhausted the Federal Savings and Loan Insurance Corporation's (FSLIC) insurance fund. The General Accounting Office estimated that the S&L debacle

3. Details of these crises are covered in Benton E. Gup, *International Banking Crises: Large-Scale Failures, Massive Government Intervention* (Westport, CT: Quorum Books, 1999).
4. L. H. Meyer, Board of Governors of the Federal Reserve System, Remarks before the Spring 1998 Banking and Finance Lecture, Widener University, PA (April 16, 1998).

cost federal taxpayers $132 billion.[5] In contrast to FSLIC, the FDIC had sufficient funds to cover the costs of the 1,617 bank failures during the 1980–1994 period.[6]

Social Goals

See http://www.bog.frb. fed.us/s-t.htm *for testimony and speeches by members of the Federal Reserve Board.*

Banks are regulated to achieve desired social goals. This public choice approach to regulation serves to reallocate resources from one group to another.[7] According to Federal Reserve Governor Edward Kelley, Jr., they are regulated "to promote an efficient and effective banking system that finances economic growth, impartially allocates credit, and meets the needs of the customers and communities that banks serve."[8] Thus, banks cannot discriminate against borrowers on the basis of race, gender, age, and other factors. Borrowers must be judged on the basis of their creditworthiness. In addition, they must supply borrowers with accurate information about the cost of borrowing.

2.2 BANK FAILURES

The focus in this section is on regulation in relation to bank failures and why banks fail. The three major reasons why individual banks fail are credit risk, interest rate risk, and foreign exchange risk. Two other potential sources of failure are bank runs and fraud. Bank runs will be explained shortly. Fraud is a legal concept, and what constitutes fraud in one country may be standard business practice in another. What was called "crony capitalism" in Indonesia (giving preferential treatment in terms of loans and grants to relatives and friends) is called fraud in the United States. Therefore, fraud is not addressed here.[9] This chapter specifically examines credit risk as a cause for failure. Interest rate risk and foreign exchange risk are addressed in later chapters.

5. For an excellent discussion of the S&L debacle, see *History of the Eighties: Lessons for the Future*, vol. 1, Federal Deposit Insurance Corporation (1997), Chapter 4 (The Savings and Loan Crises and Its Relationship to Banking). The $132 billion cost to taxpayers is from U.S. General Accounting Office, *Financial Audit: Resolution Trust Corporation's 1995 and 1994 Financial Statement*, GAO/AIMD-96-123 (July 1996).
6. *History of the Eighties: Lessons for the Future*, vol. 1, Federal Deposit Insurance Corporation (1997), Table 1.1.
7. George Stigler, "The Theory of Economic Regulation," *Bell Journal of Economics and Management Science*; Sam Peltzman, "Toward a More General Theory of Regulation," *Journal of Law and Economics*, vol. 19 (1976).
8. E. W. Kelley, Jr., "The Why, What, and How of Bank Regulation," in Federal Reserve Bank of Chicago, *Proceedings; Rethinking Bank Regulation: What Should Bank Regulators Do?* 32nd Bank Structure Conference (May 1996), pp. 24–28.
9. See Gup (1995, 1998) for a discussion of frauds that led to bank failures. Benton E. Gup, *Targeting Fraud: Uncovering and Deterring Fraud in Financial Institutions* (New York, McGraw-Hill, 1995); Benton E. Gup, *Bank Failures in the Major Trading Countries of the World: Causes and Remedies* (Westport CT.: Quorum Books, 1998).

Credit Risk

Banks' primary source of revenue is interest income from their loan portfolios, and their primary risk is credit risk. Credit risk was defined in Chapter 1 as the risk to earnings and capital that an obligor will fail to meet the terms of any contract with the bank, or otherwise fail to perform as agreed. It is usually associated with loans and investments.

Bankers know that lending is a risky business and that some of the loans will not be repaid. Therefore they set aside a reserve for expected losses, usually 1–2% of total loans and leases. If the losses exceed the amount set aside, the excess amount of losses is deducted from bank capital. If the losses are large enough to eliminate most of the banks' capital, the bank will fail unless additional capital is added.

The amount of financial leverage (bank capital relative to the assets) is important. Bank's ratio of capital to assets declined from more than 50% in the 1840s to less than 10% in the 1990s. A small capital base puts banks at greater risk of failure if it experiences large losses. Federal Reserve Chairman Alan Greenspan had the following to say about bank's financial leverage:

> No matter how regulated and supervised, throughout our history many of the benefits banks provide modern societies derive from their willingness to take risk and from their use of a relatively high degree of financial leverage. . . . But it is also that very same leverage that makes banks so sensitive to the risk that they take and aligns the stability of the economy with the critical role of supervision, both by supervisors and by the market.[10]

In order to examine the process of bank growth and failure, we make five simplifying assumptions. First, the stakeholders in a bank include shareholders, managers, employees, customers, and the communities they serve. Each of these stakeholders wants to maximize personal utility. They see higher growth of assets, loans, and profits as a means to an end. Simply stated, everyone wants the bank to grow in order to benefit their own position.

Second, some bank loans go bad over time because of factors unique to the individual borrower. Alternatively, changes in macroeconomic or international conditions might adversely affect a large number of borrowers, causing them to default. Such macroeconomic and international factors include, but are not limited to, shocks in interest rates and exchange rates, widespread asset price deflation, and global contagion.

Third, we assume that the bank in the following example has an excess concentration of loans to a single group of borrowers. In countries with developed capital market like the United States, not being adequately diversified is considered poor management. In a developing country with repressed financial markets, banks do not have the same opportunities to diversify their portfolios as banks in

---

10. Remarks by Alan Greenspan before the Annual meeting and Conference of State Bank Supervisors, Nashville, Tennessee, May 2, 1998, "Board of Governors of the Federal Reserve System (May 2, 1998).

developed capital markets. **Financial repression** implies that the government intervenes heavily in the economy and in the financial markets. In South Korea, for example, nationalized banks in the 1960s were told by the government to make loans to *chaebols*, large conglomerate business groups, to finance government-directed investment projects. The creditworthiness of the *chaebols* was not an issue because the government "encouraged" the banks to lend to them.

Fourth, the loans are not backed by collateral.

Fifth, the loan-to-value ratio is 100%. That is, the bank lends 100% of the amount of the value of the underlying asset.

Bank Growth and Failure

Consider the hypothetical bank that is shown in Table 2.1, Panel A. It has a single loan as its sole asset, which is funded by deposits and stockholder equity. The ratio of equity capital to risk assets (E/A) is sufficiently large so that the bank is well capitalized at 10%, and it has an ample loan loss reserve. In addition, the bank is profitable. It has a return on assets (ROA) of 2.88%, more than twice the 1.22% ROA for all FDIC-insured commercial banks in the United States in 1998.[11] As previously noted, the stakeholders of the bank want it to grow, which translates into higher returns on investment, higher salaries, and other perks.

In order to grow, the bank raises an additional $20 million in deposits, and it invests those funds in two loans of $10 million each (Table 2.1, Panel B).[12] No additional loan loss reserves are required. In this period, the ROA is 2.73%, and the ratio of equity to assets is 8.33%, meaning that the bank is adequately capitalized.

In the next period, which is shown in Table 2.1, Panel C, one of the $10 million loan goes into default for reasons exclusive to the borrower. The $10 million default exceeds the loan loss reserve by $8 million. That difference is deducted from stockholders' equity, leaving only $2 million in equity. After the deduction, the bank has tangible equity/risk assets of 1.79%. Now the bank is critically undercapitalized, and it fails unless additional capital is injected.[13]

What could the bank have done to reduce its credit risk? First, look at its undue loan concentration; the bank loaned too much of its capital to a single borrower. Excess concentration can also occur with particular types of loans. For example, a large number of bank failures are associated with real estate

---

11. FDIC Quarterly Banking Profile (Third Quarter 1998).
12. J. G. Haubrich, "Bank Diversification: Laws and Fallacies of Large Numbers," *Economic Review*, Federal Reserve Bank of Cleveland, vol. 34, no. 2 (1998), pp. 2–9. Haubrich (1998) provides an interesting discussion of the relationships between bank growth, diversification, and risk. In general terms, banks grow by adding risky loans. Using the weak law of large numbers, he shows that diversified banks have a reduced expected failure rate. However, they are not necessarily less risky, overall.
13. A bank is "critically undercapitalized" when its tangible equity of 2% or less.

TABLE 2.1	Bank Growth and Losses (Credit Risk)

Panel A

Assets ($ millions)				Liabilities	
Loan	$102 @ 9%			Deposits	$90 @ 7%
Loan loss reserve	− 2				
Net loans	$100				
				Stockholders' equity	$10
Totals	$100				$100
Net income	$9.18 − $6.30	=	$2.88		
Return on assets (ROA)	$2.88/$100	=	2.88%		
Equity/Assets (E/A)	$10/$100	=	10% well capitalized		

Panel B

Assets ($ millions)				Liabilities	
Loan	$102 @ 9%			Deposits	$110 @ 7%
Loan	10 @ 9%				
Loan	10 @ 9%				
Loan loss reserve	− 2				
Net loans	$120				
				Stockholders' equity	$10
Totals	$120				$120
Net income	$10.98 − $7.70	=	$3.28		
Return on assets (ROA)	$3.28/$120	=	2.73%		
Equity/Assets (E/A)	$10/$120	=	8.33% Adequately capitalized		

Panel C

Assets ($ millions)				Liabilities	
Loan	$102 @ 9%			Deposits	$110 @ 7%
Loan	10 @ 9%				
Loan default	− 10				
Loan loss reserve	2				
Net loans	$112				
				Stockholders' equity	$2
Totals	$112				$112

The defaulted loan of $10 exceeds loan loss reserve by $8, which is deducted from stockholders' equity.

Net income	$10.08 − $7.70	=	$2.38
Return on assets (ROA)	$2.38/$112	=	2.13%
Equity/Assets (E/A)	$2/$1112	=	1.79%

The bank is "critically undercapitalized," and it fails.

loans. Therefore, a bank with a portfolio that is primarily real estate loans may face more risk than a bank with a well-diversified portfolio. As previously noted, banks in repressed financial markets may not have a choice about loan concentration. Banks in developed capital markets, however, have better loan opportunities and can avoid undue concentration.

Second, the loan-to-value ratio and collateral are important determinants of a borrower's vested interest in an loan. From the borrower's point of view, a high loan-to-value ratio (i.e., 100%) is desirable. From the bank's point of view, a lower loan-to-value ratio, say 70–80%, is desirable to reduce risk. In a competitive environment, some banks will compete on the terms of the loan as well as interest rate and forego safety in order to grow.

Third, the bank could have reduced its risk by requiring collateral that could be sold in the event of default. For example, the borrower has not made monthly loan payments for the past six months. With collateral, borrowers have a positive incentive to make payments and avoid losing that valuable collateral.

Fourth, the creditworthiness of the borrower was not an issue at the time the loan was made. Nevertheless, over time, that creditworthiness deteriorated to the extent that the loan went into default. Regular monitoring of the loan may give the bank sufficient early warning to deal with the borrower's problems and avoid the default.

Fifth, the bank could have hedged some of its credit risk with credit derivatives. Credit derivatives are a new and growing part of the derivatives market. Credit derivatives include credit default contracts, total return swaps, credit spread contracts, and credit linked notes. These products are explained in a later chapter.

Bank Runs

Bank runs occur when depositors or other creditors fear for the safety or availability of their funds, and large numbers of depositors try to withdraw their funds at the same time. Banks do not keep enough cash on hand to meet large-scale unexpected withdrawals of deposits. Deposits can be withdrawn on a first-come, first-served basis. Therefore, a run reflects the herd behavior of depositors to obtain the limited amount of cash that is available. In August 1998, CNN and other television stations showed long lines of Russians citizens trying to withdraw their funds from local banks during the financial debacle in Russia. The Russian government defaulted on the payment of some of its securities, and the citizens thought that the banks were unsound. The banks were not able to pay off all depositors, and they were closed.

Similarly, a "silent run" occurs when large creditors, such as banks and investment companies, withdraw their funds in order to protect them, as happened to Continental Illinois Bank in 1974. International banks had uninsured deposits of millions of dollars in Continental. Subsequently, Continental Illinois Bank failed.

A bank run on one bank may spark bank runs on other banks and create a domino or *contagion effect*. In such a case, solvent banks that lack liquidity may be able to borrow from the Federal Reserve—the lender of last resort.

Finally, it should be noted that bank runs are not limited to uninsured deposits. On Friday, January 4, 1991, the Bank of New England announced that it expected a loss that would render it technically insolvent.[14] Depositors had a run on the bank during which they withdrew more than $1 billion. Although their deposits were insured, they did not want to be inconvenienced, and they wanted liquidity. On Sunday, January 6, 1991, the bank failed, due in part to the run. It was declared insolvent by the Office of the Comptroller of the Currency (OCC), and the FDIC was appointed as receiver.

2.3 FOUNDATION OF THE PRESENT REGULATORY FRAMEWORK

More than 14,000 banks failed between 1921 and 1929. Most were small banks in rural, agricultural communities. Failures and mergers (many of the latter serving to forestall failure) had reduced the number of commercial banks to about 25,000 in 1929. The economic collapse known as the Great Depression began that year. Legislation stemming from the economic crisis of the 1930s is responsible for our present banking structure. The following sections examine the principal laws that shaped the current banking structure.

The Banking Act of 1933 (Glass-Steagall Act)

The **Banking Act of 1933**, also known as the *Glass-Steagall Act*, did the following:

1. Separated commercial banking from investment banking (underwriting securities)
2. Established the Federal Deposit Insurance Corporation (FDIC)
3. Permitted the Federal Reserve to regulate the interest paid on time deposits, and prohibited the payment of interest on demand deposits
4. Raised the minimum capital requirements for national banks

SECURITIES POWER The Glass-Steagall Act prohibited commercial banks from engaging in **investment banking**, which is the underwriting issues of corporate securities and nonguaranteed revenue bonds of state and local governments. The separation of commercial and investment banking was regarded as a means of reducing bank risk, and was intended to help restore public

14. *History of the Eighties: Lessons for the Future*, vol. 1, Washington, D.C., Federal Deposit Insurance Corporation (1997), p. 375.

confidence in commercial banks. Further, some legislators were swayed by alleged abuses—specifically, conflict of interest—stemming from mixture of the two functions. The concern was based on the concentration of financial power in institutions that exercised commercial banking, investment banking, and trust powers. In the early 1930s, commercial and investment banking were almost totally integrated. The new law thus obliged the numerous institutions performing both functions to choose either commercial or investment banking as their line of business and divest themselves of the other.

DEPOSIT INSURANCE The Glass-Steagall Act established federal **deposit insurance** to protect small depositors, thereby reducing the incidence of bank runs. With insured deposits, depositors have less incentive to join in "runs." The creation of deposit insurance is credited with having stabilized the U.S. banking system in the wake of crises in the 1930s. At that time the deposits were insured for a maximum of $2,500, and Federal Deposit Insurance Corporation (FDIC) was funded by premiums of one-twelfth of 1% of the domestic deposits (less certain adjustments) of insured banks.

The Banking Act of 1935

The **Banking Act of 1935** was intended primarily to strengthen the Federal Reserve System and its monetary management power. It gave the Federal Reserve Board expanded reserve requirement authority. With it, the Federal Reserve could regulate discount rates of the district banks, as well as the rate of interest paid by member banks on time and savings deposits. The discount rate is the rate at which member banks can borrow from the Federal Reserve.

The 1935 act also marked the end of easy entry into banking. Congress, seeking to curb the high rate of bank failure that had long characterized the U.S. banking system, gave the Comptroller of the Currency greater discretion in the granting of national bank charters.[15] Applicants for a charter demonstrate the need for the proposed bank and make the case that the new bank would be successful without significantly injuring existing banks. If the applicant's case is not convincing to the Comptroller, or if the Comptroller's own investigation of these issues raises reasons for denial, the charter is not issued.

The effect of greater restrictions on bank entry is evident in the record of new bank charters. During the 1920s, new bank charters granted averaged about 360 per year. From 1935 until the U.S. entry into World War II an average of only about 50 new banks were chartered each year. Although this sharp reduction in

The Library of Congress keeps up to date information on current legislation, reports, laws, and so on. For further information, see http://thomas.loc.gov/.

---

15. The title "Comptroller of the Currency" originated with the National Bank Act of 1864. Notes issued by national banks were to be the circulating currency, and the Comptroller exercised some monetary control functions. Since then, the role of the Office of the Comptroller of the Currency (OCC) in the administration of currency has been reduced to "minute administrative functions." For more details on their current operations, see their web page: *http://www.occ.treas.gov.*

the rate of new bank charters largely reflected depressed economic conditions (and thus a decline in requests for charters), it also reflected the greater difficulty of obtaining a charter under the 1935 act. In the postwar expansion (1945–1960) the annual average of new bank charters remained below 100.

2.4 REVIEW OF THE 1930S

The structure and nature of U.S. banking changed dramatically in the 1930s as a result of the wave of bank failures and the reform legislation it evoked. The reduction in the number of banks proved to be enduring, partly as a result of increased entry restrictions. Deposit insurance became a salient feature of the U.S. banking system. Bank failures became rare until the 1980s.

The 1933 and 1935 banking acts, in conjunction with previously existing regulation, set in place a regulatory structure that placed the following constraints on banks:

1. *Pricing:* restrictions on pricing of deposits
2. *Geography:* restrictions on entry and geographic expansion
3. *Products:* restrictions on scope and nature of activities, especially limitations of the securities activities of commercial banks
4. *Capital:* restrictions on minimum capital requirements and on other balance sheet elements

After the reforms of the 1930s, banking entered a relatively tranquil period. Banks, like the rest of the U.S. economy, remained generally depressed until World War II. Not until the late 1940s did banking regain its pre-Depression vitality. The ratio of bank loans to assets (only 16% in 1945 compared to 63% in 1925 ratio) began to rise steadily throughout the 1950s. This resurgence of bank lending continued in the vigorous economic expansion of the 1960s, with banks becoming more aggressive, competitive, and less averse to risk. U.S. banks dramatically expanded their foreign banking activities, and sought new growth outside traditional banking avenues.

2.5 BANK REFORMS SINCE 1980

By the late 1970s, it was apparent that the severe set of restrictions imposed on commercial banks in the 1930s was inconsistent with the innovations taking place in the financial world. In particular, the limitations on the maximum rates that banks could pay on deposits (i.e., Regulation Q ceilings) had caused banks to lose substantial amounts of funds to nonbank institutions, particularly money market mutual funds. Recall that in the late 1970s, interest rates soared from about 5% to about 18%, and banks and thrifts suffered.

Limitations on the geographic area over which banks could offer their services also generated a great deal of concern as banks' customer base became increasingly mobile. All these concerns raised questions about whether the limits placed on bank activities were really achieving their objectives. As a result, a number of proposals were advanced to "deregulate" banking.

Deregulation in banking has three separate although closely related dimensions: price (e.g., deposit rate) deregulation, product deregulation, and geographic deregulation. *Price deregulation* refers to the lifting of legal restrictions on the interest rates that depository institutions may pay to obtain funds (and to a lesser extent, in terms of the importance of the restrictions, on the rates that may be charged for loans, commonly referred to as *usury laws*). *Product deregulation* refers to the removal of the restrictions placed on banks and other depository institutions regarding the types of services offered, such as investment banking services or insurance underwriting. *Geographic deregulation*, of course, refers to the removal of limitations on the geographic area in which banks (and other depository institutions) may locate and operate deposit-taking facilities.

Depository Institutions Deregulation and Monetary Control Act (DIDMCA)

The **Depository Institutions Deregulation and Monetary Control Act (DIDMCA)** was passed in 1980 and provided, among other things, for the following:

1. *Uniform reserve requirements:* Reserve requirements were extended to all depository institutions, commercial banks, mutual savings banks, savings and loan associations, credit unions, agencies and branches of foreign banks, and Edge Act corporations. Only size and type of deposit are relevant in determining reserve requirements.

2. *Federal Reserve services:* Services provided by the Federal Reserve, such as check clearing and providing vault cash, must be offered to all depository institutions and must be priced on the basis of the Fed's production costs plus a "normal" profit margin. Before this legislation was passed, the Fed provided its services only to member banks and then generally without explicit cost.

3. *Regulation Q:* The legislation began the process of eliminating interest rate ceilings on deposit accounts at all depository institutions. It created the Depository Institutions Deregulation Committee with instructions to eliminate those ceilings completely no later than March 1986.

4. *Deposit insurance:* It raised the ceiling for insured deposits from $40,000 ceiling at that time to $100,000.

5. *Negotiable order of withdrawal (NOW) accounts:* The legislation authorized all depository institutions to offer interest-bearing transactions accounts, generally in the form of NOW accounts. For the first time on

a nationwide basis the traditional monopoly by commercial banks of transaction (checking) accounts was broken. Also, for the first time in almost 50 years, explicit interest payments on transactions accounts were allowed.

6. *Savings and loans:* The lending powers of savings and loans were broadened, which allowed them to commit a substantial fraction of their assets to consumer loans. They were also given trust powers. The reforms of the powers of savings and loans contained in this legislation went a long way toward the creation of a "department store of family finance" in the form of savings and loan associations.

The Garn–St. Germain Depository Institutions Act of 1982

The provisions of The **Garn–St. Germain Depository Institutions Act** of 1982 addressed many of the problems that had not been resolved by the 1980 legislation. The DIDMCA of 1980 attempted to deal with the interest rate ceilings. By 1982 the thrift institutions problem had become a thrift institutions crisis and reflected the extraordinarily high interest rate environment of 1981–1982. As a result, the bill provided for the following:

1. *FDIC/FSLIC assistance for floundering and failing institutions:* In past years the regulatory agencies had been constrained in the purchase of floundering or failing institutions by restrictive laws on interstate acquisition of failing institutions. The new law allowed for acquisition according to the following priority schedule: (a) same type of institution, same state; (b) same type of institution, different state; (c) different type of institution, same state; (d) different type of institution, different state. For example, if the failing institution was a commercial bank in Texas, the first potential acquirer would be another bank in Texas; the second potential acquirer would be a commercial bank located outside Texas; the third potential acquirer would be another type of financial institution in Texas; and the fourth potential group of acquiring institutions would be another type of financial institution located outside Texas.

2. *Net worth certificates:* The 1982 legislation provided for an exchange of debt (called net worth certificates) between depository institutions and the regulatory agencies. Although it established substantial legal significance in maintaining an adequate capital position for floundering and failing depository institutions, this portion of the 1982 legislation was of relatively minor economic importance.

3. *Additional thrift institution restructuring:* Savings and loans and other thrifts were given even greater powers: savings and loans were permitted to offer demand deposit services to qualified commercial, corporate, and agricultural customers, and to expand consumer lending and engage in a limited amount of commercial lending.

4. *Money market deposit accounts:* Perhaps the most significant feature of the 1982 legislation was the provision instructing the Deregulation Committee to create (within 60 days) a money market deposit account equivalent to and competitive with money market mutual funds. The Deregulation Committee created such an instrument effective in January 1983.

Financial Institutions Reform, Recovery, and Enforcement Act (FIRREA) 1989

Unfortunately, neither DIDMICA nor the Garn–St. Germain Act solved all the serious problems confronting thrift institutions, especially the savings and loan industry. By early 1989 almost 500 savings and loan associations (S&Ls) were insolvent or close to failure. These failures resulted principally from credit risk problems associated with the new power given to S&Ls in the early 1980s. The growing crisis in the thrift industry led to the passage of the **Financial Institutions Reform, Recovery, and Enforcement Act (FIRREA)**, signed into law on August 9, 1989. The law sought to stem the rising tide of red ink in the thrift industry, which the General Accounting Office claims cost the taxpayers $132 billion. Other estimates of losses range up to $200 billion. Although the thrift crisis was much smaller in magnitude than bank losses during the Great Depression of the 1930s, thrift losses in the 1980s and 1990s exceeded those suffered by depositors in the Great Depression. The thrift crisis drew attention to problems in the financial system that FIRREA attempted to overcome.

REGULATORY STRUCTURE FIRREA made changes in the structure of the regulatory agencies and the deposit insurance system. First, the Federal Home Loan Bank Board (FHLBB) was closed and ceased to be the regulator for thrifts. The Office of Thrift Supervision (OTS), a bureau of the U.S. Treasury, was established to replace it. OTS is responsible for chartering federal savings institutions and examining and supervising federally insured thrifts and their holding companies. Second, the Federal Housing Finance Board was established to coordinate the activities of the 12 Federal Home Loan (FHL) banks, which provide loans to member institutions for housing finance. OTS took over the previous supervisory powers held by the FHL banks. Third, and last, the FSLIC was dissolved and replaced with the Savings Associations Insurance Funds (SAIF), which is under FDIC control. (The Bank Insurance Fund, or BIF, is also under FDIC control and insures commercial bank deposits.)

THRIFT REREGULATION FIRREA reversed some of the asset powers given to thrifts under the Garn–St. Germain Act of 1982 and increased their capital requirements. To avoid being regulated as banks, thrifts must conform to qualified thrift-lender (QTL) standards. QTLs have at least 70% of their assets in real estate-related assets (e.g., home loans and securities backed by mortgages). Junk bonds are prohibited, and commercial real estate is limited considerably, as is the amount that can be loaned to a single customer. Further, state-chartered S&Ls are generally prohibited from engaging in activities not allowed by federally chartered S&Ls.

New capital requirements for thrifts were intended to increase the stake the shareholders (owners) have invested in each thrift and, thereby, reduce insurance losses and encourage more prudent management. The ratio of core capital to total assets must be at least 3%. (Core capital is composed of stockholders' equity plus a certain amount of goodwill.) At least 50% of core capital must represent tangible capital, calculated as tangible assets minus liabilities. Moreover, S&Ls are required to meet capital standards imposed on national banks. Under an international agreement (known as the Basle Agreement), national banks must have capital, defined as stockholders' equity plus some types of debt and other items, equal to at least 8% of risk-adjusted assets and off-balance-sheet items. At least 4% of this capital ratio had to be in the form of stockholders' equity by year-end 1992. Failure to comply with these guidelines will cause an S&L to be put on a problem list, with subsequent possibility of limits on its deposit rates, asset growth, and dividend payments to stockholders. These higher capital requirements attempt to blunt the incentives for insured thrifts to take excessive risks

ENFORCEMENT POWERS Last, FIRREA enhanced the enforcement powers of bank and thrift regulators, who were given new expanded "cease-and-desist" authority and the ability to impose civil money penalties (CMPs) for violations of regulatory and statutory procedures. It also established judicial civil penalties and more stringent criminal penalties for financial institution offenses. These enforcement powers are intended to reduce risks from fraud, which played a significant role in the thrift crisis.

Another important provision of FIRREA is *cross-bank guarantees*. Congress added a statute in FIRREA that makes healthy banks in a multibank holding company (MBHC) liable to the FDIC for the losses of failed member banks. This *source of strength doctrine* means that bank holding companies act as a source of financial strength for their affiliates. Unlike the past, if a failed bank in a MBHC incurs losses for the FDIC in its closure and assistance activities, the FDIC can charge the losses against the net worth of profitable banks affiliated with the MBHC. This change in insurance liability for MBHCs should help reduce the risk of bank failures.

FIRREA also allowed bank holding companies to acquire saving and loan associations. The S&L failures plus acquisitions led to further consolidation in the S&L industry. During the 1980s the number of thrifts declined from approximately 4,000 to about 2,200. By restricting thrift activities and raising capital requirements, bank holding company (BHC) acquisitions of thrifts continued throughout the 1990s.

FIRREA represents a dramatic shift in the regulatory reform of the early 1980s. It not only completely restructured the regulatory system for savings and loans but also brought a temporary halt in the trend toward financial deregulation.

Federal Deposit Insurance Corporation Improvement Act of 1991 (FDICIA)

The **FDIC Improvement Act of 1991 (FDICIA)** focused primarily on interrelated capital requirements and deposit insurance issues in depository institutions.

Federal banking agencies are empowered to apply **prompt corrective action (PCA)** to undercapitalized institutions that are increasingly restrictive as the institution's capital declines. The risk-based capital requirements expressed as a percentage of risk-weighed assets are shown in Table 2.2. Some examples of restrictive measures that may be required are the addition of more capital, the denial of an acquisition or merger, the termination of activities posing excessive risk, replacement of directors or officers, divestiture of a subsidiary or affiliate company, or disapproval of bonuses and salary increases. Restrictions on asset growth, deposit interest rates, and dividends could be imposed under certain capital conditions. The act requires the FDIC to close an institution when it reaches a critically undercapitalized position.

Also, the act severely restricted the ability of the FDIC to protect uninsured depositors in bank failures, an issue that is particularly relevant in the failure of large banks, known as the too-big-to-fail doctrine.

It should be clear from the design of the act that capital and deposit insurance are linked to one another. Capital is needed to absorb initial losses, and deposit insurance is necessary to cover more serious losses that exhaust capital reserves. The thrust of the changes is to shift more of the burden of losses from the public to depository institutions. To the extent that more capital is required and penalties are imposed for capital shortfalls, less deposit insurance should be needed in the long run.

The FDICIA also made numerous changes in the *deposit insurance system*. The FDIC can borrow $30 billion from the U.S. Treasury (raised from $5 billion previously), and the FDIC can impose special assessments on insured institutions to repay FDIC borrowings. In a related measure the FDIC increased the

TABLE 2.2	Capital Adequacy
Capital Adequacy	**Total Risk-Based Capital %***
Well capitalized	≥ 10%
Adequately capitalized	≥ 8%
Undercapitalized	≥ 6
Significantly undercapitalized	< 6
Critically capitalized	–

*As a percentage of risk-weighted assets.

deposit insurance fees to bring federal insurance reserves up to 1.25% of all insured deposits. It also developed a risk-based deposit insurance scheme. These changes shifted the burden of failed institution losses from taxpayers to banks. Theory and practice suggest that these higher insurance costs will be shared by different parties benefiting from depository institutions' services, namely, depositors, borrowers, and shareholders.

Omnibus Budget Reconciliation Act of 1993

The **Omnibus Budget Reconciliation Act of 1993** provided that insured depositors of failed banks have a priority of claims over noninsured depositor/creditor claims. Large deposits by businesses and state and local governments are not covered by FDIC insurance. The motivation behind this provision is to encourage creditors to monitor bank risk behavior thereby instilling **market discipline** on the banks. Creditors can impose market discipline on risky institutions by not making deposits, withdrawing their funds, requiring collateral against deposits, requiring guarantees, and/or requiring interest rates that are commensurate with the risks they are taking.

Riegle-Neal Interstate Banking and Branching Efficiency Act of 1994

The **Riegle-Neal Interstate Banking and Branching Efficiency Act** opened the door for interstate banking by allowing bank holding companies to acquire banks in any state, subject to certain conditions. Beginning in 1997, the Act eased most restrictions on interstate branching. The Riegle-Neal Act was one of the factors contributing to bank mergers and increased banking concentration that was mentioned in Chapter 1.

Financial Services Modernization Act of 1999

Another catalyst for change and mergers, the **Financial Services Modernization Act** (also known as the Gramm-Leach-Bliley Act of 1999) was signed into law in November 14, 1999. It marked the end of the 1933 Glass-Steagall prohibitions concerning the separation of banks from investment banking, and the 1956 Bank Holding Company Act's prohibitions against insurance underwriting. It allows banks, brokerage firms, and insurers to merge. In addition, "financial holding companies" may engage in a wide range of financial activities including underwriting insurance and securities, merchant banking, and real estate and development. Now banks are allowed to underwrite securities in their direct subsidiaries, and use them for insurance or securities sales or other low-risk activities. Finally, national banks can underwrite municipal revenue bonds.

Despite the liberalization offered by the act, barriers between commerce and banking still prevent firms such as Wal-Mart from offering financial services by establishing new savings and loan associations known as unitary thrifts. The law also prevents unitary thrifts from being sold to commercial businesses.

The Financial Services Modernization Act of 1999 opened the door for further consolidation in the financial services industry. It is expected that banks will buy insurers, brokerage firms will buy banks, and so on. Thus, the act paved the way for the development of financial supermarkets to serve the needs of consumers. One expected benefit of consolidation is that diversification of services and geography will serve to strengthen financial institutions that heretofore served limited geographic markets with limited products.

Depending on the financial services being offered, the firms will be regulated by the Federal Reserve, the OCC, the Securities and Exchange Commission, and 50 state insurance regulators. An article in *The Economist* described this arrangement as "hopelessly fragmented and costly."[16]

2.6 BANKING AND COMMERCE ARRANGEMENTS IN OTHER COUNTRIES[17]

The banking laws in the United States differ substantially from those in other developed countries.

Germany

Universal banking exists in Germany, and banks can perform commercial and investment banking activities directly (no holding company structure is required) and insurance and real estate activities via subsidiaries. Banks can own commercial firms directly, but in practice their ownership is small. Commercial firms can own banks, although few do, given the regulations they must meet.

United Kingdom

The web site for the Bank of England reveals banking developments for one of the world's leading central banks. See http://www. bankofengland.co.uk/.

Clearing banks in the United Kingdom engage in commercial and investment banking, and in merchant banking, insurance activities, and real estate activities via subsidiaries. No formal policy separates banking and commerce, but tradition has encouraged it by restraining bank investments in nonfinancial firm equity, and such investments are not common. The Bank of England must approve firms taking a 15% or greater stake in a U.K. bank, and individuals who own more than a 5% stake in a U.K. bank must report it to the Bank of England.

16. "Killing Glass-Steagall," *The Economist* (October 30, 1999), pp. 18–19.
17. Loretta Mester, "Banking and Commerce: A Dangerous Liaison?" Federal Reserve Bank of Philadelphia, *Business Review* (May/June 1992), p. 21.

Japan

Check out the Bank of Japan at http://www.boj.or.jp/en. *The Bank of Japan is the nation's central bank.*

The Japanese banking system was modeled on the U.S. system after World War II, and commercial and investment banking were separated then. Japanese banks can perform commercial bank activities and have minority ownership (5% or less) in subsidiaries that perform leasing, insurance, credit card business, and management consulting. Until 1987, banks could hold up to 10% of the outstanding shares in any company, but through cross-holding could effectively hold much more; a bank can be a main bank in *keiretsu* (a conglomerate group) and through it have large ties to commercial firms.

European Economic Community (EEC)

Banks are allowed to engage in commercial and investment banking activities but no insurance activities. A bank is limited to 10% of its own equity as a stake in an individual commercial firm, with the total stake in commercial firm equity not to exceed 50% of bank capital. Commercial firms may own banks if such action is considered suitable by the national regulator.

In summary, at first glance, foreign banks may appear to be "commercial banks." On closer inspection, however, they may engage in activities that are considered speculative in the United States. They may take equity positions in their corporate customers, or they may be owned by corporate customers. For example, in another of the world's economic systems, industrial companies in Russia have set up most of the banks in order to finance themselves.[18]

Harmonization

The Basle Committee is located at the Bank for International Settlements in Basle, Switzerland. For the latest developments at the BIS, see http://www.bis.org/.

International banking regulators have undertaken major efforts to harmonize prudential standards. **Harmonization** refers to uniform international banking regulations. It also refers to stemming the divergent standards applied to similar activities of different financial institutions. The Basle Committee on Banking Supervision, a committee of national financial supervisors, has led the effort toward uniform standards. In 1988, the Basle Committee established uniform risk-based capital standards for banks and, later, methods for dealing with trading risks. In the European Union (EU), harmonization is reflected in a number of Directives and Recommendations. For example, the EU's Second Banking Directive, adopted in 1989, establishes home country control, and recognizes national supervisory regimes. The Second Banking Directive also established a listing of banking activities subject to mutual recognition, such as leasing, lending, guarantees, investment banks, and money brokering. Although the focus here is on

---

18. W. Jackson, "Universal Banking (Deposits and Diversified Industries in One Company?)," CRS Report For Congress, 95-579-E, Washington, D.C., Congressional Research Service (April 25, 1995).

the Basle Committee, one should recognize that other international supervisory groups coordinate some of their activities with the Basle Committee.

The EU's Own Funds Directive and Solvency Ratio Directive are generally consistent with the recommendations of the Basle Committee. With respect to services offered by different types of financial institutions, some countries eliminate the distinctions between banks and nonbank financial institutions for purposes of regulation. For example, in France, the 1984 Bank Law eliminated the distinction between commercial banks, savings banks, and medium and long-term credit banks. In 1990, the Banking Act in Switzerland was amended to put nonbank financial institutions and underwriters under the same regulations as banks.[19]

Finally, the International Monetary Fund (IMF) becomes involved in bank regulation during banking crises. In the crises in Southeast Asia that began in 1997, for example, the IMF programs included closure of nonviable financial institutions, recapitalization of undercapitalized institutions, close supervision of weak institutions, and more.[20]

2.7   THE DUAL BANKING SYSTEM

Bank Charter Type

Congress gave the Office of the Comptroller of the Currency (OCC) the authority to issue **national bank charters**. National banks have the word *National*, or the letters *N.A.* standing for "national association" in their names. However, banks can also be charted by any of the 50 state bank commissions. Thus, the United States has a **dual banking system** whereby banks can choose to have a national or a state charter.

Banks that have a national charter are required to be members of the Federal Reserve System. Banks that have state charters may elect to be members of the Federal Reserve. About 2,500 of the nation's 8,900 banks are national banks. The national banks include some of the largest banks in the country, and they accounted for 58% of total bank deposits in June 1998. State banks that were members of the Federal Reserve system held 19% of total deposits, and nonmember state banks held 23%.

See http://www.fdic.gov/bank/index.html *for data on individual banks and other banking statistics.*

Charter Type	Regulator	Member of Federal Reserve
National bank	OCC	Required
State bank	State banking commission	Optional

19. U.S. Department of Treasury, *National Treatment Study, 1994* (Washington, D.C.: December 1994).
20. "The IMF's Response to the Asian Crisis" (Washington, D.C.: International Monetary Fund, April 16, 1998).

Regulating Virtual Banks

Companies without walls are called *virtual companies*. These stripped-down companies use computer networks, phones, and fax machines to link the various parts of their businesses together. It is not necessary for all employees to be located in the same place to run a business. Much of what was formerly done by one company located in one place can be subcontracted or "outsourced." Now suppose that company provides banking services. The company could be located anywhere in the world, and operate over the Internet or by satellite network. How could such an institution be regulated, or could it?

Bank Holding Company

The process of regulation becomes more involved when bank holding companies are involved. A **bank holding company** is a corporation that holds stock in one or more banks and other financial service organizations. Bank holding companies are authorized by law or by permission of the Federal Reserve to engage in a wide variety of nonbanking activities that are closely related to banking. These activities include, but are not limited to, making and servicing loans, trust company functions, certain leasing activities, providing investment and financial advice, operating savings associations, and securities brokerage.[21]

Bank holding companies are regulated by the Federal Reserve. Therefore, the Federal Reserve regulates bank holding companies that may include both national and state chartered banks. The overlapping responsibilities led to turf battles between the Federal Reserve, the OCC, and state banks over which agency was to regulate certain banking activities under Section 20 of the Glass-Stegall Act.[22] Section 20 deals with the separation of commercial banking from certain investment banking activities. The issue was resolved with the passage of the Financial Services Modernization Act of 1999, which gave most of the regulatory power to supervise securities and insurance in holding companies to the Federal Reserve.

The turf wars extend beyond bank regulatory agencies. The Securities and Exchange Commission has concerns about bank regulators' ability to do a good job regulating the securities business of banks. Moreover, bank regulators regulating banks' securities business would water down the authority of the SEC.[23]

What's going on in terms of current banking legislation? For an answer to that question, see the House Committee on Banking and Financial Services to obtain testimony on proposed legislation. http://www.house.gov/banking/.

21. 12 CFR 225.25(b), Federal Reserve Regulation "Y."
22. The regulation of Section 20 Securities Affiliates of bank holding companies has been a source of dispute between the Federal Reserve and the OCC. For a discussion of Section 20 Securities Affiliates, see S. H. Kwan, "Securities Activities by Commercial Banking Firm's Section 20 Subsidiaries: Risk, Return and Diversification Benefits," Federal Reserve Bank of San Francisco, Working Paper 98-10 (1998).
23. M. Schroeder, "Bank Regulators, SEC Jockey to Be the New Securities Czar," *The Wall Street Journal* (February 24, 1999), pp. C1, C15.

What Bank Regulators Do

Commercial banks are private business corporations with a public role. That role includes their participation in the money supply, payments system, insured deposits, and more. Because of this public side of banking, they are regulated. Bank regulators have four primary responsibilities: chartering, regulating, supervising and examining. Additional duties are not covered here. For example, the Federal Reserve must approve bank mergers; it is specifically charged with the regulation of bank holding companies; it can lend money to banks at the "discount window"; and it acts as a lender of last resort.[24] Thus, not all bank regulators have exactly the same responsibilities.

CHARTERING As previously noted, the OCC and state banking commissions have the authority to charter banks. In doing so, they must determine whether the proposed bank will have adequate capital and proper management for its respective market area. They also have to take into account the needs and convenience of the community, competition, and other factors.

REGULATE The terms *regulation* and *supervision* are sometimes used interchangeably. However, they are technically different. Bank regulation refers to "the formulation and issuance by authorized agencies of specific rules or regulations, under governing law for the structure and conduct of banking. . . . Bank supervision is concerned primarily with the safety and soundness of individual banks, and involves general and continuous oversight to assure that banks are operated prudently in accordance with applicable statutes and regulations."[25] Today, regulations involve the types of products that banks can offer, such as investment banking, insurance, and brokerage services, enforcement of laws such as the Truth in Lending Act, and rules involving safety and soundness.

SUPERVISE Supervision is exercised by regulators to ensure that bankers comply with banking regulations. Bank examinations are one means of evaluating compliance.

Bank supervisors have a variety of techniques at their disposal to deal with problem banks not in compliance with rules and regulations. The least intrusive technique is a *memorandum of understanding* (MOU) issued by the regulator to the bank detailing the changes that must occur to put the bank back in good standing. Other techniques include *cease and desist orders* that prohibit the bank or a person from continuing a particular course of conduct. Finally, the regulators can close the bank.

24. For an overview of the Federal Reserve System, see *The Federal Reserve System: Purposes and Functions*, 8th ed. (Washington, D.C.: Board of Governors of the Federal Reserve System, 1994).
25. *The Federal Reserve System: Purposes and Functions* (Washington, D.C.: Board of Governors of the Federal Reserve, 1984), p. 88.

EXAMINATION As already noted, bank examinations are part of the supervisory process. Banks face two types of examinations. The first is to determine the *safety and soundness* of the bank. In this connection, bank examiners from the OCC, the Federal Reserve, the FDIC, and the Office of Thrift Supervision use the Uniform Financial Institutions Rating System commonly referred to as CAMELS. This acronym stands for:

Capital adequacy: refers to the amount of regulatory capital that banks are required to maintain.

Asset quality: reflects the risk associated with managing assets including the quality of loans and investments. Assets are rated by federal bank examiners as "Pass," or they are problem assets because they represent potential losses. Table 2.3 lists the problem asset categories and brief explanations of each. The worst thing that can happen to a loan is that it is classified as a loss, and it must be *charged off* (removed from the balance sheet). Lenders must charge off open-end loans (e.g., credit card loans) when they are 180 days past due, and closed-end loans (e.g., mortgage loans) when they are 120 days past due.[26]

Management: assesses to the capability of the board of directors and management's ability to measure, monitor, and control risk.

Earnings: indicates the profitability of the bank and sources of those earnings taking risk into account.

Liquidity: represents the bank's ability to meet its financial obligations when they come due, and the needs of their customers (deposit withdrawals and loans).

Sensitivity to market risk: interest rates, foreign exchange, and the ability of the bank to manage that risk.

Composite ratings of institutions range from a score of 1 to 5. A composite score of 1 is the highest rating given. It means that the administration of the institution is sound in every respect, with no cause for supervisory concern. At the other extreme, a composite score of 5 means that the institution's "fiduciary activities are conducted in an extremely unsafe and unsound manner. . . . Continuous close supervision is warranted and may include termination of the institution's fiduciary activities."[27] The composite ratings are not publicly available information, although many economists argue that such information would aid in the market discipline of banks.

Megabank mergers (e.g., Citibank and Travelers), global banking, and the expanded used of derivative securities (e.g., interest rate swaps) have increased the size and complexity of the largest banking organizations. Bank regulators

---

26. J. Seiberg, "Scrapped: Uniform 150-Day Rule for Writing Off Past-Due Loans," *American Banker* (February 11, 1999), p. 3.
27. *Federal Register*, vol. 63, no. 197 (October 13, 1998), 54707.

TABLE 2.3	Problem Asset Categories

Category	Explanation
Other Assets Especially Mentioned (OAEM)	Has potential for weakness and needs close attention. If uncorrected, it may deteriorate further.
Substandard	Inadequately protected by current worth/paying capacity of obligor, or collateral, allowing for the possibility of a loss.
Doubtful	Substandard and collection in full is highly questionable or improbable.
Loss	Uncollectible, and of such little value that it should be removed from the balance sheet.

Source: William F. Treacy, "Credit Risk Ratings at Large U.S. Banks," *Federal Reserve Bulletin* (November 1998), p. 901.

recognize that they can no longer rely on periodic examinations alone to ensure that the banks remain sound. Consequently, they look even more closely at those banks' risk management practices and internal controls.[28]

The second type of examination is to determine whether the bank is in *compliance* with all relevant regulations and laws. Banks can do only those activities permitted by laws, and how they do it is regulated too. Table 2.4 lists the Federal Reserve regulations that banks must adhere to. Banks must comply with other regulations as well.

Is Prudential Bank Regulation Effective?

One answer to the question of whether prudential bank regulation is effective depends on what one thinks prudential regulation is supposed to do. Prudential regulation ranges from safety and soundness to consumer protection. In this context, it may be successful in accomplishing some goals of prudential regulation, and less successful in other areas. One thing is clear, however; safety and soundness of the banking system are the primary objectives of prudential regulation. If banks fail in large numbers, the other objectives of prudential regulation cannot be met.

Another view is that the facts speak for themselves. During the 1980–1996 period, more than 130 IMF member countries, including the United States, had

28. "Remarks by Governor Laurence H. Meyer at the Conference Board's 1999 Financial Services Outlook Conference, New York, NY, January 11, 1999," Board of Governors of the Federal Reserve System.

TABLE 2.4	Federal Reserve Regulations

Regulation	Subject
A	Loans to Depository Institutions
B	Equal Credit Opportunity
C	Home Mortgage Disclosure
D	Reserve Requirements
E	Electronic Funds Transfer
F	Securities of Member Banks
G	Margin Credit Extended by Parties Other Than Bank, Brokers, and Dealers
H	Membership Requirements for State Chartered Banks
I	Stock in Federal Reserve Banks
J	Check Collection and Funds Transfer
K	International Banking Operations
L	Interlocking Bank Relationships
M	Consumer Leasing
N	Relationships with Foreign Banks
O	Loans to Executive Officers of Member Banks
P	Member Bank Protection Standards
Q	Interest on Demand Deposits, Advertising
R	Interlocking Relationships between Securities Dealers and Member Banks
S	Reimbursement for Providing Financial Records
T	Margin Credit Extended by Brokers and Dealers
U	Margin Credit Extended by Banks
V	Guarantee of Loans for National Defense Work
W	Extensions of Consumer Credit (revoked)
X	Borrowers Who Obtain Margin Credit
Y	Bank Holding Companies
Z	Truth in Lending
AA	Consumer Complaint Procedures
BB	Community Reinvestment
CC	Availability of Funds and Collection of Checks
DD	Truth in Savings
EE	Netting Eligibility for Financial Institutions

Source: *A Guide to Federal Reserve Regulations*, Board of Governors of the Federal Reserve System.

MANAGING RISK

Regulatory Risk and the Regulatory Dialectic

One of the risks that bank managers face is a change in the regulatory environment within which they operate. Activities that previously were prohibited may now be permissible, as was the case following the deregulation of the early 1980s. A bank that did not anticipate such a change and plan for it would find itself at a significant competitive disadvantage. Equally important, an activity that previously was permissible may now be prohibited (witness the reregulation of the late 1980s and early 1990s). Again, a bank unprepared for such a change puts itself at significant risk.

A review of the major pieces of legislation during the past 15–20 years reveals dramatic changes in the manner in which banks are regulated. To some degree these changes reflect nothing more than the relative power of special interest groups attempting to gain an advantage for their constituents (for example, commercial banks versus investment banks, large banks versus small banks, or commercial banks versus thrift institutions). Yet, Professor Edward Kane has pointed out a unifying theme to bank regulatory changes. This theme is the regulatory dialectic.*

As proposed by Kane, the regulatory dialectic (*dialectic* means "change") divides the regulatory process into three stages. The first stage (the *thesis*) refers to the proposal and enactment of legislation or regulation; for example, Regulation Q limited the ability of banks to offer competitive interest rates on deposits. The second stage (the *antithesis*) refers to the attempt by banks to avoid the regulation. For example, in the Regulation Q case, banks offered toasters rather than interest to attract deposits or developed nondeposit liabilities not subject to regulation. The third stage (the *synthesis*) refers to the adjustment of regulation in response to avoiding the antithesis, which may involve relaxing regulations, or, in the case of Regulation Q, eliminating those regulations. (Actually, Regulation Q was first related and then eliminated.)

*Edward Kane, "Good Intentions and Unintended Evil: The Case Against Selective Credit Allocation." *Journal of Money, Credit and Banking* (February 1977), pp. 55–69.

significant banking sector problems or crises.[29] During the 1997–1999 period, banking crises occurred in several Southeast Asian countries, Russia, and Brazil. The large numbers of bank failures and crises suggest that prudential regulation, at least in its present form, has limits, and that it works better in some countries than in others. Systemic causes of bank failures are one of those limits. An FDIC study of banking crises in the 1980s and early 1990s concluded by saying that "bank regulation can limit the scope and cost of bank failures, but it is unlikely to prevent bank failures that have systemic causes."[30]

Prudential regulation works best in a stable economic environment. The Basle Committee on Banking Supervision's *Core Principles*[31] states that "In the

29. C. J. Lindgren, G. Garcia, and M. I. Saal, *Bank Soundness and Macroeconomic Policy* (Washington, D.C.: International Monetary Fund, 1996).
30. G. Hanc, "The Banking Crises of the 1980s and Early 1990s: Summary and Implications," *FDIC Banking Review*, vol. 11. no. 1 (1998), pp. 1–55.
31. "Core Principles for Effective Banking Supervision," Basle, Switzerland: Bank for International Settlement, Basle Committee on Banking Supervision (April 1997).

absence of sound macroeconomic policies, banking supervisors will be faced with a virtually impossible task." Most banking crises are associated with unstable economic conditions, such as asset price deflation, interest rate shocks, foreign exchange rate shocks, and so on. The flip side of that coin is that prolonged stability and strong economic growth may lead to complacency with respect to risky lending. That, in part, is what happened in Asian countries when the stability and rapid economic growth encouraged banks to lend injudiciously resulted in overspending in the government sector.

Beyond banking crises, the growth of heterogeneous financial conglomerates that cross regulatory and national boundaries, as well as changes in information technology are testing the limits of prudential banking regulation.

SUMMARY

As Federal Reserve Chairman Alan Greenspan points out, banks are regulated to limit their incentives to take risks in order to protect the financial system and individual depositors. However, no one knows how much risk is optimal. The primary reason for bank failures is credit risk, and the failure of large banks, or large numbers of banks, can disrupt the economy. With the collapse of the banking system in the early 1930s, legislation (Banking Acts of 1933 and 1935) was put into place that dramatically circumscribed the ability of banks to take risk. However, after years with few bank failures in the post-WWII era, legislation passed in the early 1980s—DIDMCA in 1980 and the Garn–St. Germain Depository Institution in 1982—allowed banks and thrifts to have greater flexibility in their activities. Finally, in the late 1980s and early 1990s, legislation was passed (FIRREA and FDICIA) that responded to the upsurge of failures in the 1980s and again restricted the ability of banks to take risk.

Banking legislation is ever changing as are perceptions about the proper amount of risk taking at commercial banks. The expansion of banking powers and global banking became important issues in the late 1990s. Increased competition from nonbank financial institutions contributed to demand from bankers to "level the playing field."

The United States has a dual banking system whereby banks can have national charters issued by the OCC or state bank charters. In addition, the Federal Reserve regulates bank holding companies that may have banks with both national and state charters. The overlapping authority has led to turf battles over who should regulate what when it comes to banking.

The functions of the bank regulators include chartering, examination, regulation, supervision, and other tasks. Finally, when assessing the effectiveness of prudential regulation, one can quickly conclude that banking regulation must keep up with the ever-changing world in which it operates.

Key Terms and Concepts

Bank holding companies

Bank runs

Banking Act of 1933 (Glass-Steagall Act)

Banking Act of 1935

CAMELS

Deposit insurance

Depository Institutions Deregulation and Monetary Control Act of 1980 (DIDMCA)

Deregulation (price, product, geographic)

Dual banking system

Federal Deposit Insurance Corporation Improvement Act of 1991 (FDICIA)

Financial Institutions Reform, Recovery, and Enforcement Act of 1989 (FIRREA)

Financial repression

Financial Services Modernization Act of 1999

Garn–St. Germain Depository Institutions Act of 1982

Harmonization

Investment banking

Market discipline

National bank charter

Omnibus Budget Reconciliation Act of 1993

Prompt Corrective Action (PCA)

Prudential regulation

Riegle-Neal Interstate Banking and Branching Efficiency Act of 1994

Questions

2.1 Why are banks regulated? Is the regulation justified?

2.2 What is a bank run? Why is it important?

2.3 How can banks reduce their risk of failing due to credit risk?

2.4 How did the banking crisis of the 1930s change the nature of banking regulations?

2.5 What are the principal features of the Banking Acts of 1933 and 1935?

2.6 What was the DIDMCA? What were its principal provisions? Why was it enacted?

2.7 What was the principal feature of the Garn–St. Germain Depository Institutions Act?

2.8 How did the goals of FIRREA differ from those of DIDMCA and Garn–St. Germain? Why did the goals differ? Be specific.

2.9 What were the principal features of FDICIA? Why was it created?

2.10 What are the major benefits of the Riegle-Neal Act and the Financial Services Modernization Act of 1999?

2.11 How does bank regulation differ from bank supervision?

2.12 Should prudential bank regulations be harmonized? Explain your position.

The Policy Consultant (Part 2)

Jack Anderson is a policy consultant for North Information Services (NIS), a firm that specializes in lobbying Congress for banks and financial institutions that want to protect their economic interests. Mr. North, president and CEO of NIS asked Jack to prepare a brief for one of their major clients, an international bank, on the legislative issues that Congress will address during the next term, including legislation that might affect this bank. The client bank is headquartered in Zurich, Switzerland, but has global operations. To deal with the legislative part of his brief, Jack will examine information available from the Library of Congress (*http://www.loc.gov*) concerning bills under consideration by the Senate and House. Details of the bills can be found at *http://lcweb.loc.gov/global/legislative/bill.html*. Information about current legislation is also available from the Conference of State Bank Supervisors at *http://www.csbsdal.org/legreg/legregndx.html*, and from the Committee on Banking and Financial Services (*http://www.house.gov/banking*) and the Senate Banking Committee (*http://www.senate.gov/~banking/*.

1. Using these or other Internet sources, list the major banking legislative issues facing Congress.
2. Write a position paper concerning the pros and cons of the major issue.
3. If the law is passed, what impact will it have on NIS's international bank customer?

CHAPTER 3

Evaluating Bank Performance

After reading this chapter you will be able to:

■ Define the principal balance sheet and income statement items for a commercial bank.

■ Evaluate the profitability of a commercial bank to determine whether its profitability is low or high and the reasons for such difference with other banks.

■ Evaluate the risk profile of a commercial bank, including the potential for failure.

■ Describe the procedure used by the bank regulatory agencies to evaluate the quality of commercial banks.

D eregulation of interest rates, rising competition and consolidation among banks and nonbanks, continuing development of innovative ways to provide financial services, and interstate banking all contribute to a growing interest in evaluating bank performance. Banks can no longer earn legally mandated yield spreads between the average interest rates earned on sources and uses of funds. Nor can banks continue to reap monopoly rents from bank charters that naturally gave them a considerable degree of market power. Instead, in today's more competitive environment, banking institutions must evaluate carefully the risks and returns involved in serving the needs of the public.

Various groups are particularly interested in evaluating bank performance. First and foremost, *bank shareholders* are directly affected by bank performance. Investors take advantage of bank information to develop expectations concerning future performance that can be used to price common shares appropriately (in addition to capital notes and debentures that may be issued by the bank). Second, *bank management* traditionally is evaluated on the basis of how well the bank performs relative to previous years and compared with similar (or peer group) banks. Hence, employees' salaries and promotions are frequently tied to the performance of the bank. Bankers also need to be informed about the condition of other banks with which they have dealings. Loan purchases and participations from poorly managed institutions may be suspect; moreover, federal funds sold and repurchase agreements with other banks require that knowledge of their performance to prevent loss of funds in the event of their failure and subsequent closure by regulatory authorities. Third, *regulators*, concerned about the safety and soundness of the banking system and with preserving public confidence, monitor banks using on-site examinations and computer-oriented "early warning systems" to keep track of bank performance. Fourth, *depositors* may be interested in how well the bank is doing, especially if they (particularly business firms) hold deposits in excess of the insured amount (e.g., each depositor is allowed federal insurance up to $100,000), and must depend on bank funds for their continued operations. Fifth, and last, the *business community* and general public should be concerned about their banks' performance to the extent that their economic prosperity is linked to the success or failure of their bank.

The present chapter is organized into two parts. The first part provides a general framework for evaluating bank performance. This framework helps to conceptualize the nature of bank behavior and points out possible interactions between various aspects of performance. In this section we discuss the internal and external performance factors that bank management needs to evaluate.

The second part of the chapter discusses a variety of key financial characteristics that can be calculated from bank accounting statements known as *Call Reports of Income and Condition*, including profitability, capitalization, asset quality, operating efficiency, liquidity, taxes, and more. ∎

3.1 A FRAMEWORK FOR EVALUATING BANK PERFORMANCE

Omega Performance is a financial service company, specializing in service consulting and training. The site www.omega-performance.com/prod/main/comm.bank.html *contains a good example of how practitioners value a bank's performance.*

Like any corporation, the ultimate measure of a bank's performance is the value of its common shares. Maximization of shareholder wealth is a complex issue that involves both internal and external management factors. Internal factors are areas of bank management that the officers and staff of the bank have under their immediate control. By contrast, external factors are environmental aspects of the bank's market over which management has no direct control. Figure 3.1 shows the interrelationship between these two performance factors. The problem that bank management faces is allocating scarce resources to the different performance dimensions in order to maximize the total value of the bank. Interactions between different performance areas must be carefully considered. For example, increasing the bank's market share and competitiveness may compromise the bank's financial condition, due to higher operating

FIGURE 3.1   A Framework for Evaluating Bank Performance

Bank Share Price

↓

Returns/Risks

↓

Environment

- Economic conditions
- Market demand

- Political setting
- Legal setting

↓

↓

Internal Performance

External Performance

- Bank planning
  Objectives
  Budgets
  Strategies

- Market share
  Equity/Earnings
  Technology

- Technology
  Computer operations
  Communications

- Regulatory compliance
  Capital
  Lending
  Other

- Personal development
  Training
  Incentives

- Public confidence
  Deposit insurance
  Public image

- Bank condition
  Profitability
  Capitalization
  Operating efficiency
  Asset quality
  Liquidity
  Other

expenses. In turn, regulatory compliance and public confidence may be affected. Of course, changes in the bank's environment can alter the investment decisions of management with regard to the internal and external performance areas shown in Figure 3.1.

3.2 INTERNAL PERFORMANCE

In this section we discuss three aspects of internal performance: bank planning, technology, and personnel development. Bank condition is another dimension of internal performance, and is discussed in greater detail in the second part of this chapter.

Bank Planning

As a first step in planning, bank objectives should be clearly stated. Obviously, the ultimate objective of the bank (as mentioned earlier) is the maximization of shareholders' equity. Other bank objectives facilitate this result. Some examples of bank objectives are the following:

- Improve the market share of prime grade loans.
- Upgrade the quality of management expertise in the area of high-technology lending.
- Expand the financial services being offered to retail customers to increase the size and diversification of the deposit base.
- Implement an automated delivery system for payment services.
- Help the community grow so that the bank may grow with it.
- Facilitate employee training.
- Diversify the loan portfolio to a greater extent in terms of both different assets and the geographic distribution of these assets.

Once the objectives of the bank are developed, they can be translated into specific, quantifiable goals. These goals should clearly communicate the results that management seeks in both the short and long term. For example, with reference to the market share objective given earlier, the following goals could be adopted:

- Expand prime grade loans to manufacturing companies by 15% the first year and 10% thereafter annually for a period of four years.
- Maintain retail business lending at the same pace as in the past year.
- Trim lending in other areas of the bank by 5% per year across the board for the next five years.

By quantifying goals, management formalizes the planning process. This step in bank planning should involve all levels of management in order to ensure that reasonable goals are established and understood by everyone. Also, personal involvement in the process of setting goals may improve morale, increase communication between departments, and help to coordinate bank operations.

Budgets, or profit plans, are in-depth statements that are intended to bring these objectives down to the departmental level of the bank. Budgets allocate estimated labor and capital resources to various departments with the goals of the bank in mind. Typically, budgets are for a one-year period and contain quarterly and monthly refinements. The specific results expected of each department are defined in the budget, which enables periodic reviews of progress toward goals. Budgets are used to improve internal control over the bank's operations.

By contrast, strategic planning seeks to anticipate emerging internal and external conditions that could affect the bank's achievement of goals in the long run. Rather than being mechanical, strategic planning is creative in nature. It is more concerned with effectiveness in achieving goals, whereas budgeting focuses on cost efficiency. Also, strategic planning is more general than a budget plan in its content, and thus provides guidance for the future as well as a blueprint for managing the bank's environment. However, this planning must be compatible with the bank's annual budget.

The way in which the planning process is managed by officers and staff will influence the performance of the bank. Increasing competition accentuates the importance of careful planning. Institutions that do not implement comprehensive planning procedures will have lower share prices on average and be at greater risk of failure than other banks.

Technology

Automation of operations can improve internal performance in a number of ways. For example, more up-to-date and accurate information can be supplied to customers and managers alike. New financial services such as direct deposit, automatic bill paying, and Internet services can be offered to the public. Also, at least in the long run, the operating costs of the bank may be reduced as capital investment in computer and communications equipment is substituted for labor. Especially for small banks, automation may not be feasible because of low public demand for electronically produced financial services or lack of internal information needs. In this case cooperative relationships with correspondent banks, and joint ventures among banks (including franchising relationships, network sharing, and other third-party business arrangements) can be employed. Large banks typically lease or purchase equipment and spread the cost among subscribing smaller banks. However, large banks may benefit from cooperative relationships also.

Personnel Development

Because commercial banks require a highly skilled labor force, personnel development is essential. Human resources play a critical role in the achievement of bank goals and objectives. Banks must provide opportunities for ongoing training in the latest banking operations and techniques, as well as provide the means for their employees to keep up with the changes in bank regulations.

Two major challenges with personnel development are the greater emphasis on *personal selling* of financial services and the trend toward *geographic expansion* in banking. The wide variety and complexity of today's banking services require interpersonal skills to communicate with and sell to customers, which means the need for sales training and updated marketing techniques. Moreover, geographic expansion in banking has gained considerable momentum during the past decade. As a bank expands throughout its state, across state lines, and into international markets, employees need additional training to adapt to the changing geographical diversification of the institution.

Effective management of human resources is also needed to satisfy the career goals of individuals in the organization. The bank can contribute to employees' personal satisfaction through job enrichment programs and training, for example. On a more basic level, compensation for work well done is necessary to maintain motivation. Wages and salaries should be sufficient to attract and retain quality personnel, and flexible enough to recognize outstanding work and the acquisition of new skills. Employee benefits programs should also reflect differences among individuals. In summary, appropriate nonmonetary and monetary compensation for employees helps to maximize job performance.

3.3 EXTERNAL PERFORMANCE

External performance is reflected in the ability of the bank to cope successfully with customers, competitors, regulators, and the public.

Market Share

Market share is the proportion of assets, deposits, and loans held by a bank in its business region relative to other banks. Failure to meet market demands normally results in a decline in market share.

EARNINGS Market share can affect the earnings of the bank. For example, if a bank's rate of return on assets does not change while its asset size declines, then earnings per share would decline because a steady number of shares divided into lower total earnings results in lower earnings per share, which is consistent with the erosion of the asset base. Conversely, growing too fast can also lower equity returns, because assets expand but profitability may not. For example, if the bank's assets grow by 20% but the net income after taxes decrease by 10% (because higher deposit rates had to be offered to the public to attract sufficient funds to finance the relatively rapid rate of asset expansion), the earnings per share of the bank would decline. Furthermore, growth may not only affect profitability but it may change the perceived riskiness of the bank by the financial market (perhaps because of increased credit risk), which would also result in a loss of share value. Thus, growth for the sake of growth alone is not a suitable goal. Bank managers should set market share goals with the internal performance of the bank in mind.

TECHNOLOGY Through another goal, implementing new technologies, banks promote the perception of progressiveness. Hence, technology is a marketing tool that can attract customers and improve the bank's competitiveness. Technology enables the bank to reach out to customers beyond the traditional market boundaries by enhancing the convenience of the bank's financial services; that is, greater customer service and convenience increase the attractiveness of the bank. The best examples of this type of technology are credit cards, debit cards, automated teller machines (ATMs), telephone bill-paying services, point-of-sale (POS) payment services, and Internet-based payments and funds management services. See Chapter 13 on Electronic Banking for further discussion of electronic funds transfer services.

Regulatory Compliance

Another dimension of external performance is regulatory compliance. All banks must conform to the laws and regulations of the relevant federal and state authorities. Failure to comply will prompt some form of supervisory action. Such action could take the form of a simple letter explaining a problem with compliance that can be easily rectified by the bank, or it could take the form of a full-blown audit to determine the extent of a major problem. Requests for a plan of action by the bank to overcome the problem(s) could be made and then monitored over time to assess the progress of the bank. Sanctions on bank activities could be imposed by regulators to control risk taking and preserve safety and soundness. Of course, as regulatory risk increases, the costs of compliance increase for the bank. More than $10 billion is spent annually by U.S. banks in order to comply with government regulation.

Public Confidence

Public confidence relates to the market's *perception* of a bank's safety and soundness. No matter how well capitalized a bank is, a loss of public confidence can cause a run on deposits and subsequent closure by regulatory authorities. A case in point is the failure of Hartford Federal, a thrift institution in Hartford, Connecticut, in the early 1980s. By coincidence, news that regulatory authorities had placed Hartford Federal on its watch list appeared in the local paper on the same day that the movie "The Night the Money Stopped" aired on a national TV network. The timing of these two events touched off a run that lasted for a week and ended in the closure and sale of the thrift by regulators. Clearly, public confidence is necessary to maintain bank solvency.

3.4 BANK FINANCIAL STATEMENTS

Financial data on commercial banks are presented in two basic documents: the **Report of Condition** (*balance sheet*) and the **Report of Income** (*income statement*).

The Balance Sheet

At FDIC Institution Directory, http://www.fdic.gov/ bank/individual/index.html, *a search by institution name and FDIC ID number provides financial statements of any bank insured with FDIC. The site also has profit ratios and their definitions.*

Table 3.1 presents a hypothetical balance sheet for State Bank as of December 31, 2000, and December 31, 1999. A bank's **balance sheet** reports the institution's financial condition at a single point in time. Balance sheets are prepared on a particular date—usually the last day of a month, a year, or a quarter. Thus the amounts presented on a balance sheet on December 31 might be different from the same amounts on December 30 or January 1. Because balance sheets capture a condition at one time, it is useful to compare data for several accounting periods.

ASSETS Cash assets include vault cash, deposits at the Federal Reserve (primarily to meet legal reserve requirements), deposits at other banks (for clearing purposes and also to compensate the other banks for providing services such as shipping currency and coin), and cash items in the process of collection. These four categories of assets have one common feature: they earn no interest. As such, bank management should attempt to minimize its investment in these assets.

Interest-bearing bank balances, such as short-term certificates of deposit at other banks and federal funds sold are highly liquid earning assets. They are generally used as a part of the bank's liquidity management program. Most smaller banks such as State Bank have more federal funds sold than federal funds purchased, indicating relatively high liquidity.

The next major category of bank assets is investment securities. Because banks are generally prohibited from owning equity securities, the securities that appear on bank balance sheets are almost entirely debt. Regulations force banks to be lenders rather than investors. These investment securities consist of U.S. Treasury securities and U.S. government agencies' obligations (a major portion of which is generally pledged against government deposits); securities issued by states and political subdivisions in the United States (i.e., municipalities); and

TABLE 3.1	Balance Sheet for State Bank ($ thousands)	

Assets	Dec. 31, 2000	Dec. 31, 1999
Cash assets	$ 9,039	$ 10,522
Interest-bearing bank balances	0	1,000
Federal funds sold	10,500	1,500
U.S. Treasury and agency securities	54,082	44,848
Municipal securities	32,789	34,616
All other securities	0	0
Net loans and leases	90,101	81,857
Real estate loans	50,393	38,975
Commercial loans	9,615	11,381
Individual loans	8,824	10,640
Agricultural loans	20,680	19,654
Other loans and leases—domestic	3,684	4,025
Gross loans and leases	93,196	84,675
Less: Unearned income reserves	89	282
Reserve for loan and lease losses	3,006	2,356
Premises, fixed-assets, and capitalized leases	2,229	2,398
Other real estate	2,282	3,012
Other assets	4,951	4,014
Total assets	$205,973	$183,767

Liabilities & Capital		
Demand deposits	$ 23,063	$ 22,528
All NOW and ATS accounts	6,021	5,322
MMDA accounts	41,402	49,797
Other savings deposits	3,097	2,992
Time deposits <$100M	31,707	28,954
Time deposits >$100M	83,009	57,665
Total deposits	188,299	167,258
Fed funds purchase and resale	0	0
Other borrowings	0	0
Bankers' acceptance and other liabilities	3,546	3,101
Total liabilities	191,845	170,359
Subordinated notes and debentures	0	0
All common and preferred equity	14,128	13,408
Total liabilities and capital	$205,973	$183,767

all other securities, principally investment-grade corporate bonds. In addition, banks have become major buyers of mortgage-backed securities, most of which are backed by a U.S. government agency.

Loans, the least liquid of banking assets and the major source of risk, comprise the major asset category for most banking institutions as well as the primary source of bank earnings. Lease-financing arrangements substitute for loans in this section of the balance sheet. Loans and leases are classified by the following categories:

- Domestic loans secured by real estate
- Domestic commercial and industrial loans, including loans to depository institutions
- Domestic loans to individuals for household, family, and other personal expenditures
- Domestic loans to finance agricultural production
- All other loans and lease-financing receivables.

From gross loans and leases, two deductions are made—unearned income and the reserve for loan and lease losses—to arrive at net loans and leases. Unearned income represents the amount of income that has been deducted from a loan, for example, in the case of a discounted note, but has not yet been recognized as income on the income statement because it is distributed over the life of the note.

The amount in the reserve account reflects an estimate by bank management of probable **charge-offs** for uncollectible loans and leases on the balance sheet date. Although the regulatory authorities are involved in the estimation process, bank management ultimately determines the final valuation of the reserve account. Actual losses are deducted from the reserve account, and recoveries are added back to reserves. The adequacy of the valuation reserve is an important element in the analysis of a bank's risk.

Premises, fixed assets, and capitalized leases represent an important, though quantitatively minor, portion of assets. Most capitalized leases for banks involve sale-and-leaseback arrangements in which the bank "sells" property and leases it back from the buyer; terms are structured to allow the bank to maintain control over the property, and these arrangements are made primarily to generate cash. Capitalized leases are recorded as an asset rather than as a lease, as if the bank still "owns" the property, and as a liability for the indebtedness.

Other real estate is any other real estate owned by the bank and usually represents property obtained through collateral foreclosures on problem loans.

The final asset category is all other assets, and it includes intangible assets—assets without physical substance—such as goodwill recognized in business communities.

LIABILITIES Bank liabilities consist primarily of the various types of deposit accounts the institution uses to fund its lending and investing activities.

Depository accounts vary in terms of interest payments, maturity, check-writing privileges, and insurability. Demand deposits are transactions accounts payable to the depositor on demand and pay no interest. NOW accounts represent the total of all transactions accounts, less demand deposits. They are accounts that pay interest and permit check-writing but do not include money market deposit accounts. Money market deposit accounts (MMDAs) are savings accounts on which the bank pays market interest, and check-writing is limited to a certain number of checks per month. The other savings deposits category comprises all savings deposits other than money market deposit accounts and includes regular passbook accounts with no set maturity and overdraft protection plan accounts. Time deposits under $100,000 are total time deposits (with a fixed maturity). Time deposits over $100,000 are large certificates of deposit, many of which are negotiable in a well-established secondary market.

CAPITAL Subordinated notes and debentures are actually liabilities but are shown in the capital section because this type of debt has the characteristics of capital in terms of maturity and permanence and can be counted as capital in meeting certain regulatory requirements.

All common and preferred equity capital is the par value of all common and preferred stock outstanding, surplus or additional paid-in capital (the amount by which the original sale of the stock exceeded par value), undivided profits or retained earnings (all of the institution's earnings since its inception less any dividends paid), capital reserves, and cumulative foreign currency adjustments (amounts that arise from the translation of foreign subsidiary financial statements into dollars at the end of an accounting period).

The Income Statement

The **income statement**, which shows all major categories of revenue and expenditures, the net profit or loss for the period. It notes the amount of cash dividends declared, which measures a firm's financial performance over a period of time, such as a year or a quarter or a month. The income statement and the balance sheet are integrally related, and both should be evaluated when assessing bank performance. Table 3.2 presents the income statement format.

INTEREST INCOME Loans are the largest asset category for most bank balance sheets (see earlier discussion), and interest and fees on loans are the primary sources of bank income. This category of revenue, which includes all year-to-date interest and fees on loans, is presented first on the income statement. Income from lease financing is year-to-date income derived from lease-financing receivables.

The analyst must realize that income reported on loans and leases is *accrued*, meaning that it is recognized over the appropriate time period of the loan rather than when cash is actually received. A bank can recognize this income for at least 90 days before the loan goes on *nonaccrual* status.

| TABLE 3.2 | Income Statement for State Bank ($ thousands) | |

Revenues and Expenses	Dec. 31, 2000	Dec. 31, 1999
Interest and fees on loans	$ 8,931	$ 9,192
Income from lease financing	0	0
Fully taxable	8,880	9,142
Tax exempt	51	50
Estimated tax benefit	38	21
Income on loans and leases	8,969	9,213
U.S. Treasury and agency securities income	3,735	3,571
Municipal securities (tax exempt) income	3,097	3,571
Estimated tax benefit	1,882	2,103
Other securities income	13	0
Investment interest income	8,727	8,699
Interest Fed funds sold	192	83
Interest due from banks	27	5
Total interest income	17,915	18,001
Interest on CDs over $100,000	3,248	2,924
Interest on other deposits	6,757	7,167
Interest of Fed funds purchased and repos	16	59
Interest borrowed money	0	50
Interest on mortgages and leases	0	0
Interest on subordinated notes and debentures	0	0
Total interest expense	$10,021	$10,200
Net Interest Income	$ 7,894	7,801
Noninterest income	571	577
Adjusted operating income	8,465	8,378
Overhead expense	3,624	3,876
Provision for loan (and lease) losses	1,294	3,208
Pretax operating income	3,547	1,294
Securities gains (losses)	1,240	3,331
Pretax net operating income	4,787	4,625
Applicable income tax	2,267	2,133
Net Operating Income	2,520	2,492
Net extraordinary items	0	0
Net income	$ 2,520	$ 2,492

The income reported is divided into fully taxable and tax-exempt portions. The tax-exempt amount includes year-to-date income on loan obligations of state and political subdivisions, and tax-exempt income from direct lease financing. The fully taxable amount is total interest and fees on loans and income from lease-financing receivables less the tax-exempt income. The estimated tax benefit results from having tax-exempt loan and lease-financing income from municipal loans and leases. This estimate is added to income to improve the comparability of interest income among different banks over several time periods.

Investment income typically provides the next largest category of income for banking institutions. U.S. Treasury and agency securities income includes interest on U.S. Treasury securities, other U.S. government agencies, and corporate obligations. Interest on municipal securities is interest on securities issued by state and political subdivisions in the United States. Like loans to municipalities, a tax benefit results from such investments.

Other securities income includes income on federal funds sold and securities purchased under agreements to resell, interest on balances due from banks, and income on assets held in trading accounts (excluding gains, losses, commissions, and fees).

Interest expense is the largest expense for most banks. Interest expense is allocated into six categories: interest paid on time deposits of $100,000 or more; interest on other deposits; interest expense on federal funds purchased and securities sold under agreements to repurchase; interest on note balances issued to the U.S. Treasury and on other borrowed money; interest on mortgage debt and capital leases on bank premises, fixed assets, and other real estate owned; and interest on subordinated notes and debentures.

Net interest income on a tax-equivalent basis is total interest income less total interest expense. The relationship between net interest income—the amount by which interest received exceeds interest paid—and total assets is an important analytical tool in assessing a bank's ability to generate profits through the management of interest-earning assets and interest-bearing liabilities.

NONINTEREST INCOME   Noninterest income includes all other sources of income: from fiduciary activities, service charges on deposits, gains or losses and commissions and fees on assets held in trading accounts, foreign exchange trading gains or losses, and other foreign transactions. These categories of income have increased in relative importance for many banks as a result of deregulation's impact on interest-earning assets and interest-bearing liabilities and the incumbent pricing pressures that have caused banks to seek other income sources. Adjusted operating income (TE) is the total of net interest income and noninterest income.

OTHER EXPENSE   Three other types of expenses are deducted from adjusted operating income to arrive at pretax operating income. Overhead expense includes salaries and employee benefits, expenses of premises and fixed assets (net of rental income), and other noninterest operating expenses. The provision for loan and lease losses is the year-to-date amount allocated to loan and lease loss reserves (on the balance sheet). Remember that actual losses are charged against the balance sheet reserves account.

Gains or losses on the sale, exchange, redemption, or retirement of securities other than those held in trading accounts are netted against pretax operating income to determine pretax operating income on a tax-equivalent basis. Security gains and losses can be an important element in measuring bank performance. Until 1983 banks showed these amounts as a separate item after net operating income. In 1983 the Securities Exchange Commission (SEC) issued a requirement that security gains and losses be included in operating income. The analyst should be aware that a bank can influence operating profit for a period through these securities transactions.

INCOME TAX EXPENSE Income tax includes the total estimated federal, state, local, and foreign (if applicable) income taxes on operating income, including securities gains and losses.

NET INCOME Income taxes are deducted from pretax operating income to arrive at net operating income. Any extraordinary items, defined as transactions that are both unusual in nature and not expected to recur, are deducted or added, net of taxes, to determine net income.

The preceding line-by-line description of each account contained in a bank's balance sheet and income statement provides a basic understanding of the information essential to begin an evaluation of bank financial statements. But what do all of the numbers and accounts mean to a bank's operations? How can we use the information contained in a financial statement to assess a bank's historical, present, and future performance? These questions are now addressed.

3.5 ANALYZING BANK PERFORMANCE WITH FINANCIAL RATIOS

The National Information Center, or NIC, at http://www.ffiec.gov/nic/ presents searchable information on the banking system including bank performance, bank holding companies of all sizes, and history of bank acquisitions and mergers.

Financial ratios are constructed from accounting data contained in the bank's Reports of Income (profit and loss) and Condition (balance sheet). A wide variety of financial ratios can be calculated to assess different characteristics of financial performance. To evaluate a particular financial ratio for a bank, comparisons with peer group banks are often used. Also, it is beneficial to track the ratio over time relative to other banks. Even without comparison with other banks, ratio trends over time may provide valuable information about the bank's performance. A potential limitation of financial ratio analysis is that other factors are held constant. To overcome this problem, analysts use various financial ratios that provide a broader understanding of the bank's financial

MANAGING RISK

Important Terms Useful in Understanding Bank Financial Statements

Earning assets: Loans, investment securities, and short-term investments that generate interest and yield related fee income.

Federal funds sold/purchased: Excess balances of depository institutions, which are loaned to each other, generally on an overnight basis.

Interest-bearing liabilities: Deposits and borrowed funds on which interest is paid.

Interest rate spread: The difference between the average rate earned on earning assets on a taxable equivalent basis and the average rate paid for interest-bearing liabilities.

Interest-sensitive assets/liabilities: Earning assets and interest-bearing liabilities that can be repriced or will mature within specific time periods.

Interest sensitivity gap: A measure of the exposure of a bank to changes in market rates of interest, its vulnerability to such changes, and the associated effect on net interest income.

Liquidity: The ability of an entity to meet its cash flow requirements. For a bank it is measured by the ability to convert assets into cash quickly with minimal exposure to interest rate risk, by the size and stability of the core funding base, and by additional borrowing capacity within the money markets.

Net charge-offs: The amount of loans written off as uncollectible less recoveries of loans previously written off.

Net interest margin: Net taxable equivalent interest income divided by average interest-earning assets. It is a measure of how effectively a corporation utilizes its earning assets in relation to the interest cost of funding.

Nonperforming assets: Loans on which interest income is not being accrued, restructured loans on which interest rates or terms of repayment have been materially revised, and real properties acquired through foreclosure.

Provision for loan losses: Period charges against earnings required to maintain the allowance for loan losses at a level considered by management to be adequate to absorb estimated losses inherent in the loan portfolio.

Reserve for loan losses: A valuation allowance offset against total loans, which represents the amount considered by management to be adequate to absorb estimated losses inherent in the loan portfolios.

Return on average assets: A measure that indicates how effectively an entity uses its total resources. It is calculated by dividing annual net income by average assets.

Return on equity: A measure of how productively an entity's equity has been employed. It is calculated by dividing annual net income by total equity.

Taxable equivalent income: Income that has been adjusted by increasing tax-exempt income to a level comparable to taxable income before taxes are applied.

condition. Most of the remainder of this chapter discusses key ratios commonly used by bank analysts to evaluate different dimensions of financial performance, including profitability, capitalization, asset quality, operating efficiency liquidity, and interest sensitivity.

Profit Ratios

RETURN ON EQUITY (ROE) The **rate of return on equity (ROE)** is a good starting point in the analysis of a bank's financial condition for the following reasons:

1. If the ROE is relatively low compared with other banks, it will tend to decrease the bank's access to new capital needed to expand and maintain a competitive position in the market.
2. A low ROE may limit a bank's growth because regulations require that assets be (at a maximum) a certain number of times equity capital.
3. ROE can be broken down into component parts to identify trends in the bank's performance.

Because the ultimate objective of bank management should be to maximize shareholder wealth, this ratio is particularly important.

Defining equity capital as the sum of common and preferred stock, paid-in surplus (above the book value at the time of issuance), undivided profits (or retained earnings), and reserves for future contingencies, the ROE for State Bank using the data in Tables 3.1 and 3.2 is calculated as follows (numbers are in thousands of dollars):

Rate of return on equity (%) = Net income/Total equity capital × 100   3.1

Example:

| State Bank (Year 200X) | 17.8% = $2,520/$14,128 × 100 |
| Peer Group | 12.4% |

The return on equity for state bank in 200X was 17.8%, considerably higher than the peer ratio of 12.4%. If the analyst was interested in exploring the trend of earnings, the ROE for State Bank and its peer group could be calculated for earlier years.

RETURN ON ASSETS (ROA) The **rate of return on assets (ROA)** measures the ability of management to utilize the real and financial resources of the bank to generate returns. ROA is commonly used to evaluate bank management. For State Bank, ROA can be calculated as follows:

Rate of return on assets (%) = Net income/Total assets × 100   3.2

Example:

| State Bank (Year 200X) | 1.22% = $2,520/$205,973 × 100 |
| Peer Group | 0.84% |

Because the average bank in the peer group had an ROA of 0.84%, State Bank profitability was obviously above average. Again, trends in profitability as measured by the ROA could be calculated.

UNRAVELING PROFIT RATIOS In the preceding ratio analyses we found that State Bank had a relatively high ROA compared with its peer group, and also that its ROE was relatively high. The relationship between the ROE and ROA can be expressed as follows:

$$ROE = ROA \times \text{Equity multiplier} \qquad 3.3$$

$$\frac{\text{Net income}}{\text{Total equity}} = \frac{\text{Net income}}{\text{Total assets}} \times \frac{\text{Total assets}}{\text{Total equity}}$$

This formula shows the return on equity ratio as the product of ROA and a ratio indicating the extent to which the bank is using financial leverage, known as the **equity** (or **leverage**) **multiplier**. In the present example the ROE of State Bank can be broken down as follows (allowing for some degree of rounding error):

Example:
State Bank (Year 200X) $2,520/$205,973 × 100 × $205,973/$14,128
                           17.8% = 1.22% × 14.6
Peer Group   12.4% = 0.84% × 14.6

State Bank has a higher ROE than its peer group because it earns more on its assets. Its use of financial leverage (as measured by the equity or leverage multiplier) is virtually identical to that of its peer group. Another useful formula for unraveling profits is as follows:

$$ROE = \text{Profit margin} \times \text{Asset utilization} \times \text{Equity multiplier} \qquad 3.4$$

$$\frac{\text{Net income}}{\text{Total equity}} = \frac{\text{Net income}}{\text{Operating revenue}} \times \frac{\text{Operating revenue}}{\text{Total assets}} \times \frac{\text{Total assets}}{\text{Total equity}}$$

where operating revenue is the sum of total interest income and noninterest income. Notice that this formula breaks down ROA into the product of **profit margin** and **asset utilization**. The profit margin ratio provides information about the ability of management to control expenses, including taxes, given a particular level of operating income. The asset utilization ratio represents the ability of management to employ assets effectively to generate revenues. Together, these two ratios enable the bank analyst to gain insight into the derivation of ROA.

For State Bank, Eq. (3.4) can be used as follows:

Example:
State Bank (Year 200X) $2,520/($17,915 + $571) × ($17,915 + $571)/
                           $205,973 × $205,973/$14,128
                           17.8% = 1.36 × 0.90 × 14.6
Peer Group   12.4% = 0.84 × 1.00 × 14.8

State Bank generated a higher ROE than its peer group primarily because of a higher profit margin. Indeed, its asset utilization is lower than the peer group.

OTHER PROFIT MEASURES A number of other profit measures are commonly used in banking, which provide further insight into a bank's financial performance.
One of these is the **net interest margin** (NIM), which is defined as follows:

$$\text{Net interest margin (\%)} = \frac{\text{Total interest income} - \text{Total interest expense}}{\text{Average earning assets}} \times 100 \qquad 3.5$$

MANAGING RISK

Commercial Banks with Top Financial Performance

A study by Robert Clair at the Federal Reserve Bank of Dallas was conducted to identify financial strategies of banks in the Eleventh Federal Reserve District, which tended to be associated with top performance. Because strategies under the control of bank management were of primary interest, the study focused on asset and liability structure, especially reserve management, capitalization, growth, and off-balance sheet activities. Some variables that are, to a more limited extent, within the control of management were also considered, including loan losses and expense control.

The performance criterion chosen was the average annual return on assets (ROA) over the period 1981–1985, where net income excluded extraordinary income. Banks were classified into three groups: (1) small banks, with between $25 million and $100 million of assets, (2) mid-sized banks, with between $100 million and $250 million of assets, and (3) large banks, with more than $250 million of assets. Banks with ROAs in the top 10% of institutions in their asset group were defined as low performers.

Four types of strategies in particular were examined by the study. The proxies used to measure each stratgegy were as follows:

1. *Investment strategy:* percentage of total assets allocated to eight categories of loans and two categories of assets. The related ratios of loan interest income to total income were calculated also.
2. *Funding strategy:* percentage of total assets funded by transactions deposits, savings and small time deposits, large time deposits, foreign deposits, and borrowed funds.
3. *Growth strategy:* overall growth of total assets.
4. *Off-balance-sheet strategy:* percentage of total assets allocated to loan and lease commitments and letters of credit and to commitments on forward, future, and option contracts. These mea-

sures were intended to capture management's use of noninterest, service income, which was also directly measured as the ratio of noninterest income to total income.

The following results of comparisons between top and low performing banks were obtained:

- Two successful financial strategies were the commercial real estate strategy and the conservative strategy. The former involved relatively higher lending in commercial real estate, lower lending in commercial and industrial loans, and higher lending to consumers. The conservative strategy was associated with low credit risks and strong asset liquidity.
- A third group of top performers did not use any distinct financial strategy but did tend to control their expenses better than other banks.
- Regardless of financial strategy, top performers had lower loan losses than low performers.
- Among small banks, top performers acquired larger (smaller) proportions of funds from transactions accounts (small savings and time deposit accounts) than low performers.
- Among large banks, top performers tended to use a lower proportion of borrowed funds than low performers.
- Financial strategies are affected by cyclical changes in business conditions (e.g., the success of the commercial real estate strategy is related to the growth of the commercial construction business). As such, banks should adapt their strategies based on economic forecasts of the future.

Source: Robert T. Clair, "Financial Strategies of Top-Performance Banks in the Eleventh District," Federal Reserve Bank of Dallas, *Economic Review* (January 1987), pp. 1–13.

where total interest income is on a *pretax* basis. It should be noted that, in the case where municipal bond interest income is not taxable, this interest income must be "grossed up" by dividing by 1 minus the marginal tax rate of the bank to convert it to a pretax-equivalent amount. For example,

$$\text{Tax-equivalent yield (TEY)} = i/(1-t)$$

so that a bank with a 4% return on municipal securities and a 34% tax rate would report a TEY of 6.06% [4/(1 − 0.34)]. For State Bank, the net interest margin is as follows:

Example:
State Bank (Year 200X)　　　4.21% = ($17,915 − $10,021)/$187,472
Peer Group　　　　　　　　　3.90%

Because interest income and expenses make up the lion's share of total operating income and expenses, respectively, NIM is well worth calculating.

Risk Ratios

The Community Reinvestment Act, or CRA, web site at http://www.bog.frb.fed.us/DCCA/CRA/ *provides bank rating and performance evaluations, as well as approved strategic plans.*

CAPITALIZATION As shown in Eq. (3.3), *capitalization* directly influences the rate of return on equity. The leverage ratio can affect the growth rate of the bank also. For example, if the policy of the bank was to keep the equity multiplier equal to 10, then each dollar of retained earnings could be used to support $10 of assets, because $9 could be borrowed by the bank to maintain the same equity multiplier. It should be obvious that a high equity multiplier can increase both ROE and the growth rate of the bank as long as ROA is positive.

On the downside, if ROA were negative, ROE would be magnified in a negative direction. Also, in the preceding example, bank asset size would need to decline tenfold for every dollar lost to keep the equity multiplier constant. In the extreme, if losses exceeded bank capital, the bank would be insolvent and subject to closure by its chartering agency. As discussed earlier, State Bank has an equity capitalization ratio similar to that of its peers.

ASSET QUALITY Asset quality can only be assessed indirectly using financial ratios. On-site inspection of the bank's outstanding individual loans is certainly the best way to evaluate asset quality. In the absence of this opportunity, some financial ratios can provide at least a historical account of the creditworthiness of a particular bank's loan portfolio.

Each bank provides an estimate of future loan losses as an expense on its income statement. This expense may be related to the volume of loans as:

$$\text{Provision for loss ratio (\%)} = \frac{\text{Provision for loan losses}}{\text{Total loans and leases}} \times 100 \qquad 3.6$$

For State Bank the **provision for loan loss** ratio is as follows:

Example:

State Bank (Year 200X)	1.38%	= $1,294/$93,196
Peer Group	1.18%	

This ratio suggests that State Bank has provided more for losses on loans than similar banks.

The loan ratio indicates the extent to which assets are devoted to loans as opposed to other assets, including cash, securities, and plant and equipment. The ratio and results for State Bank are as follows:

$$\text{Loan ratio} = \text{Net loans/Total assets} \times 100 \qquad 3.7$$

Example:

State Bank (Year 200X)	43.74%	= $90,101/$205,973
Peer Group	48.70%	

These data suggest that the higher provision for loan losses at State Bank compared to its peer group took place despite its relatively lower exposure to loan (or credit) risk.

Additional information on the credit quality of State Bank may be obtained from the footnote to its financial statements. Two measures are particularly important: the amount of charge-offs and the amount of nonperforming assets. **Charge-offs** represent the last step in the deterioration of a loan. Once management believes that the loan is uncollectible it is "charged off" the books of the bank and therefore no longer appears as an asset. The charge-off usually reduces the reserve for loan losses and often triggers an increase in the provision for loan losses if the reserve is made inadequate by the charge-offs. The relationship between charge-offs, provision for loan losses, and the reserve for loan losses can be explained as follows (see also Chapter 11): Suppose that a bank has $5 million in the **reserve for loan loss** account on its balance sheet and suppose also that management has determined that the minimum adequate reserve is $4.8 million. Now suppose that management determines that $500,000 of loans are uncollectible and charges off these loans. The charge-off reduces the reserve for loan loss account to $4.5 million. To replenish the reserve, management would then increase the accrued expense item, provision for loan losses, by $300,000. The reserve would also be increased by recoveries of previous loan charge-offs. Algebraically, we have:

$$\begin{matrix} \text{Reserve for} \\ \text{loan losses} \end{matrix} = \begin{matrix} \text{Reserve for} \\ \text{loan losses} \end{matrix} - \begin{matrix} \text{Gross} \\ \text{charge-offs} \end{matrix} + \begin{matrix} \text{Provision for} \\ \text{loan losses} \end{matrix} + \text{Recoveries}$$

Also,

Net charge-offs = Gross charge-offs − Recoveries

In contrast to charge-offs, which are a lagging indicator of credit quality, **nonperforming assets** are a leading indicator. Nonperforming assets equal the sum of nonaccrual loans (those loans whose revenue stream is so uncertain that the bank does not recognize income until cash is received), restructured loans (for example, loans whose interest rate has been lowered or the maturity increased because of problems with the borrower), and other real estate owned (i.e., foreclosed real estate).

OPERATING EFFICIENCY A key management area that many studies have found to be the primary factor distinguishing high- and low-profit banks is operating efficiency. Operating efficiency deals with the production of outputs, such as deposit and loan accounts and securities services, at a minimum cost per dollar (or account).

A number of ratios can be calculated to provide information on cost control by simply dividing various expense accounts by total operating expenses for different expense categories.

Wages and salaries (and related employee benefits) are normally the largest noninterest expense item. The occupancy expense ratio indicates the level of fixed expenses that the bank is carrying. Relatively high fixed expenses are not always an indicator of poor expense control. In the 1960s and 1970s, for example, banks operated branch offices in part as a means of providing greater convenience to customers (assuming state laws permitted branching). Because Regulation Q prevented banks from paying market rates of interest on deposit accounts at times, branch offices represented an added (implicit) service return to customers. However, the phaseout of Regulation Q in the 1980s caused many banks to trim their branch office facilities to reduce expenses (as interest expenses began to rise dramatically). New electronic technology is also causing many banks to reshuffle the structure of their expenses. More funds are being allocated to ATMs and other automated means of delivering services, causing wage expenses to fall (as capital is substituted for labor) along with on-premise occupancy expenses for buildings and furniture.

LIQUIDITY **Liquidity** can be defined as the extent to which the bank has funds available to meet cash demands for loans and deposit withdrawals (see Chapter 9 for detailed discussion). Banks require different amounts of liquidity depending on their growth rate and variability in lending and deposit activities.

One problem in measuring liquidity is that liability management has partially replaced asset management at many banks as the way to fund liquidity needs. That is, banks, especially large banks, have decreased the quantity of liquid assets they hold for the purpose of meeting loan demands and deposit withdrawals (i.e., asset management) and increased their usage of deposit and nondeposit sources of funds paying market rates of interest (i.e., liability management). These trends have tended to affect banks in the following ways:

- Gross rates of return on assets have increased because longer-term assets normally have higher rates of return than short-term assets (due to upward-sloping yield curves).
- U.S. Treasury security holdings have declined.
- Credit risk has increased in many banks as liquid assets have been replaced by loans.

The shift away from money market assets and toward more lending was motivated in large part by the rising costs of funds in the latter 1970s and early 1980s as Regulation Q ceilings on deposits were phased out and competition for deposit funds intensified. These asset and liability changes have dramatically altered the management of bank liquidity in the last decade.

Even though liability management is becoming more prevalent as an approach to meeting liquidity needs, it is still meaningful to calculate financial ratios that focus on the asset liquidity of the bank. If a bank suffered financial distress for any reason, it is likely that other banks and the market in general would reduce their lending to the institution. In this situation the bank would need to rely on its asset liquidity to a greater extent. Thus, asset liquidity is a reserve that the bank can draw on in the event its access to purchased funds is reduced. Another reason for banks to hold liquid assets is to fund loans when interest rates are relatively high. Assuming loan demand was strong, short-term assets bearing little price risk may be a less expensive source of funds than relatively high interest rate deposits. In essence, liquid assets are an alternative source of funds that at times may be cheaper than using liability management methods to raise funds.

Two commonly used measures of liquidity are the **temporary investments ratio** and the **volatile liability dependency** ratio. Temporary investments are a bank's most liquid assets. The higher the ratio of temporary investments to total assets the greater the bank's liquidity. Temporary investments include federal funds sold, trading account assets, investment securities with maturities of one year or less, and due from banks. Volatile liabilities are brokered deposits, jumbo CDs, deposits in foreign offices, federal funds purchased, and other borrowings. Brokered deposits are a particularly important part of volatile liabilities because banks that are experiencing liquidity problems often resort to brokered deposits as their last source of funds.

The volatile liability dependency ratio is somewhat complicated but extremely useful in measuring liquidity. The ratio is calculated as volatile liabilities less temporary investments divided by net loans and leases plus long-term securities. It considers the degree to which the riskiest assets are being funded by unstable or "hot" money funds that can disappear from the bank overnight. The volatile liability dependence ratio varies inversely with liquidity.

These ratios may be calculated as follows:

$$\text{Temporary investments ratio} = \frac{\text{Federal funds sold} + \text{Investment securities with maturities of one year or less} + \text{Due from banks}}{\text{Total assets}} \qquad 3.8$$

For State Bank Fed funds sold are $10,500, and due from banks funds are $9,039. The maturities of investments are not shown in Table 3.1, and that information must be obtained from supporting financial statements. In this case, they are $11,871, so temporary investments are $31,410. Hence the temporary investments ratio is:

Example:

State Bank (Year 200X)	15.25% = $31,410/$205,973 × 100
Peer Group	43.50%

The ratio for State Bank and its peer group indicate that State Bank has much less funds invested in highly liquid assets (relative to its volatile liabilities) than does the peer group. This comparison may suggest a significant liquidity problem for State Bank. Such a problem is also implied by the volatile liability dependency ratio, which is computed as follows:

$$\text{Volatile liability dependency} = \frac{\text{Total volatile liabilities} - \text{Temporary investments}}{\text{Net loans and leases \& long-term leases}} \qquad 3.9$$

Example:

State Bank (Year 200X)	36.31% = ($83,009 – $31,410)/$142,101 × 100
Peer Group	–5.41%

State Bank funds a greater portion of its nonliquid assets with volatile liabilities. Indeed, for the peer group, the negative ratio indicates that some of its temporary assets are funded with long-term (i.e., stable) sources of funds.

Other Financial Ratios

Many more financial ratios than those discussed previously are conceivable. The analyst can construct other financial ratios if they might help to reveal the bank's strengths and weaknesses. For example, two areas that might be useful to explore are the ability of the bank to minimize taxes and the interest sensitivity of its mix of sources and uses of funds.

TAXES The tax exposure of the bank can be assessed by using the following ratio:

$$\text{Tax rate (\%)} = \frac{\text{Total taxes paid}}{\text{Net income before taxes}} \times 100 \qquad 3.10$$

where total taxes paid include the tax consequences of security gains and losses. The tax rate for State Bank was as follows:

Example:

State Bank (Year 200X)	47.4% = $2,267/$4,787 × 100
Peer Group	49.3%

Enterprise Risk Solutions, or ERS, at http://www.erisks.com *is an integrated online resource for risk professionals across all industries, providing education, best practices, benchmarking, analytics, case studies, and news via the Internet. Check out the Enterprise-wide risk management benchmarking survey, which allows banks, insurance companies, and other firms to benchmark their risk management practices against their peers.*

In general, the marginal tax rate (i.e., the tax rate applicable to the last dollar of income earned) for most banks is the maximum statutory rate.

One way that banks traditionally lowered their tax burden was to purchase municipal bonds, which in the past offered tax-exempt interest payments. Under the Tax Reform Act of 1986, this tax reduction technique was substantially lessened because interest expenses incurred on deposits subsequently invested in tax-exempt obligations can no longer be deducted from income for tax purposes. An exception to this new law is the purchase of tax-exempt securities (excluding private activity bonds, such as industrial development bonds) issued by municipalities offering $10 million or less of government obligations.

Another means of lowering taxes in the past was to deduct larger provisions for loan losses from income than anticipated charge-offs would suggest. According to the new tax law, however, deductions are allowed only as loans are actually charged off.

INTEREST SENSITIVITY   Interest sensitivity is the responsiveness of liability costs and asset returns to changes in interest rates. The difference between the quantities of **interest-sensitive assets and liabilities** is known as the **dollar gap ratio**. To compare the interest sensitivity of different banks, the following dollar gap ratio can be calculated:

$$\text{Dollar gap ratio (\%)} = \frac{\text{Interest rate-sensitive assets} - \text{Interest rate-sensitive liabilities}}{\text{Total assets}} \times 100 \quad 3.11$$

where *rate-sensitive* is defined as short-term assets and liabilities with maturities of less than one year, or that reprice in less than one year. To obtain a more complete picture of interest sensitivity, calculate gap ratios for assets and liabilities of different maturity ranges (e.g., 0–90 days, 90–120 days, and 120 days–1 year). By structuring assets and liabilities in terms of maturity ranges, or "buckets," the analyst can determine the extent to which a change in interest rates would affect bank profitability. If interest rates increased (decreased) in the future, positive gap ratios would cause the bank's profitability to increase (decrease). The opposite effects would correspond to negative gap ratios. Chapter 5 discusses interest rate sensitivity and gap management in greater detail.

Although the income statement and balance sheet do not provide sufficient information to make such calculations, in the case of State Bank, the gap ratio is as follows:

Example:

State Bank (Year 200X)	–18.25%
Peer Group	–6.00%

EVA is a registered trademark of Stern, Stewart & Co. http://www.eva.com/ checkme.html has abundant examples of valuation employing EVA methodology.

MANAGERIAL ISSUES

Internal Performance Evaluation Based on Economic Profit

In the 1990s Banker's Trust popularized a method of evaluating loans known as **RAROC** that has been expanded to include other areas of internal performance, including product lines and customers. Applied to pricing loans, RAROC allocates equity capital depending on risk of loss, calculates a required rate of return on equity, and then uses that information in pricing loans to ensure their profitability to the bank. Assume the following information:

Cost of funds	5.00%
Provision for loan losses	1.00
Direct expense	0.50
Indirect expense	0.25
Overhead	0.25
Total charges before capital charge	7.00%
Capital charge*	2.29
Total required loan rate	9.29%

*Note: The capital charge is determined by multiplying the equity capital allocated to the loan times the opportunity cost of equity and then converting to a pretax level. Assume that the allocated equity to loan ratio is 10% and the opportunity cost of equity is 16%, such that the after-tax capital charge is 1.6%. If the tax rate for the bank is 0.3, the pretax capital charge is 1.6/(1.0 − 0.3), or 2.29.

In the preceding example, if the loan rate is 9.29%, the bank will earn the target return on equity of 16%. Of course, if the bank can price the loan at a rate higher than 9.29%, it will earn profit over the target level of equity returns. In this case an *economic profit* is earned in that the value of equity is increased. Notice that economic profit is different from accounting profit. Loans with a rate of return of 8.00% likely would provide a positive return on assets, but equity returns would decline, as equity investors are disappointed by earnings rates below their expectations.

A critical step in applying RAROC is determining the capital assigned to the loan. In the example we

assumed that 10% equity would be needed to support the loan. One way to arrive at this figure is to use regulatory capital rules for the equity assignment (see Chapter 11 for details). However, capital regulations are only a minimum level, and it is possible that the bank's risk preferences require more equity be assigned to high-risk loans. In this regard, *capital-at-risk* (CAR) can be assigned to business units based on either their actual *utilized* capital or the *allocated* capital limit or capacity provided by top management (using past performance and expected earnings data). Utilized CAR is a good approach in smaller business units to avoid penalizing them for not using excess capital beyond their control. Allocated capital is more appropriate for larger business units; it enables some flexibility by managers to expand operations to the point that all capital is profitably invested.

RAROC can be extended to product lines that divide the bank into business units. For example, a large bank will typically have consumer banking, wholesale banking, and securities components. These business areas have different risk exposures that require different capital allocations. Also, operating costs can differ across product lines. It should be obvious that business units will tend to have different required rates of return in order to reach equity return targets and generate economic profits. These rates of return are minimum rates that managers need to incorporate in their pricing decisions and risk assessments. Today, many banks employ RAROC to measure managerial performance and tie compensation to earned rates of return relative to benchmark required rates of return. Hence, managers cannot simply earn accounting profits or expand market share at the expense of shareholder earnings. In this way differences between managers' versus owners' goals are mitigated to some degree. One potential drawback of applying RAROC to product lines is that it may not be possible to separate the economic costs and revenues of the different products. The production of outputs may share inputs, such as land, labor, and capital investments, which makes it impossible to individually analyze the product lines. Under these circumstances, either some assumptions on how to allocate costs and revenues must be made or the analyses must be performed on the bundle of jointly produced products.

Economic Value Added (EVA)

A performance metric that is similar in spirit to RAROC is *economic value added (EVA)*. EVA can be defined as follows:

EVA = Adjusted earnings − Opportunity cost of capital

where adjusted earnings is net income after taxes, and the opportunity cost of capital equals the cost of equity times equity capital. The consulting firm Stern Stewart & Co. developed EVA, but other consulting firms have produced similar performance measures, including Holt Value Associates' cash flow rate of return on investment (CFROI), Boston Consulting Group's total business return (TBR), and LEK/Alear Consulting Group's shareholder value added (SVA).

Managers can apply EVA to loans, projects, product lines, and so on, in order to evaluate whether the investment will be justifiable in terms of rewarding shareholders. In this context new investments should be undertaken until the marginal contribution of the last investment is zero (i.e., EVA = 0). Contrary to an accounting analysis framework in which only the investments with the highest ROEs are accepted, EVA accepts all investments that contribute to shareholder wealth.

On a practical level, managers using EVA face tradeoffs in attempting to increase the EVA for investments under their control. A higher EVA can be achieved by boosting adjusted earnings (via lowering costs, increasing sales, etc.), lowering the cost of equity, or by lowering the equity allocated to the investment. However, if earnings are increased by increasing sales, this increased production capacity will imply greater equity investment. Assuming the marginal cost of equity capital remains constant (which may not be true), EVA will only increase if the higher adjusted earnings more than offset the greater opportunity cost of capital. By focusing attention on the tradeoffs involved in the components of EVA, managers can make decisions more

consistent with creating economic value, as opposed to maximizing profits or market share. Like RAROC, EVA is beneficial in assessing managerial performance and developing incentive compensation schemes compatible with shareholder wealth goals (i.e., reducing agency costs). Also like RAROC, EVA presents some difficult challenges in allocation costs, revenues, and equity when applied to lines of business, divisions, and products that are not separate from one another due to joint production of multiple products with shared inputs.

Notice the difference between RAROC and EVA. The former compares business unit profit with the unit's capital-at-risk, whereas the latter compares business unit profit with the cost of capital. Critics of RAROC argue that it rejects profitable business opportunities when RAROC exceeds the cost of capital, which will decrease shareholder wealth. However, if the cost of capital is greater than RAROC, then use of EVA would reject profitable opportunities that would improve current performance. One way to resolve this dilemma is to recognize that the cost of capital is a longer-term concept than RAROC. Thus, short-term opportunities can be accepted with RAROC even though their rate of return is below the long-run cost of capital (and therefore would be rejected by EVA). And, investment opportunities must earn returns that exceed the cost of capital in the long run as suggested by EVA.

In sum, RAROC, EVA, and other performance measures based on economic profit help to align the managerial actions with shareholder interests. Normally, they lead to better risk management, efficient control of resources, and informed judgment on the acceptability of investments by the bank. However, they do have weaknesses, especially with respect to their application to jointly produced products in banking. In the years ahead these methods no doubt will be further refined to address these weaknesses. At present most large and regional banks internally employ one or more of these performance evaluation methods.

For an excellent discussion of bank management practice and internal performance measurement, as well as further references to related articles, see Francesco Saita, "Allocation of Risk Capital in Financial Institutions," *Financial Management* vol. 28 (1999), pp. 95–111.

RiskMetrics Group, or RMG, at http://www. riskmetrics.com/ is the world's leading provider of risk management research, data, software, and education. RMG is responsible for the creation and support of benchmark risk management products including RiskMetrics, CreditMetrics, DataMetrics, and now, CorporateMetrics. Formerly the Risk Management Products and Research group at J. P. Morgan, RMG delivers risk management technology to more than 5,000 institutions around the world.

The large negative gap ratio for State Bank relative to its peer group suggests that its profitability will be affected much more than peer banks by a change in interest rates within the next year. If interest rates increase (decrease) in the near future, State Bank's profitability will decrease (increase) dramatically because of the negative gap ratio. It is true that some amount of interest sensitivity may be desirable to take advantage of anticipated movements in interest rates, but excessive sensitivity, as in the present instance, may well be considered "betting the bank" and, therefore, is not prudent management.

Financial Performance of BankAmerica

An overview of the financial performance of BankAmerica, the second largest commercial bank in the United States, is provided in Table 3.3. As shown there, BankAmerica is compared to a peer group comprised of Citibank and Chase Manhattan Bank. BankAmerica earned a lower return on equity (ROE) than the peer group in 1998. The lower ROE for BankAmerica was not due to a difference in its return on assets, which was similar to its peers (1.19% versus 1.14%). Instead, the reason for the low ROE was a high equity to total assets ratio (9.05% versus 6.60%) that lowers the equity multiplier (or total assets to total equity ratio).

TABLE 3.3	Selected Profitability and Risk Ratios for BankAmerica (Year-End 1998)			
(in $ thousands)	BankAmerica	Citibank	Chase Manhattan Bank	Peer Group (Citi + Chase)/2
Total assets	$317,268,000	$304,316,000	$291,476,000	$297,896,000
Total liabilities	288,544,990	284,088,000	272,371,010	278,229,505
Total equity	28,723,000	20,228,000	19,105,000	19,666,500
Net income	940,000	793,000	902,000	817,500
ROA	1.19%	1.05%	1.23%	1.14%
ROE	13.26	15.88	18.80	17.34
NIM	3.53	4.15	3.00	3.58
Net charge-offs/loans	0.51%	0.89%	0.28%	0.59%
Noninterest expenses/revenues	54.17	64.68	61.66	63.17
Provision for loan loss/loans	1.40	2.46	2.00	2.23
Noncurrent loans/loans	0.98	1.99	1.04	1.52
Equity capital/assets	9.05	6.65	6.55	6.60
Purchased liabilities/assets	81.00	90.00	86.00	88.00

Note: Data were collected at the bank level, rather than for the bank holding company.

Banker's Trust web site at http://www.gis.deutsche-bank.com/gis/public/pb_index.html *presents information on RAROC 2020, an adaptation of the RAROC methodology for evaluating risk.*

Examining selected risk measures for BankAmerica suggests lower risk levels than the peer group. Both measures of credit risk—provision for loan losses and net charge-offs—reflect less credit risk for BankAmerica than the peer group. Also, BankAmerica had a smaller amount of purchased liabilities than its peer group, which implies lower potential liquidity risk. Consistent with lower risk exposures, as already mentioned, BankAmerica had a higher ratio of equity to total assets than its peers.

SUMMARY

The evaluation of bank performance is a complex process that involves assessing interactions between the environment, internal operations, and external activities. The ultimate objective of management is to maximize the value of the bank's equity shares by attaining the optimal mix of returns and risks. In this respect bank management needs to develop a comprehensive plan in order to identify objectives, goals, budgets, and strategies that will be consistent with the maximization of share values. Planning should encompass both internal and external performance dimensions. The primary method of evaluating internal performance is by analyzing accounting statements. Financial ratios of accounting items permit a historical sketch of bank returns and risks. External performance is best measured by evaluating the bank's market share, regulatory compliance, and public confidence. Because of increasing innovation and deregulation in the financial services industry, internal and external competitiveness is becoming a critical factor in performance.

Key Terms and Concepts

Asset utilization
Balance sheet
Charge-offs
Dollar gap ratio
Equity multiplier
Economic value added (EVA)
Earning assets
Federal funds sold/purchased
Income statement
Interest rate spread
Interest-bearing liabilities
Interest-sensitive assets/liabilities
Interest sensitivity gap
Liquidity
Market share

Net charge-offs
Net interest margin (NIM)
Nonperforming assets
Profit margin
Provision for loan losses
RAROC
Report of Condition
Report of Income
Reserve for loan losses
Return on average assets (ROA)
Return on equity (ROE)
Taxable equivalent income
Tax-equivalent yield
Temporary investments ratio
Volatile liability dependency

Questions

3.1 Discuss the difference between bank goals and bank objectives in the planning process. What is the ultimate objective of the bank?

3.2 Why is conserving costs by keeping employee salaries, wages, and benefits down not necessarily a good idea?

3.3 Define bank growth. Why might super growth be a problem for a bank?

3.4 Give at least three reasons for staying up to date with bank technology.

3.5 Why do you think banks are sensitive about news reports concerning them in the financial press?

3.6 ROE and ROA are two key measures of bank profitability. Discuss the importance of these ratios to (a) insured depositors, (b) bank shareholders, and (c) bank management.

3.7 If a bank has a relatively low ROA but a relatively high ROE, what factor would explain this difference? Show an equation to demonstrate your answer.

3.8 In calculating the net interest margin, why do municipal bond interest earnings have to be grossed up?

3.9 If federal regulators require that bank capital be increased to at least 10% of total assets, how would bank growth be affected?

3.10 Do loan losses reduce bank profit?

3.11 Bank A operates with an equity to assets ratio of 10% and has a return on assets ratio of 1%. What is its return on equity? What would its ROE be if it were allowed to operate with a 2% equity to assets ratio? What does this suggest about the effects of financial leverage?

3.12 Give three explanations for a bank having a lower ratio of interest expenses to total assets than its peers.

3.13 How did the Tax Reform Act of 1986 affect interest deductions on deposits?

3.14 If the dollar gap ratio is negative and interest rates are expected to rise in the near future, what will happen to bank profitability, provided all else remains the same?

3.15 Why have billion-dollar banks been less affected by deposit rate deregulations than smaller, retail banks?

3.16 What are the principal types of bank risk? Give at least one ratio for each type of risk.

3.17 What is RAROC? EVA? What are their strengths and weaknesses?

3.18 Go to the FDIC Institution Directory at *http://www.fdic.gov/bank/individual/index.html* and search for a commercial bank in your town or city. Give an overview of the financial performance of the bank in the past year.

3.19 Go to *http://www.eva.com/checkme.html* and find examples of valuation employing EVA methodology. Describe two of the examples that apply to commercial banking.

3.20 Look up the web site for a money center bank in the United States. Give a brief overview of its financial performance based on accounting data over the past three years if possible.

Problems

3.1 (a) Exhibits 3.1 and 3.2 provide year-end Reports of Condition and Income for Z-Bank in 20XX-1 and 20XX. Exhibit 3.3 shows a list of financial ratios for Z-bank's peer group. Calculate these financial ratios for Z-bank. Round your answers to the hundredths place. For the dollar gap ratio assume that all securities, one-half of loans and lease-financing receivables, and all deposits have maturities less than one year, and exclude cash and due from the calculation of this ratio.

(b) Discuss the profitability of Z-Bank by comparing its performance in 20XX-1 and 20XX and by comparing it to its peer group in these years. Break down ROE in your analysis of profitability and discuss the influence of components of ROE on Z-Bank's profitability.

(c) Discuss Z-Bank's risk ratios over time and relative to its peer group. What are Z-Bank's strengths and weaknesses?

(d) If interest rates rise in the future, what is the implication to Z-Bank's profitability?

3.2 NB bank earns 1% on its assets and has a 20% tax rate. It earns 8% on loans, and 6% on investments. It pays 4% on time deposits, and 3% on federal funds purchased. Demand deposits pay no interest. Construct an income statement for NB bank (assume a 20% tax rate). With this information construct as many ratios of bank performance as you can with the data available.

Balance Sheet for NB

Assets		Liabilities	
Cash and due from banks	$ 20	Demand deposits	$ 40
Investments	200	Time deposits	150
Federal funds sold	0	Federal funds purchased	120
Loans	120	Equity	50
Premises	20		$360
	$360		

EXHIBIT 3.1	Report of Condition: Z-Bank	

	Year-end ($ millions)	
Report of Condition Items	**20XX-1**	**20XX**
Cash and due from depository institutions	$ 200	$ 205
U.S. Treasury securities	50	40
Obligations of other U.S. governmental agencies	20	17
Obligations of state and political subdivisions	70	68
All other securities	20	18
Federal funds sold and securities purchased	35	30
Total cash and securities	$ 395	$ 378
Loans	700	600
Lease financing receivables	10	10
Banks premises, furniture, and fixtures	15	16
All other assets	70	65
Total assets	$ 1,190	$ 1,069
Demand deposits	267	138
Time and savings deposits	350	250
Deposits in foreign offices	100	100
Deposits of U.S. government	2	2
Deposits of state and political government	50	45
All other deposits	100	170
Total deposits	$ 869	$ 705
Federal funds purchased and securities sold	140	180
Interest-bearing demand notes and other borrowings	30	40
Mortgage indebtedness	5	5
All other liabilities	70	65
Total liabilities	$ 1,114	$ 995
Subordinated notes and debentures	5	5
Preferred stock—par value	1	1
Common stock—par value	40	40
Surplus	10	10
Undivided profits and capital reserves	20	18
Total capital	76	74
Total liabilities and capital	$ 1,190	$ 1,069

EXHIBIT 3.2	Report of Income: Z-Bank

	Year-end ($ millions)	
Report of Condition Items	20XX-1	20XX
Interest and fees on loans	$ 120	$ 100
Interest on balances with depository institutions	15	13
Income on federal funds sold and securities purchased	5	4
Interest on U.S. Treasury and other agencies' securities	7	7
Interests on obligations of state and political subdivisions	5	5
Interests on other securities	1	1
Income from direct lease financing	2	2
Income from fiduciary activities	1	1
Service charges on deposit accounts	3	2
Other service charges	6	5
Other operating income	4	3
Total operating income	$ 169	$ 143
Salaries and employee benefits	20	18
Interest on CDs of $100,000 or more	15	13
Interest on deposits in foreign offices	35	37
Interest on other deposits	8	14
Interest on federal funds purchased and securities sold	18	23
Interest on demand notes and other borrowings	3	3
Interest on subordinated notes and debentures	1	1
Occupancy, furniture, and fixed expenses	6	6
Provision for possible loan losses	4	4
Other operating expenses	10	10
Total operating expenses	$ 120	$ 129
Income before taxes and securities transactions	49	14
Applicable income taxes	23	7
Income before securities gains or losses	23	7
Securities gains, net of taxes	–1	–1
Net income	$ 22	$ 6
Cash dividends	12	6
Undivided profits	10	0
Recoveries credited to provision for possible loan losses	1	1
Losses charged to provision for possible loan losses	–3	–7

EXHIBIT 3.3	Financial Ratios for Z-Bank's Peer Group	

Financial Ratios	20XX-1	20XX
Profit Ratios		
Return on equity (ROE)	20.00%	18.00%
Return on assets (ROA)	1.00	0.90
Profit margin	7.00	6.50
Net operating margin	2.40	2.30
Net interest margin	5.20	5.00
Asset utilization		
Risk Ratios		
Capital		
Equity multiplier	16.00	15.50
Asset quality		
Loss rate	0.35%	0.45%
Loan ratio	55.00	53.00
Operating efficiency (% of total assets)		
Interest expense	6.50%	6.55%
Wages and salaries	1.72	1.74
Occupancy	0.48	0.49
PLL	0.30	0.32
Other expenses	0.85	0.85
Liquidity		
Cash ratio	17.00	17.00
Cash and securities ratio	36.00	37.00
Other financial ratios		
Tax rate	50.00%	50.00%
Dollar gap ratio	− 15.00	− 10.00

3.3 Using the information given here, calculate the ROA for each of the banks.

	ROE	Total Equity Capital	Total Assets
Videlia National & Trust	8.16%	$ 14.8 million	$260.5 million
York Savings and Trust	16.24	11.7 million	135.4 million
New York State	2.06	63 million	972.6 million

3.4 Capital State Bank reports total interest revenue of $86.42 million, total interest expense of $58.62 million, provision for loan losses of $3.6 million, total noninterest revenue of $15.61 million, and total noninterest expense of $28.60 million. Total assets are $842.16 million. What is Capital's net interest income? What is its net interest margin? Return on assets? Asset utilization? Profit margin?

3.5 Given the following information on Big State Bank, and on its peer group, evaluate the strengths and weaknesses of the bank. What additional information would you want in order to conduct a more in-depth analysis?

| | Big State | Peer Group |
| | For the Year Ended | |
	12/31/XX	12/31/XX
Profitability		
Return on assets	0.01%	0.75%
Return on equity	0.24	14.63
Earning assets/total assets	89.03	92.34
Noninterest expenses/average assets	1.90	1.72
Yield on Interest-Earning Assets		
Loans receivable	10.60%	9.63%
Mortgage-backed securities	5.67	5.82
U.S. government and other	3.71	4.98
Other	3.94	3.54
Total	7.28	8.27
Yield on Interest-Bearing Liabilities		
Deposits	3.99%	3.44%
Other borrowings	5.11	4.23
Total	4.54	3.86
Gross Interest Spread	2.74	4.21
Interest income/total average assets	6.44%	7.64%
Interest expense/total average liabilities & equity	4.23	3.66
Net Interest Spread	2.21%	3.98%
Capital Position		
Equity capital/total assets	4.63%	6.82%

3.6 Given the following information for First National Bank's reserve for loan loss position, answer these questions:

(a) What is the amount of net charge-offs in each year?

(b) What trend is evident in the bank's actual loan loss experience? What information is useful in making this assessment?

(c) What trend is evident in the bank's anticipated loan losses?

	20XX	20XX-1
Balance at beginning of period	$1,222	$1,206
– Loan charge-offs	61	46
+ Less loan recoveries	32	10
+ Provision for loan losses	40	52
= Balance at end of period	$1,233	$1,222

Heartland Bank Holding Company

Sandra Gonzales was recently hired by the Heartland Bank Holding Company (a $1.6 billion in assets organization with 27 operating subsidiaries) as a financial analyst. While her duties involved a variety of tasks, including some auditing of the subsidiaries, her first major task was to analyze the possible purchase of the LNB Holding Company and its sole subsidiary, the Lester National Bank. The profile of the LNB fit the policies of Heartland: a relatively small (about $200 million in assets) bank serving a rural area, but a bank that dominated its market and had been profitable throughout the years of the recent farm crisis. Indeed, Hartland had found its niche by acquiring smaller banks within a radius of 250 miles located in communities with relatively limited competition. Hence, Sandra realized that the issues here were primarily financial.

To do the analysis necessary to present a report to the senior management (specifically the Acquisitions Committee), Sandra obtained the latest Uniform Bank Performance Report on the Lester National Bank (essentially the same as a report on LNB Holding Company since the parent had no assets other than Lester National Bank and also did not have any debt on its balance sheet). While Sandra had majored in finance during her days at State U, she was overwhelmed with the numbers and the ratios provided in the UBPR. She, therefore, decided to write down a number of questions to investigate in order to focus her attention on the most relevant issues.

The initial questions she considered were the following:

1. How profitable is Lester compared to its peers? How has its profitability changed over time?
2. What are the principal differences in income and expense ratios between Lester and its peers? How have they changed over time?
3. How does Lester's credit risk compare with its peers? Is it higher? If so, does it earn an adequate compensation for taking credit risk? Is it adequately reserved?
4. How does Lester's liquidity risk compare with its peers?
5. Has Lester taken more or less interest rate risk than its peers? Has it worked?
6. Does Lester have adequate capital? Is there a significant risk that it will outgrow its capital?

Sandra knew that although the answers to these questions were important, they were not the end of her project. Assuming that Heartland wanted to bid for LNB Inc., Sandra would be asked to value the bank, that is, determine an appropriate offering price. Relevant to this issue, she knew that the owner of LNB Inc. wanted an entirely cash transaction. She pondered the valuation issue and in her analysis focused on the attached UBPR data on Lester (Exhibits 3.4 through 3.9).

EXHIBIT 3.4   Summary Ratios

	19XX LNB	19XX PEER 10[1]	19XX PCT[2]	19XX-1 LNB	19XX-1 PEER 10	19XX-1 PCT	19XX-2 LNB	19XX-2 PEER 10	19XX-2 PCT	19XX-3 LNB	19XX-3 PEER 10	19XX-4 LNB	19XX-4 PEER 10
Average assets ($000)	192419			176798			168902			172682		171255	
Net income ($000)	2520			2492			1687			1329		2748	
Number of banks in peer group	170			145			136			124		103	
Earnings and Profitability													
Percent of average assets:													
Net interest income (TE)	4.10	3.90	59	4.15	4.28	67	3.31	4.43	40	4.34	4.05	4.54	
+ Noninterest income	0.30	0.58	13	0.64	0.34	13	0.28	0.64	13	0.60	0.28	0.55	
− Overhead expense	1.88	2.56	14	2.66	2.03	23	1.63	2.60	16	2.51	1.66	2.47	
− Provision: loan/lease losses	0.67	0.68	62	1.01	1.17	82	0.66	0.73	76	0.54	0.14	0.53	
= Pretax operating income (TE)	1.84	1.45	63	1.14	1.41	35	1.30	1.76	30	1.86	2.53	2.09	
+ Securities gains (losses)	0.64	0.02	99	0.11	0.43	99	0.12	0.04	92	0.01	0.43	0.00	
= Pretax net oper inc (TE)	2.49	1.49	85	1.31	1.85	85	1.42	1.90	46	1.85	2.96	2.05	
Net operating income	1.31	0.83	79	0.67	1.00	85	0.77	1.03	42	1.05	1.60	1.12	
Adjusted net oper income	1.55	0.95	84	0.85	1.34	97	0.88	1.07	69	1.11	1.58	1.23	
Adjusted net income	1.70	0.86	91	0.72	1.31	98	0.88	1.00	70	1.03	1.51	1.10	
Net income	1.31	0.84	78	0.68	1.00	85	0.77	1.03	41	1.04	1.60	1.12	
Percent of avg earning assets:													
Interest income (TE)	10.01	9.56	74	10.49	12.28	88	12.56	11.72	84	12.55	12.00	12.21	11.44
Interest expense	5.60	5.38	67	6.03	7.43	78	8.83	6.92	81	7.88	7.66	7.25	6.48
Net interest income (TE)	4.41	4.20	59	4.48	4.85	72	3.73	4.83	55	4.71	4.34	4.95	4.96
Loan & Lease Losses, Reserves and Noncurrent Loans and Leases													
Net loss to avg tot loans & lses	0.92	1.17	52	1.73	1.73	74	1.17	1.39	72	0.85	0.34	0.87	
Earnings coverage of new loss (x)	3.54	6.20	47	3.87	2.08	31	2.38	4.93	27	9.08	7.51	9.59	
Loss reserve to net losses (x)	3.55	2.99	70	1.50	0.88	54	0.71	1.71	27	3.03	1.55	2.87	
Loss resv to tot loans & leases	3.23	1.85	89	1.67	1.41	89	0.77	1.39	62	1.26	0.49	1.10	
% Noncurrent loans & leases	2.44	3.02		3.11	1.83		3.08	2.86		2.47	2.06	1.99	

EXHIBIT 3.4   Summary Ratios (continued)

	19XX			19XX-1			19XX-2			19XX-3		19XX-4	
	LNB	PEER 10[1]	PCT[2]	LNB	PEER 10	PCT	LNB	PEER 10	PCT	LNB	PEER 10	LNB	PEER 10
Average assets ($000)	192419			176798			168902			172682		171255	
Net income ($000)	2520			2492			1687			1329		2748	
Number of banks in peer group	170			145			136			124		103	
Liquidity and Rate Sensitivity													
Volatile liability dependence	40.24	−5.41	97	34.15	−7.93	97	43.75	−1.05	98	37.32	0.22	26.07	1.20
Net loans & leases to assets	43.74	48.70	38	44.54	48.95	39	48.78	52.16	37	49.68	52.83	49.67	50.86
Net assets repricable in 1 year or less to assets	−31.68	−13.05	09	−32.70	−10.02	04	−23.07	−5.66	08	−14.31	−7.64	−17.71	−6.97
Capitalization													
Prime capital to adj avg assets[3]	8.42	8.85	45	8.73	8.82	52	8.07	8.74	36	7.76	8.60	7.52	8.54
Cash dividends to net income	71.43	45.75	71	72.23	47.30	77	106.70	45.03	90	108.35	46.83	65.50	40.19
Ret earns to avg total equity	4.78	4.72	49	4.82	2.21	48	−0.83	6.06	21	−0.82	6.13	7.26	7.79
Growth Rates													
Assets	12.08	3.51	83	2.77	4.01	42	1.88	5.43	30	−3.16	6.68	6.26	8.67
Primary capital[3]	7.46	5.98	53	14.18	5.28	88	3.37	7.27	26	0.96	7.71	7.25	9.21
Net loans & leases	10.07	1.41	75	−6.15	−1.19	36	0.03	4.36	35	−3.15	10.64	23.06	8.90
Volatile liabilities	43.95	6.27	87	−18.98	3.22	23	−2.28	9.35	36	26.12	17.15	−8.07	2.75

1. PEER 10 represents a peer group of 10 banks similar to Lester National Bank in size and regional location.
2. PCT is the percentile rank of the bank in the total number of banks in the peer group.
3. Refer to Chapter 11 for primary capital definition.

EXHIBIT 3.5 Balance Sheet—Percentage Composition of Assets and Liabilities

Assets, Percent of Avg Assets	19XX			19XX-1			19XX-2			19XX-3		19XX-4	
	LNB	PEER 10[1]	PCT[2]	LNB	PEER 10	PCT	LNB	PEER 10	PCT	LNB	PEER 10	LNB	PEER 10
Total loans	46.29	49.98	38	49.22	51.28	43	51.21	53.65	40	50.69	53.36	47.98	51.20
Lease financing receivables	0.00	0.00	74	0.00	0.00	75	0.00	0.00	75	0.00	0.01	0.00	0.00
Less: loss reserves	1.43	0.84	88	1.00	0.78	76	0.60	0.72	48	0.35	0.66	0.28	0.59
Transfer risk reserve	NA	NA	NA	NA	NA	NA	NA	NA	NA	NA	NA	NA	NA
Net loans & leases	44.86	49.20	37	48.22	50.54	43	50.61	52.99	40	50.34	52.78	47.70	50.70
Securities over 1 year	43.52	22.41	95	41.25	20.38	96	32.22	20.30	88	31.04	21.57	35.09	23.25
Subtotal	88.38	71.61	96	89.48	70.92	98	82.83	73.29	87	81.38	74.35	82.79	74.45
Interest-bearing bank balances	0.21	2.30	37	0.11	2.15	34	0.00	1.92	32	0.44	2.41	4.77	2.87
Federal funds sold & resales	1.39	6.03	13	0.39	6.86	02	0.56	5.36	05	2.50	4.35	2.74	4.36
Trading account assets	0.00	0.00	97	0.00	0.00	97	0.00	0.00	98	0.00	0.00	0.00	0.00
Debt securities 1 yr & less	0.46	8.18	05	0.37	9.70	04	6.55	9.03	40	6.92	9.26	2.48	7.78
Temporary investments	2.06	20.07	02	0.87	20.22	01	7.11	17.54	07	9.86	16.63	10.00	16.21
Total earning assets	90.44	91.78	25	90.35	91.28	32	89.94	90.92	29	91.24	90.98	92.78	90.72
Noninterest cash & due fr banks	4.77	4.22	71	4.43	4.66	52	4.34	4.82	40	3.98	4.72	2.82	5.18
Premises, fix asst, cap leases	1.17	1.38	40	1.35	1.50	49	1.49	1.57	52	1.53	1.47	1.59	1.52
Other real estate owned	1.36	0.52	87	1.45	0.53	90	1.70	0.41	96	0.51	0.27	0.02	0.17
Acceptances & other assets	2.24	1.76	82	2.42	1.92	85	2.52	2.15	75	2.75	2.26	2.78	2.14
Subtotal	9.56	8.22	74	9.65	8.72	67	10.06	9.08	70	8.76	9.02	7.22	9.28
Total assets	100.00	100.00		100.00	100.00		100.00	100.00		100.00	100.00	100.01	100.00
Standby letters of credit	0.00	0.40	23	0.00	0.48	21	0.00	0.52	22	0.01	0.46	0.01	0.52

EXHIBIT 3.5   Balance Sheet—Percentage Composition of Assets and Liabilities (*continued*)

Liabilities, Percent of Avg Assets	19XX LNB	19XX PEER 10[1]	19XX PCT[2]	19XX-1 LNB	19XX-1 PEER 10	19XX-1 PCT	19XX-2 LNB	19XX-2 PEER 10	19XX-2 PCT	19XX-3 LNB	19XX-3 PEER 10	19XX-4 LNB	19XX-4 PEER 10
Demand deposits	11.01	11.15	53	12.32	12.15	54	12.77	13.13	54	13.26	13.39	13.64	14.74
All NOW and ATS accounts	2.92	10.13	04	2.79	9.32	03	2.62	8.72	02	1.78	8.44	2.66	7.91
Super NOWS included in above	NA	NA	NA	NA	NA	NA	0.39	3.98	10	0.22	3.51	0.17	2.21
MMDA savings	21.18	12.77	91	21.29	13.50	89	16.90	11.87	83	15.65	10.83	6.96	8.19
Other savings deposits	1.54	6.07	07	1.78	4.94	11	2.01	4.74	12	2.17	5.23	4.16	7.24
Time deposits under $100M	15.30	32.23	06	15.51	32.94	06	15.54	33.55	03	19.66	33.66	27.44	32.68
Core deposits	51.97	73.73	06	53.68	73.13	04	49.85	72.29	01	52.53	71.70	54.86	71.55
Time deposits over $100M	39.04	14.70	95	36.56	15.17	97	40.61	15.55	99	37.70	15.67	34.69	15.64
Deposits in foreign offices	NA	NA	NA	NA	NA	NA	NA	NA	NA	NA	NA	NA	NA
Federal funds purch & repos	0.16	0.93	50	0.20	1.06	48	0.09	1.17	35	0.64	1.48	1.49	2.35
Other borrowing (+note opt)	0.00	0.27	45	0.134	0.31	60	0.00	0.31	43	0.00	0.33	0.00	0.26
Volatile liabilities	39.21	16.90	93	37.10	17.42	94	40.71	17.97	97	38.34	18.56	36.18	18.73
Acceptances & other liab	1.07	1.03	65	1.19	1.19	56	1.53	1.39	67	1.37	1.44	1.38	1.45
Total liabilities (incl mortg)	92.25	91.92	52	91.97	91.97	43	92.09	91.92	52	92.24	91.86	92.42	91.93
Subordinated notes & debentures	0.00	0.00	90	0.00	0.00	87	0.00	0.00	81	0.00	0.00	0.00	0.00
All common & preferred capital	7.75	8.04	47	8.03	7.95	57	7.91	8.01	52	7.06	7.92	7.58	7.91
Total liabilities & capital	100.00	100.00		100.00	100.00		100.00	100.00		100.00	100.00	100.00	100.00
Noninterest bearing deposits	11.01	11.16	53	13.41	12.30	65	14.86	13.29	70	14.23	13.56	13.64	14.74
Interest bearing deposits	80.00	77.55	66	76.84	76.30	51	75.61	75.01	48	76.01	74.17	75.92	72.42
Total brokered deposits	0.00	0.00	91	0.00	0.00	92	0.00	0.00	92	0.00	0.00	0.00	0.00

1. PEER 10 represents a peer group of 10 banks similar to Lester National Bank in size and regional location.
2. PCT is the percentile rank of LNB in the total number of banks in the peer group. (Exact numbers are provided at the beginning of Exhibit 3.4)

EXHIBIT 3.6   Analysis of Allowance for Loan and Lease Losses and Loan Mix

Change: Loans & Lease Reserve ($000)	19XX	19XX-1	19XX-2	19XX-3	19XX-4
Beginning balance	2536	1247	679	439	483
Gross loan & lease losses	1129	2084	1444	1054	337
Recoveries	305	165	33	102	53
Net loan & lease losses	824	1919	1411	952	284
Provision for loan, lease loss	1294	3208	1980	1142	241
Other adjustments	0	0	0	50	0
Ending balance	3006	2536	1248	679	440
Net ATTR charge-offs	NA	NA	NA	NA	NA
Other ATTR changes (net)	NA	NA	NA	NA	NA
Average total LNS&LS	89737	83433	81478	81568	83275

Analysis Ratios	LNB	PEER 10[1]	PCT[2]	LNB	PEER 10	PCT	LNB	PEER 10	PCT	LNB	PEER 10	LNB	PEER 10
Loss provision to avg assets	0.67	0.68	62	1.81	1.01	82	1.17	0.73	76	0.66	0.54	0.14	0.53
Loss prov to avgt total LNS&LS	1.44	1.32	66	3.89	1.91	82	2.43	1.43	79	1.40	0.96	0.29	0.98
Net losses to avg tot LNS&LS	0.92	1.17	52	2.33	1.73	74	1.73	1.39	72	1.17	0.85	0.34	0.87
Gross loss to avg tot LNS&LS	1.26	1.36	57	2.53	1.96	73	1.77	1.58	67	1.29	1.02	0.40	1.03
Recoveries to avg tot LNS&LS	0.34	0.24	72	0.20	0.22	60	0.04	0.16	24	0.13	0.16	0.06	0.13
Recoveries to prior period loss	14.64	17.91	55	11.43	20.61	40	3.13	23.74	08	30.27	23.29	12.59	24.29
Loss reserve to tot LNS&LS	3.23	1.85	89	3.00	1.67	89	1.41	1.39	62	0.77	1.26	0.49	1.10
Loss reserve to net losses (x)	3.65	2.99	70	1.32	1.50	54	0.88	1.71	27	0.71	3.03	1.55	2.87
Loss resv to nonaccrual LNS&LS (x)	1.67	1.46	47	2.01	1.06	31	0.96	1.02	27	0.31	1.47	0.33	2.12
Earn coverage of net losses (x)	3.54	6.20	47	1.24	3.87	31	2.08	4.93	27	2.38	9.08	7.51	9.59

EXHIBIT 3.6   Analysis of Allowance for Loan and Lease Losses and Loan Mix *(continued)*

	LNB	PEER 10[1]	PCT[2]	LNB	PEER 10	PCT	LNB	PEER 10	PCT	LNB	PEER 10	LNB	PEER 10
Loan Mix, % Avg Gross LNS&LS													
Construction & development	0.47	1.80	35	0.39	2.46	28	0.41	2.64	25	0.44	2.74	2.08	2.88
1–4 family residential	19.08	22.02	51	15.16	19.21	45	11.74	17.75	32	10.06	16.75	9.49	16.59
Other real estate loans	32.01	18.27	88	26.97	17.04	85	24.51	15.35	85	23.50	13.81	23.29	13.12
Total real estate	51.56	42.83	67	42.52	39.23	60	36.67	36.46	49	33.99	33.96	34.85	33.25
Financial institution loans	0.00	0.00	77	0.00	0.00	78	0.00	0.00	72	0.09	0.10	0.37	0.43
Agricultural loans	21.43	7.11	88	22.42	7.97	88	25.14	8.36	87	24.88	9.58	23.61	10.00
Commercial & industrial loans	11.17	23.41	12	14.29	26.52	13	15.68	28.37	14	20.05	29.71	21.05	31.88
Loans to individuals	11.51	18.18	21	16.18	19.19	42	17.43	19.45	46	15.35	19.21	15.89	19.30
Municipal loans	1.17	1.51	53	1.00	1.70	50	1.09	1.40	54	0.29	1.01	NA	NA
Acceptances of other banks	0.00	0.00	76	0.00	0.00	78	0.00	0.07	67	0.00	0.24	NA	NA
Loans, leases in foreign offices	0.00	0.00	99	0.00	0.00	99	0.00	0.00	99	0.00	0.00	0.00	0.00
All other loans	3.16	0.99	85	3.60	1.34	87	4.00	1.59	85	5.34	1.59	4.22	1.67
Lease financing receivables	0.00	0.00	73	0.00	0.00	75	0.00	0.00	75	0.00	0.02	0.00	0.00
Memorandum (% of avg tot loans):													
Commercial paper in loans	0.00	0.00	93	0.00	0.00	91	0.00	0.00	89	0.00	0.00	0.00	0.00
Officer, shareholder loans	0.31	0.36	57	0.21	0.37	47	0.47	0.40	65	0.38	0.31	1.54	0.59
Loan & lease commitments	17.51	5.57	92	14.75	5.05	90	16.87	4.56	95	15.42	4.35	13.13	3.62
Loans sold during the quarter	0.00	0.15	65	0.00	0.17	60	0.00	0.27	58	1.20	0.59	1.62	0.87
Composition changes:													
Asset mix	9.00	15.78	26	8.82	18.41	23	6.59	14.10	16	8.48	14.67	16.01	14.37
Loan mix (including leases)	16.24	11.64	75	11.70	13.37	53	12.44	12.51	56	12.90	14.54	15.08	14.72
Liability mix	19.14	12.72	81	26.30	24.10	65	7.87	12.29	29	57.20	84.09	53.11	76.95

EXHIBIT 3.7   Analysis of Past Due, Nonaccrual, and Restructured Loans and Leases

	19XX		19XX-1		19XX-2		19XX-3		19XX-4	
Noncurrent LNS&LS ($000)										
90 days and over past due	483		978		1446		1080		1163	
Total nonaccrual LNS&LS	1795		1766		1766		1260		1260	
Total noncurrent LNS&LS	2278		2744		3212		2340		2423	
	LNB	PEER 10	LNB	PEER 10	LNB	PEER 10	LNB	PEER 10	LNB	PEER 10
Noncurr as% of Avg LNS&LS										
Real estate loans 90+ days p/d	0.36	0.65	1.87	0.82	2.72	0.81	2.31	0.66	2.55	0.82
-Nonaccrual	3.51	2.34	4.04	2.42	3.75	2.24	2.95	2.40	3.26	2.17
-Total	3.87	3.07	5.91	3.36	6.47	3.21	5.26	3.27	5.82	3.12
Coml, other loans 90+ days p/d	0.65	0.49	0.16	0.66	0.37	0.69	0.18	0.83	0.30	0.83
-Nonaccrual	0.07	2.68	0.00	2.90	0.00	2.93	0.00	3.04	0.00	2.93
-Total	0.72	3.27	0.16	3.57	0.37	3.93	0.18	4.06	0.30	3.80
Installment loans 90+ days p/d	2.43	0.79	4.34	0.78	1.02	0.72	0.77	0.65	1.25	0.66
-Nonaccrual	0.00	0.19	0.00	0.23	0.00	0.18	0.00	0.21	0.00	0.21
-Total	2.43	1.09	4.34	1.18	1.02	1.03	0.77	0.97	1.25	0.93
Credit card plans 90+ days p/d	NA	0.36	NA	0.40	NA	0.27	NA	0.35	NA	0.24
-Nonaccrual	0.07	2.68	0.00	2.90	0.00	2.93	0.00	3.04	0.00	2.93
-Total	NA	0.37	NA	0.37	NA	0.27	NA	0.39	NA	0.26
Lease financing 90+ days p/d	NA	0.00	NA	0.00	NA	0.00	NA	0.00	NA	0.00
-Nonaccrual	NA	0.00	NA	0.00	NA	0.00	NA	0.00	NA	0.00
-Total	NA	0.00	NA	0.00	NA	0.00	NA	0.00	NA	0.00
Total LNS&LS 90+ days p/d	0.52	0.60	1.03	0.78	1.62	0.87	1.23	0.82	1.37	0.83
-Nonaccrual	1.93	2.45	1.86	2.37	1.97	2.37	1.43	2.61	1.49	2.24
-Total	2.44	3.02	2.89	3.08	3.59	3.22	2.66	3.50	2.86	3.11

EXHIBIT 3.7   Analysis of Past Due, Nonaccrual, and Restructured Loans and Leases (*continued*)

	19XX		19XX-1		19XX-2		19XX-3		19XX-4	
	LNB	PEER 10	LNB	PEER 10	LNB	PEER 10	LNB	PEER 10	LNB	PEER 10
Noncurrent LNS&LS ($000)										
90 days and over past due	483		978		1446		1080		1163	
Total nonaccrual LNS&LS	1795		1766		1766		1260		1260	
Total noncurrent LNS&LS	2278		2744		3212		2340		2423	
Memo—banks w/ag loans over 5%										
% Noncur agri loans										
90+ days p/d	0.00	0.07	0.00	0.13	0.00	0.46	0.00	0.68	0.05	0.35
-Nonaccrual	0.00	2.22	0.00	3.63	0.00	3.52	0.00	3.58	0.00	3.11
-Total	0.00	2.93	0.00	4.34	0.00	4.58	0.00	4.90	0.05	3.91
Other Pertinent Ratios										
Noncur LNS&LS										
to total assets	1.11	1.40	1.38	1.58	1.25	1.59	1.32	1.69	1.53	1.38
IENC—loans to total loans	2.51	1.24	2.51	1.39	4.18	1.34	4.18	1.29	4.71	1.38
% Current restruc debt by type										
Real estate loans	0.00	0.00	0.00	0.00	0.00	0.00	0.00	0.00	0.00	0.00
Installment loans	0.00	0.00	0.00	0.00	0.00	0.00	0.00	0.00	0.00	0.00
Credit card and related plans	NA	0.00	NA	0.00	0.00	0.00	0.00	0.00	NA	0.00
Commercial and all other loans	0.00	0.18	0.00	0.32	0.00	0.37	0.00	0.18	0.00	0.31
Lease financing receivables	NA	0.00	NA	0.00	NA	0.00	NA	0.00	NA	0.00
Agri loans included above	0.00	0.43	0.00	0.41	0.00	0.35	0.00	0.59	0.00	0.32

1. Banks under $300 million in total assets report this loan detail (by type) using their own internal categorization systems.

EXHIBIT 3.8	Liquidity and Investment Portfolio

	19XX			19XX-1			19XX-2			19XX-3		19XX-4	
	LNB	PEER 10	PCT	LNB	PEER 10	PCT	LNB	PEER 10	PCT	LNB	PEER 10	LNB	PEER 10
Temporary investments ($000)	12661			26000			1760			23276		18897	
Core deposits ($000)	105290			109593			91295			85856		107043	
Volatile liabilities ($000)	83009			57665			71173			72830		57745	
Percent of Total Assets													
Temporary investments	6.15	19.76	09	1.41	21.37	02	0.98	18.24	01	13.26	17.40	10.43	16.55
Core deposits	51.12	74.02	05	59.64	73.70	10	51.06	72.78	01	49.82	71.81	59.06	71.31
Volatile liabilities	40.30	16.76	94	31.38	17.13	88	39.80	18.07	98	41.50	18.59	31.86	19.06
Liquidity Ratios													
Volatile liability dependence	40.24	−5.41	97	34.15	ʼʼʼ−7.93	97	43.75	ʼʼʼ−1.05	98	37.32	0.22	26.07	1.20
Temp inv to volatile liab	13.25	143.50	04	4.51	149.44	02	2.47	126.12	01	31.96	120.96	32.72	114.86
Brokered deposits to deposits	0.00	0.00	92	0.00	0.00	93	0.00	0.00	93	0.00	0.00	0.00	0.00
Temp inv less vol liab to assets	−34.15	3.53	02	−29.96	4.24	02	−38.82	0.17	01	−28.23	−1.19	−21.43	−1.98
Net LNS&LS to deposits	47.85	53.79	34	48.94	54.25	34	53.95	58.60	35	54.95	59.55	54.63	57.85
Net LNS&LS to core deposits	85.57	65.10	81	74.69	66.57	67	95.53	72.60	85	101.56	73.99	84.10	71.82
Net LNS&LS to assets	43.74	48.70	38	44.54	48.95	39	48.78	52.16	37	49.68	52.83	49.67	50.86
Net loans, leases & sblc to asst	43.74	49.23	36	44.54	49.44	38	48.78	52.76	35	49.68	53.37	49.72	51.49
Percent Change In													
Temporary investments	386.96	−1.34	99	47.73	23.12	70	−92.44	18.34	01	23.17	13.50	−37.06	22.40
Securities over 1 year	6.74	11.63	46	11.07	1.69	63	56.75	6.82	91	−21.71	−7.01	6.68	7.82
Net loans & leases	10.07	1.41	75	−6.15	−1.19	36	0.03	4.36	35	−3.15	10.64	23.06	8.90
Core deposits	−3.93	2.85	12	20.04	4.82	95	6.34	5.32	54	−19.79	5.12	16.10	10.36
Volatile liabilities	43.95	6.27	87	−18.98	3.22	23	−2.28	9.35	36	26.12	17.15	−8.07	2.75
Total assets	12.08	3.51	83	2.77	4.01	42	1.88	5.43	30	−3.16	6.68	6.26	8.67

EXHIBIT 3.8   Liquidity and Investment Portfolio (*continued*)

	19XX LNB	19XX PEER 10	19XX PCT	19XX-1 LNB	19XX-1 PEER 10	19XX-1 PCT	19XX-2 LNB	19XX-2 PEER 10	19XX-2 PCT	19XX-3 LNB	19XX-3 PEER 10	19XX-4 LNB	19XX-4 PEER 10
Temporary investments ($000)	12661			26000			1760			23276		18897	
Core deposits ($000)	105290			109593			91295			85856		107043	
Volatile liabilities ($000)	83009			57665			71173			72830		57745	
Securities Mix													
Percent of total securities													
US treas & agency	62.26	61.94	41	56.44	62.90	32	60.20	59.09	93	59.55	53.28	55.62	
Municipals	37.74	29.00	73	43.56	32.19	76	36.85	40.87	83	37.56	46.72	41.34	
Foreign securities	0.00	0.00	91	0.00	0.00	93	0.00	0.00	94	0.00	NA	NA	
All other securities	0.00	7.48	09	0.00	3.23	10	0.72	0.04	16	0.69	0.00	0.79	
Debt securities under 1 year	2.49	26.31	03	0.13	29.26	02	30.31	31.32	02	31.29	7.59	29.08	
Debt securities 1–5 years	11.33	47.18	04	26.86	45.58	12	45.41	46.67	05	46.04	66.60	44.26	
Debt securities 5–10 years	64.19	14.82	98	42.57	17.47	90	16.81	14.36	94	15.28	21.28	17.80	
Debt securities over 10 years	22.00	8.39	83	30.44	6.41	93	6.08	7.64	97	5.50	4.53	7.27	
Other Securities Ratios													
Sec app (dep) to inv sec	0.17	-0.53	66	8.48	2.84	96	2.90	0.53	81	0.79	-2.45	NA	NA
Sec app (dep) to prim cap[1]	0.85	-1.09	70	42.27	9.84	99	15.22	3.58	92	3.86	-7.09	NA	NA
Taxable sec: mkt to book	92.76	99.30	01	101.04	102.03	29	108.24	102.19	99	99.80	100.94	NA	NA
Non-taxable sec:													
mkt to book	112.48	100.67	98	118.12	103.84	98	98.86	97.08	55	102.22	92.20	NA	NA
Pledged sec to total sec	80.55	41.58	88	70.72	48.40	71	69.14	49.21	70	81.81	46.49	NA	NA

1. Refer to the UBPR User's Guide for primary capital definition.

EXHIBIT 3.9 Analysis of Repricing Opportunities

Cumulative gap comparisons for interest-bearing assets and liabilities
(Excludes those categorized under "all other" on distribution)

| | 19XX | | | | | | | | | Bank Cumulative Net History | | | |
| Percent of Assets | Assets | | | Liabilities | | | Net Position | | | | | | |
Repriced Within	LNB	PEER 10	PCT	LNB	PEER 10	PCT	LNB	PEER 10	PCT	9/30/XX	6/30/XX	3/30/XX	12/31/XX-1
1 day	39.86	18.33	87	0.00	0.47	42	38.96	17.29	88	35.19	35.90	35.58	34.81
3 months	40.53	33.69	73	60.64	46.23	93	−20.11	−11.62	29	−9.57	−18.46	−12.68	−17.18
6 months	41.37	41.32	59	67.89	56.97	88	−26.52	−15.21	20	−32.69	−32.17	−26.30	−25.85
12 months	44.06	51.03	34	75.75	64.53	90	−31.68	−13.05	09	−34.64	−36.10	−35.60	−32.70
5 years	52.87	79.11	02	78.72	72.37	80	−25.85	6.74	00	−30.91	−32.06	−33.20	−21.05
Supplemental information:													
Peer group avg yield on fed funds								7.00		6.85	6.74	6.27	6.25
Bank reported futures contracts or int rate swaps								No		No	No	No	No

Repricing Distribution Comparisons for Schedule J Assets and Liabilities

| Item | Total as Percent of Assets | Percent Repriced Within 3 Months | | | Percent Repriced Within 6 Months | | | Percent Repriced Within 12 Months | | | Percent Repriced Within 5 Years | | |
		LNB	PEER 10	PCT	LNB	PEER 10	PCT	LNB	PEER 10	PCT	LNB	PEER 10	PCT
Schedule J Assets													
Residential re loans (est)[1]	NA	NA	6.72	NA	NA	13.45	NA	NA	26.90	NA	NA	69.12	NA
Consumer installment loans (est)[1]	NA	NA	15.79	NA	NA	31.58	NA	NA	58.53	NA	NA	100.00	NA
Total loans and leases	44.38	79.85	45.09	94	81.74	54.22	91	85.45	65.22	87	94.53	89.94	66
Debt securities	42.18	0.00	7.03	08	0.00	14.06	04	2.49	26.31	03	13.82	73.93	01
Other interest-bearing assets	5.10	100.00	86.01	99	100.00	94.52	99	100.00	99.44	99	100.00	100.00	99
Total schedule J assets	91.65	44.22	37.83	73	45.36	45.14	60	48.08	55.95	33	57.69	86.56	01

EXHIBIT 3.9 Analysis of Repricing Opportunities (*continued*)

Repricing Distribution Comparisons for Schedule J Assets and Liabilities

	Item Total as Percent of Assets	Percent Repriced Within 3 Months		Percent Repriced Within 6 Months		Percent Repriced Within 12 Months		Percent Repriced Within 5 Years	
		LNB	PEER 10 PCT	LNB	PEER 10 PCT	LNB	PEER 10 PCT	LNB	PEER 10 PCT
Schedule J Liabilities									
Deposits in foreign offices	NA	NA	NA	NA	NA	NA	NA	NA	NA
CDs over $100,000	27.22	80.52	59.15 89	89.88	79.87 78	99.64	92.49 83	100.00	100.00 99
Other time deposits	28.47	55.12	37.87 92	71.62	62.63 76	89.91	79.43 84	100.00	99.93 99
Other nondeposit int-bear liabs	0.00	NA	92.52 NA	NA	99.30 NA	NA	100.00 NA	NA	100.00 NA
Total schedule J liabilities	55.70	67.54	46.67 93	80.55	68.63 85	94.67	83.58 87	100.00	99.89 99

1. Presented for banks electing option #2 on Schedule J. Figures are based on estimated distribution.

Bank Valuation

After reading this chapter you
will be able to:

■ Apply the valuation
process to bank stock.

■ Describe how changes in
the amounts and riskiness
of cash flows affect the
value of a bank.

■ Discuss the determinants
of bank prices in mergers.

■ Compare the market
reaction to bank stocks of
bidders and targets in bank
mergers.

■ Identify the factors that
define investment value.

T he management of a commercial bank attempts to balance risk and
profitability in making its lending, investing, and funds-raising decisions. Issues concerning the pricing of deposits or loans and decisions about buying and selling securities, while often seemingly narrow in focus, actually should
be thought of within the risk and return framework. Yet just what should be the
goal of these decisions?

Under most situations, the goal of bank management should be to maximize
the value of the shareholder's equity. For a publicly traded bank, maximizing
shareholder's equity involves making decisions that will increase the market value
of the bank's stock. Hence, opportunities that increase the profitability of the
bank more than sufficiently to offset the risk exposure and thereby increase the
price of the stock should be pursued. In contrast, opportunities that do not
increase the profitability of the bank sufficiently to offset the increased risk and
thereby lead to a reduction in share price should be rejected. For example, a high-
risk loan could increase the profitability of the bank but it could increase its risk
even more, and therefore should be rejected.

The general rule that management should pursue opportunities that increase
the value of the stock must be tempered somewhat when discussing a bank whose
stock is not publicly traded, which is the case for most banks. Without public

market price to use as a gauge, management at these banks must rely on the income statement and balance sheet implications of various decisions. Moreover, for these closely held banks—many of which are owned by only a few individuals with a substantial portion of their wealth committed to the bank—dividend income is often a central concern as are tax considerations, both of which may lead to decisions that are different from those taken to maximize share value.

This chapter considers the determinants of the value of shareholder equity for a commercial bank and the strategies that management can follow in attempting to achieve its goals. It begins with a general discussion of the determinants of value. It then analyzes the specific determinants of bank shareholder value. It also considers the implications for shareholder value of the recent wave of mergers and acquisitions that has taken place in the banking industry over the past decade. ■

4.1 DETERMINING THE VALUE OF THE EQUITY OF A COMMERCIAL BANK

Go to www.ccbonline.com/ annualreport97/97letter-stk-val-chart.asp *for an example of bank stock valuation relative to the market proxied by S&P 500.*

Bank management should make investment, lending, deposit gathering, and other financial management decisions that will result in an increase in the stock price. The focus of these decisions then is on the investor in the stock. Given this focus, the immediate question is how does that investor obtain returns from his or her investment in the stock? To understand the answer, we need to focus on the **rate of return** concept where

$$\text{Rate of return} = \frac{D_t + (P_t - P_{t-1})}{P_{t-1}} \qquad 4.1$$

The rate of return that the investor obtains from holding a share of stock for a year or some other period is composed of two parts: (1) the **dividend return** (D_t) and (2) the **capital gain** in the value of the stock ($P_t - P_{t-1}$). For example, if the price of the stock at P_{t-1} was 50, the price at P_t equals 55, and the dividend payment was $1 per share, then the rate of return to each shareholder for the year is:

$$\text{Rate of return} = \frac{1 + (55 - 50)}{50} = \frac{6}{50} = 12\% \qquad 4.2$$

The investor who held the stock for one year obtained a 12% return (2% in the form of dividends and 10% in the form of price appreciation).

Table 4.1 provides the rates of return (sometimes called *total rates of return* or *market rates of return*) in 1998 for some of the largest U.S. banking organizations. The returns are divided into that portion due to dividend return and that part due to price change, or capital appreciation. The year 1998 was

TABLE 4.1	Rate of Return for Selected Commercial Banks 1998		

Bank	Dividend Return D_t	+ Price Change $P_t - P_{t-1}$	= Total Rate of Return
BankAmerica	2.14%	6.11%	8.25%
CitiGroup	0.85	30.94	31.79
Chase Manhattan	2.19	21.25	23.44
First Union	3.11	13.53	16.64
J. P. Morgan	3.29	1.71	5.00
Wells Fargo	2.23	9.14	11.37
Bank of New York	1.91	25.49	27.40

Source: DataStream International.

an extraordinary year for bank stocks. The rates of return for CitiGroup, Chase Manhattan, and Bank of New York exceeded 20%, while other banks had widely varying earnings rates from 5% and 20%. Banks with high earnings rates typically had low provisions for loan losses and benefited from low levels of interest rates (resulting in high net interest margins). On the other hand, lower-earning banks such as J. P. Morgan suffered temporary problems from securities losses associated with financial crises in Southeast Asia and Russia in the latter half of the 1990s.

Most of the large returns for the bank stocks in Table 4.1 reflect price appreciation. **Dividend yields** averaged less than 3%. This pattern is typical: Price changes dominate dividend yields in determining market rates of return. Because these price changes reflect reappraisals of earnings potential and risk for banks, it is the market reacting to an announcement by the bank and by others that fundamentally determines the return.

From Eq. (4.1), it is obvious that returns to investors are determined by dividend payments and price appreciation. But management can only control dividend payments directly (and dividend policies represent an important dimension of management policies). Management's influences on price changes are, at best, indirect. But what determines the stock price (and the change in the stock price) of a bank?

Although many variables enter into the determination of value, three in particular are relevant:

1. The amount of cash flow

2. The timing of cash flow

3. The riskiness of cash flow.

The value of a share of stock is determined fundamentally by the cash benefits (dividends) the buyer expects to receive from the asset. In terms of the present value concept, the value of an asset is the present value of all of its expected cash flows discounted at the appropriate discount rate that reflects the risk of those cash flows. This approach may be expressed algebraically as follows:

$$V_0 = \frac{CF_1}{(1+r)^1} + \frac{CF_2}{(1+r)^2} + \frac{CF_3}{(1+r)^3} + \ldots + \frac{CF_n}{(1+r)^n} \qquad 4.3$$

where V_0 is the present value (or price) of the asset at time zero, CF is the expected cash flow that accrues to the owner of the asset during the owner's holding period, r is the required rate of return or discount rate, and n is the amount of time the asset is held or is expected to be held. In this approach three factors will cause an increase in the value of the asset:

1. An increase in the amount of cash flow (i.e., dividends) to be received from the asset
2. Earlier receipt of the expected cash flow
3. A decrease in the required rate of return

Conversely, three factors will cause a decrease in the value of the asset:

1. A decrease in the amount of cash flow to be received from the asset
2. Later receipt of the expected cash flow
3. An increase in the required rate of return

An example of the determinants of value and how value would change can assist in an understanding of the concept. Assume that the cash benefits from holding an asset for five years are $20 per year. Further assume that the holder expected to be able to sell the asset for $100 at the end of the fifth year, and that the required rate of return is 12%. Then the value of the asset is:

$$V_0 = \frac{\$20}{(1.12)^1} + \frac{\$20}{(1.12)^2} + \frac{\$20}{(1.12)^3} + \frac{\$20}{(1.12)^4} + \frac{\$20}{(1.12)^5} + \frac{\$100}{(1.12)^5} = \$128.7 \qquad 4.4$$

What then produces changes in value? First, value obviously changes with changes in investor expectations of dividends. Any event such as a large and unexpected increase in earnings clearly changes expectations of cash dividends. Because cash dividends ultimately are paid out of the earnings created by lending, investing, and deposit gathering, any information that causes investors to change their expectations of future earnings will change the market price of a stock.

As an example, suppose that a bank has a sharp reduction in its provision for loan losses due to a strengthening in its local economy and suppose further that the bank expects the provision for loan losses to continue to be well under prior expectations. This reduction in current and future provision for loan losses will lead to an increase in current reported earnings and in the market's expectation of future earnings (and dividends). Given the announcement of the change in provision for loan losses, we would expect that the market price of the stock would rise. In terms of Eq. (4.1), P_t would go up because it would

How Bank Management Can Create Value

In the United States many of the most profitable and highest-valued banks are midsize regional banks with $250 million to $5 billion in total assets. These banks strive to create value for their shareholders by maximizing profits per unit risk from everyday operations. Based on CEO interviews and comments by industry experts, some of the ways in which bank management can boost earnings and add value to share prices are as follows:

- Minimize operating costs by keeping a careful eye on the ratio of operating expenses to operating income, an often-cited industry measure of how well a bank is managing its costs.
- Use branching systems to attract core deposits and sell profitable retail products, such as credit cards, small business loans, and trust services.
- Evaluate performance for individual units within a bank branch or office to better understand the profitability of each unit.
- Control the credit quality of the loan portfolio.
- Control the market valuation implications of

securities investments on accounting statements.
- Maintain adequate capital to satisfy regulatory requirements and enable selected acquisitions and de novo entry to take advantage of profitable market opportunities.
- Employ an aggressive sales strategy by encouraging employees to reach out to customers and their needs.
- Provide employee training on a regular basis to keep up with recent changes in products and services.
- Avoid excessive growth that can unduly stretch management resources and increase bank risk.

These lessons from past experiences of bank managers are not only important to regional banks but may well be valuable to larger institutions in the near future. The ongoing merger and acquisition wave has been driven primarily by large institutions, whose managements have been occupied with the process of restructuring. Eventually, after the consolidation process slows down, managers of large banks will need to create value from their newly acquired asset bases.

---

capture the effects of higher expected future dividends. As a result, the return to the investor in the stock would rise.

The growth rate of earnings can be incorporated into the valuation formula. Modifying Eq. (4.3) by assuming the number of periods n is infinite (i.e., in practical terms stocks do not have a maturity date), it is well known that:

$$V_0 = Div_0/(r - g) \qquad 4.5$$

where r is the nominal discount rate, and g is the nominal growth rate of earnings. The nominal discount rate or market capitalization rate equals the current dividend yield (or dividends per share divided by the market price of equity) plus the growth rate of dividends. Here, assume that the bank does not pay out all of its dividends to the shareholders; instead, the bank retains some earnings for reinvestment in capital assets that will generate increased earnings. For example, if a bank retained 40% of its earnings (i.e., the payout ratio or dividends per share divided by earnings per share equals 60%) and had a 25% return on equity (i.e., the ratio of earnings to book value of equity), its

At Fitch IBCA (www. fitchinv.com) you can find bank ratings for about 1,000 institutions in almost 70 countries. The ratings assess a bank's exposure to and management of risk.

earnings growth rate would be 10% (i.e., $0.40 \times 0.25 = 0.10$). If the current annual dividend is $5, and the discount rate is 10%, the value of the stock would be $V_0 = \$5/(0.25 - 0.10) = \$33.33$. Notice that the discount rate equals the sum of the current dividend yield (or $\$5/\$33.33 = 0.15$) plus the growth rate of dividends (or 0.10). It is clear that, as the growth rate of dividends increases, bank value increases also.

One major reason for dividends to grow over time is inflation. However, because inflation is also embedded in discount and growth rates, its effects should cancel out in Eq. (4.5). Normally, firms are slow to adjust dividend payments to changes in earnings, including those changes associated with inflation. On the other hand, investors quickly adjust discount rates for expected future inflation. According to Modigliani and Cohn, the difference in the timing of these adjustments to inflation on dividends and discount rates in Eq. (4.5) causes stocks to be undervalued during times of high inflation.[1] They point out that when inflation is low, these valuation problems are no longer present and, therefore, the real value of stocks is revealed.

The problem of valuation and inflation is relevant to the stock market boom in the 1990s. Ritter and Warr have observed that low levels of inflation in the 1990s were associated with rising stock price levels.[2] Consequently, they inferred that the bull market of the 1990s could be due in part to low inflation rates. Of course, a number of other reasons also explain high stock prices, including low and stable interest rates, technology gains, the fall of Soviet communism, increasing international opportunities for business, the baby boom generation, and so on.

In the banking industry another major reason for rising prices is the consolidation movement to be discussed shortly. Banks are expanding across product lines and geographic boundaries, increasing their size, broadening their scope of financial services, forming alliances with nonfinancial firms, developing new electronic payments systems, and upgrading employee expertise. These changes impact earnings growth rates and risk profiles, such that all of the variables in Eq. (4.5) are being altered. Today, valuation is a challenging and high stakes game in the consolidation wave of bank mergers and acquisitions.

4.2 USING THE PRICE-EARNINGS RATIO

Another approach to understanding the price of a stock and the determinants of changes in that price is in terms of its **price-earnings multiple** or **ratio**. The price-earnings ratio is calculated by dividing the current market price by earnings per share:

1. Franco Modigliani and Richard A. Cohn, "Inflation, Rational Valuation and the Market," *Financial Analysts Journal,* vol. 35, pp. 24–44.
2. Jay R. Ritter and Richard S. Warr, "The Decline of Inflation and the Bull Market of 1982 to 1997," Working paper, University of Florida (*http://bear.cba.ufl.edu/ ritter/index.html*) (1999).

$$\text{Price-earnings ratio} = \frac{\text{Price per share}}{\text{Earnings per share}} \qquad 4.7$$

For example, a bank with a market price per share of $45 and earnings per share of $3 has a price-earnings ratio of 15 times.

The price-earnings ratio summarizes the outlook for the future of the bank—the amount of its earnings and dividends, the timing of earnings and dividends, and the risk of those earnings and dividends. A bank that is expected to show rapid growth in earnings will have a higher price-earnings ratio than one with little expected earnings growth. Similarly, a bank in which earnings are highly variable and unpredictable will tend to have a lower price-earnings ratio. Hence, even if two banks have the same current earnings, their market prices can be sharply different.

Table 4.2 shows the price-earnings ratios for the same group of banks that were in Table 4.1 for the years 1996 and 1998. These two years were quite different in terms of the market perception of bank stocks. In 1996, banks were subject to market scrutiny in light of financial crises in many Southeast Asian countries, in addition to Russia and Brazil. Also, until recently Japan's financial system was under stress from prolonged economic doldrums. At that time the concern was that regional financial crises would spill over into industrialized countries and, thereby, affect U.S. and European banks. In this environment, the price-earnings ratios were generally modest or low. In contrast, due to some signs of recovery in these developing regions of the world, in 1998 bank earnings recovered sharply and the price-earnings multiple for most banks increased. However, there were significant differences in the price-earnings ratios among the individual banks, reflecting differences in the outlook for their profitability. For example, CitiGroup and First Union had large increases

TABLE 4.2	Price-Earnings Ratios for Selected Commercial Banks	
	Price-Earnings Ratios	
Bank	**1996**	**1998**
BankAmerica	12.1	15.5
CitiGroup	10.4	18.2
Chase Manhattan	13.6	15.3
First Union	11.1	20.9
J. P. Morgan	11.4	16.3
Wells Fargo	12.7	17.6
Bank of New York	11.4	19.7

Source: DataStream International.

in their price-earnings ratios relative to the other banks in those years, due in all likelihood to their high profitability and rapid expected growth in earnings. In general, most banks faired well by the end of the 1990s. Perhaps the most important uncertainty facing them as the decade closed was the ongoing merger and acquisition wave. How would this global restructuring of the banking industry affect their share values? We next turn to the empirical evidence in search of answers to this question.

4.3 BANK MERGER AND ACQUISITION PRICING

Information from prices set in bank mergers and acquisitions provides important insights into the determinants of value at commercial banks and the factors that management should focus on in attempting to increase the value of its bank. Such information is especially relevant for small, closely held banks in which no public market exists for the bank.

In forthcoming discussion it is important to recognize the difference between a bank *merger* and an *acquisition*. In the former case the target bank is absorbed into the bidding or buying bank. As such, the target loses its bank charter, does not need a CEO and board of directors anymore, and is converted to a branch office of the buying bank. By contrast, in a bank acquisition the target bank retains its bank charter, CEO, and board of directors. It becomes an affiliate member of the bank holding company (BHC) to which the buying bank belongs. Clearly, mergers are a much more drastic form of reorganization than acquisitions, especially in terms of their impact on management. Prior to the 1994 Riegle-Neal Act's deregulation of interstate banking barriers to expansion, BHC acquisitions were more common than mergers. However, after implementation of this legislation, mergers involving conversion to a branch office became the dominant form of reorganization. As cited in a paper by Smith and Walter, during the period 1985–1995, financial services M&A transactions accounted for about 44% of total global M&A activity.[3] Based on this and other evidence, the authors noted that the financial services sector of the economy experienced an unprecedented M&A wave in this period. Moreover, the second half of the 1990s has seen a continuation of this trend, with ever larger M&As taking place—creating the so-called megabanks with global market power.

One of the most comprehensive studies of the determinants of value (measured as the ratio of the market price to the book value of the target bank) was done by Stephen Rhoades of the Federal Reserve Board.[4] He examined the

3. Roy C. Smith and Ingo Walter, "Global Patterns of Mergers and Acquisition Activity in the Financial Services Industry," Working paper FIN-98-060, New York University (1998).
4. Stephen Rhoades, "Determinants of Premiums Paid in Bank Acquisitions," *Atlantic Economic Journal* (March 1987), pp. 20–30.

determinants of the **price-book ratio** for acquisitions that took place from 1973 to 1983. Only three variables were consistently related to the merger premium: the growth of the assets of the target firm, the growth of its market, and the target's capital-to-assets ratio, with a negative sign. The first two are, to a considerable extent, outside the control of the bank. The impact of the capital-assets ratio, though, is quite interesting. The negative sign suggests that management should be cautious about carrying "excess" capital above that required by the regulatory authorities.

Fraser and Kolari focus on the price-book value ratio for smaller banks involved in both mergers and acquistions. The principal financial ratios for the banks in their sample are shown in Table 4.3. The banks are first broken

TABLE 4.3	Financial Performance Ratios for Low and High Price-Book Banks			
	Banks Less Than $100 Million		Banks More Than $100 Million	
	Price/Book Ratios Less Than 1.30	Price/Book Ratios Greater Than 2.00	Price/Book Ratios Less Than 1.30	Price/Book Ratios Greater Than 2.00
Financial Ratios	$n = 77$	$n = 26$	$n = 19$	$n = 8$
Net income/total assets	.0034	.0091	.0090	.0084
Net income/total equity	.0966	.1199	.1205	.1175
Net interest income/total assets	.0395	.0428	.0339	.0414
Net operating income/total assets	.0127	.0149	.0127	.0162
Cash dividends/total equity	.0391	.0307	.0426	.0316
Total equity/total assets	.0838	.0832	.0762	.0648
Total equity/total loans	.1858	.1597	.1478	.1132
Total equity + provision for possible loan losses/total assets	.0919	.0869	.0785	.0702
Demand deposits/time deposits	.1526	.2041	.1503	.1885
Total loans/total assets	.5420	.5698	.5415	.5783
Provision for possible loan losses/total assets	.0082	.0038	.0023	.0054
Net charge-offs on loans/total loans	.0142	.0102	.0032	.0074
Commercial and industrial loans/total assets	.1310	.1244	.1238	.1199
Cash and securities/total assets	.3710	.3446	.4055	.3519

Source: Donald Fraser and James Kolari, "Determinants of Small Bank Acquisition Premiums," Federal Reserve Bank of Chicago, *Conference on Bank Structure and Competition,* May 1987, pp. 397–398.

down by size (less than or more than $100 million in total assets) and then by high price (price-book ratio greater than 2.0) and low price (price-book ratio less than 1.30). Examination of the financial ratios in this table suggest some important differences between the high-premium banks and the low-premium banks.

Net income (as a fraction of total assets) was substantially higher for the high-premium small banks, than for the low-premium small banks (0.91% versus 0.34%). Not surprisingly, highly profitable small banks were able to command higher merger premiums. The high-premium banks also had a larger fraction of their assets financed with noninterest-bearing demand deposits and also experienced sharply lower loan losses. Some evidence also indicates that the higher-premium banks made fewer commercial loans. With regard to market conditions, the high-premium small banks were located in markets experiencing greater population growth. These differences were, however, less observable for the larger banks, which are more likely to be publicly traded.

Another study of the determinants of the price-book ratio in bank mergers was done by Beatty, Santomero, and Smirlock.[5] They examined prices paid in 264 bank mergers over the period from the beginning of 1984 to the end of the third quarter of 1985. They found that the more profitable the target bank (measured by the return on equity), the higher the merger premium, and that the premium is negatively related to the ratio of U.S. Treasury investments to total assets, the ratio of loans to total assets, and the ratio of the loan loss allowance plus equity (i.e., primary capital) to total assets.

Price-book ratios in bank mergers and acquisitions have varied greatly in a range of 1.0 to more than 3.0 in the 1990s. One reason for the large fluctuation in this ratio is that the book value is historical, which means that the ratio can change merely due to target banks having different historical values, as opposed to current market values. Nonetheless, the price-book ratio is the conventional way to express the sales price of targets in the banking industry. Higher ratios imply a better price for target shareholders, and vice versa for lower ratios. Higher ratios also imply that management must earn rates of return per unit of risk that exceed historical levels—a feat that time will test in the postmerger or acquisitions years. In the early 1990s the average price-book ratio offered in deals was about 1.5, but this ratio has risen to more than 2.0 in the late 1990s. Are the prices paid in recent years too high? The old adage "time will tell" is applicable in this context. Certainly the next decade will be an interesting period in which to observe the valuation effects of the consolidation movement in the banking industry.

5. Randolph Beatty, Anthony Santomero, and Michael Smirlock, *Bank Merger Premiums: Analysis and Evidence,* Salomon Brothers Center for the Study of Financial Institutions Monograph Series in Finance and Economics, Monograph 1987–1988 (1987).

4.4 BANK EARNINGS AND STOCK PRICES

Although bank managers obviously should manage the portfolio in order to achieve those earnings that will lead to the highest share price, the question arises as to which measure of earnings is most important. Given the argument that the price of a bank's stock is a function of its earnings and some earnings multiplier (i.e., the price-earnings ratio), it is possible (perhaps likely) that the market may place a different earnings multiple on different sources of earnings. For example, one measure is composed of earnings before securities gains and losses (often referred to as operating earnings) and securities gains and losses realized when securities are sold.

Earnings before securities gains and losses stem from the fundamental deposit taking and lending activities of the bank. Changes in these earnings vary with changes in the levels of interest rates in deposit and loan markets, but, under traditional historical cost accounting, operating earnings do not change with changes in the market value of assets or liabilities. In particular, earnings before securities gains and losses do not contain any explicit revaluations of the loan portfolio or securities to reflect unrealized gains and losses. In contrast to earnings before securities gains and losses, securities gains and losses consist of changes in the market value of investment securities since their purchase date, and only those gains and losses that are realized. This income is likely to be more transitory and volatile than other components of income.

Given the difference in volatility and permanence between earnings before securities gains and losses, on the one hand, and securities gains and losses, on the other, we might expect that the market would capitalize the operating earnings at a higher multiple than the securities gains on income. But does it?

Evidence on this issue was provided by Barth, Beaver, and Wolfson.[6] They studied 150 publicly traded banks, relating the market value of their equity to the composition of earnings—operating earnings or securities gains and losses. Their study found that the market value of the stock was positively related to operating earnings. Hence, management attempts to structure the bank's portfolio in order to increase operating earnings should result in an increase in the market price of the stock. However, they found that the market value of the bank's stock was negatively related to earnings from securities gains and losses.

The negative relationship between market value and earnings from securities gains and losses is particularly interesting. It suggests that the market interprets the realization of securities gains and losses as an attempt by the bank to manage earnings, that is, to smooth earnings. Thus, management may attempt to take securities gains when operating earnings fall. However, this attempt to "fool the market" apparently does not work. Hence, in the case of earnings smoothing, it is possible that the market will view realized securities gains as bad news rather than good news.

6. Mary Barth, William Beaver, and Mark Wolfson, "Components of Earnings and the Structure of Bank Share Prices," *Financial Analysts Journal* (May/June 1990), pp. J3–J8.

4.5 DEREGULATION AND THE VALUE OF BANK STOCKS

The dramatic changes that have taken place in the economic, financial, and regulatory environment within which banks operate have raised questions about the determinants of bank stock prices. Specifically, what factors affect the price-earnings ratio of bank stocks and how have those factors changed with deregulation? Visser and Wu provide information on this question in a study of the price-earnings ratios of banks with more than one billion dollars of assets during the 1976–1985 period.[7] They were particularly interested in the effects of the passage of the Depository Institutions Deregulation and Monetary Control Act (DIDMCA) of 1980 on the determinants of bank price-earnings ratios.

Visser and Wu attempted to explain bank price-earnings ratios in terms of deposit growth rates, earnings growth rates, payout ratios, transitory earnings, and other similar variables. They found that, before DIDMCA, the growth rate of deposits, the growth rate of earnings, and the ratio of capital to assets were positively associated with the price-earnings ratio. In contrast, the volume of transitory earnings (such as through securities gains and losses) was negatively related to the price-earnings ratio.

The relative influence of these variables changed following DIDMCA. In particular, the dividend payout ratio became more significant, while the past earnings growth remained highly important. In contrast, the past five years of deposit growth became less important while the capital to assets ratio became unimportant. The transitory earnings component of profitability remained important and negatively affected the price-earnings ratio. Perhaps the most important finding is the decreased emphasis on growth in recent years as a factor that influences bank price-earnings ratios.

More recent work by Hughes, Lang, Mester, and Moon provided evidence on M&A effects of interstate banking on bank performance.[8] In this regard, the Riegle-Neal Interstate Banking and Branching Efficiency Act of 1994 permitted interstate branching in almost all states. Based on a sample of 441 U.S. bank holding companies and data collected in 1994, the authors found that within state M&As experienced fewer financial gains than M&As involving expansion across state lines. Apparently, by diversifying across different state economies, banks achieved lower operating risk. This diversification benefits not only bank shareholders but society in terms of greater bank safety and soundness.

7. John Visser and H. K. Wu, "The Effects of Deregulation on Bank Stock Price Earnings Ratios," *Financial Analysts Journal* (September–October 1989), pp. 62–67.
8. Joseph P. Hughes, William Lang, Loretta J. Mester, and Choon-Geol Moon, "The Dollars and Sense of Bank Consolidation," Working paper (1998).

MANAGING RISK

Branch Bank Valuation

The 1994 Riegle-Neal Interstate Banking and Branching Efficiency Act enables banks to branch across state lines, which previously was prohibited. More than any other deregulation in the banking industry, this act promises to drastically change the organizational structure of banks across the United States. While many banks are expanding across state lines via mergers and acquisitions, in addition to the establishment of de novo (new) banks, another approach is to purchase existing branch offices.

Valuation of branch offices is more difficult than valuation of a bank due to the lack of balance sheet and income statement data. Accounting statements for banks consolidate the data for all branches. Given this lack of accounting data, the estimation of the present value of a branch office's future earnings requires alternative methods. Because branches are normally employed to generate deposits, and these funds are transferred elsewhere in the banking organization for the purpose of making loans, it is important to focus on the deposit base of the branch. What is the mix of deposits? In this regard, branches with large proportions of core deposits (i.e., funds that are relatively stable and less interest sensitive than other liabilities) are worth more than other offices. Does the location of the branch provide a strategic advantage for the buying bank? Many times branches are used to gain a "toehold" into new markets or increase market presence in areas of previous entry. Are the physical assets of the branch up-to-date and comparable to those at other branches in the organi-

zation? A consistent marketing strategy aimed at depositors requires some degree of uniformity across physical assets. Also, what proportion of deposits will not move after the branch sale? It is likely that some customers will transfer their deposits whenever a change in bank ownership takes place.

Many times a purchasing bank will not want any of the loans managed at the branch. In this case the purchase price is based on the branch's cash and securities, physical assets, and deposit base. Typically, the premium paid on a branch is a percentage of deposits (e.g., 4% of total deposits). The premium takes into account the potential future earnings to the buyer on loaning these deposit funds. From the selling bank's standpoint, increasing the number of bidders for the branch will ensure a competitive deposit premium is obtained on sale.

The purchase of an existing branch office is many times preferable to a de novo strategy. New branches require an aggressive marketing effort to attract new customers. Consequently, it can take a number of years before a core deposit base is developed. Also, many times new offices are not very profitable in their early years due to difficulties with cost efficiency and management expertise. Existing branches have developed customer relationships, learned how to control costs, and have experienced managers with knowledge of local business conditions. These factors tend to reduce the operating risk and improve the profit potential of existing branches compared to de novo branches.

4.6 MARKET RESPONSES TO BANK M&A ANNOUNCEMENTS

Insight into the factors that affect the valuation of commercial banks can also be obtained from examining the equity market response to the announcement of a merger or acquisition among commercial banks. A number of studies have focused on the stock market response for the buyer (i.e., the **bidder**) and the seller (i.e., the **target**) banks in M&As. Generally, the studies measure the market reaction by examining a short-term period (usually a few days) around the merger announcement and calculating a measure of the difference between the actual stock price movement on those days and the movement that would have been expected given the movements in the general level of stock prices (commonly referred to as an abnormal return). Results from a study by Hawawini and Swary are representative of many other studies and provide insights useful to bank M&As.[9] They studied the stock market reaction for 123 target banks and 130 bidder banks for M&As that took place during the 1980s.

Not surprisingly, Hawawini and Swary find that targets do extremely well in a M&As. The price of a target bank's shares increases, on average, by about 11.5% during the week of the merger announcement (11.5% more than would be expected given movements in the stock market during that week). Moreover, the positive stock market response is greater for those transactions in which payment is made in cash, with the stock price increase being 5.76% higher for cash than for security transactions during the announcement week. Moreover, the target bank's share price appreciates more the larger the assets of the bidding bank.

How do the buyers fare in these mergers? Not very well, if the results of Hawawini and Swary (and other studies) are correct. The price of the bidding bank stock decreased, on average, during the week of the M&A announcement, falling generally between 1% and 2% (after adjusting for general market movements). Moreover, the market reaction was more negative when the bidding bank paid for the transaction with stock and when the bidder bank and the target bank were more similar in size.

The findings of a negative market reaction for the stock of the bidding bank raises some important questions of motivation for the management of these banks. Why do banks buy other banks if it causes their stock price to fall? Such behavior is apparently contrary to the stated goal of management to maximize shareholder value. It is, however, consistent with a number of other hypotheses regarding the motivation of management. It may be, for example, that managers are interested in maximizing their own welfare. Thus, if they expand through M&As or through other strategies they will be able to increase their salaries and benefits associated with their position. Of course, this wealth transfer represents an **agency cost** from the standpoint of shareholders, who would bear losses to the extent that management increased their salaries and perquisites (including pensions, office expenditures, vacations, bonuses, etc.). Another explanation is provided by Roll's **hubris hypothesis**.[10] According to this hypothesis, bidders invariably pay too much for targets not because they are not trying to do their best for shareholders but because they have excessive arrogance about their ability to produce profits from the merged organization.

9. Gabriel Hawawini and I. Swary, *Mergers and Acquisitions in the U.S. Banking Industry: Evidence from the Capital Markets* (Amsterdam: North Holland, 1990).
10. Richard Roll, "The Hubris Hypothesis of Corporate Takeovers," *Journal of Business* (April 1986), pp. 197–216.

They believe that their valuation of the target is correct, even though their bid overvalues the target, often by a substantial amount.

Another motive for M&As is **synergy**, or mutual benefits wherein the combined organizations exceeds the sum of its parts, which suggests that both target and acquirer experience gains. Gains could be possible immediately via cost reductions due to cutting duplicate computer, office, employee, and other expenses. Or, gains could be achieved in the long run via cost efficiency and greater management expertise. At first glance this motivation would appear to conflict with the fact that buyers do not gain from mergers. Interestingly, a paper by Zhang showed that, after taking into account losses to buyers due to agency costs and hubris, evidence in favor of synergy was found.[11]

What do these results imply for bank managers interested in maximizing the value of shareholders' equity? First, obviously be a seller, not a buyer. Sellers reap substantial gains in the value of their stock, gains that might be difficult or impossible to obtain through operations. Second, sell to a bank that is substantially larger. Third, seek to minimize agency and hubris problems and maximize synergies in M&A deals. Beyond these factors, arrange a cash transaction unless tax factors make that impossible.[12]

What are the lessons for those thinking of making an acquisition? Perhaps "don't do it" is too strong an answer. But clearly the results discussed here must give pause to any bank thinking about embarking on an aggressive M&A strategy. At the least, management should clearly understand the motivation for the structural reorganization. Is it the right motivation? Is it designed to benefit shareholders? Also, management should view with some degree of skepticism any arguments that rest on being able to operate the target bank more effectively than its existing management.

Long-Term Effects of Bank Mergers

One possible explanation for the large number of bank M&As, which is consistent with the assumption that managers are indeed attempting to increase shareholder value, focuses on the longer-term effects of these decisions. Under this view, it may indeed be the case that the announcement of a merger or acquisition does not increase (and may decrease) the bidder's stock price on the announcement date, but the longer-run improved performance of the combined entity more than offsets the temporary decline in stock price. Although only limited evidence suggests this possibility, one recent study supports the long-term benefits of bank mergers.

Cornett and Tehranian examined the post-performance of large bank acquisi-

SNL Securities is a research and publishing company that focuses on banks, thrifts, REITs, insurance companies, and specialized financial services companies. It collects corporate, market, and financial data on these companies, including bank mergers, acquisitions, and stock prices, and transmits it to business subscribers. See the Press Releases at http://www.snl.com/snl/ *for the latest banking news.*

11. Hao Zhang, "U.S. Evidence on Bank Takeover Motives: A Note," *Journal of Business Finance & Accounting* (September/October 1998), pp. 1025–1032.
12. For an excellent summary of bank mergers and performance articles, see Stephen A. Rhoades, "A Summary of Merger Performance Studies in Banking: 1980–93 and an Assessment of the 'Operating Performance' and Event Study Methodologies," Board of Governors of the Federal Reserve System, Staff Study 169 (July 1994).

tions that took place between 1982 and 1987.[13] They took a sample of 15 large interstate acquisitions and 15 large intrastate acquisitions and compared the post-acquisition performance of those banks with industry-average data. The analysis focused on the following indicators of bank performance: profitability, capital adequacy, credit quality, efficiency, liquidity, growth, and interest rate risk. They found evidence of superior cash flow performance for banks involved in acquisitions, due to their improved ability to attract loans and deposits, increases in employee productivity, and greater asset growth. This higher long-run cash flow resulting from the merger is consistent with a long-run increase in stock price.

Strategies for Increasing Stock Price: The Bank Megamerger Wave

Prior to the mid-1990s, M&As among large banks and other financial service firms (particularly insurance companies and securities firms) were relatively rare. The main reason for the sudden increase in large M&As that are creating so-called **megabanks** is the deregulation of geographic restrictions, especially interstate banking regulations, and a more favorable antitrust climate in financial services.[14] In 1985 the top ten banks had an average asset size of about $100 billion; by comparison, a similar list in 1999 would average over $300 billion. The following table gives a sample of the top five M&A deals in the banking industry in the latter half of the 1990s:

Announcement Date[a]	Effective Date[b]	Target Name	Acquirer Name	Value ($mil) of Transaction[c]	Combined Total Assets ($mil)[d]
8/95	3/96	Chase Manhattan	Chemical Banking	10,440	304,037
4/98	10/98	First Chicago NBD	Banc One	29,616	230,705
6/98	11/98	Wells Fargo	Norwest	34,353	190,914
4/98	9/98	BankAmerica	NationsBank	61,633	529,998
4/98	10/98	Citicorp	Travelers Group	72,558	716,969

Source: Securities Data Company.

a. Date when either target or acquirer makes a public announcement that it held negotiations, or received a formal proposal to combine, acquire, recapitalize, etc.

b. Date when the entire transaction is completed and effective.

c. Total value of consideration paid by the acquirer, excluding fees and expenses. The dollar value includes the amount paid for all common stock, common stock equivalents, preferred stock, debt, options, assets, warrants, and stake purchases made within six months of the announcement date of the transaction. Liabilities assumed are included in the value if they are publicly disclosed. If a portion of the consideration paid by the acquirer is common stock, the stock is valued using the closing price on the last full trading day prior to announcing the terms of the stock swap. If the exchange ratio of shares offered changes, the stock is valued based on its closing price on the last full trading date prior to the date of the exchange ratio change.

d. Combination of total assets of acquiring company and those of target company for the last 12 months. Total assets include current assets, long-term investments and funds, net fixed assets, tangible assets, and deferred charges for the acquiring company for the last 12 months.

13. Marcia Millon Cornett and Hassan Tehranian, "Changes in Corporate Performance Associated with Bank Acquisitions," *Journal of Financial Economics* (April 1992), pp. 210–234.

14. See Stephen A. Rhoades, "Bank Managers and Industrywide Structure, 1980–94," Staff study 169, Board of Governors of the Federal Reserve System (1996).

While megabank formation no doubt has agency, hubris, and synergy motivations, as already discussed, it could also be driven by diversification and **market power** in the case of the largest banks. Diversification across products and services as well as geographic areas can reduce operating risk. Also, market power may be needed to maintain a competitive position in national and international banking.

A study by Siems examined 19 bank megadeals in banking in 1995.[15] A key finding was that in-market M&As are more profitable to shareholders of buyers and targets than cross-market M&As. In-market M&As (as measured by the extent of office overlap in shared markets) were hypothesized to be driven by synergies and market power, whereas cross-market M&As were driven by diversification and growth goals. His results were as follows:

1. Evidence in favor of synergy in terms of operating cost efficiencies was found.
2. Synergy appeared to be stronger than diversification as a motivation in megadeals.
3. Banks that increase their market power do not necessarily benefit their shareholders.
4. The results support the agency cost and hubris explanations in line with studies of smaller bank M&As.

Another study by Milbourn, Boot, and Thakor argued that the magnitude of the gains in megamergers were not sufficient to explain the sudden increase in such activity.[16] Also, on a theoretical level, they observed that expansion of scale conflicts with expansion of scope. Scale economies imply greater specialization, as opposed to greater scope with a wide variety of financial services. In this context, why are megabanks expanding both scale and scope at the same time? They offer two theoretical explanations not previously considered in the literature:

1. CEOs of larger and more diverse organizations increase their reputation and possibly financial salaries.
2. When the competitive environment has considerable uncertainty, it may be advantageous for banks to expand size and scope to reduce their risk.

www.tv.cbc.ca/national/ pgminfo/banks/ mergerworld.html lists worldwide megamergers in banking and links to related newspaper articles.

These explanations are potentially useful because they have some degree of support in nonfinancial M&As.

Megadeals in banking are not confined to the United States. Instead of the fall of interstate banking restrictions triggering the megadeal wave, in the case of Europe, the key market change was the European Union banking directive that

15. Thomas F. Siems, "Bank Mergers and Shareholder Wealth: Evidence from 1995's Megamerger Deals," *Financial Industry Studies,* Federal Reserve Bank of Dallas, August 1996, pp. 1–9.
16. Todd T. Milbourn, Arnoud W. A. Boot, and Anjan V. Thakor, "Megamergers and Expanded Scope: Theories of Bank Size and Activity Diversity," *Journal of Banking and Finance* (February 1999), pp. 195–214.

allowed banks to cross national boundaries in Europe since 1993 (in addition to the monetary union begun in the late 1990s). A growing number of large European banks and nonbank financial institutions have been involved in megadeals in recent years. For example, Banque Indosuez and Credit Agricole in France, Credit Suisse and Swiss Volksbank as well as Union Bank of Switzerland and Swiss Bank Corp. in Switzerland, Generale Bank and Fortis Group in Belgium, and the intercontinental acquisition by Deutsche Bank in Germany of Bankers Trust in the United States. Other aggressive expansions in Europe have been undertaken by Santander-Royal Bank of Scotland, the Dutch banking-insurance group ING, and Lloyds Bank of the United Kingdom. In Japan a major consolidation of 21 large banks and many insurance and brokerage firms is anticipated to occur by year 2000, which would leave only seven financial holding companies. Hence, megamergers are currently tranforming the financial landscape on a global scale.[17]

It is reasonable to believe that the formation of large financial service firms will accelerate following the passage of the Financial Services Modernization Act of 1999, which allows banks, securities firms, and insurance companies to merge and acquire one another. Some experts believe that financial institutions could become so large as to be *too big to fail* (TBTF). If the failure of a large institution resulted in severe damage to the economy, it would be necessary for government to intervene to preserve economic stability as well as the safety and soundness of the financial system. TBTFs are dangerous to the extent that they might take excessive risks in view of government guarantees to cover losses—in essence, a TBTF bank is "bullet proof." This so-called *moral hazard problem* is increasingly a dilemma that governments around the world will need to address as M&A activity among large institutions continues in the years ahead.

Under the FDIC Improvement Act of 1991, a large failing institution would *not* be rescued (or deemed TBTF) unless the Treasury Department, in agreement with the president, FDIC, and the Federal Reserve Board, believes that the failure would cause systemic risk via damage to the economy. However, in 1998 the failure of Long-Term Capital Management, a hedge fund involved in securities activities, Long-Term Capital Management, was prevented by the Federal Reserve, which coordinated a bailout by that firm's creditors. It was argued that the collapse of the firm would potentially disrupt capital markets and cause other securities firms and banks to fail in a domino effect. Thus, TBTF applies not only to banks but to financial services firms in general.

The Financial Services Modernization Act charges the Fed and the Treasury to recommend ways to implement market discipline and mitigate the moral hazard problem. The most popular suggestion at this time is to require large institutions and their parent companies to issue subordinated debt. These debt

---

17. For an excellent overview of the bank M&A literature, see Allen N. Berger, Rebecca S. Demsetz, and Phillip E. Strahan, "The Consolidation of the Financial Services Industry: Causes, Consequences, and Implications for the Future," *Journal of Banking and Finance* (February 1999), pp. 135–194.

issues would not carry any government guarantees in the event of failure. As such, the financial market would discipline risky institutions by pricing their debt issues lower than other financial service firms and by not purchasing their debt securities. This *market discipline* signal could be used by regulators to implement timely measures aimed at curbing excessive risk taking and averting a financial collapse of a major, global financial institution.

SUMMARY

To achieve its goal of maximizing the value of the owner's investment, management must be able to identify those factors that produce increases in stock prices and those that produce decreases. For publicly traded banks, the equity market quickly evaluates the importance of events that affect the bank. However, most banks are not publicly traded. For those banks, management must rely more heavily on the accounting statements to provide insights into bank valuation.

Returns to shareholders include cash dividends and changes in the market price of their investments in the form of capital gains. For most banks, the total return (the sum of cash dividends plus capital gains) is dominated by stock price changes. These stock price changes reflect changes in the amount of anticipated cash flow from the stock, changes in the expected timing of the cash flow, and changes in the riskiness of the cash flow. An increase in stock price results from increases in the amount of the cash flow (i.e., dividends) to be received from the asset, earlier receipt of the cash flow, and a decrease in the riskiness of the cash flow. It is also important to consider the effects of growth in earnings and inflation on stock values. Further insight into the valuation process for bank equity can be obtained from the price-earnings ratio—the ratio of the price per share to the earnings per share. Banks with higher expected growth in cash flow or lower risk should sell at higher price-earnings ratios.

Managers can gain a deeper understanding of the bank valuation process by examining the determinants of merger and acquisition (M&A) prices in the ongoing consolidation movement. Evidence from studies of bank M&As suggests a systematic relationship between bank financial ratios such as equity to assets and net income to assets and bank valuation. Other studies suggest that targets of M&As obtain virtually all the benefits from the merger while the buyer's stock price either stays unchanged or goes down. A variety of motivations for the consolidation movement may affect bank valuation, including agency, hubris, synergy, diversification, and market power.

Key Terms and Concepts

Agency cost

Bidder

Capital gain

Dividend yield/return

Hubris hypothesis

Market power

Megabanks

Price-book ratio

Price-earnings multiple or ratio

Rate of return

Synergy

Target

Questions

4.1 What is meant by the term *rate of return*? How is it calculated? Why is it important to bank management?

4.2 What is the price-earnings ratio? What information does it provide to management?

4.3 What information is provided from studies of bank merger and acquisitions prices about the determinants of bank stock prices? What appears to be the major determinants of the price-book ratio in bank mergers and acquisitions?

4.4 Are all earnings of equal importance in determining bank stock prices? Why would operating earnings and earnings from security gains and losses differ in their effects on bank stock prices?

4.5 Are the determinants of bank stock prices different since deregulation? If so, in what ways?

4.6 If two banks today announced their agreement to merge, what would you expect to happen to the prices of the buyer's and the seller's stock? Why? What does the evidence of existing studies suggest about the motivation of management?

4.7 What are the motivations for bank mergers and acquisitions? Discuss how these motivations may affect bank value.

4.8 Use the web site *www.datachimp.com/articles/* to experiment with calculating stock value. Make up a hypothetical example, plug in the numbers, and show your calculations.

4.9 Use World Banking Merger Links at *www.tv.cbc.ca/national/pgminfo /banks/mergerworld.html* to select one megamerger in banking, and discuss details of the merger using links to related newspaper articles. What were the motives for the merger?

4.10 Go to the FDIC's web site at *http://www.fdic.gov/bank/individual /index.html* and look up one of the bank holding companies in your state. What kinds of details about the bank holding company you selected can you collect from this web site? You might also try an individual bank rather than a bank holding company if you encounter problems in your search efforts.

Problems

4.1   Capital National Bank's stock paid a cash dividend of $2.42 per share last year. During the year, the stock price changed from $52 per share at the start of the year to $62 per share at the end of the year. What was its rate of return?

4.2   Pick any five publicly traded banks. Using *The Wall Street Journal* or a similar publication, record their annual dividends, their prices one year ago, and their most recent prices. Then compute the rate of return for each bank. Finally, compute the fraction of the rate of return for each bank that reflects cash dividends paid. Do they differ significantly? If so, why?

4.3   Pick any five publicly traded electric utility stocks. Compute their rates of return as in problem 4.2. Compare the percent of the rate of return accounted for by cash dividends for these electric utilities with that of the banks from problem 4.2. Do they differ? If so, why?

4.4   The anticipated cash flow per share of stock for Capital National Bank is as follows:
Year 1 = $10
Year 2 = $12
Year 3 = $14
Year 4 = $15

In addition, it is expected that the stock will be sold at the end of year 4 at $80 per share. Assuming a required rate of return of 8%, what should be the value of the stock?

4.5   In problem 4.4, how will the value of the stock change if the required rate of return increases to 10%? Decreases to 6%? What might cause the required rate of return to increase or decrease?

4.6   Assume that the current dividend for a bank is $10, its nominal growth rate of earnings is 5% per year, and the nominal discount rate is 15%, what is the value of the bank's stock? How should changes in inflation affect this valuation? Based on this formula, how can bank management increase value?

4.7   For the five publicly traded banks you selected in problem 4.2, calculate their price-earnings ratios. Do they differ? If so, why? How do they compare with the five electric utility companies you selected in problem 4.3?

First National Bank of Smithville

As Donna Even prepared for her meeting with the president of the First National Bank of Smithville, she examined the most recent financial statements he had sent her. These included the annual report, the most recent quarterly report, and highlights of the bank operations (Exhibits 4.1 through 4.5). She noted that the bank had total assets of $106.6 million at the end of the most recent year and $107.9 million at the most recent quarter. This slow (but steady) growth had typified the bank in recent years. The bank was profitable ($625,477) in the most recent year, although his return on assets of 0.57%

was significantly below those of its peer group. With 200,000 shares outstanding, the profits fo the bank last year equaled $3.12 per share, while book value was $52.64 per share. The relatively low profitability of the bank at a time during which other banks were earning substantial profits was something of a puzzle, although Donna noted that the bank had a very small fractions (24.2%) of its assets in loans.

She thus pondered the issue of an offer price and wondered what other information she would need before setting that price.

EXHIBIT 4.1	Statement of Financial Condition December 31, 20XX

Assets		Liabilities & Capital Liabilities	
Cash on hand & due from banks	$ 6,351,751	Deposits	$ 95,635,593
Securities of U.S. government	54,398,942	Cash dividends payable	100,000
Securities of state & political subdivisions	985,567	Other liabilities	384,275
Other investments	11,988,593	Total liabilities	$ 96,119,868
Federal funds sold	7,225,000	Capital	
Commercial loans	19,551,862		
Installment loans	2,144,346	Capital stock	$1,000,000
Overdrafts	3,849	Capital surplus	1,100,000
Banking house, net	2,795,873	Undivided profits	8,429,272
Furniture & fixtures, net	59,224	Total capital	$ 10,529,272
		Total liabilities & capital	$106,649,140
Total assets	$106,649,140		

EXHIBIT 4.2	Statement of Income, Year Ended December 31, 20XX

Interest Income

Interest and discounts on loans	$1,998,945
Interest on security investments	3,764,708
Interest on other investments	168,682
Total Interest Income	$5,932,335

Interest Expense

Interest on deposits	$3,000,828
Net interest income	$2,931,507
Provision for loan losses	460,000
Net interest income after provision for loan losses & bond revaluation	$2,471,507

Other Income

Other income	$1,411,993

Other Expenses

Salaries and wages	$1,033,059
Contribution to profit-sharing trust	25,000
Other operating expenses	$1,955,506
Total other expenses	$3,013,565
Income before income taxes	$ 869,935
Federal income taxes	244,458
Net Income	$ 625,477

EXHIBIT 4.3	Statement of Changes in Capital Year Ended December 31, 20XX

Balance—Beginning of Year	$ 9,704,103
Prior period accrual adjustment	(53,808)
Changes in reserve for mutual fund valuation	225,441
Net income	625,477
Deferred tax adjustment	38,059
Cash dividends paid	(100,100)
Balance—End of Year	$10,529,272

EXHIBIT 4.4 — Highlights 20XX

Net profit	$ 625,477
Net earnings per share	$3.12
Book value per share	$52.64
Total resources	$106,649,140
Total deposits	$ 95,635,592
Total capital & reserves	$ 10,529,272
Number of stockholders	45
Number of employees and officers	49
Number of deposit accounts	9,232

EXHIBIT 4.5 — Statement of Financial Condition as of June 30, 20XX+1

Assets		Liabilities & Capital Liabilities	
Cash on hand & due from banks	$ 4,830,215.08	**Liabilities**	
Securities of U.S. government	55,186,360.24	Deposits	$ 96,582,346.79
Securities of state & political subdivisions	752,611.02	Other liabilities	458,766.81
Other investments	9,488,593.45	Total liabilities	$ 97,041,113.60
Federal funds sold	6,800,000.00		
Commercial loans	20,566,799.73	**Capital**	
Installment loans	5,590,765.90	Capital stock	$ 1,000,000.00
Overdrafts	36,998.70	Capital surplus	2,000,000.00
Banking house, net	2,344,419.12	Undivided profits	7,873,310.78
Furniture & fixtures, net	321,411.85		
Other assets	2,006,249.29	Total capital	$ 10,873,310.78
Total assets	$107,914,424,38	Total liabilities & capital	$107,914,424.38

An Overview of Asset/Liability Management (ALM)

J im Fox's first assignment at West American Bank (a $3 billion regional commercial bank) was as assistant to the asset/liability manager. In this capacity Jim was responsible for calculating the interest rate risk position of the bank. On his second day on the job, Jim's boss presented him with the following policy statement that had recently been adopted by the board of directors' asset/liability management committee.

The Board Asset/Liability Management Committee directs management to achieve an interest rate risk position that is within the following guidelines:

Change in Interest Rate	Change in Net Interest Income	Change in Market Value of Equity
+300	−80%	−40%
+200	−65	−15
+100	−40	−5
Flat	0	0
−100	−40	−5
−200	−65	−15
−300	−80	−40

The policy itself was relatively clear: if interest rates increased by 200 basis points, the bank should have its portfolio structured so that net interest income did not fall by more than 65% and the net worth (the market value of assets less the market value of liabilities) did not decline by more than 15%. Similar interpretations could be placed on other movements in interest rates. The problem facing Jim Fox was how to determine whether the interest rate position of the bank was within these guidelines. He needed to learn a good deal about dollar gap, duration gap, and simulations that test the sensitivity of income to changes in the composition of the balance sheet when interest rates change. ■

5.1 ASSET/LIABILITY MANAGEMENT

Bankers make decisions every day about buying and selling securities, whether to make particular loans, and how to fund their investment and lending activities. These decisions are based, in part, on (1) the outlook for interest rates and the potential direction of change in future interest rates, (2) the composition of the bank's assets and liabilities, and (3) the degree of risk that bank management is willing to take. Collectively, these decisions affect the bank's net interest income and balance sheet values. The process of making decisions about the composition of assets and liabilities and conducting risk assessment is known as **asset/liability management (ALM)**. Decisions are usually made by the asset/liability management committee (ALCO), which is responsible for the financial direction of the bank. The ALCO's goal is to manage the sources and uses of funds on the balance sheet and off-balance sheet activities with respect to interest rate risk and liquidity. ALM is generally viewed as short run in nature, focusing on the day-to-day and week-to-week balance sheet management necessary to achieve near-term financial goals. The traditional purpose of ALM has been to control the size of a bank's net interest income, and is associated with "dollar gap." ALM also considers the effects of the changes on the value of balance sheet items. This goal is associated with the "duration gap." Both the dollar gap and the duration gap will be explained shortly.

ALM can be illustrated with the aid of the following simplified balance sheet. Suppose that a bank has total assets consisting of $100 million in 5-year fixed-rate loans at 8%, and $90 million in liabilities consisting of 30-day time deposits at 4%. The *net interest income* (NII) of $4.4 million is the difference between the interest earned on the assets ($8 million) and the cost of the liabilities ($3.6 million). The *net interest margin* (NIM) is net interest income divided by the earning assets, or 4.4%.

$$\text{Net interest income (NII)} = \text{Interest income} - \text{Interest expense} \qquad 5.1$$
$$= \$8 - 3.6 = \$4.4$$

$$\text{Net interest margin (NIM)} = \text{Interest income} - \text{NII/Earning assets} \qquad 5.2$$
$$= \$8 - \$3.6/\$100 = \$4.4/100 = 4.4\%$$

The NIM for all FDIC-insured commercial banks in 1999 was 4.05%, down from a high of 4.4% in 1993.[1]

Assets	Liabilities
($ millions)	($ million)
$100, 5-year fixed-rate loans @8%	$90, 30-day deposits @ 4%
	Equity
	$10
Total $100	Total $100

If market rates of interest increase, the cost of short-term borrowing will increase, but the interest earned from the longer-term fixed-rate loans will remain unchanged. Assume that market rates of interest rates increase 200 basis point from 4% to 6%. When the 30-day deposits mature, the interest expense on the new deposits increases from $3.6 million to $5.4 million. However, interest income is not affected because all of the loans are at long-term fixed rates. In this case, the net interest income falls to $2.6 million ($8 million – $5.4 million = $2.6 million), and the NIM is a paltry 2.6%.

If the loans had made at a variable (floating) rate, the net interest margin would have increased to 4.6% because of the higher interest income ($10 million).

$$\text{NIM} = (\$10 - \$5.4)/\$100 = \$4.6/\$100 = 4.6\%$$

Banks make loans with a variety of maturities and interest rates. On the other side of the balance sheet, banks raise funds with different maturities and interest rates. Therefore, NII depends on (1) the interest rates earned on assets and paid for funds, (2) the dollar amount of the various earning assets and liabilities, and (3) the earnings mix of those funds (rate × dollar amount). Other things being equal, an increase in the *interest rates* earned on assets will increase the NII, whereas an increase in the interest rate paid on funding sources will reduce NII. An increase in the *dollar amount of funds* raised and invested (e.g., by increasing the size of the bank) will increase NII. Also, shifting the *earnings mix* toward higher yielding assets or less costly sources of funds will increase NII. Because all the factors involved do not remain constant, however, changes in NII will reflect changes in any of these three factors. These individual issues are only some of the decisions an ALCO must consider.

1. *FDIC Quarterly Banking Profile* (Second Quarter 1999).

5.2 HISTORICAL PERSPECTIVE

Coordinated asset/liability management is a relatively recent phenomenon. From the end of World War II until the early 1960s, most commercial banks obtained their funds from relatively stable (and interest-free) demand deposits and from small-time deposits. Interest rate ceilings on deposits (Federal Reserve Regulation Q) limited the extent to which banks could compete for funds by paying higher interest rates. Opening more branches (where permissible by law) in order to attract funds through greater customer convenience or committing more funds to the advertising budget were two of the few ways to attract more funds. As a result, **core deposits** (not sensitive to interest rates) made up the bulk of fund sources, which increased with the growth of the national and local economies. Moreover, the volatility of interest rates was quite small. In this environment, bank funds management could concentrate on the control of assets. Bank financial management principally was *asset management*. Liability management as it is known today did not exist.

During the 1960s, especially after the Vietnam War became a significant economic and political event in 1966, the demand for bank loans accelerated with the expansion in the economy. The growth in loan demands taxed the ability of commercial banks to fund the loans from existing deposit sources. As a result, banks sought to expand faster than their core deposit growth would allow by acquiring (buying at higher cost) additional funds. This process created a need for *liability management*. With liability management, commercial banks bought funds from the financial markets whenever necessary to meet loan demand, to purchase securities, or to replace reductions in other sources of their funds. The acquisition of funds at the lowest possible cost, or the management of liabilities, then became an active part of bank financial management.

During the 1970s, Regulation Q imposed deposit rate ceilings that limited banks to offering noncompetitive interest rates for many of their deposits. Therefore, liability management concentrated on *nondeposit* sources not subject to Regulation Q. The purchase of funds in the interbank or federal funds market represents perhaps the most widely used source of funds for liability management. Many large banks used the Eurodollar market (the market for dollars deposited at banks outside the United States) extensively for funds. In addition, during periods when market rates of interest were below Regulation Q ceilings, or when the regulations lifted those ceilings, banks could rely on deposit sources in their liability management.

Liability management fundamentally changed the way banks managed their funds. It provided banks with two sources of funds—core deposits and purchased funds—with quite different characteristics. For core deposits, the amount of funds remains relatively insensitive to changes in interest rate levels; that is, the demand for core deposits by bank customers is relatively interest inelastic. From the perspective of bank management, core deposits offer the advantages of stability and low cost. Although core deposit amounts do not change greatly with relatively large variations in interest rate levels, they are not overly responsive to management needs for expansion. If the bank experiences a sizable increase in loan demand, it cannot expect to fund its loan growth with core deposits.

For purchased funds, however, the bank can obtain all the funds it wants within some reasonable limit if it is willing to pay the market-determined price. Unlike core deposits, where prices are determined at the local level, interest rates on purchased funds are set in the national money market. In the money market where a bank can buy funds, it is a *price taker*, whereas it is a *price setter* in the core deposit market.

Banks that are members of the **Federal Home Loan Bank** system can borrow funds (advances) from regional FHLBanks, by using real estate loans as collateral. The maturity of the advances can range from one day to five years or more. The primary function of the Federal Home Loan Bank system is a government-sponsored enterprise (GSE) whose function is to enhance the availability of residential mortgage credit by making low-cost funds available to member institutions. Banks can become member institutions by buying stock in one of the twelve regional Federal Home Loan Banks.

The money market provides banks with flexibility in the amount of funds they are able to raise. However, the money market has two significant risks that the core deposit market does not have. First, its interest rate may be highly volatile. Second, purchased money may be unavailable for banks perceived to be in financial difficulty. This *availability risk* is particularly significant for banks that finance a large share of their assets with purchased money. Any perception that the quality of the bank is poor may eliminate this source. Then the bank would shift, perhaps overnight, from an ability to raise almost unlimited funds at the going market interest rate to a position of being unable to raise any funds. Because most purchased money sources of funds are short-term, often overnight, a change in funds availability can quickly cause a crisis if uninsured depositors who have lost confidence in the bank try to withdraw their funds. Such large-scale withdrawals of deposits, or *bank runs*, may cause the bank to fail, which happened to Continental Illinois Bank in 1984 and Bank of New England in 1991.

Liability management became the dominant method of funding asset/liabilities needs for large banks in the 1970s. Many banks significantly reduced their liquid assets and depended almost entirely on purchased funds. Unstable interest rates in the early 1980s, however, and the financial distress and failure of a large number of banks, forced many banks to move away from exclusive reliance on liability management. Today, management of bank portfolios involves managing both assets and liabilities.

5.3 ALTERNATIVES IN MANAGING INTEREST RATE RISK

Balance Sheet Adjustments

In managing the interest rate risk of a bank's portfolio, management may follow two different approaches (or some combination of the two): on-balance sheet adjustment and off-balance sheet adjustment. On-balance sheet adjustment involves changing the portfolio of assets and liabilities in order to change the manner in which the profitability of the bank or dollar amount of its assets and liabilities changes as interest rates change. For example, management may adjust the maturity, repricing, and payment schedules of its assets and liabilities. Suppose that a small bank or thrift has a substantial amount of long-term fixed rate mortgages funded by short-term CDs. If interest rates rise, the cost of funds will increase but the earnings on the asset will not, thereby reducing the net interest margin. One approach to dealing with this problem is to shift to adjustable rate mortgages on the asset side of the balance sheet or to longer-term CDs on the liability side of the balance sheet. Both of these portfolio management decisions represent on-balance sheet portfolio adjustments.

In addition, a bank could securitize some of its assets and sell them to other investors. As noted in previous chapters, securitization is the packaging and selling of otherwise unmarketable loans, such as home mortgage loans. Alternatively, the bank could buy tranches (parts) of securitized loans or participations (parts) of large loans to adjust its loan portfolio.

Off-Balance Sheet Adjustments

A bank can change its interest rate risk position without changing the portfolio of assets and liabilities by using off-balance sheet derivatives, such as interest rate swaps and futures. In an **interest rate swap contract** a bank and another party (referred to as a counterparty) trade payment streams but not principle amounts. For example, a bank with a long-term fixed rate mortgage portfolio could agree to receive a floating rate payment stream and to pay the counterparty an equivalent fixed rate payment stream. Such a transaction would reduce the interest rate risk from holding this fixed rate mortgage because rising rates would produce a higher payment to the bank from the swap.

As an alternative, the bank could engage in a futures transaction. An **interest rate futures contract** is an agreement between two parties to buy (or sell) a commodity (an interest-bearing instrument) for a fixed price at a specified time in the future. Various financial instruments, such as Treasury bonds and Eurodollars, are packaged as interest rate commodities, and they are actively traded.[2] The holder of the contract earns a gain or incurs a loss based on movements in the price of the contract after purchase. For example, if interest rates fall subsequent to the purchase of a Treasury bond contract, the price of the contract will rise (because bond prices and interest rates move inversely), and, conversely, if interest rates rise the price of the contract will fall. Because the concern of the bank with a long-term fixed rate mortgage portfolio is that it will be harmed by rising interest rates, it could sell a Treasury bond contract (i.e., take a short position). If interest rates did rise, its profit from the sale of the bond futures contract would offset some or all of the loss on its holdings of fixed rate mortgages. The use of off-balance sheet adjustment is covered in greater detail in Chapter 6.

5.4 MEASURING INTEREST RATE SENSITIVITY AND THE DOLLAR GAP

Three techniques of dealing with interest rate risk are examined in this chapter: the dollar gap, duration gap, and simulation. The dollar gap is the oldest technique, and the easiest to understand. It also provides a foundation for understanding the other two techniques.

The most commonly used measure of the *interest sensitivity* position of a financial institution is **gap analysis.** Under this approach, all assets and liabilities are classified into groups—interest rate sensitive or noninterest rate sensitive—according to whether their interest return (in the case of assets) or interest cost (in the case of liabilities) varies with the general level of interest rates. Thus, the focus of gap analysis is on net interest income.

Gap analysis classifies assets or liabilities according to their interest sensitivity. Interest-sensitive assets and liabilities are those that reprice within some defined period (e.g., 0–30 days, 31–60 days, 61–90 days, and so on).

Rate sensitivity is determined by how often assets or liabilities are repriced, rather than by their maturity. Of course assets and liabilities with short-term maturities (less than 90 days) are more rate sensitive than those with longer maturities. However, assets and liabilities with longer-term maturities, but variable rates of interest, which are repriced when changes in the general level of interest rates occur (such as a floating rate, 5-year CD), also are rate sensitive. Therefore, rate sensitivity depends on the frequency of repricing.

Classification of Assets and Liabilities

Table 5.1 presents the classification of the assets and liabilities of a financial institution according to their interest rate sensitivity. Those assets and lia-

2. See the *Wall Street Journal* for a listing of interest rate commodities and other types of commodities.

TABLE 5.1	Classification of Assets and Liabilities by Interest Rate Sensitivity		

Assets			Liabilities and Equity		
Vault cash	NRS	$ 20	Demand deposit	NRS	$ 5
Short-term securities	RSA	15	NOW accounts	NRS	5
Long-term securities	NRS	30	Money market deposits	RSL	20
Variable rate loans	RSA	40	Short-term savings	RSL	40
Short-term loans	RSA	20	Long-term savings	NRS	60
Long-term loans	NRS	60	Federal funds borrowing	RSL	55
Other assets	NRS	10	Equity	NRS	10
		$195			$195

Note:
NRS = Nonrate-sensitive asset or liability
RSA = Rate-sensitive asset
RSL = Rate-sensitive liability

bilities whose interest return or costs vary with interest rate changes over some given time horizon are referred to as **rate-sensitive assets (RSAs)** or **rate-sensitive liabilities (RSLs)**. Assets and liabilities whose interest return or cost *does not* vary with interest rate movements over the same time horizon are referred to as **nonrate-sensitive (NRS)**. In other words, assets and liabilities that reprice within the time horizon are rate sensitive.

Note that the selection of the time period over which to measure the interest sensitivity of the asset or liability is crucial. An asset or liability that is interest rate sensitive in one time period (e.g., 90 days) may not be rate sensitive in a shorter time period (e.g., 30 days). The time periods are sometimes referred to as **maturity buckets** or *planning horizons*. Over a sufficiently long time period virtually all assets and liabilities are interest-rate sensitive. As the time period is shortened, however, the ratio of rate-sensitive to nonrate-sensitive assets and liabilities falls. At some sufficiently short time period (one day, for example), virtually all assets and liabilities are nonrate sensitive. The industry does not establish standard time periods. Each bank decides on those time periods that match its needs.

In the classification of assets and liabilities used in Table 5.1, short-term securities and short-term deposits are those with a maturity of one year or less. Under this criterion, interest rate-sensitive assets are all those assets with a maturity of one year or less (short-term securities and short-term loans) *and* variable rate loans (assuming that the rates on those loans adjust with interest rate changes within a year). All other assets are noninterest rate-sensitive, and include vault cash, long-term securities, and long-term loans. Interest rate-sensitive assets in Table 5.1 are $115, and noninterest rate-sensitive assets total $120. Thus, slightly more than half of the earning assets is rate sensitive.

The total effect of any change in the general level of interest rates on the net interest income of a financial institution depends on *both* the effects on interest revenue *and* interest expense. The effect on interest expense depends, in turn, on the interest sensitivity of liabilities. In the example given in Table 5.1 interest rate-sensitive liabilities are short-term savings deposits, money market deposits (whose interest rates are generally adjusted each week), and federal funds borrowings (whose rates change daily with the federal funds rate). Noninterest rate-sensitive liabilities are demand deposits (whose interest rate is fixed at zero by federal law), *NOW* accounts (negotiable order of withdrawal, or checking accounts that pay a positive interest rate but whose interest rate changes infrequently), and long-term savings, such as three- or four-year CDs. Interest rate-sensitive liabilities total $115, whereas noninterest rate-sensitive liabilities are $70.

Definition of the Dollar Gap

The total effect of interest rate changes on profitability can be summarized by its dollar gap. The **dollar gap** (also referred to as the *funding gap* or the *maturity gap*) is the difference between the dollar amounts of interest rate-sensitive assets (RSA) and interest rate-sensitive liabilities (RSL).

$$Gap\$ = RSA\$ - RSL\$ \qquad 5.3$$

Comparison of the interest sensitivity position of different financial institutions using the gap is not meaningful because of differences in the sizes of the institutions. Such a comparison requires some type of "common size" calculations.

$$\text{Relative gap ratio} = \frac{Gap\$}{\text{Total assets}} \qquad 5.4$$

$$\text{Interest rate-sensitivity ratio} = \frac{RSA\$}{RSL\$} \qquad 5.5$$

The **relative gap ratio** expresses the dollar amount of the gap (dollar RSAs – dollar RSLs) as a percentage of total assets. The *interest-sensitivity* ratio expresses the dollar amount of RSAs as a fraction of the dollar amount of RSLs.

Asset and Liability Sensitivity

A financial institution at a given time may be *asset or liability sensitive*. If the financial institution were asset sensitive (for example, it had $100 million in rate-sensitive assets and $50 million in rate-sensitive liabilities), it would have a positive gap, a positive *relative gap ratio*, and *interest-sensitivity ratio* greater than 1. Conversely, an institution that was liability sensitive (for example, it had $50 million in rate-sensitive assets and $100 million in rate-sensitive liabilities) would have a negative gap, a negative relative gap ratio, and an interest-sensitivity ratio less than 1.

Financial institutions that are asset sensitive (they have a positive gap, positive relative gap, or interest rate sensitivity ratio greater than 1) will experience an increase in their net interest income when interest rates increase and a decrease in their net interest income when interest rates fall. In contrast, financial institutions that are liability sensitive (they have a negative gap, negative relative gap, or interest rate-sensitivity ratio less than 1) will experience a decrease in their net interest income when interest rates increase and an increase in their net interest income when interest rates fall. As previously noted, the bank shown in Table 5.1 has rate-sensitive assets of $75 and rate-sensitive liabilities of $115. Therefore, its dollar gap is a negative $40. The negative gap means that the bankers believe interest rates will decline, and they hope to benefit from the lower cost of funds.

$$Gap\$ = RSA\$ - RSL\$$$
$$-\$40 = \$75 - \$115$$

The relative gap is

$$Relative\ gap = Gap\$/Total\ assets$$
$$-0.21 = -\$40/\$195$$

The interest rate-sensitivity ratio is

$$Interest\ rate\text{-}sensitivity\ ratio = RSA\$/RSL\$$$
$$0.65 = \$75/\$115$$

Gap, Interest Rates, and Profitability

The effects of changing interest rates on net income for banks with different gap positions are illustrated in Eq. (5.6):

$$(\Delta NII) = RSA\$(\Delta i) - RSL\$(\Delta i) = Gap\$(\Delta i) \qquad 5.6$$

where (ΔNII) is the expected change in the dollar amount of net interest income, and (Δi) is the expected change in interest rates in percentage points. An example may help to illustrate the effects of changing interest rates on the net interest income of a financial institution. Suppose a financial institution has RSAs of $55 million and RSLs of $35 million, and thus has a GAP of $20 million. If interest rates were to rise from 8% to 10%, the net interest income of the institution would rise by $0.4 million.

$$Gap\$(\Delta i) = \$20\ million\ (0.02) = \$400,000\ expected\ change\ in\ NII$$

Of course, the effect of this interest rate change on net interest margin (net interest income divided by earning assets) depends on the previous level of net interest income as well as the size of earning assets of the financial institution.

Which way are interest rates going? Each Federal Reserve Bank gathers anecdotal information on current economic conditions in its district through reports from bank and branch directors and interviews with key business contacts, economists, market experts, and other sources. The Beige Book summarizes this information. See http://www.federalreserve.gov/FOMC/BeigeBook/.

Interest rate data can be obtained from the Federal Reserve at http://www.federalreserve.gov/.

Conversely, if RSAs of the institution were $35 million and RSLs were $55 million, the institution would have a negative gap and would be liability sensitive. An increase of 2 percentage points in interest rates would, in this situation, *lower* net interest income by $0.4 million.

The effects of changing interest rates on net interest income is summarized in Table 5.2. For commercial banks with a positive gap, net interest income will rise or fall as interest rates rise or fall. For banks with a negative gap, net interest income will rise or fall inversely with interest rate changes; that is, net interest income will increase with falling interest rates and fall with rising interest rates. In contrast, banks with a zero gap should experience no change in their net interest income because of changing interest rates.

Incremental and Cumulative Gaps

The gap between interest rate-sensitive assets and interest rate-sensitive liabilities can be measured either incrementally or in cumulative terms. The *incremental gap* measures the difference between rate-sensitive assets and rate-sensitive liabilities over increments of the planning horizon. The **cumulative gap** measures the difference between rate-sensitive assets and liabilities over a more extended period. The cumulative gap is the sum of the incremental gaps. Of course, in the case of only one planning horizon, the incremental gap and the cumulative gap are the same.

Table 5.3 illustrates the calculation of incremental and cumulative gaps, with a one-year planning horizon broken down into four increments: 0–30 days, 31–90 days, 91–180 days, and 181–365 days. Note that during the entire 365-day period, the institution has a gap of zero, but over a shorter period the institution is not balanced. It has a positive gap for the first gap period (0–30 days), a positive gap also for the second gap period (31–90 days), but it has negative gaps for the other two gap periods.

TABLE 5.2	Gap, Interest Rate Changes, and Net Interest Income	
Gap	**Change in Interest Rates**	**Change in Net Interest Income (NII)**
Positive RSA > RSL	Increase	Increase
Positive RSA > RSL	Decrease	Decrease
Negative RSA < RSL	Increase	Decrease
Negative RSA < RSL	Decrease	Increase
Zero RSA = RSL	Increase	No change
Zero RSA = RSL	Decrease	No change

TABLE 5.3	Incremental and Cumulative Gaps ($ millions)			
Days	Assets Maturing or Repriced Within	Liabilities Maturing or Repriced Within	Incremental Gap	Cumulative Gap
0–30	$50	$30	+$20	+$20
31–90	25	20	+$ 5	+$25
91–180	0	20	–$20	+$ 5
181–365	0	5	–$ 5	$ 0
	$75	$75		

Gap Analysis: An Example

Table 5.4 provides a comprehensive dollar gap for City Bank, a community bank with total assets of slightly more than $300 million. In this gap analysis, the interest sensitivity of the bank is divided into five increments or "maturity buckets": daily floating rate, 1–30 days, 31–60 days, 61–90 days, 181–360 days, and 360+ days. Each asset and liability of the bank is then allocated to one (or more) time horizons. For example, federal funds sold reprice every day. Hence, the $34 million that the bank has outstanding as federal funds sold shows up in the daily floating rate column. Similarly, the $200,000 that the bank has as federal funds purchased shows up in the same column (as a liability). For many asset and liability items, however, the amount of the outstanding balance is distributed among several time horizons. For example, fixed rate commercial loans are distributed as follows (based on their maturity and repricing characteristics): $1,109,000 in the 1–30 day time horizon, $469,000 in the 31–60 day column, $549,000 in the 61–90 day time horizon, $1,766,000 in the 91–180 day time horizon, $1,954,000 in the 181–360 day time horizon, and $2,202,000 in the 360+ day time horizon. Similarly, on the liability side of the balance sheet, CDs under $100,000 are distributed as follows (based on their maturity): $6,495,000 in the 1–30 day position, $6,741,000 in the 31–60 day time horizon, $5,164,000 in the 61–90 day time horizon, $17,161,000 in the 91–180 day time horizon, and $13,347,000 in the 181–360 day time horizon.

It is important to note the following in understanding the construction of this gap matrix. First, because each asset and liability item must be allocated entirely among the incremental gap positions, reading across each row must produce a sum in each asset or liability category that is the same as the amount shown in the balance sheet. For that reason, the final column in Table 5.4 on the right side of the gap matrix equals the total balance shown on the left side of the matrix.

Second, and more important in understanding the construction of a gap matrix, a considerable amount of judgment is required in the allocation of many balance sheet items among the different maturity positions, especially the liability

TABLE 5.4 Gap Analysis for City Bank March 31, 20XX

	Total Balance	Daily Floating Volume	1–30 Day Position Volume	31–60 Day Position Volume	61–90 Day Position Volume	91–180 Day Position Volume	181–360 Day Position Volume	360+ Day Position Volume	Total Volume
Assets									
Var rate comm lns	—	—	8,778	—	—	—	—	—	8,778
Fix rate comm lns	8,049	—	1,109	469	549	1,766	1,954	2,202	8,049
Var rate real estate lns	12,890	—	12,890	—	—	—	—	—	12,890
Fix rate real estate lns	66,949	—	949	1,420	558	8,879	17,578	37,565	66,949
Installment loans	10,618	—	641	523	503	1,389	2,096	5,466	10,618
Student loans	8,934	—	3,311	3,145	2,478	—	—	—	8,934
Credit card loans	1,203	—	—	—	—	—	—	1,203	1,203
Nonaccrual loans	471	—	—	—	—	—	—	471	471
Overdrafts	883	—	—	—	—	—	—	883	883
Loan lnss reserve	8,599	—	—	—	—	—	—	8,599	8,599
FNMA/FHLMC ARMs	7,592	—	113	3,808	1,717	1,954	—	—	7,592
Agency issue CMOs/REMICs	64,752	—	1,324	1,289	1,188	8,208	21,771	30,972	64,752
Other U.S. government agency—Fix	8,709	—	1,001	—	—	—	—	2,717	8,709
Other U.S. government agency—Var	5,257	—	1,759	1,756	1,742	—	—	—	5,257
GNMA ARMs	4,840	—	38	38	38	4,726	—	—	4,840
State & political subdiv	60	—	—	—	—	—	5	55	60
Private issue CMOs/REMICs	27,282	—	2,819	1,779	1,304	8,732	4,931	7,717	27,282
Other debt securities	16,414	—	2,375	—	200	4,753	2,375	6,711	16,414
Other marketable securities	8,080	—	673	673	673	2,019	4,038	4	8,080
Investment CDs	291	—	—	—	—	291	—	—	291
Federal funds sold	34,800	34,800	—	—	—	—	—	—	34,800
Cash & due from banks	24,774	—	—	—	—	—	—	24,774	24,774
Fixed assets	6,393	—	—	—	—	—	—	6,398	6,398
Other real estate	4,284	—	—	—	—	—	—	4,284	4,284
Other assets	3,738	—	—	—	—	—	—	3,738	3,738
Total Assets	327,547	34,800	37,780	19,891	10,950	42,717	54,748	126,661	327,547

TABLE 5.4   Gap Analysis for City Bank *(continued)*
March 31, 20XX

	Total Balance	Daily Floating Volume	1–30 Day Position Volume	31–60 Day Position Volume	61–90 Day Position Volume	91–180 Day Position Volume	181–360 Day Position Volume	360+ Day Position Volume	Total Volume
Liabilities									
Demand deposits IPC	48,095	—	—	—	—	—	—	48,095	48,095
Demand deposits public Fn	12,136	—	—	—	—	—	—	12,136	12,136
NOW	52,482	—	—	—	—	—	—	52,482	52,482
Money market	21,375	—	21,375	—	—	—	—	—	21,375
Super money market	43,197	—	43,197	—	—	—	—	—	43,197
Regular savings	19,268	—	—	—	—	—	—	19,268	19,268
Variable rate IRAs	5,400	—	5,400	—	—	—	—	—	5,400
Fixed rate IRAs	6,411	—	709	909	420	697	1,846	1,830	6,411
CDs < 100M	55,679	—	6,495	6,471	5,164	17,161	13,347	6,771	55,679
CDs > 100M	27,652	—	2,136	1,460	1,512	18,458	2,960	1,126	27,652
Federal funds purchased	200	200	—	—	—	—	—	—	200
Accrued interest payable	781	—	—	—	—	—	—	781	781
Miscellaneous liabilities	1,739	—	—	—	—	—	—	1,739	1,739
Capital stock	2,800	—	—	—	—	—	—	2,800	2,800
Certified surplus	10,200	—	—	—	—	—	—	10,200	10,200
Undivided profits	19,324	—	—	—	—	—	—	19,324	19,324
Current net earnings	808	—	—	—	—	—	—	808	808
Total liabilities	327,547	200	79,312	9,110	7,096	36,316	18,153	177,360	327,547
Gap	—	34,600	−41,532	10,781	3,854	6,401	36,595	−50,699	
Cumulative Gap	—	34,600	−6,932	3,849	7,703	14,104	50,699	0	
RSA/RSL	—	174.00%	0.48	2.18	1.54	1.18	3.02	0.71	
Cumulative RSA/RSL	—	174.00%	0.91	1.04	1.08	1.11	1.34	1.00	
Gap/Total Assets	—	0.11	−0.13	0.03	0.01	0.02	0.11	−0.15	
Cum. Gap/Total Assets	—	0.11	−0.02	0.01	0.02	0.04	0.15	0.00	

size of the balance sheet. For example, City Bank has chosen to allocate all $21,375,000 of the money market deposit accounts (MMDA) to the 1–30 day time horizon. For these accounts, interest rates changes are at the discretion of management, though management responds to changes in open market interest rate in the decisions (made each week) concerning rate adjustments on these deposits. In fact, despite some small changes in market interest rates, management had not changed the rates offered on MMDAs in the three months proceeding the date of this gap matrix. Demand deposits also present a difficult problem for the asset/liability analyst. Because these accounts pay no interest, they are by definition not interest sensitive. Hence City Bank has allocated the $48,095,000 in Demand Deposits IPC (Individuals, Partnerships, and Corporations) and the $12,136,000 in Demand Deposits Public Funds (mostly local government) to the 360+ day time horizon. Yet rising rates will cause customers to shift into interest-bearing accounts such as MMDAs, which will affect the bank's interest expense.

The gap position for City Bank is given at the bottom of Table 5.4. Calculations are made of the gap for each time period, and the cumulative gap. Also, each of the gap measurements is expressed as a fraction of total assets. For example, City Bank's gap for the daily floating rate period is +$34,600,000, reflecting its large amount of federal funds sold. It is thus highly asset sensitive for the one-day period, and its earnings will be significantly affected by changes in the federal funds rate. However, its gap over the 2–30 day period is a negative $41,532,000, producing a cumulative gap of a negative $6,930,000 for the first two periods. The gap then turns positive for each of the remaining periods until the last days when, by definition, the cumulative gap must be one over the entire gap period.

See http://www.fdic.gov/ *for the FDIC's Quarterly Banking Profile providing data about net interest income and other statistics.*

Managing Interest Rate Risk with Dollar Gaps

The principal purpose of asset/liability management traditionally has been to control the size of the net interest income. The control can be achieved through defensive or aggressive asset/liability management. The goal of **defensive asset/liability management** is to insulate the net interest income from changes in interest rates, that is, to prevent interest rate changes from decreasing or increasing the net interest income. In contrast, **aggressive asset/liability management** focuses on increasing the net interest income through altering the portfolio of the institution. The success of aggressive asset/liability management depends on the ability to forecast future interest rate changes. For example, a strategy that anticipates rising interest rates and that restructures the portfolio to benefit from the anticipated rate increase would fail if interest rates remain unchanged or decline. In contrast, defensive asset/liability management does not require the ability to forecast future interest rate levels.

No one has perfect foresight with respect to interest rates. However, high-risk strategies combined with imperfect forecasts of interest rate movements can result in disaster. Be sure to read the following Managing Risk feature about how one bank misjudged interest rates, took a high degree of risk, and failed.

> ## MANAGING RISK
>
> ## *How Not to Manage Interest Rate Risk*
>
> First Pennsylvania Corporation provides an excellent case example of how a bank should not manage its interest rate risk. Management of the bank violated one of the basic rules of asset/liability management: Although taking some risk is an acceptable management practice, never bet the bank on any interest rate forecasts. Failure to follow this simple principle resulted in massive losses for the bank, the threat of failure, and ultimately a rescue by the Federal Deposit Insurance Corporation. Existing management was dismissed, and for a considerable period of time, the bank was in effect managed by the FDIC.
>
> In the mid and late 1970s, First Pennsylvania began to increase markedly their securities portfolio, especially their long-term holdings. Securities as a fraction of total assets ranged from 12% in 1972 to 28% in 1978. Financially, this expansion in longer-term securities with longer-term sources of funds would not have produced any interest rate risk problem. However, the buildup in long-term securities was financed primarily with short-term purchased funds. Federal funds purchased (as a percent-
>
> age of total assets) increased from 8% in 1972 to 26% in 1978. The bank thus had a large negative gap; it was liability sensitive.
>
> If interest rates had stayed unchanged, First Pennsylvania would have done reasonably well with its strategy of borrowing short and lending long. If interest rates had fallen, First Pennsylvania would have made large profits. Unfortunately, interest rates exploded upward in late 1970s . Interest rates on 3-month Treasury bills soared from about 5% in 1977 to over 10% in 1979, and over 14% in 1981. The combination of soaring rates and the negative gap virtually destroyed the bank. Profits turned into losses, the bank experienced a liquidity crisis because it was unable to roll over its short-term purchased funds. The problem was further intensified by large loan losses that produced an unwillingness on the part of large depositors and other creditors to put funds in the bank. The financial crisis at First Pennsylvania was stemmed only by an FDIC rescue effort in April 1980 that included a $500 million assistance program from the FDIC and a group of private banks.

Balance Sheet Adjustments

A commercial bank may use any of the financial instruments currently on its balance sheet or potentially on the balance sheet in adjusting its assets and liabilities. Banks generally use money market instruments to adjust their asset and liability portfolios, including federal funds, short-term Treasury securities, federal agency securities, Eurodollar time deposits and certificates of deposit (CDs), domestic negotiable CDs, and repurchase agreements. *Federal funds* are overnight interbank loans. Shifting funds into federal funds sales tends to shorten the maturity of the bank's assets and make the assets more interest sensitive. *Short-term Treasury* (or agency) securities allow the bank to earn interest on highly liquid, credit risk-free securities that are available in a wide variety of maturities. Bank management can also vary the interest sensitivity of assets by making deposits at other banks in domestic or Eurodollar CDs. The purchase of a short-term security such as a Treasury bill with the obligation to sell it back in the near term serves as a means of adjusting the maturity of the bank's assets.

On the liability side of the balance sheet, the bank may issue certificates of deposit in various sizes and maturities or may borrow in the federal funds market. Federal funds borrowing, or overnight funds, are the most interest sensitive and least stable source of funds. Shifting from CDs to federal funds shortens the maturity of the liability size of the balance sheet, makes it more interest sensitive, and increases the risk of the bank's portfolio.

How Much Interest Rate Risk Is Acceptable?

One of the most difficult decisions that bank managers face is determining the appropriate degree of interest rate risk to assume. At one extreme, referred to as defensive interest rate risk management, the bank would attempt to structure its assets and liabilities in order to eliminate interest rate risk. The other extreme would follow an aggressive strategy and bet the bank on expectations of interest rate changes. Few banks follow either extreme. Most limit their interest rate risk according to their operating strategy. In making decisions about the appropriate amount of interest rate risk, bank management should consider a number of factors.

The profitability of a bank that does not take some interest rate risk might be inadequate. If the bank matches the interest sensitivity of its assets with the interest sensitivity of its liabilities, the spread between the cost of its funds and the amounts that can be earned by investing the funds may be inadequate. Large banks in particular may be unable to earn an adequate return in competitive loan markets unless they accept both credit and interest rate risk.

A policy of eliminating all interest rate risk on the balance sheet may be incompatible with the desires of the bank's loan customers. Suppose that loan customers want fixed rate loans at a time when the bank wants to increase the amount of interest-sensitive assets on its books, or customers want long-term deposits at a time when the bank wants to issue short-term deposit. The bank could ignore the desires of its customers, but if it did so, it would face the substantial risk of them taking their business elsewhere. Within reasonable limits, the bank must accommodate the desires of its customers. Adjustments to the interest sensitivity of its portfolio must then be made elsewhere.

The expertise and risk preference of management are also significant. Managing the assets and liabilities of a bank to achieve a desired risk position often requires extensive knowledge of sophisticated financial market instruments such as futures, options, and swaps. It also requires a management that is comfortable with accepting interest rate risk. Many bankers feel less comfortable in assessing and managing interest rate risk than in dealing with credit risk.

Aggressive Management

The management of a bank may choose to focus on the dollar gap (also called *maturity* or *funding gap*) in controlling the interest rate risk of its portfolio. With an aggressive interest rate risk management program, such a strategy would involve two steps. First, the direction of future interest rates must be predicted. Second, adjustments must be made in the interest sensitivity of the assets and liabilities in order to take advantage of the projected interest rate changes. The prediction of rising interest rates generally results in shifting the portfolio to a positive gap position.

RISING INTEREST RATES If interest rates were expected to increase, a financial institution with a positive gap (i.e., more rate-sensitive assets) would increase interest return more than the liabilities would increase their cost.

A financial institution that expected interest rates to increase but was not in a positive gap position would need to make adjustments in its portfolio. It might, for example, shorten the maturity of its assets by selling long-term securities and using the funds to purchase short-term securities. It could also make more variable rate loans. Either of these actions would increase the amount of rate-sensitive assets and would thereby allow the higher level of interest rates to be reflected in higher interest income. Another strategy that could be used either as a substitute for the asset portfolio shift or as a complement to it would be to lengthen the maturity of the liabilities of the financial institution. One way to lengthen liability would be to sell longer-term CDs and use the funds to replace federal funds borrowings. With such a strategy, the impact of rising interest rates on the cost of funds of the institution would be reduced, thereby contributing to an increase in the net interest income and net interest margin.

FALLING INTEREST RATES Expectation of falling interest rates would produce just the opposite adjustment in the portfolio under an aggressive portfolio management strategy. Management would want to shift to a negative gap position to benefit from the falling rates. The maturity of fixed rate assets should be lengthened, its dollar amount increased, and the amount of variable rate assets should be reduced. Finally, the gap position could be shifted to a negative one by shortening the maturity of liabilities through, for example, replacing CDs with federal funds borrowings.

See http://www.stls.frb. org/publications *for trends in interest rates and other economic data.*

Defensive Management

The appropriate gap management policy under a defensive strategy is quite different. As discussed earlier, in contrast to an aggressive strategy that seeks to profit from anticipated interest rate movements, a defensive strategy attempts to prevent interest rate movements from reducing the profitability of the financial institution. *An aggressive strategy thus seeks to raise the level of net interest income, whereas a defensive strategy attempts to reduce the volatility of net interest income.*

By keeping the dollar amount of rate-sensitive assets in balance with the amount of rate-sensitive liabilities over a given period through a defensive strategy, the dollar gap will be near zero. If the strategy proves successful, increases in interest rates will produce equal increases in interest revenue and interest expense, resulting in no change in net interest income and net interest margin. Similarly, falling interest rates will reduce interest revenue and interest expense by the same amount and leave net interest income and the net margin unchanged if the amounts of rate-sensitive assets and liabilities are balanced.

A defensive strategy is not necessarily a passive one. Many adjustments in the asset and liability portfolio under a defensive strategy are often necessary in order to maintain a zero gap position. For example, suppose that a variable rate loan was paid off unexpectedly. If the gap was zero prior to the loan pay-off, it would be negative afterward. To restore a zero gap, the asset/liability manager would have to add to short-term securities or loans or increase the amount of variable rate loans. Similarly, a large and unexpected inflow of funds into short-term CDs would shift the portfolio from a zero gap to a negative gap. Again the asset/liability manager would have to make portfolio adjustments even under a defensive strategy.

Three Problems with Dollar Gap Management

TIME HORIZON Although widely used in practice, dollar gap management has a number of important deficiencies that have caused its modification and, in some cases, abandonment. The first problem concerns the selection of a time horizon. As discussed earlier, separation of the assets and liabilities of a financial institution into rate-sensitive and nonrate-sensitive ones requires the establishment of a time or planning horizon. Although necessary, selecting a time horizon can cause problems because it ignores the time at which the interest rate-sensitive assets and liabilities reprice within the time period, implicitly assuming that all rate-sensitive assets and liabilities reprice on the same day. As an example of the problems caused by such an implicit assumption, suppose that a financial institution had a zero gap (rate-sensitive assets = rate-sensitive liabilities), that the maturity of the rate-sensitive assets was one day, that the maturity of the rate-sensitive liabilities was 30 days, and that the planning horizon was 30 days. Given these assumptions, interest rate changes clearly would affect the net interest income of the financial institution even though the institution had a zero gap. Increases in interest rates would lead to an immediate repricing of the assets upward, whereas the liabilities would reprice upward only after 30 days. Conversely, decreases in interest rates would be reflected in an immediate decrease on earnings on the assets but would produce a decrease in the cost of funds only with a lag.

One solution to this problem is to divide the portfolio of assets and liabilities into separate subcategories, referred to as maturity buckets, and to manage each maturity bucket separately. With the maturity bucket approach, gap analysis becomes the analysis of multiple gaps. Balance sheet items are grouped into a number of maturity buckets and the gap is computed for each one of these buckets. For example, the gap might be computed for one month, one to three months, three to nine months, and so on. The gap for each maturity bucket is referred to as an incremental gap, and the incremental gaps sum to the total gap. The maturity bucket approach would not fully solve the problem, however, unless the time horizon were shortened to a one-day period. Further, expansion of the number of maturity buckets itself causes problems, because it becomes difficult to determine the overall interest-sensitivity position of the institution.

CORRELATION WITH THE MARKET   A second problem with traditional gap analysis is the implicit assumption that the correlation coefficient between the movement in general market interest rates and in the interest revenue and cost for the portfolio of the financial institution is one; that is, when interest rates in the market rise (or fall) by 10%, the interest revenue on rate-sensitive assets and the interest cost for rate-sensitive liabilities will rise (fall) by precisely 10%. The estimated change in net interest income from the calculations will occur only if this assumption implicit in the calculation is correct. Yet some reasons indicate that belief that the assumption is incorrect. For example, many variable rate assets are not truly variable, that is, they do not adjust quickly and fully to changes in market interest rates. Residential real estate loans provide an excellent example of the limitations that often exist in variable rate loans. Variable rate loans usually adjust their interest rates only over an extended period, sometimes two or three years after the adjustment in market interest rates, and usually have a limit or ceiling on how far upward they can adjust regardless of the changes in market interest rates. Similar constraints exist for a variety of other types of loans. As a result, it would be unusual for the interest returns on rate-sensitive assets to change at the same time by exactly the amount of the change in the general level of market interest rates.

One method of dealing with the problem of imperfect correlation of interest rates is the use of the *standardized gap*. This measure of the gap adjusts for the different interest rate volatilities of various asset and liability items. It uses historical relationships between market interest rates and the interest rates of the bank's asset and liability items in order to alter the maturity and therefore interest sensitivity of the portfolio items. For example, a variable rate asset whose interest rate has been shown to be rather insensitive to market interest rate movements might be considered as a fixed-rate asset for purposes of short-run gap analysis.

The benefits of the standardized gap approach can be illustrated by looking at Figure 5.1. The rate-sensitivity gap shown in the figure is –30% (interest-sensitive assets are 20% of total assets, whereas interest-sensitive liabilities are 50% of total liabilities). If it is assumed that rate-sensitive assets are $200 and rate-sensitive liabilities are $500, then the dollar gap is –$300. This difference may be referred to as the "naive" gap, because it ignores the correlation between the interest rate changes of the individual assets and of the market. But if the interest rate-sensitive liabilities are 90-day CDs and the interest rate-sensitive assets are 30-day commercial paper, they may, and probably will, respond differently to market rate movements. For example, if the CD rate is 105% as volatile as the 90-day T-bill, whereas the 30-day commercial paper

FIGURE 5.1 **Rate-Sensitivity Gap**

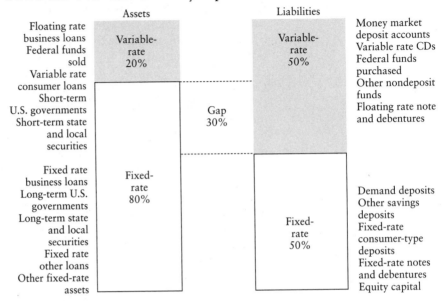

Source: Elijah Brewer, "Bank Gap Management and the Use of Financial Futures," Federal Reserve Bank of Chicago, *Economic Perspectives* (March/April 1985), p. 16.

rate is 30% as volatile, then the standardized gap is –$460. This gap figure is computed as follows: The standardized volatility of the 90-day CDs is 1.05 × 500 = 525, and the standardized volatility of the commercial paper is 0.30 × 200 = 60. Comparing the standardized assets with the standardized liabilities produces a standardized gap of -$460. As a result, the potential interest rate risk for this bank is considerably greater than would be indicated by the "naive" gap. An increase in interest rates would produce a much larger fall in net interest margin than the naive gap and would indicate.

FOCUS ON NET INTEREST INCOME The final and perhaps the most significant problem with the use of traditional gap analysis is its focus on net interest income rather than shareholder wealth. The asset/liability managers of a financial institution may adjust the portfolio of the institution so that net interest income increases with changes in interest rates, but the value of shareholder wealth may decrease. Aggressive asset/liability management based on predictions of interest rate movements increases the risk of loss. Even if asset/liability management does not "bet the bank" through extremely high gap positions (negative or positive) and allows the gap to exceed some desired amount, the attempt to restructure the portfolio still will add some degree of risk to the earnings flow of the financial institution. If successful, aggressive gap management may increase the level of net interest income, but it is also likely to add to the volatility of that income. As a result, aggressive gap management may lessen the value of the institution because of its focus on the wrong goal.

It is possible to take an aggressive position on the balance sheet through positioning of assets and liabilities and yet minimize interest rate risk by using derivatives (such as futures, options, and swaps) to guard against interest rates moving in the wrong direction. However, such techniques have costs and are similar to the costs involved in taking out hazard insurance. Chapter 8 provides insights into these techniques.

Even defensive gap management may produce a decline in shareholder wealth by creating an illusion that an institution is protected from interest rate changes just because it has a zero gap. But, because of the less-than-perfect correlation between asset earnings, liability costs, and general market interest rate movements, it actually was at risk in its net interest income. A more complex but equally valid problem would arise if the dollar amount of rate-sensitive assets equaled the amount of rate-sensitive liabilities, and the amount of non-rate–sensitive assets equaled the amount of nonrate-sensitive liabilities. In that case, even if the interest earnings and costs moved precisely with market interest rate movements, the market value of the institution could drop with rising rates because, despite a constant net interest income, the market value of the assets could fall more than the market value of the liabilities. The market value of the assets would fall more than the market value of the liabilities if the duration of assets exceeded the duration of liabilities. Ultimately the market value of the equity is equal to the market value of assets less the market value of liabilities, and therefore such a policy would lessen the value of the organization to its shareholders.

One final note in the discussion of gap analysis: As the use of financial derivatives (e.g., interest rate swaps, futures, and options, floors, and caps) and simulation models becomes more widespread, the value of dollar gap report will diminish. More will be said about these other technologies shortly.

5.5 DURATION GAP ANALYSIS

The deficiencies of traditional gap analysis, especially the focus on accounting income rather than on equity, have encouraged a search for alternative approaches to measuring and managing the interest rate exposure of a financial institution. One such approach is duration gap analysis. *Duration* is defined as the weighted average time (measured in years) to receive all cash flows from a financial instrument. The **duration gap** is the difference between the duration of a bank's assets and liabilities.[3] It is a measure of interest rate sensitivity that helps to

3. For further details about duration and its application to financial institutions, see Gerald O. Bierwag, *Duration Analysis: Managing Interest Rate Risk* (Cambridge, MA: Ballinger Publishing Company, 1987).

explain how changes in interest rates affect the market value of a bank's assets and liabilities, and, in turn, its net worth. The net worth is the difference between assets and liabilities (Eq. 5.7). It follows that changes in the market value of assets and liabilities will change the value of the net worth (Eq. 5.8). By using duration, we can calculate the theoretical effects of interest rate changes on net worth.

$$NW = A - L \qquad\qquad\qquad 5.7$$

$$\Delta NW = \Delta A - \Delta L \qquad\qquad 5.8$$

where

NW = Net worth
A = Assets
L = Liabilities
Δ = Change in value

A word of caution is in order. The concept of net worth, or value of the equity, as used in the context of duration analysis, is the *not* the same as the market value of the firm's outstanding stock. Stock market prices reflect the present value of expected cash flows in the form of dividends. In contrast, duration net worth or duration equity value is the *theoretical value of the bank's equity*, taking into account the market value of its assets and liabilities. Stated otherwise, stock prices reflect future cash flows rather than the market values of balance sheet assets and liabilities.

The actual value of a bank's liabilities cannot be less than the amount owed to its creditors. By way of illustration, suppose that you have a $1,000 fixed rate 5-year deposit in a bank. Further suppose that interest rates increase from 5% to 6%. Duration theory tells us that market value of the deposit should decline to say $950. While that may be true in theory, the bank's obligation to you is still $1,000. Thus, while the value of marketable liabilities (e.g., some notes and debentures) may decline when interest rates increase, the value of transaction accounts and other liabilities is insensitive to such changes. For simplicity in the remaining discussion of duration, we will assume that the value of bank liabilities is interest rate sensitive.

Despite the difference between the theoretical and legal value of some bank liabilities, the duration gap concept provides a valuable guide to bank managers and regulators. The theoretical value of a firm's net worth is one indicator of its solvency. If interest rates increase, and the market value of a bank's assets decline sufficiently, some creditors and regulators may consider it insolvent.

Measurement of the Duration Gap

The interest-sensitivity position of a financial institution with duration gap analysis may be illustrated with the information in Table 5.5. The financial institution whose balance sheet is shown there has three assets: cash, business loans with 2.5-year maturities (amortized monthly), and mortgage loans with 30-year maturities (amortized monthly). On the liability side of the balance

TABLE 5.5	Balance Sheet Duration				
Assets	$	Duration (years)	Liabilities	$	Duration (years)
Cash	100	0	CD, 1 year	600	1.0
Business loans	400	1.25	CD, 5 year	300	5.0
			Total Liabilities	$ 900	2.33
Mortgage loans	500	7.0	Equity	100	
Total assets	$1,000	4.0	Total Liabilities and Equity	$1,000	

sheet, the institution has CDs with two different maturities as well as equity capital. It is assumed that the CDs pay interest only once—at maturity. The interest rate on the loans is assumed to be 13%, 11% on deposits, and the cash assets are assumed to earn no interest.

The duration of each of the assets and liabilities is also given in Table 5.5. Cash has a zero duration. The durations of both the business loans and the mortgage loans are shorter than their maturities. Except for zero-coupon securities where only single payment occurs, duration is always less than maturity. The durations of the CDs are the same as their maturities, because they are single-payment liabilities.

Interest Rates, the Duration Gap, and the Value of Equity

Given the preceding information, the duration of the asset portfolio (the weighted duration of the individual assets) is 4.0 years and the duration of the deposits (the weighted duration of the individual types of deposits) is 2.33 years. How will the value of the assets and deposits and theoretical value of the net worth change as interest rates change?

The effect of changing interest rates on the net worth is related to the size of the duration gap, where the duration gap is measured as follows:

$$DGAP = D_a - WD_L \qquad\qquad 5.9$$

where

$$DGAP = \text{Duration gap}$$
$$D_a = \text{Average duration of assets}$$
$$D_L = \text{Average duration of liabilities}$$
$$W = \text{Ratio of total liabilities to total assets}$$

In the example given in Table 5.5, if interest rates were to increase, the value of net worth would decline. Conversely, if interest rates were to decline, the value of net worth would increase. For rising interest rates, the value of the assets would drop more than the value of liabilities, and thus the value of the net worth would drop. For falling interest rates, the value of the assets would rise more than the value of the liabilities and the value of the net worth would increase.

The change in the net worth can be determined by measuring the size of the duration gap and by specifying the amount of the change in interest rates. In the preceding example, the duration gap may be determined as follows:

$$DGAP = 4.0 - (.9)(2.33) \qquad\qquad 5.10$$
$$= 4.00 - 2.10 = 1.90 \text{ years}$$

Eq. (5.11) gives an approximation for the expected change in the market value of the equity relative to total assets (TA) for a given change in interest rates:

$$\frac{\Delta \text{Net worth}}{\text{Total assets}} \cong -DGAP \frac{\Delta i}{1 + i} \qquad\qquad 5.11a$$

For the dollar amount of the change in net worth, the equation can be rewritten as:

$$\$\Delta \text{Net worth} \cong -DGAP \frac{\Delta i}{1 + i}(TA) \qquad\qquad 5.11b$$

Suppose that current interest rates are 11%, are expected to increase by 100 basis points (1 percentage point), and the duration gap is as given in Eq. (5.11). Then the percentage change in the net worth will be

$$\%\Delta \text{Net worth} \cong (-1.90)\left(\frac{1}{1.11}\right) \cong -1.7\%$$

From Eq. (5.11b), we can determine the dollar amount of the change in equity by multiplying the percentage in net worth by total assets (*TA*):

$$\%\Delta \text{Net worth} \cong (-1.90)\left(\frac{1}{1.11}\right)(TA) \cong -1.7\%(\$1,000) = -\$17$$

Defensive and Aggressive Duration Gap Management

If the duration gap is positive (i.e., the duration of assets exceeds the duration of liabilities), then increases in interest rates will reduce the value of net worth, and decreases in interest rates will increase the value of the net worth. Conversely, if the duration gap is negative, with the duration of assets less than the duration of liabilities, rising interest rates will increase the value of the net worth, whereas falling interest rates will lead to a reduction in it. If the institution is immunized from changes in interest rates through a zero duration gap, changes in the values of assets will be exactly offset by changes in the value of liabilities. (These relationships are summarized in Table 5.6).

An aggressive interest rate risk management strategy would alter the duration gap in anticipation of changes in interest rates. For example, if interest rates

TABLE 5.6	Duration Gap, Interest Rates, and Changes in Net Worth	
Duration Gap	**Change in Interest Rates**	**Change in Net Worth**
Positive	Increase	Decrease
Positive	Decrease	Increase
Negative	Increase	Increase
Negative	Decrease	Decrease
Zero	Increase	No change
Zero	Decrease	No change

were expected to increase, management would want to shift from a positive to a negative gap position. It could do this by reducing the duration of assets and/or increasing the duration of liabilities. The expectation of falling interest rates would, of course, precipitate the opposite portfolio management adjustments. Note that the portfolio strategy in response to the expectation of higher interest rates for both duration and dollar gap are similar—more short-term assets and more long-term liabilities. However, such a strategy would produce a positive dollar gap, where the gap is measured as the difference between the dollar amount of interest-sensitive assets and liabilities, and a negative duration gap, where the gap is measured as the difference in the number of years of the duration of assets and liabilities.

Defensive interest rate risk management within this context would seek to keep the duration of assets equal to the duration of liabilities, thereby maintaining a duration gap of zero. When changes in the demand for loans or in the quantity of CDs occurs at the institution, changing the makeup of the portfolio, the interest rate risk manager would make adjustments in the duration of assets and liabilities in order to keep the duration gap at or near zero.

Problems with Duration Gap Management

Although duration gap measurement provides insights that are useful to asset/liability managers, it also has a number of problems. For example, the **immunization** or isolation of the market value of equity to interest rate changes will be effective only if interest rates for all maturity securities shift up or down by exactly the same amount (i.e., only if the yield curve moves upward or downward by a constant percentage amount). In fact, yield curves seldom move in this way. In periods of rising interest rates, short-term rates usually move up more than long-term rates, whereas in periods of falling interest rates short-term interest rates usually fall more than long-term rates. In addition, the earlier discussion of the price changes that occur in the value of a financial asset due to interest rate changes was only an approximation. The relationship

Duration

Duration is a widely accepted measure of a financial instrument's interest rate sensitivity. In its most basic form, *Macaulay duration*, it is a measure of the effective maturity of an instrument. Specifically, duration is the weighted average maturity of an instrument's cash flows, where the present values of the cash flows serve as the weights. The Macaulay duration of an instrument can be calculated by first multiplying the time until the receipt of each cash flow by the ratio of the present value of that cash flow to the instrument's total present value. The sum of these weighted time periods is the Macaulay duration of the instrument. Mathematically,

$$\text{Macaulay duration} = \sum_{t=1}^{n} \frac{PV\,(CF_t)}{TPV} \times t$$

where

t = number of periods remaining until the receipt of cash flow CF_t

CF_t = cash flow received in period t

PV = present value function $1/(1 + R)^t$, where R is the per-period internal rate of return of the instrument

TPV = total present value of all future cash flows (including accrued interest)

n = number of periods remaining until maturity

Because a zero coupon instrument has only one cash flow, its Macaulay duration is equal to its maturity. It contrast, instruments with periodic cash flows, such as coupon bonds and amortizing mortgages, have durations smaller than their maturity.

Duration is measured in units of time, typically years. Relative to the more traditional measure of term to maturity, duration represents a sophisticated measure of the effective life of a financial instrument. Moreover, when modified to reflect an instrument's discrete compounding of interest, duration measures the instrument's price volatility relative to changes in market yields. Modified duration is calculated as follows:

$$\text{Modified duration} = \frac{\text{Macaulay duration}}{1 + R/c}$$

between interest rate changes and bond price changes is, in reality, not linear, so that the calculation discussed earlier provides only an approximation of the true relationship for small changes in interest rates. The extent to which bond prices change asymmetrically relative to yield changes is called *convexity*.[4] Negative yield changes have a greater impact on bond prices than positive yield changes. If the asset and liability have considerably different duration, comparing the effects of interest rate changes on their values may be unwarranted.

Finally, asset/liability managers must deal with the problem of **duration drift**. Assume, for example, that a financial institution finances a long-term (7-year duration) portfolio with a mixture of 5- and 10-year duration deposits. After 3

4. For a concise discussion of duration, immunization, and convexity, see William F. Sharpe, Gordon J. Alexander, and Jeffrey V. Bailey, *Investments*, 5th ed. (Prentice Hall, 1995), Chapter 16.

where *R* is the per-period internal rate of return of the instrument and *c* is the number of times per period that interest is compounded (for example, 2 for a semiannual coupon bond when *R* is an annual rate).

Modified duration is the price elasticity of an instrument with respect to changes in rates. It represents the percentage change in the present value of a financial instrument for a given percentage point change in market yields; this relationship is defined as follows:

$$
\begin{array}{c}
\text{Percentage} \\
\text{change} \\
\text{in price}
\end{array}
=
\begin{array}{c}
\text{−Modified} \\
\text{duration}
\end{array}
\times
\dfrac{
\begin{array}{c}
\text{Basis point} \\
\text{change in yield}
\end{array}
}{100}
$$

For example, with a modified duration of 10, a bond changes 10% in price for every 100 basis point change in the market yield of that bond.

In the preceding equation, the inverse relationship between the price of a bond and its market yield is established by the minus sign proceeding the term for modified duration. Modified duration acts as a multiplier in translating the effect of changing interest rates on the present value of an instrument: The larger the duration, the greater the effect for a given change in interest rates; and for a given duration, large changes in market rates lead to large percentage changes in price. Therefore, to the extent that the riskiness of an instrument is equated with its price sensitivity, *modified duration acts as a measure of interest rate risk.*

Modified duration provides a standard measure of price sensitivity for different instruments. The standardization allows the duration of a portfolio to be calculated as the weighted average of the durations of its individual components. Because a financial institution can be thought of as a portfolio of assets and liabilities, the duration of an institution's net worth is simply a weighted average of the durations of assets and liabilities. Therefore, by weighting assets, liabilities, and off-balance sheet positions by their estimated durations, a single measure of interest rate risk exposure can be derived.

Modified duration is a powerful concept for measuring interest rate risk, but it does have several limitations. The most noteworthy is that the accuracy of duration depends on the assumption of small, instantaneous, parallel shifts in the yield curve. Errors in its use as a measure of interest rate risk increase as actual changes in market yields diverge from these assumptions.

Source: J. Houpt and J. Embersit, "A Method for Evaluating Interest Rate Risk in U.S. Commercial Banks," *Federal Reserve Bulletin* (August 1991), p. 637.

The Office of Thrift Supervision (http://www.ots. treas.gov/) publishes the Quarterly Review of Interest Rate Risk where duration is used as one measure of risk. This site provides examples of how this measure is used in practice.

years the duration of the assets has declined very little, but the duration of the deposits has declined substantially. After 4 years the duration mismatch is even larger, which happens because maturities were not matched initially even though durations were. This problem raises the question of how often you should rebalance the portfolio (annually, quarterly, monthly, etc.). Such rebalancing is costly and is not generally undertaken unless clearly defined benefits are indicated.

5.6 SIMULATION AND ASSET/ LIABILITY MANAGEMENT

The availability of simulation techniques not only has substantially reduced the mechanical burdens involved in asset/liability management, but has also broadened the scope of possible management techniques. In particular, **simulated asset/liability management models** have made possible the evaluation of various balance sheet strategies under differing assumptions. Most simulation models require assumptions about the expected changes and levels of interest rates and the shape of the yield curve, pricing strategies for assets and liabilities, and the growth, dollar amounts, and mix of assets and liabilities. Alternative assumptions allow for the creations of various "what if" projections. These projections can include current and expected dollar gaps, duration gaps, balance sheet and income statements, various performance measures such as net interest margin, and return on equity and complete balance sheet and income statement date.

Many larger banks depend primarily on simulations, and they set limits for their interest rate exposure, and then test those limits. For example, a bank may limit its interest rate exposure to a 5% change in net interest income. Given this limit, it models the balance sheet that will constrain it to that limit when interest rates change by, say, 200 basis points.

In addition, simulation can be used for **stress testing** to reveal the effects on income and capital of larger changes in interest rates. Stress testing can be thought of as testing the implications of a "worst case" scenario.

Simulation models allow bank management to determine the risk/return trade-offs for different balance sheet strategies. Because of their flexibility in testing different scenarios, they are a superior tool for asset/liability management.

They can combine the best features of dollar gap analysis, duration analysis, and other inputs that management wants to consider. Although simulations are used primarily at large banks, their use will spread as the cost of such models declines.

5.7 CORRELATION AMONG RISKS

The focus of asset/liability management is on interest rate risk. As discussed in Chapter 1, however, bank management is concerned with managing the entire risk profile of the institution, including interest rate risk, credit risk, and other dimensions of risk. If risks were unrelated or uncorrelated, then management could concentrate on one type of risk, making appropriate decisions, and ignoring the effects of those decisions on other types of risk. However, the different types of risk exhibit considerable interrelationships, with a particularly significant connection between interest rate risk and credit risk, especially for commercial banks that use their loan portfolio as the principal vehicle to adjust their interest rate risk exposure.

Credit Risk

A simple example may best illustrate the relationship between interest rate risk and credit risk. Suppose, for example, that asset/liability management strategy concludes that the bank should increase its emphasis on variable rate loans. Suppose also that interest rates increase dramatically after a large number of these loans have been made. Rising interest rates lead to higher payments for borrowers, especially if the loans are long term, such as home mortgages and some automobile loans. The heavier cash outflows burden might reasonably be expected to produce a greater number of defaults in the bank's loan portfolio. The converse situation would arise if asset/liability strategy increased the emphasis on fixed rate loans and interest rates fell dramatically. Unless borrowers were able to refinance these loans at acceptable costs, the incidence of defaults would be likely to increase substantially. And even if refinancing were easy enough to reduce the default rate, the bank would still find its asset/liability management strategy thwarted because assets that were considered fixed rate would in fact be rate sensitive.

Liquidity

Interest rate risk management focuses on the effects of alternative portfolio strategies on the net interest margin (or some other goal) of the bank. Even though interest rate risk and liquidity risk are different types of risk, they are closely related. Liquidity management focuses on the effects of alternative portfolio strategies on the bank's ability to meet its cash obligation to depositors and borrowers. The two are in fact inextricably intertwined. A few examples may assist in understanding the relationship.

Suppose bank management decides to pursue a liability-sensitive position, that is, to have more interest-sensitive liabilities than assets. This interest rate management strategy necessarily reduces the liquidity position of the bank. More liabilities come due in a shorter period, which creates potential funds strains, and fewer short-term highly liquid assets are available to meet those funding needs. Under most circumstances, this mismatch would not be a problem. However, any concern about the bank's ability to meet its obligations may exacerbate funding problems as liabilities mature.

As another example, suppose that bank management structured the portfolio in order to achieve a positive duration gap—the duration of assets exceeded the duration of liabilities. In that case, the ability to realize liquidity from the assets of the bank has been reduced. Long-duration assets will decline more than short-duration assets if interest rates increase. In that case, the sale of assets to raise funds, although still possible, will cause severe losses—losses management would rather avoid.

The coordination of interest rate risk and liquidity management is complex, but it is obvious also that they are too interrelated to be managed independently.

SUMMARY

Asset/liability management refers to short-run balance sheet management designed to achieve near-term financial goals. The focus of asset/liability management in connection with the dollar gap is on net interest income, which is defined as the difference between total interest income and total dollar interest expense. Expressed in relative terms, the focus is on net interest margin, where net interest income is divided by earning assets. Active and aggressive asset/liability management is a relatively recent phenomenon and reflects the increase in volatility of interest rates, the elimination of interest rate ceilings on deposits, and the growth of purchased money, as opposed to "core" deposits.

Net interest income is affected by the interest rates earned on assets and paid on liabilities, by the dollar amount of assets and liabilities, and by the earnings mix of assets and liabilities. Changes in net interest income (and margin) from one period to the next may be partitioned into those caused by interest rate changes, those caused by changes in the amount of funds, and those caused by changes in the mix of assets and liabilities. Asset/liabilities management generally focuses on the effects of interest rate changes on net interest income.

The most commonly used measure of a bank's interest sensitivity position is its dollar gap, defined as the difference between the dollar amount of interest-sensitive assets and interest-sensitive liabilities. Interest-sensitive assets and liabilities are those whose interest earnings or costs change with the general movement of interest rates within some planning horizon. The gap may be calculated for a variety of time periods and subperiods, resulting in both incremental and cumulative gap.

In managing risk, bank management may adopt a defensive strategy to insulate net interest margin from interest rate fluctuations or an aggressive strategy to increase net interest margin by predicting interest rate changes and restructuring the portfolio accordingly.

If the focus of interest rate risk management were on net interest margin, a defensive strategy would seek to balance the amount of interest-rate sensitive assets and interest rate-sensitive liabilities. Properly done, interest revenues and interest expenses would rise and fall together with changing interest rates, so that net interest margin would remain unchanged under this dollar gap strategy. With an aggressive dollar gap program, management would establish a positive gap (rate-sensitive assets greater than rate-sensitive liabilities) when interest rates were expected to rise and a negative gap when interest rates were expected to fall. If the interest rate forecast was correct, the bank would benefit through a higher net interest margin. Of course, if the interest rate forecast was incorrect, the net interest margin would be reduced.

Although widely used, the dollar gap approach has a number of limitations, including the difficulty in selecting a single, appropriate time horizon; the implicit assumption that interest revenue and costs on rate-sensitive assets and liabilities are perfectly correlated with general interest rate movements; and the myopic focus on net interest margin rather than the goal of maximizing shareholder wealth. Such a limited focus may produce portfolio strategies that, although they increase profitability, may reduce the market value of the equity.

The deficiencies of traditional dollar gap analysis have given rise to duration gap analysis, an alternative approach that focuses on the market value of the assets, liabilities, and equity of the bank. The duration of assets is compared with the duration of liabilities. A defensive duration gap management would balance the duration of assets and liabilities. With an aggressive strategy, management would establish a negative duration (duration of assets shorter than the duration of liabilities) if interest rates were expected to increase and a positive duration if interest rates were expected to fall.

The use of simulation models allow banks to examine alternative interest rate scenarios and to stress test their portfolios.

Many banks—especially the larger banks—deal with interest rate risk by making their adjustments off-balance sheet through futures, options, and swaps. If bank policy leads to sizable interest rate risk in the balance sheet, this risk can be offset by taking an appropriate position off-balance sheet through derivatives such as futures, options, and swaps.

Key Terms and Concepts

Aggressive asset/liability
   management
Asset/liability management (ALM)
Core deposits
Cumulative gap
Defensive asset/liability management
Dollar gap
Duration drift
Duration gap
Federal Home Loan Bank
Gap analysis

Immunization
Interest rate futures contract
Interest rate swap contract
Maturity buckets
Nonrate-sensitive assets/liabilities
Rate-sensitive assets/liabilities
Relative gap ratio
Simulated asset/liability management models
Stress testing

Questions

5.1   What is asset/liability management?

5.2   What is the difference between defensive and aggressive asset/liability management?

5.3   Why is it advantageous for banks to accept some amount of interest rate risk? How much interest rate risk should a bank take?

5.4   What kind of aggressive gap management would be appropriate if interest rates are expected to fall?

5.5   Briefly explain the influence of rate, dollar amount, and mix on net interest income.

5.6 Distinguish between the incremental gap and the cumulative gap. Why is this distinction important?

5.7 How would an increase (decrease) in interest rates affect a bank with a positive dollar gap? Negative dollar gap?

5.8 If a bank has a positive duration gap and interest rate risk, what will happen to bank equity? Explain your answer.

5.9 What is immunization in the context of bank gap management?

5.10 What assumptions are made using duration gap analysis?

5.11 How should a bank change its dollar gap as the yield curve changes?

5.12 What is simulated asset/liability management? What benefit is it to a bank?

5.13 How is interest rate risk linked to liquidity risk? Give an example.

5.14 Explain your position on the following statement: Precise identification of the repricing characteristics of each of the assets and liabilities of a bank is possible.

5.15 The ALM committee of your bank is concerned about the recent trends in the secondary market for CDs. Using monthly, weekly, and daily data from the Federal Reserve Statistical Release H. 15, Selected Interest Rates (available from the web site *http://www.bog.frb.fed.us/ releases/*), explain what has been happening to interest rates.

Problems

5.1 Given the following information:

Assets	$	Rate	Liabilities & Equity	$	Rate
Rate-sensitive	$3,000	10.0%	Rate-sensitive	$2,000	8.0%
Nonrate-sensitive	1,500	9.0	Nonrate-sensitive	2,000	7.0
Nonearning	500		Equity	1,000	
	$5,000			$5,000	

(a) Calculate the expected net interest income at current interest rates. Assuming no change in the composition of the portfolio, what is the net interest margin?

(b) Assuming that all interest rates rise by 1 percentage point, calculate the new expected net interest income and net interest margin.

5.2 Given the following information:

ABC National Bank ($ millions)

Assets		Liabilities and Equity	
Rate-sensitive	$200 (12%)	Rate-sensitive	$300 (6%)
Nonrate-sensitive	400 (11%)	Nonrate-sensitive	300 (5%)
Nonearning	100	Equity	100
Total Assets	$700	Total Liabilities and Equity	$700

(a) What is the gap? Net interest income? Net interest margin? How much will net interest income change if interest rates fall by 200 basis points?

(b) What changes in portfolio composition would you recommend to management if you expected interest rates to increase. Be specific.

5.3 The ALCO has obtained the following information on the interest rate sensitivity of your bank:

	Amount	Rate
90-day interest rate-sensitive assets	$80,000	8.0%
90-day interest rate-sensitive liabilities	$120,000	6.0%

The consensus of forecasting is for interest rates to increase by 50 basis points during the 90 days. But a significant minority of forecasters expects rates to fall by 50 basis points.

(a) How could the bank eliminate its interest rate risk?

(b) What could happen to net interest income if the minority forecast turned out to be the correct one?

5.4 A bank recently purchased at par a $1,000,000 issue of U.S. Treasury bonds. The bonds have a duration of 3 years and pay 6% annual interest. How much would the bond's price change if interest rates fell from 6 percent to 5 percent? If interest rates rose from 6 percent to 7 percent? What would your answer be if the duration of the bond was 6 years?

5.5   Calculate the duration gap of the following bank.

Assets				Liabilities/Equity			
	Amount	%	Duration (years)	Transaction		%	Duration
Cash	$ 1,000			Deposits	$ 3,000	4.0%	0.5
U.S. government securities	2000	4.0%	5.0	CDs	$ 9,000	6.0%	4.0
Loans	10,000	8.0%	4.0	Equity	1,000		
	$13,000				$13,000		

Calculate the percentage and dollar change in the value of equity if all interest rates increase by 200 basis points. How could the bank protect itself from this anticipated interest rate change?

5.6   Assume that the ABC National Bank has the following structure of assets and liabilities:

Assets		Liabilities	
Floating rate business loans	$ 250	Variable rate liabilities	
Federal funds	50	(floating rate CD and money	
Fixed rate loans and investments	700	market deposit accounts)	$ 200
		Federal funds purchased	200
		Fixed rate liabilities	500
		Equity	100
Total Assets	$1,000	Total Liabilities and Equity	$1,000

(a) What is the dollar or maturity gap of the bank?
(b) Assuming that floating rate business loans are 20 percent as volatile as Treasury bills, that federal funds are 200 percent as volatile as Treasury bills, and that variable rate liabilities other than federal funds purchased are 10 percent as volatile as Treasury bills, what is the standardized gap?
(c) Does the standardized gap suggest a different conclusion about interest rate risk?

5.7   If a bank has a duration gap of 4.0 years, and interest rates increase from 6 percent to 8 percent, what is the change in the dollar value of equity (assume that assets are $1 billion)?

5.8   As a management trainee assigned to the bank's asset/liability management committee, you have been asked to calculate the duration of each of the following loans:

(a) $20,000 principal, $4,500 payments per year for five years.
(b) $20,000 principal, $4,200 payments per year for five years.
Assume that the bank's current required return on these types of loans is 8%.

5.9   The balance sheet of Capital Bank appears as follows:

Assets		Liabilities and Maturities	
Short-term securities and		Short-term and floating	
adjustable rate loans	$ 220	rate funds	
Duration: 6 months		Duration 6 months	$ 560
Fixed rate loans		Fixed rate funds	
Duration: 8 years	700	Duration: 30 months	270
Nonearning assets	80	Equity	170
Total Assets	$1,000	Total Liabilities & Net Worth	$1,000

(a) Calculate the duration of this balance sheet.
(b) Assuming that the required rate of return is 8%, what would be the effect on the bank's net worth if interest rates increased by 1%?
(c) Suppose that the expected change in net worth is unacceptable to management, what steps could management take to reduce the effects?

5.10 Consider the following bank balance sheet:

Assets		Liabilities	
3-year Treasury bond	$275	1-year CD	$155
10-year municipal bond	$185	5-year note	$180

Assume that the 3-year Treasury bond yields 6%, the 10-year municipal bond yields 4%, the 1-year certificate of deposit pays 4.5%, and the 5-year note pays 6%. Assume that all instruments have annual coupon payments.
(a) What is the weighted average maturity of the assets? Liabilities?
(b) Assuming a 1-year time horizon, what is the dollar gap?
(c) What is the interest rate risk exposure of the bank?
(d) Calculate the value of all four securities on the bank's balance sheet if interest rates increases by 2 percentage points. What is the effect on the value of the equity of the bank?

5.11 A bank issues a $1,000,000 1-year note paying 6% annually in order to make a $1,000,000 corporate loan paying 8% annually.

(a) What is the dollar gap (assume a 1-year time horizon)? What is the interest rate risk exposure of the bank?

(b) Immediately after the transaction, interest rates increase by 2 percentage points. What is the effect on the asset and liability cash flows? On net interest income?

(c) What does your answer to part (b) imply about your answer to part (a)?

Madison National Bank[5]

Judy Langer, vice-president of funds management for Madison National Bank, was reviewing Madison's loan position during a coffee break at the asset/liability management committee (ALCO) meeting. The ALCO decides the composition of earning assets, which include loans, time deposits at other banks, federal funds sold, and security investments. The committee also decides the different funding options of the liability side of the balance sheet. Examples are the amount of CDs versus transaction accounts. Members of the committee include the vice-presidents of funds, bonds, and securities (which include all nonbond security investments) management as well as commercial lending. The chairperson of the committee is the executive vice-president of investments and financial planning.

Madison has a reputation for having conservative lending policies. Madison's loan position, established by the board of directors, is governed by two lending policy guidelines. First, total loans cannot exceed 100 percent of core deposits, which are defined as demand, savings, and time deposits as well as certificates of deposit less than $100,000. Second, earning assets cannot exceed 140% of core deposits. (See Exhibit 5.1.)

ALCO Meeting

Sam Rogers, chairman of the committee, started the meeting by discussing the bank's current posture with respect to transaction-based loans. He informed the members that several large companies are in the market for these transaction-based loans that are to be repriced. They want quotes from Madison as well as other banks. Sam then asked for

5. The original field-based research for this case was conducted by graduate students taking Dr. Gup's banking classes.

comments and opinions on what Madison's position should be regarding these opportunities.

Mike Clayman, vice-president of commercial lending, started the discussion by raising the issue of strong commercial loan demand. Mike stated that in the past year the demand for loans has been increasing. In addition, it is expected to remain strong in the months ahead due to the continued economic expansion in such areas as housing construction as well as commercial and industrial modernization of plant and equipment. Judy Langer wanted more information about both points and wrote herself a note on the pad in front of her.

Willie Morgan, vice-president of securities management, then pointed out that these loan requests are for transaction-based loans. Transaction-based loans are short-term loans to large corporate borrowers for the purpose of meeting inventory and other operational needs. The typical size of such loans is about $10 million.

He also stated that these corporations are interest rate-sensitive; that is, they will shop around for the lowest loan prices and borrow from banks offering the best terms. He stressed the fact that losing such a loan is not disastrous because the corporations will come back to shop for prices again when their loans are repriced.

Denise Wright, vice-president of bonds management, asked about the bank's current pricing policy. Judy Langer told her that the borrower selected the maturity of the loan. Three maturity options currently available at Madison are 30, 90, and 180 days. In addition, the borrower selects the pricing base to be used in pricing the loan, with four choices: the "all-in" CD rate, the federal funds rate, the prime rate, and the London Interbank Offered Rate (LIBOR). However, LIBOR was not considered in this case. The "all-in" CD rate is the market rate plus the cost of deposit insurance and the reserve requirement on CDs. The insurance fee and reserve requirement adds about 8

EXHIBIT 5.1	Balance Sheet

($ millions)	2004	2003
Assets		
Cash and due from banks	$ 820,268	$ 676,448
Earning assets		
Time deposits in other banks	-0-	398,000
Federal funds sold and securities purchased under agreement to resell	418,550	16,900
Trading account securities	19,606	15,292
Investment securities	1,211,300	1,330,017
State & local gov't. securities	352,462	452,689
Loans	5,419,424	4,187,428
Less: Allowance for loan losses	73,488	56,478
Unearned income	152,622	153,258
Net loans	5,193,314	3,979,692
Total earning assets	7,195,232	6,192,590
Premises and equipment, net	170,060	155,628
Customer's acceptance liability	126,694	23,232
Accrued interest receivable and other assets	251,504	255,262
Total Assets	$8,563,758	$7,273,160
Liabilities and Shareholders' Equity		
Deposits and interest-bearing liabilities		
Deposits:		
Noninterest-bearing transaction	$1,698,846	$1,846,068
Interest-bearing transaction	1,173,072	977,844

basis points to the market rate of CDs. Finally, the maturity of the pricing option is matched with the maturity of the loan. Thus, a 30-day loan is priced off a 30-day CD, for example.

Judy also reviewed the spread set for each pricing option. The spread when using the prime rate, which is more stable than other pricing options, averages about 100 basis points. When the bank wants the loan, the spread is lowered 5–10 basis points. On the other hand, when the bank does not want the loan, the spread is increased.

The CD and federal fund rates, being more volatile than the prime rate, usually have a premium of 5–10 basis points, respectively. For example, if the spread is set off a prime of 10%, the "all-in" CD rate of 8.5%, and federal funds rate of 8.0% with a

EXHIBIT 5.1	Balance Sheet *(continued)*		

Savings		465,610	494,398
Time		1,431,344	1,107,208
Certificates of Deposits less than $100,000		715,670	553,600
Certificates of Deposits of $100,000 or more		952,610	643,856
Total deposits		6,437,152	3,622,974
Federal funds purchased and securities sold under agreement to repurchase		866,808	799,224
Commercial paper		32,530	36,990
Other interest-bearing liabilities		457,124	162,600
Total deposits and interest-bearing liabilities		7,793,614	6,621,788
Acceptances outstanding		126,662	23,158
Accrued expenses and other liabilities		121,676	115,004
Total liabilities		$8,041,952	$6,759,950
Shareholders' equity:			
Preferred stock		$ -0-	$ 800,000
Common stock		22,782	22,612
Capital surplus		274,710	271,200
Retained earnings		270,196	224,038
		567,688	525,850
Less cost of common stock in treasury		45,882	12,640
Total shareholders' equity		521,806	513,210
Total Liabilities and Equities		$8,563,758	$7,273,160

100-basis point spread to start with, the following loan prices would be derived: The prime would not have any additions other than the 100 basis point spread, making its related price 11.0%. The "all-in" CD rate would have the 100 basis points and 5 additional basis points added due to the volatility of such rates, giving a price of 9.55%. The federal funds rate would have the 100 basis points and 10 additional points added giving a price of 9.10%.

Available Options

After hearing the information presented at the meeting, Sam Rogers stated that the committee must decide what to do about the demand for transaction-based loans. He went on to present the following options.

A. *Run off the loan:* By pricing the loan above competitive rates, Madison can avoid absorbing a large volume of transaction-based accounts as the potential borrower will go elsewhere for available funds. Plus, funds would become available for possible higher-yielding lending opportunities of longer maturity. Experience indicates that an increase in spread of 8–10 basis points above the market rate will remove Madison from consideration by the borrowers.

B. *Accept the loan using purchased funds:* This method, which has been used in the past, generally involves purchasing funds and setting the desired spread off the average monthly rate. For December, the federal funds rate ranged between 8.83 percent and 7.95 percent for an average monthly rate of 8.38 percent. (See Exhibit 5.2.)

C. *Accept the loan and sell participations:* This arrangement allows Madison to make these loans and share the principle funding responsibility (and interest income generated) with other interested banks that buy parts of the loan. This option may be done either upstream (sharing with larger banks) or downstream (through a network of smaller correspondent banks). Additionally, Madison could sell off a portion of its current loan portfolio already on the books to other banks through a participating agreement, thereby freeing up a portion of current funds tied up in transaction-based lending for alternative uses.

D. *Liquidate securities:* Madison could exchange assets by selling securities and making loans from the funds generated by the sale.

Sam Rogers instructed the committee to take a short recess and think about the alternatives discussed for handling transaction-based loans. Judy Langer contemplated these options relative to Madison's current loan position and tried to decide what to do.

Case Questions

1. What is the bank's status with respect to its ALM policy guidelines?
2. What options are available to management for handling the increased loan demand?
3. How does the loan pricing suggested here affect interest income?
4. What is your recommendation for this situation?

EXHIBIT 5.2	Pricing Options for Transaction-Based Loans*

| | Prime | Fed Funds | Certificates of Deposit | | |
			1-mo.	3-mo.	6-mo.
Sept.	12.97	11.30	11.20	11.29	11.47
Oct.	12.58	9.99	10.18	10.38	10.63
Nov.	11.77	9.43	9.09	9.18	9.39
Dec.	11.06	8.38	8.47	8.60	8.85
Jan.	10.60	8.35	8.05	8.14	8.45
Feb.	10.50	8.45	8.15	8.23	8.49

*Predicted monthly averages

CHAPTER 6

Techniques of Asset/ Liability Management: Futures, Options, and Swaps

After reading this chapter you will be able to:

■ Describe the nature of interest rate futures, options, and swaps.

■ Discuss the ways in which a bank can use interest rate futures, options, and swaps to hedge against interest rate risk.

■ Compare the advantages and disadvantages of interest rate futures, options, and swaps in managing interest rate risk.

Three techniques used by banks (and other financial institutions) to manage interest rate risk include futures, options, and swaps. Although recent in development and application, they have enjoyed explosive growth as significant tools for management. Although commonly used in defensive asset/liability management, these techniques may also be used in a more aggressive mode. This chapter discusses each technique separately and then compares and evaluates them as alternative devices for managing interest rate risk.

Banks may deal with interest rate risk by either reducing that risk through dollar and duration gap management of the balance sheet as discussed in previous chapters or by transferring risk to another party. Buying insurance is one device used by individuals, nonfinancial businesses, and banks for transferring risk. Another commonly used method of transferring interest rate risk is the use of **derivative securities**. These securities derive their characteristics from previously existing securities. This chapter focuses on three types of derivatives—futures, options, and swaps—and how they may be used to transfer interest rate risk. ■

6.1 FINANCIAL FUTURES

Sydney Futures Exchange (SFE) (http://www.sfe. com.au/) is the largest open-entry futures exchange in the Asia-Pacific region. This web site contains information on futures, including an introduction to futures contracts, futures FAQs, and benefits of futures.

Using Financial Futures Markets to Manage Interest Rate Risk

The adjustments to a bank's portfolio that were discussed in the previous chapter—changing the dollar gap and/or the duration gap—involve alterations in the current cash, or spot, market positions in the portfolio of assets and liabilities.

Equivalent adjustments in the interest sensitivity position of the bank can be achieved through transactions in the futures markets. These transactions, in effect, create new or synthetic assets and liabilities with interest sensitivity positions different from those currently held in the portfolio.

Nature of Futures Contracts

A **futures contract** is a standardized agreement to buy or sell a specified quantity of a commodity (financial instrument) on a specified future date at a set price. The buyer of a futures contract agrees to take delivery at a future date of the specified quantity of the financial instrument at today's determined price, whereas the seller agrees to make delivery of that quantity of the financial instrument at the future date at today's established price. The buyer is said to have established a **long position** in the futures market and will benefit if the price of the commodity rises. The seller is said to have established a **short position** in the futures market and will benefit if the price of the commodity falls. The futures market transaction may be contrasted with a cash or spot market transaction. In the futures markets, pricing and delivery occur at different times—pricing occurs today, delivery (if it takes place) occurs at some point in the future. In the cash or spot market, pricing and delivery occur at the same time.

Futures contracts are traded on a number of organized exchanges, with most U.S. activity occurring at the Chicago Board of Trade (CBOT), Chicago Board Options Exchange (CBOE), and the Chicago Mercantile Exchange (CME). Growing markets in Europe (i.e., Eurex, a German-Swiss electronic exchange, and the London International Financial Futures and Options Exchange, or LIFFE) are also becoming significant. Trading involves a large number of different types of short- and long-term financing instruments, including Treasury bills, notes, and bonds; municipal bonds (munis); Eurodollar time deposits; 30-day federal funds; and one-month LIBOR contracts. In each case, the contract traded specifies the precise nature of the financial instrument to be delivered at the maturity of the contract. For example the Treasury bill futures contract traded on the CME is for $1 million par value of U.S. Treasury bills with 90 days to maturity.

New York Mercantile Exchange (NYMEX), the world's largest physical commodity futures exchange, has charts and graphs for a wide variety of futures contracts, including electricity, propane, and palladium. You can learn about the functioning of the Exchange, futures and options contract specifications, and other information of public interest at http://www.nymex.com.

Although futures contracts differ somewhat by type of financial instrument traded and also by exchange, all futures contracts have the following characteristics in common. First, the contracts are for a specified, standardized amount of a financial instrument, with other identical features, such as the date of delivery. Because the contracts are identical, they are easily traded among market participants at low transaction costs.

Second, the **exchange clearinghouse** is a counterpart to each contract. Once a futures contract is traded the exchange clearinghouse steps in. The buyer and seller never need to have any relationship with each other. Rather, their relationship is with the exchange clearinghouse. By this device, the risk of default on the contract is minimized. Third, the contracts may be bought and sold with only a small commitment of funds relative to the market value of the contract itself. This commitment of funds is known as the **margin**, a performance bond that guarantees the buyer and seller of the contract will fulfill their commitments. The fact that the margin is a small fraction of the contract value creates great "leverage," thereby magnifying the potential gain or loss from a futures market transaction.

Fourth, futures contracts are **marked-to-market** each day; that is, market participants must recognize any gains or losses on their outstanding futures positions at the end of each day. Gains are added to the margin balance of traders each day and losses are subtracted from the margin balance each day. If the margin balance falls below the exchange-mandated minimum, the trader will be required to add funds to the margin account.

Exhibit 6.1 provides an example of a simple futures market transaction.

In most cases contracts are closed prior to the delivery date (i.e., the buyer would offset the long position by selling the identical contract), with the result that no delivery actually occurs. In fact, delivery of the underlying financial instrument seldom occurs in most futures market transactions.

Professor Campbell Harvey at Duke University has set up a web page called "Harvey's A Guide to Futures and Options Quotations," at http://www.duke.edu/~charvey/options/index1.htm, *which provides futures and options prices. Case-by-case examples of various derivatives used in the capital markets are provided.*

Techniques in Using Financial Futures

Although futures may be used both to speculate on future interest rate movements and to hedge against interest rate risk, regulatory policies limit bank use of the futures market to a hedging role. A few examples can clarify the ways in which banks are permitted to use the futures markets.

Using Interest Rate Futures to Hedge a Dollar Gap Position

A long or buy hedge may be used to protect the bank against falling interest rates. For example, suppose that the bank has a positive dollar gap—that is, it has more interest-sensitive assets than liabilities. If interest rates increased, the bank would benefit through higher net interest margins. If interest rates fell, however, the bank's net interest margin would deteriorate. In short, the bank is exposed to interest rate risk. The bank could reduce this interest rate risk by transactions in the spot or cash market such as reducing the interest sensitivity of assets. As an alternative, the bank could engage in a **long hedge** by purchasing one or more T-bill contracts for future delivery. In that case, if interest rates fell, the reduction in the net interest margin would be offset by the gain on the long hedge in the futures market. Of course, if interest rates increased, the gain in the net interest margin would be offset by the loss on the futures transaction.

EXHIBIT 6.1	Example of a Treasury Bill Futures Transaction

Suppose that on October 2, 2000, a trader buys one December 2000 Treasury bill futures contract at the opening price of $94.83. Once the transaction is complete the trader is contractually obligated to buy a $1 million (face value) 13-week Treasury bill yielding 100 − 94.83 = 5.17% on a discount basis on the contract delivery date in late December 2000. At the time of the initial transaction, however, the trader pays only a commission and deposits the required margin with a broker.

Effects of Price Changes

Suppose that the final index prices fell two basis points during that day's trading session, meaning that the discount rate on bills for future delivery rose after the contract was purchased. Because each basis point change in the T-bill index is worth $25 dollars the trader would lose $50 if he or she were to sell the contract at the closing price.

The practice of marking futures contracts to market at the end of each trading session means that the trader is forced to realize this loss even though the bill is not sold; thus, $50 is subtracted from the margin account. That money is then transferred to a seller's margin account.

Final Settlement

The contract is marked to market one last time at the close of the last day of trading. The final settlement or purchase price implied by the IMM index value is determined as follows: First calculate the total discount from the face value or $1,000,000 of the bill using the formula

$$\text{Discount} = \text{Days to maturity} \times \frac{[(100 - \text{Index}) \times 0.01] \times \$1,000,000}{360}$$

where $[(100 - \text{Index}) \times 0.01]$ is the future discount yield expressed as a fraction. Second, calculate the purchase price by subtracting the total discount from the face value of the deliverable bill. Note that it is essentially the same procedure used to calculate the purchase price of a bill from the quoted discount yield in the spot market rate.

Suppose that the futures price is $94.81. Then the settlement price for the first delivery day is

$$\$986,880.83 = \$1,000,000 - 91 \times \frac{.0519 \times \$1,000,000}{360}$$

This calculation assumes that the deliverable bill will have exactly 91 days to maturity, which will always be the case on the first contract delivery day except in special cases when a bill would otherwise mature on a national holiday.

Because buying a futures contract during the last trading session is essentially equivalent to buying a Treasury bill in the spot market futures prices tend to converge to the spot market price of the deliverable security on the final day of trading in a futures contract. Thus, the final futures discount yield should differ little, if at all, from the spot market discount yield at the end of the final trading day.

A bank may also adjust its interest sensitivity position through the sale of futures contracts, or a **short hedge**, to reduce the interest rate risk associated with a negative dollar gap. If interest rates increased, the unhedged bank would suffer a reduction in its net interest margins. With a short hedge position, however, the bank would experience a gain from the futures hedge that would offset the reduction in the net interest margin. Of course, if interest rates fell, the increased net interest margin would be offset by the loss on the futures contracts.

The number of contracts to be bought (long hedge) to hedge an asset-sensitive position or sold (short hedge) to hedge a liability-sensitive position can be calculated using Eq. (6.1):

$$\text{Number of contracts} = \left[\frac{V \times M_C}{F \times M_F} \right] b \qquad 6.1$$

where V is the value of the cash flow to be hedged, F is the face value of the futures contract, M_C, is the maturity of the anticipated cash asset, M_F is the maturity of the futures contract, and b is the ratio of variability of the cash market to the variability of the futures market.

Suppose that a bank wishes to use T-bill futures to hedge a $48 million positive dollar gap over the next six months. The number of futures contracts to be purchased would be (assuming a correlation coefficient of 1):

$$\text{Number of contracts} = \left[\frac{48 \times 6 \text{ mos.}}{1 \times 3 \text{ mos.}} \right] \qquad (1)$$

$$= 96 \text{ contracts}$$

Balance Sheet Hedging Example. To illustrate the use of financial futures in hedging the dollar gap, consider the problem of a bank with a negative dollar gap facing the expected increased interest rates in the near future. Assume that bank has assets comprised of only one-year loans earning 10% and liabilities comprised of only 90-day CDs paying 6%. If interest rates do not change, the following cash inflows and outflows would occur during the next year:

Day	0	90	180	270	360
Loans:					
Inflows					$1,000.00
Outflows	$909.09				
CDs:					
Inflow	909.09	$922.43	$935.98	$949.71	
Outflows		922.43	935.98	949.71	963.65
Net cash flows	0	0	0	0	$ 36.35

Notice that for loans $1,000/(1.10) = $909.09. Also notice that CDs are rolled over every 90 days at the constant interest rate of 6% [e.g., $909.09 $(1.06)^{0.25}$, where 0.25 = 90 days/360 days]. Of course, the negative dollar gap of the bank exposes it to the risk that interest rates will rise and CDs will have to be rolled over at higher rates. As a hedge against this possibility, the bank may sell 90-day financial futures with a par of $1,000. To simplify matters, assume only one T-bill futures contract is needed. In this situation the following entries on its balance sheet would occur over time:

Day	0	90	180	270	360
T-bill futures (sold)					
Receipts		$985.54	$985.54	$985.54	
T-bill (spot market purchase)					
Payments		985.54	985.54	985.54	
Net cash flows		0	0	0	

It is assumed here that the T-bills pay 6% and interest rates will not change (i.e., $1,000/(1.06)^{0.25} = $985.54).

If interest rates increase by 2% in the next year (after the initial issue of CDs), the bank's net cash flows will be affected as follows:

Day	0	90	180	270	360
Loans:					
Inflows					$1,000.00
Outflows	$909.09				
CDs:					
Inflow	909.09	$922.43	$940.35	$958.62	
Outflows		922.43	940.35	958.62	977.24
Net cash flows	0	0	0	0	$ 22.76

Thus, the net cash flows would decline by $13.59. In terms of present value, this loss equals $13.59/1.10 = $12.35.

The effect of this interest rate increase on net cash flows from the short T-bill futures position would be as follows:

Day	0	90	180	270	360
T-bill futures (sold)					
Receipts		$985.54	$985.54	$985.54	
T-bill (spot market purchase)					
Payments		980.94	980.94	980.94	
Net cash flows		$ 4.60	$ 4.60	$ 4.60	

The total gain in net cash flows is $13.80. In present value terms, this gain equals $4.60/(1.10)^{.25} + 4.60/(1.10)^{.50} + 4.60/(1.10)^{.75} = $13.16. Thus, the gain on T-bill futures exceeds the loss on spot bank loans and CDs. As a check on your understanding, work the case problem entitled "Hedging the Balance Sheet" at the end of the chapter.

Using Interest Rate Futures to Hedge a Duration Gap

Interest rate futures can also be used to hedge a mismatch in the duration of a bank's assets and liabilities. For example, suppose that the bank has a negative duration gap in which the duration of assets is less than the duration of liabilities. In that case, the bank could extend the duration of its assets or reduce the duration of its liabilities, thereby reducing the duration gap. As an alternative, it could establish a long position in the financial futures market. Similarly, if the bank had a positive duration gap, it could either reduce the duration of assets, increase the duration of liabilities, or execute a short or sell position in financial futures.

Suppose the bank's portfolio appears as in Table 6.1. It is assumed that the assets are single-payment loans repayable in 90, 180, 270, and 360 days and are rolled over for 360, 270, 180, and 90 days, respectively. The loan portfolio is financed with a 90-day CD at 10%, providing the bank, initially, with a two percentage point spread (the loans carry an interest rate of 12%).

The present value of the loan portfolio is $3,221.50 = [\$500/(1.12)^{1/4} + \$600/(1.12)^{1/2} + \$1,000/(1.12)^{3/4} + \$1,400/(1.12)]$. To finance the loan portfolio, the bank borrows \$3,221.50 in 90-day CDs at 10%. [This is the present value of the amount that the bank will owe in 90 days, or ($3,299.18 = 3,221.50 (1.10)^{1/4}$.]

The bank bears considerable interest rate risk in this example. The duration of its assets is considerably longer than the duration of its liabilities. The duration of the loan portfolio is 0.73 years, whereas the duration of the liabilities is 0.25 years. The bank has a positive duration gap. An increase in interest rates will reduce the value of the equity of the bank; the bank can reduce or eliminate this positive duration gap by a short hedge. Financial futures should be sold until the duration of the assets falls to 0.25, at which point the bank is perfectly hedged.

TABLE 6.1	Interest-Sensitive Assets and Liabilities	
Days	Assets	Liabilities
90	$ 500	$3,299.18
180	600	
270	1,000	
360	1,400	

Source: Elijah Brewer, "Bank Gap Management and the Use of Financial Futures," Federal Reserve Bank of Chicago, *Economic Perspectives* (March/April 1985), p. 19.

The duration of a portfolio containing both cash or spot market assets and futures contracts may be calculated with Eq. (6.2):

$$D_p = D_{rsa} + D_f \frac{N_f FP}{V_{rsa}} \qquad 6.2$$

where D_p is the duration of the entire portfolio, D_{rsa} is the duration of the rate sensitive assets, D_f is the duration of the deliverable securities involved in the hypothetical futures contract from the delivery date, N_f is the number of futures contracts, FP equals the future price, and V_{rsa} is the market value of the rate-sensitive assets.

The goal is to reduce the duration of the assets to 0.25 years. With this goal in mind, the bank should sell 64 T-bill futures contracts, assuming that T-bills are yielding 12% [such that their price is $\$100/(1.12)^{1/4}$]. In that case, the number of T-bill futures contracts to be sold is calculated as:

$$0.25 = 0.73 + 0.25 \ N_f \frac{(\$97.21)}{\$3{,}221.50} \qquad 6.3$$

$$N_f = -64$$

Steps Involved in Hedging

To hedge the interest-sensitivity position of a bank, either its dollar gap or its duration gap, the following seven steps are used:

1. Determine the total interest rate risk either on or off the balance sheet.
2. Select a futures contract. The futures contract selected should be the one most highly correlated with the cash market instrument being hedged. Normally, it would be the same instrument. If the cash market instrument does not have a futures market equivalent then the bank executes a cross hedge using a futures contract in an asset with the highest correlation with the spot market asset.
3. Determine the number of contracts needed, taking into account the less-than-perfect correlation that may exist between the cash market instrument and the futures market instrument.
4. Determine the maturity of the hedge.
5. Place the hedge.
6. Monitor the hedge.
7. Lift the hedge.

Perfect and Imperfect Futures Short Hedges

Although it normally does not take place, the following example shows a "perfect hedge" with financial futures contracts (assuming margin and brokerage costs are not considered). In this example the securities firm has agreed in June to purchase long-term municipal bonds (munis) at a fixed yield in October issued by a local city. The securities firm plans to immediately sell these securities into the financial marketplace. If interest rates rise between the commitment and sale dates, the firm will incur a loss of principal value on the munis. The derivatives strategy is to use a short hedge to offset this potential loss and enable a profitable sale of muni bonds in October. Of course, if interest rates fall, the firm foregoes the gain in the munis' principal value because the futures position would have an offsetting loss. The fact that the firm's profits are not influenced by changes in interest rates is indicative of a true hedge.

Month	Cash Market	Futures Market
June	Securities firm makes a commitment to purchase $1 million of muni bonds yielding 8.59% (based on current munis' cash price at 98-28/32) for $988,750.	Sells 10 December muni bond index futures at 96-8/32 for $962,500.
October	Securities firm purchases and then sells $1 million of muni bonds to investors at a price of 95-20/32 for $956,250.	Buys 10 December muni bond index futures at 93, or $930,000, to yield 8.95%.
	Loss: ($32,500)	Gain: $32,500

Now consider an imperfect short futures hedge for a securities dealer. The dealer holds long cash positions in a bond trading account. The maintenance of these bonds implies that a rise in interest rates will reduce their price. Suppose that the dealer owns corporate bonds purchased on October 4 and then sells an equal amount of Treasury bond futures contracts maturing in March of the following year. The following results of the short hedge are obtained:

Date	Cash Market	Futures Market
October/YearX	Purchase $5 million corporate bonds maturing Aug. 2005, 8% coupon at 87-10/32: Principal = $4,365,625	Sell $5 million T-bonds futures contracts at 86-21/32: Contract value = $4,332,813
March/Year X+1	Sell $5 million corporate bonds at 79.0: Principal = $,950,000	Buy $5 million T-bond futures at 79-21/32: Contract value = $3,951,563
	Loss: ($415,625)	Gain: $381,250

Here we see that the dealer suffered a loss of $34,375 even with the short hedge but this loss is much less than the loss of $415,625 that would have been incurred if no hedge had been employed.

Complications in Using Financial Futures

Although financial futures are designed to allow banks to reduce interest rate risk, a number of complications must be considered:

1. The bank must use the futures markets within the limits prescribed by accounting and regulatory guidelines. These guidelines generally limit a bank's financial futures activities to those transactions that relate to a bank's business needs and the bank's capacity to meet its obligations.

2. For **macro hedges**, in which the bank is hedging the entire portfolio, the bank cannot, under current guidelines, defer gains and losses from marking the futures contract to market daily. As a result, earnings are likely to be less stable in the short term with the practice of macro hedging. However, if the hedge is a **micro hedge**, whereby the hedge is linked directly to a specific asset, then gains and losses can be deferred until the maturity of the contract. Hence, accounting policies favor micro hedges even though a macro hedge is generally more appropriate for portfolio management. See Chapter 10 on Investments Management for recent accounting standards applied to securities (including derivatives) activities. In general, derivatives held for trading purposes must be reported at their average fair value or current value balance in the accounting period, in addition to their net gains and losses.

3. The bank faces a number of risks in implementing a hedging strategy using financial futures. Perhaps the most important is **basis risk**. Basis refers to the difference between the cash and futures price of the financial instrument used for the hedge. Generally, the cash and futures prices move together, which provides the opportunity for risk reduction through hedging. Yet the cash and futures prices are not perfectly correlated. As a result, when the basis changes, as it usually does during the period of the hedge, the ability to reduce interest rate risk is compromised. Interest rate risk may be eliminated only if basis does not change, and basis usually does change over the life of the hedge because the cash and futures prices are not perfectly correlated.

4. Bank management also must recognize that the existing gap position of the bank may change due to deposit inflows or loan repayments over which the bank has little control. Consequently, a hedge that was appropriate for the portfolio at the time the hedge was created may be inappropriate as the period of the hedge unfolds.

Using the Futures Options Markets to Manage Interest Rate Risk

Buying and selling options on futures contracts offers an alternative means to manage interest rate risk. **Futures option contracts** provide their holders with the right (but not the obligation) to buy or sell a particular financial instrument at a specified price on or before a specified date. In contrast, futures contracts convey both the right and the obligation to buy a financial instrument at a specified price on or before a specified date.

Options on a number of futures contracts trade on various exchanges. The most actively traded contracts are for Treasury note and bond futures, munis bond index futures, Eurodollar time deposit futures, and one-month LIBOR futures.

6.2 OPTIONS

Characteristics of Options

The Chicago Board Options Exchange (CBOE) at http://www.cboe.com/tools/ *has market statistics, such as option index statistics for the past four years, the most active options of the day, including price, volume, and closing figures, as well as active puts and calls.*

A **call option** gives the buyer the right (but not the obligation) to buy an underlying instrument (such as a T-bill futures contract) at a specified price (called the *exercise* or *strike price*), and it gives the seller the obligation to sell the underlying instrument at the same price. For this right the buyer pays a fee, referred to as a **call premium,** to the seller determined by supply and demand conditions in the options market.

A **put option** gives the buyer the right (although not the obligation) to sell a specified underlying security at the price stipulated in the contract and the seller the obligation to buy the underlying security. As with calls, the premium is determined by the interplay of supply and demand in the options market. Like futures markets, options contracts are standardized contracts that trade on organized exchanges. Fulfillment of the contract is guaranteed by the market clearing corporation. Unlike futures contracts, however, buyers are not required to put forward a margin (because their loss is limited to the premium paid for the option). Due to their uncertain potential for losses, sellers of put and call options must maintain margin positions.

Call and put options on Treasury bill and Eurodollar futures are traded on the International Monetary Market (IMM). When the contract is exercised, the buyer agrees to take delivery of a T-bill or Eurodollar contract at some future date and the seller agrees to make delivery on a contract. The buyer has a long futures position, whereas the seller has a short futures position. Contract specifications for options in the IMM are given in Table 6.2.

Stock index options have become increasingly popular since the October 19, 1987, stock market crash. These options provide ways to hedge stock portfolios of institutional investors, especially when the market is turbulent. Index contracts based on the S&P 500, Nasdaq 100, Russell 2000, Value Line, Wilshire, NYSE, and more are available. To reduce hedging costs institutions

TABLE 6.2	Contract Specifications for Options on IMM Money Market Futures

Options on Treasury Bill Futures

IMM Treasury bill futures options were first listed for trading in April 1986. The underlying instrument for these options is the IMM three-month Treasury bill futures contract. Expiration dates for traded contracts fall approximately three to four weeks before the underlying futures contract matures. IMM futures options can be exercised anytime up to the expiration date.*

Strike Price Intervals

Strike price intervals are 25 basis points for IMM index prices above 91.00 and 50 basis points for index prices below 91.00. Strike prices are typically quoted in terms of basis points. Thus, the strike prices for traded Treasury bill futures options can be 90.50 or 92.25, but not 90.25 or 92.10.

Price Quotation

Premium quotations for Treasury bill futures options are based on the IMM index price of the underlying futures contract. As with the underlying futures contract, the minimum price fluctuation is one basis point, and each basis point is worth $25. Thus, a quote of 0.35 represents an options premium of $875 (35 basis points × $25). The minimum price fluctuation for put and call premiums is one basis point, with no upper limit on daily price fluctuations.

Options on Eurodollar Futures

IMM options on Eurodollar futures began trading in March 1985. Eurodollar options expire at the end of the last day of trading in the underlying Eurodollar futures contract. Because the Eurodollar futures contract is cash settled, the final settlement for Eurodollar options follows the cash settlement procedure adopted for Eurodollar futures. To illustrate, suppose the strike price for a bought Eurodollar futures call option is 91.00 and the final settlement price for Eurodollar futures is 91.50. Exercising the call option at expiration gives the holder the right, in principle, to place $1,000 in a three-month Eurodollar deposit paying an add-on rate of 9%. But because the contract is settled in cash, the holder receives $1,250 (50 basis points × $25) in lieu of the right place to place the Eurodollar deposit paying 9%.

Strike Price Intervals

Strike price intervals for Eurodollar futures options are the same as Treasury bill strike price intervals.

Price Quotation

Premium quotations for Eurodollar options are based on the IMM index price of the underlying Eurodollar futures contract. As with the underlying futures contract, the minimum price fluctuation is one basis point, and each basis is worth $25.

*The precise rule used to determine IMM Treasury bill futures options expiration dates is as follows. The expiration date is the business day nearest the underlying futures contract month that satisfies the following two conditions: First, the expiration date must fall on the last business day of the week. Second, the last day of trading must precede the first day of the futures contract month by at least six business days.

Legal and Regulatory Entanglements of Derivatives

As interest rates rose in Spring 1994, Gibson Greetings and Procter & Gamble suffered large losses in derivatives. The firms blamed their dealer, Bankers Trust, for misleading them and therefore sued the bank. Shortly thereafter, the Federal Reserve Bank of New York, the Commodity Futures Trading Commission, and the Securities Exchange Commission added to the furor by taking regulatory actions against the bank. In early 1995 Bankers Trust estimated the losses on derivatives contracts executed on behalf of its clients at $423 million. This announcement triggered Moody's Investors Service to put the bank on its credit watch list. In eventual legal settlements Bankers Trust absorbed $14 million of the $20 million owed to it by Gibson Greetings and $160 million of $190 million owed to it by Procter & Gamble. Also, it paid $10 million in civil fines to the regulatory agencies and hired an independent consultant to review its derivatives operations.

In response to these legal and regulatory problems, Bankers Trust has changed its derivatives strategy from a transactions-driven to a relationship approach. The high volume transactions approach was suitable for homogeneous derivatives products sold with low profit margins. The new relationship approach seeks to provide derivatives products tailored to specific customer needs. While profit margins are higher on these more complex products, total revenues will likely decline due to lower business volume. To offset this potential shortfall, sales staff are encouraged to use the relationships to cross-sell other risk management products to client firms. Importantly, this more comprehensive approach to offering risk management services no doubt decreases the chance of another client mishap with adverse legal and regulatory implications.

will often use a "zero-cost collar." In this strategy a portfolio manager will sell call options on an index and use the proceeds to purchase put options. This combination of options protects the stock portfolio from downside risk but places a cap on upside market gains if stock prices rise. Such a collar can help protect previous gains that an institution had earned.

Payoffs for Futures and Futures Options Contracts

Figure 6.1 provides a comparison of payoff possibilities for futures and futures options contracts. Figure 6.1(a) shows the payoff for unhedged long and short futures positions. The horizontal axis measures the price of the futures contract (F), and the vertical axis measures any profits or losses due to changes in the prices of the futures contracts. Because the buyer of a futures contract gains or loses one dollar for each dollar the contract rises or falls, the 45-degree line passed through F_0 in Figure 6.1(a) provides a representation of the payoff. The payoff from an unhedged short futures position is, of course, the opposite of an unhedged long position.

Figure 6.1(b) shows the payoff for an unhedged futures call option bought and held until expiration. The buyer pays the amount of the call premium (C), which is the maximum that can be lost. As the value of the futures contract

FIGURE 6.1 Options Payoffs

(a) Payoffs for Unhedged Future Contracts

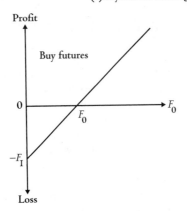

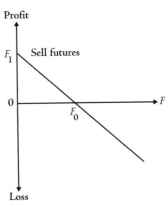

(b) Payoffs for Unhedged Call Options

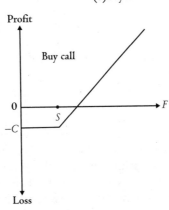

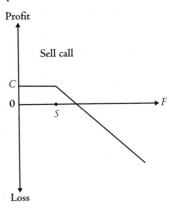

(c) Payoffs for Unhedged Put Options

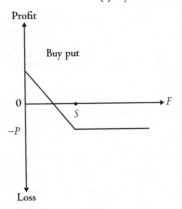

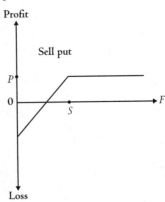

rises, the value of the option increases. At a futures price above F_0, the option buyer has a profit. The logic is reversed for the seller of a call option. The seller receives the call premium. However, the profit from the transaction is diminished as the price of the futures contract falls. At a price of F_0, the loss on the futures contract offsets the receipt of the call premium, whereas at higher prices the seller of the call experiences a loss on the futures contract that exceeds the call premium.

Payoffs for put options are shown in Figure 6.1(c). The buyer of a put option pays a premium (P) and receives the right to sell the underlying futures contracts (at strike price S). As the price of the futures contract drops, the premium is recouped and at some (lower) price the buyer of the put has a gain. The logic is comparable although reversed for the seller of a put.

Hedging with Futures Options

If a bank measured its interest rate-sensitive assets and liabilities and found that it had a negative dollar gap, without hedging, the bank would experience a declining net interest income if interest rates were to increase. In that case, the interest rate risk could be reduced by selling a futures call option. If interest rates did increase, the prices of futures contracts would fall. Through selling the call, however, the bank has, in effect, locked in the higher price. It can then take its profit on the call option (i.e., the call premium) and use it to reduce or eliminate the loss from the negative gap. Conversely, a bank with a positive dollar gap could buy call options in order to hedge its interest rate risk. If interest rates fall, the bank would lose on its cash or spot market portfolio, but the gain from its options position would partially or completely offset that loss.

Micro and Macro Hedge

The preceding discussion is focused on the macro hedge, where management attempts to hedge the entire portfolio. The bank may also wish, however, to hedge specific portions of the portfolio using a micro hedge. For example, suppose that the bank has funded a loan that reprices every six months with Eurodollar CDs that reprice every three months. In that case, the bank could lose considerably if interest rates increase. To protect itself from such a risk, the bank could sell call options on Eurodollar futures. If interest rates increase, the gain from the call options (i.e., the call premium) would offset the loss on the funding of the loan.

Caps and Floors

Caps and floors are widely used to transfer interest rate risk. An interest rate **cap** is a contract that reduces the exposure of a floating rate borrower (or a liability-sensitive bank) to increases in interest rates. It is essentially a series of interest rate call options in which the writer guarantees the buyer (i.e., the

The Harvard Business School library has an excellent compilation of explanations, sites, and sources about hedge funds—called "Baker Library's Guide to Hedge Funds" at http://www.library.hbs.edu/hedgefunds.htm—*which uses a variety of derivative securities in its risk management services.*

bank) that the writer will pay the buyer any additional interest cost that results from rising interest rates. In contrast, an interest rate **floor** is a contract that limits the exposure of the buyer to downward movements in interest rates. An interest rate floor is a series of interest rate put options by which the writer guarantees the buyer (i.e., the bank) that the writer will pay to the bank an amount that increases as the level of interest rates fall. Remember that the strike price of debt instruments varies inversely with the level of interest rates, because their prices and interest rates move opposite to one another. Thus, a call option on a Treasury bill rate is equivalently a put option on its price. Here we use interest rates to discuss the option characteristics of caps and floors. In Chapter 14's Off-Balance Sheet Activities, we discuss caps and floors in terms of options on prices of debt securities.

A few examples may provide insight into the use of caps and floors for bank asset/liability management. Suppose that a bank has a portfolio of fixed rate assets that are financed with variable rate (or short-term) sources of funds. Suppose that this liability-sensitive bank has a $10 negative gap. It might choose to purchase an interest rate cap with a strike price of 8% with a principal of $10 million. The cap could be purchased with varying maturities, perhaps ranging from three months to five years. The writer of the cap could be an investment bank, a large commercial bank, or another party.

Comparisons are made between market interest rates and the strike price—often using a T-bill or London Interbank Offered Rate (LIBOR) reference rate—at regular intervals (six months is common), referred to as the determination date. If the market yield has risen above the strike price, the cap holder is entitled to receive the difference between the current market interest rate and the strike price multiplied by the principal value of the contract. For example, assuming that on the determination date the relevant market rate for the contract is 9%, the writer of the call would be obligated to pay to the bank:

$$(9\% - 8\%)(\$10,000,000)(0.5) = \$50,000$$

This payment could be used to offset the increased net interest cost produced by the liability-sensitive position of the bank's balance sheet. Of course, if rates do not increase, the bank does not collect on its insurance policy, or cap, but also does not lose from a liability-sensitive balance sheet.

Suppose on the other hand that the bank is asset sensitive because it has short-term assets financed with longer-term liabilities. In this case, the bank will benefit if rates rise but will be harmed if rates fall. The bank might then purchase a floor with a $10,000,000 principal, a strike price of 7%, and a six-month determination date. If the interest rate on the appropriate market instrument (say, the three-month Treasury bill) was 6% as of the determination date, the bank would be entitled to receive from the writer of the contract:

$$(\$10,000,000)(1\%)(0.50) = \$50,000$$

This payment could then be used to offset the reduced profitability associated with an asset-sensitive position in a falling rate environment. Of course, if rates

MANAGING RISK

Are Interest Rate Risk and Communication Risk Related?

The Board of Directors' Asset/Liability Management Committee for Metropolitan National Bank faced a particularly difficult decision during its meeting on the afternoon of February 22. This $4 billion regional bank, unlike many similar-sized commercial banks, had decided to become active in originating, packaging for resale, and holding various types of single-family mortgages. As a result, it had established a mortgage lending division under the organizational control of the lending division, had hired a number of new personnel, and had established relationships with correspondents to facilitate the acquisition of mortgages.

The ALCO committee had expressed concern about the potential impact of this strategy on the interest rate risk of the bank. Reflecting this con-

cern, it had adopted a policy at its December meeting that the "bank would originate or purchase fixed rate mortgage loans with a maturity greater than 5 years only up to a total of $20 million." It was thus with great surprise that one of the committee members noted at the February meeting that the bank's portfolio of 30-year fixed rate mortgages totaled $218 million. Moreover, because interest rates had increased because December, the market value of that portfolio was $208 million, a loss of $10 million. When confronted about this violation of policy, the head of the mortgage division said "No one told me." Moreover, given the embryonic stage of development of his division, the bank was left with no easy way to get rid of the mortgages.

stay the same, this insurance policy expires without producing any benefit, but the bank has not experienced any loss due to being asset sensitive.

6.3 INTEREST RATE SWAPS

One of the most recent techniques devised to manage interest rate risk and for other purposes is the **interest rate swap**. First developed in Europe in 1981, swaps have literally exploded in volume since then, and now total more than $20 trillion. In an interest rate swap, two firms that want to change their interest rate exposure in different directions get together (usually with the help of some financial intermediary) and exchange or swap their obligations to pay or receive interest (just the interest payment obligations are swapped, not the principal). Table 6.3 provides year-end information on the tremendous growth of interest rate swaps compared to currency swaps and interest rate options (i.e., caps, collars, floors, and swaptions) in the OTC market, as well as exchange-traded instruments such as interest rate futures and options and currency futures. Interestingly, the notional amounts of OTC instruments is now comparable to total cash positions in global banking and securities markets.

Assume that one firm has long-term fixed assets financed with short-term

TABLE 6.3	Selective Derivative Market Data ($ trillions)					
Derivatives Contract	1993	1994	1995	1996	1997	1998
Exchange-traded instruments:						
Interest rate futures	$7.7	$8.8	$9.2	$9.9	$12.2	$13.5
Interest rate options	5.0	5.8	5.9	5.9	7.5	7.7
Currency futures	2.3	2.6	2.7	3.3	3.6	4.6
OTC instruments:						
Interest rate swaps	6.2	8.5	12.8	19.2	22.3	n.a.
Currency swaps	0.9	0.9	1.2	1.6	1.8	n.a.
Interest rate options	1.4	1.6	3.7	4.7	4.9	n.a.

Source: International Swap Dealers Association (ISDA) Market Survey, *http://www.isda.org/*. Excluded from exchange-traded instruments are currency options and stock market index futures and options due to their smaller volume.

variable rate liabilities. Further assume that another firm has short-term variable rate assets financed with long-term fixed rate liabilities. Both firms are exposed to interest rate risk but their exposure is quite different. The first firm gains if interest rates fall, whereas the second firm loses if interest rates decline. Of course, if interest rates increase, the first firm loses and the second firm gains.

For firms having this type of interest rate exposure (e.g., a bank and a savings and loan), the swap of interest payments allows each firm to benefit. The first firm substitutes fixed rate liabilities for its floating rate liabilities and thereby reduces its interest rate risk. The second firm substitutes variable rate liabilities for fixed rate liabilities and also reduces its interest rate risk.

Figure 6.2 provides an illustration of a swap transaction for a liability-sensitive institution. The liability-sensitive institution has fixed rate assets (bonds) financed by floating interest rate notes. It arranges a swap with a counterparty in which it pays a fixed rate and receives a floating rate. (Fixed rate cash payments are shown as straight lines, whereas floating rate cash payments are shown as wavy lines.) The bottom portion of the illustration shows the net result of the swap, which is that the swap receipt of floating rate cash payments goes to lower the payment on the floating rate liabilities on the balance sheet, and the firm is left with the fixed rate earnings on the bonds financed with fixed rate payments on the swap.

Figure 6.3 shows a similar example, except that the institution is a bank with floating rate assets and fixed rate liabilities. This institution arranges a swap in which it pays floating rate and receives fixed rate. The net result of the swap is that the fixed receipts from the swap counterparty are used to pay the

FIGURE 6.2 Using an Interest Rate Swap to Hedge a Liability-Sensitive Position

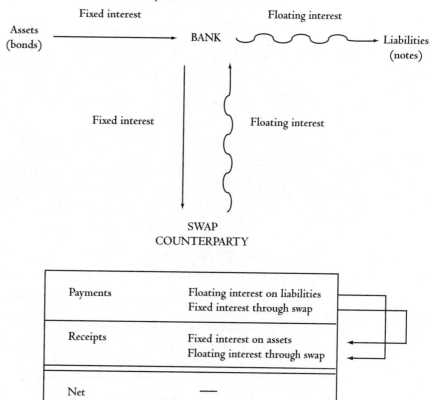

Green Interest Rate Swap Management at http://home.earthlink.net/~green/whatisan.htm *is a financial service company that offers interest rate swap services to corporate treasurers, fund managers, government entities, and bankers. Their web site gives detailed explanations of swaps and cross-comparisons with other financial derivatives such as futures.*

fixed payments on the on-balance-sheet liabilities, so that the floating interest rate earnings are matched with the floating interest rate swap payments.

Exhibit 6.2 provides more detailed information on the mechanics of a swap.

A further evolution of the swap concept is embodied in the so-called **swaption**. A swaption is an option on a swap. The buyer of a swaption has the right (but not the obligation) to enter into an interest rate swap at terms specified in the contract. As with any option, the buyer pays a premium to the seller of the option.

With a call swaption, the buyer has the option to enter into an interest rate swap in which the buyer pays floating and receives fixed. (The writer or seller of the option obviously agrees to enter into a swap in which it receives floating and pays fixed.) In contrast, with a put option, the buyer has the option to enter into an interest rate swap in which the buyer pays fixed and receives floating (and the seller receives fixed and pays floating).

FIGURE 6.3 Using an Interest Rate Swap to Hedge
an Asset-Sensitive Position

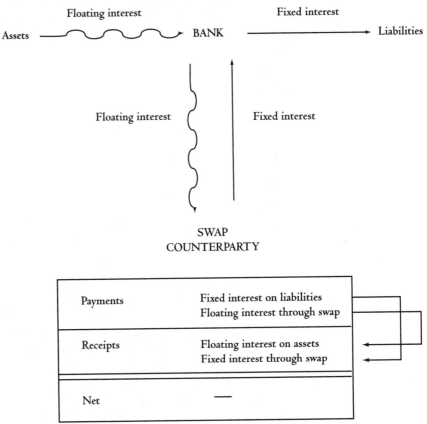

Interest Rate Swaps, Quality Spread, and Cost of Funds

The principal purpose of an interest rate swap is to reduce the degree of interest rate risk by more closely synchronizing the interest sensitivity of cash inflows and outflows. However, under certain conditions, the interest rate swap may also result in a reduction in the cost of funds for each of the two parties to the swap. As an example, consider the following:

	High-Quality Bank	Low-Quality Bank	Quality Spread
Floating rate debt	LIBOR + 1.0%	LIBOR + 2.5%	1.5%
Fixed rate debt	8%	11%	3.0%

EXHIBIT 6.2   How a Swap Works

The following example is based on an actual transaction arranged by an investment bank between a large thrift institution and a large international bank. "Thrift" has a large portfolio of fixed-rate mortgages. "Bank" has most of its dollar-denominated assets yielding a floating rate return based on LIBOR (the London Interbank Offered Rate).

On May 10, 1999, the "Intermediary," a large investment bank, arranged a $100 million, seven-year interest rate swap between Thrift and Bank. In the swap, Thrift agreed to pay Bank a fixed rate of 11% per year on $100 million, every six months. This payment covered exactly the interest Bank had to pay on a $100 million bond it issued in the Eurodollar market. Thrift also agreed to pay Bank the 2% underwriting spread that Bank itself paid to issue this bond. In exchange, Bank agreed to make floating-rate payments to Thrift at 35 basis points (0.35%) below LIBOR. Intermediary received a broker's fee of $500,000.

Twice a year, Intermediary (for a fee) calculates Bank's floating rate payment by taking the average level of LIBOR for that month (Col. 2), deducting 35 basis points, dividing by 2 (because it is for *half* a year), and multiplying by $100 million (Col. 3). If this amount is larger than Thrift's fixed rate payment (Col. 4), Bank pays Thrift the difference (Col. 5). Otherwise, Thrift pays Bank the different (Col. 6).

The swap allows both Bank and Thrift to reduce their exposure to interest rate risk. Bank can now match its floating rate assets priced off LIBOR with an interest payment based on LIBOR, while the fixed rate interest payments on its bond issues are covered by Thrift. At the same time, Thrift can hedge part of its mortgage portfolio, from which it receives fixed interest earnings, with the fixed rate payment it makes to Bank. However, the floating rate payment that Thrift receives is linked to LIBOR while its cost of borrowing is more closely linked to the T-bill rate. Because LIBOR and the T-bill rate do not always move in tandem, Thrift is still exposed to fluctuations in the relation between LIBOR and the T-bill.

The most common type of swap is the one described here: a dollar fixed rate loan swapped for a dollar floating rate loan, otherwise called the "plain vanilla" swap. However, several variations on this basic swap have emerged in the market. One such variation is a floating-to-floating swap where parties agree to swap floating rates based on different indices. For example, a bank with assets tied to the prime rate and liabilities based on LIBOR may want to swap the interest payments on its

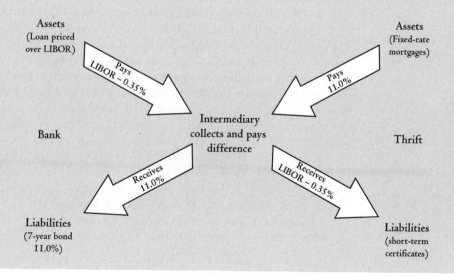

EXHIBIT 6.2	How a Swap Works *(continued)*				

Date	LIBOR	Floating Rate Payment 1/2 (LIBOR – 0.35%)	Fixed Rate Payment 1/2 (11%)	Net Payment from Bank to Thrift	Net Payment from Thrift to Bank
May 1999	8.98%	—	—	—	—
Nov 1999	8.43	$4,040,000	$5,500,000	0	$1,460,000
May 2000	11.54	5,595,000	5,500,000	$95,000	0
Nov 2000	9.92	4,785,000	5,500,000	0	715,000
May 2001	8.44	4,045,000	5,500,000	0	1,455,000

liabilities with payments on a prime-tied, floating rate loan. Another type of arrangement involves currency swaps such as a swap of a sterling floating rate loan for a dollar fixed rate loan. For firms whose assets are denominated in a different currency than are its liabilities, this type of swap may be more appropriate. Finally, rather than exchanging interest payments on liabilities, swaps can also be used to exchange yields on *assets* of different maturities or currencies.

The interest rate swap market has proven to be flexible in adjusting its product to new customer needs. This innovativeness all but guarantees that swaps will remain a permanent feature of international capital markets.

Source: Adapted from Jan Loeys, "Interest Rate Swaps, A New Tool for Managing Risk," Federal Reserve Bank of Philadelphia (May/June 1985), p. 20.

High-Quality Bank is assumed to be able to borrow at LIBOR + 1.0% in the short-term floating rate debt market or at 8% in the long-term fixed rate debt market. Low-Quality Bank is assumed to be able to borrow on the short-term floating rate market at LIBOR + 2.5% or at 11% in the long-term fixed rate debt market. Notice that while High-Quality Bank can borrow cheaper in both markets it has a *relative* or *comparative* advantage in the long-term market, as shown by the **quality spread** differentials. High-Quality Bank can borrow on the fixed rate market at 300 basis points (3%) less than Low-Quality Bank but at only 1.50 basis points (1.5%) in the short-term market. But how can an interest rate swap both reduce their interest rate risk and lower their costs of funds?

Suppose that Low-Quality Bank has a negative gap and High-Quality Bank has a positive gap. Both can reduce their interest rate risk if Low-Quality Bank pays fixed to High-Quality Bank and if High-Quality Bank pays floating to Low-Quality Bank. Further, assume that High-Quality Bank pays LIBOR + 1.0% to Low-Quality Bank and, in return, receives 9% fixed from Low-Quality bank.

What is the cost of funds for both banks after the swap?

Cost of funds for Low-Quality Bank =	Borrow floating in market	−	Receive LIBOR + 1% from High-Quality Bank	+	Pay 9% fixed to High-Quality Bank
=	LIBOR + 2.5%	−	(LIBOR + 1%)	+	9%
=	10.5%				

With the swap, Low-Quality Bank has matched its interest rate risk (it now has more fixed rate liabilities) *and* has lowered its cost of those fixed rate liabilities (10.5% with the swap as compared to 11% without the swap). But High-Quality Bank has also benefited. Its cost of funds is:

Cost of funds for High-Quality Bank =	Borrow fixed in market	−	Received fixed from Low-Quality Bank	+ Pay LIBOR + 1% to Low-Quality Bank
	8%	−	9%	+ (LIBOR + 1%)
=	LIBOR			

High-Quality Bank has obtained the floating rate debt that it wanted in order to offset a positive gap *and* has lowered its cost for this floating rate debt by 1% with the swap as compared to LIBOR + 1% without the swap.

Notice that the gain of 1.5% (0.5% for Low-Quality Bank and 1.0% for High-Quality Bank) to the two parties in the swap exactly equals the difference in the quality spreads of the two parties in the floating and fixed rate market of 1.5% (3.0% − 1.5%). This difference in relative access to the two markets creates the opportunity to lower the cost of money for both parties. If the quality spreads had been the same, then both parties could use the swap to reduce interest rate risk but both could not reduce their costs of funds.

Swaps and Futures

Interest rate swaps provide an alternative to futures (and options) as a device banks can use to manage interest rate risk. Swaps have both advantages and disadvantages when compared with futures. The principal advantages of swaps over futures are twofold. First swaps may be customized to meet the exact needs of the bank. Because interest rate swaps are negotiated contracts, the terms of maturity and other dimensions of the swap can be tailored to the needs of the bank. Second, the swap can be established for a long-term arrangement; most swaps have maturities of 3–10 years. In contrast, financial futures are standardized contracts that have a limited number of specified delivery dates and deliverable types of financial instruments. Most important, futures contracts generally are available only for delivery dates at three-month intervals that extend only up to 2.5 years in the future, making hedging interest rate risk with futures contracts impossible over the long term.

Swaps do present some disadvantages, however, relative to futures. Most of these disadvantages stem from the customized nature of the swap contracts.

The lack of standardization of swaps increases the search cost of finding counterparts to the swap. In monetary terms, also, it is more costly to close out a swap contract prior to maturity than a futures contract. Equally significant, the bank that enters into a swap agreement faces the possibility that the counterparty may default. Although the bank has no principal at risk, it does have credit risk in the interest payment obligation.

As the swap market has evolved, the importance of these disadvantages has been diminished by the intervention of intermediaries into the market. These intermediaries (generally investment or commercial banks) have been willing (for a fee) to guarantee the payment of interest on a swap contract. Also, to reduce the problems associated with the customized nature of the swap contract, these intermediaries now more frequently standardize the contract terms, such as the type of floating rate interest, the repricing dates, and collateral requirements. Secondary markets for swaps have also developed, thereby increasing the liquidity of the swap contracts.

SUMMARY

Recent innovations in financial markets have created new instruments that banks can use in managing their interest rate risk. Three in particular have great importance to bank management: futures, options, and swaps. Each allows bank management to alter interest rate exposure, and each has certain advantages and disadvantages when compared with the other. Taken together, however, they give bank managers enormously improved flexibility in managing interest rate risk.

A bank may hedge its interest rate risk in the futures market by taking a position that is the opposite of its existing portfolio position. If, for example, the bank was asset sensitive, it could take a long position in the futures market to hedge risk. If interest rates were to fall, it would suffer a loss with its existing portfolio because it was asset sensitive, but it would incur an off-setting gain in its futures position. Conversely, a liability-sensitive bank could protect itself against interest rate movements by establishing a short position in the futures market. Futures market positions could also be used to hedge positive or negative duration gaps. An alternative way of managing interest rate risk is to buy or sell an option on a futures contract. A call option gives the buyer the right (but not the obligation) to buy an underlying instrument (such as a T-bill futures contract) at a specified price (called the exercise or strike price), and it gives the seller the comparable right to sell the underlying instrument at the same price. A put option gives the buyer the right (although not the obligation) to sell a specified underlying security at the price stipulated in the contract and the seller the obligation to buy the underlying security. Options on futures would be used similarly to the futures themselves in order to hedge interest rate

MANAGERIAL ISSUES

The Risk That Won't Go Away

Although derivatives (futures, options, and swaps) provide important vehicles by which bank managers can hedge their interest rate risk, they present a number of challenges to those same managers and to bank regulators. The challenges derive both from the size and the complexity of the market. Significant dimensions of the derivatives market include:

- The notional value of U.S. banks' holdings in derivative securities (excluding credit derivatives) at year-end 1997 exceeded $25 trillion.
- Large banks are the dominant players in the derivatives markets. More than 99% of these derivatives positions are held by the top 100 banks, and more than 90% are held by the top 10 banks.
- Even though most banks generally apply derivatives to the problem of hedging a mismatch in asset and liability interest rate sensitivities, derivatives are also employed to increase income, rather than control interest rate risk. Assume a bank made a six-month loan yielding 10%, financed by a six-month CD costing the bank 6%. If the bank "paired" a short futures contract against the six-month loan, it would move from a "hedged" position to an "unhedged" position, at least on an overall basis. Thus, paired derivatives positions should not be used to determine the bank's overall

hedging strategy. From a regulatory standpoint, the Federal Reserve requires that bank holding companies engage only in risk reducing derivatives activities; however, dealer subsidiaries are permitted to use derivative contracts as trading substitutes for cash market instruments to produce income and not necessarily reduce risk.

- A growing history of blunders in derivatives management has resulted in the failure of large financial institutions. For example, one of the oldest banks in England, Barings, collapsed in July 1995 due to unauthorized derivatives trading in options and futures by a single trader. The losses were estimated to be about $1 billion. Also, in the United States one of the nation's largest credit unions, Capital Corporate Federal Credit Union, suffered about $100 million of losses from derivative investments, which required regulatory intervention.
- In recent years accounting standards for disclosure of information have increased and new risk-based capital guidelines related to derivatives activities have been implemented (see Chapter 11). While derivatives are powerful tools to manage interest rate and currency risks, they always involve the potential for abuse in terms of seeking to magnify returns without properly considering the risks.

exposure, although options have the advantage of smaller initial outlay in order to accomplish the interest rate risk management.

The third technique for managing interest rate risk without actually altering the existing portfolio is the swap. With a swap, the bank swaps its obligation to pay interest (but not principal) to another party. The bank agrees to pay the interest of the other party (e.g., fixed rate interest), whereas the counterparts agree to pay the bank's interest. Whether asset sensitive or liability sensitive, then, the bank is able through the swap to reduce its exposure to interest rate fluctuation.

Key Terms and Concepts

Basis risk	Long hedge
Call option	Long position
Call premium	Margin
Cap	Marked-to-market
Derivative securities	Micro/macro hedge
Exchange clearinghouse	Put option
Floor	Quality spread
Futures contract	Short hedge
Futures option contract	Short position
Interest rate swap	Swaption

Questions

6.1   What are financial futures contracts? What similarities exist among all futures contracts?

6.2   What is meant by a short position in financial futures? A long position? How is each affected by changes in interest rates?

6.3   Why can buyers and sellers of futures contracts ignore possible default by the other party?

6.4   What does marked-to-market mean?

6.5   Distinguish between a micro hedge and a macro hedge. Are there any inherent conflicts in using both simultaneously in managing interest rate risk?

6.6   How would a bank use interest rate futures to hedge a positive dollar gap? A negative dollar gap?

6.7   How would a bank use interest rate futures to hedge a positive duration gap? A negative duration gap?

6.8   What complications exist in using financial futures to hedge a bank portfolio?

6.9   What is a futures options contract? Compare and contrast a futures options contract with a futures contract.

6.10   Compare and contrast the characteristics and use of put and call futures options contracts.

6.11   Explain how futures options contracts can be used to hedge interest rate risk.

6.12   What is an interest rate swap? How can it be used to hedge interest rate risk?

6.13   Compare a swap with a swaption.

6.14   Compare the pros and cons of futures, futures options, and swaps as devices to hedge interest rate risk.

6.15   What is an interest rate cap? How is it used? Compare it with a floor.

6.16 Your bank is liability sensitive. To protect itself against rising interest rates, management purchased 10 caps from a large investment banking firm. Each contract had a notional value of $1,000,000, a strike price (based on three-month Treasury bill rates) of 7% (current rate = 6%), and a one-year maturity. Over the next year interest rates in Treasury bills fell, reaching 3% at the end of the year, the cap expired without benefit, and the bank lost the full premium of $46,000. Did management err in its decision to purchase the cap?

6.17 After reviewing Baker Library's Guide to Hedge Funds at *http://www.library.hbs.edu/hedgefunds.htm*, write a one-page description of hedge funds and their risk management operations.

6.18 The International Swap Dealers Association's (ISDA) web site at *http://www.isda.org/* contains the information on futures, options, and swaps. Print out the latest statistics on the volume of these contracts and discuss the derivatives market trends.

6.19 Go to the Chicago Board of Trade's web site at *http://www.cbot.com/ourproducts/financial/index.html* to see the list of financial contracts traded there. Pick one of the products in the list and print out its contract specifications.

Problems

6.1 Suppose that an investor holds a $1,000,000 91-day T-bill futures contract. It is marked to market on the close of the last day of trading at $95.00. What is the settlement price?

6.2 Assume that on April 1 your bank plans to issue a three-month Eurodollar CD in July. On April 1, the bank could issue a three-month Eurodollar CD for 7.02%. The corresponding rate for the six-month Eurodollar contract (due in September) was 7.58%.
   (a) What position should the bank take in the Eurodollar market?
   (b) Suppose that the bank took a position in Eurodollar futures on April 1, and that it closes out its position in July when the futures rate is 7.82%. In that situation, has the bank achieved its objective with the hedge?

6.3 Suppose that your bank has a commitment to make a fixed rate loan in three months at the existing interest rate. To hedge against the prospect of rising interest rates, the bank takes a position in the futures options market. What position should it take? The relevant information is as follows:

$$T\text{-bill futures prices} = \$89$$
$$Put\ option = \$90$$
$$Premium = \$2,500$$

What will be the net gain to the bank if T-bill futures prices fall to $85? If they increase to $93?

6.4   A bank has a spot market asset duration of 1.0 and a liability side duration of 0.50. It seeks to reduce the duration of the asset side to 0.25 using a short T-bill futures hedging strategy. The present value of cash flows on assets is $4,000. If the selling price of the futures contracts is $98.00, how many T-bill futures contracts are needed to achieve a duration equal to 0.50 for the portfolio containing both spot market assets and futures contracts?

6.5   Corporation XYZ obtains a ceiling agreement from a bank for a five-year loan of $20 million at a rate of 7% (tied to LIBOR). An upfront fee of 2% is paid by XYZ for the guarantee that rates will not exceed 10%.

  (a) If LIBOR goes to 12%, calculate the quarterly compensation the bank must pay XYZ.

  (b) What kind of option is it for the bank? XYZ? When is it "in-the-money"?

6.6   Given a forward rate agreement (FRA) on bonds purchased by a bank at 90 for delivery in three months:

  (a) If the price of the bonds is 100 on the delivery date, what is the profit (loss) of the bank?

  (b) What type of option is analogous to this example?

6.7   Bank A and Bank B have the following opportunities for borrowing in the short-term (floating rate) and long-term (fixed rate) markets:

	Bank A	Bank B
Floating rate	T-bill + 1.0%	T-bill + 2.0%
Fixed rate	8%	10.5%

Bank A has a positive gap and Bank B has a negative gap. Show that both banks can benefit from a swap in the sense of lowering their interest rate risk. Can they also lower their cost of funds?

6.8   State Bank purchased a $10,000,000 floor from a large investment banking firm. The floor has a 4% strike price (based on the three-month Treasury bill) and a three-month determination date. Assuming that the three-month Treasury bill rate is 2.5% at the determination date, what is the payment under the contract? Does the bank receive or make payments? Assuming that the bank paid $50,000 for the contract, has the bank gained from the transaction?

6.9   Consider a fixed-for-floating LIBOR swap with a notional principal of $200 million and a fixed rate of 7%. Suppose that the swap cash flows are determined at six-month intervals ($t = 0, 1, 2, 3$, etc.). Suppose that LIBOR turns out to be:

t	LIBOR
0	4.25
1	5.25
2	6.75
3	7.25
4	8.00
5	9.00
6	10.00

What would be the net payments for the counterparties on each of the settlement days?

6.10 Assume the date is August 7, Year X and the you have the following information: (1) the September 13-week T-bill futures discount is 10.49% and matures on December 20, and (2) the spot quote on September 20 for 13-week T-bills maturing December 20 is 10.39%.

(a) Assuming a long position in the futures market, what is the purchase price of the T-bill futures contract? (Note: There are 43 days from August 7 date to September 20, and 9.91% is the applicable 13-week T-bill rate in this period.)

(b) Assuming a long position in the spot market, what is the purchase price of the T-bills using the spot quote?

(c) What would happen if the futures and spot prices of T-bills differed by an amount larger than the transactions costs of buying and selling them?

CASE STUDY

Hedging the Balance Sheet

Janet Chilton and George Stephens joined World Trust Corporation (WTC) a few years ago as trainers in the derivatives products group. Part of their responsibilities is to explain to potential clients how their derivatives services could help manage their risk exposures. A small depository institution, First Savings Association, recently contacted World Trust about hedging its net worth against a possible increase in interest rates based on regular speculation that the Federal Reserve would continue raising interest rates to hold down incipient inflation in the economy. During its latest board of directors meeting, First Savings decided that the probability of a significant increase in interest rates was sufficient to warrant the implementation of a derivatives hedging strategy. However, the board wanted the selected dealer to clearly present its hedging plan at its meeting the following month, because a number of the board members expressed concern due to past news stories of major blunders by derivatives dealers in properly managing client risk.

Janet and George collected the latest reports on the maturities of assets and liabilities held by First Savings. After checking the data, they agreed that First Savings did indeed face interest rate risk due to a positive maturity gap; that is, the maturity of assets exceeded the maturity of liabilities on average. They decided to set up a simple example of this type of mismatch and present it to the board of First Savings.

Assume the institution made a 1-year loan at 10% with receipts of $1,000 (i.e., its present value is $909.09). This loan is funded with 90-day CDs paying 8%. Put together a schedule of receipts and payments for the loan and CDs in each quarter for the upcoming year.

Assume further that the preceding date is September 15 and that you sell 13-week T-bill futures in December, March, and June as a hedge on the CDs. Calculate the price of the T-bill futures contract using a 10% discount rate. Assuming further that interest rates do not change, show the results of First Savings' purchase of T-bills in the spot market and sale of T-bills in the futures market on the delivery date.

We are now ready to demonstrate the effects of an interest rate increase of 2% on the receipts and payments associated with the balance sheet and the futures hedge strategy. Assume that interest rates increase after the first 90-day T-bill contract is sold at 8%, such that all subsequent CDs must pay the higher interest rate of 10%. Assume also that First Savings has already sold T-bill futures for the upcoming year prior to the interest rate increase and therefore has locked in its sales price.

As a member of the staff at World Trust, you have been asked by Janet and George to show how the net receipts on the balance sheet and futures hedge are affected. In anticipation of their upcoming meeting with the board of First Savings, they also want you to write some short answers to the following questions for distribution to the members of the board.

- What is the present value of the net receipts if interest rates rise 2%?
- How does this change in net receipts compare with the result assuming no change in interest rates?
- If interest rates decline rather than increase, what would be the effect on the balance sheet and futures hedge results?
- How might the bank use an option on a futures contract to achieve the same result?
- What are the advantages of using the option on a futures contract over a futures contract alone? What is the disadvantage of the options approach compared to using only a futures contract?
- Finally, should World Trust seek to pair a hedge contract to each individual asset or liability on the balance sheet of First Savings, or should it seek to look at the "big picture" and hedge the overall risk of the balance sheet?

CHAPTER 7

Commercial and Industrial Lending

After reading this chapter you will be able to:

- Understand how competition affects lending.
- Evaluate the lending process.
- Describe the various types of loans.
- Analyze financial statements.

I n this chapter and the next, the discussion will focus on lending and managing loan portfolios. This chapter deals primarily with **commercial and industrial loans** (C&I loans) and the process of lending. C&I loans are those made to businesses to finance their day-to-day activities (e.g., inventories and receivables), longer-term needs (e.g., plant and equipment), and for other business purposes. The next chapter deals with real estate and consumer loans. ■

7.1   THE ROLE OF ASYMMETRIC INFORMATION IN LENDING

The three theoretical concepts examined in this section describe the relationships between banks and the customers who borrower from them. These concepts underlie much of the material presented here and in in the next chapter.

Asymmetric Information and Adverse Selection

Before banks make loans, they must evaluate imperfect information about prospective borrowers to determine whether they are creditworthy. Information is difficult and costly to obtain. Information about large firms that are publicly traded, such as Microsoft, is easier to obtain than information about small, privately held firms. The information that prospective borrowers provide to the banks may be sufficient to make a credit decision. However, it is usually incomplete in the sense that borrowers know more about the risk of their proposed investment projects than they reveal to the bank. We are using the term *investment project*, but the concept applies to the use of any funds borrowed from the bank including consumer loans. The inequality of information between the bank and the borrower is called **asymmetric information**. Simply stated, asymmetric information means that the borrowers have more information about themselves than is available to the bank.

Because of asymmetric information, banks tend to charge an interest rate that reflects the average rate of risk of all borrowers. The average interest rate is too high for borrowers with low-risk investment projects, and too low for borrowers with high-risk investment projects.

ADVERSE SELECTION **Adverse selection** means that high-risk borrowers try to obtain loans from banks willing to pay the average rate of interest, which is less than they would have to pay if their true condition were known to the bank. It also follows that low-risk creditworthy borrowers may be able to borrower directly from the money and capital markets at lower rates than those offered by banks. Market rates of interest confirm this relationship. In February 1999, the prime rate was 7.75%. The rate is the base rate on corporate loans made by banks. However, the rate on Aaa (top quality) corporate bonds was 6.27%, and the rate on 30-day commercial paper (short-term paper issued by major corporations) was 4.80%.[1] The banks tend to attract higher-risk borrowers that do not have direct access to the money and capital markets. Note that adverse selection occurs before the loan is made.

---

1. Interest rate data are from the Federal Reserve Bank of St. Louis, *USFinancialData* (February 4, 1999).

MORAL HAZARD The asymmetric information also gives rise to a moral hazard problem after the loan is made. **Moral hazard** is the risk that the borrower, who now has the loan, might use the funds to engage in higher-risk activities in expectation of earning higher returns. The higher-risk activities increase the probability of default on the loan. The moral hazard problem is most likely to occur when the lender is unable to monitor the borrower's activities.

7.2 THE COMPETITIVE ENVIRONMENT

The Business of Lending

Lending money can be profitable, but it is risky. The profits come from collecting the interest income and fees earned on the loans. To the extent possible, banks and other lenders try to charge high-risk borrowers higher interest rates than low-risk borrowers. Therefore lenders have an incentive to take greater risks in expectation of earning higher returns. The major risk they face is credit risk.

Credit risk is "the risk of repayment, i.e., the possibility that an obligor will fail to perform as agreed," and adversely affect earnings and capital.[2] Credit risk applies to loans, derivatives, foreign exchange transactions, the investment portfolio, and other financial activities. With respect to loans, it is the risk that borrowers may default on their loans causing losses to the lender.

Banks do not intentionally make bad loans. They do, however, make loans that can go bad over time. For example, two years after granting a loan, a severe recession may adversely affect a borrower's ability to repay the loan, the borrower defaults. The fact that economic conditions changed the borrower's ability to repay helps to explain why banks must monitor their loans.

The decision to default on a loan belongs to the borrowers. In theory, borrowers have a "put option" to put the loan back to the lender when it is to their advantage to do so, usually when they are unable to make the required loan payments or meet other terms of the loan agreement. If a large number of borrowers exercise their put options to default, and the losses are sufficiently large, the lender may fail. Fearing losses and failure, lenders try to control their credit risk.

Increasing Competition

Economic theory tells us that the expectation of high returns attracts competition, and the loan business is no exception. In the past, banks dominated

---

2. *Loan Portfolio Management: Comptroller's Handbook*, Washington, D.C., Office of the Comptroller of the Currency (April 1998), p. 4.

commercial and consumer lending, because many assumed that banks had particular expertise in making, monitoring, and collecting loans. However, the banks did not have a sustainable competitive advantage, and today they face increasing competition from nonbank lenders such as General Electric Capital Services (total assets of $255.4 billion at year-end 1997), Ford Motor Credit Company, ($121.9 billion), Commercial Credit Company ($109.3 billion), Merrill Lynch, credit unions, and others.[3] In an effort to retain their share of the debt markets and compete with investment bankers, banks syndicate large loans. Loan syndication is explained in Chapter 15.

Because of information problems, specialized institutions have developed. For example, venture capital firms played an important role in the development of high-technology firms in the Silicon Valley of California. Specialized lenders have developed to deal with "subprime" (high credit risk) consumer lending, and "monoline" (one line of business) banks have developed expertise in credit card lending.

The growth of nonbank lenders has resulted in highly competitive terms of lending on loans and the standards used to make those loans.[4] Stated otherwise, some lenders who are trying to maximize revenue, or market share, may not give credit risk the weight it deserves in their lending decisions. Nevertheless, some differential in pricing risk remains. The average interest rate on C&I loans at all commercial banks in a 1998 Federal Reserve survey was 6.87%. The lowest risk loans were charged 6.10% and the highest were charged 7.33%.[5] No data were available for nonbank lenders. Competition also affects the nonprice terms of loans, such as the degree of "tightness" in loan covenants, and the releasing of guarantees to make easier to obtain loans. Loan covenants are conditions in the loan contract that the borrower must meet. For example, the borrower must provide audited financial statements annually.

Both nonbank and bank lenders have shifted their portfolios to higher yielding, higher-risk loans in recent years. During the 1988–1997 period, C&I loans for all U.S. banks declined from 23.36% to 16.90% of interest-earning assets, while 1–4 family real estate loans increased from 5.83% to 11.02%.[6] In

3. Data on total assets are from "Top 25 Finance Companies in the U.S. in Total Capital Funds," *American Banker* (September 9, 1998), p. 8.
4. "The Significance of Recent Changes in Bank Lending Standards: Evidence from the Loan Quality Assessment Project," Board of Governors of the Federal Reserve System, Division of Supervision and Regulation SR 98-18 (SUP), (June 1998).
5. "Terms of Lending at Commercial Banks," *Federal Reserve Bulletin* (May 1998), p. A66.
6. William B. English and William R. Nelson, "Profits and Balance Sheet Developments at U.S. Commercial Banks in 1997, *Federal Reserve Bulletin* (June 1998), Table A2, p. 412. Home equity loans accounted for 1.70% of total interest-earning assets in 1997. In a study of bank failures in various countries, Gup found that real estate loans were more commonly associated with bank failures than any other category of loan. Benton E. Gup, *Bank Failures in the Major Trading Countries of the World: Causes and Remedies* (Westport, CT: Quorum Books, 1998), Chapter 4.

the past, most banks had loan policies that limited them to 80% of price or value of the homes, because percentage was considered prudent. That practice has changed. Consider the market for home equity loans (second mortgages). Because of competition, many banks have raised their loan-to-price ratios on home equity loans, and they may be as high as 100%. This policy means that they are operating in a higher-risk environment to meet competition from finance companies that make home equity loans for 125% or more of the value of the homes.[7]

Changes in Technology

Recent developments in financial technology are changing the way that banks operate their lending activities. These developments are the securitization of loans, credit scoring, and measuring portfolio risks. Other changes in technology, such as the use of credit derivatives to manage portfolio risks are emerging, but their use is not widespread.

SECURITIZATION Securitization is the packaging and selling of otherwise unmarketable loans to other financial institutions and investors. For example, residential mortgage loans are packaged in large volumes and sold as mortgage pools, some of which are guaranteed by government agencies. Other securitized loans include automobile loans, credit card loans, and small business loans. The small business loans may be guaranteed the Small Business Administration. Alternatively, the issuer may "overcollateralize" the loans—putting up more collateral loans than is required—to enhance the package.

The growth of securitization means that loans formerly funded in local markets are now being funded in global capital markets. Removing geographic financial constraints for borrowers and lenders allows demand for such loans and the supply of funds to grow and provides increasing liquidity for the secondary loan market. It also provides lenders and investors who buy those loans a means of diversifying their portfolios.

Prior to the development of securitization, the loan market tended to clear more on quantity (i.e., the dollar amount of the loan) than on price. With the development of the secondary market, securitized loans behave more like bonds, where the quantity is set by the issuer and the price by the market.[8]

7. F. R. Bleakley, "A 125% Solution to Credit Card Debt Stirs Worry," *Wall Street Journal* (November 17, 1997). Check your local telephone book for advertisements under "mortgages." Mortgage lenders may show what percentage of value they are willing to lend.

8. For additional discussion of credit portfolio issues, see Elliot Asarnow, "Goldman Sach's Risk Wranglers: An Interview with Allen J. Levinson," *Journal of Lending and Credit Risk Management* (November 1998), pp. 8–21.

UNBUNDLING OF LOANS The growth of securitization has contributed to the unbundling of loans. Traditionally, banks made and held loans in their portfolios. Today, the lending process can be divided into the following activities:

1. Originating loans
2. Packaging loans for sale to others
3. Servicing loan portfolios
4. Investing in loan-backed credit instruments

A bank, or some other organization, can do any one or all of these activities. Accordingly, one firm may originate the loans, another package them for resale, and so on.

CREDIT SCORING **Credit scoring** is the use of statistical models to determine the likelihood that a prospective borrower will default on a loan. Credit scoring models are widely used to evaluate business, real estate, and consumer loans. In the case of small business loans, for example, the models may be based on data from credit applications, personal financial statements, business financial statements, business and credit bureau reports. Other factors may include the Standard Industrial Classification (SIC) codes, time in business, annual revenues, average checking account balance, and previous payment experience. For example, if the payments are always current, the score may be 25. If they are frequently 30 days past due, but never 60 days past due, the score may be 12. If they were ever 90 days past due, the score is zero. The scores for each of the items used are summed to generate a numerical score used by lenders to determine who qualifies for loans. The higher scores indicate a greater creditworthiness. The cutoff scores used by lenders depends on the degree of risk they are willing to take. Therefore different lenders use different scores, and they have override policies. A customer who receives a low score may still receive a loan if the lender decides to override the model because of other considerations.

See http://www.fairisaac. com *for information about small business credit scoring models.*

The major advantages of credit scoring models are the reduced time and lower cost of processing loans. Fair Isaac, a leading supplier of data analysis software, claims that the processing time can be reduced from 12 hours to 15 minutes.[9] The cost of processing can be reduced from say $650 per loan to $160 per loan. Another advantage is that the same measures are applied to all customers, thereby demonstrating a consistent credit policy.

Banks and other lenders use credit scoring models. However, because of economies of scale and the "standardized" treatment of loans, the use of credit scoring encourages automated lending decisions on a large scale from a single location, such as the monoline banks mentioned previously.

9. "Fast Turnaround Still Mostly a Dream, But Technology May Make it Happen," *American Banker* (February 13, 1995), p. 11; James C. Allen, "Small Business Banking: A Promise of Approvals in Minutes, Not Hours," *American Banker* (February 28, 1995). Estimates on the time savings and cost reductions vary widely, but they all show significant savings in both. Also see: L. J. Mester, "What's the Point of Credit Scoring?" Federal Reserve Bank of Philadelphia, *Business Review* (September/October 1997), pp. 3–16.

Some lenders preapprove loans, and solicit large numbers of customers. Typically, this method is used in connection with unsecured loans (not backed by collateral). Lenders making such loans can diversify their loan portfolio risk by making a large number of relatively small loans spread over large geographical areas.

MEASURING CREDIT PORTFOLIO RISK In 1997, J. P. Morgan announced Credit-Metrics™, a statistical model used to assess the credit portfolio risk, including bonds, loans, letters of credit, commitments, derivatives, and receivables. CreditMetrics is a value-at-risk (VaR) approach to credit risk management. That is, it incorporates the volatility of value due to changes in obligor's credit quality, defaults, upgrades, and downgrades to estimate the probability of decline in portfolio value, or losses, in a given period of time. The probability of losses usually ranges from 1–5%, and the time horizon may be any length, but it is usually short term. Since the introduction of CreditMetrics, other firms have developed competing models with different features. Dealing with the technical aspects of any of the statistical models is beyond the scope of this text.[10]

See http:\\www.jpmorgan.com *for information about risk management and CreditMetrics.*

Figure 7.1 shows a detailed roadmap of the analytics with CreditMetrics. In a simplified form, it computes exposure profiles for each asset, the volatility due to changes in value caused by upgrades or downgrades and defaults, and the correlations. All this information is used to determine the portfolio VaR due to credit exposure.

FIGURE 7.1 Simplified "Road Map" of the Analytics with CreditMetrics

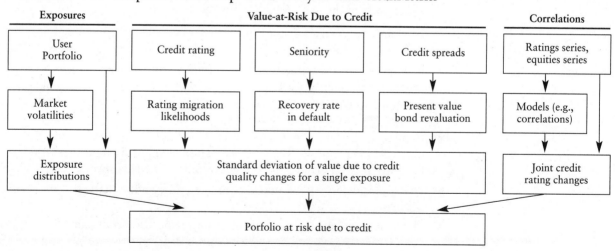

Source: J. P. Morgan, *Introduction to CreditMetrics* (1997). Reprinted with permission.

10. See Katerina Simons, "Value at Risk—New Approaches to Risk Management," *New England Economic Review*, Federal Reserve Bank of Boston (September/October 1996), pp. 3–13.

Banks also use internal credit risk ratings and models to manage their credit risk. A Federal Reserve study concluded that "No single internal rating system is best for all banks. Banks' systems vary widely because of differences in *business mix* and in the *uses* to which the ratings are put."[11] The business mix depends on the composition of large corporate loans and smaller loans. Internal rating systems can be used for profitability analysis and product pricing.

7.3 BOARD OF DIRECTORS WRITTEN LOAN POLICY

The Role of Directors

The board of directors has the ultimate responsibility for all of the loans made by their bank. Because the board delegates the task of making loans to others, it must have a **board of directors written loan policy** that establishes the guidelines and principles for the bank's lending activities.

Loan policies vary widely from bank to bank. The loan policies for a small bank that lends primarily to local consumers is going to differ from the policies of a large bank that specializes in lending to business concerns. In either case, the policy would state that the bank is in the business of making sound and profitable loans. Therefore, the loan policy must make it clear that an important part of the lending process is that all loans should have a repayment plan at the time the loan is made.

Other parts of the loan policy deal with:

- Loan authority: who has the authority to make loans, the lending limits relative to capital, deposits, or assets, and the loan approval process.

- Loan portfolio: the types of loans the bank wants to make, such as consumer loans, loans to start up businesses, loans to large businesses, farm loans, international loans, and so on. The policy should also put limits on the concentration of particular types of loans.

- Geographic limits of the bank's trade area where it may grant loans. The overwhelming majority (97%) of small and medium-sized business use financial institutions within 30 miles of their principal office.[12]

- Policies for determining interest rates, fees, and contractual terms of the loans.

- Limits and guidelines for off-balance sheet exposures from loan

11. William F. Treacy, "Credit Risk Rating at Large U.S. Banks," *Federal Reserve Bulletin* (November 1998), p. 921.
12. Comments by Joseph E. Stiglitz, *Bank Lending to Small Business*, Washington, DC, Office of the Comptroller of the Currency (November 15, 1994), p. 9.

commitments, letters of credit, securitized loans, and derivative products (swaps, options, futures, etc.).

- A loan review process to evaluate lending procedures and the quality of the loan portfolio.

Although this listing is incomplete, it is sufficient to give you an overview of some of the key topics that are covered in a loan policy. The policy also may specify the types of loans that the board considers undesirable. For example, the bank should not make loans to persons whose integrity or honesty is questionable. It should not make capital loans to a business where the loan cannot be repaid within a reasonable period except by liquidation of the business. And finally, it should not make loans secured by stock in a closed corporation where there is no market for that stock.

Reducing Credit Risk

Banks use a wide variety of techniques to reduce their credit risk. Some of the techniques are listed here:

1. *Avoid making high-risk loans.* For example, a small bank located in Cincinnati, Ohio, should reject a loan proposal to buy deep sea fishing boats in New England. While this loan might be good for a bank in New England that is familiar with that industry, it would be a high-risk loan for a midwestern bank that has no expertise in lending on deep sea fishing boats.

2. *Require the use of collateral.* Collateral reduces the risk to the lender, and the threat of loss of the collateral provides an incentive for the borrower to repay their loans. Collateral is considered a secondary source of repayment in the event of loan default.

3. *Diversify the loan portfolio.* Diversification means making loans to a variety of borrowers whose cash flows are not perfectly positively correlated, and avoiding undue concentration to a borrower, or in a particular type of loans whose returns are related. For example, when domestic crude oil prices increased from about $18 dollars a barrel in 1980 to $35 dollars a barrel in 1981, businesses throughout Texas, Oklahoma, Louisiana and Alaska prospered, and so did the banks in those states that lent to them during the oil boom. Then oil prices declined to about $9 a barrel by 1986. The sharp decline in oil prices produced a regional recession that resulted in large numbers of loan defaults and bank failures. The point here is that many of the loans that defaulted were tied directly and indirectly to the oil industry. The problem was exacerbated because interstate banking was not allowed at that time, and the banks could not diversify their portfolios geographically, neither were securitization and credit derivatives. Interstate banking became a reality in 1997.

4. *Document all information needed to legally enforce a loan contract and to protect a bank's interest.* Documents typically include promissory notes, guarantees, financial statements, UCC (Uniform Commercial Code) filings for collateral, notes about meetings with the customers, and so on. An unsigned promissory note is not enforceable. Moreover, failure to renew a UCC filing on collateral can turn a secured loan into an unsecured loan. The successful collection of loans may depend on documentation.

5. *Remember that guarantees do not eliminate default risk or the riskiness of a loan portfolio.* In fact, they may contribute to increased risk as banks substitute financial guarantees for high credit standards or higher rates charged on risky loans. Nevertheless, the federal government loan guarantees pay important roles in agriculture, commerce, and housing. The Small Business Administration (SBA), for example, assists small businesses by guaranteeing all or parts of qualifying loans made by banks and other lenders. Government guaranteed loans are one way that the government channels benefits to targeted sectors in the economy. Direct loans are another method. A Federal Reserve Bank of Richmond study revealed that guaranteed loans do not make the economy more efficient because the government does not have better information or a technical advantage over private lenders.[13] Private guarantees (those not backed by government) are also widely used by borrowers. A parent company guaranteeing the loan of a subsidiary is one example.

6. *Limit the amount of credit extended to any single borrower, or groups of borrowers with related cash flow patterns.* To avoid undue loan concentration, for example, banks that are members of the Federal Reserve System are limited in the amount of their capital that they can lend to a single borrower. The maximum amount is 15% of the total capital in the case of a loan that is not fully secured, and an additional 10% for loans that are secured by readily marketable collateral.[14]

7. *Monitor the behavior of the borrower after the loan is made to ensure compliance with the loan agreement.* Recall that the decision to default on a loan is a put option held by the borrower. Some borrowers have a moral hazard problem and take excessive risks. Other borrowers may be adversely affected by external factors such as oil price shocks, recessions, floods, droughts, and so on. Therefore, the monitoring should take into account those external factors that might impede the borrower's ability to repay the loan.

   The outside monitor may know that the borrower has used the loan funds to buy assets, such as inventory or equipment. However, the

13. W. Li, "Government Loan, Guarantee, and Grant Programs: An Evaluation," Federal Reserve Bank of Richmond, *Economic Quarterly* (Fall 1998), pp. 25–51.
14. The limits apply to a bank's total unimpaired capital and surplus, which equals their Tier 1 and Tier 2 capital. For additional details, see 12 USC 84 and 12 USC 1817.

monitor may not be able to verify the value of those assets.[15] The difference between what the monitor knows and what they can verify contributes to the agency problems between the lender and borrower. *Agency problems* as used here refer to the ability of the lender (the principal) to influence the behavior of the borrower (the agent).

Outside Monitor	
What They "Know"	**Is It "Verifiable?"**
What is there	Yes
The value of what is there	No

8. *Transfer risk to other parties by selling securitized loans and loan participations, and by hedging with interest rate and credit derivatives.*[16]

7.4 SEVEN WAYS TO MAKE LOANS

Banks have a number of different methods in which to make loans.

Banks Solicit Loans

Banks actively solicit loans in person, by mail, and on the internet, offering loans and other services provided by their respective banks. These sales efforts are typical of banks seeking new customers and those trying to cross-sell their services. For example, a branch manager or loan officer may explain to a prospective borrower how the bank's cash management services, including lock boxes and cash concentration accounts, can improve the firm's cash flow. Lock boxes are mail boxes where retail customers send their payments for goods and services purchased. The lock boxes are serviced by the bank, and funds can be concentrated and forwarded to the firm's treasury for investment.

Buying Loans

Banks buy parts of loans, called *participations*, from other banks. The acquiring banks have pro rata shares of the credit risk. Participations by three or more unaffiliated banks in loans or formal loan commitments in excess of $20 million

15. This view of agency problems is based on an unpublished paper by Stewart C. Myers, "Outside Equity Financing" (March 14, 1998), presented at a seminar at the University of Alabama, February 19, 1999.
16. For a discussion of credit derivatives, see: J. T. Moser, "Credit Derivatives: Just-in-time Provisioning for Loan Losses," Federal Reserve Bank of Chicago, *Economic Perspectives* (Fourth Quarter 1998), pp. 2–11.

MANAGERIAL ISSUES

Illusory Collateral, or What You See Ain't What You Get

What bankers "know" about the collateral and what they can "verify" may be two different things. Unscrupulous borrowers find many ways to give bankers the illusion that their loans are protected by collateral. In one instance, the collateral was salad oil that was supposed to be held in large storage tanks. Large storage tanks can hold 700,000 gallons or more of oil, gas, and other liquids. The storage tanks were located near a waterway in New Jersey.

The bankers used a long dipstick to determine how much salad oil was in the tanks. What they didn't know until it was too late is that most of the salad oil had been drained from the storage tanks and taken elsewhere on tankers. The oil was replaced with seawater. Because oil floats on water, the dipstick measured the upper level of the oil-covered water. Banks and other business concerns lost millions of dollars on "The Great Salad Oil Scandal."

are called *shared national credits*.[17] Suppose that a large bank is making a $100 million loan to an airline, but the originating bank does not want to keep such a large loan in its loan portfolio. It may sell parts (participations) of that loan to other banks. The sale of participations downstream to smaller banks allows those banks to participate in loans that they could not originate. In addition, it is one way for a bank with slack demand for loans to increase its loan portfolio. It also allows all of the banks involved to diversify their loan portfolios. Participations can originate from small banks too. Suppose that a small bank wants to make a loan that exceeds its lending limits. It can make the loan and sell participations upstream to larger banks. Banks also buy and sell securitized loans.

Commitments

About three-fourths of all commercial and industrial loans are made under loan commitments.[18] A **loan commitment** is an agreement between a bank and a firm to lend funds under terms agreed upon in writing. Loan commitments specify the amount of the commitment fee, the amount of funds to be borrowed, but the cost of borrowing depends on the prevailing rates at the time the loan is made. The pricing on the loan is usually specified when the commitment is made. For example, the bank may charge the *prime rate* (the base rate on corporate loans) plus two percentage points when the funds are borrowed.[19]

17. Shared National Credits are defined fully in the FDIC press release PR-67-99 (November 10, 1999).
18. See the "Terms of Lending at Commercial Banks," *Federal Reserve Bulletin* (May 1998), p. A66.
19. The *Wall Street Journal* section on "Money Rates," gives the current prime rate, LIBOR, and short-term rates.

Firms pay a commitment fee to banks for the call option of borrowing at some future date. Commitment fees range from 0.25% to 0.50% per annum of the total amount to be borrowed. Commitment fees contribute to bank's income, and they do not require immediate funding. For example, assume a 45-day commitment for $5 million, with a commitment fee of 0.50% per annum, computed on a 360-day basis. The bank earns $3,125 without investing any assets, but it does have a contingent claim.

$$\text{Commitment} \times 0.50\%$$
$$\$5,000,000 \times 0.005 = \$25,000$$
$$\text{Daily fee} = \text{total fee}/360$$
$$\$69.444 = \$25,000/360$$
$$\text{Fee for 45 days} = \text{daily fee} \times 45 \text{ days}$$
$$\$3,125.00 = \$69.444 \times 45$$

Banks may compute the fee on a 365-day basis. Using 365 days, the daily fee is $68.493 and the bank earns $3,082.19. The bank is better off using 360 days.

Customers Request Loans

A customer asks for a commercial loan. Unfortunately, many potential borrowers are denied loans or do not get what they need because they do not know what information the bank needs in order to grant a loan request. Some borrowers, for example, do not know what type of loan (i.e., line of credit, term loan) will meet their financial needs, or what type of collateral (i.e., accounts receivable, bill of lading, second mortgage) is suitable for their loans. Good loan officers work with prospective borrowers who do not know the procedures, by explaining to them what information they must provide to the bank.

Loan Brokers

Loan brokers sell loans to banks and other lenders. Loan brokers are individuals or firms who act as agents or brokers between the borrower and the lender. For example, a loan broker may contract with a real estate developer to find financing for a particular project. The broker will seek out lenders and arrange for the loan. Once the loan is made and the fees are paid, the broker is out of the picture.

Overdrafts

An **overdraft** occurs when a customer writes a check on uncollected funds, or when an account contains insufficient funds to cover the withdrawal. If a bank pays on a check written against insufficient balances, it is extending an unsecured loan.

Some overdrafts are written with prior permission of the bank, but most are not. In the latter case, the overdraft represents a loan that the bank may not want to make. The borrower did not ask the bank for the funds in advance.

Overdrafts can be for less than one day (daylight overdraft) when a check is written or funds transferred out by wire in the morning and the deposit to cover that check or wire transfer is not made until that afternoon. Suppose that a firm located in New York City deposits a check drawn on a bank located in El Paso, Texas. It will take about two days for the check to be collected by the New York bank from the bank in Texas. Although the New York firm's balance has increased, it cannot use those funds to write checks without the bank's permission. Many banks analyze their customer's "out of town" checks and permit them to write checks only on their average collected balances. Under the Competitive Banking Equality Act of 1987, no more than one business day may intervene between the deposit of a local check and the availability for withdrawal of those funds, and four business days for nonlocal checks.

Refinancing

Borrowers refinance loans. Suppose that interest rates on loan have declined from 14% to 10%, and that borrowers with high fixed rate loans want to take advantage of the lower rates. They can make a new loan at the lower rate and pay off the high-rate loan. The refinancing is at the borrower's option, and only occurs when it is to their advantage.

Collecting Loans

Making loans is the easy part of the lending process. Collecting the loans is the hard part. The two primary sources of repayment lenders consider when they make loans are (1) cash flow, such as earnings, and (2) the sale of the assets being finance, or inventory. Collateral serves as a secondary source of repayment.

In the event that neither the primary nor the secondary sources of loan repayment satisfy the debt, the bank will have to take appropriate action to protect its interests. If the loan is guaranteed (such as a guarantee from the Small Business Administration), the bank will turn to the guarantor for repayment. Alternatively, the bank may force the borrower into bankruptcy, which is generally the least effective method of repayment. When the loan is no longer of sufficient value to be considered creditworthy, it is removed or **charged-off** the balance sheet.

7.5 PRINCIPAL LENDING ACTIVITIES

Principal lending activities include loans and leases. Banks make a variety of types of loans, but the loans presented include lines of credit, revolving loans, term loans, and bridge loans. Each type of loan has its own purpose. Figure 7.2 illustrates this concept of "different types of loans for different purposes." As shown in the figure, the total assets of a firm can be divided into two categories, permanent assets and temporary assets. Permanent assets include plant

FIGURE 7.2 **The Financing Mix**

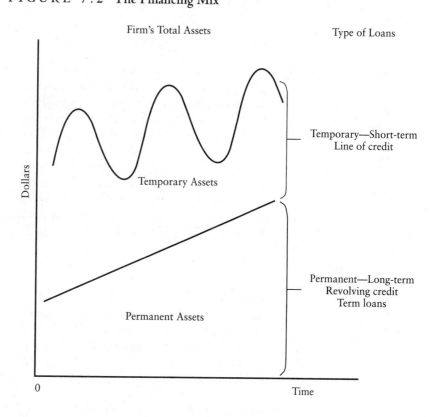

and equipment as well as that portion of working capital (cash, accounts receivable, and inventory) that will be sustained over time. Temporary assets include that portion of working capital that fluctuates with periodic changes in sales and revenues. For example, the inventory of The Toy Store is expected to increase before Christmas. When the toys are sold, the inventory will be reduced but the accounts receivable will increase. As the receivables are collected and the cash is used to repay debts or acquire new long-term assets, working capital will be reduced.

The figure also shows that temporary assets should be financed with temporary loans and permanent assets with permanent loans. Stated otherwise, a safe lending strategy is to match the maturity of the asset being financed with the maturity of funds used to finance it. For example, it makes sense to finance The Toy Store's seasonal inventory loan for up to one year, although one would expect it to be repaid in less time. It does not make sense to provide funds for five years to finance an inventory of toys for one Christmas season. Sometimes this kind of a mismatch occurs when funds are lent to finance both temporary and permanent assets in one loan rather than being treated as separate loans.

Line of Credit

A **line of credit** is an agreement between a customer and the bank, that the bank will entertain requests from that customer for a loan up to a predetermined amount. The line of credit is established when the bank gives a letter to the customer stating the dollar amount of the line, the time it is in effect (i.e., one year), and other conditions or provisions such as the relationship the customer must maintain with the bank and the customer's financial condition. If the borrower does not meet all of the terms and conditions of the letter, the bank is not obligated to make the loan or continue the line of credit.

The line of credit is the maximum amount that can be borrowed under the terms of the loan. The loans are typically made for periods of one year or less, and should be used to finance seasonal increases in inventory and accounts receivable. When the inventory is sold, receivables are collected, and the funds are used to reduce the loan. The loans are usually payable on demand by the bank, or within 90 days.

Revolving Loan

Revolving loans are similar to a line of credit because they too are used to finance borrowers' temporary and seasonal working capital needs. One difference between a revolving loan and line of credit is that the bank is obligated to make the loans up to the maximum amount of the loan, if the borrower is in compliance with the terms of the agreement. Revolving loans commonly specify the minimum amount of the increments that may be borrowed. For example, the loan could be for $30,000 increments up to a maximum limit of $3 million. Another difference is that revolving loans usually have a maturity of two years or more, while lines of credit are usually for shorter periods.

Term Loan

A **term loan** is usually a single loan for a stated period of time, or a series of loans on specified dates. They are used for a specific purpose, such as acquiring machinery, renovating a building, refinancing debt, and so forth. They should not be used to finance day-to-day operations.

Term loans may have an original maturity of five years or more. From the lender's point of view, the maturity of the loan should not exceed the economic life of the asset being financed if that asset is being used as collateral for the loan. Equally important, the value of the asset being financed always should exceed the amount of the loan. The difference between the value of asset and the amount being financed is the borrower's equity. The borrower's equity represents the borrower's investment in the asset being financed. It also provides the bank with a "cushion" in the event of default. The borrower will lose his or her funds before the bank experiences a loss. Borrowers not wanting to lose their equity investment have an incentive to operate their business so that the loan will be repaid.

Term loans may be repaid on an amortized basis or at one time. Recall, that the planned repayment of loans should come from the borrower's operating revenues, or from the sale of assets. These concepts are illustrated in the top panel of Figure 7.3. The point of these concepts is to help protect the bank's security interest in the loan.

The lower panel illustrates improper lending procedures—a loan that exceeds the value of the asset that it is financing. In addition, the maturity of the loan

FIGURE 7.3 Term Loans for Machinery

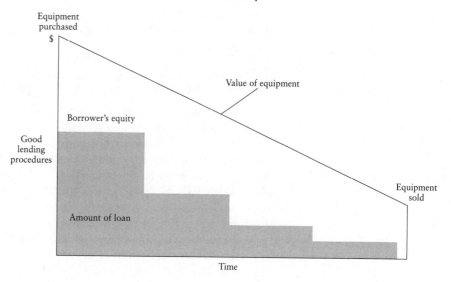

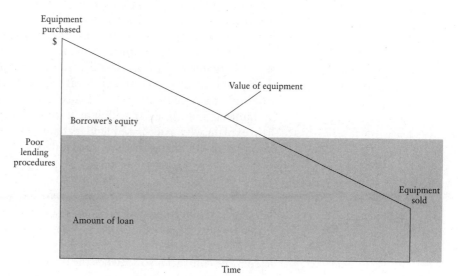

exceeds the life of the asset. If the borrower defaults when the value of the equipment is less than the amount of the loan, the bank will incur a substantial loss.

Bridge Loan

Bridge loans "bridge a gap" in a borrower's financing until some specific event occurs. For example, a firm wants to acquire a new warehouse facility, but needs funds to finance the transaction until the old warehouse can be sold. A bridge loan can be used to finance the firm's operations in the interim.

Similarly, a firm needs working capital now; next week it is going to issue commercial paper to provide those funds. A bank can provide this week-long temporary financing as a short-term substitute for other debt financing by the firm.

Asset-Based Lending

Asset-based lending is a form of commercial lending where the assets of a company are used to secure the company's obligation to the lender. Most asset-based lenders are finance companies, although some banks do asset-based lending too. In the broadest sense, all secured loans could be classified as asset-based lending. Asset-based loans have as their collateral base accounts receivable, inventory, machinery and equipment, and real estate, individually or packaged in various combinations, such as receivables and inventory or receivables and machinery or inventory and equipment, and so forth.

The major distinctions between asset-based loans and other secured loans is that much greater weight is given to the market value of the collateral in asset-based lending than in regular C&I loans. In addition, asset-based lenders place greater emphasis on monitoring than do bank lenders. Moreover, if the borrower defaults, the asset based lenders are more willing to liquidate the borrower's collateral than is the case for regular C&I loans.

Asset-based loans require a higher level of monitoring than do other secured commercial loans. The degree of monitoring to ensure the existence, value, and integrity of the collateral further differentiates asset-based loans from other secured commercial loans. The combination of a higher level of monitoring and a greater willingness to liquidate in the event of default may help explain why asset-based lenders tend to have higher spreads and fees and lower write-offs than other secured lenders.

Leasing

Leasing are used to finance tangible assets such as cars, airliners, and ships. A lease is contract that enables a user—the lessee—to secure the use of a tangible asset over a specified period of time by making payments to the owner, the lessor. The contract also specifies the details of the payments, the disposition of income tax benefits, provisions for maintenance, renewal options, and other clauses that permit the contract to qualify as a true lease under the Internal Revenue Code. We will consider two types of leases, operating leases, and financial leases.

Operating leases are short-term leases used to finance equipment such as computers, where the term of the lease is a fraction of the economic life of the asset. The asset is not fully amortized over the term of a lease. Operating leases may be canceled.

Financial leases are used in connection with financing long-term assets and have a term equal to the economic life of the asset. For example, a communications satellite may be leased for 12 years. Such leases are usually not canceled.

7.6 COLLATERAL

Sound banking practices require that certain types of loans be backed by collateral. **Collateral** refers to an asset pledged against the performance of an obligation. If a borrower defaults on a loan, the bank takes the collateral and sells it. Therefore, it is frequently referred to as a secondary source of repayment.

Collateral reduces the bank's risk when it makes a loan. However, collateral does not reduce the risk of the loan per se. The risk of the loan is determined by the borrowers ability to repay it and other factors. Even though collateral reduces the bank's risk, it increases the costs of lending due to the need for documentation and monitoring the collateral. In an effort to cut costs, some banks are not requiring collateral on lines of credit issued to small businesses. However, without collateral some borrowers could not obtain loans.

Collateral benefits both borrowers and lenders in certain type of loans. In other types of loans collateral is not used. For example, a large creditworthy corporation borrowed $20 million for one day until it sold its own commercial paper. The minimal risk and the large volume of paperwork to obtain liens against specific assets mitigated the need for collateral in this case.

Characteristics of Good Collateral

Almost anything that is lawful may be used as collateral, but some things are better than others. The following five factors determine the suitability of items for use as collateral.

1. **Durability.** The ability of the assets to withstand wear, or its useful life, is referred to as durability. Durable goods make better collateral than nondurables. Stated another way, crushed rocks make better collateral than fresh flowers.

2. **Identification.** Certain types of assets are readily identifiable because they have definite characteristics or serial numbers that cannot be removed. Two examples are a large office building and an automobile that can be identified by make, model, and serial number.

3. **Marketability.** In order for collateral to be of value to the bank, the collateral must be marketable, meaning it can be sold. Specialized equipment that has limited use is not as marketable as trucks that have multiple uses.

4. **Stability of value.** Bankers prefer collateral whose market values are not likely to decline dramatically during the period of the loan. Common stocks, for example, are not as desirable as real estate for collateral because the stock prices are more volatile than real estate prices.

5. **Standardization.** Certain types of grains have been graded by the Department of Agriculture. For example, soybeans are graded as No. 1 yellow, No. 2 yellow, or No. 3 yellow. These grades indicate the quality of the beans. Likewise, other types of commodities and merchandise have been graded to facilitate their use in trade and as collateral. The standardization reduces the ambiguity between the borrower and the lender as to nature of the asset that is being used as collateral.

Types of Collateral

The most common types of collateral that are used in commercial lending are examined here.

ACCOUNTS RECEIVABLE The three ways that accounts receivable can be used as collateral are pledging, factoring, and bankers' acceptances.

1. **Pledging:** A borrower can pledge accounts receivable with his or her bank. In this case the borrower retains ownership of the receivables; usually no notification is made to the buyer of the goods for which the receivables have been pledged. The percentage of face value of the accounts receivable that the banker is willing to advance depends on the size, number, and quality of the receivables. Most bankers prefer to advance funds from receivables from a few well-established firms with good credit ratings.

2. **Factoring:** Factoring is the sale of accounts receivable usually to a bank or finance company, or factor. When the receivables are sold, the buyer of the goods is usually notified to make payments to the factor. Like pledging, factors prefer receivables from well-established firms. One important difference between the two methods is that factors usually buy receivables on a nonrecourse basis. Nonrecourse means that it cannot be returned to the firm that is selling the receivables. Thus, the factor accepts the credit risks for the receivables that they purchase. To reduce their risk, the factor may only advance 80–90% of the face value, with the remainder held in reserve until the receivables are collected or until some predetermined date. In addition, the factor charges a commission ranging from 1% to 3% of the total face value, as well as monthly interest charges on the advances. For example, suppose that Southern Mill Outlet wants to factor $100,000 in receivables. The factor holds a reserve of 10% (advances 90%), charges a 3% commission, and a 2% monthly interest charge. The

Southern Mill Outlet receives $85,260 and the factor earns $4,740 plus what they can earn on investing the reserve.

Face value of the accounts receivable	$100,000
Reserve held by factor (10%)	10,000
Commission (3%)	–3,000
Funds that may be advanced	$87,000
Less monthly interest charge (2%)	–1,740
Funds available to Southern Mill Outlet	$85,260

3. **Bankers' Acceptance: A bankers' acceptance** usually arises from foreign trade. Suppose that a U.S. exporter sells computer parts to a French concern. The French importer agrees to pay for the parts 30 days after they have been delivered. The means of payment is a *time draft*, which is similar to a predated check. The U.S. manufacturer can send the time draft, which from the manufacturer's point of view is the same as an account receivable, to the French importer's bank and have it accepted. The French bank then becomes responsible for the payment of the draft, and will collect the funds from the importer when the draft becomes due. In other words, the French bank is guaranteeing payments of the French importer's obligation. The accepted draft is called a bankers' acceptance. It is a negotiable instrument that can be traded in the securities markets. The U.S. manufacturer can sell the bankers' acceptance at a discount to compensate investors who bought it and cannot collect the full value until it matures.

INVENTORY Inventory is widely used as collateral against commercial loans. The inventory may consist of raw materials or finished goods, such as automobiles. Other types of inventory may include natural resources, livestock and crops, and so on.

MARKETABLE SECURITIES Marketable securities, including corporate stocks and bonds, certificates of deposit, U.S. Treasury securities, and others, may be used as collateral for business loans. The amount of credit extended on such securities varies widely. One problem with securities as collateral is that the market value of publicly held stocks and bonds can vary widely from day to day. The value of publicly traded securities is readily available in the press. In contrast, the market value of privately held companies may not be determinable without considerable effort and expense.

REAL PROPERTY AND EQUIPMENT Real property refers to real estate that includes houses, office building, shopping centers, factories, and so on. Such property is widely used as collateral. In addition, equipment of various sorts may be used. Equipment includes trucks, fork lifts, drill presses, robotics, and other items.

Bond and stock prices are volatile. The latest price information and causes of the volatility can be found on CNN's Financial Network at http://cnnfn.com/.

The Small Business Administration provides funding and guarantees for certain types of loans for small businesses. To find out more about their loan and guarantee programs, see http://www.sba.gov/.

Appraisals by qualified real estate appraisers and equipment appraisers are essential before the loan is made.

GUARANTEES Bankers can improve their security by having a third party guarantee the payments. The third party may be an individual, insurance company, or U.S. government agency such as the Small Business Administration. For example, a parent company may guarantee a loan made by a subsidiary. Without the guarantee, the loan would not have been made. With the exception of the government agencies, the quality of guarantee depends on the financial strength of the guarantor.

In summary, many banks require collateral and/or a guarantee when they make business loans. Small businesses frequently use the personal assets of the principals as collateral. Personal assets include real estate, cars, the surrender value of life insurance policies, or anything else of value.

7.7 THE LENDING PROCESS

The process of lending begins before a loan is made. The board of directors establishes a loan policy and considers the risk reduction techniques previously described. The process ends when the loan is repaid or when it is determined to be uncollectible. At that point, if it no longer has value, it is removed as an asset from the bank's balance sheet. Even then, the bank still may be able to collect some of the proceeds. Both the lender and the borrower perform certain tasks over the term of the lending process.

Evaluating a Loan Request

A key part of the lending process involves the *6 Cs of credit*. Banks that use credit scoring models incorporate data from credit reporting agencies and other sources that cover some of the 6 Cs. While the use of credit scoring models is growing in importance, many loans must be evaluated using the following traditional methods.

1. Character: personal characteristics of the borrower, honesty, and attitudes about willingness, and commitment to pay debts.
2. Capacity: the borrower's success in running a business, or cash flows.
3. Capital: the financial condition of the borrower, or net worth.
4. Collateral: pledged assets.
5. Conditions: economic factors.
6. Compliance: compliance with laws and regulations.

For details about the information provided in Dun and Bradstreet reports and to view sample reports see http://www.dnb.com/prods_svcs/samples.htm.

CHARACTER Banks must "know their customer" before they make loans, and character is the place to start. Character refers to a combination of qualities that distinguishes one person or a group from another. To some extent, the words *character* and *reputation* overlap in meaning. We use the term *character* here to refer to a borrower's honesty, responsibility, integrity, and consistency as the basis on which we can determine their willingness to repay loans. Evidence of character traits can be found in reports from credit bureaus and credit reporting agencies, such as the Dun and Bradstreet (D&B) report shown Figure 7.4. The D&B report provides vital information about the firm, with particular emphasis on its history of payments and its financial condition.

CAPACITY Success of the borrower's business as reflected in its financial condition and ability to meet financial obligations via cash flow and earnings is referred to as capacity. Banks generally require prospective borrowers to submit their financial statements and/or federal and state income tax statements in order to determine their creditworthiness. Appendix 7A provides a detailed description of financial analysis.

Credit scoring is widely used to aid in decision making. In addition, credit analysts may use analytical software programs that provide a wide range of financial ratios and comparative data to evaluate the data and to do pro forma projections and stress testing. However, the results of a recent Federal Reserve survey reveal that projections of borrower's future performance were present in only 20–30% of the loans they observed, and stress testing was even less common.[20] These findings may reflect the fact that most loans are for relatively small amounts, which do not warrant the cost of doing pro forma statements or stress testing.

CAPITAL Capital represents the amount of equity capital a firm can liquidate for payment if all other means of collection of the debt fail. Equity capital is equal to total assets less total liabilities. However, a substantial difference may exist between the *book value* and the *market value* of assets and liabilities. For example, land purchased 20 years ago can be carried on the books at its historical cost. However, the present market value of the land could be substantially higher or lower than the book value.

COLLATERAL Collateral refers to assets that are pledged for security in a credit transaction. The fact that borrowers may lose their collateral if they default on their loans typically serves as an incentive for them to perform in accordance with the loan contract.

---

20. "The Significance of Recent Changes in Bank Lending Standards: Evidence from the Loan Quality Assessment Project," Board of Governors of the Federal Reserve System, Division of Supervision and Regulation, SR 98-18 (SUP) (June 1998).

FIGURE 7.4 A Typical Credit Report

Dun & Bradstreet, Inc.		This report has been prepared for
BE SURE NAME, BUSINESS AND ADDRESS MATCH YOUR FILE	ANSWERING INQUIRY	SUBSCRIBER 008-001042

THIS REPORT MAY NOT BE REPRODUCED IN WHOLE OR IN PART IN ANY MANNER WHATSOEVER

CONSOLIDATED REPORT	{FULL REVISION}

DUNS: 00 007 7743
GORMAN MFG CO INC
(Subsidiary of Gorman Holding Companies Inc.)
492 KOLLER ST
AND BRANCH(ES) OR DIVISION(S)
SAN FRANCISCO CA 94110
         TEL: 415-555-0000

DATE PRINTED:
OCT 30 199-

COMMERCIAL PRINTING
SIC NO.
2752

SUMMARY

RATING	3A3
STARTED	1965
PAYMENTS	SEE BELOW
SALES F	$13,007,229
WORTH F	$2,125,499
EMPLOYS	500 (150 here)
HISTORY	CLEAR
FINANCING	SECURED
FINANCIAL CONDITION	FAIR

CHIEF EXECUTIVE: LESLIE SMITH, PRES

SPECIAL
EVENTS
10/20/9-
On Oct. 13, 199-, the subject experienced a fire due to an earthquake. Damages amounted to $35,000, which was fully covered by its insurance company. The business was closed for two days while employees settled personal matters due to the earthquake.

PAYMENTS   (Amounts may be rounded to nearest figure in prescribed ranges)

REPORTED	PAYING RECORD	HIGH CREDIT	NOW OWES	PAST DUE	SELLING TERMS	LAST SALE WITHIN
10/9-	Ppt-Slow 90	1000	500	-0-	N30	1 Mo
09/9-	Ppt	250	100			4-5 Mos
	Ppt-Slow 30	2500	2500	1000		1 Mo
	Slow 30	500	500			2-3 Mos
	Slow 30-60	70000	70000	65000		1 Mo
08/9-	Disc	2500	1000			1 Mo
	Disc-Ppt	25000	25000	-0-	2 10 Prox	1 Mo
	Ppt-Slow 15	1000	500	250		1 Mo
	Ppt-Slow 30	15000	10000	5000		1 Mo
	Ppt-Slow 30	1000	-0-	-0-	N30	4-5 Mos
07/9-	Ppt	250000	250000	-0-		1 Mo
	Ppt	7500	250	-0-	N15	1 Mo
	Ppt	500	-0-	-0-	N30	6-12 Mos
	Ppt	100	50	-0-	Regular terms	1 Mo
	Ppt-Slow 30	100000	100000	40000		1 Mo
	Ppt-Slow 30	70000	70000	50000	2 15 Prox	1 Mo
	Slow 30	7500	-0-	-0-		1 Mo
	Slow 30		-0-	-0-	N30	6-12 Mos
06/9-	Disc-Slow 30	30000	30000	7500		1 Mo
05/9-	Ppt	250	-0-	-0-		6-12 Mos
	Ppt-Slow 60	200000	200000	90000		1 Mo
04/9-	(022)	100	100		N30	

*Payment experiences reflect how bills are met in relation to the terms granted. In some instances payment beyond the terms can be the result of disputes over merchandise, skipped invoices etc.

*Each experience shown represents a separate account reported by a supplier. Updated trade experiences replace those previously reported.

Changes
03/17/9-
Subject moved from 400 KOLLER ST. to 492 KOLLER ST. on March 11, 199-.

Update
08/17/9-
On August 17, 199- KEVIN J. HUNT SEc-Treas stated for the six months ended June 30, 199- profits were up compared to same period last year.

FIGURE 7.4 **A Typical Credit Report** (*continued*)

		Fiscal Dec 31, 1989		Fiscal Dec 31, 1990		Fiscal Dec 31, 1991
			This report has been prepared for			
	BE SURE NAME, BUSINESS AND ADDRESS MATCH YOUR FILE		ANSWERING INQUIRY		SUBSCRIBER 008-001042	

THIS REPORT MAY NOT BE REPRODUCED IN WHOLE OR IN PART IN ANY MANNER WHATSOEVER

CONSOLIDATED REPORT   {FULL REVISION}

FINANCE 09/11/9-		Fiscal Dec 31, 1989	Fiscal Dec 31, 1990	Fiscal Dec 31, 1991
	Curr Assets	4,643,821	4,825,611	5,425,125
	Curr Liabs	3,595,821	3,625,000	4,125,718
	Current Ratio	1.3	1.3	1.3
	Working Capital	1,048,000	1,200,611	1,299,407
	Other Assets	1,468,291	1,485,440	2,191,690
	Worth	1,879,451	1,912,112	2,125,499
	Sales	9,321,118	10,325,582	13,007,229
	Net income	32,661	213,387	26,014

Fiscal statement dated Dec. 31, 1991:

Cash	$ 925,000	Accts Pay	$ 2,125,114
Accts Rec	1,725,814	Notes Pay	450,000
Inventory	1,643,311	Bank Loan	1,100,000
Other Curr Assets	1,131,000	Other Curr Liabs	450,604
	-----------------		-------------------
Curr Assets	5,425,125	Curr Liabs	4,125,718
Fixt & Equip	1,667,918	L.T. Liab-Other	1,365,598
Other Assets	523,772	CAPITAL STOCK	50,000
		RETAINED EARNINGS	2,075,499
	-----------------		-------------------
Total Assets	7,616,815	Total	7,616,815

From JAN 1, 1991, to DEC 31, 1991 sales $13,007,229; cost of goods sold $9,229,554. Gross profit $3,777,675; operating expenses $3,751,661. Operating income $26,014; net income before taxes $26,014. Net income $26,014.

Submitted SEPT 11, 199- by Leslie Smith, President. Prepared from statement(s) by Accountant: Ashurst & Ashurst, PC. Prepared from books without audit.

--0--

Accounts receivable shown net less $12,586 allowance. Other current assets consist of prepaid expenses $64,471 and $1,066,529 of a loan from an affiliated concern. Other assets consist of deposits. Bank loans are due to bank at the prime interest rate, are secured by accounts receivable and inventory, and mature in 3 years. Notes payable are due on printing equipment in monthly installments of $37,500. Other current liabilities are accrued expenses and taxes. Long term debt consists of the long term portion of the equipment note.

On SEPT 11, 199- Leslie Smith, president, submitted the above figures.

Leslie Smith submitted the following interim figures dated JUNE 30, 199-.

Cash	$ 1,011,812	Accts Pay	$ 1,932,118
Accts Rec	1,932,118	Owe Bank	1,100,000
Mdse	1,421,112	Notes Pay	350,000

Sales for 6 months were $7,325,001. Profits for 6 months were $103,782. Projected annual sales are $14,000,000.

The financial condition at DEC 31, 1991 was fair. Total debt was heavy in relation to the net worth. Total debt exceeded net worth by 2.6 to 1 vs an industry median of 2.3 to 1.

Current assets were centered in a slow moving inventory, while profitability has been below average the past three years. The median return on sales for this industry is 1.9%. Return on sales for the past three years has been 0.2%, 2.1% and 0.4% respectively.

Total equity represented 27.9% of the total capitalization which compared unfavorably to the industry average of 37.7%. On SEPT 11, 199-, Leslie Smith, president, stated profits were below average due to heavy price competition in the industry, higher operating expenses, and decreased advertising budgets following the nationwide move towards cost containment. Net worth increased due to additional paid in capital.

FIGURE 7.4   A Typical Credit Report (*continued*)

Dun & Bradstreet, Inc.		This report has been prepared for
BE SURE NAME, BUSINESS AND ADDRESS MATCH YOUR FILE	ANSWERING INQUIRY	SUBSCRIBER 008-001042

THIS REPORT MAY NOT BE REPRODUCED IN WHOLE OR IN PART IN ANY MANNER WHATSOEVER

CONSOLIDATED REPORT		{FULL REVISION}

The following data is for information purposes only and is not the official record. Certified copies can only be obtained from the official source.

PUBLIC FILINGS

If it is indicated that there are defendants other than the report subject, the lawsuit may be an action to clear title to property and does not necessarily imply a claim for money against the subject.

* * * SUIT(S) * * *

DOCKET NO.: 21211
SUIT AMOUNT: $1,000
PLAINTIFF: MAZZUCA & ASSOC.
DEFENDANT: GORMAN MANUFACTURING CO. INC.
CAUSE: Goods sold and delivered
WHERE FILED: SAN FRANCISCO, CA

STATUS: Pending
DATE STATUS ATTAINED: 03/25/199-
DATE FILED: 03/25/199-
RECEIVED BY D & B: 03/31/199-

* * * UCC FILING(S) * * *

COLLATERAL: Accounts receivable - inventory including proceeds and products
FILING NO.:   86188586
TYPE: Original
SEC. PARTY: A.C. Paper, Palo Alto, CA
DEBTOR: Gorman Manufacturing Co., Inc.

DATE FILED: 07/24/199-
RECEIVED BY D & B: 10/04/199-
FILED WITH: SECRETARY OF STATE/
              UCC DIVISION, CA

There are additional UCC's in D&B's file on this company available by contacting 1-800-DNB-DIAL.

The public record items contained in this report may have been paid, terminated, vacated or released prior to the date this report was printed.

BANKING
09/9-

Account(s) averages high 6 figures. Account open over 10 years. Loans granted to low 7 figures on a secured basis. Now owing low 7 figures. Collateral consists of accounts receivable and inventory. Matures in 1 to 5 years. Borrowing account is satisfactory. Overall relations are satisfactory.

HISTORY
09/11/9-

LESLIE SMITH, PRES   KEVIN J. HUNT, SEC-TREAS
DIRECTOR(S): THE OFFICER(S)

BUSINESS TYPE: Corporation - Profit
AUTH SHARES - COMMON: 200
PAR VALUE - COMMON: No Par Value

DATE INCORPORATED: 05/21/1965
STATE OF INCORP: California

Business started May 21, 1965 by Leslie Smith and Kevin J. Hunt. 100% of capital stock is owned by parent company. SMITH born 1926. Married. Graduated from the University of California, Los Angeles, CA in June 1947 with a BS degree in Business Management. 1947-65 general manager for Raymor Printing Co., San Francisco, CA. 1965 formed subject with Kevin J. Hunt.

HUNT born 1925. Married. Graduated from Northwestern University, Evanston, IL in June 1946. 1946-1965 general manager for Raymor Printing Co., San Francisco, CA. 1965 formed subject with Leslie Smith.

RELATED COMPANIES: Through the financial interest of Gorman Holding Company Inc., the Gorman Manufacturing Co. Inc., is related to two other sister companies:

1. Smith Lettershop Inc., San Diego, CA; commercial printing, started 1972.
2. Gorman Suppliers Inc., Los Angeles, CA; commercial printing, started 1980.

Intercompany relations consists of loans.

OPERATION
09/11/9-

Subsidary of Gorman Holding Company Inc., Los Angeles, CA, started 1965 which operates as a holding company for its underlying subsidiaries. Parent company owns 100% of capital stock. Parent company has 2 other subsidiaries. Intercompany relations: consist of loans and advances.

A consolidated financial statement on the parent company dated Dec. 31, 1991 showed a net worth of $4,125,112, with an overall fair financial condition.

Commercial printing specializing in advertising posters, catalogs, circulars, and coupons.

Net 30 days. Has 175 accounts. Sells to commercial concerns. Territory: United States. Nonseasonal.

EMPLOYEES: 500 including officers. 150 employed here.
FACILITIES: Rents 55,000 sq. ft. on first floor of one story cinder block building in good condition. Premesis neat.
LOCATION: Central business section on well traveled street.
BRANCHES: Subject maintains a branch at 1073 Boyden Road, Los Angeles, CA.

Source: Dun & Bradstreet, a company of The Dun & Bradstreet Corporation, 1998.

CONDITIONS Conditions are the external factors that are beyond the control of a firm, but that may affect their ability to repay debts. Excess capacity in commercial real estate is one example. A lender needs to take into account excess capacity in that market before granting a loan to add to the capacity. These types of changes in conditions, such as recessions, interest rate shocks, and asset price deflation, can adversely affect borrowers and contribute to their defaulting on loans.

COMPLIANCE While the previous Cs concerned the borrower, compliance applies to the lender. Compliance with court decisions, laws, and regulations is an increasingly important part of the lending process. Banks must comply with the Community Reinvestment Act (CRA), the Environmental Superfund Act, and dozens of other laws to operate in accordance with the law and bank regulations, and to avoid lender liability. **Lender liability** means that the lender may be sued by borrowers or others for losses and damages. For example, in the case of *U.S. v. Maryland Bank and Trust Company*, the Environmental Protection Agency (EPA) sued the bank for reimbursement of cleanup costs of a hazardous waste dump after the bank foreclosed on the property. However, in *U.S. v. Fleet Factors*, the Eleventh Circuit Court of Appeals ruled that a secured lender can be liable under federal environmental laws, even absent foreclosure, if the lender participates in management to a degree that it influences the firm's treatment of hazardous waste.

Structuring Commercial Loan Agreements

When the bank decides to grant a loan, the terms of the loan are put into a contract called a *loan agreement*. The contract is structured to control the borrower to the extent necessary to assure timely repayment of the loan. All commercial loans have the following elements:

1. The type of credit facility (e.g., term loan) and amount to be borrowed

2. The term of the loan (e.g., 2 years)

3. The method and timing of repayment (e.g., repaid monthly from the sale of inventory)

4. Interest rates and fees to be paid by the borrower to the banker (fixed rates, or floating rates based on the prime rate or the London interbank offered rate, LIBOR, etc.)

5. Collateral if required

6. Covenants, or promises by the borrower to take or not to take certain actions during the term of the loan (e.g., the borrower will provide the bank with quarterly financial statements; the borrower will not incur additional long-term debt without the bank's prior permission).

See http://www.bog.frb.fed.us/boarddocs/surveys/ *for senior loan officers' opinions of bank lending practices.*

Know Your Customer—Especially If He or She Is an Illegal Drug Trafficker

Banks must "know their customers." What it means is that the bank must make reasonable efforts to determine who the borrower is, a credit history, the purpose of the loan, and other relevant information. Consider the following case. A bank made a one-year, $800,000 first mortgage loan to a Panamanian corporation. The loan was collateralized with a $1.1 million home owned by the corporation. After the loan was made, a government investigation discovered that the Panamanian corporation was owned by an illegal drug trafficker. The government seized the property claiming that it had probable cause to believe that the house was purchased with the proceeds from illegal drug sales. The government also claimed that the bank's president, who made the loan, should have known that the owner of the property was a drug trafficker.

Under federal laws, property that has been purchased with laundered money is subject to government seizure and forfeiture, even when it is collateral for a bank loan. Laundered money refers to money obtained by illegal means, such as through illegal drug sales, and converted into legitimate uses

without revealing it source. If the bank was an "innocent" lienholder in the loan, the court may "pardon" the property. However, the bank must first prove it had no knowledge of the illegal activity that led to the forfeiture. In the case of the loan to the Panamanian corporation, the court ruled that the bank was "willfully blind" to a number of obvious facts that it should have taken into account in making the loan. These facts were that the borrower was a Panamanian shell corporation whose sole asset was the property, which was vacant and up for sale. The bank did not know the purpose of the loan or how it was going to be repaid. It did do a title search on the property. The loan proceeds were transferred to Switzerland. Some of the loan proceeds were used to buy expensive gifts for the bank president's family, and more. The bank lost $800,000 plus attorney fees.

Source: Cliff E. Cook, "Complying with the Spirit of BSA: 'Know Your Customer' Policies and Suspicious Transactions Reporting," *ABA Bank Compliance* (Summer 1991), reprinted in U.S. Senate, *Current Trends in Money Laundering*. Hearing before the permanent subcommittee on investigations of the committee on governmental affairs, 102 Cong. 2nd. Sess. (February 27, 1992), pp. 328–329.

Pricing Commercial Loans

One key element in the process of commercial lending is **loan pricing**—determining what interest rate to charge the borrower and how to calculate that rate. The interest rate may be determined by using a *loan pricing model*. The purpose of loan pricing models is to determine the minimum price that a bank should charge on a commercial loan. Before we examine loan pricing, let's consider the effective yield.

How to Calculate Effective Yield The difference between the *nominal interest rate*—the interest rate stated in the loan agreement—and the *effective yield* takes into account the payment accrual basis and the payment frequency. The method for calculating effective yields is explained after some terms have been defined.

The *payment accrual basis* refers to the number of days used in the interest rate calculation. One part of the calculation involves the number of days in a year. Interest may be calculated on the basis of a 365-day year or a 360-day year. To illustrate the difference, consider a $1 million loan at a 10% nominal rate of interest. The daily interest payment (interest income to the bank and interest expense to the borrower) of the loan is determined by multiplying the amount of the loan by the nominal interest rate and then dividing by the appropriate number of days (365 or 360), and multiplying that figure by the amount of the loan. Accordingly, the cost of a $1 million loan at 10% interest is $273.97 per day on a 365-day basis and $277.78 on a 360-day basis.

Another part of the calculation involves the number of days that the loan is outstanding. One can use the actual number of days the loan is outstanding, or one can use a 30-day month base.

The final variable is the frequency of interest payments. Typically, term loans are structured with monthly, quarterly, or annual payments. Because of the time value of money (money is worth more today than if the same amount is received in the future), frequent payments are favored by bankers but harder to sell to borrowers. The effect of payment frequency on interest earned and yields will be explained shortly.

To illustrate the effective yield, let's consider a 345-day term loan beginning on January 1 and ending on December 11. The principal amount is $1 million and the interest rate is 10%. The calculations for a 360-day year and 30-day month are as follows:

$1,000,000	Principal amount	7.1
× 0.10	Annual interest rate	
$100,000	Annual interest amount	
360	Divided by number of days in year (360 or 365)	
$277.78	Daily interest payment	
× 341	Times (11 months × 30-day months + 11 days)	
$94,722.22	Total interest paid	

$$\text{Effective yield} = \frac{\text{Total interest paid}}{\text{Principal amount}} \times \frac{365}{\text{Term of loan in days}}$$

$$= \frac{\$94,722.22}{\$1,000,000.00} \times \frac{365}{345} = 10.02\%$$

The same process may be used to calculate the effective yields for 360-day years with actual number of days and 365-day year with actual number of days. The effective yield for the three methods are as follows:

	Effective Yield
360-day year/30-day month	10.02%
360-day year/actual number of days	10.14%
365-day year/actual number of days	10.00%

EFFECT OF PAYMENT FREQUENCY ON INTEREST EARNED AND YIELDS The frequency of loan payments has a major impact on interest earned and the yield received on loans. Suppose that a bank is considering making a one-year $100,000 loan at 12%. The $100,000 loan will be repaid at the end of the year. The bank earns $12,000.00 if interest is paid annually, and $12,747.46 if it is paid daily. The bank earns more when interest is collected frequently.

Payment Periods	Interest Earned on $100,000 Loan	Yield
Continuous	$12,748.28	12.748%
Daily	$12,747.46	12.747%
Monthly	$12,682.50	12.683%
Quarterly	$12,550.88	12.551%
Annually	$12,000.00	12.000%

The amount that the bank receives at the end of the period may be determined by the equation for the future value of $1:

$$FV_n = PV_0(1 + i/m)^{nm} \qquad 7.2$$

where

FV_n = future value at end of n periods
PV_0 = present value ($100,000 in this example)
i = interest rate
n = number of periods
m = number of interyear periods (days, months, quarters)

Thus, the amount earned if interest is collected monthly is:

$$FV_{12} = \$100,000(1 + 0.12/12)^{1 \times 12}$$
$$= \$112,682.50$$

Interest earned is the difference between FV_{12} and PV_0, which is:

$$\$112,682.50 - \$100,000 = \$12,682.50$$

It follows that the annual yield is[21]

$$FV_n = PV_0(1 + 0.12/12)^{n \times 12}$$
$$= 12.683\%$$

---

21. The continuous yield is determined by calculating $e^{in} = (2.718)^{0.12 \times 1} = 12.7483\%$, where e = Euler's constant, and where e^{in} is the limit of $(1 + i/m)^{nm}$.

Many loans are amortized, which means that the principal is reduced with periodic payments. Methods for computing the annual interest rates (APR) on such loans are explained in connection with consumer loans in Chapter 8.

LOAN PRICING When profit margins on commercial loans are razor thin, precise estimates of cost are necessary to price the loans correctly. Overpricing of loans results in some borrowers going elsewhere to obtain loans. Underpricing of loans results in banks earning less than they should for a given level of risk. Consistent underpricing could adversely affect both the profits and the value of banks making that error.

Many banks price commercial loans by using an index rate (i.e., prime rate) plus a markup of one or more percentage points. Other banks use the cost of borrowed funds (i.e., 90-day CD rate) plus a markup. The advantage of using markups above prime of the cost of CDs is that they are simple and easy to understand. Markups are supposed to compensate the bank for the risk it takes in making a loan, as well as providing a return on its investment. The disadvantage of using markups is that they may not properly account for risk, the cost of funds, and operating expenses. The result may be that some loans are mispriced. The alternative is to use loan pricing models that properly account for risk, costs, and returns.

RETURN ON NET FUNDS EMPLOYED Of the many types of loan pricing models, the one presented here illustrates some of the factors going into loan pricing. This loan pricing model establishes the required rate of return that the bank wants to earn on the loan, and then it determines the net income that the loan must generate to provide that return. If the loan cannot generate sufficient net income to earn the required rate of return, the bank should consider rejecting it. We will examine each of the components of the model and then solve for loan income.

$$\text{Marginal cost of funds} + \text{Profit goal} = \frac{\text{Loan income} - \text{Loan expense}}{\text{Net bank funds employed}} \qquad 7.3$$

REQUIRED RATE OF RETURN In this model, the required rate of return is equal to the marginal cost of funds plus a profit goal. The marginal cost of capital (funds) is the rate of return required by debt and equity investors on newly issued funds they provide to the bank.[22] That rate may differ from the rate of return required by the bank's management. We make the simplifying assumption that the marginal cost of capital is the *weighted average cost of capital* (WACC).[23] In this example, we further assume that WACC is 6%. A detailed

22. Risk-based capital weights are not considered here because commercial loans have a 100% risk weighting.
23. If the increased equity results in the bank being perceived by investors as being less risky, the cost of borrowing may be reduced, which may lower the WACC.

explanation of how to calculate WACC for a bank appears in appendix 7B at the end of this chapter.

$$k_w = k_d(1 - T)L + k_e(1 - L)$$ 7.4

where

k_w = weighted average cost of capital of new funds
k_d = cost of interest-bearing liabilities
k_e = cost of equity
T = corporate tax rate
L = ratio of liabilities to assets

PROFIT GOAL Although the cost of capital takes into account the average risk of the bank, the profit goal must consider the specific risk of each loan, including the risk of bankruptcy as measured by a loan's Z (zeta) score.[24]

The percentages we discuss here reflect the profit goal and are added to the WACC. The size of the markup is directly related to the risk of the loan under consideration. High-risk loans require larger markups than low-risk loans. The criteria for classifying the riskiness of the loan may include the strength of the financial statement, relative position the firm holds in the industry, collateral, and other factors. When all the factors are considered, the firms may be classified as having, say, very low, low, average, or high risk.

Liquidity, measured in terms of years, must be considered when evaluating the profit goal. Short-term loans are more liquid than long-term loans.

The combination of risk and liquidity can be used to determine a profit goal. For example, the profit goal shown here for a very low risk loan made for one year or less is 1.0%. If the loan had a maturity of three to five years, a 1.2% return would be required. The profit goal increases with the risk and the maturity of the loan. The profit goals based on risk and liquidity are determined by management's judgment. Thus, they will vary from bank to bank.

Profit Goal for Term of Loans

Class of Risk	Under 1 Year	3–5 Years
Very low	1.0	1.2
Low	1.5	1.8
Average	2.0	2.4
High	2.6	3.1

24. For additional discussion of the use of the Z (zeta) score in loan pricing, see Edward I. Altman, "Valuation, Loss Reserves, and Pricing of Commercial Loans," *The Journal of Commercial Lending* (August 1993), pp. 8–25.

LOAN EXPENSE Loan expense includes all direct and indirect costs associated with making, servicing, and collecting the loan. However, it does not include the bank's cost of funds. Making effective cost estimates to be used in a pricing model is difficult to do. To illustrate the difficulty, suppose that a loan officer spent 35 hours of working time trying to attract a new loan customer. Let's consider only the officer's time, which is worth $100 per hour. The cost is $3,500. If the customer borrows $10,000 for 90 days, the equation suggests that the bank would have to charge more than $3,500 (35%) to cover that cost alone. Obviously, the bank would not attempt to charge that amount. To pay for the loan officer's time, the bank uses cost accounting data in trying to make reasonable estimates about the cost of making, servicing, and collecting loans.

NET BANK FUNDS EMPLOYED The net bank funds employed is the average amount of the loan over its life, less funds provided by the borrower, net of Federal Reserve System reserve requirements. Borrowers provide funds in the form of compensating balances or other balances held at the bank. The bank cannot use the entire amount on deposit because it is required by the Federal Reserve System to maintain a specified amount of reserves against those balances.

To illustrate the use of Eq. (7.4), let's make the following assumptions:

1. Marginal cost of funds is 6%.
2. Profit goal is 2%.
3. Loan expense is $2,000.
4. Net bank funds employed are $100,000.

Given these assumptions, we use Eq. (17.4) to solve for loan income:

$$(6\% + 2\%) = (\text{Loan income} - \$2,000)/\$100,000$$
$$\text{Loan income} = \$10,000$$

The $10,000 is the amount of income this loan must generate in order for the bank to earn its required rate of return. This figure understates the correct amount because it does not take the time value of money into account. Nevertheless, it is a good "ballpark" estimate of the income that is needed.

This loan pricing model is best suited for banks that have effective cost accounting data and can estimate the order data that are required. If this model is used to price variable rate loans, the rate of return to the bank will change whenever the loan rate changes. This problem is resolved in the next model.

RELATIONSHIP PRICING The loan pricing model that was examined did not take into account other business relationships that the borrower may have with the bank. For example, the borrower may be using cash management services, have a pension fund managed by the bank, and use the other bank facilities. Each of these activities generates positive income. When, and under what circumstances, should a borrower's relationships be considered?

To answer that question, we must think of making a loan as a new investment opportunity. All relevant cash flows must be evaluated. If the loan is the only business that the borrower has with the bank, then only the cash flows associated with the loan are relevant. However, if the loan is one of many services provided by the bank, then all cash flows associated with that borrower's relationship with the bank must be evaluated. The projected cash flow from each service, including the loan, should be adjusted to take risks into account. In *relationship pricing*, the rate charged on a loan may differ from the rate indicated by the loan pricing model presented previously.

MINIMUM SPREAD   Some banks price loans by determining the minimum spread they will accept between their lending rate and their costs plus a profit margin. For example, assume that a bank's costs are 12% and the profit margin is 2%. If the bank wants to encourage lending, it will accept a smaller profit margin and charge borrowers 13%. If the bank wants to retard lending, it will increase the spread and charge borrowers 15%. Encouraging and discouraging lending is a common practice and reflects banks' changing financial needs. The banks know that many large commercial loans are repriced every day or every 30, 60, or 90 days. Large borrowers regularly shop for the lowest rates. A bank that increases its lending rate in one period to discourage a borrower may decide to make the loan the next time it is repriced. Loans to corporations waiting to sell commercial paper are an example of loans that are repriced frequently.

AVERAGE COST VERSUS MARGINAL COST   The costs used in this model include the cost of funds and operating costs. Here too the problems in determining the relevant costs arise. Because operating costs have been discussed previously, let's focus on the cost of funds. Should the bank use the *average cost of funds* or the marginal cost of funds? In the explanation of the cost of capital, the marginal and average costs were the same, which is not always the case. To illustrate this problem, suppose that a firm wants to borrow $1 million for 90 days. The bank's lending rate is the cost of funds plus 1 percentage point per annum. The hypothetical bank raised $0.5 million by selling a 90-day CD at 12%. In addition, the bank has $0.5 million in other interest-rate sensitive liabilities that cost 8%. For simplicity, we ignore equity. The average cost of borrowed funds, which is determined by dividing total interest cost by total funds employed, is 10%. The marginal cost of funds, or the 90-day CD rate, is 12%.

Should the bank use the average cost of funds or the marginal cost of funds to price the loan? When market rates of interest are rising, the bank is better off using the marginal cost of funds because it is higher than the average cost of funds. However, when market rates of interest are falling, it is better off using the average cost of funds, which is higher than the marginal cost.

Another consideration is how the loan is funded. If the $1 million, 90-day loan was *match-funded* by selling a $1 million, 90-day CD, the CD rate could be used to represent the borrowed funds. Although not mentioned previously, the bank would have to raise more than $1 million in order to cover reserve requirements. Suppose that reserve requirements are 5%. The bank would have to raise $1,052,632 ($1,000,000/0.95 = $1,052,632) in order to lend $1 million.

If the bank views all its deposits as a "pool" of funds used to finance loans, the answer is still the marginal rate. In theory, the marginal loan (the next loan to be made) should be charged the marginal cost of funds including the cost of equity.

All of the examples used here suggest that in order to make a profit, a bank's lending rate should be greater than its cost of funds, including equity.

PERFORMANCE PRICING The price of a loan reflects the riskiness of the borrower. When the borrower's riskiness changes, the price of the loan should be changed accordingly. One way to reprice a loan is through *performance pricing*, which allows banks and borrowers to change the price of a loan without renegotiating it. The price can be tied to specific financial ratios, the amount of the loan outstanding, the borrower's debt ratings, or other criteria that are mutually agreeable.

Monitoring and Loan Review

After the loan has been granted, the bank must monitor the loan to determine whether the borrower is complying with the terms of the loan agreement. Part of the monitoring process is a loan review, which is an internal audit system for the lending functions of the bank. Loan reviews help to identify potential problems with particular loans and weaknesses in loan procedures. In addition, it is used to help quantify the risk in the loan portfolio.

Payoffs or Losses?

One of four things can happen to an outstanding loan: (1) it can be repaid on schedule; (2) it can be renewed or extended; (3) it can be sold by the bank to another investor; or (4) it can go into default, causing the bank to sustain losses. Items 1–3 are desirable outcomes. Item 4 is the worst-case scenario for the bank.

SUMMARY

Banks make most of their money by lending, and lending accounts for most of their risk, or credit risk. Recall from Chapter 1 that credit risk is the primary cause of bank failure. Simply stated, credit risk is the risk to earnings and capital that an obligor will fail to meet the terms of a contract with the bank. The asymmetric information and adverse selection play important roles in credit risk. With asymmetric information, borrowers know more about their business prospects than banks, and the banks tend to attract the higher-risk borrowers. Asymmetric information, coupled with increased competition for lending from nonbank lenders, has resulted in banks shifting their portfolios to higher-risk loans in hopes of increasing their profitability. Changes in technology, such as securitization and credit scoring, also have affected the ways loans are made and serviced.

The process of lending begins with the board of director's written loan policy that sets out the guidelines within which the bank must operate. Given those limits, which will vary from bank to bank, various techniques can be used to reduce credit risk (avoiding high risk loans, diversification, etc.). Against this background, the ways (soliciting loans, buying loans, commitments, etc.) that banks make C&I loans was explained. Loans should be made with the expectation that it will be repaid from earnings or the sale of assets. Collateral is a secondary source of repayment.

Banks make different types of C&I loans for different purposes. Lines of credit, for example, are used to finance temporary or seasonal working capital needs. Term loans are used to finance the acquisition of real assets and for other purposes. The use of collateral is a common practice in C&I lending. Collateral reduces the risk to the bank and serves as an incentive to the borrower to repay the loan. Almost anything that is legal can be used as collateral. However, the most common forms of collateral include accounts receivable, inventory, equipment, and real estate.

Before loans are granted, the lender must evaluate the creditworthiness of the prospective borrower. The borrower's character, financial condition, and ability to repay the loan from future income or the sale of assets are of primary importance. A detailed description of financial analysis appears in Appendix 7A. The bank must also comply with numerous federal regulations before and after credit is extended. In addition, the bank must price the loan so that it is fair to the customer and profitable for the bank. Different pricing models result in different interest earnings. Once the request is evaluated and accepted, the loan agreement is developed that provides details about how the funds will be used, how they will be repaid, and other terms. After the loan is granted, the bank must monitor the loan to assure repayment. The best outcome is that the loan is repaid in full. The worst outcome is that it is charged off as a loss.

Key Terms and Concepts

Adverse selection
Asset-based lending
Asymmetric information
Bankers' acceptance
Board of directors written loan
   policy
Bridge loan
Charged-off (loan)
Collateral
Commercial and Industrial Loan
   (C&I)
Credit risk
Credit scoring

Factoring
Financial leases
Leasing
Lender liability
Line of credit
Loan commitment
Loan pricing
Moral hazard
Operating leases
Overdraft
Pledging
Revolving loan
Term loan

Questions

7.1 How can banks reduce their credit risk?

7.2 Explain the concepts of asymmetric risk and adverse selection in connection with commercial lending.

7.3 What is credit scoring and how is it used in commercial lending?

7.4 Explain the difference between a line of credit and a revolving loan.

7.5 What type of loan should be used to finance:
(a) seasonal inventory needs?
(b) construction of a warehouse?
(c) refinancing debt?
(d) Acquiring equipment?

7.6 What are the sources of repayment of term loans?

7.7 How does asset-based lending differ from other types of lending?

7.8 Explain the role of documentation in the lending process.

7.9 Does the payment of a commitment fee and a loan commitment guarantee that a bank will make funds available to a borrower?

7.10 List the five characteristics of good collateral.

7.11 How does collateral benefit lenders?

7.12 True or false: The quality of a loan guarantee depends on the quality of the guarantor. Explain your answer.

7.13 How does pledging accounts receivable differ from factoring?

7.14 What is the role of the board of directors in the lending process? Why is a written loan policy important?

7.15 How does the effective yield differ from the nominal interest rate on a loan?

7.16 Why do many loan pricing models ignore the cost of equity?

7.17 Many banks use relationship pricing. What does that mean? What is the implication for loan pricing?

7.18 Under what circumstances is a loan charged-off, and what does that mean? What is the effect on earnings?

7.19 Carla Fernandez owns a fleet of taxi cabs. The cabs are leased to taxi drivers for periods of one year or longer. The cabs are used for about two years before they are sold. She asked her attorney for advice on borrowing money from a bank to acquire more cabs. He recommended a line of credit so that she could borrow the funds when she needed them. He further suggested that the lease agreements could be used as collateral for the loans. If you were a bank loan officer, what would you tell Carla about her attorney's suggestion?

7.20 The key performance objectives established by the Board of Directors of Commonwealth Bank include (1) achieving a secure and sustainable return on shareholder's investment, (2) achieving a profit performance that compares well within the industry, and (3) managing our business with prudence to avoid levels of risk that could threaten our profitability. Are these performance objectives consistent? Explain your answer.

7.21 Suppose that you served on a large bank's management committee. Issues facing the committee today are how to fund a $15 million, three-year loan and whether the interest rate charged on the loan should be floating or fixed. The loan request has been approved, but the details of the credit facility have not yet been worked out. Given the current economic and financial outlook, what is your recommendation?

7.22 According to the Survey of Term of Lending (Federal Reserve statistical release E.2, which can be found on the web at *http://www.bog. frb.fed.us/releases*), what is the average size and maturity for all C&I loans? What percentage of the C&I loans are secured by collateral? What is the most common base pricing rate?

Problems

7.1 Alpine Cotton Mill wants to factor $312,500 in accounts receivable. The Northern Bank is willing to factor 80% of that amount. Northern charges a 3% commission, requires 8% of the factored amount to be held in reserve, and charges 18% per annum on the amount advanced. Northern can invest its funds at a 7% per annum return. How much will Northern earn during the first month of factoring?

7.2 Newton Mfg. is shopping for a loan commitment for $10 million for 60 days. Bank A is willing to make the commitment for 3.33 percent on a 360-day year basis. Bank B is offering the same rate but uses a 365-day year. Which one should Newton take, and how much will be saved?

7.3 A $500,000 loan is made for 90 days at 8% per annum. Compute the effective yield using
(a) 360-day year/30 day months.
(b) 365-day year/actual number of days.

7.4 Using the net bank funds employed pricing model, determine how much loan income the following loan must generate to produce the required returns. Marginal cost of funds is 12%, profit goal is 3%, loan expense is $5,000, and the amount of the loan is $220,000.

7.5 Compute the annual interest earned on a $350,000 loan, at 10% interest compounded monthly, quarterly, and annually.

7.6 Compute the weighted average cost of capital for a bank using the following information: equity = 8%, tax rate = 25%, cost of debt 8%, cost of equity = 12%.

7.7 A 5% commitment fee on a $1 million loan for 6 months (180 days) is equal to what return?

Financial Analysis

7A.1 REASONS FOR USING FINANCIAL ANALYSIS

Financial analysis is used by commercial banks for two reasons. The first reason is to determine the financial condition and creditworthiness of potential and existing customers. For banks, making loans results in credit risk. Credit risk means that the customers to whom credit has been extended may default on their payment for the goods and services they received resulting in a loss to the bank. Credit risk is represented by loans, which account for about 60 percent of banks' total assets.

The second reason we use financial analysis is to monitor the financial behavior of customers after credit has been extended. Monitoring is necessary to detect activities that could impair customers' ability to pay their loans and accounts payable or to honor commitments to buy products that take a long time to produce. For example, retail firms in distress might liquidate inventory at unprofitable prices in order to increase their cash flow in the short run. An increase in sales at unprofitable prices can only result in bankruptcy over time. ■

7A.2 GENERAL OBSERVATIONS AND CAVEATS ABOUT FINANCIAL ANALYSIS

Comparisons Are Relative

Suppose that you read that the score of a football game was 32 for your team. The problem is that your team's 32 points could be a winning or losing score, depending on what the other team scored. Thus, scores are relative. Similarly, analysis of data, such as the growth of sales or profitability, cannot be examined in isolation. The data must be judged relative to (1) historical trends, and (2) other firms that are peers.

Historical Trends

Analysis of historical data is important. While data for one or two years may be an aberration, data for five years or longer provide a good basis for trend analysis. Substantial deviations from a trend may be considered red flags, or warning signs that something is happening that warrants further investigation. The deviation from the trend may be good or bad.

The red flag tells what happened—the figures deviated from a trend, some important figure such as total assets experienced a large change. The important issue is *why* the deviation occurred. The key to meaningful financial analysis is explaining both *what* and *why* significant changes occurred.

Comparisons with Other Firms

Financial data should be compared to firms of similar size, in the same industry, and located in the same geographic region. By way of illustration, let's compare the return on assets of small and large commercial banks, and banks located in the Midwest and Northeast in 1999. The return on assets is a broad measure of profitability that will be defined shortly. As shown in Table 7A.1, the return on assets for small banks is substantially lower than that for large banks. Similarly, banks located in the Midwest were more profitable than those in the Northeast. These numbers reveal that size and geographic location should be considered when selecting peer banks for comparison. When making comparisons in other industries, similar factors pertinent to those industries should be taken into account.

AVERAGE DATA   Comparing data for a firm to an average for other firms can be misleading too. Average is a measure of central tendency, and comes in different types: arithmetic mean, median, mode, and geometric. By definition, half of the firms are more profitable than the median average return, and the other half are less profitable. The real issue is not whether a firm is above or below average, but how much the firm deviates from the average. A small deviation is no cause for concern. A large deviation is a *red flag*, something that warrants further investigation.

TABLE 7A.I	Commercial Bank's Return on Assets	
		Return on Assets (%)
Bank Size		
Small banks (assets of less than $100 million)		1.08
Large banks (assets of more than $10 billion)		1.21
Geographic Region		
Midwest		1.57
Northeast		1.15

Source: FDIC, *Quarterly Bank Profile* (First Half 1999).

LIFO/FIFO Differences in accounting practices between firms may distort comparisons. For example, some firms use the LIFO (last in, first out) method of inventory valuation, and others use FIFO (first in, first out). During periods of inflation, FIFO can result in overstating profits and, thus, in overstating profitability. Even during periods of price stability, the two methods yield substantially different profits. By way of illustration, suppose that a firm purchases 10 items of inventory at $5 each and then 10 more items at $8 each. For simplicity, we assume that the firm has no other inventory. If the firm uses the FIFO method, items are sold in the order in which they were purchased. If 15 items are sold, 10 items will be assigned a cost of $5 each, and 5 items will be assigned a cost of $8 each. The total of goods sold is $90. Because inventory purchases total $130, and the cost of goods sold is $90, the remaining inventory is valued at $40. Let's say the 15 items sold were priced at $12 each, giving a gross sales figure of $180. With the cost of goods sold at $90, the profit is $90.

If, instead, the firm uses LIFO, the results are quite different. With LIFO the cost of the last items purchased is assigned first. Profit under the LIFO method is $75. Similarly, different methods of depreciating fixed assets can affect profitability and financial ratios (see Table 7A.2).

LIFE CYCLE CONSIDERATIONS The life cycle of a firm should be kept in mind when analyzing financial data.[1] It is common practice to use industry average to make financial comparisons. However, firms that are just beginning to grow are not going to have the same financial characteristics as mature firms. For example, mature firms are expected to pay cash dividends, but start-up firms

1. For additional discussion of this topic, see Benton E. Gup and Pankaj Agrrawal, "The Product Life Cycle: A Paradigm for Understanding Financial Management," *Financial Practice and Education* (Fall/Winter 1996), pp. 41–48.

TABLE 7A.2	Comparison of LIFO Versus FIFO Inventory Methods		
		FIFO	**LIFO**
First inventory purchase			
(10 items at $5 each)		$ 50	$ 50
Second inventory purchase			
(10 items at $8 each)		80	80
Total inventory purchases		$130	$130
Cost of goods sold (15 items)			
10 at $5 = $50; 10 at $8 = $80		$ 50	$ 80
5 at $8 = $40; 5 at $5 = $25		40	25
Total cost of goods sold		$ 90	$105
Inventory Balance at End of Period			
Beginning inventory (assumed)		$ 0	$ 0
Total inventory purchases		130	130
Less total cost of goods sold		90	105
Value of ending inventory		$ 40	$ 25
Profit			
Gross sales (15 items at $12 each)		$180	$180
Less total cost of goods sold		90	105
Gross profit		$ 90	$ 75

are not in a financial position to do so. Without understanding the life cycle concept, one could misinterpret the data to mean that the new firm is performing poorly in comparison to the industry average; whereas in reality, it may be doing relatively well, given its stage of development.

7A.3   RATIO ANALYSIS

To illustrate the process of financial analysis, we will refer to the financial statements for Ajax Manufacturing Corporation. Ajax Manufacturing Corporation designs and produces parts used in household appliances and industrial equipment. Ajax's true identity has been disguised to eliminate any prior knowledge that the readers may have concerning the company or its operations.

Our analysis will be from point of view of a loan officer who wants to evaluate the overall condition of Ajax, to assess its strengths and weaknesses, before he visits the firm to offer them his bank's services.

Balance Sheet

The balance sheet shown in Table 7A.3 represents a statement of financial condition on one particular date. It is analogous to a snapshot of Ajax's financial condition on one day, December 31. Assets represent resources that the company owns or controls. Assets include *financial assets* (cash, investments, receivables, etc.), *real assets* (property, plant, and equipment), and some firms have *intangible assets* (patents, trademarks, etc.). Assets that are expected to be converted into cash within one year, or an operating cycle, are called *current assets*. An *operating cycle* refers to the time when inventory is purchased until cash is collected after the goods are sold.

Ajax had total assets of $818,219,575 at the end of 2004, compared to $794,521,255 at the end of the previous year. The increase in assets indicates that Ajax is growing in size. But bigger may not be better. More analysis is required.

Liabilities represent what the company owes to others. It is the amount that various creditors have invested in the business. Liabilities due to be paid within one year, or within an operating cycle, are called *current liabilities*. The remainder of the liabilities includes long-term debts and leases and deferred liabilities. *Deferred taxes*, for example, represent amounts that may be owed in taxes due to timing differences in income earned but not yet recognized for tax purposes.

Not all liabilities are shown on the balance sheet. For example, post-retirement benefits are described in the notes at the end of the financial statements. Financial Accounting Standards Board Statement No. 106 requires employers that provide certain post-retirement benefits to recognize those costs and to report them. Other firms may have commitments, contingent liabilities, or be engaged in hedging (buying and selling futures contracts), all of which are described in the notes. (The point is that you must read all of the notes!)

Stockholders' equity represents the owners' investment in the business. It is a claim against assets. It is not funds that the stockholders can withdraw from the firm. For Ajax, stockholders' equity includes the value of the stock purchased by the stockholders, earnings that have been retained, stock that has been repurchased by the company (treasury stock), and an accounting adjustment representing changes in the value of foreign currencies in connection with their foreign operations.

By definition, total assets must equal total liabilities plus stockholders' equity.

Income Statement

The *income statement* represents a firm's revenues and expenses during an accounting period such as a year or a quarter. The statement is reported on an accrual basis rather than a cash basis. An *accrual basis* means that revenues are recognized in the accounting period when they are earned, regardless of when the

TABLE 7A.3	Consolidated Balance Sheets for Ajax Manufacturing Corporation and Subsidiaries (Years Ended December 31, 2004, 2003)		
($ millions)		**2004**	**2003**
Assets			
Current Assets			
Cash		$ 3,344,075	$ 1,487,676
Temporary investments		10,073,726	11,734,261
Trade accounts receivable, less allowances		137,299,371	35,065,650
Inventories		162,086,784	173,168,270
Prepaid expenses and other current assets		7,896,024	7,269,878
Future income tax benefits		6,406,485	5,725,166
Total Current Assets		327,106,465	334,450,901
Other Assets		35,976,963	36,815,088
Property, Plant, and Equipment			
Land		2,593,311	3,223,368
Buildings		173,661,175	151,716,975
Machinery and equipment		546,629,604	504,747,066
Construction in progress		46,727,823	32,118,483
		769,611,913	691,805,892
Less allowances for depreciation and amortization		(314,475,766)	(268,550,626)
		455,136,147	423,255,266
		$ 818,219,575	$ 794,521,255

cash is received. Similarly, expenses are recognized in the accounting period when they are incurred, regardless of when the cash is paid. This practice explains why deferred taxes are included on the balance sheet. A *cash basis* means that revenues and expenses are recognized when they are received or paid.

Table 7A.4 reveals that Ajax's net sales increased during the three-year period shown. The major categories of expenses include cost of goods sold; selling, general, and administrative expenses; interest expense; and taxes. When the expenses were deducted from the revenues, net income declined. This result suggests that Ajax is doing some things that appear to be beneficial to stockholders, such as increasing sales. However, Ajax has problems too, as evidenced by the decline in income. We will use data from these and other tables to analyze Ajax and try to find the cause of its problems. Selected indus-

TABLE 7A.3	Consolidated Balance Sheets for Ajax Manufacturing Corporation and Subsidiaries (Years Ended December 31, 2004, 2003) *(continued)*

($ millions)	2004	2003
Liabilities and Stockholders' Equity		
Current Liabilities		
Notes payable	$ 7,167,285	$ 6,684,796
Accounts payable and accrued expenses		
Trade accounts	23,896,090	38,826,568
Employee compensation	14,355,414	10,523,668
Other	4,456,928	4,921,527
	42,708,432	54,271,763
Federal and state income taxes	10,709,170	11,528,267
Current maturities of long-term debt and capital lease obligations	11,129,575	12,283,430
Total Current Liabilities	71,714,462	84,768,256
Long-Term Debt and Capital Lease		
Obligations (less current maturities and unamortized debt discount)	180,338,551	191,257,695
Deferred Liabilities		
Federal and state income taxes	48,656,564	49,727,625
Accrued pension and other	9,424,669	6,815,997
	$ 58,081,233	$ 56,543,622
Redeemable Cumulative Preferred Stock		
Par value $.01 per share; authorized 10,000,000 shares; issued and outstanding 558,443 shares in 2004 and 559,943 shares in 2003	5,584,430	5,599,430
Stockholders' Equity		
Common stock, par value $.01 per share; shares outstanding: 40,889,909 in 2004; 40,919,638 in 2003	414,200	414,200
Paid-in capital	47,383,897	48,494,262
Retained earnings	465,552,899	422,221,703
Treasury stock	(13,601,818)	(15,811,931)
Currency translation adjustment	2,751,721	1,034,018
	502,500,899	456,352,252
	$ 818,219,575	$ 794,521,255

TABLE 7A.4	Consolidated Statements of Income for Ajax Manufacturing Corporation and Subsidiaries (Years Ended December 31, 2004, 2003, 2002)		
	2004	2003	2002
Net sales	804,584,939	$713,821,344	$687,954,312
Cost of goods sold	553,159,643	461,280,501	457,874,872
	251,425,296	252,531,843	230,079,440
Selling, general, and administrative expenses	142,773,638	126,269,548	109,724,386
	108,651,658	126,262,295	120,355,054
Other deductions (income)			
Interest expense incurred	18,096,696	18,884,674	15,643,287
Other, net	(310,980)	(2,294,670)	1,983,444
	17,785,716	16,590,004	17,626,731
Income Before Taxes	90,865,942	109,672,291	102,728,323
Federal and state income taxes			
Currently payable	35,779,380	38,897,000	32,314,689
Deferred	(1,752,380)	2,828,000	5,678,891
	34,027,000	41,725,000	37,993,580
Net income	56,838,942	67,947,291	64,734,743
Preferred stock dividends	559,568	568,943	571,943
Net Income Applicable to Common Shareholders	$ 56,279,374	$ 67,378,348	$ 64,162,800
Net income per common and common equivalent shares	$ 1.38	$ 1.65	$ 1.57
Dividends per share	$ 0.32	$ 0.32	$ 0.28

try data will be used for comparisons. Only two consecutive years of balance sheet data are presented here for ease of exposition. However, the use of longer periods, such as five years, is recommended for trend analysis.

Average Versus Year-End Data

Ratios, using data from both the balance sheet and income statement, can be calculated in two ways. Because the balance sheet represents one day (December 31), and the income statement may represent one year (365 days), the first method uses the same time period when computing ratios that involve both statements by averaging data from two balance sheets so that the data cover the same period as the income statement. For example:

Assets at Year-End December 31 (from Table 7A.3)	
2004	$ 818,219,575
2003	794,521,255
Total	$1,612,740,830
Average	$ 806,370,415

This amount represents the average assets of the firm during the course of one year. This figure can be used when comparing, say, net income to average total assets:

$$\frac{\text{Net Income 2004}}{\text{Average total assets}} = \frac{\$56,838,942}{\$806,370,415} = 0.0705 \text{ or } 7.11\%$$

The second method uses year-end balance sheet data instead of average balance sheet data. Computing the same ratio for 2004 using year-end data yields a different result:

$$\frac{\text{Net Income 2004}}{\text{Year-end assets 2004}} = \frac{\$56,838,942}{\$818,219,575} = 0.0695 \text{ or } 6.95\%$$

The first method is more accurate because the average balance sheet data and the income statement cover the same time period. One drawback of this method is that it requires the use of two years of balance sheet data to calculate one average balance sheet figure. Because many publicly held companies provide only two years of balance sheet data in their annual and quarterly reports, comparisons are difficult. Therefore, some credit analysts use year-end data because (1) they can calculate the ratio for two years, and (2) it's easier to calculate. Both methods provide similar insights into the financial condition of a firm as long as they are used consistently. Only two years of balance sheet data are shown in the examples given here. Therefore, we will use year-end balance sheet data for the computations.

Profitability Ratios

Profitability is the ultimate test of the effectiveness of management. Profitability can be measured in terms of returns on assets, net assets, equity, and sales. The measures presented here indicate that Ajax's profitability declined.

RETURN ON ASSETS The *return on assets* (ROA) is the most comprehensive measure of profitability, measuring the productivity for shareholders, bondholders, and other creditors. ROA is calculated by dividing net income (NI) by total assets. Recall that we are going to use year-end balance sheet figures in our computations. The ratios reveal that overall profitability declined and was less than the industry average. The industry average is based on the results of three similar firms.

$$\text{ROA} = \text{NI/Total assets} \qquad\qquad 7A.1$$

$$\frac{\text{Net income 2004}}{\text{Year-end assets 2004}} = \frac{\$56,838,942}{\$818,219,575} = 0.0695 \text{ or } 6.95\%$$

$$\frac{\text{Net income 2003}}{\text{Year-end assets 2003}} = \frac{\$67,947,291}{\$794,521,255} = 8.55\%$$

Industry average = 7.83%

RETURN ON EQUITY *Return on equity* (ROE) measures the rate of return on the stockholders' investment in the corporation, which includes their paid-in capital as well as retained earnings. ROE is calculated by dividing net income by total stockholders' equity.

If a firm has large amounts of preferred stock outstanding, a similar ratio may be computed by dividing income available to common stockholders by common equity. Notice that Ajax has redeemable cumulative preferred stock outstanding (see Table 7A.3). The preferred stock is redeemable at the stockholder's option, and all of the dividends due to the preferred stockholders must be paid to them before any dividends can be paid on common stock. Technically, preferred stockholders are owners of the corporation. However, they have limited voting rights, and they receive fixed cash payments (dividends), similar to the fixed interest payments on debt. Thus, this hybrid preferred stock has some features of both debt and equity investments. Therefore, it is listed in the liability section of the balance sheet, and it is not considered part of stockholders' equity.

$$\text{ROE} = \text{NI/Common stockholders' equity} \qquad\qquad 7A.2$$

$$\text{ROE 2004} = \frac{\$56,838,942}{\$502,500,899} = 11.31\%$$

$$\text{ROE 2003} = \frac{\$67,947,291}{\$456,352,252} = 14.89\%$$

Industry average = 12.54%

Let's examine the ROE and ROA in further detail. The ROE is equal to the ROA times LR, which is a leverage ratio. The LR is one indicator of financial leverage. It indicates the dollar amount of assets that are financed by each dollar of equity:

$$\text{ROE} = \text{ROA} \times \text{LR} \qquad\qquad 7A.3$$
$$\text{NI/E} = (\text{NI/A})(\text{A/E})$$

where

$$NI = \text{net income}$$
$$E = \text{stockholders' equity}$$
$$A = \text{total assets}$$
$$LR = \text{leverage ratio (A/E)}$$

Using 2004 data for Ajax companies, we see that the leverage ratio is 1.63. In other words, every dollar of equity finances $1.63 dollars in assets. The remainder of the assets are financed by debt (including current liabilities). The relationship between debt and equity is called *financial leverage*. More will be said about financial leverage shortly.

$$ROE = ROA \times LR$$
$$NI/E = (NI/A)(A/E)$$
$$11.31\% = 6.95\% \times 1.63 \text{ times}$$

Suppose that the leverage ratio was 1.00, which means that every dollar of equity finances only $1 dollar in assets. If net income remains the same, ROE will decline to 6.95%. It means that ROE is a function of both financial leverage and net income. Observe that ROA is not affected directly by financial leverage. Both measures are affected indirectly because interest expense affects NI.

$$ROE = ROA \times LR$$
$$6.95\% = 6.95\% \times 1.00 \text{ times}$$

NET PROFIT MARGIN As previously mentioned, profitability can be measured in terms of returns on assets, net assets, equity, and sales. The *net profit margin* on sales, computed by dividing net income by net sales, is the percent of profit earned for each dollar of sales. Both the numerator and the denominator in this ratio come from the income statement. The sharp decline in the profit margins is a red flag telling us that further analysis of the income statement is required. We do this analysis when we examine common-size financial statements.

$$\text{Net profit margin} = \frac{\text{Net income}}{\text{Net sales}} \qquad \text{7A.4}$$

$$\frac{\text{Net income 2004}}{\text{Net sales 2004}} = \frac{\$56,838,942}{\$804,584,939} = 7.06\%$$

$$\frac{\text{Net income 2003}}{\text{Net sales 2003}} = \frac{\$67,947,291}{\$713,812,344} = 9.52\%$$

$$\text{Industry average} = 9.48$$

EARNINGS PER SHARE *Earnings per share* (EPS) is the statistic often quoted when profitability is discussed. The reason for its popularity is that it is relatively easy to understand and easy to relate to stock prices. Earnings per share is derived by dividing income available for common stock by the number of shares outstanding. The EPS can be reported as "basic EPS" and "diluted EPS." Basic EPS represents the income from continuing operations and net income. Diluted EPS takes into account the effect of conversion of convertible securities, warrants, and stock options.[2]

Because the number of shares outstanding can change from year to year, a firm with no change in income could have higher EPS if the number of shares declined. Many firms buy their own stock for Treasury stock, employee stock option plans (ESOP), and for other purposes. One effect of such purchases is to increase EPS.

If a firm has an extraordinary charge to earnings, such as a one-time adjustment for a change in accounting methods, earnings before and after the charge should be examined to gain a better understanding of the trend.

Net income available for common stockholders is net income less preferred stock dividend payments. Some companies have sinking fund payments that must be deducted too. Sinking fund payments are periodic payments made to retire debts.

The number of shares outstanding for Ajax is listed in the Stockholders' Equity portion of the balance sheet (Table 7A.3). The data reveal that the EPS has $1.38 in 2004 compared to $1.65 in the previous year.

$$\text{Earnings per share} = \frac{\text{Net income available for common stock}}{\text{Number of shares outstanding}} \qquad \text{7A.5}$$

$$2004 \qquad = \frac{\$56,279,374}{40,889,909} = \$1.38 \text{ per share}$$

$$2003 \qquad = \frac{\$67,378,348}{40,919,638} = \$1.65 \text{ per share}$$

DIVIDEND PAYOUT RATIO Earnings may be retained by the firm to help finance growth, or they may be paid out to the shareholders in the form of cash dividends. The extent to which earnings are paid to common stockholders in the form of cash dividends is called the *dividend payout ratio*. Strictly speaking it is not a measure of profitability, but it does relate to the distribution of profits. The payout ratio is computed by dividing cash dividends per share on common stock by earnings per share. The cash dividends per common shares are listed in Table 7A.4.[3] Ajax paid a cash dividend of $0.32 cents per share in both years. Because the dividend remained unchanged and earnings per share declined in 2004, the payout ratio increased from 19% to 23%, slightly above the industry average.

2. The terminology used here is based on Financial Accounting Statement No. 128, adopted in February 1997.
3. If "per share" data are not available, then divide cash dividends by net income available for common stockholders.

The average payout ratio for this industry is far below the national average for all corporations. The ratio of dividends to profits after taxes for all corporations ranges from about 60% to 70%.[4] Ajax's relatively low payout ratio indicates that management believes that it has growth opportunities that they want to fund, in part, with retained earnings. Equally important, it suggests that this industry is still in the expansion stage of the life cycle, while the national average may be dominated by mature firms.

$$\text{Payout ratio} \quad = \frac{\text{Cash dividends per share}}{\text{Earnings per share}} \qquad \text{7A.6}$$

$$2004 \qquad = \frac{\$0.32}{\$1.38} = 23\%$$

$$2003 \qquad = \frac{\$0.32}{\$1.65} = 19\%$$

$$\text{Industry average} = 20\%$$

As noted at the beginning of this section, all of the measures indicate that Ajax's profitability declined, which is *what* happened. Now we will try to determine *why* it happened.

Liquidity Ratios and Measures

A company must survive the short run in order to prosper in the long run. If a firm does not have sufficient liquidity, it may not survive the short run, which is why liquidity measures are so important. The following measures of liquidity assess the ability of a firm to meet its short-run, or current, obligations—those due within one year.

NET WORKING CAPITAL As a general rule, companies use current assets to pay their current liabilities. For example, cash is used to pay accounts payable. The arithmetic difference between current assets and current liabilities is called *net working capital (NWC),* and it represents a cushion for creditors' short-term loans. In other words, creditors view more working capital as being better than less. However, too much working capital may be a detriment to the company, because it may indicate that funds are not being used effectively. Holding excess nonearning assets, such as cash and accounts receivable, can hold down profits. Cash, for example, might be better employed in inventory or fixed assets. An examination of Ajax's balance sheet (Table 7A.3) reveals that net working capital increased from about $250 million in 2003 to $255 million in 2004:

4. For details on such data, see the monthly *Economic Indicators,* U.S. Government Printing Office, Corporate Profits.

$$\text{Net working capital = Current assets – Current liabilities} \qquad 7A.7$$

$$\text{NWC 2004} \quad = \$327{,}106{,}465 - \$71{,}714{,}462$$
$$= \$255{,}392{,}003$$

$$\text{NWC 2003} \quad = \$334{,}450{,}901 - \$84{,}768{,}256$$
$$= \$249{,}682{,}645$$

CURRENT RATIO The *current ratio* is a broad measure of liquidity derived by dividing current assets by current liabilities. It is considered a broad measure because it includes all current assets and all current liabilities. The current ratio for Ajax increased sharply in 2004 and was well above the industry average. It is another red flag that requires further analysis. The high current ratio suggests that Ajax may be too liquid.

$$\text{Current ratio} \quad = \frac{\text{Current assets}}{\text{Current liabilities}} \qquad 7A.8$$

$$\text{Current ratio 2004} = \frac{\$327{,}106{,}465}{\$71{,}714{,}462} = 4.56 \text{ times}$$

$$\text{Current ratio 2003} = \frac{\$334{,}450{,}901}{\$84{,}768{,}256} = 3.95 \text{ times}$$

$$\text{Industry average} \qquad\qquad = 2.97 \text{ times}$$

ACID TEST RATIO The *acid test ratio* is a narrow measure of liquidity derived by dividing cash, marketable securities, and accounts receivable by current liabilities. It is considered narrow because it excludes the least liquid current assets—inventory, prepaid expenses, and future tax benefits—from the numerator of the equation. The acid test ratio for Ajax increased in 2004, which may account for the high current ratio and lower profits.

Notice that Ajax's acid test ratio is high when compared to the industry average. Sometimes a high acid test ratio is due to conservative financial policies. Alternatively, the firm may be building its cash and investments in anticipation of capital expenditures or an acquisition. Finally, the firm may not be collecting its receivables. Further analysis is required to determine which explanation is correct.

$$\text{Acid test ratio} \quad = \frac{\text{Cash + Securities + Accounts receivable}}{\text{Current liabilities}} \qquad 7A.9$$

$$\text{Acid test 2004} \quad = \frac{\$150{,}717{,}172}{\$71{,}714{,}462} = 2.10 \text{ times}$$

$$\text{Acid test 2003} \quad = \frac{\$148{,}287{,}587}{\$84{,}768{,}256} = 1.75 \text{ times}$$

$$\text{Industry average} = \qquad\qquad 1.48 \text{ times}$$

AVERAGE COLLECTION PERIOD The *average collection* period indicates the average number of days that a firm waits before receiving cash from sales made on credit. All of Ajax's sales are made on credit, so it is important for the firm to minimize the collection period in order to be paid as soon as possible.

Two steps are required to calculate the average collection period. Step 1 involves determining the dollar amount of credit sales per day, by dividing net sales (Table 7A.4) by 360 days. The use of 360 days to represent a financial year was developed in an era before hand-held calculators and computers, but is still widely used by analysts. Either 360 or 365 days may be used as long as they are used consistently. Step 2 is to divide accounts receivable by credit sales per day. The data revealed that the average collection period declined from 68 to 61 days, indicating that Ajax is doing a better job of collecting its funds. Therefore, the high level of the acid test ratio noted earlier is either a result of conservative management policies or they are increasing liquid assets for future expansion.

$$\text{Credit sales per day} \quad = \quad \frac{\text{Net sales}}{360 \text{ days}} \qquad \text{7A.10a}$$

$$\text{Credit sales per day 2004} \quad = \quad \frac{\$804,584,939}{360 \text{ days}} \quad = \$2,234,958$$

$$\text{Average collection period} \quad = \frac{\text{Accounts receivable}}{\text{Credit sales/Day}} \qquad \text{7A.10b}$$

$$\text{Average collection period 2004} = \frac{\$137,299,371}{\$2,234,958} \quad = 61.42 \text{ days}$$

$$\text{Credit sales per day 2003} \quad = \quad \frac{\$713,812,344}{360 \text{ days}} \quad = \$1,982,812$$

$$\text{Average collection period} \quad = \quad \frac{\$135,065,650}{\$1,982,812} \quad = 68.11 \text{ days}$$

$$\text{Industry average} \qquad\qquad = \quad 63 \text{ days}$$

AVERAGE PAYMENT PERIOD The *average payment period* is one indicator of how a firm is managing its current liabilities. This ratio is computed using two steps. Step 1 determines the dollar amount of credit purchases per day. Credit purchases amount to 80% of the cost of goods sold for Ajax. Step 2 divides accounts payable by the credit purchases per day. The sharp decline in the dollar amount of accounts payable and in the average payment period put Ajax far below the industry average. We don't have the information here to explain the sharp reduction in time. Nevertheless, we can guess that if they had sufficient liquidity, the reduction in the payment period may be to allow Ajax to take advantage of trade discounts for early payment of bills.

$$\text{Average payment period} = \frac{\text{Accounts payable}}{\text{Credit purchases/day}} \qquad \text{7A.11}$$

$$\text{Credit purchases/day 2004} = \frac{0.80(\$553{,}159{,}643)}{360 \text{ days}}$$

$$= \$1{,}229{,}244$$

$$\text{Average payment period 2004} = \frac{\$23{,}896{,}090}{\$1{,}229{,}244} = 19 \text{ days}$$

$$\text{Credit purchases/day 2003} = \frac{0.80(\$461{,}280{,}501)}{360 \text{ days}}$$

$$= \$1{,}025{,}068$$

$$\text{Average payment period 2003} = \frac{\$38{,}826{,}568}{\$1{,}025{,}068} = 38 \text{ days}$$

$$\text{Industry average} = 35 \text{ days}$$

Measuring Efficiency

Efficiency indicators measure how effectively certain assets and liabilities are being used in the production of goods and services. The average collection period can be thought of as both a measure of liquidity and efficiency.

INVENTORY TURNOVER RATIO The objective in managing inventories is to hold the minimum amount necessary in order to serve customers' needs and make sales. The *inventory turnover ratio* is calculated by dividing the cost of goods sold by inventory.

As a general rule the higher the turnover, the faster the company can realize profits. Inventory turnover ratios vary widely from industry to industry. One would expect a daily newspaper to have a high inventory turnover ratio (about 365 times per year), because few people want to buy last month's newspaper. In contrast, the inventory turnover ratio for a jewelry store may be relatively low, perhaps once or twice per year.

$$\text{Inventory turnover ratio} = \frac{\text{Cost of goods sold}}{\text{Inventory}} \qquad \text{7A.12}$$

$$\text{Inventory turnover 2004} = \frac{\$553{,}159{,}643}{\$162{,}086{,}784} = 3.41 \text{ times}$$

$$\text{Inventory turnover 2003} = \frac{\$461{,}280{,}501}{\$173{,}168{,}270} = 2.66 \text{ times}$$

$$\text{Industry average} = 3.00 \text{ times}$$

AGE OF INVENTORY Another way to examine inventories is to determine the average number of days that the inventory remains on hand, which is accomplished by dividing 360 days by the inventory turnover ratio. The age of the inventory declined in 2004, reflecting the higher inventory turnover ratio and more efficient use of inventories.

$$\text{Age of inventory} \quad = \frac{360 \text{ days}}{\text{Inventory turnover ratio}} \qquad \text{7A.13}$$

$$\text{Age of inventory 2004} = \quad 360/3.41 = 106 \text{ days}$$

$$\text{Age of inventory 2003} = \quad 360/2.66 = 135 \text{ days}$$

$$\text{Industry average} \quad = \quad 120 \text{ days}$$

ASSET TURNOVER RATIO The *asset turnover ratio* is a broad measure of efficiency because it encompasses all assets. It is computed by dividing net sales by total assets. The ratios indicate that Ajax is using its assets more efficiently. This result is consistent with the improvements noted in the management of accounts receivable and inventory.

$$\text{Asset turnover} \quad = \frac{\text{Net sales}}{\text{Total assets}} \qquad \text{7A.14}$$

$$\text{Asset turnover 2004} = \frac{\$804,584,939}{\$818,219,147} = 98.33\%$$

$$\text{Asset turnover 2003} = \frac{\$713,812,344}{\$794,521,255} = 89.84\%$$

$$\text{Industry average} \quad = \quad 93.15\%$$

Financial Leverage

Financial leverage refers to the relationship between borrowed funds, such as loans and bonds, and common stockholders' equity. Some analysts consider preferred stock to be in the same category as debt because of the obligation to pay preferred dividends. We will follow that practice because the balance sheet for Ajax (Table 7A.3) does not include the preferred stock in stockholders' equity.

Companies with a high proportion of borrowed funds are said to be highly leveraged. Financial leverage increases the volatility of earnings per share and the risk of bankruptcy. Several measures of financial leverage are described here.

DEBT RATIO The *debt ratio* indicates the proportion of a firm's total assets that is financed with borrowed funds. It is calculated by dividing total liabilities by total assets. The easy way to compute total liabilities is to subtract common stockholders' equity from total assets. Recall that we are not considering the preferred stock as equity.

The data reveal that the debt ratio declined in 2004. An examination of the balance sheet reveals both an increase in equity and a decrease in liabilities. The principal changes in liabilities were lower accounts payable and long-term debts.

$$\text{Debt ratio} \quad = \frac{\text{Total liabilities}}{\text{Total assets}} \qquad\qquad 7A.15$$

$$\text{Debt ratio 2004} = \frac{\$315,718,676}{\$818,219,576} = 38.59\%$$

$$\text{Debt ratio 2003} = \frac{\$338,169.003}{\$794,521,255} = 42.56\%$$

$$\text{Industry average} = \quad 40.18\%$$

LONG-TERM DEBT AS A PERCENT OF TOTAL CAPITAL Total capital includes long-term debt and equity. In 2004, for example, total capital for Ajax was:

Long-term debt	$180,338,551
Preferred stock	5,584,430
Stockholders' equity	502,500,899
Total capital	$688,423,880

$$\text{Long-term debt as a percent of total capital} = \frac{\text{Long-term debt}}{\text{Total capital}} \qquad 7A.16$$

$$\text{Long-term debt/capital 2004} = \frac{\$180,338,551}{\$688,423,880} = 26.19\%$$

$$\text{Long-term debt/capital 2003} = \frac{\$191,257,695}{\$652,939,377} = 29.29\%$$

$$\text{Industry average} \quad = \quad 32.13\%$$

Ajax reduced its long-term debt and is currently below the industry average.

TIMES INTEREST EARNED By reducing the amount of debt outstanding, Ajax was better able to cover (i.e., pay) its outstanding debts, thereby reducing its financial risk. Debt coverage is measured by *times interest earned*, which is computed by dividing earnings before interest and taxes (EBIT) by interest expense. In 2004, EBIT was:

Income Before Income Taxes	$90,865,942
Interest Expense	18,096,696
EBIT	$108,962,638

The decline in the coverage ratio in 2004 reflects the lower EBIT. Nevertheless, the firm still has ample coverage and is above the industry average by a substantial margin.

$$\text{Times interest earned} = \frac{\text{EBIT}}{\text{Interest expense}} \qquad 7A.17$$

$$\text{Times interest earned 2004} = \frac{\$108,962,638}{\$18,096,696} = 6.02 \text{ times}$$

$$\text{Times interest earned 2003} = \frac{\$128,556,965}{\$18,884,674} = 6.81 \text{ times}$$

$$\text{Industry average} = 5.38 \text{ times}$$

Review of Financial Indicators

Table 7A.5 provides a review of the financial indicators as well as the results for Ajax Manufacturing Corporation. The financial indicators reveal that Ajax's profitability declined. The liquidity measures indicate that Ajax is highly liquid, but its high degree of liquidity did not account for the decline in profitability. The efficiency measures show that Ajax has become more efficient in the most recent period. Finally, the firm has reduced its financial leverage. The reason for the decline in profitability will be revealed shortly.

7A.4 COMMON-SIZE STATEMENT ANALYSIS

Balance Sheet

Common-size financial statements present each item listed on the balance sheet as a percent of total assets, and each item listed on the income statement as a percent of net sales. This format facilitates comparisons of financial statements because the data are expressed as percentages instead of dollar amounts. Consider Ajax's balance sheet (refer back to Table 7A.3). Total current assets for Ajax decreased from $334.4 million in 2003 to $327.1 million in the following year, while total assets increased from $794.5 million to $818.2 million. Although it is difficult to comprehend the significance of these changes, it is easy to understand that total current assets declined from 43% of total assets to 39.9%. Similarly, common-size statements are useful in comparing financial statements of different companies, and for comparing financial data from large and small companies because all of the data are expressed as percentages of total assets or sales.

Table 7A.6 is the common-size balance sheet for Ajax Manufacturing. The common-size balance sheet and income statement for Ajax are based on the balance sheet and income statements presented in Tables 7A.3 and 7A.4. As

TABLE 7A.5	Review of Financial Indicators

$$\text{ROA} = \text{NI/Total assets} \qquad 7A.1$$

$$\frac{\text{Net income 2004}}{\text{Year-end assets 2004}} = \frac{\$56,838,942}{\$818,219,575} = 0.0695 \text{ or } 6.95\%$$

$$\frac{\text{Net income 2003}}{\text{Year-end assets 2003}} = \frac{\$67,947,291}{\$794,521,255} = 8.55\%$$

$$\text{Industry average} = 7.83\%$$

$$\text{ROE} = \text{NI/Common stockholders' equity} \qquad 7A.2$$

$$\text{ROE 2004} = \frac{\$56,838,942}{\$502,500,899} = 11.31\%$$

$$\text{ROE 2003} = \frac{\$67,947,291}{\$456,352,252} = 14.89\%$$

$$\text{Industry average} = 12.54\%$$

$$\text{ROE} = \text{ROA} \times \text{LR} \qquad 7A.3$$
$$\text{NI/E} = (\text{NI/A})(\text{A/E})$$
$$11.31\% = 6.95\% \times 1.63 \text{ times (for 2004)}$$

$$\text{Net profit margin} = \frac{\text{Net income}}{\text{Net sales}} \qquad 7A.4$$

$$\frac{\text{Net income 2004}}{\text{Net sales 2004}} = \frac{\$56,838,942}{\$804,584,939} = 7.06\%$$

$$\frac{\text{Net income 2003}}{\text{Net sales 2003}} = \frac{\$67,947,291}{\$713,812,344} = 9.52\%$$

$$\text{Industry average} = 9.48$$

TABLE 7A.5	Review of Financial Indicators *(continued)*

$$\text{Earnings per share} = \frac{\text{Net income available for common stock}}{\text{Number of shares outstanding}} \qquad 7A.5$$

$$2004 \quad = \quad \frac{\$56,279,374}{40,889,909} \qquad = \$1.38 \text{ per share}$$

$$2003 \quad = \quad \frac{\$67,378,348}{40,919,638} \qquad = \$1.65 \text{ per share}$$

$$\text{Payout ratio} \quad = \quad \frac{\text{Cash dividends per share}}{\text{Earnings per share}} \qquad 7A.6$$

$$2004 \quad = \quad \frac{\$0.32}{\$1.38} \qquad = 23\%$$

$$2003 \quad = \quad \frac{\$0.32}{\$1.65} \qquad = 19\%$$

$$\text{Industry average} \qquad\qquad\qquad = 20\%$$

$$\text{Net working capital} = \text{Current assets} - \text{Current liabilities} \qquad 7A.7$$

$$\text{NWC 2004} \quad = \$327,106,465 - \$71,714,462$$
$$= \$255,392,003$$

$$\text{NWC 2003} \quad = \$334,450,901 - \$84,768,256$$
$$= \$249,682,645$$

$$\text{Current ratio} \quad = \quad \frac{\text{Current assets}}{\text{Current liabilities}} \qquad 7A.8$$

$$\text{Current ratio 2004} = \frac{\$327,106,465}{\$71,714,462} \quad = 4.56 \text{ times}$$

$$\text{Current ratio 2003} = \frac{\$334,450,901}{\$84,768,256} \quad = 3.95 \text{ times}$$

$$\text{Industry average} \qquad\qquad\qquad = 2.97 \text{ times}$$

TABLE 7A.5	Review of Financial Indicators *(continued)*

$$\text{Acid test ratio} \quad = \quad \frac{\text{Cash + Securities + Accounts receivable}}{\text{Current liabilities}} \qquad \text{7A.9}$$

$$\text{Acid test 2004} \quad = \quad \frac{\$150,717,172}{\$71,714,462} \qquad = 2.10 \text{ times}$$

$$\text{Acid test 2003} \quad = \quad \frac{\$148,287,587}{\$84,768,256} \qquad = 1.75 \text{ times}$$

$$\text{Industry average} \qquad\qquad\qquad = 1.48 \text{ times}$$

$$\text{Credit sales per day} \quad = \quad \frac{\text{Net sales}}{360 \text{ days}} \qquad \text{7A.10a}$$

$$\text{Credit sales per day 2004} \quad = \quad \frac{\$804,584,939}{360 \text{ days}} \qquad = \$2,234,958$$

$$\text{Average collection period} \quad = \frac{\text{Accounts receivable}}{\text{Credit sales/day}} \qquad \text{7A.10b}$$

$$\text{Average collection period 2004} = \frac{\$137,299,371}{\$2,234,958} \qquad = 61.42 \text{ days}$$

$$\text{Credit sales per day 2003} \quad = \quad \frac{\$713,812,344}{360 \text{ days}} \qquad = \$1,982,812$$

$$\text{Average collection period 2003} = \frac{\$135,065,650}{\$1,982,812} \qquad = 68.11 \text{ days}$$

$$\text{Industry average} \qquad\qquad\qquad = 63 \text{ days}$$

TABLE 7A.5	Review of Financial Indicators *(continued)*

$$\text{Average payment period} = \frac{\text{Accounts payable}}{\text{Credit purchases/day}} \qquad 7A.11$$

$$\text{Credit purchases/day 2004} = \frac{0.80(\$553,159,643)}{360 \text{ days}}$$

$$= \$1,229,244$$

$$\text{Average payment period 2004} = \frac{\$23,896,090}{\$1,229,244} = 19 \text{ days}$$

$$\text{Credit purchases/day 2003} = \frac{0.80(\$461,280,501)}{360 \text{ days}}$$

$$= \$1,025,068$$

$$\text{Average payment period 2003} = \frac{\$38,826,568}{\$1,025,068} = 38 \text{ days}$$

$$\text{Industry average} = 35 \text{ days}$$

$$\text{Inventory turnover ratio} = \frac{\text{Cost of goods sold}}{\text{Inventory}} \qquad 7A.12$$

$$\text{Inventory turnover 2004} = \frac{\$553,159,643}{\$162,086,784} = 3.41 \text{ times}$$

$$\text{Inventory turnover 2003} = \frac{\$461,280,501}{\$173,168,270} = 2.66 \text{ times}$$

$$\text{Industry average} = 3.00 \text{ times}$$

$$\text{Age of inventory} = \frac{360 \text{ days}}{\text{Inventory turnover ratio}} \qquad 7A.13$$

$$\text{Age of inventory 2004} = 360/3.41 = 106 \text{ days}$$

$$\text{Age of inventory 2003} = 360/2.66 = 135 \text{ days}$$

$$\text{Industry average} = 120 \text{ days}$$

TABLE 7A.5	Review of Financial Indicators *(continued)*

$$\text{Asset turnover} \quad = \quad \frac{\text{Net sales}}{\text{Total assets}} \qquad \qquad \text{7A.14}$$

$$\text{Asset turnover 2004} \quad = \quad \frac{\$804,584,939}{\$818,219,147} = 98.33\%$$

$$\text{Asset turnover 2003} \quad = \quad \frac{\$713,812,344}{\$794,521,255} = 89.84\%$$

$$\text{Industry average} \qquad \qquad = 93.15\%$$

$$\text{Debt ratio} \quad = \quad \frac{\text{Total liabilities}}{\text{Total assets}} \qquad \qquad \text{7A.15}$$

$$\text{Debt ratio 2004} \quad = \quad \frac{\$315,718,676}{\$818,219,576} = 38.59\%$$

$$\text{Debt ratio 2003} \quad = \quad \frac{\$338,169.003}{\$794,521,255} = 42.56\%$$

$$\text{Industry average} \qquad \qquad = 40.18\%$$

$$\text{Long-term debt as a percent of total capital} \quad = \quad \frac{\text{Long-term debt}}{\text{Total capital}} \qquad \text{7A.16}$$

$$\text{Long-term debt/capital 2004} \quad = \quad \frac{\$180,338,551}{\$688,423,880} = 26.19\%$$

$$\text{Long-term debt/capital 2003} \quad = \quad \frac{\$191,257,695}{\$652,939,377} = 29.29\%$$

$$\text{Industry average} \qquad \qquad = 32.13\%$$

$$\text{Times interest earned} \quad = \quad \frac{\text{EBIT}}{\text{Interest expense}} \qquad \qquad \text{7A.17}$$

$$\text{Times interest earned 2004} \quad = \quad \frac{\$108,962,638}{\$18,096,696} = 6.02 \text{ times}$$

$$\text{Times interest earned 2003} \quad = \quad \frac{\$128,556,965}{\$18,884,674} = 6.81 \text{ times}$$

$$\text{Industry average} \qquad \qquad = 5.38 \text{ times}$$

previously noted, total current assets declined in both absolute and relative terms. Keeping in mind that we know that sales increased during the period under review, the reduction in current assets is consistent with the improvement in the average collection period of accounts receivable and the higher inventory turnover that we observed. In other words, Ajax is using these assets more efficiently. Also note that Ajax increased its investments in property, plant, and equipment.

On the other side of the balance sheet, a substantial decline in both total current liabilities and long-term debt was noted, whereas total equity increased. This result is consistent with the downward trend in the debt ratio that we observed. We did not find any surprises in examining the common-size balance sheet.

Income Statement

Table 7A.7 is the common-size income statement. It shows that the net profit margin [Eq. (7A.4), net income expressed as a percent of net sales], declined from 9.5% in 2003 to 7.1% in 2004. We examined this ratio previously, but we were not able to determine the reason for its decline. Now, by using the common-size income statement, we can delve into the problem further. A careful examination of Table 7A.2 reveals that the reason for Ajax's poor performance is the increase in the cost of goods sold. The cost of goods sold is the total cost of the finished goods inventory in a period (annual in our example). The cost of goods sold is the cost of goods available for sale less cost of finished goods in inventory. In manufacturing accounting, the cost of goods sold includes direct materials and work-in-process. Work-in-process includes labor and manufacturing expenses. Some manufacturing concerns have high levels of fixed operating and financial costs, or high operating and financial leverage. Fixed costs are those costs incurred regardless of the level of short-term production. Over the long term, such costs may change if, for example, new plant and equipment are acquired.

The cost of goods sold increased from 64.6% of net sales in 2003 to 68.7% in 2004. The reason for the higher cost was explained in footnotes and in management's discussion and analysis of its financial condition that were attached to the financial statements, but were not presented here. The higher cost of goods sold was due to a reduced production schedule. In the first half of 2004, unit sales had increased, but prices had declined, and Ajax had excess inventory. By the second half of the year, the imbalance was corrected and improved sales resulted in the higher inventory mentioned previously.

Net sales less cost of goods sold is the gross margin, which is the profit before all of the other expenses are considered. The other expenses listed in the table did not change appreciably.

Let's review the process of financial analysis. We began by examining the raw data listed in Ajax's balance sheet and income statement. The raw data revealed that Ajax was growing, but its net income had declined. The ratio analysis showed that Ajax was operating more efficiently and that it had

TABLE 7A.6   Common-Size Consolidated Balance Sheets for Ajax Manufacturing Corporation and Subsidiaries (Years Ended December 31, 2004, 2003)

	2004	2003
Assets		
Current Assets		
Cash	0.41%	0.19%
Temporary investments	1.23	1.48
Trade accounts receivable, less allowances	16.78	17.00
Inventories	19.81	21.80
Prepaid expenses and other current assets	0.97	0.93
Future income tax benefits	0.78	0.72
Total Current Assets	39.98	43.35
Other Assets	4.39	4.63
Property, Plant and Equipment		
Land	0.32	0.41
Buildings	21.22	19.11
Machinery and equipment	66.81	63.53
Construction in progress	5.71	4.04
	94.06	87.07
Less allowances for depreciation and amortization	(38.43)	(33.80)
Total Assets	55.63	53.27

reduced its financial leverage. However, it was not until we examined the common-size income statement that we discovered that the increased cost of goods sold was one of the principal factors that contributed to the lower earnings. For this reason, computing common-size statements was essential in this case.

Questions

7A.1 Which financial ratio is the most important?

7A.2 Consider the saying: In order to survive in the long run, you have to survive in the short run. What ratios can be used to determine whether a firm can meet its current financial obligations?

7A.3 What ratio provides the best measure of liquidity?

TABLE 7A.6	Common-Size Consolidated Balance Sheets for Ajax Manufacturing Corporation and Subsidiaries (Years Ended December 31, 2004, 2003) *(continued)*	

	2004	2003
Liabilities and Stockholders' Equity		
Current Liabilities		
Notes payable	0.88%	0.84%
Accounts payable and accrued expenses:		
Trade accounts	2.92	4.89
Employee compensation	1.75	1.33
Other	0.55	0.62
	5.22	6.81
Federal and state income taxes	1.31	1.45
Current maturities of long-term debt and capital lease obligations	1.36	1.55
Total Current Liabilities	8.77	10.67
Long-term debt and capital lease obligations (less current maturities and unamortized debt discount)	22.04	24.07
Deferred liabilities		
Federal and state income taxes	5.95	6.26
Accrued pension and other	1.15	0.86
	7.10	7.12
Redeemable cumulative preferred stock		
Par value $.01 per share, authorized 10,000,000 shares, issued and outstanding 558,443 shares in 2004 and 559,943 shares in 2003	0.68	0.71
Stockholders' Equity		
Common stock, par value $.01 per share, shares outstanding: 40,889,909 in 2004; 40,919,638 in 2003	0.05	0.05
Paid-in capital	5.79	6.10
Retained earnings	56.90	53.14
Treasury stock	(1.66)	(1.99)
Currency translation adjustment	0.34	0.13
	61.41	57.44
Total Liabilities and Equity	100.00%	100.00%

Note: Figures may not add to totals due to rounding.

TABLE 7A.7	Common-Size Consolidated Statements of Income for Ajax Manufacturing Corporation and Subsidiaries (Years Ended December 31, 2004, 2003)		
	2004	2003	2002
Net Sales	100.0%	100.0%	100.0%
Cost of goods sold	68.7	64.6	66.5
Gross Margin	31.3	35.4	33.5
Selling, general and administrative expenses	17.7	17.7	15.9
Other deductions (income)			
Interest expense incurred	2.2	2.6	2.2
Other, net	0.0	(0.3)	0.3
	2.2	2.3	2.5
Income before income taxes	11.3	15.4	14.9
Federal and state income taxes			
Currently payable	4.4	5.4	4.6
Deferred	(0.2)	0.4	0.9
	4.2	5.8	5.5
Net Income	7.1	9.5	9.4

Note: Figure may not add to totals due to rounding.

7A.4 The inventory turnover ratio measures how many times an inventory is sold each year. What would be the expected turnover ratios for TIME magazine and for Zales Jewelry Stores?

7A.5 When comparing a firm's ratios to an industry, is it bad to be below average?

7A.6 Is it possible to make a meaningful comparison of the financial statements of Ford Motors and a small company?

7A.7 Why is a high degree of financial leverage considered risky?

7A.8 Why are high degrees of financial leverage more acceptable in some industries than in others?

7A.9 What does an increase in the average collection period suggest?

7A.10 What does an increase in the average payment period suggest?

The Cost of Capital

T his appendix explains how to calculate the weighted average cost of capital for banks. We make the simplifying assumptions that total liabilities are interest-rate sensitive and that interest expense divided by total liabilities represents the marginal cost of borrowed funds. Considering liabilities to be interest-rate sensitive means that they are repriced when market rates of interest change. In this example, the marginal cost of capital is the *weighted average cost of capital* (WACC).[5]

$$k_w = k_d(1 - T)L + k_e(1 - L) \qquad \text{7B.1}$$

where

k_w = weighted average cost of capital of new funds
k_d = cost of interest-bearing liabilities
k_e = cost of equity
T = corporate tax rate
L = ratio of liabilities to assets

Eq. (7B.1), which is the same as Eq. (7.4), reveals that the cost of capital for all new funds raised is equal to the proportionate after-tax cost of liabilities, plus the proportionate cost of equity. The WACC is expressed as a percentage.

The cost of equity may be computed by the *capital asset pricing model*

5. If the increased equity results in the bank being perceived by investors as being less risky, the cost of borrowing may be reduced, which may lower the WACC.

(CAPM)[6] The CAPM asserts that the cost of equity capital is equal to the risk-free rate of interest plus beta times a market premium. The risk-free rate of interest refers to the rate paid on default-free Treasury securities. Beta is a measure of systematic risk—risk that is common to all stocks.

The market premium is the difference between the expected return on the stock market and the risk-free rate of interest. The CAPM may be expressed as:

$$k_e = rf + b(k_m - rf)$$ 7B.2

where

rf = risk-free rate of interest on Treasury bills
b = stock market beta of a stock
k_m = expected return on the stock market

To illustrate the use of these equations, we will computer the cost of capital of Major Bank, a large money center bank. Using the following data, Major Bank's cost of equity capital is estimated to be 11.45%.

$$rf = 0.0412$$
$$b = 1.2$$
$$km^7 = 0.1120$$
$$kd = 0.0858$$
$$T = .040$$
$$L = 0.955$$
$$ke = rf + b(k_m - rf) = 0.0412 + 1.2 (0.1120 - 0.0412)$$
$$= 12.62\%$$

Using the 12.62% cost of equity, the WACC for Major Bank is 5.49%:

$$k_w = k_d(1 - T)L + k_e (1 - L)$$
$$= (0.0515 \times 0.955) + (0.1262 \times 0.045)$$
$$= 5.49\%$$

Although the cost of equity is relatively high (12.62%), it only accounts for a small portion (4.5%) of the total capital structure. Therefore, the proportionate cost of equity ($0.1262 \times 0.045 = 0.0057$) in the WACC is relatively small, but nevertheless important.

6. The cost of equity may be computed by using the CAPM, the dividend valuation model, or by using a bond yield plus a risk premium. Although questions have been raised about the validity of the CAPM, as well as questions about the other methods, the CAPM is still widely used.
7. The expected return on the market may be estimated by several methods. For simplicity, we used 11.2%. From 1926–1998, the geometric return on common stocks was 11.2% on large company stocks according to Roger G. Ibbotson and Rex A. Sinquefield, *Stocks, Bonds, Bills and Inflation: Historical Returns (1926–1998)* (Chicago: Ibbotson Associates), Table 2-1.

CHAPTER 8

Real Estate and Consumer Lending

After reading this chapter you will be able to:

■ Explain the characteristics of residential mortgage loans.

■ Understand alternative mortgage instruments.

■ Understand how commercial real estate loans differ from residential loans.

■ Explain the various types of consumer loans.

■ Understand how finance charges on consumer loans are computed.

■ Explain the major federal laws governing real estate and consumer credit.

Times have changed. In the past, people who wanted to obtain mortgage loans or personal loans had to go to the bank and ask for them. Today, they can do it from the comfort of their homes by using the Internet, or they can do it from anywhere using their cellular phones. Technology is changing the ways that home buyers and consumers borrow money. The other side of that coin is how it affects the ways that lenders make real estate and consumer loans. In this chapter, we examine the real estate and consumer lending from the lender's point of view. ■

8.1   REAL ESTATE LENDING

Mortgage Debt Outstanding

The term **mortgage** is used in connection with real estate lending. In general terms, a mortgage is a written conveyance of title to real property. It provides the lender with a security interest in the property, if the mortgage is properly recorded in the county courthouse. It also provides that the property being used as collateral for the loan will be sold if the debt is not repaid as agreed. The proceeds from the sale of the property are used to reimburse the lender. As shown in Table 8.1, 1–4 family mortgage debt accounts for 76% of the total mortgage debt outstanding. Nonfarm, nonresidential mortgage debt, which we will call *commercial mortgage loans* is the second largest category of mortgage loans. Multifamily residences and farm mortgages account for the remainder.

Mortgage loans are originated by commercial banks and other financial institutions. The originating institutions may hold the mortgages in their loan portfolios or sell them in the secondary market. The *secondary mortgage market*, in which securities representing pools of mortgage loans are purchased and sold, increases the liquidity of residential mortgages and lessens the cyclical disruptions in the housing market. The pools of mortgage loans are referred to as *asset-backed securities*.

The process of transforming individual loans into marketable asset-backed securities is called *securitization*. The process involves the issuance of securities that represent claims against a pool of assets (i.e., mortgages, car loans, credit card receivables, and small business loans) that are held in trust. The originator of a loan sells the assets to a trust. It must be a *true sale*, which means that the assets cannot be returned to the originator's balance sheet. The trustee then issues securities through an investment banker (underwriter) to investors. Some banks act as packagers of asset-based loans, and they take on the risk of an underwriter. Some act as originators, packagers, and they service (collect loan payments, deal with delinquencies, etc.) the loans too. As the principal and interest payments are made on the loans, they are paid out to investors by the trustee or servicer who

TABLE 8.1	Mortgage Debt Outstanding by Type of Property 4th Quarter 1998 ($ millions)	
1–4 family residences	$4,375,730	76%
Multifamily residences	362,092	6
Nonfarm, nonresidential (commercial)	949,230	16
Farm	94,974	2
Total	$5,782,027	100%

Source: Mortgage Debt Outstanding, *Federal Reserve Bulletin* (July 1999), p. A 35.

retains a small transaction fee. In most cases, the cash flows to investors are guaranteed (*enhanced*) by bank guarantees (standby letters of credit), by government agency guarantees (e.g., Government National Mortgage Association), or by having more loans than necessary to secure the value of the pools (*overcollateralize*). Credit rating agencies, such as Standard and Poor's, assign ratings to asset-backed securities just as they do for stocks and bonds. The quality of the credit enhancement is an important part of the rating. The credit enhancements, credit ratings, and the reputations of the investment banker or packager help to standardize the quality of asset-backed loans.

One benefit of the secondary mortgage market is that it permits lenders to increase the liquidity of their mortgage portfolio. Stated otherwise, they can package otherwise unmarketable individual mortgage loans and sell them to investors. Another benefit is that the secondary market has attracted investors from outside the traditional mortgage investment community who want to buy mortgage-backed securities. Thus, the secondary mortgage market has increased the breadth, depth, and liquidity of the capital market that is available for mortgage financing.

The three major participants in the secondary market are the Federal National Mortgage Corporation (Fannie Mae), the Government National Mortgage Association (Ginnie Mae), and the Federal Home Loan Mortgage Association (Freddie Mac). These three organizations were created by Congress, and they developed a secondary mortgage market. They issue mortgage pools or trusts of 1–4 family, multifamily real estate, and certain other properties. Congress also created the Farmers Home Administration, but it is a small factor in the secondary mortgage market. Some private organizations also operate in the secondary mortgage market. As shown in Table 8.2, mortgage pools and trusts hold almost half of the total mortgage debt outstanding. The table also reveals that commercial banks hold more mortgage debt than savings institutions, life insurance companies, and federal and related agencies.

TABLE 8.2	Mortgage Debt Outstanding by Type of Holder 4th Quarter 1998 ($ millions)
Commercial banks	$1,337,378
Savings institutions	643,773
Life insurance companies	211,940
Federal and related agencies	291,858
Mortgage pools and trusts	2,631,790
Individuals and others	665,001
Total	$5,782,027

Source: Mortgage Debt Outstanding, *Federal Reserve Bulletin* (July 1999), p. A 35.

Characteristics of Mortgage Loans

Table 8.3 lists selected characteristics of new home mortgages in April 1999. The average purchase price of a new home was $209,400, and average amount of the loan was $162,400. The difference between those two amounts, $47,000, represents the *down payment*, or borrower's equity. *Equity* is the difference between the market value of the property and the borrower's mortgage debt. From the lender's perspective, the percentage loaned to the borrowers, or the loan-to-price ratio was 79.5%. Bank regulators have established loan-to-price (value) limits for different categories of loans. For example, the loan-to-value limit for raw land is 65%, for 1–4 family residential construction it is 85%, but no limit is put on owner-occupied homes.[1] In fact, some lenders are writing mortgages for up to 125% of a property's value, and securitizing them.[2] This practice is risky for the investors who hold those mortgages.

In option pricing theory, bank loans are considered compound options containing the rights to prepay (call options) and to default (put options) on each of the scheduled payment dates.[3] When the put options are in the money (the value of the asset is less than the loan amount), borrowers have an incentive to exercise their put options and default on the loans. The lower the loan-to-price ratio (i.e., the higher the borrower's equity), the less likely it is that borrowers will default.

When market rates of interest rates decline, borrowers with fixed interest rate loans may exercise their call options and prepay the loans. That is, they

TABLE 8.3	Selected Characteristics of New Home Mortgages, April 1999
Purchase price	$209,400
Amount of loan	$162,400
Loan-to-price	79.5%
Contract interest rate	6.74%
Fees and charges	$1,250 (0.77% of loan amount)
Maturity	28.9 years

Source: *Federal Reserve Bulletin,* Mortgage Markets (July 1999), p. A 34.

1. K. Spong, *Banking Regulation: Its Purposes, Implementation, and Effects,* Federal Reserve Bank of Kansas City (1994), p. 96–97.
2. Karen Talley, "Small Banks Stepping Up High-LTV Securitizations," *American Banker* (January 20, 1998), p. 7.
3. For additional discussion of this point, see B. W. Ambose and C. A. Capone, Jr., "Cost-Benefit Analysis of Single Family Foreclosure Alternatives," *Journal of Real Estate Finance and Economics,* vol. 13 (November 1996), pp. 105–120.

refinance their loans at lower rates. For example, Table 8.3 shows that the average contract interest rate on mortgage loans was 6.74%, and borrowers paid fees, commissions, discounts, and points to make the loan amounting to $1,250. The fees and the interest earned on the loan are income for the lenders. If interest rates and fees decline sufficiently, say 200 basis points, many borrowers with fixed rate mortgages will refinance at the lower rates.

The average maturity of new home mortgage loans is about 29 years. However, because borrowers may sell their home or refinance when rates decline, the average life of a mortgage portfolio is about 12 years.

The Real Estate Portfolio

Banks make an investment decision as to the percentage of their loan portfolio that they want to invest in various types of real estate loans. The decision takes into account risks and returns of the various types of real estate loans they make (residential, commercial, etc.). The risks include defaults, declining real estate values, prepayments, and lack of liquidity. Bankers also must decide what proportions of their loans should be made at fixed rates, or at adjustable rates. These decisions reflect the characteristics of the lender, the market, and the borrowers. Lenders mitigate some of these risks by raising their credit standards and excluding less creditworthy borrowers, by requiring borrowers to make larger down payments (lower loan-to-price ratios), by selling real estate loans in the secondary market, and by charging origination fees to influence borrowers' behavior. The returns banks receive on real estate lending come from interest earned on the loans, fees for transaction, settlement and closing costs, and fees for servicing loans that are sold. In addition, they charge *points* that are fees paid to the lender and they are often linked to the interest rate. One point equals 1% of the loan. Finally, some lenders require *private mortgage insurance* (PMI) when the down payment is less than 20%. The PMI protects the lender in the event of default.

COLLATERAL Residential real estate is good collateral because it is durable, easy to identify, and most structures cannot be moved elsewhere. Despite these fine qualities, the value of real estate can go up or down. During periods of inflation, residential real estate in many parts of the country appreciated in value, thereby enhancing its value as collateral. During deflation and recessions, however, the value of residential real estate in some areas declined. When real estate values decline during periods of economic distress, such as the early 1990s in the southwestern parts of the United States, delinquencies and default rates on real estate loans increased to such an extent that many banks and thrifts failed.

The fact that real estate has a fixed geographic location is both good and bad. It is good in the sense that the collateral cannot be removed. It is bad in the sense that its value is affected by adjacent property. If a toxic waste dump site were to locate in what was previously a golf course, the value of the adjacent residential property would decline. Finally, real estate is illiquid. That is, it is difficult to sell on short notice at its fair market value. These comments on residential real estate also apply to commercial real estate.

Residential Mortgage Loans

Residential mortgage loans differ from other types of loans in several respects. First, the loans are for relatively large dollar amounts. As shown in Table 8.3, the average loan for a new home was $209,400. Second, the loans tend to be long term, with original maturities as long as 30 years. Third, the loans are usually secured by the real estate as collateral. However, real estate is illiquid, and its price can vary widely.

The two basic types of 1–4 family residential mortgage loans are **fixed rate mortgages** and **adjustable rate mortgages (ARMs)**. The interest rate charged on fixed rate mortgages does not change over the life of the loan. In contrast, ARMs permit lenders to vary the interest rate charged on the mortgage loan when market rates of interest change. The basic idea behind ARMs is to help mortgage lenders keep the returns on their assets (mortgage loans) higher than the costs of their funds. However, it is the borrowers who decide what type of mortgage loans they want, and that choice is influenced by the level of interest rates. ARMs accounted for 41% of conventional first mortgage loans on new single-family homes in 1994 when mortgage rates were relatively high compared to 21% in 1997 when rates were lower.[4] *Conventional mortgage loans* are those that are not insured by the Federal Housing Administration (FHA) or guaranteed by the Veterans Administration (VA). Mortgage loans that are insured by the FHA or guaranteed by VA are called *government-backed or insured mortgages*. However, some conventional mortgages are insured against default by private mortgage insurance companies.

FIXED RATE MORTGAGES Fixed rate, fully amortized, level payment mortgages are the predominant form of financing residential mortgage loans. *Fixed rate, fully amortized, level payment mortgage* means that the interest rate does not change and the debt is gradually extinguished through equal periodic payments on the principal balance. In other words, the borrower pays the same dollar amount each month until the mortgage loan is paid off. *Partially amortized, fixed rate mortgages* also are used for financing home loans. In this case, only a portion of the debt is extinguished by level periodic payments over a relatively short period, say five years, and the unamortized amount is paid in one large lump sum payment—a balloon payment. Alternatively, the loan can be refinanced when it matures.

Monthly Mortgage Payments The dollar amount of monthly payments

---

4. U.S. Department of Commerce, *Statistical Abstract of the United States, 1998,* Table 815.

depends on the size of the loan, the interest rate, and the maturity. Table 8.4 shows the monthly mortgage payments for a $1,000 mortgage loan with selected annual interest rates and maturities. A close examination of the body of the table reveals two important facts. First, the dollar amount of the monthly mortgage payment increases as the interest rate increases. For example, the monthly mortgage payment for a loan with 10 years to maturity ranges from $11.10 when the interest rate is 6 percent to $16.76 when the interest rate is 16 percent. Second, the dollar amount of the monthly mortgage payment declines as the maturity of the loan is extended. When the interest rate is 6 percent, the monthly mortgage payment declines from $11.10 when the maturity is 10 years maturity to $6.00 when the maturity is 30 years.

The monthly mortgage payments shown in Table 8.4 can be determined by using Eq. (8.1) to solve for the present value of an annuity. By way of illustration, we will compute the monthly mortgage payment for a $1,000 mortgage loan at 6 percent interest for 10 years.[5] Because we are solving for a monthly payment, the number of payments over the 10 years is 120 (10 years $\times$ 12 months per year). Moreover, only one-twelfth of the 6 percent annual interest rate (0.06/12 = 0.005) is charged each month. The present value of the annuity is the $1,000 mortgage loan in this example. The monthly payment is $11.10.

TABLE 8.4	Monthly Payments for a $1,000 Mortgage Loan				

Annual Interest Rate	Years to Maturity				
	10 years	15 years	20 years	25 years	30 years
6%	$11.10	$8.44	$7.16	$6.44	$6.00
8	12.13	9.56	8.36	7.72	7.34
10	13.22	10.75	9.65	9.09	8.78
12	14.35	12.00	11.01	10.53	10.29
14	15.35	13.32	12.44	12.04	11.85
16	16.76	14.69	13.92	13.59	13.45

5. To solve the problem on a financial calculator, such as a Hewlett-Packard 12C, clear the calculator then enter n = 10 years (multiplied by 12 monthly payments, blue key), i = 6 (divided by 12 monthly payments, blue key), PV = $1,000, (also press END button, blue key) and then press PMT. The monthly payment PMT = – $11.10. Each model and brand of calculators has unique features. Your operator's manual should explain how to compute loan payments for amortized loans.

$$\text{PV of annuity} = PMT\left[\frac{1 - (1 + i)^{-n}}{i}\right] \qquad 8.1$$

$$\$1,000 = PMT\left[\frac{1 - (1 + 0.005)^{120}}{0.005}\right]$$

$$\text{PMT} = \$11.10$$

where

PV = present value of the annuity
PMT = payment per period
i = interest rate per period
n = number of periods

Maturity Don't be fooled by low monthly payments. For a given interest rate and maturity, the total cost of the loan is higher with longer maturities (smaller monthly payments) than shorter maturities (higher monthly payments). The total cost is determined by multiplying the mortgage payment per $1,000 of loan for each interest rate by the dollar amount of the loan (in thousands) and the number of months. By way of illustration, consider an $100,000 mortgage loan at 12 percent with a maturity of 10 years. The monthly payment is $1,435 ($14.35 × 100 = $1,435) and the total cost over the life of the loan is $172,200 ($1,435 × 120 months = $172,200). If the maturity were 25 years, the monthly payment would be reduced to $1,053, but the total cost would be $315,900, which is $143,900 more than the cost of the shorter-term loan.

Principal and Interest Let's examine the monthly mortgage payment in greater detail and consider the amount that is allocated to principal and to interest. Table 8.5 shows the breakdown between principal and interest for the first year's payments of an $100,000 loan at 12 percent for 25 years. The striking feature of this table is the disproportionate amount of the monthly payment that is applied to interest payments. Total mortgage payments amounted to $12,636 ($1,053 × 12 = $12,636) during the first twelve months of the loan. Of that amount, $11,963.83 was applied to interest and only $672.17 was used to reduce the principal amount of the loan.

The implication of the data presented in Table 8.5 is that lenders earn most of their interest income during the early years of a mortgage loan. Therefore, all other things being equal, a high turnover of the mortgage loans contributes more interest income to earnings than having mortgage loans remain in their portfolio until they mature.

See http://mortgage.quicken.com/ *for current mortgage rates and terms.*

ADJUSTABLE RATE MORTGAGES An adjustable rate mortgage is one in which the interest rate changes over the life of the loan. The change can result in changes in monthly payments, the term of the loan, and/or the principal amount.

Index The idea behind ARMs is to permit lenders to maintain a positive spread between the returns on their mortgage loans (assets) and their cost of

TABLE 8.5	Mortgage Amortization, $100,000 @ 12% for 25 years, Months 1–12, Monthly Payment = $1,053.00		
Month	Principal	Interest	Principal Balance
1	$53.00	$1,000.00	$99,947.00
2	53.53	999.47	99,893.47
3	54.07	998.93	99,839.40
4	54.61	998.39	99,784.79
5	55.15	997.85	99,729.64
6	55.70	997.30	99,673.94
7	56.26	996.74	99,617.68
8	56.82	996.18	99,560.86
9	57.39	995.61	99,503.47
10	57.97	995.03	99,445.50
11	58.54	994.46	99,386.96
12	59.13	993.87	99,327.83
Totals	$672.17	$11,963.83	

borrowed funds (liabilities) when benchmark interest rates change. In ARMs the mortgage rate is linked to a standard benchmark rate, such as the rate on one-year Constant Maturity Treasury yield or the Federal Reserve's District Cost of Funds.

When an index changes, the lender can (1) make periodic changes in the borrowers monthly payments, (2) keep the monthly payment the same and change the principal amount of the loan, (3) change the maturity of the loan, or (4) any combination of the above. Some mortgage loans have fixed rates for 3 years, 5 years, 7 years, or 10 years, but may adjust one time, or annually after that.

The best adjustment, from the lender's point of view, depends on whether interest rates are expected to rise or fall over the life of the mortgage. If they are expected to rise, increased monthly payments will increase the lender's cash flow. If they are expected to fall, the second option will permit the lender to more or less maintain their spread between earning assets and costs of funds. The adjustment period may be monthly, annually, or any other time period, according to the terms of the contract.

Caps ARMs have *caps* that limit how much the interest rate or monthly payments can change annually or over the term of the loan. For example, the interest rate may change no more than 2 percentage points annually nor more than 6 percentage points over the life of the loan. Alternatively, a $50 payment cap means that the monthly payment cannot increase more than $50 per year.

Margin   Margin is the number of percentage points that the lender adds to the index rate to determine the rate charged on the ARM each adjustment period. The equation for the ARM rate that is charged is:

$$\text{ARM interest rate} = \text{Index rate} + \text{Margin} \qquad 8.2$$

Suppose the index rate is 10% and the margin is 2%. The interest rate that will be charged on the ARM is 12% (10% + 2% = 12%). The margin usually remains constant over the life of the loan. However, the size of the margin can vary from lender to lender.

Rates   Lenders may offer prospective home buyers a lower interest rate or lower payments for the first year of the mortgage loan to induce the buyer to use an ARM. After the discount period, the ARM rate will be adjusted to reflect the current index rate. The lower rate is commonly called a *teaser rate*, because lenders expect it to increase in future years.

Even without teaser rates, the initial interest rates charged on ARMs are lower than the rates charged on fixed rate mortgages. The extent to which they are lower depends on the maturity of the loans, and varies widely, but differences of 100 or more basis points are not uncommon. For example, in October 1999, the lowest 1-year ARM available in California was 6.250%, while the lowest 15-year fixed rate mortgage was 7.125% and the 30-year rate was 7.625%.[6]

Shifting the Risk   Lenders shift some of their interest rate risk of holding mortgage loans from themselves to borrowers by using ARMs. However, the lenders may have traded reduced interest rate risk for increased default risk and lower income. First, ARMs are riskier than fixed rate mortgages because they generate less interest income during periods of declining interest. Second, ARMs have higher delinquency and default risk than fixed rate mortgages. The Federal National Mortgage Association (Fannie Mae) reported that ARMs in their portfolio and mortgage-backed securities had a delinquency rate of 0.98% in August 1999 compared to a rate of 0.46% for fixed rate mortgages.[7] One reason for this difference may be that loan-to-value ratios are higher for ARMs than for fixed rate mortgages. Another may be that ARMs are used more frequently by younger, first-time buyers. The delinquency rates reported here occurred during a period of falling interest rates. The delinquency rates may get worse if interest rates increase because the borrower's ability to repay the loan may be diminished; the borrower's disposable income may not increase sufficiently to cover the higher interest payments. These risks are reflected in the relatively narrow spread between the effective rates charged on fixed rate mortgages and ARMs.

The Office of Thrift Supervision (http://www.ots.treas.gov/) publishes the Quarterly Review of Interest Rate Risk.

6. The mortgage rates are from CNNfn on the Internet. For current mortgage rates in a wide variety of cities, credit card rates, and other financial data, see: *http://www.cnnfn.com.*

7. Fannie Mae Monthly Summary (October 13, 1999). The loans are three or more months delinquent, in relief, or in foreclosure process as a percent of the number of loans. Data are for June 1998.

Lenders can reduce their risk by requiring the borrowers to have *private mortgage insurance* (FMI) on their loans. PMI is usually required when the down payment, or borrowers equity is less than 20%. Private mortgage insurance companies consider ARMs riskier than their fixed rate counterparts, and the insurance premiums on ARMs are higher than those on fixed rate mortgages.

ADDITIONAL TERMS Some additional terms and concepts are important to a discussion about mortgages.

Assumable Mortgage Some mortgage loans, such as Veterans Administration (VA) backed home loans are assumable, which means that they can be passed on to a new owner if the property is sold. Most mortgage loans are not assumable.

Buydown A high mortgage interest rate is offset by paying points at the time of closing.

Due-on-Sale Clause Some mortgage loans contain a *due-on-sale clause*, which means that the mortgage loan is not transferable to the new buyer, and the balance of the loan must be paid to the lender when the house is sold. The clause is exercised at the option of the lender. Other loans, however, are *assumable*, which means that the mortgage loan can be transferred to the buyer, if the buyer meets the lender's credit requirements and pays a fee for the assumption.

Late Charges Borrowers are required to make their monthly payments by a certain date or pay a late charge. Late charges cover the costs of handling delinquent accounts and adds to the lender's fee income.

Mortgage Insurance Private mortgage insurance for conventional mortgage loans is required by some lenders to reduce the default risk by insuring against loss on a specified percentage of the loan, usually the top 20–25%.

Points In addition to paying interest on the borrowed funds, lenders charge both fixed rate and adjustable rate mortgage borrowers additional fees or points, to increase their income, and to cover the costs of originating and closing mortgage loans. A *point*, is one percent of the principal amount of a mortgage loan, and points are prepaid interest. One point on an $100,000 mortgage is $1,000. The points usually are paid by the borrower at the time of the closing. They may be deducted from the face amount of the loan or paid as a cash cost. If they are deducted from the face amount of the loan, a one point closing cost on an $100,000 mortgage loan would result in a disbursement to the borrower of $99,000. Points are charged on government-backed (FHA, VA, FmHA) mortgages when the market rate of interest on conventional mortgage loans exceeds the rate permitted on such mortgages. The points make up the difference in rates between the two types of mortgages.

Points increase the *effective interest rate* of a mortgage loan. The effective interest rate is contract interest rate plus points and other costs amortized over the payback period of the loan. As a rule of thumb, each point (1% of the loan amount) increases the interest charge by one-eighth (1/8 or 0.125) of one percent. The ⅛ factor corresponds to a *payback period* (number of years until the loan is paid off) of about 15 years. For example, suppose that the contract interest rate on a mortgage loan is 13 percent and 4 points are charged at the closing. The effective interest rate for a 15 year payback is 13.5 percent (13% + 0.125 × 0.04 = 0.135). If the loan is repaid before or after 15 years, the rule of thumb does not apply.

Settlement Charges Settlement is the formal process by which ownership of real property, evidenced by the title, is transferred from the seller to the buyer. The settlement process for most residential mortgage loans is governed by the Real Estate Settlement Procedures Act (RESPA). Part of the settlement costs may include fees that enhance the lender's income. Examples of such fees include:

- Loan discounts or points.
- Loan origination fees, covers the lender's administrative costs.
- Lender's inspection fees, to inspect the property.
- Assumption processing fees, may be charged when the buyer takes on the prior loan from the seller.
- Escrow, funds held to ensure future payment of real estate taxes and insurance. No interest is paid on the funds.
- Settlement or closing fee, a fee paid to the settlement agent.

These settlement fees and others not mentioned here may amount to three percent, or more, of the total amount borrowed.

Alternative Mortgage Instruments

Alternative mortgage instruments are generic terms that cover a smorgasbord of mortgage instruments where the terms of the contract can change or where they differ from the traditional mortgage loan. The principal types of alternative mortgage instruments are discussed here.

BALLOON MORTGAGE **Balloon mortgage** loans are relatively short-term loans, such as five years. At the end of that period, the entire amount of the loan comes due and a new loan is negotiated. The initial payments are usually based on a 20- to 30-year amortization. This process is similar to the *Canadian rollover mortgage or renegotiable mortgage*, where the maturity is fixed, but the interest payments are renegotiated every three to five years.

GRADUATED PAYMENT MORTGAGE Because of the high cost of housing, many young buyers cannot afford large monthly mortgage payments. **Graduated payment mortgages** address this problem by making a fixed-rate loan where monthly payments are low at first and then rise over a period of years.

Because the monthly payments on GPMs are so low in the early years, the loan experiences *negative amortization* in which the monthly payments are insufficient to pay the interest on the loan. The unpaid interest accrues, and borrowers pay interest on the interest. If the borrowers decided to sell their residence in the early years, and it did not appreciate in value, the principal balance on the loan would have increased due to negative amortization. In other words, they would owe more than they originally borrowed on the house, and the sale of the mortgaged property might not provide sufficient funds to pay off the loan.

GROWING EQUITY MORTGAGE **Growing equity mortgages** (GEMs) are 15-year fully amortized home mortgage loans that provide for successively higher debt service payments over the life of the loan. They are made a fixed rate and the initial payments are calculated on a 30-year schedule. However, they are paid off more rapidly because an annual increase in the monthly payments goes to reduce the principal balance of the loan. In addition, the interest rate is made below the prevailing rate for 30-year loans. Borrowers who can afford the increased payments can save thousands of dollars in interest payments over the term of the loan.

SHARED APPRECIATION MORTGAGE A **shared appreciation mortgage** (SAM) is a mortgage loan arrangement whereby the borrower agrees to share in the increased value of the property (usually 30% to 50%) with the lender in return for a reduction in the fixed interest rate at the time the loan is made. The increased value of the property is determined at some specified date in the future when the loan can be refinanced or when the property is sold. Sharing a decline in value is not part of the loan agreement.

The Internal Revenue Service considers the bank's portion of the appreciation as contingent or residual interest, which means that it is ordinary income. Thus, the bank has no equity position in the property. Similar arrangements can be applied to other types of mortgage loans, such as large commercial mortgage loans and reverse annuity mortgages. While such arrangements between banks and real estate borrowers are not common, they are used by insurance companies and other long-term lenders making commercial real estate loans.

REVERSE ANNUITY MORTGAGE The **reverse annuity mortgage** (RAM) is designed for senior citizens who own their houses free and clear and want to increase their incomes by borrowing against the equity in their houses. In this case, the lender pays the property owner a fixed annuity based on a percentage value of the property. The owner would not be required to repay the loan until his or her demise, at which time the loan would be paid from the proceeds of the estate, or until the house is sold. The interest rate on the loan may be adjustable and the loan may have a refinancing option.

SECOND MORTGAGE/HOME EQUITY LOAN Many homeowners use a second mortgage when they need funds for business or as a substitute for consumer loans. Other than selling their homes, a home equity loan is the only way homeowners can convert their equity into funds they can spend. As previously noted, *equity* is the difference between the market value of the property and the mortgage debt, A traditional second mortgage is made in addition to the first mortgage and uses the same property as collateral. Second mortgages usually provide for a fixed dollar amount to be repaid over a specified period of time requiring monthly payment of principal and interest. Second mortgages have a subordinated claim to property in the event of foreclosure.

A **home equity loan** can be a traditional second mortgage, or a revolving line of credit that has a second mortgage status, but would be the first lien if the borrower has no mortgage debt outstanding when the credit line was established.[8] The line of credit has more a flexible repayment schedule than the traditional second mortgage. Under the home equity line of credit, the borrower with a fixed credit line can write checks up to that amount. In the case of a home equity loan, the loan is a lump sum that is paid off in installments over time.[9] Interest charges on home equity loans may be tax deductible, unlike the interest on consumer loans. Moreover, because home equity loans have the borrower's home as collateral, the interest rate charged on such loans may be less than the interest rate on credit cards. The home equity loan can be for a fixed amount, or it can be line of credit. Some lenders lend up to 125% to 150% of the value of the property on such lines. Banks usually have lower loan-to-value ratios, but may succumb to competitive pressures. An FDIC study of these high loan-to-value loans revealed that their charge-off rates and are increasing and the severity and frequency of defaults was much higher than for traditional home equity loans.[10]

See http//www.banking. state.ny.us/ *to compare credit card rates and terms and* http://www. lendingtree.com/ *for rates on credit cards, mortgages, and other types of loans.*

Credit Scoring Loan Requests

Credit scores have been in use since the 1950s to evaluate automobile and credit card loans. However, it has only been in recent years that Fannie Mae and Freddie Mac have used credit scores as a credit determinant in real estate lending. The real estate and consumer credit scoring models take into account credit bureau data, loan-to-value ratios, and information provided by the applicant. The models do not include any factors prohibited by the Equal Credit Opportunity Act (Federal Reserve Regulation B). These prohibitions will be explained later in this chapter. Data from credit bureaus account for about two-thirds to three-fourths of the predictive power of the model depending on the model used.[11] The credit score rank orders (from high to low) borrowers into categories based on the default risk they pose to lenders. Because lenders have different risk preferences, a score that is unacceptable to a low-risk lender may be acceptable to a lender willing to take higher risks.

For more information on credit scoring models, see Fair Isaac http://www. fairisaac.com/servlet/ SiteDriver/Content/3.

8. Glenn B. Canner, Thomas A. Durkin, and Charles A. Luckett, "Recent Developments in Home Equity Lending," *Federal Reserve Bulletin* (April 1998), pp. 241–251.
9. These definitions are based on the Bank Rate Monitor as they appear in the New York State Banking Department web site: *http//www.banking.state.ny.us/.* Also see: *http://www.bankrate.com* for additional terms.
10. FDIC News Release, PR-12-99, "FDIC Analysts Review High Loan-to-Value Lending: Evaluate Trends in Commercial Real Estate Markets" (March 17, 1999).
11. Sally Taylor-Shoff, "Shedding New Light on Credit Scoring," *Mortgage Banking* (March 1997), *http://www.fairisaac.com/html/pa_1.html.*

According to one article, a prospective home buyer spent 20 minutes on the phone providing a loan officer with financial information that was then used in a credit scoring model. Later that same day, the loan was approved.[12] Manually processing the loan application may take several days or longer. The article goes on to say that while credit scoring is a great tool, many lenders also consider other factors, such as collateral, credit reputation, and the ability to repay the loan.

The role of technology in mortgage lending is not limited to credit scoring. Automated underwriting technology at the Federal National Mortgage Association (Fannie Mae) has reduced the time it takes to originate a mortgage loan from four weeks to four minutes, and has cut the cost of origination by $800.[13]

Because substantial economies of scale can come from having large numbers of applications scored in one place, specialized or limited purpose banks or monoline banks have developed that deal primarily in credit cards, and to a lesser extent in mortgage lending. Nevertheless, small institutions may acquire generic credit scoring models for as little as $10,000, although custom models cost more.[14]

Commercial Real Estate Loans

Commercial mortgage loans are made for land, construction, and real estate development, and commercial properties such as shopping centers, office buildings, or warehouses. Commercial real estate loans often are linked to commercial loans. For example, suppose a delivery firm wants to expand and buy new trucks and build a warehouse. The bank would make a term loan to finance the trucks, a construction loan to build the warehouse, and then refinance it with a mortgage loan when it is completed. The mortgage loan on the warehouse cannot be pooled and sold like home mortgage loans. Nevertheless, it is a profitable loan. It is financed on a floating rate basis for seven years, and it is cross-collateralized with the trucks.

After land is acquired and financed, *construction loans* call for the bank to make irregular disbursements to the borrower/builder. One method of making the disbursements is based on completion of certain phases of construction. For example, 30% may be paid when the foundation is completed, 30% when the project is under roof and the plumbing and wiring have been completed,

12. Connie Potter, "Credit Scores: Number Crunching Can Mean Fast Moves for Spring Home Buyers," *Fair Isaac Press* (March 2, 1997), *http://www.fairisaac.com/html/pa_3.html*.

13. J. A. Johnson, "Remarks by James A. Johnson, Chairman and Chief Executive Officer, Fannie Mae, before the New York Society of Security Analysts, New York (October 28, 1998).

14. Ann Hayes Peterson, "Credit Scoring: Predictive Models Should Make Recommendations—Not Decisions—About Loan Approvals," *Credit Union Magazine* (January 1998), *http://www.fairisaasc.com/html/pa_4.html*.

and the remainder when the structure is completed and it is ready for occupancy. Another method is to pay the builder upon presentment of bills from suppliers and subcontractors as the building progresses. Construction loans have to be flexible to meet the needs of the borrower and the lender.

Construction and development loans are considered "interim" financing. That is, the loans are only in effect during the development and construction phase of the real estate project. When the project is complete, the builder is expected to get "permanent," or long-term, financing. The permanent financing is usually determined before interim financing is provided.

In the case of home loans, the permanent financing will be provided when the homes are sold and the buyers obtain mortgage loans. In the case of commercial property, long-term financing can be obtained from life insurance companies, Fannie Mae, Freddie Mac, pension and retirement plans, as well as banks. It is common practice of life insurance companies to share in the equity or profits from large commercial real estate ventures they finance.

During the development and construction phase of development, the land and partially completed structures serve as collateral for the loan. If the developer/builder is unable to complete the project for one reason or another, and defaults on the loan, the lender may take possession of the partially completed structure. Then the lender has to consider finishing the structure or liquidating it. Because considerable risk may be involved with interim financing, the interest rates charged are relatively high for some borrowers. Interest rates on construction loans are frequently priced a the prime rate plus one or more percentage points depending on the risk involved. In addition, an origination fee of 1–3% of the amount of the loan may be charged. This fee covers the cost of the paperwork involved and increases the effective yield on the loan to the bank.

8.2 CONSUMER LENDING

Consumer credit outstanding was $1.3 trillion in March 1999. Commercial banks held 37% of total, and the remainder was held by finance companies, savings institutions, credit unions, and others. **Consumer credit** consists of loans to individuals for personal, household, or family consumption. Consumer lending is the heart of *retail banking*—banking services provided to individuals and to small business concerns. Services provided to medium-sized and large business concerns and governments is called *wholesale banking*. Most banks do both retail and wholesale banking, although some specialize more than others. Small banks tend to specialize in retail banking because they do not have sufficient assets to do large-scale wholesale lending.

MANAGERIAL ISSUES

Clean Up Your Act

Under the Environmental Superfund Act of 1980, and the amendments in 1986, banks may be held responsible for cleaning up environmental damage done by their borrowers. In the case of *U.S. v. Maryland Bank Trust Co.*, for example, the Environmental Protection Agency (EPA) sued the bank for reimbursement of cleanup costs of a hazardous waste dump after the bank had foreclosed on the property.* The bank had held the property for four years, and the court held that the bank should pay for the cleanup cost.

However, foreclosure was not a necessary condition in *U.S. v. Fleet Factors Corporation*. The Eleventh Circuit Court of Appeals held that a secured leader can be liable under federal environmental laws, even absent foreclosures, if the lender participates in the financial management of the borrower's facility to a degree indicating a capacity to influence the corporation's treatment of hazardous waste.**

*632F. Supp. 573 (D.Md. 1986).

**U.S. v. Fleet Factors Corp. 724 F. Supp. 955 (S.D. Ga. 1988); 111 S.Ct. 752 (1990).

Types of Consumer Loans

Consumer loans differ from commercial and real estate loans (including home equity loans) in several respects. First, except for automobile and mobile home loans, most consumer loans are for relatively small dollar amounts compared to a home or car loan. Second, most consumer loans are not secured by collateral because they are used to buy nondurable goods and services where collateral is not practical. Airline tickets, food, gasoline, and doctor bills are examples of such goods and services. Third, with the same exceptions, many consumer loans are *open-end* (no maturity) lines of credit whereby consumers may increase their loans and pay off the loans over an indefinite period of time. Credit card loans are one example of open-end loans. Loans with definite maturities are called *closed-end loans*. Automobile loans that must be repaid within 48 months are an example of closed-end loans.

The greatest risk associated with consumer installment credit is default risk—the risk that the borrower will not repay the loan. Defaults tend to increase with the size of the loan, with longer-term maturities, and are inversely related to the value of the collateral relative to the size of the loan. Defaults also tend to increase during recessions when unemployment is high. The average delinquency rate for all types of closed-end bank installment loans was 2.43% in 1997.[15] Within this group of closed-end loans, mobile home loans had the highest delinquency rate (4.91%) and home equity loans had the lowest rate (1.49%). Bank credit card loans had a delinquency rate of 3.04%.

15. U.S. Department of Commerce, *Statistical Abstract of the United States, 1998,* Table 820.

The market for consumer loans is highly competitive in the areas of interest rates, amounts loaned, fees, and noncredit services provided by issuers of credit cards. The services offered include liability insurance on automobile rentals, frequent flyer mileage on airlines, travel accident insurance, discounts on long-distance phone calls, extended warranties on items purchased, and other benefits. The Discover card has a cashback bonus that pays its card-holders a small percentage of the items charged on their credit card. In addition, *affinity card plans* offer bank credit cards to members of a particular organization (i.e., universities, clubs, unions). Affinity cards carry the organization's logo, and the organization may benefit financially from members' card usage.

Consumer installment loans can be profitable. One obvious reason is that the rates charged on such loans are relatively high when compared to rates charged on commercial and real estate loans. A credit card loan, for example, may have an interest rate of 15%, while the commercial loan my have a 10% rate and the real estate loan an 8% rate. Of course the size, risk, and maturity of each of the loans differ substantially. Another reason for the high profitability is that much of the processing and monitoring work concerning consumer loans (i.e., credit cards) can be automated. The automation provides economies of scale when managing large portfolios of such loans. Large consumer loan portfolios consist of many small loans over a wide geographic area, which allows the lender to diversify its risk of lending. It also means that the few loans that default will not have a major impact on the bank's capital. In contrast, banks that have small loan portfolios of large commercial real estate loans may not have sufficient capital to withstand the failure of a few large commercial real estate loans. Failures of real estate loans were one of the primary causes of bank failures in the last two decades in the United States and other major countries.[16] More will be said about income from the credit card business shortly.

AUTOMOBILE LOANS As shown in Table 8.6 automobile loans accounted for 35% of consumer loans from all lenders. Automobile loans may have an original maturity of 60 months and some lenders will finance 90% or more of the cost. The average loan-to-value ratio is 91% for new cars and 99% for used ones. Although most automobile loans are paid off in installments, some are balloon loans with a repurchase agreement that makes them look like a closed-end lease from the customer's point of view. Closed-end leases will be discussed shortly. Under a *repurchase agreement*, the bank (or some other third party) will repurchase the automobile at the end of the term of the loan, at the customer's option, for a price that is equal to the balloon obligation. In other words, the bank takes the automobile instead of the final payment. Suppose that the amount borrowed for the loan is $18,000 and the automobile is expected to have a value of $10,000 at the end of the loan period, which is the

16. Benton E. Gup, *Bank Failures in the Major Trading Countries of the Word: Causes and Remedies* (Westport CT: Quorum Books, 1998).

same dollar amount as the balloon payment. At the end of the loan period, the customer can choose one of the following options:

1. Sell or trade-in the car and pay off the balance of the loan
2. Keep the car and payoff or refinance the balance
3. Exercise the repurchase agreement instead of paying off the loan

The repurchase agreement stipulates that the vehicle must be within certain standards for mileage and wear and tear. The mileage limit may be 15,000 miles per year, and the buyer is required to provide normal maintenance. The trade-in value of the automobile is usually supported by an insurance policy, thereby reducing the risk to the bank.

The monthly payments on balloon loans are often 300 to 500 basis points higher than the monthly payments on a lease payments because the lender does not get the tax advantage of the depreciation from the vehicle.

Like mortgage loans, automobile loans can be pooled and sold to investors. In March 1999, asset-backed/securitized consumer loans (automobile, credit cards, and other types of loans) amounted to $381 billion, or about 29% of total consumer installment credit.[17]

REVOLVING CONSUMER LOANS **Revolving consumer loans** accounted for 43% of consumer credit (Table 8.6). With *revolving loans*, or *open-end credit*, the borrower has a line of credit up to a certain amount, and may pay off the loans and credit charges over an indefinite period of time. Revolving loans have no definite maturity. The terms of repayment are flexible and are largely at the discretion of the borrower. Most revolving loans only charge interest on the amount borrowed if the borrower pays less than the full amount of the loan at the end of a grace period of 25–30 days or less. The grace period does not apply to cash advances, which may incur finance charges beginning on the

TABLE 8.6	Consumer Credit, March 1999	
Type	**Amount ($ millions)**	**Percentage**
Automobile	$462,860	35%
Revolving	568,338	43
Other	293,562	22
Totals	$1,324,760	100%

Source: *Federal Reserve Bulletin*, Consumer Credit (July 1999), p. A36.

17. *Federal Reserve Bulletin* (July 1999), p. A36.

transaction date. Bank credit cards, such as VISA and MasterCard, account for most of the revolving loans.

Credit Cards A **credit card** is any card, plate, or device that may be used from time to time and over and over again to borrow money, or buy goods and services *on credit*.[18] A credit card should not be confused with a debit card, or prepayment card. A *debit card* looks like a plastic credit card, and may be used to make purchases, but no credit is extended. The funds are withdrawn or transferred from the cardholder's account to pay for the purchases. In the case of *prepayment (stored-value) cards*, a certain dollar amount is prepaid, and deductions are made for each transaction. They are widely used to make telephone calls, and in New York, San Francisco, and Washington in lieu of coins for subway fares. *Smart cards*, cards containing silicon chips and capable of storing data and making simple computations, are being introduced into the payments system in China, Europe, and the United States.

A Federal Reserve study revealed that in 1995, 66% of households had credit cards, up from 56% in 1989.[19] The growth of credit card-related consumer debt is attributable to automation, and the fact that credit cards are mass marketed like a commodity. That is, credit cards are sold as a cluster of services at one price, without personal contact with the issuer. Mass mailings of credit card applications are sent to selected segments of the population based on demographic criteria, such as income and housing. The applications are evaluated by computer programs using credit scoring. Qualified applicants receive cards, and their accounts are monitored by computer programs. The use of automation keeps labor costs at a minimum for the large number of transactions processed. This process allows credit card issuers located in Delaware, North Dakota, or elsewhere to sell their cards anywhere in the United States. Obviously, they must be sold in sufficient quantity to justify the cost of credit card operations.

See http://www. onlinebankingreport.com/ *for rates on mortgages, car loans, CDs, and more.*

In addition to the mass marketing of credit cards, individual banks issue them to their customers. Of the three types of credit card plans used by banks, the first type of plan utilizes a single principal bank to issue the credit card, maintain accounts, bill and collect credit, and assume most of the other functions associated with credit cards.

In the second type of plan, one bank acts as a limited agent for the principal bank. The principal bank issues the card, carries the bulk of the credit, and performs the functions described in the first plan. The functions of the agent bank are to establish merchant accounts and accept merchant sales drafts; it receives a commission on the business it generates without incurring costs of a credit card operation. The limited agent bank may have its own name and logo

18. Credit cards are defined by Regulation Z, and in 12 CFR 226.2 (a)(15).
19. Sandra E. Black and Donald P. Morgan, "Meet the New Borrowers," *Federal Reserve Bank of New York, Current Issues in Economics and Finance* (February 1999); U.S. Department of Commerce, *Statistical Abstract of the United States 1998,* Table 823.

on the card. Cardholders assume that the card is issued and managed by that bank, which is not the case.

In the third plan, a bank affiliates with one of the major *travel and entertainment card* (T&E) plans such as American Express. A travel and entertainment card is a credit card, but cardholders must pay the amount owed when billed. They do not have the option of making small payments over time. However, American Express also issues the Optima card, which is a credit card in the true sense of the word.

All bank credit cards have the following common features:

1. The credit cardholder has a prearranged line of credit with a bank that issues credit cards. Credit is extended when the credit cardholder buys something and signs (or approves) a sales draft at a participating retail outlet. The retail merchant presents the sales draft to its bank for payment in full, less a *merchant discount* that is based on one of the following:
    a. The retail outlet's volume of credit card trade
    b. The average size of each credit card sale
    c. The amount of compensating balances kept at the bank
    d. Some combination of the above factors

    The merchant discounts range from nothing to 6% or more. Some merchants do not accept certain credit cards that have high merchant discounts. Thus, not all credit cards are equal in the eyes of merchants.

    The merchant's bank will get part of the merchant discount for handling the transaction and routing it to the major credit card company, such as VISA, that issued the card. The credit card company determines the amount that the card-issuing bank owes. The card-issuing bank pays the credit card company, and the credit card company pays the merchant bank. Finally, the card-issuing bank presents the sales draft to the credit cardholder for payment.

Current information on credit card interest rates, fees, and other terms is available from the New York State Banking Department Credit Card Survey at http://www.banking.ny.us.

2. Most banks allow the credit cardholder to pay for the draft in full within a grace period (say 25 days from the billing date), and not be charged interest on the outstanding balance, or pay some minimum amount each month on an installment basis. However, some banks have no grace period, and they state in their contracts, "There is no period during which credit extended can be repaid without incurring a finance charge." Banks depend on interest income earned on these credit balances as the major source of income from their credit card operations.

    Banks also earn *fee income* from credit cards. For example, a bank may charge an annual fee, say $50, for the privilege of having a credit card. However, for competitive reasons, some banks charge no annual fees.

    Fees are also charged for other account activities, including the following:

    - Cash advances: 3% of the cash advance or a minimum of $3 and no maximum amount
    - Late payments: the issuer will add $20 to the purchase balance

for each billing period the borrower fails to make the minimum payment due

■ Exceeding the credit line: the issuer will add $20 to the purchase balance for each billing period the balance exceeds the line of credit

■ Returned check charges: when payments are not honored, the issuer may add $20

Finally, banks earn fees for the sale of products, vacation packages, magazine subscriptions, and insurance in connection with their credit cards.

3. The final feature is the plastic credit card itself, which serves special purposes. First it identifies the customer to the merchant. Some Citibank credit cards have the customer's picture on the card in order to enhance its security. This identification aspect does not apply to credit transactions by Internet, mail, or telephone. Second, it is used to transfer account information to the sales draft by use of a machine. Finally, the card may be encoded with a magnetic strip or computer chip that provides additional information about the cardholder's financial condition.

About 52% of credit card debt outstanding is *convenience* use, in which the cardholder uses the credit card instead of cash or checks and pays the amount owed in full when billed, thereby avoiding interest charges.[20] Therefore, the amount of consumer credit shown in Table 8.6 is overstated.

OTHER LOANS The "other" type of credit listed in Table 8.6 is a catchall category that includes all other consumer loans made to individuals. Loans for mobile homes, boats, vacations, debt consolidation, and for other purposes are included here.

Mobile Home Loans Because of their origins as trailers being pulled behind cars, mobile home loans are included in consumer credit. Mobile home loans are direct and indirect loans made to individuals to purchase mobile homes. A mobile (manufactured) home is a moveable dwelling unit, 10 feet or more wide and 35 feet or more in length, that may be moved on its own chassis. They are not considered the same as travel trailers, motor homes, or modular housing. In the case of indirect loans, banks may require the dealers from whom they purchased loans to stand behind them in the event of default, which can be accomplished by the dealer keeping a reserve account at the bank until the loan is repaid. Additional protection for the lender can be obtained in the form of insurance. Mobile home loans may be guaranteed by the FHA or VA. Mobile (manufactured) home loans that are backed by FHA/VA qualify as collateral in GNMA mortgage-backed securities. In addition, the Department of Housing and Urban Development (HUD) insures approved lenders against losses on manufactured home loans, lots and parks for manufactured homes,

20. U.S. Department of Commerce, *Statistical Abstract of the United States 1998*, Table 823. The latest data are for 1995.

made in accordance with the National Housing Act (Titles I and II, and Section 207). The loan must be for the purchase of a manufactured home to be used as the principal single-family residence, or for manufactured home lots and parks. The manufactured homes must meet certain design, construction, and performance standards.

Noninstallment Loans   Commercial banks also make noninstallment consumer loans. These loans are scheduled to be repaid in a lump sum. The largest component of the noninstallment loans are single payment loans that are used to finance the purchase of one home while another home is being sold. Loans used for this purpose are called bridge loans. Other noninstallment loans are used to finance investments, and for other purposes.

Leases

Leasing is an alternative method of financing consumer durables such as automobiles, trucks, airplanes, and boats. In the case of cars, low monthly costs and getting a new car every few years are two reasons for their popularity.

Under a lease, the bank owns the automobile and "rents" it to the customer.[21] The lease may be *open-end*, in which case the bank is responsible for selling the automobile at the end of the lease period. If the amount received is less than a previously agreed upon residual value the customer pays the difference in a balloon payment. Suppose that an automobile is leased under a three-year open-end lease. The lessor estimates that the car will be worth $15,000 after three years of normal wear. If the auto is returned in a condition that reduces its value to $12,000, the lessee may owe a balloon payment of $3,000. The value can be determined by an independent appraiser, but the lessee must pay the appraisal fee. The balloon payments are usually no more than three times the usual monthly payment. If the monthly payment is $600, the balloon payment would not be more than $1,800, unless the auto sustained unusual wear and tear. If the appraised value is more than the residual value, the customer receives the difference.

Under a *closed-end* lease, the bank assumes the risk of the market value being less than the residual value of the automobile. National banks must have insurance on the residual on closed-end leases. The monthly payments for closed-end leases are higher than those for open-end leases because the bank has a greater risk, but the lease has no balloon payment. However, because the bank owns the automobile and gets the tax benefit (depreciation), the monthly payments may be less than that of a loan of an equivalent amount to buy the automobile outright.

Under the Consumer Leasing Act of 1976 and Federal Reserve Regulation M, consumer leases must meet the following criteria:

---

21. When a customer leases a car, he or she pays a monthly rental use tax in lieu of a sales tax had the car been purchased.

MANAGING RISK

History of Consumer Credit in the United States

During the eighteenth century and first half of the nineteenth century, the principal nonbank agencies that extended credit were small merchants, physicians, and pawnbrokers. The Industrial Revolution brought about changes in credit demands and institutions. Industrialization made more goods available for consumers and created a class of wage earners, which was bolstered by large-scale immigration into the United States. The credit needs of the industrial wage earners differed from the credit needs of farmers, who generally borrowed on "open-book" accounts (without formal agreements) and paid off their debts with the crops that were sold. In contrast, industrial wage earners received steady incomes and could pay their debts on a regular basis throughout the year. Accordingly, the concept of installment credit evolved, because many workers received low wages and required credit to raise their standard of living above subsistence levels.

These credit needs were partially satisfied by *small loan companies* that concentrated on making personal loans secured by personal property and wage assignments. Those who could not obtain credit from legitimate small loan companies borrowed from *loan sharks*, individuals who charged excessive rates of interest—sometimes in excess of 200 percent—and sometimes required the borrower's physical well-being as collateral. Today such interest rates are a violation of the federal extortion and credit statutes (Title 18, U.S.C. 891-896).

By the turn of the twentieth century, installment credit and loan sharks were widespread throughout the United States. The first legislation concerning installment credit and the abuses of loan sharks was enacted in Massachusetts in 1911. This law permitted lenders to make loans of up $300 and charge an interest rate of 42% per year. Other states enacted similar legislation. A direct result of the effort to curb and regulate loan sharks was the development of consumer finance companies.

After World War I, new types of credit institutions developed. The availability of consumer durables such as automobiles and washing machines expanded the demand for consumer credit. Sales finance companies, which buy consumer installment credit contracts from retail dealers and provide wholesale financing to those dealers, grew from this demand. Commercial banks were the next institution to enter the consumer loan field. The National City Bank of New York opened the first personal loan department in 1928. Revolving retail credit appeared when John Wanamaker, a large Philadelphia department store, introduced it in 1938. The next major innovation was the development of the credit card. In 1951, Franklin National Bank of New York issued the first bank credit card. This plastic money was the forerunner of the credit cards issued by banks, retailers, oil companies, and others.

- The lease covers personal (not real) property.
- The term of the lease must exceed four months.
- It must be made to a natural person, not a corporation.
- The total lease obligation must not exceed $25,000.
- The lease must be for personal, family, or household purposes, and covers cars, furniture, and appliances, but not daily car rentals or apartment leases.

Finance Charges

The Truth-in-Lending Act (Title I of the Consumer Protection Act of 1968), which is implemented Federal Reserve *Regulation Z*, requires lenders of consumer loans to provide borrowers with written information about finance charges and annual percentage rates (APR), before they sign a loan agreement, so that they may compare credit costs.[22] The extent to which consumers use the information to make intelligent decisions is not clear. Few consumers have the time or the knowledge to compare the nuances of the costs of financing. As we will see shortly, costs are not always what they appear to be.

The **finance charge** is the *total dollar amount* paid for the use of credit. It is the difference between the amount repaid and the amount borrowed. The finance charge includes interest, service charges, and other fees the borrower must pay as a condition of or incident to the extension of credit. For example, a customer borrows $1,000 for one year and pays $80 in interest, a $10 service charge, and a $10 origination fee, The finance charge is $100.

Four methods of assessing finance charges on revolving credits are presented here. As previously mentioned, some methods of computing charges have a higher profit potential for lenders than others. To illustrate the differences in potential profits, or costs to consumer, consider the following transactions.

On June 5, Andrew Earl receives a statement with the total amount due of $100 for the billing period ending May 31. No finance charge will be assessed if the balance is paid by June 30. On June 1, Andrew made a $100 purchase that will appear on his next monthly statement. On June 15, he made a $20 payment on the loan. The interest rate charged on the unpaid balance is 1½ percent monthly (18% annually).

ADJUSTED BALANCE METHOD Using this method, the finance charge is applied against the amount that has been billed less any payments made prior to the due date. Purchases are not counted. The amount billed in this example is $100 and the payment was $20, resulting in $80. The finance charge is 1½ percent times $80, which amounts to $1.20.

PREVIOUS BALANCE METHOD According to this method, the finance charge is applied against the original amount billed and no consideration is given to the $20 payment. The finance charge is 1½ percent times $100, which amounts to $1.50.

AVERAGE DAILY BALANCE METHOD EXCLUDING CURRENT TRANSACTIONS According to this method, the finance charge is based on the average daily balance outstanding over the current 30-day period, but does not include current transactions. The average daily balance is $90 ($100 for 15 days and $80 for 15 days) and the finance charge is $1.35 ($90 × 1½% = $1.35).

---

22. In the case of automobile leases from banks, the interest cost is referred to as a "money factor," and may be converted to an APR.

AVERAGE DAILY BALANCE METHOD INCLUDING CURRENT TRANSACTIONS According to this method, the finance charge is based on the average daily balance outstanding during the current 30-day period, including new purchases made during that time. The average daily balance is $200 for the first 15 days ($100 from April and $100 purchased on June 1) and the $180 for the last 15 days ($200 less $20 = 180), so the average balance for the entire period is $190. The finance charge is 1½ percent times $190, which amounts to $2.85.

If borrowers skip a payment on a month's purchases, or make a partial payment, they may lose the "grace period." The grace period is the time in which the bill can be paid in full to avoid interest on the most recent month's charges. The reason is that many card issuers calculate interest on the account's average daily balance retroactive to the first purchase. The average daily balance including the current transactions method illustrates the impact a grace period has on finance charges. Some banks, which promote their low interest rates, use the most expensive methods of computing their finance charges.

Methods	Finance Charge
Adjusted balance	$1.20
Previous balance	1.50
Average daily balance excluding current transactions	1.35
Average daily balance including current transactions	2.85

In review, by using different methods for determining the unpaid balance, finance charges on the same transaction based on an 18% annual interest rate (1½% monthly) ranged from a low of $1.20 to a high of $2.85! All these methods for determining unpaid balances are widely used.

The Truth-in-Lending Act does not tell creditors how to calculate the finance charges, it only requires that they inform borrowers of the methods that are used and provide them with information about the annual percentage rate.

Annual Percentage Rate

SINGLE PAYMENT, END OF PERIOD The **annual percentage rate (APR)** is the percentage cost of credit on an annual basis. The APR may be used to compare credit costs of loans of various sizes and maturities.[23] The APR is the annualized *internal rate of return* (IRR) on the loan. Readers who are familiar with financial management will recognize that the IRR is that rate of interest that equates the present value of the periodic payments with the principal amount of the loan.

23. For detailed information about interest rate calculations, see David Thorndike, *Thorndike Encyclopedia of Banking and Financial Tables, Revised Edition* (Boston: Warren, Gorham & Lamont, 1980).

The APR for a given series of payments can be calculated easily by calculators programmed to calculate the IRR. For textbook exercises, we recommend such calculators. Most banks use computer programs or tables to compute the APR. Finally, the IRR may be determined by using the following equation when the payments are the same in each period:

$$P = \sum_{t=1}^{n} \text{PMT}[1/(1 + i)^t] \qquad\qquad 8.3$$

     P = original principal amount ($), or the amount received by the borrower in the case of discount loan rate

PMT = periodic payments ($)

    i = periodic interest rate (%)

    n = number of periodic payments

Other equations (methods) also may be used to calculate APRs.[24] The Federal Reserve allows some flexibility in how to compute APRs. The APRs are considered acceptable as long as they are within ⅛ of 1 percent of one of the two "actual APRs" computed by the Federal Reserve. The Federal Reserve uses the internal rate of return (actuarial method) and/or the U.S. Rule method (not described here) to compute the actual APR. The methods give slightly different results.

By way of illustration of the use of the IRR to compute APRs, assume that a customer wants to borrow $1,000 for one year at 10%. The bank can offer the customer monthly amortization, an add-on rate, or a discount rate. The APRs for each method are substantially different.

MONTHLY AMORTIZATION Amortization refers to the gradual repayment of debt over time. In this example, the loan is amortized by 12 monthly payments of $87.92 each. Using Eq. (8.3), we determine that the IRR/periodic rate is

$$P = \sum_{t=1}^{n} \text{PMT}[1/(1 + i)^t]$$

$$\$1,000 = \sum_{t=1}^{12} \$87.92[1/(1 + i)^t]$$

$$i = 0.83407$$

$$\text{APR} = 0.83407 \times 12 = 10.01\%$$

24. An alternative method for computing APR is presented in Chapter 13, Electronic Banking.

Because the periodic rate is monthly, the nominal annual rate is determined by multiplying the periodic rate by 12 to get the percentage. Accordingly, the APR in this example is 10.01% ($12 \times 0.83407 = 10.01\%$). percent.

ADD-ON LOAN RATE The term *add-on* means that the finance charge is added on to the amount borrowed. Consider a $1,000 loan for one year at 10% add-on interest. For purposes of illustration, the finance charge, *FC*, is determined by multiplying the amount borrowed, *P*, by the add-on interest rate expressed as a decimal, *R*, times the life of the loan in *years*, *T*. The *FC* may include fees and charges not considered in these examples. In this example, one year is used so $T = 1$. If the loan had been for 15 months, *T* would be equal to 1.25; if it were for 18 months, *T* would be equal to 1.5, and so on.

$$FC = P \times R \times T \qquad\qquad 8.4$$
$$= \$1,000 \times .10 \times 1$$
$$= \$100$$

The $100 finance charge is added on to the amount borrowed, so that the total amount owed is $1,100. The monthly payments, PMT, are determined by dividing the total amount owed, which is principal amount plus the finance charge, by the number of payments *n*.

$$\text{PMT} = (P + FC)/n \qquad\qquad 8.5$$
$$= (\$1,000 + \$100)/12 = \$91.67$$

Using Eq. (8.3), the APR is 17.98%.

$$P = \sum_{t=1}^{n} \text{PMT}[1/(1 + i)^t]$$

$$\$1,000 = \sum_{t=1}^{12} \$91.67[1/(1 + i)^t]$$

$$i = 1.498$$

$$\text{APR} = 1.498 \times 12 = 17.98\%$$

DISCOUNT LOAN RATE In a discount loan, the creditor deducts the finance charge from the principal amount of the loan and the borrower receives the difference. Consider a $1,000 loan discounted at 10%. The creditor deducts the $100 finance charge from the $1,000 principal amount and the borrower receives $900. Nevertheless, the borrower must repay $1,000 in 12 monthly payments of $83.33 ($1,000/12 = $83.33). When calculating the APR on discount loans, *P*, the amount received by the borrower ($900), is set equal to the discounted monthly payments. The APR for the discount loan is 19.90%.

$$P = \sum_{t=1}^{n} \text{PMT}[1/(1+i)^t]$$

$$\$900 = \sum_{t=1}^{12} \$83.33[1/(1+i)^t]$$

$$i = 1.6587$$

$$\text{APR} = 1.6587 \times 12 = 19.90\%$$

In summary, the APRs are

Monthly amortization	10.01%
Add-on rate	17.97%
Discount rate	19.90%

From the bank's point of view, the discount method produces the highest returns followed by the add-on method.

As mentioned previously, the APR may be used to compare the cost of credit. The concept of *cost of credit* is multidimensional, and it includes the amount of the monthly payments, the amount of the down payment, method of payment (i.e., cash, payroll deduction, etc.), and other factors. By way of illustration, consider loans A and B, each for $6,000, and each having an APR of 14%. Loan A has a maturity of 3 years and loan B has a maturity of 4 years. Because loan B has a longer maturity, the monthly payments are lower than those of loan A. However, the total finance charge and total payments of loan B is higher than that of loan A. Although the finance charges are lower with loan A, consumers who prefer lower monthly payments may choose loan B.

	APR %	Maturity Years	Monthly Payments	Finance Charge	Total Payments
Loan A	14	3	$205.07	$1,382.52	$7,382.52
Loan B	14	4	163.96	1,870.08	7,870.08

Real Estate and Consumer Credit Regulation

Federal laws prescribe certain terms and conditions under which lenders can make residential real estate and consumer loans. Highlights of selected laws are presented here. The legislation and regulations impose substantial costs on lenders. They must maintain detailed records of their actions and submit to examinations to review their compliances with legislation and relevant regulations. A recent study revealed that the costs of complying with *all bank regulations* is about 12–13% of banks' noninterest expense.[25]

25. Gregory Elliehausen, "The Cost of Bank Regulation: A Review of the Evidence," *Federal Reserve Bulletin* (April 1998), pp. 252–253.

COMMUNITY REINVESTMENT ACT (CRA) The Community Reinvestment Act is directed at federally regulated lenders that take deposits and extend credit. Such institutions are required to serve the needs and convenience of their respective communities. The intent of the legislation is to facilitate the availability of mortgage loans and other types of loans to all qualified applicants, without regard to their race, nationality, or gender.

EQUAL CREDIT OPPORTUNITY ACT (ECOA) AND THE FAIR HOUSING ACT The Equal Credit Opportunity Act (Federal Reserve Regulation B) and Fair Housing Act collectively prohibit lenders from discriminating against borrowers on the basis of age (provided that the applicant has the capacity to contract), color, family status (having children under age 18), handicap, marital status, national origin, race, receipt of public assistance funds, religion, gender, or the exercise of any right under the Consumer Protection Act.

FAIR CREDIT BILLING ACT If a customer believes his or her bill contains an error, he or she must contact the lender, *in writing*, within 60 days after the first bill in which the error appears is sent. A telephone call to the lender does not preserve the customer's rights. The amount in dispute, including finance charges, accrues until the issue is resolved. The lender has 90 days to correct the error or explain why the bill is correct.

HOME MORTGAGE DISCLOSURE ACT The HMDA (Federal Reserve Regulation C), enacted by Congress in 1975, and amendments were intended to make available to the public information concerning the extent to which financial institutions are serving the housing credit needs of their communities. HMDA data are also used by government officials to assess public sector investments in housing, and to identify possible discriminatory lending patterns.

REAL ESTATE SETTLEMENT PROCEDURES ACT (RESPA) *Settlement* is the process by which the ownership of real estate, which is represented by the title, passes from the seller to the buyer. The intent of RESPA is to provide buyers and sellers with information about the settlement process. RESPA covers most residential real estate loans including lots for houses or mobile homes. When a buyer applies in writing for a loan covered by RESPA, the lender must send the borrower "good faith estimates" of the settlements costs within three business days of the application, and a booklet, called *Settlement Costs—A HUD Guide*, describing the settlement and charges. One day before settlement, the borrower has the right to see the completed Uniform Settlement Statement that will be used.

TRUTH-IN-LENDING ACT The purpose of the Truth-in-Lending Act (Federal Reserve Regulation Z) is to assure that creditors disclose to individual consumers who are borrowers (not business borrowers) the amount of the finance charge and the annual interest rate (APR) they are paying to facilitate the comparison of finance charges from different sources of credit. In addition, credit card issuers are required to disclose, in written applications or their telephone solicitations, fees, grace period, and the method of calculating balances. Finance charges and APR were discussed earlier in this chapter. The law requires that the disclosures be clear and conspicuous, grouped together, and segregated from other contractual matters to make it easier for consumers to understand.

IF CREDIT IS DENIED Credit denial must be based on the creditworthiness of the applicant. If credit is denied, the creditor must notify the applicant within 30 days. The notification must be in writing and explain the reasons for the denial, or tell you that you have the right to ask for an explanation if one is not provided. Frequently, the denial is based on information received from a credit bureau, a firm that provides credit information for a fee to creditors. Credit bureaus obtain their information from creditors, and sometimes errors are made or information is out of date. For example, bankruptcies must be removed from credit histories after 10 years, and suits, judgments, tax liens, and arrest records must be removed after 7 years.

Under the Fair Credit Reporting Act, applicants who have had credit denied based on information from a credit bureau have the right to examine the credit file and correct errors or mistakes in it. If the request is made within 30 days of the refusal, the credit bureau may not charge a fee for providing the information. The credit bureau is required to remove any errors that the creditor who supplied the information admits are there. If a disagreement still remains, the applicant can include a short statement in his or her file with their side of the story. However, removal of incorrect information from one credit bureau does not change the files of the other credit bureaus.

SUMMARY

Real estate and consumer lending are the heart of retail banking. Mortgage lending for 1–4 family homes accounts for about 76% of the mortgage debt outstanding, and revolving credit accounts for 43% of consumer credit.

Changes in technology are having a major influence in the conduct of retail banking. The use of credit scoring to make lending decisions and securitization to manage portfolios are changing the way that lenders operate. The economies of scale in both credit scoring and securitization favor both increased concentration (size) of lenders, and increased specialization. In addition, an increasing number of lenders are using the Internet to sell their products, thereby expanding the geographic markets in which they operate from local market to global markets.

This chapter examined some of the details of real estate and consumer lending. One significant difference between commercial and industrial loans that were examined in the previous chapter, and real estate and consumer loans is that the latter are becoming standardized commodity products that can be securitized. Nevertheless, a large number of real estate and consumer loans still are not securitized and remain on the lender's books.

Finally, retail banking is more heavily regulated than wholesale banking in order to help consumers make informed credit decisions, to protect their financial interests, and to meet social goals mandated in the CRA and other acts.

Key Terms and Concepts

Adjustable rate mortgage (ARM)	Graduated payment mortgage
Annual percentage rate (APR)	Growing equity mortgage
Balloon mortgage	Home equity loan
Commercial mortgage loans	Mortgage
Consumer credit	Residential mortgage loans
Credit card	Reverse annuity mortgage
Finance charge	Revolving consumer loans
Fixed rate mortgage	Shared appreciation mortgage

Questions

8.1   Is real estate good or bad collateral?

8.2   What are the two basic types of 1–4 family residential mortgage loans? Which is the most widely used? Why?

8.3   What is a balloon loan?

8.4   What factors affect monthly payments on a residential mortgage loan? Explain the effect of each factor.

8.5   Why do lenders charge points on mortgage loans?

8.6   Explain the following terms: settlement charges, RESPA, buydown, and due-on-sale clause.

8.7   What are the advantages and disadvantages of an ARM from the lender's point of view?

8.8   Briefly distinguish between the following types of loans: graduated payment mortgages, shared appreciation mortgages, reverse annuity mortgages, and home equity loan.

8.9   In what respects are the Home Mortgage Disclosure Act and the Community Reinvestment Act similar?

8.10   Describe the secondary mortgage market.

8.11   Explain the meaning of the term *consumer installment credit*.

8.12   Distinguish between open-end and closed-end consumer loans. Give an example of each.

8.13   Explain what is meant by nonprice competition in credit cards.

8.14 What is the difference between a debit card, a credit card, and pre-payment card?

8.15 Distinguish between open-end and closed-end leases for automobiles.

8.16 Explain the intent of the Truth-in-Lending Act.

8.17 What is the difference between a finance charge on a loan and the APR?

8.18 Which method produces the highest APR on a $50,000 loan, an add-on rate or a discount loan rate? Why?

8.19 What method of computing interest charges on credit cards produces the largest finance charges? Explain why.

8.20 What is the purpose of CRA?

8.21 The Truth-in-Lending Act protects consumers against unauthorized use of their credit cards, if the loss or theft is reported. What happens if the loss or theft is not reported?

Problems

8.1 On August 31, the amount outstanding from the previous billing period is $500. No interest, which is computed at 18% annually, is due if the bill is paid by September 30. On September 15, an additional charge of $500 is made. On September 20, a $100 payment is made. Compute the finance charges due at the end of the billing period using:
(a) adjusted balance method
(b) previous balance method
(c) average daily balance method excluding current transactions
(d) average daily balance method including current transactions

8.2 Compute the APRs for the following loans. Which yield the highest return on investment to the lender?

	Principal	Maturity	Periodic Payment
a)	$1,000	12 months	$88.85
b)	$5,000	15 months	$360.62
c)	$10,000	18 months	$609.82

8.3 What is the APR on the following loans?
(a) 9.33%, 18 month, $1,000 add-on-loan
(b) 7.95%, 15 month, $1,000 add-on loan

8.4 What is the APR on the following loans?
(a) 9.33%, 18 month, $1,000 discount loan
(b) 7.95%, 15 month, $1,000 discount loan

8.5   An advertisement for a $25,000 installment loan provided the following information:

Loan amount: $25,000	Loan Payments
36 months	$825
48 months	$653
60 months	$550
72 months	$483
84 months	$435

(a) Compute the APR.
(b) What is the total interest payment for each of the maturities?
(c) What is the interest cost as a percent of the loan amount for each maturity? Divide the total interest payment by $25,000.
(d) Which maturity would you recommend if you were a borrower? If you were a lender?

What's It Going to Cost?

Bloch Realty Inc. is headquartered in the city where you are now. It owns and manages commercial real estate properties in the surrounding states. The company specializes in large-size multifamily units. Germaine Bloch, the principal stockholder in Bloch Realty, has decided to expand the scope of the firms operations and is considering some properties in New York City. Germaine knows that cost of living in New York City is different from her current location, but she does not know what it's going to cost to live and operate there. She asks you to prepare a brief report comparing some of the costs of living in your city with those in New York City. Give her some comparative data, especially with respect to mortgage rates, credit card rates, and other costs. She suggests the following Internet sites that may be helpful in writing your report:

- For information about credit cards, mortgage rates, and home equity loans, see the State of New York Banking Department's web site at *www.banking.state.ny.us* and look at "Consumer Services." Also see the Bank Rate Monitor and CNNfn on the Internet: *http://www.cnnfn.com*.
- The U.S. Department of Housing and Urban Development: *http://www.hud.gov*.
- Mortgage surveys and data from the Federal Home Loan Mortgage Corporation (Freddie Mac) at *http://www.freddiemac.com* and the Federal National Mortgage Association (Fannie Mae) at *http://www.fanniemae.com*.
- Bureau of the Census, for economic surveys and other data, at *http://www.census.gov*.

CHAPTER 9

Liquidity Management

After reading this chapter you will be able to:

- Define the basic liquidity problem facing banking institutions.
- Describe how banks can estimate their liquidity needs.
- Discuss the resources available to meet bank liquidity needs.
- Compare alternative management approaches to meeting liquidity needs.
- Consider liquidity problems of public confidence, bank runs, and government intervention.
- Identify measures of bank liquidity and their trends over time in the banking industry.

The concept of liquidity is well known in business; it is the ability to sell assets on short notice with minimal loss in value. However, bank liquidity management is a much more complex concept than liquidity per se. In general, liquidity management consists of two interrelated parts. First, management *must estimate funds needs*, which is related to deposit inflows and outflows and varying levels of loan commitments. Deposit flows are affected by movements of interest rates relative to other financial instruments, as well as the competitive rates posted by banks in their respective geographic markets. For example, the mid to late 1990s was marked by low interest rates and strong economic growth. These business conditions made it difficult for banks to attract transactions deposits. Also, the economic expansion put considerable pressure on banks to supply credit, even though deposit sources of funds were shrinking. At least for large banks, another credit problem is competition for loans from other financial institutions and even nonfinancial firms. Also, loan commitments, letters of credit, and other off-balance sheet activities are creating new liquidity demands on large banks. Thus, recent market trends have challenged bankers to accurately estimate liquidity needs.

The second part of liquidity management involves *meeting liquidity needs*. Two types of liquidity are available to meet potential liquidity requirements: asset management and liability management. **Asset management** refers to meeting liquidity needs by using near-cash assets, including net funds sold to other banks and money market securities.[1] Also, asset-backed securities derived from securitizing loans is a growing source of asset liquidity in the banking industry. **Liability management** refers to meeting liquidity needs by using outside sources of discretionary funds (e.g., fed funds, discount window borrowings, repurchase agreements, certificates of deposit, and other borrowings). However, in order to access these sources of liquidity a bank must maintain sound financial condition. In general, smaller banks tend to emphasize asset management in meeting liquidity needs, in contrast to large banks with an emphasis on liability management.

From a policy standpoint, bank management should develop a liquidity plan or strategy that balances risks and returns. Excessive asset liquidity offers safety but can decrease bank profits, because liquid assets are shorter term and lower risk than other assets, both of which cause their rate of return to be lower than could be earned on investment securities and loans. On the other hand, aggressive liability management can increase bank profits via shifting funds to longer-term and higher-earning assets; however, this strategy can expose the bank to unexpected risks that could trigger sudden withdrawals of interest-sensitive deposit and non-deposit funds. Indeed, in the early 1990s some experts estimated that nearly one-third of banks with assets exceeding $2 billion faced either a temporary liquidity problem or a sustained liquidity crisis that threatened their solvency. Each bank must determine the appropriate level of asset versus liability management in view of liquidity risk and associated tradeoffs in terms of bank profitability.

Finally, liquidity management is related to prudential regulation of the banking industry. Suppose that depositors perceive future loan losses will exceed available capital on a bank's balance sheet. Even though bank insolvency cannot be predicted with certainty, simply the prospect of bank failure could trigger panic among depositors and a full-blown bank run. Most countries, including the United States, have implemented government-backed deposit insurance programs to help prevent such liquidity crises. However, government implementation of deposit insurance requires regulatory oversight of bank risk taking due to the fact that the insuring agency and taxpaying public are liable for bank losses. As government intervention via regulation of banking practices increases, bank competitiveness may be compromised. Financial service firms not subject to regulation but competing with banks may well offer more services at better prices due to limited constraints on their risk taking. Thus, a tradeoff exists between regulation and competitiveness in terms of safety and soundness in the context of liquidity crises. ∎

1. Cash and due from banks is not a near-cash asset. Cash and due is comprised of Fed reserves, float, and vault cash, all of which are frozen assets and not available for purchasing other assets or decreasing liabilities.

9.1 ESTIMATING LIQUIDITY NEEDS

The first step in any analysis of bank liquidity is the estimation of liquidity needs. These needs arise primarily from deposit withdrawals and loan demands (including off-balance sheet commitments), and to estimate them, the bank must forecast the level of future deposit and loan activity. Although loan growth generally will not exceed deposit growth in a community, differences can arise temporarily, especially in urban areas. Forecasting month-to-month or seasonal liquidity needs is a process based normally on the experience of the bank, with appropriate adjustments for specific future events that would alter typical liquidity needs. A recent trend in liquidity management is the ability to meet cash needs arising from securities activities, which in many cases are off-balance sheet exposures for hedging or market-making purposes. Admittedly, the complexity of liquidity management involves considerable subjectivity due to uncertainty in forecasting the future. Consequently, it is prudent to adjust the estimated need upward to some extent to avoid a liquidity squeeze in the form of a cash shortage that could result in lost lending opportunities, reduced depositor confidence, and/or regulatory agency suspicions concerning safety and soundness.

Sources and Uses of Funds Method

One method of estimating future liquidity needs is to develop a **sources and uses of funds statement**. To compile this statement, bank management must evaluate potential future changes in its individual asset and liability accounts. For example, the loan portfolio would have to be divided into its component parts: commercial and industrial loans, residential real estate loans, consumer loans, agricultural loans, and other loans. The demand for funds by businesses and individuals in these different lending areas could be estimated from past loan histories and future economic projections. Commercial and industrial loan demand, for instance, would be influenced by past and anticipated production and growth of the business sector. In 1991 the rate of growth of business loans declined by about 9% due to a sluggish economy. However, by 1995 the economy was on the rebound and business loan growth had increased by more than 12%. Throughout the second half of the 1990s demand for credit was strong, and banks responded by increasing business loans on average about 8% per year. Although it is not easy to forecast the amount of bank financing needed by business firms, experience and judgment of local and regional loan demands, in addition to information on national and international economic trends, are valuable guides to follow in obtaining estimates of loan demands.

Similarly, deposit levels are influenced by economic and competitive market conditions. As interest rates rise, corporate treasurers move funds out of demand deposits and into interest-bearing assets and, therefore, banks will tend to experience increasing competition for deposit funds from nonbank financial service companies such as money market mutual funds. Also, during periods of relatively low interest rate levels, as in the 1990s, depositors are motivated to "reach" for higher yields by investing their funds in bonds and stocks, thereby increasing liquidity demands at banks. Other variables may periodically influence deposit levels also, such as changes in monetary policy and international financial markets. If the Federal Reserve moves to decrease the money supply, deposit levels in the banking system as a whole will contract. Also, if U.S. money market securities are viewed in global markets as a safe haven relative to other countries experiencing financial crises (i.e., a scenario repeated a number of times in the 1990s due to periodic problems in emerging market countries), foreign investors would transfer holdings of dollars into CDs issued by U.S. banks, in addition to other U.S. money market instruments, thereby increasing domestic deposit levels.

As an example, Table 9.1 gives a hypothetical *sources and uses funds statement* for a bank over a six-month period. The expected increase in total loan demand in the spring and subsequent decline in early summer are part of a common seasonal trend in agricultural banking. When loan demands increase, deposit balances often decline as many bank customers obtain both deposit and loan services from the same bank. Notice that *decreases* in loans and *increases* in deposits are sources of funds; conversely, increases in both loans and deposit withdrawals are uses of funds. Subtracting deposit changes from loan changes provides an estimate of liquidity needs. In regard to sources and uses of funds, discretionary items and nondiscretionary items are based on the ability of management to control the flow of funds. Obviously, deposit withdrawals are nondiscretionary because the bank cannot control depositors' activities; however, loans (and securities sales and purchases) are discretionary for the most part due to the fact that management can affect their quantity.

To estimate the figures shown in Table 9.1, past seasonal trends are reviewed by bank management. Next, these trends are adjusted for cyclical movements in economic and financial conditions. For example, a bank with a large proportion of its assets invested in commercial and industrial loans needs to adjust loan estimates downward if a recession in the business sector is forecasted. Although loan demand will fall and therefore ease liquidity needs, rising unemployment will tend to depress deposit balances, offsetting the decline in loans. A bank with a relatively high proportion of residential real estate loans would be particularly affected by movements in interest rates. As interest rates rise to relatively high levels, loan demand can be expected to fall at some point, as many potential home buyers can no longer qualify to meet the higher interest expenses. As rates fall, demand for home loans increases and is aggravated by homeowners seeking to refinance at lower rates of interest.

Local and regional economic factors must also be evaluated and used to adjust estimated liquidity needs. A dramatic example is the passage of the North American Free Trade Agreement (NAFTA) in the late 1980s and its impact on U.S. border states with Mexico. Increased traffic and business trade on the border greatly increased infrastructure needs, including roads, bridges, warehouse facilities, water treatment facilities, etc. Loan demands far surpassed deposit growth, which forced many border banks to seek assistance

TABLE 9.1	Estimating Liquidity Needs Based on a Sources and Uses of Funds Statement				
End of Month	Estimated Total Loans	Estimated Total Deposits	Estimated Loans	Change Deposits	Estimated Liquidity Need
Dec.	$68,000	$85,000	$ —	$ —	$ —
Jan.	70,000	90,000	2,000	5,000	(3,000)
Feb.	79,000	86,000	9,000	(4,000)	13,000
March	89,000	83,000	10,000	(3,000)	13,000
April	96,000	78,000	7,000	(5,000)	12,000
May	95,000	79,000	(1,000)	1,000	(2,000)
June	88,000	80,000	(7,000)	1,000	(8,000)

from other banks in the form of loan syndications, fed funds, and correspondent relationships. In some cases bank mergers and acquisitions were motivated by liquidity pressures that only larger organizations could manage. Another example is the economic slowdown in the northeastern region of the United States in the late 1980s and early 1990s that resulted in large loan losses, especially in real estate loans. Faced with the onset of new risk-based capital requirements, many banks were forced to raise their equity and cut back on liabilities, thereby reducing their ability to borrow funds to meet liquidity needs and causing cutbacks in loans to some degree. These examples make clear that local and regional business conditions can have a significant impact on the sources and uses of bank funds.

The Basle Committee has proposed a framework for assessing and managing bank liquidity among large international banks along certain major dimensions: (A) measuring and managing net funding requirements, (B) managing market access, and (C) contingency planning. Under part (A), the analysis of net funding requirements involves the construction of a detailed sources and uses of funds statement referred to as a *maturity ladder*. The maturity ladder gives a daily calculation of the cumulative net excess or deficit of funds at selected dates in the future (e.g., days 1, 2, 3–5, 6–10, 1–30, etc.). A variety of maturity ladders can be constructed to take into account alternative scenarios, such as normal business conditions, institution-specific problems, and general market problems. These detailed daily liquidity analyses are most appropriate for large banks but the same concepts can be applied to smaller banks by using less elaborate weekly or monthly analyses as in Table 9.1. Part (B) addresses the methods the bank employs to meet liquidity needs identified in part (A). Finally, part (C) considers contingency plans to meet emergency liquidity needs that exceed normal sources of funds to meet those unexpected needs.

Structure-of-Deposits Method

Another way to estimate liquidity needs is the **structure-of-deposits method**. The basic idea of this approach is to list the different types of deposits that the bank is using to acquire funds and then assign a probability of withdrawal to each type of deposit within a specific planning horizon. High-risk, or unstable, deposits require substantial liquidity to support them, whereas low-risk, or stable, deposits require relatively less liquidity. It should be noted that large-dollar liabilities are necessarily unstable. Most large deposits are uninsured, as are nondeposit unsecured creditors of the bank, and, therefore, are more prone to cause a liquidity drain than insured deposits and secured creditors. However, banks under $2 billion in size typically have loyal customers that provide "core" funds for the bank. These funds are stable to the extent that a strong and positive relationship exists between the bank and its customers. Also, core deposits are much less interest sensitive than other deposits. Examples of core deposits are demand deposits, NOW accounts, MMDAs, and small time deposits that are stable over time.

The major strength of the structure-of-deposits method is that it directs management attention to the probable cause of liquidity pressures (i.e., deposit withdrawals). On the other hand, its main weakness is ignoring other liquidity demands stemming from loans. Despite this drawback as well as the subjectivity of the deposit classification process, the structure-of-deposits method is a useful technique for controlling liquidity risk.

As a simple example, bank management might have structured its deposit sources as shown in Table 9.2. Notice that the bank has relatively small amounts of short-term and long-term deposits. The major deposit source is medium-term

TABLE 9.2	Deposit Sources		
	Amount Held ($ millions)	$\times$ Probability of Withdrawal in Next Three Months $=$	Expected Withdrawals ($ millions)
Short-term (unstable):			
Demand deposits	$ 2	0.90	$ 1.8
Other transactions accounts	10	0.60	6.0
Medium-term:			
Small time and savings deposits	50	0.30	15.0
Long-term (stable):			
Large time deposits	10	0.20	2.0
Expected deposit withdrawals			$24.8

small time and savings deposits, which are relatively stable components of core deposits. In this case liquidity demands from deposit withdrawals should be fairly modest. Of course, this same structuring method may be applied to nondeposit funds sources also, particularly if these sources are important to the bank. In any application the evaluation of the probability of withdrawal, or volatility, of various sources of funds must be determined on a case-by-case basis. A careful examination of the stability characteristics of each source of funds by management is essential due to the large differences that can exist among banks in this respect.

Funding and Market Liquidity Needs

Banks with significant investment portfolios are exposed to liquidity needs that arise from trading activities. **Funding-liquidity risk** refers to maintaining sufficient cash to meet investment objectives. For example, suppose that a bank has large holdings of securities on its balance sheet and that interest rates are expected to increase in the near future. In this case the price of the securities will fall and the bank will incur a capital loss. To hedge the price risk in this spot position, the bank sells short Treasury bill contracts. If interest rates later increase as expected, the bank can simultaneously buy T-bills at the now lower price and sell T-bills at the earlier contracted higher price. Netting out the spot and futures positions, the losses in the spot position will be offset by the futures position (see Chapter 6 for numerical examples). However, T-bill futures contracts are marked-to-market daily, which means that gains and losses are reckoned at the end of each day. Losses in the futures position that prompt margin calls must be paid in cash, whereas the profits on the spot position are simply paper gains unless the securities are actually sold. This mismatch in cash outflows versus inflows in many securities activities creates a liquidity problem. For large banks the funding-liquidity risk attached to their considerable exposures to securities risks involved in derivatives and foreign-exchange trading operations puts constant pressure on their cash flows. Indeed, the sheer complexity of multifaceted derivatives strategies can make liquidity needs difficult to measure for many large banks. Because such banks are continuously either putting up or unwinding different parts (or legs) of complex securities strategies, they are always exposed to some degree of cash flow imbalance.

   Market-liquidity risk is another source of potential cash flow problems for banks with sizeable securities activities. Consider the liquidity effects of a market disruption (e.g., the October 1987 stock market crash). Sudden shifts in supply and demand forces in the financial markets cause bid/ask spreads to widen—that is, the price difference between what buyers and sellers are seeking in the market. Given that bid/ask spreads are normally representative of the depth of a market, market participants could have difficulty closing out open positions in derivatives, securities, etc., without sustaining losses. At such times large institutional investors may pull out of the market and further widen bid/ask spreads. Thus, volatile financial markets can cause temporary illiquidity in securities positions held by banks.

9.2 ASSET LIQUIDITY

Historically, **asset liquidity** was the primary means by which banks met cash demands. Money market instruments, such as Treasury bills and short-term obligations of state and political subdivisions (municipal securities), are "liquid" in the sense that they can be sold readily with minimal loss of capital. Relatively large loan demands and deposit withdrawals were typically met by liquidating the required quantity of these near-money instruments. This approach to liquidity management traditionally fell under the rubric of *asset management*.

Asset management was the dominant method of bank management until the 1960s, when *liability management* became popular as an alternative means of meeting cash needs. Liability management involves the acquisition of external funds from deposit and nondeposit sources as liquidity needs arise. As discussed later in this chapter, liability management substantially altered the role of liquidity management in banking.

Role of Asset Liquidity

Asset liquidity management in modern banking fills two basic roles. First, liquid assets serve as an alternative source of funds for the bank; the bank can use either assets or liabilities to meet cash needs. Its selection of sources of funds will depend heavily on their relative costs. If it is less costly to sell off some liquid assets than to issue certificates of deposit (CDs), internal liquidity will be favored over external liquidity to acquire funds. Consider a situation in which interest rates are relatively high. Increased loan demand at this time might be better met by selling Treasury bills than by issuing CDs with interest rates at or near the Treasury bill rate. By selling Treasury bills, funds effectively are shifted to higher-earning assets such as commercial loans, which will boost bank profitability.

The second role of asset liquidity management is as a reserve. If the financial market loses confidence in a bank's safety and soundness, it is likely that borrowed sources of funds would become inaccessible. In this case, the bank would have to rely upon its liquid assets to maintain business operations. Thus, asset liquidity is a reserve to forestall problems that threaten bank solvency. In keeping with this rationale, regulators impose **primary reserve** requirements that apply to cash held in their vaults and on deposit at a Federal Reserve district bank. **Secondary reserves** are near-money financial instruments that have no formal regulatory requirements and provide an additional reserve of liquid assets to meet cash needs. Although bank regulators impose no formal liquidity requirements, it is considered in the on-site examination process. Also, professional analysts compare the asset liquidity of banks to their large, uninsured liabilities to see how many times these liabilities are "covered" in the event of a loss of market confidence and rapid funds withdrawals. Finally, one should note that use of liability management increases the asset size of the bank and so requires appropriate increases in capital reserves to stay within regulatory guidelines. By contrast, liquidating money market assets (with no capital requirements) does not change bank size and, therefore, does not affect bank capital reserves, unless the funds are used for loans or investments that require capital backing.

Primary Reserves

Most primary reserves are cash assets held to satisfy legal reserve requirements. Banks seek to minimize cash accounts because of the opportunity cost of holding idle funds. That is, cash does not earn interest.[2] Thus, total cash reserves generally equal legal reserves. Today, banks must maintain a 3% reserve against transactions accounts less than or equal to $50.6 million and a 10% reserve for transactions accounts greater than $50.6 million. The first $3.8 million of transactions balances is exempt from reserve requirements. To the extent that legal reserves exceed the cash reserves banks would hold in the absence of these requirements, banks are *taxed* by the government. Taxation is an appropriate interpretation here because the Federal Reserve invests banks' deposits held at its district banks in Treasury securities, and most of the resultant earnings are transferred to the U.S. Treasury to help pay the fiscal budget. This reserve tax has been opposed by bankers. Indeed, an exodus of member banks from the Federal Reserve system occurred in the 1960s and 1970s, as bankers complained of relatively high reserve requirements imposed on member compared with nonmember banks. In the 1990s banks' legal reserves declined considerably, due in large part to banks' efforts to avoid noninterest (or idle) funds. In this regard, banks increased their usage of sweep accounts that transferred customer deposit accounts exposed to reserve requirements to savings accounts that have no reserve requirements. In part to address this issue, the Depository Institution Regulatory Streamlining Act of 1999 proposed (among other things) to pay depository institutions interest on reserve deposits held at the Reserve Banks.

In 1980 the Monetary Control Act was passed under Title I of DIDMCA. This legislation requires all depository institutions to carry legal reserves set by the Federal Reserve under Regulation D. It eliminated any reserve requirement incentive for banks to leave the system, while establishing uniform reserve rules for banks. Moreover, it tightened the linkage between reserves and money supply and thus served to facilitate monetary control (because reserve requirements are a fulcrum used by the central bank in an attempt to achieve its monetary and economic objectives). To further enhance its ability to control the money stock and so rein in inflation, in 1984 the Federal Reserve began using **contemporaneous reserve requirement (CRR) accounting** methods on transactions deposits, as opposed to **lagged reserve requirement (LRR) accounting** previous to that time. Under CRR rules, the computation and maintenance periods overlap to a great extent, such that from a banking perspective reserve

2. Cash assets include vault cash, bank deposits at Federal Reserve banks, bank deposits at other banks, and other available cash (e.g., cash items in the process of collection, in addition to cash and due from banks, which are holdings of other banks' certificates of deposit).

management was a daily activity. Due to difficulties encountered by depository institutions in managing reserves under CRR, in 1998 the Federal Reserve returned to a lagged system of reserve accounting.

Currently, required reserves using LRR under Regulation D are computed on the basis of daily average balances of transactions deposits during a 14-day period ending every second Monday (the *computation period*). Figure 9.1 provides an example for illustrative purposes. Reserve requirements are computed by applying the ratios shown in Table 9.3 (to be discussed shortly). It should be noted that average daily vault cash held in a subsequent 14-day computation

FIGURE 9.1 Lagged Reserve Requirement Accounting

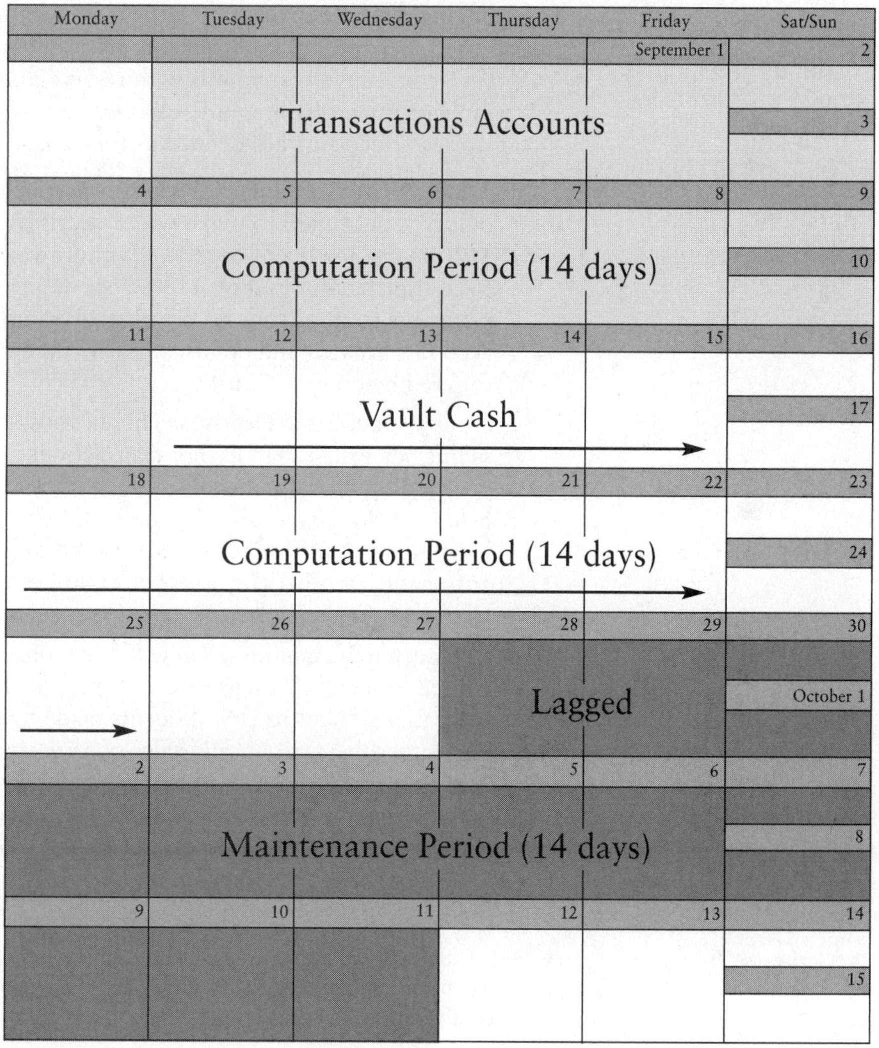

The Federal Reserve, the central bank of the United States, founded by Congress in 1913, announces changes in reserve requirements through press releases at http://www.bog.frb.fed.us/boarddocs/press/BoardActs/1999/.

period are counted as reserves, which means they are deducted from the amount required based on transactions accounts to get the required reserve balance. The reserve balance that is required must be maintained with the Federal Reserve during a 14-day period (the *maintenance period*) that begins on the third Thursday following the end of the transactions computation period. Thus, a 17-day lag separates the end of the transactions computation period and the beginning of the maintenance period. This lagged reserve accounting procedure is advantageous in terms of allowing banks and the Federal Reserve to lower management costs and improve the quality of information on required reserve balances.

Managing the Money Position

Managing the money position of a bank relates to minimizing cash holdings. Because legal reserve requirements exceed bank preferences in general, the money position is synonymous with reserve management.[3] Table 9.3 shows an example of how a bank would calculate its required reserves. The three basic categories of deposits are defined as follows:

1. **Transactions Accounts.** All deposits are included on which the account holder is permitted to make withdrawals by negotiable or transferrable instruments, payment orders of withdrawal, and telephone and preauthorized transfers (in excess of three per month) for the purpose of making payments to third persons or others. Examples of these types of deposit accounts are demand deposits, NOW accounts, and share draft accounts (offered by credit unions).

2. **Nonpersonal Time Deposits.** These deposits are time deposits, including savings deposits, that are not transactions accounts and that in general are not held by an individual. However, certain transferable time deposits held by individuals and other obligations are included. For example, MMDA (and similar accounts) with no more than six preauthorized, automatic, or other transfers per month (of which no more than three can be checks) are included.

3. **Eurocurrency Liabilities.** These funds represent net borrowings from related foreign offices, gross borrowings from unrelated foreign depository institutions, loans to U.S. residents made by overseas branches of domestic depository institutions, and sales of assets by U.S. depository institutions by their overseas offices. Eurocurrencies (or so-called Eurodollars) are used mainly by large banks as an alternative source of deposit funds.

Total reserves required according to the calculations in Table 9.3 are $3,268,000. Because the bank has an average daily vault cash balance of

---

3. For this reason cash reserves are not liquid assets for most banks. However, the money position is still relevant to liquidity management due to its short-term nature and daily adjustment using internal and external liquidity sources.

$418,000 (which is based on the 2-week period ending 3 days prior to the beginning of the 2-week maintenance period under LRR), it needs to increase its reserves by $2,850,000 to comply with Regulation D.

If a bank has excess reserves, it can carry over 4% of the average daily minimum reserve balance to the next maintenance period. If it has deficient reserves, as in Table 9.3, it must correct this shortfall or face penalties. In the latter case, the Federal Reserve banks are authorized to assess charges for deficiencies or require additional reserves be maintained in subsequent reserve maintenance periods.

If the bank had a deficiency (or excess) in reserves, the federal funds market is a likely source (use) of funds. Also, the Federal Reserve's **discount window** is another source of funds that banks commonly tap for cash needs.[4] Sometimes unexpected payments on loans and deposits will cause cash balances to increase substantially above legal requirements. In this event, the money manager would seek first to evaluate the nature of this increase. If the increase in reserves is strictly temporary, short-term money market instruments (such as Treasury bills, bankers' acceptances, or commercial paper) could be

TABLE 9.3   Calculating Reserve Requirements for Commercial Banks

Type of Deposit and Deposit Interval	Average Dollar Amount ($ millions) in Computation Period	Reserve Requirement	Average Dollar Amount ($ millions) in Maintenance Period
Net transactions accounts:			
$0–$46.5 million[a]	$46.5	3%	$1.248
Over $46.5 million	20.2	10	2.020
Nonpersonal time deposits	25.0	0	0
Eurocurrency liabilities	5.0	0	0
Total reserves required			$3.268
Less vault cash			(0.418)
Federal Reserve District Bank			$2.850

a. The first $4.9 million of transactions accounts is exempt from reserve requirements. The cutoffs for exemptions and the 3% reserve requirement regularly change as amendments are made by the Board of Governors of the Federal Reserve System. For the latest details on applicable cutoffs, see the Federal Reserve Bank of Chicago's web site at *http://www.frbchi.org/banker/regulatory_update/*.

4. Regulation A restricts banks from using the discount window to "supplement capital," which means that chronic use of the window to meet liquidity needs is not permitted.

purchased to earn interest on the excess cash. If the increase in cash appears to be more permanent, the money manager would consider longer-term investment opportunities, such as capital market securities (e.g., longer-term government securities, including municipal securities and corporate bonds) and loans. On the other hand, significant drains on cash balances could be met either by selling short-term, liquid securities or by purchasing deposit and nondeposit funds in the market. The deregulation of interest rate ceilings on deposits has made the latter strategy more feasible than it was in the past, because posting relatively competitive deposit rates can rapidly attract funds.

Small and large banks generally differ in their approach to managing their money positions. During the beginning of the reserve maintenance period, small banks will tend to run a surplus volume of reserves at the Federal Reserve. After this point, they will sell their excess reserves in the federal funds market. By contrast, large banks tend to experience an increasing shortfall in reserves as the maintenance period proceeds. They become purchasers of fed funds later in the maintenance period, which are supplied primarily by small banks. This general pattern of reserve holdings at large banks does not always occur, however. It may be altered because of anticipated fed funds rates—for example, if a money manager believed interest rates in the fed funds market were going to rise substantially near the end of the maintenance period (perhaps due to tight money conditions), it would be less costly to purchase fed funds at the beginning of the maintenance period and to sell any surplus at the end of the period or use the discount window later. Alternatively, larger banks may experience relatively volatile reserve levels throughout the maintenance period because of changes in loan demands and deposit activity that occur as the bank reacts aggressively to changing market conditions.

Secondary Reserves

Once future liquidity needs have been estimated, the bank must decide what sources of liquidity will be tapped to cover these needs. If deposits are forecasted to decline in the near future, some amount of cash reserves is likely to become available for use because reserve requirements will decline. Remaining liquidity needs must be covered either with liquid assets or by borrowing funds.

Assuming liquid assets are to be used, banks normally seek to match the maturities of their assets with specific future liquidity needs. This **money market approach** enables the bank to avoid transactions costs, as well as price risk, while maximizing interest revenues. Table 9.4 gives a brief description of the principal money market instruments used by banks for liquidity purposes.

Secondary reserves can also be used to provide collateral for repurchase agreements, discount window borrowings, and public deposits by the government. Pledging requirements in the form of near-cash assets for these purposes must follow regulatory guidelines. Once pledged, these secondary reserves cannot be employed for other liquidity needs. Thus, pledged securities should be netted out to determine unencumbered liquid securities.

TABLE 9.4	Principal Money Market Instruments

Treasury bills (T-bills) are direct obligations of the U.S. government that have an original maturity of one year or less. T-bills are discount instruments that are sold at a weekly auction. The minimum denomination is $10,000, with larger denominations available in multiples of $5,000 above this minimum. Original maturities of T-bills are three months, six months, and one year.

Federal agency securities are issued by various government agencies (e.g., Federal Land Banks, Federal Home Loan Banks, Banks for Cooperatives, Federal National Mortgage Association, Federal Home Mortgage Loan Association, and Tennessee Valley Authority). These securities have little or no default risk, because the issuing agencies are acting in the public interest to finance sectors of the economy that the government wishes to support (e.g., housing, agriculture, and small business). Some agencies are backed directly by the federal government whereas others carry the implicit assumption of government support (e.g., government-sponsored entity or GSE status). Agency securities are interest-bearing instruments with varying maturities and minimum denominations of $50,000 or more.

Repurchase agreements (RPs or repos) are securities purchased (sold) under agreement to resell (repurchase) with a securities dealer. RPs may or may not have a set maturity date, but generally their term does not exceed three months. They have low default risk because T-bills are normally pledged as collateral. Interest is paid on transactions that involve at least $1 million.

Bankers' acceptances are time drafts used in international trade that are "accepted" by a large bank. For example, an importer may obtain a letter of credit from a bank, which is used by the exporter to draw a draft on the bank for payment of goods. Upon accepting the draft, the bank can market it if desired. Maturities normally extend throughout the transit period for shipment of goods (i.e., from 30 to 180 days).

Negotiable certificates of deposit (CDs) are interest-bearing liabilities of banks and other depository institutions that may be sold to third parties and carry minimum denominations of $100,000. Maturities range from about 1 to 18 months, and rates may or may not vary with interest rate conditions. Eurodollar CDs are dollar-denominated securities issued by foreign branches of major U.S. banks and foreign-owned banks. Yields on CDs can differ depending on the size and risk of issuing banks and exceed Treasury yields on instruments of equal maturity.

Federal funds (fed funds) are immediately available funds that represent interbank loans of cash reserves, either held on deposit at Federal Reserve district banks or elsewhere (including correspondent banks). Government intervention may cause fed fund rates to move sharply in response to monetary policy operations of the Federal Reserve. Fed funds "sold" are liquid assets of the lending institution that appear as fed funds "purchased" on the borrowing institution's liability side of the balance sheet. Fed funds are not considered deposits and, therefore, do not require that reserves be held against them. Most fed funds' transactions are "overnight loans" and expire in a single day. Typically, fed funds flow from small respondent banks with excess liquidity to larger correspondent banks with liquidity demands.

Commercial paper is a short-term, unsecured promissory note issued by major U.S. corporations. Denominations normally are in multiples of $1,000, with a minimum of $25,000. Maturities range from three days to nine months. Commercial paper may or may not be a discount instrument, and rates closely track the prime rate quoted by major U.S. banks. Little or no secondary market exists for this security.

Cyclical monetary policies to restrain strong inflationary pressures can cause liquidity pressures that force banks to rely more on their internal liquidity than on their external liquidity. This possibility influences the decision concerning the choice of liquid assets to hold. For example, Treasury bills (and notes and bonds nearing maturity) are most liquid because of an active secondary market with large trading volume. By contrast, commercial paper has a thinner secondary market, such that it may have to be discounted depending on buyer demand. Bankers' acceptances and negotiable certificates of deposit (CDs) have a good secondary market and, thus, fall somewhere between these two extremes. Of course, the bank must trade off liquidity risk against interest earnings in selecting the asset securities it will purchase.

Although timing securities to mature in order to meet liquidity demands is the most common approach to managing asset liquidity, an **aggressive liquidity approach** may allow an opportunity to take advantage of yield curve relationships. For example, if the yield curve were upward-sloping, as shown in Figure 9.2, and expected to remain at the same level in the near future, the purchase of longer-term securities would not only offer higher yields than shorter-term securities but also could offer the realization of capital gains if they were sold before maturity to meet liquidity needs. Capital gains are possible because, as time passes and the securities' maturities shorten, their interest rate declines in line with the upward slope of the yield curve. To demonstrate, suppose a bank knows that it will have a cash deficiency in six months. Further, assume that the yield curve now is upward sloping and is forecast to have approximately the same shape and level in six months. If $500,000 of one-year Treasury securities were purchased now at a price of 92 (or 92% of par value) and six-month Treasury securities have a price of 94 due to upward sloping yield curve-year, the expected capital gain on the sale of the Treasury securities in six months would be $0.02 \times \$500,000 = \$10,000$. These potential earnings' gains would have to be weighed against transactions costs and risks associated with this aggressive approach. If the level of the yield curve rose over the next six months, instead of remaining about the same, the sale of the one-year bonds after holding them six months would result in a reduced capital gain and perhaps even a capital loss. Note that a capital loss may not completely offset the higher interest earnings on one-year securities compared to six-month securities earned over the past six months.

A recent innovation that is affecting bank liquidity is the securitization of certain types of loans. For example, a bank may sell securities to investors that represent claims on a pool of auto loans. If they are sold without recourse, the bank is not liable to security holders. Instead, the security investors obtain a pro rata share of the monthly payments on auto loans, net of a service fee charged by the bank. This type of asset-backed financing (via securitization) is most likely to be feasible for loans that can be standardized and do not require the bank to obtain confidential, nonpublic information on borrowers. It is possible that the bank could, in effect, certify the quality of business loans without divulging sensitive

FIGURE 9.2 Aggressive Liquidity Management and the Yield Curve

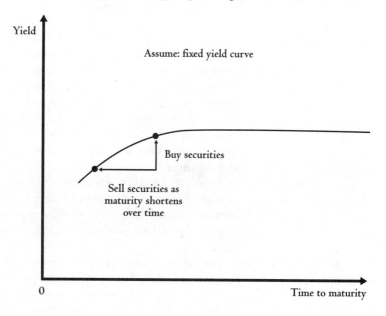

information to security investors, but the bank may then expose itself to some degree of liability should investors lose funds due to loan defaults. The securitization of commercial loans is in its initial stage of development as some banks have begun to package large numbers of small business loans. The main effect on bank liquidity of securitization is the increase in marketability of these loans in the financial marketplace. In effect, asset liquidity is improved with the added benefit that credit risk can be geographically diversified and, therefore, reduced. Whether the reduction in credit risk is passed on to borrowers (in the form of, say, lower auto loan interest rates compared to no securitization of such loans), holders of the securities, or bank shareholders is an issue for further study. It is logical to believe that these different parties in the securitization process will share the risk benefits in some way.

9.3 LIABILITY MANAGEMENT

An alternative approach to liquidity management is to purchase the funds necessary to meet loan demands and deposit withdrawals. This approach falls under the heading of liability management, a topic that was covered in the more general context of asset/liability management in Chapter 5. In this section our purpose is to discuss liability management as applied to the more general problem of liquidity management.

Substantial differences distinguish small and large banks in their use of liabilities to manage liquidity. Large banks that are active in the money market have a natural advantage over smaller banks in terms of their ability to cost-effectively raise funds through federal funds, the discount window, repurchase agreements, negotiable CDs, Eurocurrency deposits, and other types of purchased funds. By contrast, smaller banks often obtain purchased funds in the money market through their larger correspondent banks. Because smaller banks tend to have deposits in excess of loan demands, they will deposit excess funds at correspondents in exchange for money market services. **Correspondent balances** thus serve as an additional source of asset liquidity for smaller banks and as an additional source of borrowed liquidity for larger banks.

The primary advantage of liability management is that assets can be shifted from lower-earning money market instruments to higher-earning loans and longer-term securities. Greater asset diversification also may be possible in this instance.

On the downside, risks are involved in liability management. If interest rates increase suddenly, the cost of funds could rise substantially as purchased funds come due and must be rolled over at higher rates of interest. If the bank's assets are less sensitive to interest rate changes than its liabilities are, profit margins would suffer and capital may become inadequate. As profit margins decline, the bank could be forced to sell off assets to reduce its need for purchased funds and improve its capital ratios. Capital losses on the sale of assets could further squeeze profit margins, however. Because liquid assets would minimize capital losses, larger banks need to carry some amount of money market instruments to help offset *interest rate risk*. Furthermore, in the event that the public loses confidence in the bank's safety and soundness, deposit withdrawals may increase temporarily, and liquid assets will help absorb these withdrawals.

Liability management also increases the bank's financial risk. As discussed in Chapter 11, *financial risk* is the increase in the variability of earnings per share associated with an increase in debt as a proportion of total assets (i.e., financial leverage). Bank managers thus need to consider the risk preferences of shareholders when using liabilities to meet liquidity needs.

Finally, a new risk that is related to liability management is **capital market risk**. This risk occurs due to low interest levels that motivate investors to transfer deposit funds to the capital market in an attempt to earn higher rates of return. Throughout much of the 1990s, interest rate levels remained at low levels and caused CD rates to drop to around 3%. Banks lost billions of dollars of "hot money" (i.e., sources of funds sensitive to interest rates) to the capital markets due to this dip in the interest rate cycle. During such times banks must find alternatives to retain deposits and, more importantly, customers. For example, many banks have recently offered customers mutual funds managed by the bank (i.e., proprietary funds) or by nonbanking institutions (i.e., nonproprietary funds). Investment consultants have been retained by banks to assist customers in portfolio decisions concerning deposits, mutual funds, and individual stocks and bonds. The main idea of this relationship banking is to view the customer as a client of the bank and, therefore, encourage future deposits when interest rates move up again.

It should be obvious that one of the greatest difficulties in using liabilities to meet liquidity needs is estimating the availability and cost of external funds. The quantity and cost of deposit and nondeposit funds depends on many factors, including monetary policy actions by the Federal Reserve, economic conditions, and the bank's financial strength. Uncertainties associated with these factors require that banks have more than sufficient access to different kinds of liabilities to make sure that liquidity needs are adequately covered.[5] Chapter 10 provides detailed discussion of different sources of bank funds.

Recognizing the growing difficulties of liability management for banking organizations, the Federal Home Loan Bank (FHLB) System in 1990 began offering credit services to member depository institutions and insurance companies in an effort to support the housing finance industry.[6] Due to the decline of thrift institutions in the 1980s, banks now play a more important role in the home loan market than in the past. While most banks have access to fed funds, the Federal Reserve's discount window, and lines of credit from other banks, these sources can be costly at times due to tight money conditions or simply increased demands for cash around days near the end of the reserve maintenance period. As a federal agency, the FHLB prices its credit competitively based on Treasury rates and has a broad range of maturities to fit any liability need. Loans from the FHLB are normally collateralized with a "blanket pledge" of mortgage-related assets, such as residential mortgages and mortgage-backed securities, and deposits held at the FHLB, U.S. Treasury, and other agency obligations.

5. The 1984 Continental Illinois National Bank liquidity crisis caused not only a deposit drain on Continental Illinois but increased deposit interest rates at large Chicago banks. Some experts observed that the five largest Chicago banks, including Continental, experienced an average increase in CD risk premia of 100 basis points in the weeks following announcements of Continental's problems. This swift market reaction is a good example of the risks inherent in liability management of liquidity, particularly its linkage to bank condition and market confidence.
6. To become a member of the FHLB System, an institution must have at least 10% of total assets in home loan-related assets. Also, stock in the regional FHLB must be purchased in the amount of the greater of either 1% of residential assets or 0.3% of total assets. Additional stock purchase requirements are linked to the quantity of FHLB borrowings, which usually are based on $1 of stock for every $6 or $7 of borrowings. This requirement could be lessened for institutions with larger holdings of residential assets. FHLB pay competitive dividend yields but must be evaluated in terms of the bank's opportunity costs of not investing in other securities or loans.

MANAGING RISK

New Liquidity Sources: Collateralized Commercial Paper Programs and Medium-Term Notes

A popular way for large banks to securitize assets is by setting up a *special purpose corporation* (SPC). This unconventional approach to securitization allows the bank to raise funds for credit card loans, consumer loans, commercial loans, leases, and other uses by issuing commercial paper through an entirely independent firm. The SPC is not legally linked to the bank or its holding company, but for all practical purposes is another way to practice asset securitization and, thereby, generate fee income. SPCs essentially are off-balance sheet entities for accounting purposes and under Regulation D of the Federal Reserve. Investors in commercial paper of SPCs hold claims on the portfolio loans originated by the bank.

Medium-term notes (MTNs) is jargon for debt securities that are continuously offered by a firm (either financial or nonfinancial), as opposed to underwritten debt securities sold within a relatively short time period. MTNs have maturities ranging from nine months to 30 years, can be counted as senior or subordinated debt by bank holding companies, and can be issued by banks themselves as deposits or senior debt. While large banks have been most active in MTNs, they also could be attractive to smaller banks that either want to raise small amounts of funds not sufficient to justify underwriting costs of new debt issues or do not have access to traditional debt markets. Also, MTNs help to avoid price risks in underwriting that could affect the cost of debt to the bank. Best of all, MTNs can be sold in the exact quantities and maturities demanded by investors. These advantages help to explain the growing popularity of MTNs among both financial and nonfinancial firms.

9.4 FUNDS MANAGEMENT OF LIQUIDITY

As suggested by the preceding discussion, management of liquidity is best handled by combining asset liquidity and liability management, or a **funds management approach**. Funds management involves comparing total liquidity needs with total liquidity sources.

Liquidity Ratios

From the standpoint of bank analysts, bank liquidity can only be roughly estimated using Call Reports of Condition. Four common ratio measures of bank liquidity include the following:

- Loans/deposits
- Loans/nondeposit liabilities
- Unencumbered liquid assets/nondeposit liabilities
- Near-cash assets/large-denomination liabilities

These ratios must be evaluated together in order to gain insight into a bank's liquidity position. For example, if the loans/deposits ratio is high, we can infer that the bank either has a large loan portfolio or is using large amounts of non-deposit, or purchased, funds to finance assets. If the loans/nondeposit liabilities ratio is also high, it must be that the loan portfolio is large, rather than a heavy reliance on nondeposit funds. To examine liquidity further, the unencumbered (nonpledged) liquid assets/nondeposit liabilities ratio is valuable. If it is relatively high, the bank has considerable secondary reserves; alternatively, if this ratio is fairly low, it would imply that the bank had used up a large part of secondary reserves and was borrowing funds to finance loans and investments. The last ratio, or near-cash assets/large-denomination liabilities, was mentioned earlier and is a good measure of the ability of the bank to use liquid assets to cover wholesale funds that are for the most part uninsured. It should be clear that bank liquidity is a multidimensional concept that requires management to consider many factors and their interrelationships.

Table 9.5 gives the average values of these liquidity ratios for all U.S.-insured commercial banks from 1990 to 1998. Loans/deposits ratios increased from 0.98 to 1.33 over this period, which was due to strong loan demand and falling interest rates that caused deposit funding to decline and nondeposit funding to increase. This latter trend is supported by the decline in the loans/nondeposit liabilities ratio from 2.01 in 1990 to 1.61 in 1998. Because the large denomination time deposits/total assets ratio decreased from 1.37% to 0.42% during these years, as did the small denomination time deposits/total assets ratio from 1.57% to 0.73%, it is evident that banks were having difficulty in attracting CDs in the low interest rate environment of the 1990s. As noted earlier, low interest rates in the early 1990s caused deposit withdrawals. On the whole, these changes suggest that U.S. banks' liquidity deteriorated to some extent in the 1990s.

Another approach to measuring liquidity is to account for changes over time in both liquidity needs and sources. This approach is superior to focusing on one or the other parts of the liquidity problem because it evaluates liquidity relative to bank needs. For this evaluation, the following ratio can be calculated:

$$\frac{\text{Liquid assets and liabilities in period } t}{\text{Estimated liquidity needs in period } t} \qquad 9.1$$

The main business of Skypak Service Specialist (http://www.skyserve.com/ cash.htm) is to assist banks in funds management of simultaneously meeting loan demands and managing deposit sources of funds.

Table 9.6 calculates this ratio for a hypothetical bank using the estimated liquidity needs from Table 9.1 and other information on the bank's liquid assets and estimated access to liability sources of funds (i.e., detailed information of this kind is probably only available internally to bank management). Asset liquidity is restricted to unencumbered assets, and liability sources are based on estimates of low-cost external funding sources. Notice that estimated liability sources are assumed to stay the same from month to month. It is possible, however, that changing economic and financial market conditions could affect the ability of the bank to access purchased funds over time. Asset liquidity is under greater management control and can be varied to ensure that adequate total liquidity is available to meet deposit and loan needs. As shown in Table

TABLE 9.5	Liquidity Ratios of All Insured Commercial Banks Over Time								

Liquidity Ratio	1990	1991	1992	1993	1994	1995	1996	1997	1998
Loans/deposits	0.98	0.92	0.91	0.93	0.98	1.04	1.07	1.07	1.33
Loans/nondeposit liabilities	2.01	2.06	1.92	1.76	1.61	1.64	1.67	1.61	1.61
U.S. government securities[a]/nondeposit liabilities	0.40	0.49	0.55	0.56	0.49	0.42	0.39	0.36	0.30
U.S. government securities[a]/large denomination time deposits	1.67	2.09	3.17	4.37	4.64	3.80	3.27	2.88	1.65
Other Ratios:									
Large denomination time deposits[b]/ total assets	1.37%	1.15%	0.83%	0.50%	0.39%	0.41%	0.44%	0.44%	0.42%
Small denomination time deposits[b]/ total assets	1.57%	1.79%	1.59%	1.31%	1.00%	1.06%	0.97%	0.84%	0.73%

a. Information on the amount of unencumbered U.S. government securities is not publicly available.
b. These deposits are domestic only and exclude foreign deposits.
Source: William B. English and W. Nelson, "Profits and Balance Sheet Developments at U.S. Commercial Banks in 1997," *Federal Reserve Bulletin,* July 1998, p. 664.

9.6, the bank has negative liquidity needs (or excess liquidity) in January, May, and June, such that negative liquidity ratios result in these months. In the other months the ratio exceeds one, indicating that sufficient liquidity was available to meet normal operating needs. If the ratio had been in the range between zero and one, the bank could experience a potential liquidity problem and should begin developing a plan to overcome this shortfall.

Optimum Bank Liquidity

A question that bank management must ultimately face is whether the liquidity ratio is optimal. Optimality in this context is a dynamic concept because liquidity conditions in a bank change from day to day and week to week. For this reason bank liquidity must be regularly monitored and adjusted to reflect changing bank financial condition and market demands.

Optimum liquidity is achieved by balancing risks and returns. To be more

	TABLE 9.6	Evaluation Bank Liquidity by Comparing Needs and Sources Over Time

End of Month	(1) Estimated Liquidity Needs[a]	Asset Liquidity	Estimated Liability Sources	(2) Total Liquidity	(2)/(1) Liquidity Ratio
Jan.	(3,000)	5,000	10,000	15,000	–5.00[a]
Feb.	13,000	6,000	10,000	16,000	1.23
March	13,000	7,000	10,000	17,000	1.31
April	12,000	7,000	10,000	17,000	1.42
May	(2,000)	4,000	10,000	14,000	–7.00[a]
June	(13,000)	3,000	10,000	13,000	–1.00[a]

a. A negative liquidity need causes the bank liquidity ratio to be negative, which can be interpreted to mean that the bank has sufficient liquidity.

specific, measures of liquidity need to be high enough to meet even *unexpected* changes in liquidity needs and sources. On the other hand, liquidity should not be too high because of the opportunity cost of excessive near-cash assets that could be earning higher rates of return if sold and funds were invested in other assets. Also, liquidity management can conflict with other management goals in areas such as interest sensitivity management, loan management, and portfolio management. As a case in point, excessive use of liability management could force the bank to use relatively high cost funding if interest rates unexpected surged upward.[7] Thus, the bank must trade off the cost of maintaining excessive liquidity and the cost of insufficient liquidity. As shown in Figure 9.3, at some point, an optimum liquidity level is reached at which liquidity costs are minimized.

Because of the reliance on forecasted needs and sources, a reasonable margin for error should be considered. Greater uncertainty tends to increase the potential costs of maintaining liquidity, as well as the potential costs of insufficient liquidity. As such, the optimum quantity of bank liquidity is increased by uncertainty. To evaluate uncertainty and its effects on bank liquidity more formally, a graphical comparison of the probability distributions of both liquidity needs and sources can be constructed as shown in Figure 9.4. The shaded area is proportional to the probability that the bank will use up all of its liquidity; that is, liquidity needs could exceed liquidity sources. As the amount of overlap in these

7. Evaluating the costs of various liabilities sources involves an all-in-cost approach. Deposits have interest payments, FDIC insurance premiums, and operating costs. Commercial paper has interest payments, underwriting fees, and (at times) credit enhancement costs (through standby letters of credit and other guarantees). Likewise, costs of repurchase agreements, bankers' acceptances, fed funds, and other external funding sources need to be fully assessed.

FIGURE 9.3   Trading Off the Cost of Maintaining Liquidity
Against the Cost of Insufficient Liquidity

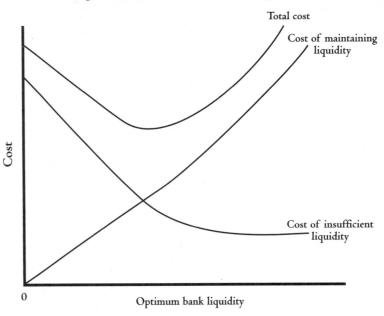

The Federal Reserve Bank of Chicago has generously provided a database (http://www.frbchi.org/ RCRI/rcri_database.html) of all insured U.S. banks' and bank holding companies' balance sheet and income statements. The data series is quarterly and starts in 1976. Using the information contained in the database, liquidity data for individual banks can be obtained to calculate liquidity ratios. Numerous other links to other federal regulators and related web sites are available.

two distributions increases, it becomes more likely that the bank will be illiquid at some point during the period of time under consideration.

It should be obvious that liquidity management is a complex balancing of risks and returns over time. Banks today differ considerably not only in their liquidity needs and sources but also in the extent to which they use different liquidity management strategies. As banks expand their asset base, changes in liquidity management should be assessed. Also, changes in bank condition could require management to modify its approach to liquidity. Less liquidity is necessary if the bank has large amounts of (unpledged) long-term securities, loan cash flow, and marketable loans. Also, as alluded to earlier, the bank may be using a considerable quantity of large denomination liabilities, but the risk associated with these funds would depend on their apportionment between core funding and volatile funding.

Regulatory View of Bank Liquidity

Regulators are concerned with the adequacy of a bank's liquidity, in contrast to the least cost liquidity strategy. The criteria used by the three federal regulatory agencies (Federal Reserve, Comptroller of the Currency, and FDIC) to evaluate bank liquidity—under the 1978 Uniform Interagency Bank Rating System—are as follows:

FIGURE 9.4 Graphical Analysis of Bank Liquidity

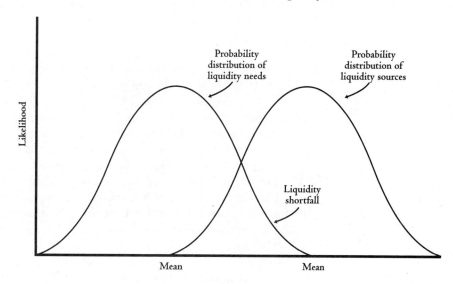

The Federal Financial Institutions Examination Council or FFIEC (http://www.ffiec.gov) *is a formal interagency body empowered to prescribe uniform principles, standards, and report forms for the federal examination of financial institutions by the Board of Governors of the Federal Reserve System (FRB), the Federal Deposit Insurance Corporation (FDIC), the National Credit Union Administration (NCUA), the Office of the Comptroller of the Currency (OCC), and the Office of Thrift Supervision (OTS), and to make recommendations to promote uniformity in the supervision of financial institutions. The FFIEC web site contains information services on banking industry data.*

- The availability of assets readily convertible into cash
- The structure and volatility of deposits
- The reliance on interest-sensitive funds, including money market instruments and other sources of borrowing
- The ability to sustain any level of borrowings over the business cycle or to attract new sources of funds
- The bank's formal and informal commitments for future lending or investment
- The ability to adjust rates on loans when rates on interest-sensitive sources of funds fluctuate

The **Uniform Bank Performance Report (UBPR)** published by the Federal Financial Institutions Examination Council gives liquidity analyses of individual banks, as well as different groupings of banks. Table 9.7 shows selected figures from UBPR liquidity analyses for all insured U.S. commercial banks during the period 1995–1998. *Temporary investments* are money market instruments, *core deposits* are relatively stable sources of deposits normally under $100,000, and *volatile liabilities* are large CDs and purchased deposits (or brokered deposits) and nondeposit sources of funds. Banks with larger percentage holdings of temporary investments and core deposits, and lesser percentage holdings of short-term noncore liabilities, would generally be considered more liquid. Applying these criteria to Table 9.7, asset liquidity declined in 1996 (due to surging loan demands) but recovered later in the 1990s, core deposits decreased by about 4%

from 1995 to 1998, and the use of short-term volatile liabilities did not change over time. A variety of other liquidity ratios give information on the extent of asset versus liability management of liquidity. Notice that core deposits are not sufficient to fund loans and leases; thus, banks must resort to noncore sources of funds to meet credit demands. The UBPR is a practical resource for analyzing bank liquidity and other management areas due to the availability of reports for individual banks, asset size groups, and the nation as a whole.

The decline in these liquidity sources exceeds the decline in the rate of growth of assets. The sharp decreases in liquid assets and volatile liabilities can be explained by (1) historically low interest rates motivating holders of interest-sensitive volatile liabilities to shift their funds to the capital market for higher returns, and (2) similar behavior by banks themselves to transfer funds out of low-earning assets and into higher-earning loans and long-term securities. Clearly, bank liquidity is seriously challenged during low interest rate periods.

Although not shown in Table 9.7, regulators also consider the loan risk of the bank in judging liquidity, as well as other potential factors that could be relevant. For example, a bank with a relatively risky loan portfolio financed by large CDs could be prone to extreme liquidity risk in the sense that it is "reaching" for interest income on risky loans with "hot" deposits, which are relatively expensive and can disappear overnight. If loan problems arose such that the CDs could not be rolled over, the bank would suffer a severe liquidity crisis. It is therefore important to distinguish between **operational liquidity** and **crisis liquidity** management. The former term applies to liquidity practice in normal everyday operations, whereas the latter type of liquidity relates to a temporary or enduring problem situation that threatens the bank's solvency. Crisis liquidity can be differentiated further into problems specific to the institution versus systemic problems that affect all institutions. Referring to the preceding example, the bank may be considered operationally liquid but relatively illiquid in a crisis situation.

Almost all banks employ a staff to oversee **management information systems** to measure and respond to liquidity needs. Such systems collect information both on- and off-balance sheet and are especially helpful for institutions with global operations. They also are valuable tools to forecast operational and crisis liquidity positions under alternative scenarios in a simulation setting. As a further check on liquidity management, banks routinely audit their information systems and their management success in achieving the bank's liquidity goals and policies. And, yet another layer of protection is afforded by **comprehensive contingency funding plans**. These plans outline courses of action to various liquidity problems and define coincident management responsibilities.

The wide variety of data collected by federal regulators to gauge bank liquidity amply suggests that it is a multidimensional concept. No single index is currently available that captures all of the factors included in an evaluation of liquidity, including the liquidity of assets, stability of liabilities, access to borrowed funds, and liquidity needs. Instead, each bank must be analyzed on an individual basis. In this regard, an extenuating circumstance could be bank holding company (BHC) membership. Under FDICIA of 1991, banks that are members of holding

TABLE 9.7	UBPR Liquidity Analysis of All Insured U.S. Commercial Banks			
Percent of Total Assets	**12/31/98**	**12/31/97**	**12/31/96**	**12/31/95**
Temporary investments	9.46%	9.96%	8.33%	9.50%
Core deposits	49.38	50.14	52.48	53.55
Short-term noncore deposits	25.91	26.05	24.82	NA
Short-term assets to short-term liabilities	75.86	75.91	77.62	NA
Temporary investments less volatile liabilities to assets	8.71	8.81	8.01	NA
Net loans and leases to deposits	86.44	85.00	86.19	84.01
Net loans and leases to core deposits	118.42	115.88	114.76	110.29
Net loans and leases to assets	62.96	62.71	64.84	63.48

Source: Adapted from Federal Financial Institutions Examination Council, *Uniform Bank Performance Report* (1999).

The FDIC's web site (http://www.fdic.gov/bank/ individual/index.html) carries a summary of financial results from all insured commercial banks and savings institutions, along with current and historical banking statistics, including liquidity ratios.

companies are liable for the losses of failed banks in their organization, which means that a liquidity crisis at a member bank could threaten the holding company itself. Furthermore, because most banks are members of bank holding companies, it means that crisis liquidity is best evaluated for the holding company as a whole, rather than for an individual banks as in the case of operational liquidity.

Bank Liquidity: A Hypothetical Example

Southwest National Bank and Rocky Mountain Bank are two medium-sized, regional banks located in a city with a population of approximately 5 million people. Southwest is oriented primarily to serve large commercial and industrial business firms in the area, while Rocky Mountain has sought to meet the needs of both individuals and businesses, most of which are smaller retail and light manufacturing firms. The two banks are not in direct competition with one another due to emphases on different market niches but do share a common economic base in the same city.

In the last two years the local economy has experienced a sharp downturn due to cutbacks in military spending that have seriously affected some large electronic components firms in the area. The slowdown has caused losses of jobs and outflows of workers, which triggered failures of retail merchants, restaurants, and a decline in real estate values due to a rising supply of homes for sale.

These events have affected the financial condition of both Southwest and Rocky Mountain. Table 9.8 on page 336 shows a number of financial ratios over the past three years for these banks. Both institutions have been under some degree of financial distress, as net income/total asset ratios have markedly slipped

Financial Panics and Liquidity Crises

Periodic bouts with bank failures have marked past as well as more recent U.S. financial history. Prior to the Great Depression in the 1930s, more than 30,000 banks existed in the United States. Due to bank closures by regulatory authorities, only about 15,000 banks remained after the economic crisis of this period. Prudential regulation and the introduction of deposit insurance stabilized the banking industry. Indeed, in 1980 the number of U.S. commercial banks remained at about 15,000 banks Regional economic woes throughout the 1980s further reduced the number of banks to about 12,000 by 1990, which subsequently dwindled to about 9,000 in 1999 due to a merger and acquisition wave. While bank failures in the 1930s were primarily small institutions, the 1980s witnessed numerous large bank failures: First Pennsylvania Bank, Philadelphia (1980), First National Bank, Seattle (1983), Continental Illinois Bank, Chicago (1984), First Republic Bank, Dallas (1987), MCorp, Dallas (1988), and the Bank of New England, Boston (1990).

A common problem in failing banks, whether small or large in size, is liquidity. Because demand deposits can be readily withdrawn, and other sources of bank funds are short term and can be withdrawn fairly rapidly, a "run" can quickly precipitate a fatal liquidity drain. This Achilles' heel in the viability of banks has caused regulators to take action in some circumstances to prevent a financial panic that would threaten multiple banks at a single point in time. The Great Depression aptly demonstrated the ill consequences of no regulatory intervention to bolster liquidity in the bank system. To stop the swelling run contagion, President Roosevelt declared a banking "holiday" in March 1933. Insolvent banks were placed in government receivership and solvent banks reopened with the approval of the government. Thereafter the banking system gradually recovered over a 10-year period.

From a societal viewpoint, history has shown that run contagions can be destructive to public confidence, to credit contracts outstanding at banks, and to the creation of money in the financial system. For these reasons the Federal Reserve today practices a "lender of last resort" policy intended to prevent runs that may have serious implications to the efficient operation of the financial system. Of course, the failure of a large bank could have the financial impact of many small bank failures. Consequently, the Federal Reserve has made available discount window borrowings to some large banks believed to be "too big to fail" (TBTF). Also, at times the Fed will

and equity capital/total assets ratios have declined also. Southwest appears to have experienced a sharper downturn in profit rates and capital ratios than Rocky Mountain.

Comparing their loan portfolios, Southwest has tended to increase business lending, as well as consumer lending, on a percentage of assets basis. These changes could be due to a desire by bank management to increase asset risk and, therefore, loan yields in an effort to make up for declining earnings. Rocky Mountain has maintained its business loan activity, cut back on home loans, and shifted to greater consumer lending. These changes likely had little or no effect on its overall credit risk.

Finally, and most relevant to our discussion, Southwest and Rocky Mountain clearly have different approaches to liquidity management. Southwest has intervene and seek to merge a large, failing institution that could threaten public confidence in the banking system with one or more healthy banks. The TBTF policy was officially announced by federal regulators in the wake of the Continental Illinois liquidity crisis in 1984. At the time the eighth largest U.S. bank with over $40 billion in total assets, Continental suffered from losses on foreign and oil and gas loans. Heavy reliance on large foreign depositors worsened Continental's liquidity problems. A federal bailout package totaling $4.5 billion was arranged by the Federal Reserve Bank, FDIC, and a consortium of banks.

Some degree of controversy surrounds this TBTF practice, however. Smaller banks complain that large banks receive unlimited deposit insurance for free. That is, uninsured depositors with balances exceeding the $100,000 insurance limit are effectively receiving protection under the TBTF doctrine. In some cases uninsured depositors have lost some amount of funds upon a large bank's collapse (e.g., First Republic and MCorp cited earlier), but in the past at least, the total losses to uninsured depositors has been small due to both TBTF actions by the Federal Reserve and FDIC support of uninsured depositors.

Some experts have argued that, with the exception of Continental Illinois, most large bank failures previously treated as TBTFs did not have systemwide potential for damage and, therefore, should not have been bailed out. In regard to failing banks, the FDIC Improvement Act of 1991 set forth guidelines for pro-viding assistance to banks (and other financial institutions) and prohibits the FDIC from covering uninsured deposit losses or losses of creditors other than depositors. These changes will diminish but not eliminate the TBTF issue. The liquidity problem of financial panics is sudden, large in magnitude, and unpredictable. Also, financial markets respond well to government intervention in times of crisis, as demonstrated by numerous episodes over the past two decades. For example, on the day of the October 1987 stock market crash, Federal Reserve Chairman Alan Greenspan promptly announced that the central bank stood ready to supply needed liquidity to the financial system. That simple announcement quelled fears that the stock market panic would spread to banks and appeared to contribute to the rebound and stabilization of the stock market in subsequent weeks. More recently, banking panics in Mexico in 1994 and 1995, as well as southeast Asian countries (i.e., Indonesia, Malaysia, South Korea, Thailand) and Russia in the period 1996–1999, have reaffirmed the necessity of government intervention to preserve the safety and soundness of a banking system. Also, as discussed previously at the end of Chapter 4, the Federal Reserve coordinated a bailout of a multi-billion dollar hedge fund named Long-Term Capital Management in 1998 that was deemed TBTF. These events remind us of the fragility of institutional liquidity and its linkage to solvency and, in turn, the need for competent management in this area of bank liquidity.

---

relatively higher temporary investments than Rocky Mountain, but it uses much larger proportions of assets funded by volatile liabilities and much smaller proportions of assets funded by core deposits than Rocky Mountain. These differences are not unexpected, as greater use of volatile liabilities naturally should be backed up with higher secondary reserves. However, notice that Southwest has decreased its temporary investments while increasing volatile liabilities and decreasing core deposits. Rocky Mountain has also drawn down its temporary investments somewhat, but its mix of core deposits and volatile liabilities has stayed about the same over time.

We can infer that Southwest has significantly weakened its liquidity position. It is reasonable to believe that this change was prompted by a shift to higher-risk loans, as funding for these loans was essentially purchased as

TABLE 9.8	Financial Condition of Southwest National Bank and Rocky Mountain Bank Over Time					
	Southwest			Rocky Mountain		
Financial Ratios	1998	1999	2000	1998	1999	2000
Net income/Total assets	2.1%	1.0%	0.5%	1.2%	0.9%	0.8%
Equity capital/Total assets	6.5	6.0	5.5	6.0	5.6	5.5
Business loans/Total assets	50	52	53	20	22	19
Home loans/Total assets	5	5	4	30	28	26
Consumer loans/Total assets	6	8	9	15	16	18
Temporary investments/Total assets	20	18	16	15	14	12
Core deposits/Total assets	50	48	45	80	82	83
Volatile liabilities/Total assets	40	42	44	12	11	12

needed. By contrast, Rocky Mountain has been under earnings and capital pressures but has not compromised its safety and soundness by increasing credit risk or substantially altering its liquidity. Instead, Rocky Mountain is using some of its secondary reserves for meeting liquidity needs otherwise covered by bank earnings. This hypothetical example helps to illustrate that liquidity is a relative concept that varies not only from bank to bank but over time.

SUMMARY

Banks are under constant liquidity pressures. Because no bank can function without adequate liquidity, it is one of the most fundamental aspects of bank management. While adequate liquidity to avoid a crisis is one dimension of the problem, for most ongoing banks it is operational liquidity that is the real challenge. In this respect the central issue that management must evaluate is the risk and return tradeoffs.

Liquidity management involves estimating future expected liquidity needs and then planning to meet those needs by converting assets to cash, acquiring external funds, or both. To estimate liquidity needs the sources and uses approach can be used to evaluate the effects of deposit inflows and outflows and changing loan demands on bank liquidity. The structure-of-deposits method is another way to estimate liquidity needs, and focuses on the stability of deposits as a source of funds. Another major bank liquidity consideration is meeting the Federal Reserve's legal reserve requirements under Regulation D. Contemporaneous reserve requirement (CRR) accounting procedures must be used for transactions deposits as specified by the Federal Reserve.

Once liquidity needs are estimated, bank management must plan to meet those needs. Asset liquidity is a traditional approach, whereas liability management is a more modern approach. Asset liquidity refers to holding secondary reserves of money market instruments that may be quickly converted to cash with little or no capital loss. Use of cash and short-term financial instruments to meet liquidity needs does not affect the capital position of the bank, while liability management can affect the bank's capital position, which must be sufficient to satisfy regulatory requirements.

Liability management of liquidity enables the bank to shift funds from lower-earning money market instruments to higher-earning loans and investment securities. It also tends to increase the financial flexibility of the bank in dealing with liquidity needs. If it is cheaper to acquire funds than it is to liquidate assets to finance new loans, the former should naturally be used, barring the influence of other factors in the decision. However, this liquidity approach is not without risks. Debt interest obligations rise as a percentage of total assets, which tends to increase the bank's exposure to interest rate risk, as well as its financial risk because of increased financial leverage.

Optimally, bank managers must weigh the cost of maintaining excessive liquidity against the cost of insufficient liquidity in an attempt to minimize the total costs of liquidity management. By contrast, regulators are more concerned with the adequateness of the bank's liquidity, as measured in the Uniform Bank Performance Report (UBPR) and by bank examiners.

Key Terms and Concepts

Aggressive liquidity approach
Asset liquidity
Asset management
Bankers' acceptances
Capital market risk
Commercial paper
Comprehensive contingency funding plans
Contemporaneous reserve requirement accounting
Correspondent balances
Crisis liquidity
Discount window
Eurocurrency liabilities
Federal agency securities
Federal funds
Funding-liquidity risk
Funds management approach
Lagged reserve requirement accounting

Liability management
Management information systems
Market-liquidity risk
Money market approach
Negotiable certificates of deposit
Nonpersonal time deposits
Operational liquidity
Optimum liquidity
Primary reserves
Repurchase agreements
Secondary reserves
Sources and uses of funds method
Sources and uses of funds statement
Structure-of-deposits method
Treasury bills
Transactions accounts
Uniform Bank Performance Report (UBPR)

Questions

9.1   What is the first step in any bank liquidity analysis? Discuss two methods of accomplishing this first step.

9.2   Why has asset management been less emphasized over the past 20 years?

9.3   When would asset liquidity be preferred to liability management of liquidity?

9.4   Why are legal reserves considered a tax on banks?

9.5   What are collateralized commercial paper programs and medium-term notes? How do they help meet liquidity needs?

9.6   What are lagged reserve requirements? How is vault cash counted in maintaining reserves using LRR?

9.7   How are reserve requirements calculated for MMDAs?

9.8   How do small and large banks differ in the management of their money positions?

9.9   What is the money market approach to liquidity management?

9.10   Discuss the risks and returns associated with using liability management to meet liquidity needs.

9.11   What is funds management? What does it seek to do?

9.12   Discuss optimality in bank liquidity management. How does uncertainty affect optimal bank liquidity?

9.13   How do regulators evaluate bank liquidity? How much liquidity is adequate?

9.14   How does operational liquidity management differ from crisis liquidity management?

9.15   If the ratio of liquid assets and liabilities in period *t* divided by estimated liquidity needs in period *t* is between 0 and 1, might there be a problem with bank liquidity?

9.16   Why is government interested in supporting bank liquidity in the face of a financial panic? Should large banks be prevented from failing by the government?

9.17   What is funding-liquidity risk and market-liquidity risk? How might banks use management information systems to control these risks?

9.18   Review the Federal Financial Institutions Examination Council's (FFIEC) "User's Guide for the Uniform Bank Performance Report *(http://www.ffiec.gov/UBPR.htm)*. What is contained in the report? How is it useful to banking institutions?

9.19   Go to the FDIC's web site overviewing different bank rating services available in the United States at *http://www.fdic.gov/bank/individual/ bank/index.html*. Pick one of the private firms listed there and write a summary of its financial services.

9.20 Go to the National Information Center (NIC) web site at *http://www.ffiec.gov/nic/default.htm* and look up an individual bank, and collect data on its liquidity. Write a short report based on your data.

Problems

9.1 (a) Given the Sources and Uses of Funds Statement in Exhibit 9.1, calculate the estimated changes in loans and deposits from month-to-month, as well as the estimated liquidity need.

  (b) Given the results of part (a), in which months does the bank have excess or deficient liquidity? What sources of liquidity are there to meet the liquidity need in case of a deficiency? In the month(s) having excess liquidity, what uses of funds are available to avoid holding too much idle cash?

  (c) Given the information in Exhibit 9.2, calculate the bank's ratio of estimated liquidity sources to liquidity needs. Will the bank have a liquidity problem at some time in the coming months?

9.2 Given the following deposit data, calculate the total reserves required:

	Average Dollar Amount ($ millions) in Computation Period
Net transactions accounts	
0–$46.5 million	$46.5
Over $46.5 million	30.0
Nonpersonal time deposits	25.0
Eurocurrency liabilities	
All types	2.0

Note: The first $4.9 million of transactions deposits are exempt from reserve requirements.

EXHIBIT 9.1	Sources and Uses of Funds Statement	
End of Month	**Estimated Total Loans**	**Estimated Total Deposits**
June	$180,000	$190,000
July	190,000	180,000
Aug.	210,000	190,000
Sept.	240,000	200,000
Oct.	200,000	210,000
Nov.	180,000	200,000
Dec.	170,000	190,000

EXHIBIT 9.2	Estimated Sources of Liquidity	

End of Month	Estimated Asset Liquidity	Estimated Sources of Liabilities
June	$3,000	$5,000
July	4,000	10,000
Aug.	4,000	5,000
Sept.	3,000	3,000
Oct.	2,000	5,000
Nov.	3,000	10,000
Dec.	4,000	10,000

9.3   You are given the responsibility by top management to review your bank's liquidity position, as reflected by balance sheet and income statement information. Your assistant assembled the following financial data per your request:

Financial Ratios	Metropolitan Bank			Peer Group of Banks		
	1998	1999	2000	1998	1999	2000
Net income/Total assets	0.8	0.9	1.1	0.8	0.9	0.9
Equity capital/Total assets	5.5	5.7	6.0	5.6	5.7	5.9
Business loans/Total assets	50	53	56	48	47	48
Home loans/Total assets	10	9	8	12	13	13
Consumer loans/Total assets	9	8	6	10	9	9
Temporary investments/ Total assets	20	18	15	20	21	20
Core deposits/Total assets	55	50	45	53	55	54
Volatile liabilities/ Total assets	35	39	45	37	36	37

CASE STUDY

Northeast National Bank

The last few years had been quite profitable for Northeast National Bank, despite increasing competition from out-of-state competitors in its home state. Northeast had increased total assets over the last five years from $300 million to $500 million and was starting to enjoy some scale economies from the larger size of operations and recent organizational changes. Five years ago changes in federal banking laws had opened up interstate branching in the nation. A low-cost opportunity to enter new markets presented itself—branch offices did not require (1) applying for new bank charters, (2) a CEO or board of directors, and (3) high operating and overhead costs. Instead, branch offices could be operated with a manager and many operations of the branch channeled through the main bank office, including paperwork on mortgage loans, most computerized record keeping, wire transfers of funds, payrolls, etc. The cost savings of branch banking had enabled Northeast to increase its profits despite growing competition and use the retained earnings to expand its reach in the area. At the present time, Northeast had five branch offices located within a 20-mile radius of the main office, with two of these offices located across a nearby state line.

The larger size and different configuration of operations of Northeast had changed its liquidity management. It had become essential that the main office for a branch network work closely with the branch managers on their liquidity needs and sources. Unfortunately, no formal system of control over the liquidity function had formally developed over the last five years, because most liquidity issues were overcome by strong cash flows from recent cost savings on branch operations.

However, other banks in the state also have been modifying their organizational structure to take advantage of operating cost savings from branching. A competitive trend that has been emerging in the last year is the use of these savings by other banks to lower loan rates and raise deposit rates relative to

Treasury rates of interest. Thus, profit margins are beginning to return to levels that existed prior to the federal relaxation of branch banking laws.

John Thorpe, vice-president of operations for Northeast, arrived at work Monday morning to find a memorandum from CEO George Schindler requesting a strategic report on liquidity management issues that would need more in-depth analyses in the next six months. Mr. Schindler asked that the following questions be discussed in the report:

- How is liquidity defined?
- How is liquidity measured at the branch office level in relation to the bank organization as a whole?
- How does the branching structure change liquidity risks for the main office?
- How does the branching structure affect the liquidity risks of each individual branch office?
- Does it make sense to evaluate the liquidity of the consolidated branching organization or should liquidity analyses focus on each operating branch as well as the main office?
- How can the bank communicate its liquidity strengths to outside observers who can obtain data only on the consolidated bank organization?

After calling the branch managers, John learned that each branch had a different market niche and normally (but not always) referred larger customer needs for credit and other services to the main office. The main office was located in a large suburb of a major U.S. city. One branch was located near a university and specialized in small, retail deposit accounts for students with few credit services, except for auto loans and some other consumer installment loans. A second branch was located on the main street of a small nearby community and offered small business deposit and loan services for the most part. A third branch was not far from the main office at a convenient customer location that helped support both retail and commercial services for the main office. The fourth branch tended to emphasize auto loans due to its close proximity to a number of automobile dealerships that were concentrated in one part of town. The fifth, and last, branch office was larger than the other branches and offered a full line of financial services, with the exception of wholesale banking services to large corporate clients.

With this information in mind, John Thorpe has asked you, as his assistant, to write a two-page report briefly addressing each of the CEO's questions. He has encouraged you to stick to fundamentals but, at the same time, show some creativity in handling the issue of branch offices.

Investment Management

The second largest asset item on a bank's balance sheet is investments, or the securities held by the bank. As a general rule, investment securities are purchased to produce income in the form of interest paid and capital gains, but liquidity is another role that these securities can fulfill. During recessionary periods when demand for commercial credit is relatively low, investment securities are a good alternative source of income. As economic recovery proceeds and loan demand increases, maturing investment securities can be rolled into loans, or shorter-term securities may be sold to fund higher-earning loan and investment security opportunities. To some extent, therefore, investment securities provide an additional reserve of funds over and above secondary reserves to meet the liquidity need of banks.

Investment securities also play other roles in bank management. For example, they may be pledged as collateral on public deposits of federal, state, and local governments, borrowing from Federal Reserve banks, and securities sold under agreement to repurchase. Some municipal securities can be used to reduce income taxes. Moreover, investment securities may be purchased to increase the diversification of the bank's total asset portfolio or to take advantage of interest rate movements that would yield capital gains, both of which are portfolio adjustments that attempt to maximize return per unit risk. More recently, banks have been using securities to adjust their interest rate risk and to help meet risk-based capital standards. In the present chapter we overview investment policies and goals, types of investment securities, methods of evaluating investment risk, and investment strategies. As we will see, securities investments play an important role in bank risk management and profitability. ■

10.1 DEVELOPING INVESTMENT POLICIES AND GOALS

Bank **investment policy** should be formally established so that managers can make decisions that are consistent with the overall goals of the organization. In general, investment policy seeks to maximize the return per unit risk on the investment portfolio of securities, although regulatory requirements, lending needs, tax laws, liquidity sources, and other factors can limit return/risk performance. Bank policy should have sufficient flexibility to enable it to shift investment goals in response to changes in financial and economic conditions and competition from rival institutions. For example, the bank must decide how to divide assets between liquidity and securities investment. Higher asset liquidity reduces the risk of missing profitable lending opportunities because of a shortfall of available funds; however, higher returns on longer-term investment opportunities are normally sacrificed. Liability management tends to decrease the emphasis on asset liquidity (as discussed in the previous chapter), which implies that investment securities are more likely to comprise a significant part of the asset base of today's banks. Furthermore, the volatile interest rate environment of the 1970s and early 1980s, as well as stock and bond market turbulence in the late 1990s, serve as potent reminders that the potential risks and returns on investment securities can be substantial. In this context investment policies are essential to successfully managing the inherent risks and potential returns in a securities portfolio.

The investment policy should be written out as a guide to managers in allocating responsibilities, setting investment goals, directing permissible securities purchases, and evaluating portfolio performance. Tables 10A.1 and 10A.2 in the appendix contain an actual investment policy of a major U.S. bank. In Table 10A.1 securities are broken into different risk types or categories. Table 10A.2 gives the regulatory guidelines for each security, in addition to bank-imposed guidelines for investment size, quality, and maturity. Notice that securities are classified into three categories under rules for members of the Federal Reserve System:[1]

1. The Office of the Comptroller of the Currency (OCC) revised their investment-securities regulation in 1996 to identify five basic types of securities. Interested readers can find details in the assets section of the *Commercial Bank Examination Manual* for Federal Reserve examination personnel at the following Federal Reserve web site: *http://www.federalreserve.gov/boarddocs/SupManual/default.htm#cbem.*

- **Type I:** low-risk securities such as U.S. Treasuries, federal agencies, and general obligation municipals with no limitations on their purchases
- **Type II:** moderately low-risk securities issued by various federal and state agencies with regulatory and self-imposed limitations on purchases
- **Type III:** higher-risk securities issued by corporations and asset-backed securities of various kinds with more stringent regulatory and self-imposed limitations on purchases

This example clearly demonstrates that a well-defined investment policy is an invaluable guideline to everyday investment practices.

Banks with assets of more than $500 million or so need to devote greater effort toward developing investment policies and goals than do smaller institutions. Larger banks typically manage trading accounts that conduct a variety of securities services, including diversification, liquidity, expert advice to clients, government securities management, and speculation in price movements. Many times smaller banks follow the investment recommendations of larger "correspondent" banks. Smaller banks also subscribe to a variety of other investment services that correspondent banks offer (e.g., safekeeping of financial instruments, trading services, and computer portfolio analyses).

The following list includes some examples of different investment goals:

- Income
- Capital gains
- Interest rate risk control
- Liquidity
- Credit risk
- Diversification
- Pledging requirements

Income can be achieved by either purchasing bonds with high coupon rates or when loan demand is weak and securities represent an alternative source of revenues. If foregoing current income for future income is desired, *capital gains* are an appropriate investment goal. Deeply discounted bonds have relatively low coupon rates and emphasize capital gains. Moreover, interest rate conditions can affect these two earnings goals. For example, if interest rate levels are declining, income will also decline, but this loss of earnings on securities can be more than offset by purchasing long-term securities that will increase in price (yielding a capital gain) as interest rates fall.

Interest rate risk control is another factor for management to consider. Loans cannot easily be sold in many cases, which decreases management's ability to adjust dollar and duration gaps, as discussed in Chapter 5.[2] By contrast,

2. The growing securitization of loans is changing their flexibility of maturity composition and risk taking. Credit card and automobile loans are commonly securitized today and some signs indicate that small business loans could become another popular area of securitization in the future.

securities can be sold at management's discretion, so that if management expected interest rates to change in the near future, it could buy and sell securities with various maturities to diminish interest rate risk effects on the bank.

As an example, in low interest rate periods, depositors will be hesitant to purchase long-term CDs, and borrowers will prefer longer-term loans than usual to take advantage of the low interest rates. This difference in deposit and loan demands would tend to cause the average maturities of deposits to be less than the average maturity of loans. An increase in interest rates would squeeze profit margins, as deposit accounts would be rolled over more rapidly than loan accounts—in effect, interest costs rise more rapidly than earnings on assets over time. Also, an increase in interest rates would diminish the value of bank equity due to the greater price risk of assets compared to liabilities. (For an illustration of these concepts, see the Managing Risk box.) To offset these potentially harmful interest rate risk effects, the maturity of the investment securities portfolio could be shortened to lower the average maturity of assets comprised of loans and securities. An excellent choice to accomplish this defensive strategy is adjustable-rate agency securities.

While longer-term securities are not liquid, they have some liquidity in the sense that management has the option of selling them to meet cash needs. Because balance sheets reflect book values (or purchase prices) of securities, banks at times "cherry pick," or sell securities with large gains. This practice became controversial in the 1990s, however. The Securities Exchange Commission (SEC) argued that by using book values, rather than market values, bank financial condition is distorted. Cherry picking left securities selling below book value on the balance sheet and therefore overstated their value, further implying that the level of bank capital was lower than reflected by its book value. Others defended book value accounting by pointing out that market valuation of securities would give investors and depositors a false impression of bank risks. The greater balance sheet volatility associated with market value accounting could hamper bank lending, especially in the face of a large, unanticipated increase in interest rates that significantly decreased securities prices.

In recent years the Financial Accounting Standards Board (FASB) approved **market value accounting** rules that require banks to classify securities as "assets held for sale" (or trading) and "assets held for maturity." Whereas investment securities can be carried at book (or historical) value if the holder has no intention (at least at the time of purchase) to sell them prior to maturity, assets held for sale must be carried at book value or market value, whichever is lower. Thus, if liquidity is a goal, banks must set aside securities in assets held for sale. (See the Managerial Issues box for a chronology of recent events concerning market value accounting.)

The Bankers Administration Institute (BAI) surveyed bankers about the management effect of market value accounting on their investment practices.[3]

3. See Lizbeth S. Berquist, "Trends in Investment Portfolio Management," *Bank Management* (January 1991), pp. 64, 66–67.

MANAGING RISK

A Simple Example of Interest Rate Risk and Securities Management

Assume that a bank funds $100 of two-year securities with $100 of one-year deposits. To simplify matters also assume that both securities and deposits are discount instruments that pay par at maturity so that there are no interest payments during the year. The securities earn a yield of 10%, and the deposits cost 8%. The income and expenses for the bank for the bank over these two years is as follows:

	Year 1	Year 2
Income	$0	$121 (= $100 × 1.10 × 1.10)
Expense	−8	− 108
Profit	−$8	$ 13

Discounting all cash at 8%, which is the cost of funds, we get $13/(1.08)^2 − $8/(1.08) = 3.74, such that the net present value of the investment portfolio is positive.

Suppose that interest rates rise to 10% for deposits in the second year. Given that the securities purchased and deposits acquired in the first year have their interest rates locked in at the rates that prevailed at the beginning of the first period, the income and expenses for the bank would now be:

	Year 1	Year 2
Income	$0	$121 (= $100 × 1.10 × 1.10)
Expense	−$8	− 110 (= 100 × 1.10)
Profit	−$8	$ 11

Discounting all cash at 8% in the first period and 10% in the second period, we get $11/(1.10)^2 −

$8/(1.08) = $1.68. Notice that the net present value of the investment portfolio has declined by more than 50% from $3.74 before the rise in interest rates. This drop in profitability was due to the decrease in profits in year 2 from $13 to $11 (before discounting to present values).

We can also calculate the effect of the increase in interest rates on the equity value of the bank in year 2. For this purpose we make use of Eq. (10.3) covered later in this chapter. That equation shows how the concept of duration can be employed to estimate changes in asset values in response to interest rate changes (see also Chapter 5). In the preceding example, securities have a duration equal to 2, while deposits have a duration equal to 1. Substituting this information into Eq. (10.2), the change in the value of securities is $-(2)$100(.02/1.10) = −3.64, while for deposits the change is $-(1)$100(.02/1.08) = −1.85. So, the net change in equity must be −$1.79 in year 2.

The bank could have avoided the negative profit and capital implications of the increase in interest rates with an accurate interest rate forecast in year 1 of the 2% increase in year 2. In this event some of its securities could have been sold and the resultant funds used to purchase shorter-term securities with less price risk. Rearranging the maturity structure of deposits or loans is also possible but it is more difficult from the standpoint that, while bank pricing of deposits and loans with different maturities can influence their maturities, depositor and borrower preferences for different maturity ranges also comes into play. With securities investments, interest rate risk can be adjusted without taking into account deposit and loan demands.

MANAGERIAL ISSUES

Recent Steps Toward Market Value Accounting (MVA) for Banks

- For years, banks have been required to designate a separate trading account for those securities they do not intend to hold to maturity and to mark such securities to market.
- The FDIC Improvement Act of 1991 required regulators to develop "methods for institutions to provide supplemental disclosure on estimated fair market value of assets and liabilities, to the extent feasible and practicable."
- The Federal Reserve Board's Supervisory Policy Statement on Securities Activities, developed under the auspices of the Federal Financial Institutions Examination Council, took effect in February 1992. It extended the original trading account requirements by requiring banks to report loans and securities "held for sale" at the lower of cost or market value.* In addition, it stipulated that stripped mortgage-backed securities, residuals,

and zero-coupon bonds "may only be acquired to reduce an institution's interest rate risk and must be reported in the trading account at market value, or as assets held for sale at the lower of cost or market value."

- The Financial Accounting Standards Board (FASB) adopted Statement 115 for MVA in February 1993 that would apply to banks as well as to other companies. The new rule was effective in 1994. Other recent actions by FASB that affected banks include Statement 105 requiring disclosure of off-balance-sheet risk and Statement 107 requiring disclosure of fair (market value) of all financial instruments.

*A bank must be well capitalized and have strong earnings and adequate liquidity to be permitted to maintain a trading account.

Some of the findings were that managers believed the new accounting rules would tend to:

- decrease securities sales due to possible adverse balance sheet effects.
- increase emphasis on a buy and hold investment strategy.
- decrease the maturities of securities to lessen price risk.
- decrease aggressive or active management of the securities portfolio.
- increase documentation demands on managers to fully explain reasons for sales and purchases.

Interestingly, the survey respondents perceived interest rate risk management and liquidity management as the most important investment objectives at their bank. These objectives help explain the growing use of swaps and off-balance sheet derivative products in banking today. Also, they account for the fact that most securities held by banks are in the form of assets held for sale, rather than held for maturity.

One problem for investment managers under market value accounting is that many times securities are held for sale to meet liquidity demands, rather than to maximize yields or to trade at a profit. For many small banks this problem is particularly troublesome. To minimize the effect of market value accounting, shorter-term securities should be held for sale and longer-term securities can be held for maturity. In this way liquidity needs are met without exposing the investment portfolio to considerable interest rate risk.

Credit risk and *diversification* are important aspects of securities investment that are discussed in further detail later in this chapter. In the context of investment goals, bank management needs to consider the risk preferences of shareholders. Risk by itself is not undesirable; instead, it is risk in excess of some level appropriate for the shareholders that is unsatisfactory. Thus, bank management must understand shareholder risk preferences in order to establish investment goals.

Securities held to meet *pledging requirements* mentioned earlier should be selected with other goals in mind to avoid conflicts among investment goals. For example, if U.S. government deposits must be collateralized with Treasury securities, or state government deposits require pledged municipal securities, bank management should purchase instruments with income and capital gains earnings that coincide with goals in these particular areas. Other liabilities, such as repurchase agreements (RPs) and discount window borrowings, must also be collateralized with qualifying assets.

Development of an investment policy that maximizes returns per unit risk involves defining the various goals already discussed. Even though policies generally are oriented toward a long-run perspective, the investment policy should incorporate some degree of management flexibility to accommodate changing market conditions. If tax laws or regulatory standards change to more favorably treat a particular type of security (e.g., new risk-based capital standards have zero capital requirements on some types of securities and higher capital requirements on other securities), management should take such changes into account in their investment decisions. Because internal and external conditions change over time for banks, management must periodically review and update investment goals.

10.2 TYPES OF INVESTMENT SECURITIES

Investment securities can be arbitrarily defined as those securities with maturities exceeding one year. Two categories of securities dominate more than 90% of bank investment portfolios—U.S. government and agency securities, and obligations of state and political subdivisions, or municipal securities. Other bonds and equity securities are heavily restricted by regulations; for example, high-quality corporate bonds are allowed but are subject to restrictions, and common stock investment is allowed in subsidiaries of banks or bank holding companies that are legally separate entities under the Financial Services Modernization Act of 1999.

U.S. Government and Agency Securities

U.S. TREASURY SECURITIES Most **Treasury notes** and **treasury bonds** purchased by banks have maturities ranging from 1 to 5 years. Unlike Treasury bills, which are sold at a discount and pay no coupon interest, Treasury notes and bonds are coupon-bearing instruments, consistent with their income function.[4] Because the market for Treasuries in the 1–5 year range is relatively deep and broad, these securities provide an extra measure of bank liquidity. Additionally, these securities serve to secure both deposits of public money (e.g., tax and loan accounts of the U.S. Treasury) and loans from Federal Reserve banks, and they are widely accepted for use in repurchase agreements.

Freddie Mac (http://www. freddiemac.com/), the Federal Housing Administration (FHA) (http://www. c21homepros.com/faq/88. html), and other related federal agencies can be readily accessed on the Internet.

AGENCY SECURITIES Many federal agencies issue securities, called **agency securities**, that are not direct obligations of the U.S. Treasury but nonetheless are federally sponsored or guaranteed. Some examples of federal agencies are the Government National Mortgage Association (GNMA or Ginnie Mae), Federal Home Loan Mortgage Corporation (FHLMC or Freddie Mac), Federal Housing Administration (FHA), Veterans Administration (VA), Farm Credit Administration (FCA), Federal Land Banks (FLB), and Small Business Administration (SBA). Ginnie Maes, for instance, represent a claim against interest earnings on a pool of FHA and VA mortgages issued by private mortgage institutions. The principal and interest on these so-called "pass through" bonds are guaranteed by the full faith and credit of the U.S. government. Similarly, securities issued by the Federal National Mortgage Association (FNMAs or Fannie Maes), the Mortgage Guarantee Insurance Corporation (MGICs or Maggie Maes) and other agencies represent claims on mortgage pools; however, because FNMA is

---

4. Discount money market instruments, such as Treasury bills, commercial paper, repurchase agreements, and bankers' acceptances, have a peculiar convention of using discount basis yields, otherwise simply referred to as the *discount rate* (DR):

$$DR = [(\text{Par value} - \text{Discounted sale price})/\text{Par value}](360/n),$$

where n is the days to maturity. For a $1 million, 90-day T-bill selling at 98 16/32 (or $985,000), we have

$$DR = [(100 - 98.5)/100](360/90) = 0.06 \text{ or } 6\%.$$

This yield is lower than normal due to using 100 in the denominator of the rate of return calculation in brackets, as well as due to using 360 days instead of 365 days. To obtain a coupon equivalent rate (CER), the following formula is used:

$$CER = [\text{Par value} - \text{Discounted sale price})/\text{Discounted sale price}](365/90)$$
$$CER = [100 - 98.5)/98.5](365/90) = 0.062 \text{ or } 6.2\%.$$

An effective annual rate (EAR) can be estimated by assuming that the security will be rolled over at the same CER, or 6.2%, each quarter during the year: $EAR = \{1 + [0.062/(365/90)]\}^{365/90} - 1 = 0.063 \text{ or } 6.3\%$.

a federally sponsored agency and MGIC is a private mortgage bank, FNMA securities have lower interest rates than do MGIC securities. A modest risk distinction separates federally guaranteed issues (e.g., GNMAs) and federally sponsored issues (e.g., FNMAs and FHLMCs).

Other mortgage-backed securities (MBSs) include participation certificates (PCs), guaranteed mortgage certificates (GMCs) and collateralized mortgage obligation (CMOs). PCs are ownership claims on conventional mortgages held by Freddie Mac with monthly payments of interest and principal. GMCs are also claims on a pool of mortgages held by Freddie Mac, but the interest payments are made semiannually like a corporate bond, and principal is paid once a year. CMOs are an important innovation that repackages the cash flows from both pooled mortgages and MBSs (with standardized terms of payment and maturity) into different payment combinations—for example, interest only (IO), principal only (PO), and mixed payment streams—and different maturity ranges. In so doing CMOs are designed to appeal to diverse investor demands.

All mortgage-derivative securities are exposed to **prepayment risk**. For example, when interest rates decline, refinancings of mortgages by homeowners to take advantage of the lower interest payments can cause prepayments of outstanding mortgages.[5] While homeowners clearly benefit from refinancing at lower interest rates, MBS investors now must reinvest at lower interest rates as MBSs effectively mature. In turn, as interest rates fall to low levels, the prices of MBSs can decline due to negative investor reaction to prepayment risk. This price behavior is known as "reverse convexity"[6] (i.e., prices decline as interest rates decline, which is opposite of normal experience in which prices rise in response to falling interest rates). Interestingly, one advantage of CMOs is that investors can select bonds with varying levels of prepayment risk, for shorter-term bonds have lower risk than longer-term bonds in this respect.

In recent years banks have increased their purchases of agency securities relative to U.S. government securities. In 1985 only 5% of total assets in the banking industry was invested in U.S. government agencies, but in 1998 the percentage had doubled to almost 10%. The major reason for this increasing trend is that agencies earn a slightly better yield than Treasuries without sacrificing much liquidity, as secondary markets for agencies have become well developed over the last decade.

---

5. Prepayment of home loans can occur for other reasons also, such as moving to a new home due to family, economic, and other conditions.

6. Convexity measures the second derivative of prices with respect to interest rates, or $d^2P/di^2(1/P)$, while duration represents the first derivative, of dP/di. Because convexity is the nonlinear slope of the price curve (where price is the y-axis and interest rates are the x-axis), reverse convexity simply means that the slope of the price curve is positive rather than negative. See footnote 11 for the formula for duration. For further discussion of convexity and its relationship to duration, see G. O. Bierwag, George G. Kaufman, and Cynthia M. Latta, "Duration Models: A Taxonomy," *Journal of Portfolio Management*, vol. 14 (Fall 1988), pp. 50–55.

Municipal Bonds

Municipal bonds are issued by state and local governments to finance various public works, such as roads, bridges, schools, fire departments, parks, and so on. They normally offer higher yields than do U.S. governments and agency securities because they are exposed to default risk. *General obligation municipal bonds* (GOs) are backed by the "full faith and credit" of the taxing governmental unit. *Revenue bonds* are somewhat riskier than GOs because they are backed by the earning power of a public project, such as a toll road. In the event of default, bondholders would likely suffer large losses, because the physical assets are not marketable, especially if construction is not completed. The supply of revenue bonds has risen in recent years because of the desire by communities to borrow funds and thereby avoid further taxation of local residents.

TAXES Historically, due to the exposure of banks to federal (and state) income taxes, the primary advantage of "munis" compared with other securities was their exemption from federal income taxes (as well as from state income taxes if issued by a governmental unit within the state). In this case, a munis yielding 7% before taxes may well have had an after-tax yield that exceeded a comparable risk corporate bond yielding 10% before taxes. To see how the interest tax exemption on munis affected the income statement, assuming only federal income taxes, consider the following short-form income statement for a bank:

	($ thousands)
Total interest on securities	$1,000
Municipal bond interest	600
Other interest on securities	400
Total interest on loans	2,000
Total operating income	3,000
Total interest expenses	(2,100)
Total noninterest expenses	(300)
Total operating expenses	(2,400)
Net operating income (NOI)	600
Less municipal bond interest	(600)
Taxable income	0
Less taxes	(0)
Net income after taxes	0

Notice that net operating income (NOI) is just offset by municipal interest earnings such that the bank does not have any taxable income. If NOI were less than municipal interest earned, the bank would obtain no benefits from the tax exemption on munis.[7] This type of situation occurred for many U.S. banks in the 1980s, because profit margins narrowed due to deregulation, regional economic doldrums, and farming sector problems.

However, under the Tax Reform Act of 1986 (TRA86), the attractiveness of munis as investments for banks was substantially reduced. Generally, banks no longer can deduct interest expenses on borrowed funds used to purchase tax-exempt securities.[8] The loss of this deduction offsets the tax exemption on munis' interest earnings for the most part. In the previous example, if interest paid on funds acquired to purchase munis was $400, interest expenses would be reduced to $1,700 from $2,100, and taxable income would rise to $400 from $0. Note that banks are permitted to deduct 80% of the interest paid to acquire funds to purchase munis issued by local governments with no more than $10 million of new issues in any one year (so-called "bank qualified" munis[9]).

To compare the yields on munis with yields on taxable bonds, the following tax equivalent yield for munis with comparable risk and maturity can be applied:[10]

$$YTM_m/(1 - T) - (1.0 \times \text{Average cost of funds} \times T)/(1 - T) = YTM_{TE} \quad 10.1$$

where YTM_m = the yield-to-maturity on the muni bond, T = the tax rate of the bank, the average cost of funds is calculated based on IRS rules, and YTM_{TE} = the tax equivalent yield-to-maturity on munis. The factor of 1.0 in the numerator of the second term indicates that 100% of interest is nondeductible under

---

7. As another example, suppose that a bank issues $10,000,000 in CDs. The CDs require no reserves so the full amount can be invested. The cost of CD money is 5.4% and the marginal tax rate of the bank is 35%. At the moment taxable security interest rates are equal to 9%, while tax-exempt rates are equal to 7%, such that the latter are more attractive than taxable securities. We can now calculate the dollar amount of taxable and tax-exempt securities to purchase as $[(.09 \times \text{Taxable}) + (.07 \times \text{Tax-exempt})] - \$540,000 - (.07 \times \text{Tax-exempt}) = 0$, where the term in brackets is the total interest income, $540,000 is total interest expense, and the last term in parentheses subtracts out tax-exempt interest income to get zero taxable income. This equation simplifies to $(.09 \times \text{Taxable}) = 0$, such that $6,000,000 is the quantity of taxable securities to purchase, which implies that $4,000,000 of tax-exempt securities should be purchased. If the bank purchases more than this amount of tax-exempt securities, it will not benefit from further tax exemptions. By contrast, at $4,000,000 of tax-exempt securities it will maximize the value of the interest tax exemption.
8. Also, not all munis are exempt from taxes under TRA85 (e.g., securities classified as private activity bonds, which are used by communities to support private companies, are taxable).
9. To be classified as "bank qualified," the bonds must also be used to finance essential government services, such as schools, water and sewer utilities, highways, and so forth. Most munis are issued for these purposes, such that most small muni issues are bank qualified.
10. This formula assumes that the bonds are sold at par and held to maturity. In this case all income is earned in the form of interest payments with no capital gains.

TRA86 rules. For qualified muni bonds this factor would be 0.20. To demonstrate the use of this formula, assume $YTM_m = 8\%$, tax rate = 34%, average cost of funds = 7%, and 100% of interest is nondeductible. The tax equivalent muni yield is:

$$[0.08/(1 - 0.34)] - [(1.0 \times 0.07 \times 0.34)/(1 - 0.34)] = .0852$$

or 8.52 percent. As a check, if we consider (for example) a $1,000,000 corporate bond, the after-tax earnings would be the same as the muni bond:

	Taxable Bond	Muni Bond
Interest	$85,200	$80,000
– Taxes	(28,968)	0
Nondeductible interest	0	(23,800)(=1,000,000 $\times$ 0.07 $\times$ 0.34)
After-tax earnings	$56,200	$56,200

Another relevant tax item under TRA86 is that banks pay the higher of (1) regular income tax, or (2) alternative minimum tax at a 20% tax rate. Today, the maximum corporate tax rate is 39%. The alternative minimum tax prevents banks from paying no taxes, as in the preceding example. If the alternative minimum tax method is used, one-half of muni interest will be exposed to taxes (i.e., a 10% tax rate on muni interest). Clearly, the net effect of these changes in tax laws is a reduction in the attractiveness of munis for commercial banks.

Additionally, risk-based capital rules effective December 1992 (see Chapter 11) have altered banks' interest in GO versus revenue bonds. The new rules require 1.6% capital backing for GOs compared to 4.0% for revenue bonds. For every $100 of investment, this implies that $4.00 of capital is needed for revenue bonds but only $1.60 for GOs. Clearly, bank investment in revenue bonds will decrease, and investment in GO bonds conversely will increase, due to risk-based capital requirements.

Of course, at least from a tax management perspective, bank management should not hold municipal securities beyond the point where their after-tax yield to the bank (after taking into account lost interest deductions) is less than the after-tax corporate bond yield of comparable risk. However, even if munis yields exceed corporate yields, for various reasons, such as liquidity needs and capital regulations, management may opt to invest in corporate securities. Also, it is possible that taxes can be reduced by other means than municipal securities, such as utilizing leasing, making loans subject to foreign tax credits, timing loan and security losses, and accelerating depreciation.

Smith Breeden Associates Inc. at http://www. smithbreeden.com/research/ res.htm *is an investment management company specializing in the analysis and management of investment-grade fixed-income portfolios. Their web site contains an example of its investment strategies, portfolio selection standards, and risk management methods.*

Corporate Bonds

A **corporate bond** is a long-term debt security issued by a private corporation. Because the historical failure rate of corporations far exceeds the default rate by state and local governments on their debt obligations, it is necessary to evaluate carefully the default risk of this type of bond. Bond ratings and financial analysis of firms' accounting statements are two approaches to evaluating this risk.

Recent Portfolio Composition

Table 10.1 shows the composition of the securities portfolio of all insured U.S. commercial banks during the nine-year period 1990–1998. The mix of total securities was dominated by U.S. Treasury and government agency securities, which normally accounted for 10% to 17% of total assets during this period. State and local government (or municipal) securities accounted for only about 1% to 2% of total assets. In this regard, investment in municipal securities has gradually diminished from a level of about 6% since 1986, when the Tax Reform Act was signed as discussed earlier. All other securities, which are corporate bonds and private mortgage-backed securities for the most part, were 2% to 3% of total assets, with a downward trend in the 1990–1997 period and increase in 1998. Over this period of time, purchases shifted toward U.S. government agencies comprised of government-backed mortgage pools (MBSs) and collaterized mortgage obligations (CMOs). Notice that securities investments grew from 16% of total assets in 1990 to 22% in 1993 but thereafter gradually declined to about 17% percent in 1998. The increase in securities holdings in the early 1990s was due to weak loan demand, rising deposit flows, and higher capital standards on loans than securities. The subsequent decrease in securities investments in the mid to late 1990s was no doubt related to the low interest rates and rising loan demands during those years.

Of total securities held, about 25% had maturities of less than 1 year and, therefore, were purchased primarily for liquidity purposes. The majority of securities, about 75%, had maturities exceeding 1 year and may be considered the investment portfolio. Of these securities, about one-half had maturities in the range of 1–5 years, and one-half had maturities exceeding 5 years. Thus, most investment securities will mature at different times within one business cycle. This provides banks with some degree of flexibility in their allocation of funds throughout the business cycle.

Table 10.1 indicates a slight decrease in the percentage of assets devoted to loans. Given the fact that loan demand was weak in 1990 and increased considerably throughout the 1990s, the failure of the loan ratio to increase is surprising. One reason for this lackluster loan growth is that banks were increasingly securitizing loans (especially credit card loans) and moving them off the balance sheet. This trend in asset-backed securities is being driven by liquidity and default risk considerations, not to mention the lower risk-based capital standards on off-balance sheet items compared to loans. Additionally, noninterest-earning assets expanded in the second half of the 1990s due to the growth in the gross positive fair value of derivatives (i.e., forward and option contracts) held by banks. This new trend on bank balance sheets tended to

TABLE 10.1	Composition of Securities Portfolio for All U.S. Commercial Banks: 1990–1998								
As a Percent of Total Assets	1990	1991	1992	1993	1994	1995	1996	1997	1998
Securities	16.19	17.38	20.38	21.97	21.19	18.64	16.87	15.80	16.65
U.S. Treasury	3.42	3.78	5.88	7.05	6.85	4.82	3.34	2.81	2.24
U.S. government agencies	7.42	8.43	9.26	9.55	9.28	9.40	9.12	8.98	9.93
State and local government	2.03	1.63	1.46	1.31	1.21	1.11	0.99	0.88	0.92
Other	2.27	2.19	2.39	2.43	2.15	2.18	2.17	1.91	2.49
Total loans	62.22	60.08	58.30	56.33	58.56	62.68	64.24	63.89	64.40

Source: Antulio N. Bomfim and William R. Nelson, "Profits and Balance Sheet Developments at U.S. Commercial Banks in 1998," *Federal Reserve Bulletin* (June 1999), p. 390.

lower both securities and loans as a percentage of assets. Virtually all derivative investments are concentrated in the top 100 U.S. banks.

Figure 10.1 graphically displays the percentage holdings of banks by asset size. As bank size increases, the percentage of total assets in securities decreases.

10.3 EVALUATING INVESTMENT RISK

The investment risk involved in purchasing securities can be evaluated either on an individual security basis or in the context of the total asset portfolio of the bank. Thus, both security-specific and portfolio considerations should be taken into account to understand the risk of investment securities. Lastly, an important consideration is potential inflation effects on investment values.

Standard & Poor Rating Service (http://www.ratings. com/) *and Moody's Investment Company* (http:// www.moodys.com/) *are private firms with global rating services. Investors use their ratings to gauge the general level of default risk associated with bond issuers.*

Security-Specific Risk

DEFAULT RISK Default risk is the probability that promised payment of interest and principal will not be made on time. In general, municipal and corporate bonds (and some agency bonds) have greater credit risk than do federal government securities. Standard and Poor's and Moody's both provide credit risk ratings that indicate the long-run probability of timely payment of promised interest and principal. **Investment grade bonds** are assigned letter ratings by Moody's/S&P's as follows:

FIGURE 10.1 Securities Holdings of U.S. Banks by Asset Size

Ten Largest Banks: Asset Holdings

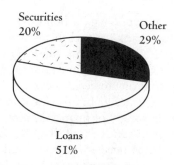

Securities
20%

Other
29%

Loans
51%

Banks Ranked 11th through
100th by Assets

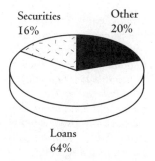

Securities
16%

Other
20%

Loans
64%

Banks Ranked 101st through
1,000th by Assets

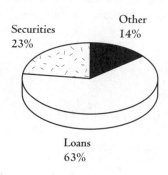

Securities
23%

Other
14%

Loans
63%

Banks Not Ranked among the
1,000th by Assets

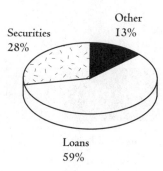

Securities
28%

Other
13%

Loans
59%

Source: *U.S. Treasury Bulletin,* Washington, D.C. (1999).

Aaa/AAA Highest-grade bonds have almost zero probability of default.

Aa/AA High-grade bonds have slightly lower credit quality than triple-A bonds.

A/A Upper-medium-grade bonds are partially exposed to possible adverse economic conditions.

Baa/BBB Medium-grade bonds are borderline between definitely sound and subject to speculative elements, depending on economic conditions.

Junk bonds are rated as follows:

Ba/BB Lower-medium-grade bonds bear significant default risk should difficult economic conditions prevail.

B/B, Caa/CCC, Ca/CC, C/C Speculative investment of varying degree have questionable credit quality.

DDD, DD, D Bonds with these ratings are in default and differ only in terms of their probable salvage value.

Bonds-Online (http://www. bondsonline.com/) *provides various information related to bond investment, such as news related to bonds, yield indexes for Treasuries, and bond products. The web site also has links to a variety of educational topics, including bond basics, bond ratings, and investing basics.*

Except in rare instances (e.g., a bond may have been downgraded subsequent to its purchase), banks restrict themselves to investment-grade securities, which fall within the "prudent man" rule of law.

Bond ratings provide general guidelines for gauging default risk. However, what if a bank is attempting to decide between three different firms' bonds and all have the same bond rating? In this situation financial analysis can be helpful. Typically, a wide variety of financial ratios are calculated from the firms' accounting statements. Ratios should be calculated over time to gain insight into trends. Also, ratios need to be compared to industry averages or peer group averages. Industry averages are reported by a number of sources, including Robert Morris Associates, Dun & Bradstreet, the Federal Trade Commission, and trade associations. Alternatively, a peer group of firms that one considers to be close competitors of the firm can be sampled by the analyst.

Table 10.2 gives an example of financial ratios for three hypothetical firms that we will assume have the same bond rating. Firm B has the highest rate of

TABLE 10.2	Example of Financial Ratio Analysis*		
Financial Ratios	**Firm A**	**Firm B**	**Firm C**
Profitability			
Net profits/Net sales	0.04	0.05	0.03
Net profits/Net worth	0.15	0.12	0.18
Net profits/Total assets	0.06	0.07	0.06
Liquidity			
Current assets/Current liabilities	2.00	2.30	2.40
(Current assets – Inventory)/Current liabilities	1.30	1.40	1.30
Leverage			
Total debt/Total assets	0.40	0.35	0.50
Gross income/Interest charges	4.00	4.20	3.00
Activity			
Sales/Inventory	10.00	8.50	9.00
Sales/Total assets	1.50	2.00	1.40

* All ratios are calculated using book values as reported on accounting statement.

return on assets (net profits/total assets), firm C has the highest rate of return on equity (net profits/net worth), and firm A is in the middle of this peer group. Firm C has the highest current ratio (current assets/total liabilities) but its quick or acid test ratio ([current assets – inventory]/current liabilities) is not the highest. Higher activity ratios reflect stronger short-term solvency, as more liquid assets are available to cover short-term creditor claims. Because inventory commonly is not as liquid as other current assets, and losses can occur on inventory if liquidated, the quick ratio is a stronger (acid) test of liquidity than the current ratio. The data in Table 10.2 show that firm C is more highly levered (indebted) than firms A and B. This difference explains the high rate of return on net worth for firm C (i.e., lower net worth in the denominator of this ratio). Finally, firm C has a moderate level of inventory turnover (sales/inventory) but has low total assets turnover (sales/total assets). The latter low figure suggests that it does not produce as much in sales per dollar of assets as the other firms. Thus, assuming equal bond yields, firm C should be dropped from consideration due to higher financial risk associated with relatively higher leverage and lower ability to generate sales to pay debt charges. Comparing firms A and B, firm B has lower leverage, stronger activity, more liquidity, and higher profitability than A. Firm B is favored over firm A for these reasons.

Our purpose here is to simply introduce some basic concepts within the context of investment decisions. In general, a complete financial ratio analysis involves analyses of trends over time, a broader set of financial ratios and other financial information, and industry or peer group comparisons. If the bank is planning to purchase large quantities of bonds issued by an individual entity where default risk is a relevant concern, an in-house analysis by bank investment managers would be warranted.

BONDHOLDER LOSSES IN DEFAULT Readers should recognize that both bond ratings and financial analyses capture default risk but not potential losses to bondholders in the event of default. Potential losses to bondholders arise from two sources: (1) priority of claims and (2) bankruptcy costs. In bankruptcy court proceedings, bondholders receive the prorated cash flows of the firm, depending on their order of claim. Importantly, nonsubordinated bonds have more senior claims than subordinated bonds. The amount paid out to bondholders depends largely on various bankruptcy costs, such as the administrative costs of legal, accounting, and court procedures. Another bankruptcy cost relates to the value of the firm's assets. If the court sells off portions of the firm, merges it out with a solvent firm, or liquidates all of its assets, bondholders receive returns based on proceeds of any such "distressed" sale. If a firm's assets are easily transferred to other firms and are valued highly due to market demand (e.g., commercial airplanes), then bondholders will have lower default losses. It is essential that bank management assess potential default losses before making bond investments. Thus, although firm C was dropped from consideration in the preceding financial analysis, this decision may well be reversed by relatively higher expected values of assets than firms A and B in the event of default. Unfortunately, no agency or firm supplies publicly available information on distressed sale values of assets held by firms. This information could either be purchased from consultants or researched by investors by studying recent (or historical) liquidation results of comparable firms with similar assets.

BOND PRICES AND DEFAULT RISK Bond prices are inversely related to credit risk, which means that lower-quality bonds have higher yields on average than do higher-quality bonds. This difference in yields between low- and high-quality bonds (or **yield spread**) tends to vary with economic conditions. During recessionary periods, when default is perceived to be most likely to occur, yield spreads are greater than during economic expansions. For bank management, this cyclical behavior of yield spreads implies that lower-quality bonds offer relatively favorable yields per unit of risk during recessionary periods (when loan demand is depressed and the bank has greater excess cash to invest). While interest rates normally increase after a recession, which would depress bond prices, bonds purchased during an economic downturn could be timed to mature at different points in the future in order to both avoid capital losses and provide added liquidity throughout the expansionary phase of the business cycle.

PRICE RISK *Price risk* refers to the inverse relationship between changes in the level of interest rates and the price of securities. This relationship is particularly relevant to bank managers of investment securities, because securities purchased when there is slack loan demand and interest rates are relatively low may need to be sold later at a capital loss (to meet loan demand) in a higher interest rate environment. In light of this potential pitfall, securities should be timed to mature during anticipated future business-cycle periods of increased loan demand. Bonds maturing beyond five years normally fall outside of this range and so are not generally emphasized in the investment portfolio. Moreover, because the yield curve tends to be upward sloping and to flatten out after about five years, banks typically have little income incentive to purchase securities beyond the five-year range.

When interest rates are relatively high and the expansionary phase of the business cycle is peaking, purchasing securities with terms longer than five years may well be justified. At such times loan demand is beginning to fall as business firms decide that interest rates are so high that borrowing would not be profitable (i.e., the net present value of projects declines as interest rates rise and expectations for future business revenues fall). The next-best income-producing alternative is to purchase long-term securities. Earning high yields for an extended period of time is clearly one benefit of purchasing such securities, because interest rates will probably decline during a downturn in business activity. Another, although perhaps less obvious, benefit is that, if these long-term securities are later sold to meet load demand, for example, a capital gain could be realized, because interest rates will likely be lower than they were when the securities were originally purchased. The longer the term-to-maturity of the securities that are sold, the larger this capital gain would be. Thus, longer-term securities can be purchased as an aggressive approach toward price risk. Such an approach is not without its potential pitfalls, for uncertainties are inherent in forecasting both expected future interest rates and business cycle movements. Bank management needs to weigh the expected returns against the expected risks in order to evaluate price risk properly in this situation.

To evaluate the amount of price risk on a bond, it is necessary to consider not only the expected change in interest rates but also the duration of the bond. As previously discussed in Chapter 5, duration is a measure of bond maturity that considers the timing of cash flows. Relevant to the current discussion, duration is a proxy for price risk. The following formula shows how duration links interest rate changes to bond price changes:

$$\Delta P = -D \times B \times \Delta i/(1 + i) \qquad\qquad 10.2$$

where ΔP is the change in the price of the bond, D equals the duration (in years),[11] B is the original price of the bond, Δi is the change in interest rates from some original level i. To demonstrate, if a bond currently selling for $1,000 has a duration of five years and interest rates are expected to increase from 5% to 7% in the coming year, the bond's price will decline by approximately $95, that is $-5 \times \$1,000 \times .02/1.05$. Because high-coupon bonds have shorter durations than do low-coupon bonds of the same yield and term-to-maturity, high-coupon bonds have relatively less price risk. For example, consider two five-year bonds with equal yield to maturity and risk. One bond is a zero coupon bond and the other a high coupon bond. The "zero" would have a duration equal to its maturity, or five years, whereas the high-coupon bond, say, has a duration of three years. If interest rates increase by 2%, this change is multiplied by 5 for the zero-coupon versus 3 for the high-coupon bond in calculating their respective price declines. Clearly, duration is a valuable price

11. More specifically, $D = [\Sigma \text{ (Coupon payment} \times t)/(1 + i)^t + \text{(Principal value} \times m)/(1 + i)^m]/B$, where t is the time a coupon payment is paid, m is the maturity date, i is the discount rate, and B is the price of the bond. Notice that time is weighted by the cash flows such that duration is a weighted average of time to maturity. It is obvious that, if a bond has no coupon payments, then $D = m$ (i.e., the duration reaches a maximum limit equal to the maturity of the bond). As coupon payments increase, duration decreases in line with greater weighting of earlier time periods. As mentioned in footnote 6, for a typical bond paying coupons over time and principal value at maturity, taking the partial derivative of bond price with respect to a change in interest rates results in Eq. (10.2), including the aforementioned formula for duration. Some investors prefer to use a modified duration calculated as $MD = D/(1 + i)$. Now $\Delta P = -MD \times B \times \Delta i$, which simplifies the relationship between changes in interest rates and prices. Finally, we should note that duration is a fairly good measure of price risk for small Δi. Due to the nonlinear relationship between interest rates and prices, however, large changes in interest rates (e.g., $\Delta i = 2\%$ or more) will cause price changes that are considerably different from Eq. (10.2) predictions. For further discussion and an example, see James C. Van Horne, *Financial Market Rates and Flows*, 5th ed., (London, UK: Prentice-Hall International, 1997), pp. 103–113.

risk measure that management can use to gauge its exposure to potential future changes in interest rates.

Duration analysis can be used to "immunize" the investment portfolio from the opposing forces of price risk and reinvestment risk. If interest rates increase, prices of securities decline but periodic coupon returns on bonds can be reinvested at higher rates of return. Conversely, if interest rates decrease, prices of securities rise but earnings on bonds must be reinvested at lower rates of return. Assuming coupon-bearing securities on average are sold at about their duration date, these opposing risks will approximately offset one another. The net result is that the promised yield-to-maturity is earned on a security. Alternatively, if the holding period for a bond is other than the duration date, it is unlikely that the promised yield will be realized. For example, suppose a manager purchases a five-year bond with a promised yield-to-maturity equal to 10% and plans to hold the bond to its maturity date. In the calculation of the promised yield, it is assumed that all coupons earned over time on the bond are reinvested at the promised yield of 10%. However, it is almost impossible that interest rates will not change over time; thus, it is obvious that holding a bond to maturity will likely not result in a realized yield of 10%. In order to more accurately estimate ahead of time the actual yield to be earned on securities, duration must be set equal to the holding period. In this way the bank can immunize itself from price and reinvestment risks and thereby increase control over the returns per unit risk on securities.

Even if a bank uses duration to immunize securities' risks, market value accounting for securities held for sale requires that duration analysis be employed to evaluate the expected future prices of securities in the investment portfolio in response to potential changes in interest rates. Of course, a key ingredient to such an analysis is the estimation of expected future changes in interest rates. In this regard, market analysts examine the **yield curve**. Figure 10.2 shows the yield curve for U.S. Treasury securities as of December 1, 1999. Normally, the yield curve has an upward slope, with longer-term securities offering higher yields than shorter-term securities.

Figure 10.3 shows how the yield curve typically changes its level and shape over the business cycle. In a recession, interest rate levels are low due to the weak demand for funds by business firms, and the shape is more steeply upward sloping than at other times. During a business expansion, the level of the yield curve will rise in response to increased demand for funds by business firms and will gradually flatten in shape but remain generally upward sloping. Finally, at the end of an economic expansion, the yield curve will be at its highest level and take on a variety of shapes. Figure 10.3 shows an inverted shape at this point, but humped shapes and a flat shape are also possible. At some point high interest rates will precipitate a business slowdown, and the yield curve can collapse in a matter of months.

Many observers have attempted to explain the shape and dynamics of the yield curve throughout the business cycle. Four theories that have gained favor over the years are the expectations theory, liquidity premium theory, market segmentation theory, and preferred habitat theory.

FIGURE 10.2   Yields on U.S. Treasury Securities, December 1, 1999

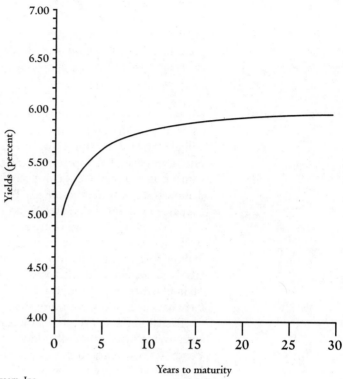

Source: Datastream, Inc.

FIGURE 10.3   The Yield Curve and the Business Cycle

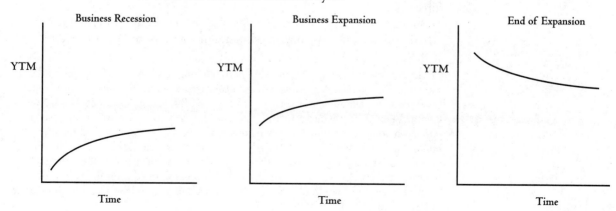

According to the **expectations theory** of the yield curve, investors earn the same rate of return regardless of their holding period. Therefore, an investor would earn the same amount by either purchasing a two-year bond and holding it for two years or purchasing a one-year bond now and another one-year bond next year. Formally stated, the following geometric average relationship is hypothesized to hold between long- and short-term interest rates over time:

$$(1 + {_0}R_2)^2 = (1 + {_0}R_1)(1 + {_1}r_2) \qquad\qquad 10.3$$

where ${_0}R_2$ is the two-year (spot) rate at the present time, ${_0}R_1$ is the one-year (spot) rate at the present time, and ${_1}r_2$ is the one-year future implicit rate that will exist one year from now. In effect, the future implicit rate is a forecasted rate of interest. The future implicit rate is not known with certainty at time 0 (now) but it nonetheless is reflected in the two-year spot rate of interest. To demonstrate, assume that ${_0}R_2 = 10\%$ and ${_0}R_1 = 9\%$. Given this information, the rate ${_1}r_2$ can be calculated to be 11%; that is, $1 + {_1}r_2 = (1 + .10)^2/(1 + .09) = 1 + .11$ or ${_1}r_2 = 11\%$. Thus, one-year interest rates are expected to increase by about 2% within the next year. Naturally, market expectations are not always correct and this forecasted interest rate may well be in error. But we would anticipate that the forecasts of future implicit rates would be too high 50% of the time and too low 50% of the time. On average, it should not matter what the holding period of the investor is.[12]

Based on the expectations theory, interest rate forecasts in any period and for any maturity range of bonds can be estimated. To forecast the two-year bond rate two years from now, or ${_2}r_4$, four-year and two-year spot rates could be gathered and used as follows:

$$(1 + {_0}R_4)^4 = (1 + {_0}R_2)^2 (1 + {_2}r_4)^2$$

To forecast the one-year bond rate three years from now, or ${_3}r_4$, four-year and three-year spot rates could be used:

$$(1 + {_0}R_4)^4 = (1 + {_0}R_3)^3 (1 + {_3}r_4).$$

Equations of this form can be readily developed to derive other interest rate forecasts.

Empirical evidence has repeatedly shown that future implicit rates in Eq. (10.3) provide upwardly biased estimates of actual future rates of interest. For

12. The geometric average relationship between long- and short-term interest rates shown in Eq. (10.3) holds because of the arbitrage activities of investors. Arbitrage takes place, for example, in the two-year rate, or 0R2, was greater than 10%. Now investors could earn higher returns by purchasing the two-year bond, as opposed to purchasing one-year securities in two consecutive years. Investors would sell one-year bonds and purchase two-year bonds. As this process proceeds, the price of the one-year securities would fall, causing their yield to rise, and the price of the two-year bonds would rise, causing their yield to fall. Eventually, an equilibrium would be reached in which it would no longer be advantageous to purchase two-year bonds. At this point Eq. (10.3) would hold once again.

this reason, it is advisable to adjust the interest rate forecast based on the expectations theory for other possible influences on yields over time. One factor is the liquidity preference of lenders in the financial market. Risk-averse lenders prefer to lend funds for short periods of time, unless a premium is paid for foregoing greater liquidity and lending funds for longer periods. This added return, or premium, is known as a **liquidity premium**.[13]

Many analysts believe that liquidity premiums cause expectations theory forecasts to be biased upward; that is, the actual yield curve is a summation of the expectation yield curve plus liquidity premiums. For example, in our previous example, $_0R_2$ = expected yield on two-year bonds + liquidity premium. If the liquidity premium were 0.5%, the expected two-year rate would equal 9.5% (i.e., 10 = 9.5 + 0.5). Substituting this adjusted long-term rate into Eq. (10.3), the new forecast for the one-year rate next year is 10%, which means interest rates can be expected to increase by only 1%, rather than 2% before accounting for the potential liquidity premium.

Another factor that could affect yields over time is the relative supplies and demands for short- and long-term financial instruments by various market participants, especially government and institutional investors. It is generally acknowledged that **segmented markets** exist in the financial system because of the different participants and needs in the money and capital markets. Commercial banks, the Federal Reserve, and corporations requiring inventory and other working capital are the key participants in the money market, whereas life insurance companies, pension funds, and corporations demanding capital funds for investment projects dominate the long-term bond market. This segmentation occurs due to the desire by firms to maintain maturity structures of assets and liabilities that are matched for the most part. Generally speaking, short-term interest rates tend to be more volatile than long-term rates. Apparently, short-term variations in supply and demand factors will have the greatest influence on the shape of the yield curve and, therefore, on forecasts of expected future interest rates. Adjusting for liquidity preferences, for example, we earlier estimated one-year interest rates to increase by about 1% next year. This short-term forecast could be adjusted further for anticipated changes in Federal Reserve monetary policy, corporate working capital needs, and commercial bank effects on the supply and demand for money.

Finally, the **preferred habitat theory** takes into account all three of these yield curve factors. It hypothesizes that investors will switch from their normal maturity preference (or habitat) to a different maturity range of securities if yield differentials are sufficiently high to compensate for the potential price risks associated with mismatched asset and liability maturities. As such, interest rate forecasts would be based on market expectations, liquidity preferences, and market segmentation. Forecasts of potential future changes in interest rates enable investment managers to evaluate the influence of these changes on

13. For a more complete discussion of liquidity premiums, see J. R. Hicks, *Value and Capital*, 2nd ed. (London: Oxford University Press, 1946).

security prices. These estimates can be valuable in making purchase and sale decisions, particularly if the bank is seeking aggressively to manage the investment portfolio throughout the business cycle.

Table 10.3 shows an example of how price risk can affect the investment portfolio at two points in time. Assume that all securities are held for sale, such that market value accounting is a key concern of bank management. Further assume that at time 0 information contained in the yield curve forecasted a 1% in interest rates. Given that the forecast was accurate, notice that at time 1 (i.e., one quarter later) the market values of securities declined, with larger declines associated with longer-term securities. Because these securities are marked-to-market, losses must be subtracted from retained earnings to obtain the net addition (loss) to equity on the balance sheet. It is possible that the securities losses could diminish equity capital sufficiently to fall below regulatory standards. In this event the bank would be under regulatory and market pressure to maintain adequate capital. A common solution to this problem is to purchase a short (or sell) position in financial futures contracts. As interest rates rise, the futures contracts can be sold at higher prices than their later purchase prices, with resultant gains on sale. Thus, the gains on shorting futures offset losses on long (buy) cash positions in securities held on the balance sheet (see examples in Chapter 6).

TABLE 10.3   Example of Price Risk in a Securities Portfolio ($ millions)

Quarter 1 Values:

Quarters to Maturity	One-Year U.S. Bonds Par Value	One-Year U.S. Bonds Market Value	Five-Year U.S. Bonds Par Value	Five-Year U.S. Bonds Market Value	State and Munis Bonds Par Value	State and Munis Bonds Market Value
2	5.000	5.000	15.000	15.000	10.000	10.000
3	5.000	5.015	15.000	15.050		
4	10.000	10.061	15.000	15.089	5.000	5.011
8					27.000	27.085
12			15.000	15.412	1.250	1.197

Quarter 2 Values (after a 1% increase in the level of interest rates):

Quarters to Maturity	One-Year U.S. Bonds Par Value	One-Year U.S. Bonds Market Value	Five-Year U.S. Bonds Par Value	Five-Year U.S. Bonds Market Value	State and Munis Bonds Par Value	State and Munis Bonds Market Value
1	5.000	5.000	15.000	14.945	10.000	9.978
2	5.000	4.997	15.000	15.001		
3	10.000	9.993	15.000	14.985	5.000	4.979
7					27.000	26.635
11			15.000	14.929	1.250	1.160

Duration analysis and interest rate cycles can be useful in estimating the **value-at-risk (VAR)**. VAR considers the maximum amount that could be lost in investment activities in a specified period of time. More specifically, given a certain probability and holding period, VAR gives the amount by which the investment portfolio will decline in value. Based on the historical movements in interest rate series over time, a distribution of interest rate changes over a chosen holding period can be constructed. Assuming the distribution is normal, the probability of any particular change in interest rates can be selected. For example, based on an historical distribution of interest rate changes, suppose that the probability of a 50 basis point (large) increase in interest rates in a 10-day period is 5%. Using this interest rate increase in Eq. (10.3), in combination with the average duration of securities held for sale, an estimate of the maximum loss in market value of these securities that will occur in one-out-of-20 ten-day holding periods can be calculated. If the average duration is 3 years, the securities are worth $1 billion at the present time, and interest rates are currently at 6%, this data would yield a VAR of $0.0156 billion (= −3 × $1 billion × 0.0050/1.06) or $15.6 million.

Obviously, the application of VAR in measuring price risk in the investment portfolio offers considerable flexibility. The selection of probabilities and holding periods is *ad hoc* and subject to manager judgment. Volatility can change over time and cause the historical analyses to be invalid. If interest rate forecasts suggest an increasing trend in market volatility, VAR estimates could be adjusted to reflect these changing conditions. Of course, banks can buy and sell futures contracts to either offset long cash positions or change their duration and thereby alter their VAR. Due to the dynamic nature of VAR estimates, it is now routine for banks to simulate the performance of their securities portfolios under alternative conditions. Assumptions are changed and input parameters in calculating VAR are altered to reflect the latest market conditions and hedging strategies. These *stress tests* consider normal and worst-case scenarios in order to give management a complete picture of securities portfolio risks. Despite the inherent subjectivity of VAR due to uncertainty in financial markets, it is a popular tool in investment practice that is rapidly developing as experience is accumulated.

Barry Schachter's personal web site (http://www. gloriamundi.org/) contains all kinds of information on VAR, with important links to papers, software, educational resources, etc.

MARKETABILITY RISK Not all bonds can be sold quickly without loss of principal. If the bank has to sell investment securities to meet liquidity demands, it will likely sell U.S. government securities before municipal and corporate bonds because the secondary market for the former securities is deeper and broader than for the latter bonds. Viewed from another perspective, to guard against **marketability risk**, investment managers should evaluate the likelihood of liquidity demands exceeding secondary (or liquid) reserves and then purchase investment securities to take into account this potential added liquidity.

For both municipal and corporate bonds the *volume* of outstanding securities by a particular borrower can significantly affect marketability. Small issue size reduces marketability simply due to the fact that the issue is unknown to most investors. By purchasing widely traded bond issues, bank management can reduce marketability risk.

CALL RISK Municipal and corporate bonds issued when interest rates are relatively high commonly have a call provision in their indenture agreements. The call provision gives the borrowing firm or institution the right to redeem the bond prior to maturity. The bond is callable only if the call deferment period has expired and the current price of the bond has risen to at least the call price, which exceeds the original price of the bond. As interest rates decline over time, the bond's price rises and eventually "strikes" the call price. If the call deferment period has lapsed, the bond can be redeemed. The bank's **call risk** in this situation is the reinvestment of the par value in bonds bearing lower interest yields. As compensation for this reinvestment risk, the indenture agreement will state call premiums—an added "sweetener" paid to the bondholder—payable on various dates in the future. When bonds are called early, the call premium is higher, which offsets in part or whole the call risk.

When banks attempt to purchase bonds during high interest rates periods and later plan to sell them for sizable capital gains as rates fall, call risk is especially worth evaluating. Because callable bonds have an additional element of uncertainty, they tend to offer higher yields than other bonds.

Portfolio Risk

According to portfolio theory, the riskiness of any security should not be evaluated in isolation but in the broader context of all assets held by an investor. In this way the effect of a security on the risk per unit of return of the bank's total portfolio of assets can be considered. It is possible for a securities portfolio to decrease the **portfolio risk** of the bank's assets, especially if the returns on securities over time are not perfectly correlated (or synchronized) with the returns on loans over time. As a descriptive example, if loan rates of return are falling due to declining interest rates, but rates of return on securities are rising due to increasing capital gains, the overall pattern of earnings of the bank are smoother over time and therefore less risky due to the securities portfolio than if all bank assets were loans. This type of risk reduction is known as a diversification effect. Notice that diversification is a more complicated concept than merely purchasing a bundle of different assets. It also is necessary that the returns of the assets follow different patterns over time with less than perfect positive correlation to obtain diversification benefits.

Few banks make a conscious effort to set up a securities portfolio to decrease the total risk of bank assets due to greater emphases on interest rate risk and liquidity risk objectives. However, most banks consciously purchase securities outside of their loan area to help protect themselves from a potential economic downturn that could increase loan defaults. In this circumstance out-of-area securities offset to some extent falling earnings in the loan portfolio.

This income stream smoothing is an important benefit of diversification in bank asset portfolios. For those interested, Appendix 10B gives a more detailed treatment of modern portfolio theory, as well as an example of its application to bank management.

Inflation Risk

Another potential risk in purchasing securities that is not security-specific is inflation. Here the investor is concerned that the general price level will increase more than expected in the future. Unanticipated increases in inflation lower the purchasing power of earnings on securities. An unexpected surge in inflation can cause interest rates on bonds to suddenly increase with potentially large price declines. In this case securities held for sale would suffer losses that could diminish bank liquidity and lower trading profits. Such losses would increase as the average maturity of the investment portfolio increases. For these reasons banks should be cautious about long-term investments subject to substantial price risk in periods of inflation uncertainty.

In the period from the 1960s to the early 1980s, periodic bouts with inflation motivated investment managers to shorten security maturities and seek securities with sufficiently high yields to offset **inflation risk**. However, the 1990s witnessed historically low rates of inflation in the United States and other industrialized countries. As nominal interest rates declined due to lower inflation rates, long-term securities experienced strong capital gains. In recent years the Federal Reserve and other central banks around the world have raised concerns about a resurgence of inflation rates due to tight labor markets and the long economic expansion of the 1990s. Consequently, investors are evaluating their potential inflation risk in the years ahead.

10.4 INVESTMENT STRATEGIES

Investment strategies should be guided by the principle that income be maximized within the constraints of regulations, taxes, liquidity needs, correspondent banking relationships, management expertise, and various types of investment risk. Management can choose between **passive investment strategies** that do not require active management and **aggressive investment strategies** that are specially designed to take advantage of prevailing or expected market conditions.

Passive Investment Strategies

Two passive strategies used in managing the investment portfolio are the *spaced-maturity*, or *ladder*, approach and the *split-maturity*, or *barbell*, approach. Smaller banks commonly use these methods because they are simple to implement, and thus conserve management resources. Also, the investment goals of many small banks are often of secondary importance because the majority of their excess funds is transferred upstream to larger correspondent banks in return for competitive money market rates of interest in addition to financial services, such as wire transfers, foreign exchange, etc.

SPACED-MATURITY APPROACH Otherwise known as the *ladder approach*, the spaced-maturity investment strategy involves spreading available investment funds equally across a specified number of periods within the bank's investment horizon. For example, if the bank had an investment portfolio of $10 million, and its investment horizon was five years, then it would purchase $2 million one-year securities, $2 million of two-year securities, and so on until the $10 million was evenly distributed over the five-year planning period.

This strategy is not only simple to set up but also to maintain, as principal redeemed on one-year securities coming due would be rolled over into five-year securities to keep an evenly spaced maturity of securities over five years. Other advantages of this approach are that trading activity and, therefore, transactions costs are minimized, and that an average rate of return is earned because investment securities are spread out evenly at different points in time on the yield curve. The major drawbacks of this approach are that the bank is passive with respect to interest rate conditions, and that liquidity is sacrificed to some extent should loan demands exceed short-term investment securities.

SPLIT-MATURITY APPROACH Another relatively conservative strategy is to purchase larger proportions of short- and long-term securities and smaller proportions of intermediate-term securities. This *so-called barbell approach* offers a balance of higher income on the long-term securities (assuming the yield curve is upward-sloping) and good liquidity through substantial purchases of short-term securities. One way to maintain the barbell strategy is to reinvest matured short-term securities in the longest-maturity, short-term securities and sell shortest-maturity, long-term securities and reinvest in the longest-maturity, long-term securities. The periodic sales of securities result in modest capital gains or losses depending on changes in the level or shape of the yield curve. Of course, management must consider the tradeoff between transactions costs versus both liquidity and income benefits from using the barbell strategy relative to the spaced-maturity strategy. Variations on the barbell strategy include holding fewer longer-term securities, which is known as *a front-end loaded approach*, and holding fewer shorter-term securities, or a *back-end loaded approach*. These strategies may be implemented by the bank to stress either liquidity or income, respectively, in the investment strategy.

Aggressive Investment Strategies

Larger banks with sizable investment portfolios and more volatile loan demands than smaller banks typically engage in one or more aggressive investment strategies intended to maximize their investment income. Because these strategies require a certain level of management expertise and trading activity, management must weigh the added costs against the potential benefits when selecting an appropriate strategy. In general, aggressive strategies may be classified into two groups: yield-curve strategies and bond-swapping strategies.

YIELD-CURVE STRATEGIES "Playing the yield curve" is a widely used phrase that means the bank is attempting to take advantage of expected future changes in interest rates by coordinating investment activities with the shape and level of the yield curve. When the yield curve is at a relatively low level and is upward sloping, short-term securities are usually purchased. As interest rates rise in the months (or years) ahead, the securities are repeatedly rolled over into higher-earning securities. At the same time, they provide added liquidity should investment securities be needed to meet loan demands. When the yield curve is at a relatively high level, the bank would switch to longer-term securities. This strategy provides higher yields to maximize interest income. Liquidity is not as relevant at this point in the business cycle because it is expected that loan demand will decline because of the high interest rates. As interest rates in future periods decline, capital gains are earned on these long-term securities because of favorable price risk. When interest rates are believed to have bottomed out, the long-term securities are sold and the principal and capital gains are rolled over into short-term securities.

This *switching* strategy in playing the yield curve is not without its potential problems, however. Market timing is pivotal to success. For example, if interest rates continued to rise after the maturity of investment securities is lengthened (in anticipation of a decline in rate levels), the bank would be forced to meet liquidity needs either by purchasing funds at increasingly higher costs or selling the long-term securities at a capital loss, plus transactions costs. Such a mistake could have a significant impact on the bank's profitability. Thus, it is recommended that some amount of short-term securities not be rolled over into longer-term securities to maintain an element of liquidity in the investment portfolio.

Another approach to playing the yield curve is known as *riding the yield curve*. For this strategy to work, (1) the yield curve must be upward sloping, and (2) the level of interest rates must not be expected to move upward as much as indicated by the shape of the yield curve in the near future. According to this strategy, the investment manager would purchase securities with a longer maturity than the investment horizon of the bank. With an upward-sloping yield curve, as time passes and the term-to-maturity of the securities declines, their yields fall in line with the upward shape of the yield curve. The increasing prices of the securities yield a capital gain when they are sold at the end of the investment horizon.

To estimate the holding period yield of riding the yield curve, the following formula can be used:

$$Y_h = Y_o + T_r(Y_o - Y_m)/T_h \qquad\qquad 10.4$$

where Y_h = the holding period yield, Y_o = the original yield on the security purchased, Y_m = the security's market yield at the end of the holding period when it is sold, T_r = the remaining maturity of the security when sold, and T_h = the holding period (or investment horizon) equal to the lapsed time between the purchase and sale of the security. As an example, suppose that Yo = .10, Tr = 1 year, T_h = 1 year, and Y_m = .09, the holding period yield obtained from riding the yield curve is 0.10 + 1 (0.10 − .09)/1 = .11 or 11%, which exceeds the original yield by one percent. As long as the yield on the security declines from its original yield on the purchase date such that $Y_m < Y_o$, the second term on the right-hand side of Eq. (10.4) gives an estimate of the approximate capital gain earned by riding the yield curve. On the other hand, if interest rates increased in line with the expectations theory of the yield curve, then $Y_m > Y_o$ and $Y_h < Y_o$, or a capital loss would cause the holding period yield to fall short of the original yield.

Obviously, playing the yield curve by using a switching strategy or by riding the yield curve requires considerable market forecasting expertise. According to expectations theory, the expected return is identical across all maturities for any holding period. Thus, playing the yield curve involves forecasting changes in interest rates that are not expected by the market as a whole. In this regard, although "outguessing" the market is surely possible, such an aggressive strategy may well be imprudent on a large scale. For this reason, playing the yield curve is a strategy that should not be overemphasized in investment management and should be coupled with one or more other investment strategies.

BOND-SWAPPING STRATEGIES Exchanging one bond for another for return and risk reasons is known as a bond swap. A swap may be undertaken in anticipation of future changes in interest rates or simply because the swap would clearly be a superior choice. For example, management may perform a *tax swap* if the corporate bond yield is higher than the pretax equivalent municipal bond yields currently held by the bank. If the municipal bond is sold at a capital loss, tax savings equal to the bank's marginal tax rate multiplied by the capital loss are realized. Thus, even if the corporate and municipal pretax yields are comparable, a tax swap may still be initiated to lower the bank's tax burden. Alternatively, if the bank's marginal tax rate declined from some reason (e.g., a decline in earnings or change in applicable tax laws), the bank might choose to swap municipal bonds for corporate bonds. Opposite reasoning would apply to swapping corporate for municipal bonds.

A *substitution*, or *price, swap* entails selling securities comparable to the ones being purchased because the latter have a lower price. In an efficient market, where securities' prices reflect all publicly available information, it is not common to find imbalances of this sort, but it is possible to find mispriced securities at times (i.e., a temporary market disequilibrium).[14] Trading banks that have day-to-day market operations in various securities are most likely to execute substitution swaps. A trading account must be maintained for regulatory purposes, and the resultant trading profits (and losses) must be reported as a separate account in the bank's operating earnings. It should be mentioned that other portfolio profits (and losses) and associated taxes on securities are reported after net operating earnings are adjusted for federal income taxes.

A *yield-pickup*, or *coupon*, *swap* involves the exchange of a low-coupon bond for a high-coupon bond, or vice versa. The tradeoff between coupon earnings and capital gains in such a swap could be influenced either by interest rate risk (duration) differences or tax differences.

A *spread*, or *quality*, *swap* implies the exchange of two bonds with unequal risk. As in the case of substitution swaps, an abnormally low or high price for a security must prevail for this swap to be profitable. The bank would seek to sell (buy) securities that are overpriced (underpriced) and purchase (sell) securities that are correctly priced in the market. When market equilibrium is restored, the reverse market purchase and sale activities would be executed.

Finally, a *portfolio shift* (bond swap) strategy entails selling securities with low yields and replacing them with higher yielding instruments. If a bank purchased securities during a period of low interest rates, as interest rates gradually rise over time, the cost of funds at the bank would increase until a negative spread developed between security yields and average interest costs. In this case the bank might opt to sell the old securities, take the capital loss due to increased interest rate levels, deduct the loss from taxes, and purchase new higher-yielding securities with the sale proceeds plus tax savings. As an example, suppose that the bank purchased at par value $1 million of five-year Treasury bonds with an annual coupon rate of 6%. Also, initially average deposit costs are 3% but rising interest rates push up this cost to 5% two years after the bonds are purchased. Assume that allocable operating expenses equal 1.5%. Under these circumstances, the following cash flows are available to the bank:

	Year 1	Year 2	Year 3	Year 4	Year 5
Interest income	$60,000	$60,000	$60,000	$60,000	$60,000
Average deposit expense	(30,000)	(30,000)	(50,000)	(50,000)	(50,000)
Allocable operating expense	(15,000)	(15,000)	(15,000)	(15,000)	(15,000)
Net profit on bonds	$15,000	$15,000	$(5,000)	$(5,000)	$(5,000)

14. Fischer Black, in "Bank Funds Management in an Efficient Market," *Journal of Financial Economics*, vol. 2 (1975), pp. 323–339, gives an excellent discussion of the implications of an efficient market to bank management in general.

It is clear that after year 3 the bond is an unprofitable investment that cumulates larger losses over time. Now consider the possibility of selling the bond at the beginning of year 3. The 2% increase in interest rates would decrease the value of the Treasury bond to say $950,000. Given the bank's marginal tax rate equals 30%, the tax savings earned by the bank on the capital loss would be $50,000 (1 – .30) = $35,000. Thus, the bank could invest $950,000 + $35,000 = $985,000 in three-year Treasury bonds selling at par value and offering a 8% coupon yield. The cash flows with this portfolio shift are as follows:

	Year 1	Year 2	Year 3	Year 4	Year 5
Interest income	$60,000	$60,000	$78,800	$78,800	$78,800
Average deposit expense	(30,000)	(30,000)	(50,000)	(50,000)	(50,000)
Allocable operating expense	(15,000)	(15,000)	(15,000)	(15,000)	(15,000)
Net profit on bonds	$15,000	$15,000	$13,800	$13,800	$13,800

The new higher coupon earning Treasury bonds purchased at the beginning of year 3 generate a net profit stream that is $1,200 less than the initial years of the five-year investment horizon but boost net profits from $5,000 losses to $13,800 gains in the later years.[15] Hence, changes in interest rate levels can force banks to undertake portfolio shifts to protect profit margins. It is important in this and other types of bond swaps to also factor in transactions costs.

SUMMARY

Investment securities provide an alternative source of income for commercial banks, especially when loan demand is relatively low during slowdowns in economic activity. Bank policy should aim to maximize the return on the securities portfolio per unit of risk within regulatory and market constraints. In this regard, bank management needs to consider the tax implications of municipal securities, default risk and call risk of municipal and corporate bond securities, interest rate risk of longer-term securities, and marketability of securities. The effects of investment policy on the risk and return of the bank's total assets should also be evaluated in a portfolio context, where diversification benefits can be gained by purchasing securities with return patterns that are not perfectly positively correlated with the return patterns of other bank assets.

Once bank policy is established, an investment strategy needs to be chosen.

15. Losses on bonds held for more than 12 months must be used to first offset long-term capital gains, and losses in excess of long-term capital gains can then be applied to short-term gains. Likewise, losses on bonds held for less than 12 months must first be applied to short-term gains. This distinction can be significant as short-term gains are taxed as ordinary income with rates as high as 39.6% compared to the 20% top rate for long-term gains.

Passive strategies, such as the spaced-maturity, or ladder, approach and the split-maturity, or barbell, approach do not require much expertise, conserve management resources, and are inexpensive to implement. Aggressive strategies, such as playing the yield curve and bond swapping, require more management expertise, involve more trading activity, and are riskier in nature than passive strategies but offer higher earnings potential.

Key Terms and Concepts

Agency securities	Municipal bonds
Aggressive investment strategies	Passive investment strategies
Call risk	Portfolio risk
Corporate bond	Preferred habitat theory
Expectations theory	Prepayment risk
Inflation risk	Segmented markets
Investment grade bonds	Treasury bonds
Investment policy	Treasury notes
Junk bonds	Value-at-risk (VAR)
Liquidity premium	Yield curve
Market value accounting	Yield spread
Marketability risk	

Questions

10.1 Why are Treasury bills not considered to be investment securities?

10.2 Why might agency securities be preferred to Treasury notes and bonds?

10.3 How do municipal bonds reduce taxes for a bank?

10.4 What do bond ratings indicate? How do bond yields vary with these ratings?

10.5 Why is investment policy affected by the interest rate cycle?

10.6 Why do most investment securities have maturities in the range of 1–5 years?

10.7 Why do banks generally avoid junk bonds?

10.8 Discuss two components of bond risk premiums.

10.9 Define price risk. How can a bank take advantage of price risk in a relatively high interest rate period?

10.10 Why might forecasts of future interest rates using the expectations theory of the yield curve be wrong? How would you adjust for other interest rate influences?

10.11 Why do bonds issued in relatively low interest rate periods have low call risk?

10.12 Why is call risk an important factor for an investment manager purchasing bonds in a relatively high interest rate period?

10.13 How does diversification affect portfolio return? How does it affect portfolio risk?

10.14 Show a graph of two assets that offer no diversification benefit. Also draw graphs illustrating both partial and complete diversification of risk.

10.15 What is the key to diversification?

10.16 Why might the split-maturity approach to investment management be preferred to the spaced-maturity approach?

10.17 What does "playing the yield curve" mean? How is it different from "riding the yield curve"?

10.18 Briefly discuss four kinds of bonds swaps.

10.19 Pick two of the following web sites and explore them. Write a short summary of information located there.
- E*Trade: *www.etrade.com* Online services by online brokers are provided.
- Hollywood Stock Exchange: *www.hsx.com* A stock-trading game can be found here.
- The Motley Fool: *www.fool.com* One of the original stock-trading communities, this site contains message boards, tips, and investing philosophy.
- FinanCenter: *www.financenter.com* Calculators for solving typical financial problems can be accessed.
- ClearStation: *www.clearstation.com* Stock trends, technical analysis, charts and graphs, and more can be viewed.
- Morningstar: *www.morningstar.com* One-stop shopping for mutual funds where ratings, top holdings, returns, and more are available.

10.20 Go to the Securities and Exchange Commission web site at *http://www.sec.gov/* and look under "What's Hot." Select an article concerning recent securities market news and write an abstract on its content.

10.21 Go to the Bankers Administration Institute web site at *http://www.bai.org/* and search for "investments." Under "BAI Research Briefings," select a research topic and write an abstract on its content.

10.22 Go to the International Finance and Commodities Institute's (IFCI) web site at *http://risk.ifci.ch/index.htm* and find the case study, "Lessons from the Collapse of Hedge Fund, Long-Term Capital Management, by David Shirreff. Write a two-page paper summarizing the activities of LTCM, its problems, and eventual resolution.

Problems

10.1   (a) Given a five-year municipal bond yielding 10%, a comparable five-year corporate bond yielding 15%, and a federal income tax rate of 34%, which bond should be preferred by the bank?

(b) Given the following income statement information, calculate the bank's net income after taxes. Assume a tax rate of 34%. What if $400 of interest tax deductions are lost due to the municipal bond purchases?

	($ thousands)
Total interest on securities	$2,000
Municipal bond interest	500
Other securities' interest	1,500
Total interest on loans	4,000
Total operating income	6,000
Total interest expense	(4,100)
Total noninterest expense	(900)
Total operating expense	(5,000)

10.2   A muni bond selling at par has a yield-to-maturity equal to 10%. A bank investment manager wishes to calculate its tax equivalent yield. Assume that it is a qualified bond, the bank's tax rate is 34%, and the average cost of funds for the bank is 8%. If the bond was not qualified, what would be the answer?

10.3   Given the following information about security j in states of nature i:

State of Nature	P_i = Probability	R_{ji}
1	.10	.08
2	.25	.10
3	.30	.12
4	.25	.14
5	.10	.16

(a) Calculate the mean and variance of security j's rate of return.

(b) Given further the rate of return on the bank's portfolio of assets is as follows:

State of Nature	P_i = Probability	R_{pi}
1	.10	.16
2	.25	.14
3	.30	.12
4	.25	.10
5	.10	.08

Find the mean and variance of the rates of return on the bank's port-folio of assets.

(c) If the bank invests in security j such that 10% of its funds are allocated to security j and 90% of its funds are allocated to its previous portfolio of assets, what will be the mean and variance of rates of return for the bank?

10.4   You are given the responsibility by your bank to conduct a financial analysis of three firms issuing bonds. All three firms are regional manufacturing firms in the same industry. Your bank's loan officer has requested that you evaluate their potential default risk. After collecting accounting statements from last year, you construct the following table of financial ratios for the three firms:

	Firm X	Firm Y	Firm Z
Profitability:			
Net profits/Net sales	0.08	0.05	0.06
Net profits/Net worth	0.20	0.24	0.13
Net profits/Total assets	0.10	0.06	0.08
Liquidity:			
Current assets/Current liabilities	2.50	2.00	2.60
(Current assets – Inventory)/Current liabilities	1.50	1.20	1.50
Leverage:			
Total debt/Total assets	0.50	0.75	0.40
Gross income/Interest charges	3.80	2.50	5.00
Activity:			
Sales/Inventory	8.00	10.00	9.00
Sales/Total assets	2.00	1.80	2.20

The Case of the Missing Gap

Jack Brothers had recently taken over the management of the securities portfolio at Community Bank & Trust, a bank with $100 million in assets in a suburb of a large U.S. city. Previously, Jack worked in the loan portfolio department of a bank in another state. He had gained favorable recommendations from his prior employers due in large part to his innovative work in securitizing loans, a new and growing area of management in the banking industry. A meeting with CEO George Willis the day before had raised some unsettling evidence concerning the gap management of the bank. The accounting department reported that, while the dollar gap of the bank over the past year was zero, with equal dollar holdings of interest rate-sensitive assets and liabilities, the bank had lost $500,000 in interest income over the last year as interest rates had rapidly fallen 300 basis points. Mr. Willis asked Jack to identify the "missing gap" problem that appears to exist and make recommendations in the securities portfolio that would help solve the problem. He wanted a fast turnaround on these questions, with a preliminary report due tomorrow afternoon. He also made clear that, according to investment policy, securities portfolio management was a means to effective and efficient asset and liability management. The recommendations made by Jack to Mr. Willis would be forwarded to the asset/liability committee in order to coordinate activities in the bank.

Jack reviewed asset/liability materials that evening in his study at home and decided to go forward with a standardized gap analysis (see Chapter 5). The short period of time allowed for the preliminary report required that only a general analysis of the problem be attempted at this stage.

In the morning he visited the accounting department staff, who helped him obtain some rough historical figures from the past year on the interest rate sensitivity of broad asset and liability accounts in response to a change of 100 basis points in the prime rate of interest (see Exhibit 10.1).

It occurred to Jack that the rapid decline in interest rates this past year may imply that interest rates will increase in the future. Consequently, he also checked the financial newspaper in the morning and found that the two-year Treasury bond rate was 5.0% and the one-year Treasury rate was 4.0%. He estimated that approximately a 50 basis point liquidity premium likely exists in the two-year bond rate to compensate investors for the added price risk of these bonds relative to the one-year bonds.

Based on standardized gap analysis, why did the 300 basis point drop in interest rates so adversely affect the bank's net interest earnings in the past year? How could securities management have reduced or eliminated the recent loss of $500,000? What is the interest rate forecast using expectations and liquidity premium theories of the yield curve? What are the implications of anticipated future interest rate movements for net interest earnings, the bank's gap position, and securities management in the near future?

EXHIBIT 10.1	Summary of Interest Rate Sensitivity: Community Bank & Trust	

Accounts	Change per 100 Basis Points in the Prime Rate	Dollar Holdings
Liabilities:		
Retail deposits	25 basis points	$40,000,000
Wholesale deposits	100 basis points	30,000,000
Nondeposit funds	100 basis points	23,000,000
Assets:		
T-bills (< 1 year)	91 basis points	$10,000,000
Gov't. (1 year)	77 basis points	10,000,000
Gov't. (5 year)	20 basis points	10,000,000
Munis (1 year)	60 basis points	3,000,000
Munis (5 year)	20 basis points	2,000,000
Loans	80 basis points	70,000,000

Note: While interest rates on five-year government and munis securities are fixed, a portion of the portfolio either matures or is sold during the year, most of which is normally replaced by rolling over the funds in investments of the same type. Also, while most loans have variable rates, some portion of fixed rate loans mature and are replaced each year with new fixed rate loans.

Investment Policy of a Major U.S. Bank

This appendix contains an actual investment policy of one of the largest banks in the United States. Two steps are required. First, securities are classified by risk level into three categories (i.e., Type I, II, and III), as is done in Table 10A.1. Second, the investment policy itself specifies for each asset type in the investment portfolio both regulatory guidelines and internal management guidelines (see Table 10A.2). ■

TABLE 10A.1	Definitions or Types of Securities (Nonexhaustive)

Type I Securities (No Limitation)

Treasury and Agency
U.S. Treasury Bills, notes and bonds
Government National Mortgage Association
Community Development Corporation
Farmers Home Administration
Federal Financing Bank
General Services Administration
Maritime Administration
Small Business Administration
Student Loan Marketing Association
Federal National Mortgage Association
Federal Home Loan Mortgage Corporation
Federal Home Loan Bank System
Bank for Cooperatives
Federal Land Bank
Federal Intermediate Credit Banks
Federal Farm Credit Banks

Municipals
General obligation of any state or any political subdivision

Type II Securities (4% of Capital Limitation)

Agencies
Asian Development Bank
Inter-American Development Bank
International Bank for Reconstruction & Development
Tennessee Valley Authority

Municipals
Obligations issued by any state, political subdivision or any agency of a state of political subdivision for housing, university, or dormitory purposes

TABLE 10A.I	Definitions or Types of Securities (Nonexhaustive) *(continued)*

Type III Securities (4% of Capital Limitation)

Corporate Notes and Bonds

Industrial Revenue Bonds

Limited to purchasing for bank's account.

Corporation Shares or Stock

A bank may not purchase for its own shares or stock of any corporation unless authorized by federal regulation.

A bank may not deal in or underwrite Type III securities.

Acceptable Asset-Backed Security Types

Automobile loans/leases

Credit card receivables

Manufactured housing

Mobile homes

Home equity loans

Equipment leases

Boat loans

Recreational vehicles

TABLE 10A.2	Acceptable Investments

Investment Portfolio Asset Type	Regulatory Guidelines	Size[a] Quality/Issuer	Maximum Maturity Repricing Freq.
U.S. Treasury bills, obligations, notes, Type I bonds	No limitation	No limitation	No limitation
Agency obligations	No limitation	No limitation	No limitation for Type I notes/bonds. 30 yr WAM[b] and 10 years WAL[c] for mortgage-backed pass-throughs. Limitations for mortgage derivative products are described elsewhere.
Tax-exempt general obligation securities	No limitation >S&P BBB	<10% of capital[d] per issuer for state obligations	20 years
Type I	>Moody's Baa	<4% of capital[d] per issuer for all other >Moody's A/P-1 >S&P A/A-1	
Secondary Mortgage Market Enhancement Act (SMMEA) eligible securities (nonagency issued)	No limitation	<10% of capital[d] if Moody's Ass/P-1 or S&P AAA/A-1+ <4% of capital[d] if Moody's Aa/P-1 or S&P AA/A-1 Not to exceed 50% of affiliate capital per issuer	30 years WAM[b] and 10 years WAL[c] mortgage-backed pass-throughs Limitations for mortgage derivative products described elsewhere
Taxable obligations, Type II	<10% of capital[d] >S&P BBB >Moody's Baa	<4% of capital[d] >Moody's A/P-1 or >S&P A/A-1	Notes/bonds 20 years. 30 years WAM[b] and 10 years WAL[b] for mortgage-backed pass-throughs Limitations for mortgage derivative products described elsewhere
Tax-exempt housing, university or dormitory, Type II	<10% of capital[d] >S&P BBB >Moody's Baa	<4% of capital[d] >Moody's A/P-1 or >S&P A/A-1	20 years
Tax-exempt revenue, Type III	<10% of capital[d] >S&P BBB >Moody's Baa	<4% of capitald >Moody's As/P-1 or >S&P AA2/A-1	20 years

TABLE 10A.2	Acceptable Investments (continued)		
Investment Portfolio Asset Type	Regulatory Guidelines	Size[a] Quality/Issuer	Maximum Maturity Repricing Freq.
Corporate notes and bonds, Type III (see definition of Type III for a listing acceptable asset-backed security types)	<10% of capital[d] >S&P BBB >Moody's Baa	<4% of capital[d] >Moody's A/P-1 or >S&P A/A-1 Subject to credit approval if >$50MM and less than Moody's Ass/P-1 or S&P's AAA/A-1+	10 years. 30 yrs WAM[b] and 10 years WAL[c] for mortgage backed pass-throughs Limitations for mortgage derivative products described elsewhere
Overnight federal funds sold	No limitation	$ limit bank No higher than 10% of corporate capital per issuer subject to approved credit lines Aggregate corporate subject to 200% of corporate capital	Overnight
Term federal funds sold	<15% of capital[d]	<4% of capital[d] Subject to approved credit lines	1 year
Commercial paper	<15% of capital[d]	<4% of capital[d] >Moody's P-1 and >S&P A-1 (short-term) and Moody's A and S&P A (long-term) A list of eligible issuers must be preapproved by corporate credit Subject to credit approval if >$100MM and less than Moody's Aaa/P-1 or S&P AAA/A-1	270 days
Eligible bankers' acceptances	<15% of capital[d]	<10% of capital[d]	182 days
Negotiable CDs (Domestic, Eurodollar, Yankee)	No limitation (10% of capital for non-Federal Reserve banks)	10% of corporate capital	<6 months against short-term line >6 months against long-term line

TABLE 10A.2	Acceptable Investments *(continued)*		
Investment Portfolio Asset Type	**Regulatory Guidelines**	**Size[a] Quality/Issuer**	**Maximum Maturity Repricing Freq.**
Eurodollar time deposits	No limitation	10% of corporate capital	<6 months against short-term line >6 months against long-term line
Money market preferred stock	15% of capital	Total aggregate exposure to any one issuer limited to parent company at 4% of corporate capital Subject to credit approval if >$50MM and less than Moody's Aaa/P-1 or S&P's AAA/A-1 >Moody's A or S&P A	
Money market mutual funds (limited to U.S. Treasury securities)		Subject to approved list and mutual funds No more than 5% of corporate capital in one fund; investment in any one <5% of the total fund	90 days

a. Short-term ratings must be accompanied by the corresponding long-term rating when extending short-term (<6 months) credit. Issues by entities not bearing a corresponding long-term rating must be approved by the Chief Credit Officer and the Chief Investment Officer.

b. WAM: weighted average maturity. WAM is calculated by multiplying the maturity of each mortgage in a given pool by its remaining balance, summing the products, and dividing the result by the total remaining balance.

c. WAL: weighted average life. WAL is the weighted average retirement date of a bond, the average amount of time each dollar of principal amount will be outstanding. WAL is computed by multiplying each principal repayment by the time of repayment (months, or years from the evaluation date), summing these products, and dividing the sum by the total amount of principal repayments.

d. Capital is defined as capital stock and surplus plus undivided profits and refers to corporate capital.

Modern Portfolio Theory and Bank Securities Management

Markowitz's (1959) now famous work on individual investment choice under uncertainty established modern portfolio theory as a foundation of financial market investment behavior. Markowitz believed that investors not only evaluate the expected rates of return on investment but their risks as well. In the forthcoming discussion, we assume for simplicity that the bank holds two general classes of assets—securities and loans—and desires to examine the effect of the securities portfolio j on the total risk of the bank's assets after taking account the loan portfolio k. Note that the same portfolio concepts apply to individual securities and loans. ■

10B.1   MEASURING EXPECTED RATES OF RETURN

To estimate *expected* rates of return, the following equation can be used:

$$E(R_j) = \sum_{i=1}^{n} P_i R_{ji} \qquad\qquad 10B.1$$

where P_i = the probability that a particular (random) state of nature i will occur (with a total of n states of nature considered), R_{ji} = the rate of return on the security portfolio in the ith state of the nature, and $E(R_j)$ = the expected rate of return on the securities portfolio. By "state of nature," we refer to a possible future business environment from among all possible scenarios that may exist. A rough approach is simply specifying pessimistic, average, and optimistic business scenarios. Table 10B.1 provides an example of this calculation using hypothetical data.

10B.2   MEASURING VARIABILITY

The total risk of an investment is directly linked to the variability of its rates of return over time. To measure the risk of the securities portfolio, the variability of the rate of return in different states of nature can be proxied by their standard deviation, or σ. The standard deviation is calculated by taking the square root of the variance of returns, or $\sigma^2(R_j)$, where

$$\sigma^2(R_j) = \sum_{i=1}^{n} P_i[R_{ji} - E(R_j)]^2 \qquad\qquad 10B.2$$

TABLE 10B.1   Hypothetical Calculation of the Expected Rate of Return

State of Nature	P_i = Probability	R_{ji}	P_jR_{ji}	$R_{ji} - E(Ri)$	$[Rji - E(R_j)]^2$	$P_i[R_{ji} - E(R_j)]^2$
1	.10	.05	.005	−.02	.0004	.00004
2	.20	.06	.012	−.01	.0001	.00001
3	.40	.07	.028	.00	.0000	.00000
4	.20	.08	.016	.01	.0001	.00001
5	.10	.09	.009	.02	.0004	.00004
	1.00	$E(R_j)$	= .070			$\sigma^2(R_j)$ = .00010
						$\sigma(R_j)$ = .010

and

$$\sigma(R_j) = \sigma^2(R_j)^{1/2} \qquad \qquad \text{10B.3}$$

Based on these equations, Table 10B.1 shows that the standard deviation of rates of return is 1.0%.

Assuming that rates of return are normally distributed, $E(R_j)$ and $\sigma(R_j)$ can be used to understand the risk and return characteristics of the securities portfolio. Figure 10B.1 graphically depicts the probability of rates of return on the vertical axis and rates of return themselves on the horizontal axis. Notice that 65% (95%) of the normal distribution falls within one (two) standard deviations of the mean, or $E(R_j)$. Given $E(R_j) = 7\%$ and $\sigma(R_j) = 1.0\%$, we can infer that 65% of the security portfolio's rate of return will fall within the range of 6.0% to 8.0% and 95% of the time it will be from 5.0% to 9.0%.

10B.3   PORTFOLIO EFFECTS

With these risk and return concepts in hand, consider the effect of the securities portfolio on the expected return and risk of all bank assets including the loan portfolio. We define the expected return and standard deviation of the bank's portfolio of loans as $E(R_k)$ and $\sigma(R_k)$. The bank's expected rate of return and variance of rates of return *after* purchasing securities can be calculated as follows:

$$E(R_{\text{bank}}) = aE(R_j) + (1 - a)E(R_k) \qquad \qquad \text{10B.4}$$

where a = the proportion of funds invested in the securities portfolio with expected rate of return $E(R_j)$, and $(1 - a)$ = the proportion of funds invested in the loan portfolio with expected rate of return $E(Rk)$, and

$$\sigma^2(R_{\text{bank}}) = a^2\sigma^2(R_j) + (1 - a)^2\sigma^2(R_k) + 2a(1 - a)\,\text{Cov}(R_j,R_k) \quad \text{10B.5}$$

where $\text{Cov}(R_j, R_k)$ = the covariance of the rates of return of securities portfolio j and loan portfolio k, or

$$\text{Cov}(R_j,R_k) = \sum_{i=1}^{n} P_i[R_{ji} - E(R_j)]\,[R_{ki} - E(R_k)] \qquad \text{10B.6}$$

Table 10B.2 shows an example of how the securities portfolio might affect the expected rate of return and risk of bank assets as a whole. The loan portfolio is calculated to have $E(R_k) = 6\%$ and $\sigma(R_k) = 2.2\%$. If the securities portfolio is considered in combination with the loan portfolio, then $E(R_{\text{bank}}) = 6.1\%$ and $\sigma(R_{\text{bank}}) = 1.9\%$. Thus, the securities portfolio would not only increase the bank's total expected rate of return above that earned by the loan portfolio, it would also reduce the bank's risk by decreasing the standard deviation of rates of return below that of the loan portfolio.

FIGURE 10B.1   Normal Distribution of Hypothetical Investment Opportunities

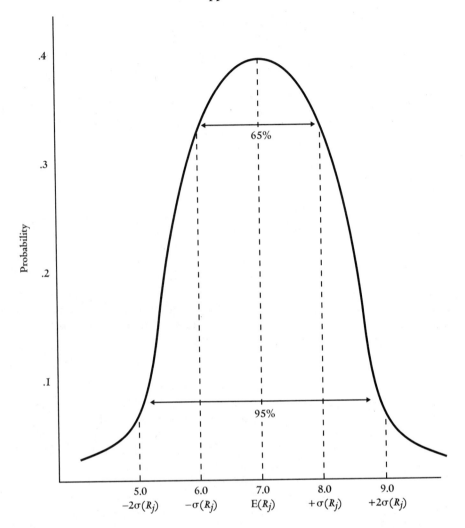

Notice that bank risk declines both because the standard deviation of the securities portfolio was less than the loan portfolio's standard deviation and because the covariance term was negative. Hence, we can infer that the effect of the securities portfolio on the risk of the bank's portfolio of assets is not a simple weighted average of the loan portfolio and securities portfolio risks (where weights are the proportional investment), instead, an adjustment must be made for the relationship of the securities portfolio's pattern of rates of return to the loan portfolio's rates of return in different states of nature (i.e., the covariance term affects the bank's total risk).

TABLE 10B.2 Hypothetical Example of Securities Portfolio Effects on the Risk and Return of Total Bank Assets Including Loans

State of Nature	P_i = Probability	$a = 10\%$ R_{ji}	$(1-a) = 90\%$ R_{ki}	$P_i[R_{ki} - E(R_k)]^2$	(1) $R_{ji} - E(R_j)$	(2) $R_{ki} - E(R_k)$	(3) (1) × (2)	P_i × (3)
1	.10	.05	.10	.00016	−.02	.04	−.008	−.00008
2	.20	.06	.08	.00008	−.01	.02	−.0002	−.00004
3	.40	.07	.06	—	—	—	—	—
4	.20	.08	.04	.00008	.01	−.02	−.0002	−.00004
5	.10	.09	.02	.00016	−.02	−.04	−.0008	−.00008

$$E = (R_j) = .07 \quad E(R_k) = .06 \quad \sigma^2(R_k) = .00048$$

$$\sigma(R_k) = .022 \qquad \mathrm{Cov}(R_j, R_k) = -.00024$$

$$
\begin{aligned}
E(R_{bank}) &= aE(R_j) + (1-a)(E(R_k)) \\
&= (.10)(.07) + (.90)(.06) \\
&= .061
\end{aligned}
$$

$$
\begin{aligned}
\sigma^2(R_{bank}) &= a^2\sigma^2(R_j) + (1-a)^2\sigma^2(R_k) + 2a(1-a)\mathrm{Cov}(R_j,R_k) \\
&= (.10)^2(.00012) + (.90)^2(.00048) + 2(.10)(.90)(-.00024) \\
&= .0003468
\end{aligned}
$$

$$\sigma(R_{bank}) = .019$$

To elaborate on covariance adjustment, we can redefine the last term in the variance formula shown in Eq. (10B.5) as

$$2a(1-a)\mathrm{Cov}(R_j,R_k) = 2a(1-a)\rho_{jk}\sigma(R_j)\sigma(R_k) \qquad \text{10B.7}$$

where ρ_{jk} = the correlation of the securities portfolio with the loan portfolio. If $\rho_{jk} = 1$, we say that the two patterns of rates of return are perfectly positively correlated. If $\rho < 1$, the variance measure of risk is reduced, with maximum variance reduction occurring at $\rho = -1$, which is perfectly negative correlation. The reduction of variance caused by less than perfect positive correlation is technically known as *diversification*.

Figure 10B.2 graphically depicts three different correlation possibilities and their effects on risk. The rates of return patterns for two assets (or portfolios) of equal value considered separately in different states of nature are shown by thin lines, and their combination is shown by the bold line. The variability, or risk, of each rate of return pattern can be visually compared by observing the amount of its movement up and down over different states of nature. Panel A in Figure 10B.2 shows that combining perfectly positively correlated assets does not reduce risk. At the other extreme, panel B shows the total elimination of risk by combining perfectly negatively correlated assets. In the real world,

FIGURE I 0 B . 2   Correlation of Assets' Rates
of Return and Risk Reduction

A. Perfect positive correlation: $\rho_{12} = I$

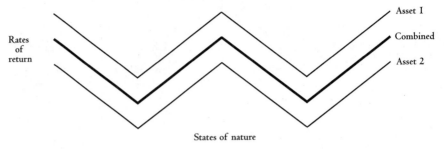

B. Perfect negative correlation: $\rho_{12} = -I$

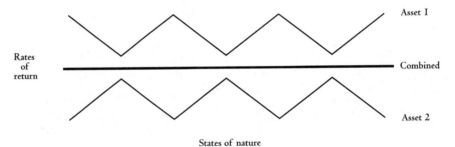

C. Positive but not correlation: $0 < \rho_{12} < I$

correlations between financial assets are normally positive but not perfectly so. Panel C shows that risk is reduced by combining assets with less than perfect positive correlation; that is, the combined pattern is flatter in shape than either asset alone.

While we have discussed the diversification effects of the securities portfolio on the bank as a whole, investment managers could also consider the effect of individual securities on the bank. Because most bank assets are debt instruments, and these assets' yields tend to follow interest rate changes, the correlations among bank assets' rates of return are usually highly positive. Evidence reported by the Federal Reserve, for example, has indicated that securitization of home loans by commercial banks and other financial institutions has caused mortgage rates to follow U.S. Treasury security rates more closely. A partial offset to this trend is that differences in maturity cause prices (and therefore yields) of bank assets to be less than perfectly positively correlated as interest rate levels change over time. Because investment securities are longer-term than most other bank assets, they tend to have a significant diversification effect on the bank's portfolio. Also, many loans—for example, consumer and commercial loans—likely have different rate of return patterns than Treasury and agency securities that dominate the investment portfolio.

CHAPTER II

Capital Management

After reading this chapter you will be able to:

- Define the components of bank capital, which differ from nonfinancial firms' capital.

- Describe the role of bank capital in the banking industry.

- Discuss the capital adequacy of banking institutions from the perspectives of both regulators and shareholders.

- Compare the different capital standards utilized by regulators over the years, including those standards applied today.

- Identify trends in the capitalization of U.S. commercial banks and their relationship to regulatory standards.

Bankers and regulators view bank capital differently. From the banker's perspective, using less capital is a way to magnify (or leverage) asset earnings and so earn higher equity rates of return. By contrast, regulators prefer that banks increase their capital to ensure their safety and soundness in the event earnings become negative. Despite these disparate views, on one point they come together—namely, capital is a fundamental building block of the banking business and essential to its survival and growth.

This chapter begins by defining bank capital and then discusses its role in managing both bank operations and financial risk. With these basics in hand, we cover the issue of capital adequacy from the alternative viewpoints of bank regulators and bank shareholders. The international risk-based capital requirements applicable to banks today are presented in some detail. Finally, capital trends over time for U.S. commercial banks are presented and discussed. ■

11.1 DEFINITION OF BANK CAPITAL

Like nonfinancial firms, capital in banking includes equity plus long-term debt. Equity is a residual account in the sense that it is the difference between total assets on the left-hand side of the balance sheet and total liabilities on the right-hand side of the balance sheet. Unlike nonfinancial firms, however, **bank capital** also includes reserves that are set aside to meet anticipated bank operating losses from loans, leases, and securities. Moreover, bank capital is subject to detailed regulatory requirements that attempt to ensure adequate capital to absorb normal levels of operating losses. In so doing, depositors are protected, as well as the deposit insurer.

Equity

Equity is comprised of common stock, preferred stock, surplus, and undivided profits. The accounting value of **common stock** (and **preferred stock**) is equal to the number of shares outstanding multiplied by their par value per share. **Surplus** is the amount of paid-in capital in excess of par value realized by the bank upon the initial sale of stock. Finally, **undivided profits** equal retained earnings, which are the cumulative net profits of the bank not paid out in the form of dividends to shareholders. The sum of these components is the **book value of equity**.

An alternative way to measure common stock and preferred stock is in terms of the **market value of equity**. Market values reflect not only the past, such as the historical book value of equity, but also the expected future of the bank. Indeed, stockholders are most concerned about future earnings available to them and the associated risks of those earnings. Thus, it is not surprising that the book value and market value of equity differ from one another.

As an example, suppose that a newly chartered bank sold 1 million common shares with a par value of $9 per share for $10 per share. During the first 3 years of business, the bank had undivided profits of $100,000, $110,000, and $120,000, respectively. Equity capital, as indicated in the Report of Condition would be as follows:

Preferred stock	$ 0
Common stock	9,000,000
Surplus	1,000,000
Undivided profits	330,000
Total equity	$10,330.00

Normally, the market value of equity would exceed the ex-post book value of equity, because most banks expect to have positive earnings per unit of risk in the future. Unfortunately, the equity stock of most banks is not traded in the open market either because they are closely held by a small group of investors or because trading activity is too low to warrant listing on a stock exchange. In this case the historical accounting (or book) value traditionally has served as a benchmark in comparing the equity positions of different banks. However, as discussed in Chapter 10, intense debate surrounds the use of market value accounting of assets and liabilities, which would enable a more accurate measure of a bank's equity position than the historical (book) value. Even though market value accounting has its pros and cons, it clearly provides a measure closer to the value of traded bank equity. As such, current and prospective shareholders, in addition to regulators and bankers, would benefit.

Long-Term Debt

Subordinated notes and debentures are sources of long-term debt that banks can utilize to raise additional external funds. Because this debt is second in priority to depositor claims in the event of bank failure, it is said to be "subordinated." Banks use far less long-term debt than do nonfinancial firms because most of their debt is in the form of short- and intermediate-term deposit and nondeposit funds, which essentially are money market sources of funds. Nonetheless, long-term bank debt increased substantially in the 1960s, especially among large banks. This increase was motivated by a change in regulatory requirements that allowed notes and debentures (with maturities of at least 7 years) to be used to meet capital standards for national banks. In the context of regulatory capital, however, it should be noted the long-term debt only serves to absorb operating losses in the event of failures.

A major advantage of using debt capital (as opposed to equity capital) is that interest payments are tax deductible, whereas equity earnings are fully exposed to federal income taxes. Consequently, debt is a less expensive after-tax source of external capital than equity in general.

For small banks the use of long-term debt is much more costly than it is for large, billion-dollar banks. Fixed transactions costs can raise the marginal cost of small debt issues to an unreasonably high level. Moreover, small issues normally are less liquid than larger issues, causing investors to demand a higher rate of return, which raises the cost of borrowing for small banks. Nonetheless, under regulatory capital standards banks have incentives to issue long-term debt. By inducing banks to issue long-term debt, regulators intend to increase "market discipline," whereby creditors monitor bank safety and soundness and reflect their views in bond prices. Of course, for small banks, scanty trading activity for bonds would diminish market discipline to some extent.

Reserves

Banks set aside earnings for loan (and lease) loss reserves. When a loan defaults, the loss does not necessarily reduce current earnings because it can be deducted from the reserve account. To establish reserves to meet anticipated loan losses, banks expense an account known as the **provision for loan losses** (PLL) in the income statement. By expensing PLL, banks reduce their tax burden. In the past banks used either the experience method or the percentage method to calculate their PLL. The experience method involves using the average loan losses over the previous six years. The percentage method simply takes 0.6% of eligible loans. Since the passage of the Tax Reform Act of 1986, however, banks with more than $500 million in assets can only expense actual losses from pretax income. This change prevents banks from overstating loss reserves to reduce their income.

Another reserve account is the **reserve for loan losses**. This account is reported on the asset side to the balance sheet and is also known as the allowance for loan losses. The reserve for loan losses is calculated as the cumulative PLL minus net loan charge-offs. Because this reserve is subtracted from total loans to get net loans, it is a contra-asset account. Part of the reserve for loan losses is counted as capital reserves on the right-hand side of the balance sheet. These reserves are employed by regulators in measures of capital adequacy. Typically, **capital reserves** are comprised of funds set aside to pay dividends or retire stocks and bonds outstanding, as well as funds held for unexpected losses.

As an example of what happens when banks charge off loans, assume that a bank has a PLL equal to $1,000,000 and the reserve for loan losses is $3,000,000. Given that the bank charged off $800,000 in loan losses during the year, but recovered $80,000 on previous charge-offs, the reserves for loan losses is calculated as follows:

Reserves for loan losses, beginning of 199X	$3,000,000
Less: Charge-offs during 199X	800,000
Plus: Recoveries during 199X on loans previously charged off	80,000
Plus: Provision for loan losses, 199X	1,000,000
Reserves for loan losses, end of 199X	$3,280,000

Because reserves absorb most losses in the banking industry, they are a key component of bank capital. Losses that exceed these reserves would have to be absorbed by stockholder's equity.

11.2 ROLE OF BANK CAPITAL.

Bank capital serves three basic roles. The first, and most obvious, is that it is a source of funds. A new bank requires funds to finance start-up costs of capital investment in land, plant, and equipment. Established banks require capital to finance their growth, as well as to maintain and modernize operations. They normally rely upon internal capital (retained earnings) to a much greater extend than external capital (long-term debt and equity stock). However, external capital is often used to finance major structural changes, such as acquisitions and mergers.

The second function of capital is to serve as a cushion to absorb unexpected operating losses. Relatively high loss rates on loans that surpass the loan loss provisions covering anticipated operating losses are charged against capital. Banks with insufficient capital to absorb losses are declared insolvent by their regulatory agency and are handled by the Federal Deposit Insurance Corporation (to be discussed in greater detail later in this chapter).

Long-term debt instruments as a capital source of funds cannot be used to absorb losses except in a liquidation of a failed institution. Thus, in contrast to reserves and equity sources of capital, long-term debt only weakly satisfies the role of capital as a cushion to absorb losses.

The third function of bank capital addresses the question of adequate capital. Unlike nonfinancial firms with capital/asset ratios commonly in the 40% to 60% range, banks generally have less than 10% of assets funded by capital, meaning that relatively small (unanticipated) asset losses can significantly affect bank capital and threaten bank solvency. As discussed in the forthcoming section, "adequate capital" to maintain a reasonable margin of safety is a difficult concept in practice. Bank regulators establish minimum requirements to promote safety and soundness in the banking system. They also seek to mitigate the moral hazard problem in deposit insurance by using capital requirements to increase the exposure of bank shareholders to potential losses and so motivate prudent management. Additionally, market confidence is another factor in evaluating adequate capital. If the market perceives a shortage of bank capital, bank stock prices will be adversely affected. Conversely, a record of strong and stable capital over time tends to favorably impact bank stock prices.

Depository Institution Failures and Capital

The Federal Deposit Insurance Corporation or FDIC (http://www.fdic.gov/) issues regulations governing federally insured bank and savings association procedures and performance. It conducts several kinds of banking examinations in connection with its regulatory powers.

Depository institution failures sharply increased in the 1980s and caused substantial losses to taxpayers as losses outstripped insurance reserves. Over 4,000 federally insured depository institutions failed from 1980 to 1991 (e.g., 1,381 commercial and savings banks, 1,073 savings and loans, and 1,707 credit unions). After reckoning up the damage, it is now believed that taxpayers will have to pay over $200 billion in losses (or about 20 percent of these depository institutions' assets). Also, while most failures in the past were small institutions, large banks are increasingly at risk. For example, in 1992 the number of failed banks declined to 120 from more than 200 in 1989, but their combined total assets exceeded $42 billion, which is the third highest in terms of total assets since the FDIC was formed under the 1930s banking acts.[1]

Many reasons have been cited for these catastrophic losses, including interest rate management problems, high and volatile interest rates, local regional economic declines, deregulation that expanded risk-taking opportunities, changes in tax laws that adversely affected real estate investments, and illegal

---

1. Throughout the remainder of the 1990s net interest margins in the banking industry much improved due to relatively low interest rates. These profits bolstered capital levels and strengthened bank condition. Consequently, the failure rate declined to relatively low levels by the late 1990s.

or unethical practices. Central to the debate concerning the reasons for these losses at depository institutions is deposit insurance. Deposit insurance at fixed rates or premiums creates incentives for bank managers and shareholders to take excessive risks, as losses are paid by the insuring agency, such as the FDIC. It is known as the **moral hazard problem**. In nonfinancial firms creditors monitor asset and other risks and use this information to constrain borrowing. By contrast, in depository institutions, insured depositors are indifferent to bank risks so that risk must be monitored by regulators. With more than 15,000 depository institutions in the United States, the regulatory tasks of measuring risks and invoking disciplinary actions is formidable. Indeed, this regulatory approach to controlling risk in depository institutions clearly is deficient in view of the record losses in the 1980s and early 1990s.

For these reasons capital has become a centerpiece of regulatory policy. The basic idea is that shareholders with significant stakes in the institution will act to control risk taking to protect their investment. Thus, greater capital requirements are being imposed on depository institutions. Also, as already mentioned, banks are being encouraged to issue long-term bonds, which would improve market discipline from the standpoint of creditor monitoring. While some institutional losses can be explained by other reasons—regulatory forbearance in terms of keeping insolvent institutions with negative net worth open and able to incur further losses—the moral hazard problem can be diminished via equity and debt investment in the banking industry.

The web site http://www.law.cornell.edu/topics/banking.html is maintained by the Cornell University law school and is an excellent resource for laws related to the banking business.

11.3 CAPITAL ADEQUACY

As mentioned earlier, bank regulators and bank shareholders tend to have differing views about the adequacy of capital. Regulators normally are concerned about the downside risk of banks; that is, they focus on the lower end of the distribution of bank earnings. By contrast, shareholders are more concerned with the central part of the earnings distribution, or the expected return available to them. Both regulators and shareholders also consider the variability of bank earnings, albeit from different perspectives once again. Regulators perceive earnings variability in the context of the likelihood that earnings will fall so much that capital is eliminated and the bank becomes insolvent. Shareholders require higher earnings per share as the bank profitability becomes more variable. Of course, shareholders receive compensation for bank risk, whereas regulators do not.

Regulators' Viewpoint

From the viewpoint of regulators, financial risk increases the probability of bank insolvency. Greater variability of earnings after taxes means that interest and noninterest expenses are more likely to exceed bank earnings and that capital

As a regulator for nationally chartered banks, the Office of the Comptroller of the Currency or OCC (http://www.occ.ustreas.gov/) charters, regulates, and supervises national banks to insure a safe, sound, and competitive banking system. The OCC web site has a wide variety of banking information, in addition to risk-based capital requirements for banks.

will be required to absorb potential losses. If a bank has insufficient capital to absorb losses, regulators must close the bank due to **capital impairment**.

The problem faced by regulators is that, although requiring banks to maintain higher capital tends to lower financial risk, such requirements may inhibit the efficiency and competitiveness of the banking system; that is, capital requirements that exceed unregulated levels act as a constraint on the lending operations of banks. In this instance, banks may not allocate loanable funds in the most efficient way. The productivity of the economic sector could therefore be lessened by this constraint on the financial system. Regulatory restrictions on bank capital could also hinder their competitiveness relative to other sellers of financial services. For example, relatively high capital requirements tend to constrain the rate at which bank assets may be expanded. Unable to grow as rapidly as other financial service companies, banks would be at a competitive disadvantage. Thus, regulatory policy regarding **capital adequacy** must weigh the potential benefits of safety and soundness against the potential costs of efficiency and competitiveness.

Capital Standards

In general, regulators favor added capital as a buffer against insolvency to promote the safety and soundness of the financial system. "Safety and soundness" in this instance implies protecting depositor funds and preventing financial panics through the provision of a stable money supply. Regulators historically have maintained different standards for capital adequacy and have changed those standards many times. For example, because deposit runs were the major threat to bank soundness in the early 1900s, the **Office of the Comptroller of the Currency (OCC)** required banks to have capital-to-deposit ratio to measure capital adequacy, because risky assets (e.g., defaults on loans) were perceived to be the major cause of failure. During World War II, banks accumulated large proportions of default-free government securities to help finance federal debt, which caused regulators to utilize a capital-to-risk-asset ratio, where the term *risk assets* was defined as total assets minus cash and government securities.

Over the last 50 years, a wide variety of methods for assessing capital adequacy has been applied by regulators. In the 1950s for example, the **Federal Reserve Board (FRB)** began using the **Form for Analyzing Bank Capital (FABC)** to classify assets into six different risk categories. Banks were required to hold a different percentage of capital against each asset category (e.g., 0.4% capital against U.S. Treasury bills and 10% capital against business loans). Also, smaller banks had higher capital requirements because of the perception that their portfolio diversification was less than larger banks. By contrast, the OCC abandoned the use of strict guidelines in the early 1960s in favor of more subjective evaluations based on many factors, including management quality, asset liquidity, ownership, operating expenses, deposit composition, and so on. Because OCC standards applied to national banks, FRB standards applied to state member banks and banks affiliated with holding companies, and FDIC

The extensive web site of the Board of Governors of the Federal Reserve Board (http://www.federalreserve. gov/) is an excellent resource for anyone interested in commercial banking to follow the latest changes in regulations, banking data, research, and more.

standards applied to state-chartered banks, the capital adequacy of an individual bank was determined to a certain degree by its particular regulatory agency. Of course, for banks subject to multiple federal regulatory agencies (e.g., national banks in bank holding companies), compliance with capital requirements could become confusing.

Another problem with capital standards has been their enforceability. In the past, regulators relied primarily upon persuasion to enforce capital standards. Seldom were cease and desist orders employed to obtain compliance, because regulators were not supported by force of law. A steady decline in capital/asset ratios in the banking industry in the 1960s and 1970s made clear that this approach to capital regulation was not working. This problem was solved by the **International Lending Supervision Act** of 1983 under which regulators were given legal authority to establish minimum capital requirements and enforce them. Normally, the regulator requires violating banks to submit a plan to correct the capital shortfall, which is now enforceable in the courts.

Yet another problem with previous capital standards is the question of fairness. In the past, small banks had more restrictive capital requirements than large banks. Presumably bank size was directly related to safety and soundness according to this dichotomy. However, the historical evidence on bank failures in the United States has not proved failure risk to be negatively related to asset size.

Uniform Capital Requirements

In 1981 federal bank regulators established minimum primary capital-to-asset ratios. Primary capital was defined as common stock, perpetual preferred stock, capital surplus, undivided profits, capital reserves, and other nondebt instruments. The FRB and OCC adopted a 6% minimum for banks with less than $1 billion in assets and 5% for banks over $1 billion assets. The FDIC applied a 5% minimum ratio to all banks. Multinational banks, which are the 15–20 largest banks in the United States, were evaluated on a case-by-case basis. Under the 1983 International Lending and Supervision Act, however, multinationals were required also to meet the 5% minimum primary capital requirement.

To further improve uniformity, in 1985 the three federal bank regulators settled on a 5.5% primary capital ratio for all banks. In this regard, regulators established zones for billion-dollar banks that consider ranges of ratios for primary and total capital (defined to also include debt instruments), as well as asset quality and other factors that are relevant to capital risk. Finally, if a bank was judged to be undercapitalized, it had to make up the shortfall under the supervision of its regulatory agency. Progress toward compliance with capital standards was monitored over time.

In response to this uniform capital/asset ratio measurement of capital adequacy, undercapitalized, larger banks generally raised new capital, reduced their holdings of liquid assets, and increased off-balance-sheet activities (because only booked assets were counted in the calculation of the capital ratio). Some larger institutions, forced to increase capital, also sought to cut operating costs, raise service prices, and make riskier loans. These changes tended to offset the advantage of added capital in many cases and so defeated to some extent the capital adequacy goals of regulators.

Risk-Adjusted Capital Requirements

The Bank for International Settlements or BIS (http:// www.bis.org/publ/) is a central banking institution which is unique at the international level. BIS was established in 1930 to provide improved international central bank cooperation and achieve international financial stability. Owned and controlled by central banks, it provides a number of highly specialized services to central banks around the world. All banks with international operations must meet BIS capital requirements.

In 1987, U.S. federal regulatory agencies, in conjunction with the Bank of England and authorities from 10 other leading industrial countries, agreed to release for public comment proposed **risk-based capital rules**.[2] The major rationale for this proposal was that historical evidence indicated no obvious relationship between bank capital and failure risk. In the Great Depression, for example, capitalization was not linked directly to failures. Not only would the proposed standards be more closely related to failure risks, they would also promote convergence of supervisory policies on the adequacy of capital among countries with major banking centers. This convergence was needed due to the rising competition in international banking. If U.S. regulators raised capital standards for U.S. banks, but other counties did not do so, U.S. banks would be disadvantaged relative to international competitors. In June 1988 the so-called **Basle Agreement** was signed by 12 industrialized nations under the auspices of the Bank for International Settlements (BIS). By year-end 1992 all U.S. banks were required to comply with the new rules.

The international risk-based capital rules maintain a minimum threshold for all banks, which is consistent with previous uniform standards, and classify assets into four credit risk categories that have different capital requirements, not unlike the Federal Reserve's previous FABC approach. Additionally, beginning no later than January 1998 an amendment by the Basle Committee was implemented to extend previous rules to new market risk capital requirements that focus on securities trading by commercial banks. The two categories of capital are: (1) Tier 1 or "core" capital, and (2) Tier 2 or "supplemental" capital. **Tier 1 capital** measures equity holdings and is equal to the sum of tangible equity, including common stock, surplus, retained earnings, and perpetual preferred stock. Unlike primary capital under uniform rules, capital reserves are excluded from equity. This exclusion is reasonable because loan loss reserves reflect anticipated actual losses, while equity indicates the ability of the bank to

---

2. The proposal was adopted in 1988 by the Basle Committee on Banking Regulations and Supervisory Practices, which is comprised of representatives of the central banks and supervisory authorities of Belgium, Canada, France, Germany, Italy, Japan, Netherlands, Sweden, Switzerland, United Kingdom, United States and Luxembourg. The Committee continues to work toward strengthening the capital resources of international banks.

absorb unexpected losses.[3] **Tier 2 capital** is comprised of loan loss reserves, subordinated debt, intermediate-term preferred stock, and other items counted previously as primary capital (e.g., mandatory convertible debt and cumulative perpetual preferred stock with unpaid dividends). Since year-end 1992, the minimum capital levels are:

Capital	Risk-Adjusted Assets	Total Assets
Tier 1	4%	3%
Tier 1 + Tier 2 (**Total Capital**)	8%	No requirement

Table 11.1 gives further details of the minimum requirements for Tier 1 and Tier 2 capital. It should be recognized that the 3% leverage ratio is only applicable to the lowest risk institutions. Depending on risk factors, this ratio can be increased 100–200 basis points.

Table 11.2 provides the weighting scheme for calculating risk-adjusted assets for purposes of **credit risk capital requirements**. Weights for on-balance sheet assets increase as credit risk increases: zero default risk items have a 0% weight; mortgaged-backed bonds issued by U.S. government and U.S. government sponsored agencies and general obligation municipal bonds have a 20% weight; home loans, revenue bonds, and some other mortgage-backed securities carry a 50% weight; and all other assets have a 100% weight. To calculate the minimum capital requirements for a bank in dollar terms, the following formula can be used:

$$K = \text{Minimum ratio} \times [0.00(A_1) + 0.20(A_2) + 0.50(A_3) + 1.00(A_4)] \quad 11.1$$

where minimum ratio = the Tier 1 or total capital minimum requirement, and $A_1 \ldots, A_4$ = the dollar amounts held in four asset categories. The term is brackets is known as **risk-adjusted assets**.

As an example, assume a bank has the following assets:

Assets	(1) Amount ($ thousands)	(2) Risk Weight	(1) × (2) Risk-Adjusted Assets
Cash	$ 100	0.00	$ 0
FNMA securities	1,000	0.20	200
GO municipal bonds	1,500	0.20	300
Home loans	3,000	0.50	1,500
Commercial loans	5,000	1.00	5,000
	$10,600		$7,000

3. Using the primary capital ratio, some failing banks posted record highs for primary capital prior to their collapse in the early 1980s. The reason for this high capital ratio was that loan-loss reserves were high but equity capital was low. Thus, a high primary capital ratio was not necessarily associated with sound financial condition.

TABLE 11.1	Components and Rules Governing Qualifying Capital Under Risk-Based Capital Rules

Components	Minimum Requirements
Tier 1 (Core) Capital	Must equal or exceed 4% of risk-weighted assets (RWAs)
Common shareholder's equity and retained earnings	No limit
Qualifying noncumulative perpetual preferred stock and related surplus[a]	No limit, but regulatory warning against "undue reliance"
Minority interests in equity accounts of consolidated subsidiaries	No limit, but regulatory warning against "undue reliance"
Less:	
Goodwill and some intangible assets[b]	
Subsidiaries of S&Ls engaged in activities not permitted national banks	
Tier 2 (Supplementary) Capital	Limited to 100% of Tier 1
Allowance for loan and lease losses	Limited to 1.25% of RWAs
Perpetual preferred stock not qualifying for Tier 1 capital	No limit within Tier 2
Hybrid capital instruments and equity-contract notes[c]	No limit within Tier 2
Subordinated debt and intermediate-term preferred stock	Limited to 50% of Tier 1
Deductions from Total Capital	
Investments in unconsolidated subsidiaries	
Reciprocal holdings of other depositories' capital securities	
Other activities of S&Ls not permitted national banks	
Other deductions required by supervisory agents	
Total Capital	Must equal or exceed 8% of RWAs
= Sum [Tier 1 + Tier 2] − Deductions	

a. Bank holding companies can include both cumulative and noncumulative perpetual preferred stock in Tier 1, but the total amount is limited to 25 percent of Tier 1 capital.

b. Other intangible assets are those that do not meet a three-part test (see 54 FR 4168, 4179, January 27, 1989).

c. Hybrid capital instruments include instruments that are essentially permanent in nature and that have characteristics of both equity and debt.

TABLE 11.2	Components of On-Balance Sheet Risk-Weighted Asset Categories

Risk-Weight Category	On-Balance Sheets Assets
0%	Cash
	Securities backed by the full faith and credit of U.S. and OECD governments and some U.S. government agencies
	Balances due from Federal Reserve banks and central banks in other OECD countries
20%	Cash items in the process of collection
	Mortgage-backed U.S. government or U.S. government-sponsored agency securities
	U.S. and OECD interbank deposits and guaranteed claims
	Assets collateralized by securities backed by the full faith and credit of U.S. and OECD governments
	Assets conditionally guaranteed by U.S. and OECD governments
	Securities issued by and direct claims on U.S. government-sponsored agencies
50%	Loans fully secured by first liens on 1–4 and multifamily properties
	Mortgage-backed securities backed by home mortgage loans with at least 80% loan-to-value ratios
	U.S. state and local government revenue bonds
100%	All other claims on private obligers, including consumer and commercial loans
	Long-term claims on, or guaranteed by, non-OECD banks
	Residential construction loans
	Premises, plant, and equipment; other fixed assets; and other real-estate owned
	Commercial paper and most private-issue debt
	Investments in unconsolidated subsidiaries, joint ventures, or associated companies not deducted from capital
	Mortgage-related securities with residual characteristics
	All other assets, including intangible assets not deducted from capital

The minimum capital requirements using the risk-adjusted assets procedure would be:

$$\text{Tier 1 capital} = 0.04(\$7,000) = \$280$$
$$\text{Total capital} = 0.08(\$7,000) = \$560.$$

Tier 1 capital would also have to be greater than 3.0% of total assets, or $318. In this case the capital required under the risk-adjusted assets procedure of

$280 is irrelevant because at least $318 Tier 1 capital is required on total assets. Thus, the risk adjusted method of calculating primary capital is only important for banks with larger amounts of risky assets. For less risky banks Tier 1 capital ratios are based on the uniform 3.0% requirement.

Table 11.3 shows the risk-weighting scheme for **off-balance sheet activities**. These items must first be converted to on-balance sheet "credit equivalent" amounts. The items are assigned to the appropriate on-balance sheet risk category, and the capital requirements can then be calculated as before. For example, assume that a bank has the following off-balance sheet items:

Items	(1) Amount ($ thousands)	(2) Conversion Factors	(3) Risk Weight	(1) × (2) × (3) Risk-Adjusted Assets
Performance standby letters of credit	$1,000	0.50	0.20	$ 100
Commercial letters of credit	2,000	0.20	1.00	400
Guaranteed letters of credit	1,500	1.00	1.00	1,500
Total off-balance-sheet items	$4,500			$2,000

Tier 1 capital and total capital requirements under the risk-adjusted assets procedures would now be:

$$\text{Tier 1 capital} = 0.04\ (\$7,000 + \$2,000) = \$360$$
$$\text{Total capital} = 0.08\ (\$7,000 + \$2,000) = \$720.$$

Including off-balance sheet items, Tier 1 capital of $360 exceeds the minimum using total assets of $318. Thus, the risk-adjusted requirement for Tier 1 capital is binding. It should be mentioned that a more complicated formula is used for interest rate swaps, forward contracts, and options as well as foreign exchange contracts (see Table 11.3).

As already mentioned, **market risk capital requirements** were fully implemented in January 1998. These rules supplement the credit risk capital requirements by invoking some adjustments to the risk-based capital ratio. Insured state member banks and bank holding companies with significant trading activity are exposed to market risk rules; namely, institutions with more than 10% of total assets or $1 billion or more in trading account positions. The trading account includes both on- and off-balance sheet positions in financial instruments, currencies, and commodities held for profitable resale in the event of price and rate changes. These assets are marked-to-market daily and banks must hold on a daily basis a minimum 8% risk-adjusted capital ratio adjusted for market risk. Two types of market risk adjustments are necessary: (1) **general market risk** associated with the financial market as a whole, and (2) **specific risk** due to other risk factors (including credit risk of the securities

TABLE 11.3	Components of Off-Balance Sheet Risk-Weighted Asset Categories

Conversion Factor	On-Balance Sheets Assets
	20% Risk Weight
50%	Performance standby letters of credit conveyed to others
	Participations in commitments with an original maturity exceeding one year conveyed to others
100%	Financial standby letters of credit conveyed to others
	50% Risk Weight
0%	Unused commitments with an original maturity of one year or less
	Other unused commitments if unconditionally cancelable and a separate credit decision is made before each draw
20%	Commercial letters of credit and similar instruments
50%	Performance standby letters of credit less those conveyed to others
	Unused portion of commitments with an original maturity exceeding one year less those conveyed to others
	Revolving underwriting facilities, note issuance facilities, and similar arrangements
100%	Financial guarantee standby letters of credit less those conveyed to others
	Participations in acceptance acquired
	Securities loaned
	Farmer Mac loans (Farm Credit Administration)
	Other off-balance sheet items
	Sale and repurchase agreements and assets sold with recourse
	Forward agreements and other contingent obligations with a specified draw down
	Subordinated portions of senior/subordinated mortgage-pool securities

Note: The notional value of off-balance sheet items are converted to on-balance sheet "credit-equivalent" amounts. These "credit-equivalent" amounts are then assigned the risk weights that would be applicable to the counterparty or underlying collateral. Interest-rate and exchange-rate contracts are converted to on-balance-sheet credit equivalent amounts by summing the current credit exposure and the potential credit exposure. Current credit exposure is the replacement cost of the contract (in U.S. dollars). The potential credit exposure is an estimate of the potential increase in credit exposure over the remaining life of the contract.

issuer). A "covered position" implies that adequate capital is held to support these two market risks.

The primary adjustment to the risk-adjusted capital ratio due to market risk takes place in the denominator. In the denominator the value of market-risk equivalent assets must be added to an adjusted value of credit-risk-weighted assets (i.e., the previous value of credit-risk-weighted assets less covered positions in the trading account). Thus, in the previous example, assume that the $1,500 in GO municipal bonds is all in the trading account of the bank. Given the risk-adjusted assets for these securities was $1,500 × 0.20 = $300, the adjusted value of credit-risk-weighted assets would be $7,000 – $300 = $6,700. The calculation of market-risk equivalent assets is determined by individual banks using their own internal risk model. As discussed in Chapter 10, such a model estimates the daily value-at-risk (VAR) for the trading account assets. VAR is normally calibrated to the 10-day 99th percentile standard. As an example, assume that on a particular day a bank calculates from past records over the last year a 1-in-100 chance of losing $66.67 in any 10-day period. This VAR is typically multiplied by a scaling factor of 3 (but it can be higher if required by regulators), such that market-risk equivalent assets equals $66.67 × 3 = $200 on the chosen day in the present case. Under the new rules, banks must use (1) an average VAR over the last 60 business days times 3, or (2) the previous day's VAR. Because the second criterion is only relevant to periods in which the financial markets are extremely volatile, the first criterion is more commonly employed. Banks must use a minimum of one year in their historical calculations of VAR on any particular day. Assuming that $200 is the average VAR over the last 60 business days, the new value for risk-adjusted assets in the denominator of the risk-adjusted capital ratio is $6,700 + $200 = $6,900.

Specific risk can be calculated either using standardized measurement methods or using the bank's individual internal model. Capital charges for specific risk are intended to cover losses not captured by the VAR model estimates. Recall that general market risk captures movements in prices and interest rates; consequently, it does not reflect risk in a trading position involving securities that are illiquid due to infrequent trading. In the context of our previous example, if specific risk was estimated at $50, the capital charge would be $50 × 4 = $200 and, in turn, the denominator of the risk-adjusted capital ratio would become $6,900 + $200 = $7,100. We can see that the new market risk capital requirements have increased risk-adjusted assets from $7,000 for credit risk alone to $7,100 for credit risk and market risk. If total capital was 9% of credit-risk-adjusted assets (or $630), it would decline to about 8.9% due to market risk. Most experts believe that total capital ratios will likely decline 30–40 basis points due to market risk.

All banks must implement control procedures in market risk assessments. Each bank must have a risk-control unit that is separate from the business-trading function. The risk-control unit is required to regularly perform back-tests to determine the accuracy of the internal VAR model and specific risk estimates. Internal models should be updated at least every three months, and (as mentioned in Chapter 10) stress tests of simulated changes in various risk factors checked against actual trading experience. Backtesting results enable VAR models to evolve over time and provide regulators with important information on changing risk levels in banks' trading accounts. While criticisms about the *ad hoc* application of scaling factors and potential risks of turning over some degree of regulatory control to banks themselves are certainly warranted, market risk capital requirements represent a major advance in both regulatory oversight and bank risk management.

For banks with abnormal risk levels, capital in excess of minimum requirements is needed. Banks judged to be capital deficient need to take corrective action by restructuring or decreasing assets, increasing equity by reducing dividends or issuing new stock, or some combination of these alternatives. Most banks have had no difficulty in meeting the new capital rules. Figure 11.1 shows the average Tier 1, Tier 2, and leverage ratios of all U.S. insured commercial banks for the period 1991–1998, as well as the share of industry assets at well-capitalized banks. The general trend for all three ratios is that a noticeable increase in capital levels took place in the years after the implementation of the Basle Agreement for all sizes of banks. Thus, the new capital rules prompted an increase in capital levels in the U.S. banking industry. By 1994 more than 90% of U.S. banks were classified as "well-capitalized" with total capital ratios exceeding 10%, a Tier 1 ratio greater than 6%, a leverage ratio greater than 5%, and high composite CAMEL ratings of 1 or 2 (on a 5-point scale).[4] In 1998 the percentage of well-capitalized banks rose to about 95%, which indicates that most banks exceed the minimum capital standards.

In general, risk-based capital requirements should tend to decrease risk by forcing equity holders to take a greater stake in banks. However, some potential weaknesses are present in the current approach. First, related to credit risk, differences in the default probabilities and potential recovery rates in default are generally not addressed (see Managerial Issues, "Refining Credit Risk Capital Standards"). Another problem is that book values rather than market values are used in the weighting scheme and could impact the allocation of bank funds. By favoring (nontrading) securities over loans in the weighting scheme, risk-based capital requirements may curtail bank credit, as banks shift more funds to investments. Then, the possibility that savings are not being channeled to their best uses arises, which means that allocational efficiency is diminished. In effect, from a public policy standpoint, safety and soundness in the banking system is being traded off against allocational efficiency. Second, the new rules do not account for other kinds of bank risk, such as operating, liquidity, and legal risks. Of these, operating risk is increasingly being discussed by regulators. Operating risk considers the competitive risks the bank faces in its market, as well as payments and accounting system failures and fraud. Third, a lack of portfolio diversification is another consideration that is not explicitly taken into account. It is possible that banks' internal models could be employed to develop capital charges for these risks. Because some of these risks are already being addressed in banks' treatment of specific risk in market risk capital requirements, further adjustments to capital rules will likely be implemented in the future. Despite these weaknesses, the combination of credit risk and market risk capital

---

4. CAMEL ratings (discussed in Chapter 2) are based on on-site bank examinations and reflect capital adequacy, asset management, management expertise, earnings, and liquidity. Ratings range from 1 (high) to 5 (low).

FIGURE II.I Regulatory Capital Ratios at Insured
Commercial Banks and Share of Industry Assets
at Well-Capitalized Banks, 1991–1998

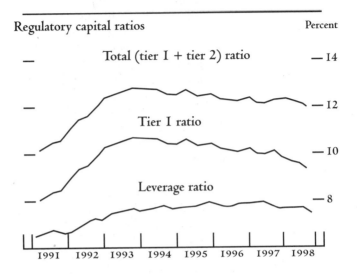

Regulatory capital ratios   Percent

Total (tier I + tier 2) ratio

Tier I ratio

Leverage ratio

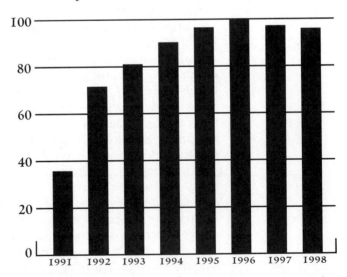

Share of industry assets
at well-capitalized banks

Source: Antulio N. Bomfim and William B. English, "Profits and Balance Sheet Developments at U.S. Commercial Banks in 1998," *Federal Reserve Bulletin* (June 1999), p. 377.

requirements is a significant improvement over previous capital rules. The new capital rules (1) are sensitive to some extent to differences in bank risk taking; (2) incorporate off-balance sheet activities into risk assessments; (3) do not penalize banks for holding low-risk, liquid assets; and (4) increase the consistency of rules applied to large banks around the world.

FDIC

The **Federal Deposit Insurance Corporation (FDIC)** has a vested interest in bank capital adequacy. It insures deposits held by approximately 98% of all U.S. commercial banks. Banks are required to pay premiums to insure deposit accounts up to $100,000. Rebates in the past have been paid to sound institutions at the end of the year that are determined by the FDIC's collections minus disbursements and operating expenses.

Created in 1933, the FDIC has two policy objectives. First, deposit insurance is intended to protect depositors of modest means against bank failures. Second, the insurance is supposed to protect communities, states, or the nation from the economic consequences of a breakdown in the payments system. The record shows that since its inception the FDIC has effectively met these objectives, with 100% recovery of insured deposits and about 99% recovery of total deposits.

When a distressed bank situation arises, the FDIC handles it in one of five ways: (1) depositor payoff, (2) purchase and assumption, (3) provision of financial aid, (4) charter of a Deposit Insurance National Bank (or bridge bank), or (5) reorganization. In a depositor payoff, each insured depositor receives up to $100,000 from the FDIC within one week. Liquidated proceeds from the bank are used for this purpose, and remaining funds are used to pay off other deposit and nondeposit claims, as well as the FDIC itself. It is normally less costly, however, for the FDIC to use the purchase and assumption (P&A) method of disposition. Under this approach, the bank is merged with a healthy bank. The FDIC accepts the lower-cost bid for the bank and pays off part (or all) of the acquiring bank's losses in the merger.

If the closure of a bank would severely disrupt banking services to a community or cause creditors to suffer extraordinary losses, the FDIC can choose among the latter three approaches cited previously. Financial aid can be used temporarily to assist a distressed bank. A **Deposit Insurance National Bank (DINB)**, or so-called bridge bank, can be chartered by the FDIC to take over operations until the bank is either closed or acquired by another bank. Finally, the major creditors can reorganize the bank with or without regulatory intervention. Of these five alternative approaches, P&A's (mergers) are most commonly used.

Deregulation of financial institutions over the last decade has caused new problems for the FDIC. Deregulation has enabled banks to choose among a broader opportunity set of risks and returns in their liability and asset management. Intuitively, it is inappropriate for all banks to pay the same deposit insurance costs but prior to 1993 premium rates were fixed for all banks.

Refining Credit Risk Capital Standards

As discussed in the text, the 1997 Market Risk Amendment to the Basle Capital Accord implemented a refined system of capital requirements for bank securities. Market risk exposures are measured by internal bank models based on value-at-risk (VAR). Recently, the International Swap Dealers Association (ISDA) and Institute of International Finance Working Group on Capital Adequacy (IIF) have argued that credit risk models should be developed to more precisely calculate risk-adjusted capital requirements. At the present time only two weights are possible for bank loans—namely, 0.50 for 1–4 family and multi-family loans and 1.00 for all other loans.

Default risk can be defined in the terms of the volatility of debt instrument value in response to changes in the credit quality of borrowers. One problem in measuring and forecasting default risk is that many debt instruments are not actively traded. VAR methods are easily applied to traded securities due to ready calculation of fluctuations in market prices on a daily basis. However, bank loans are generally not traded such that no daily pricing data are available. In this case the only way to measure default risk is to observe the default histories of bank loans, which implies that it takes a long time to develop enough observations to assess default risk. In turn, it is difficult to validate a credit risk model because it may only be an accurate measurement tool for the period under analysis and not useful in forecasting default risk in future periods.

One alternative way to measure default risk is to track credit ratings over time. Credit ratings or scores for loans generated on a quarterly basis enable banks to track the credit quality of their loan portfolio over time. Internal credit risk models attempt to forecast changes in average rating levels over time. The models seek to link changes in credit ratings with changes in the value of the loan portfolio, which is the key variable from the perspective of bank capital management. The probability that capital will be impaired by any particular decline in credit ratings can then be estimated. The bank can then take appropriate actions with regard to its allowance for loan loss account to ensure than capital does not become impaired by credit losses.

Regulatory capital requirements for credit risk would use internal credit risk models of banks to establish weights for different levels of credit risk. Also, they could take into account the risk reducing effects of diversification in the loan portfolio. While model validation is an ongoing problem in measuring default risk, an accumulation of experience for many banks over a number of business cycles should strengthen the reliability of the credit risk estimates. Such backtests can be used to periodically make adjustments to credit risk models and further refine their accuracy.

Note: For readers interested in the technical details of credit risk modeling, see Jose A. Lopez and Marc R. Saidenberg, "Evaluating Credit Risk Models," Working Paper, Federal Reserve Bank of San Francisco and Federal Reserve Bank of New York, respectively (April 1999), and citations to other literature therein.

Indeed, it is believed that some banks took excessive risks in an attempt to exploit the mispricing of deposit insurance by the FDIC, part of the moral hazard problem mentioned previously. For these reasons, the FDIC implemented a **risk-based deposit insurance** scheme in 1994—the strongest institutions would pay 0 cents per each $100 of domestic deposits, while the weakest would pay 27 cents. Premiums can vary within this range for institutions depending on capital levels and supervisory ratings (see Managing Risk, "Variable-Rate Deposit Insurance" for further details). In effect, the variable-rate premiums

MANAGING RISK

Variable-Rate Deposit Insurance

The FDIC adopted in September 1992 a **variable-rate deposit insurance** pricing scheme effective January 1, 1993. The following range of premiums is currently applied to banks and savings banks: 0–27 cents per $100 of domestic deposits. Only about 2% of banks and 7% of savings banks are estimated to pay the highest insurance rate. A number of amendments in the pricing system have taken place since its implementation in January 1994.

A matrix with nine different risk categories is used. The first step is to assign each institution to one of three capital groups:

- *Well capitalized:* total capital to risk-adjusted assets greater than or equal to 10%, minimum 6% Tier 1 capital to risk-adjusted assets, *and* minimum 5% Tier 1 capital to total assets (leverage ratio)
- *Adequately capitalized:* minimums of 8% for the total capital ratio, 4% for the Tier 1 ratio, *and* 4% for the leverage ratio
- *Undercapitalized:* below average standards

The second step is to assign each institution to one of three risk groups;

- *Group A:* financially sound and only a few minor weaknesses; composite ratings of 1 or 2.
- *Group B:* weaknesses that, if not corrected, could cause serious financial distress over time and increased risk to the insurance fund; composite rating of 3 normally
- *Group C:* substantial probability of loss to the insurance fund unless effective corrective measures are taken. Composite ratings of 4 or 5

Based on these capital and risk groups, the matrix of insurance rates (in cents per $100 domestic deposit) is:

| | Risk | | |
Capital	A	B	C
Well capitalized	0	3	17
Adequately capitalized	3	10	24
Undercapitalized	10	24	27

Supervisory ratings and financial data are employed in evaluating institutions' risk level. An appeals process is available for institutions that disagree with their risk group classification. The supervisory "prompt corrective action" gives mandatory and discretionary guidelines to regulators as bank capital falls below specific "tripwires." All banks are not allowed to make capital distributions or pay management fees if they would cause the bank to become undercapitalized. Undercapitalized banks must submit a capital plan within 45 days to remedy their capital shortfall. Depending on the level of capital, restrictions on asset growth, acquisitions, branches, new business activities, salaries, deposit rates, as well as increased monitoring, can be imposed on undercapitalized banks. Further restrictions can apply to banks deemed significantly undercapitalized. Critically undercapitalized banks, with tangible equity ratios below 2%, can be placed in regulatory receivership.

According to historical statistics, more than 95% of U.S. banks are typically classified as well capitalized, about 3% fall into the adequately capitalized range, and slightly more than 1% are undercapitalized. Critically undercapitalized banks ranged from 10 to 50 banks per year during the 1990s. Thus, most U.S. banks meet capital standards but some banks are at risk of government seizure.

increase deposit (debt) costs as the probability of failure and deposit losses increase. This pricing system mimics to some extent the higher interest costs of debt demanded by creditors of nonfinancial firms as risk increases. Of course, deposit premiums reduce earnings available to shareholders, which exerts further control on bank managers, who are accountable to shareholders. On the other hand, some banks may be willing to pay higher insurance premiums if risky investments are well managed and earn relatively high returns.

It may seem that risk-based capital requirements and risk-based deposit insurance are redundant. However, while capital forces shareholders to "co-insure" (with the FDIC) against bank losses, deposit insurance pays for losses beyond the coinsurance level. Naturally, banks with higher coinsurance (equity capital) should pay lower premiums. Therefore, capital adequacy and deposit insurance pricing are interrelated rather than redundant.

11.4 SHAREHOLDERS' VIEWPOINT

Shareholders view bank capitalization in a substantially different way than do regulators. Shareholders seek an optimal mix of debt and equity financing to maximize the value of their common stock. Because share values are a function of both expected future cash flows available to equity owners and their associated risks, shareholders focus on the expected value of rates of return on equity and their variability. In this section we review some of the major factors that influence capital structure decisions of bank shareholders.

Financial Risk and Share Valuation

Financial risk is associated with borrowing funds to finance assets. Banks that substitute debt (including both deposit and nondeposit liabilities) for equity give themselves less margin for error in lending, liability management, investment, and other bank operations. This financial risk is reflected in the variability of **earnings per share (EPS)**. Table 11.4 gives an example of the effect of financial risk on EPS. It is clear from the results there that greater use of debt, or **financial leverage**, causes the percentage change, or variability, of EPS to increase. More specifically, the relationship between debt usage and EPS variability can be written simply as:

$$\% \text{ change in EPS} = \% \text{ change in EBIT} \times \frac{\text{EBIT}}{\text{EBIT} - \text{Interest}} \qquad 11.2$$

where EBIT equals expected net operating earnings before interest expenses and taxes. In Table 11.4, for the low debt scenario, the percentage change in EPS for a 10% change in EBIT is 10% × ($10,000)/($10,000 − $7,000) = 10% × 3.33 = 33.33%, which agrees with our findings shown there. As a check, the same result can be calculated for the high debt scenario.

TABLE 11.4   Financial Risk and Variability of Earnings per Share ($ thousands)

	Low Debt			High Debt		
	Bad	Expected	Good	Bad	Expected	Good
Net earnings before interest and taxes	$9,000	$10,000	$11,000	$9,000	$10,000	$11,000
Interest expenses	(7,000)	(7,000)	(7,000)	(9,000)	(9,000)	(9,000)
Net earnings	2,000	3,000	4,000	0	1,000	2,000
Taxes (@34%)	(680)	(1,040)	(1,360)	0	(340)	(680)
Earnings after taxes	$1,320	$1,960	$2,640	$0	$ 660	$1,320

Common Shares Outstanding = 1 Million

Earnings per share	$1.32	$1.96	$2.64	$0	$0.66	$1.32
Percentage change in EBIT relative to expected outcome	–10%	0%	+10%	–10%	0%	+10%
Percentage change in EPS relative to expected outcome	–33%	0%	+33%	–100%	0%	100%

Although shareholders must bear more variation in earnings if they use greater financial leverage, tax deductions on interest payments lower the costs of making loans. For example, suppose debt and equity rates were equal to 10% (after adjusting for risk differences) and the bank's marginal tax rate was 40%. The after-tax cost of debt to the bank would be only 6% because of the tax deductibility of interest expenses, or 10% × (1 – 0.40). The relatively lower cost of debt compared to equity on an after-tax basis causes a preference for debt financing by shareholders.

In nonfinancial corporate enterprises, shareholders cannot necessarily increase their wealth by using debt to obtain tax deductions beyond some leverage point. As compensation for the increased probability that the firm will be unable to pay the higher debt load, debt claimants can be expected to raise the required interest rate that the firm must pay. Also, debtors use covenants to place limits on the extent to which corporations can borrow in the future, as well as on the kinds of debt that can be used and other restrictions on business operations. At some level of financial leverage, the tax gains on leverage are offset by higher interest payments and restrictions on debt usage.

In banking, however, because of deposit insurance, the debt usage of share-holders normally is not limited by debtors, many of whom are bank deposi-tors. Depositors of insured banks generally do not require a higher rate of interest depending on the bank's leverage, nor do they place restrictions on the issuance of new debt. In the absence of these forms of market discipline, regulators must control bank leverage by setting capital standards and imposing compliance costs on banks that violate those standards. Also, as mentioned earlier, risk-based deposit premiums increase debt costs as leverage increases. We can formally state the effects of debt, taxes, and regulation on bank valuation (and therefore shareholder wealth) as follows:

$$V_L = V_U + tD - C \qquad\qquad 11.3$$

where

V_L = value of the levered bank
V_U = value of the unlevered (no debt) bank
t = tax rate on bank income
D = market value of debt (insured deposits)
C = costs imposed by regulators, such as deposit insurance premiums, reporting requirements, and other compliance costs of regulation

To simplify matters, we have assumed all debts (deposits) are insured and, consequently, are riskless. Without any regulatory costs (or $C = 0$), the maximum value of the bank is obtained by borrowing as much as possible by expanding deposits and reducing equity capital. This result is consistent with the famous Modigliani and Miller (1963) model of corporate valuation; however, Buser, Chen, and Kane (1981) have argued that regulatory costs cause banks to temper their use of deposits to finance assets.[5] At some point, further use of deposits will impose such high regulatory costs that bank valuation will decline. Under the new risk-based capital rules, exceeding the minimum requirements will cause C to rise substantially, thereby reducing bank (and stock) value. As banks approach the minimum equity capital boundary, management must be increasingly careful not to make decisions that will later decrease equity capital below the regulatory standard. Moreover, deposit insurance premiums are tied to equity capital levels. Thus, C gradually increases as banks approach minimum equity capital levels. The optimal use of debt occurs where V_L is maximized. Of course, bank management seeks to use an optimal financing mix of debt and equity to maximize the value of the firm.

As an example, assume the bank has made investments in loans and securities

5. See Franco Modigliani, and Merton Miller, "Corporate Income Taxes and the Cost of Capital: A Correction," *American Economic Review* (June 1963), pp. 433–443 and Stephen A. Buser, Andrew H. Chen, and Edward J. Kane, "Federal Deposit Insurance, Regulatory Policy, and Optimal Capital Structure, *Journal of Finance* (March 1981), pp. 51–60.

that are expected to earn $1 million per year based on a rate of return of 10%. The unlevered value of the firm, or V_U, equals $1 million/0.10 = $10 million. The bank borrows $12 million in insured deposits and has a 30% income tax rate, such that $tD = 0.30 \times 12 million = $3.6 million. Regulatory costs are as follows: (1) deposit insurance premium is $0.10 \times ($12,000,000/$100) = $12,000; (2) management compliance costs are $200,000 per year (e.g., compliance officer salary, office space, equipment, etc.), and reporting requirements are $300,000 per year (e.g., loan officers must document that loans are consistent with regulatory guidelines). The value of the bank then is $V_L = 10 million + $3.6 million – $12,000 – $200,000 – $300,000 = $13,088,000. Clearly, the tax deductions of deposit interest exceeds regulatory costs, such that the bank would likely benefit from further increasing its use of deposits and decreasing equity capital. Figure 11.2 summarizes this analysis and shows an optimal debt level corresponding to bank value maximization. The equity position of the bank currently equals $S = V_L - D = $13,088,000 – $12,000,000 = $1,088,000, such that the equity/total assets ratio is $1,088,000/$13,088,000 = 0.083 or 8.3%. Because this equity ratio well exceeds regulatory minimums of 3%, assuming the bank does not have abnormally high asset-risk levels, increased leverage likely would boost bank (and share) valuation.

Corporate Control

It is possible that greater debt usage increases stockholders' **corporate control** of management and, therefore, the bank's operations. That is, more concentrated ownership in the hands of fewer shareholders tends to enhance management control. In closely held banks, because the owners are often the executive officers, minimal conflicts of self-interest arise. In banks that are not closely held, however, it is possible, for example, that managers may make decisions to protect and enhance their careers at the expense of shareholders. This potential conflict between principals (shareholders) and agents (managers) is known as an "agency cost" problem.

Although shareholder meetings should normally resolve conflicts of this kind, management might dominate such meetings under some circumstances. For example, if equity ownership is diluted among a large number of owners, individual owners might view themselves as having a negligible effect on the outcome of stockholder meetings. Faced with the costs of collecting information necessary to vote intelligently on issues raised at meetings, many owners may opt out of bank control. This likelihood does not necessarily mean that bank managers can act imprudently. Poor performance will tend to stir interest among shareholders concerning management capability. Also, the bank may become a **hostile takeover** target—that is, if its shares are undervalued, well-managed banks might seek to purchase a controlling interest in the bank and remove existing management. If shareholders finance bank assets with a greater proportion of debt, individual owners have a greater vested interest in

FIGURE 11.2   Bank Valuation with Interest Tax Deductions on Debt
as Well as Regulatory Costs ($ million)

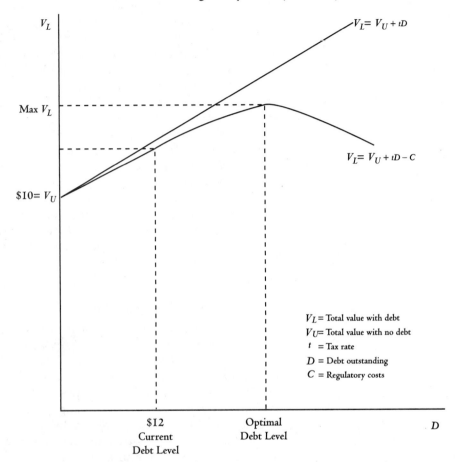

stockholder meetings and, in turn, management control is more easily achieved.[6]
Agency costs also can be reduced by linking management compensation to
stock prices by offering stock options and bonuses. Finally, shareholders have
preemptive rights that enable them to maintain their proportionate ownership

6. For banks using large amounts of nondeposit liabilities, it is possible that the degree
of financial leverage employed by shareholders could be limited. Uninsured debtholders seeking to protect their claims from new debtholders' claims as well as from potential bankruptcy costs incurred in failure can be expected to require debt covenants
that place an upper bound on bank leverage. To this extent, concentration of ownership would tend to be reduced, as well as the associated control of bank management
by shareholders.

share in the event a new issue to stock is made. This right reduces dilution of ownership across many owners and increases the vested interest of existing shareholders. In doing so, the agency cost problem is mitigated to some degree.

Market Timing

Cyclical price movements in the debt and equity markets can affect bank financing decisions. If the level of interest rates is relatively high and debt prices are depressed, it may be cheaper to use equity financing, even accounting for the tax deductibility of interest. Thus, general market conditions may at times favor equity over debt. Alternatively, if inflation is expected to increase in the near future, debt may be preferred over equity because interest payments could be made in "cheaper" dollars as the nominal value of currency falls over time.

Bank income can also affect debt usage by banks. For example, the marginal tax rate of the bank may be sufficiently low to warrant the use of equity over debt, as in the case of considerable income earned from municipal bonds not exposed to ordinary income taxes, loan losses, depreciation, and other noncash expenses. Alternatively, marginal tax rates may decline due to low net operating income.

Asset Investment Considerations

Bank asset and capitalization decisions are interrelated to some extent. For example, under the Garn–St. Germain Act of 1982, banks can lend no more than 15% of their capital, plus an additional 10% of loans secured by marketable collateral, to any individual borrower (i.e., the previous limitation was 10% of capital). Restrictions also exist on the purchase of various securities investments held by the bank (as opposed to a securities subsidiary). Additionally, as asset risk increases, more bank capital is needed to absorb potential losses. As already discussed, risk-based capital rules (see Tables 11.2 and 11.3) tie capital closely to the risks of different bank assets and commitments.

Dividend Policy

Shareholders usually desire the payment of some proportion of bank earnings in the form of cash dividends, because they either wish to consume part of their investment income or because they want to diversify their investment holdings. Most owners also want regular and predictable dividend payments. A sudden decrease in dividends would likely raise questions among shareholders concerning the bank's profitability and cause share prices to decline. Thus, bank management should establish and maintain a dividend policy.

In developing a dividend policy, the bank needs to determine its payment strategy. One approach is to use fixed dividend payments. This strategy satisfies shareholder demands for consistent returns, but if earnings decline, this approach may force the bank to raise external debt and equity to finance operations, regardless of their costs. Alternatively, a fixed dividend payout ratio strategy could be implemented, which means that a specific percentage of net income is distributed to owners. This strategy does not constrain the bank's financing choice as much as the fixed dividend strategy; however, it causes dividends to vary with net income over time.

Considerable controversy surrounds the question of why shareholders wish to receive income in the form of dividends instead of capital gains. If shareholders sold shares of stock to consume income or diversify more fully, they could do so when they wished to rather than when the firm distributed dividends. Also, receiving income in capital gains form defers income taxes until such gains are realized, which is a clear advantage relative to receiving periodic dividends. Despite these (and perhaps other) disadvantages of dividends, it is generally true that a sizeable proportion of earnings is paid out as dividends to shareholders. A long-standing rationale for this is practice that individuals simply prefer to receive cash returns sooner rather than later because of risk aversion concerning uncertainty in the future. In this way the duration of the stock is reduced to reflect lower price risk. Alternatively, some individuals may prefer the convenience of regular dividends, which involve no transactions cost. In general, differences in individuals' preferences cause "clienteles" to exist, which firms attempt to attract by appropriately setting dividend policy. A more recent argument is that firms pay dividends as a way to signal shareholders of expected future changes in earnings. Unfortunately, the "optimal" dividend policy in the sense of maximizing share price remains somewhat of a puzzle. Perhaps management's best approach here is historical experience and keeping in touch with the needs of the bank's shareholders.

Debt Capacity

It is generally preferable to avoid using the maximum amount of debt possible in order to preserve some amount of financial flexibility. If a bank borrowed to the limit of capital regulations, for example, it may be unable to take advantage of an unexpected investment opportunity. Some amount of borrowing capacity provides slack that can be used to meet unanticipated liquidity problems. Also, an unexpected loss could push borderline capital below regulatory requirements, thereby provoking added compliance costs. Thus, a reasonable amount of debt capacity is needed as a reserve to help cover potential capital demands.

Transactions Costs

Costs of issuing securities can affect bank financing plans. The acquisition of debt is normally much more costly for nonfinancial corporations than it is for banking institutions. Banks have easier access to credit markets than do nonfinancial firms, mainly because of their intermediary role as depository institutions and their access to insured deposits.

In contrast to most nonfinancial firms, however, all but the largest banks would find the transactions costs of equity issues relatively high. High transactions costs are due to the generally smaller size of bank issues of equity stock as compared to nonfinancial, corporate issues. Transactions costs, including registration with the Securities and Exchange Commission (SEC), underwriting expenses, legal fees, and other expenses, have a large fixed component that raise the per-share cost of smaller issues. Thus, economies of scale in transactions costs make public offerings of equity fairly expensive for most banks. To sidestep the costs of a public offering, banks can use a private stock issue to raise new equity capital. Other reasons for private sale of stock are that the funds can be raised in a relatively short period of time, no SEC registration is required, and underwriter fees can be avoided.

Mergers and Acquisitions

External growth through mergers and acquisitions generally requires raising new capital to purchase a controlling equity interest in the target institution(s). The mix of debt and equity used to finance external growth is complicated by the existing capital structures of the bank itself and the target institution(s). The consolidated banking organization must meet regulatory capital requirements, be consistent with the desires of the acquiring (and possibly the target) shareholders, and fulfill other management criteria previously discussed. For example, a common-for-common (stock) exchange in an acquisition would dilute the earnings per share of the buyer (or bidder), if the seller's (target) stock had a relatively high price-earnings ratio. If a buyer could use excess debt capacity plus cash to purchase the seller's shares, however, no dilution of earnings per share would occur.

On the other hand, banks anticipating a takeover attempt by another institution may repurchase equity. By repurchasing equity and increasing concentration of ownership, the ability of outsiders to seize voting control through buying publicly available shares is diminished. However, such a capital strategy could compromise other factors influencing the capital position of the bank, such as excessive financial risk due to higher leverage.

Experts anticipate continued consolidation of the banking industry in the years to come, especially in view of the recent passage of the Financial Services Modernization Act of 1999. Mergers and acquisition (M&A) activity can be broken down into mega, middle market, and small bank deals. As previously covered in Chapter 4, megamergers involve the world's largest banks. M&As involving purchases of institutions with assets in the $500 million to $5 billion range represent the middle market. At least in the United States, the major buyers have been large national organizations that are taking advantage of interstate banking deregulation, in addition to the fact that internal growth is more expensive under the more restrictive risk-based capital requirements. In the 1990s the pace of M&A activity among small and medium-sized banks pushed up their stock prices from market/book ratios in the range of 1.0–1.5 to a range of 2.0–2.5. In combination with the high stock market level at the end of the 1990s, these lofty stock prices tended to slow the speed of middle market consolidation in the banking industry. Finally, many small banks are being purchased by middle market banks, who are seeking to become regional level banks. Together, mega, middle market, and small bank M&A activities are reshaping the structure of the banking industry.

Internal Expansion

The rate at which a bank can internally expand its assets and still maintain its capital ratio is known as the **internal capital generation rate (ICG)**. This rate can be calculated as follows:

$$\text{ICGR} = \frac{1}{\text{Capital ratio}} \times \frac{\text{Return on}}{\text{assets}} \times \frac{\text{Earnings}}{\text{retention ratio}} \qquad 11.4$$

where the capital ratio is total equity/total assets, return on assets is net income after taxes/total assets, and the earnings retention ratio is net income available to shareholders minus preferred and common stock dividends/net income available to shareholders.

According to the ICGR ratio, decreasing the capital ratio allows a more rapid expansion of bank assets, all other things being equal.[7] Conversely, higher capital requirements increase the role of internally generated profits, as opposed to externally borrowed funds, in growing the asset base of the bank. It should be recognized that management's approach to financing asset growth is a function not only of the ICGR but regulatory rules concerning capital adequacy, competitive pressures, financial market conditions, and various internal factors, such as shareholder preferences for debt.

As an example of management usage of ICGR, assume that the bank has a total equity/total assets ratio of 4%. If the return on assets ratio is 1% and the retention ratio is 0.50, then ICGR = (1/.04) × 0.01 × 0.50 = 0.125 or 12.5%. Thus, total assets can be expanded 12.5% within the next year with no decrease in the capital ratio. In view of regulatory requirements on bank capital, ICGR is a useful tool for maintaining adequate capital. Also, it highlights the importance of capital in management planning of profit rates, growth rates, and dividend policy.

11.5 TRENDS IN BANK CAPITAL

Figure 11.3 shows trends in the ratio of equity capital to total assets, equity growth rates, and asset growth rates for all insured U.S. commercial banks during the period 1988–1998. As mentioned earlier, the Basle Agreement had

---

7. From a regulatory viewpoint, higher capital requirements are favored for this same reason, as rapid rates of growth increase the risk of bank failure according to historical evidence.

FIGURE 11.3   Trends in Bank Capital

Equity Capital to Total Assets Ratio

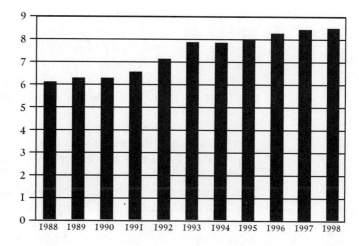

Percentage Growth in Total Assets and Equity Capital

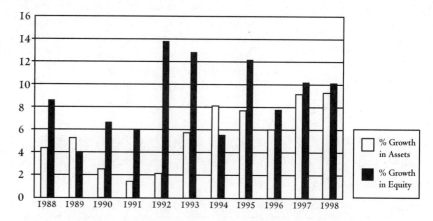

Sources: William B. English and W. Nelson, "Profits and Balance Sheet Developments at U.S. Commercial Banks in 1997," *Federal Reserve Bulletin* (July 1998); Antulio N. Bomfim and William B. English, "Profits and Balance Sheet Developments at U.S. Commercial Banks in 1998," *Federal Reserve Bulletin* (June 1999).

a favorable impact on bank capital ratios. In Figure 11.3 we see that average equity ratios among U.S. banks increased from the 6% range in the early 1990s to around 8% in the middle and late 1990s. The continued increase in equity ratios implies that equity was growing faster than assets, as documented in the lower part of Figure 11.3. Notice that the growing equity base enabled banks to gradually increase the rate of growth of their assets throughout the 1990s. This association highlights the fact that bank asset growth is constrained by equity capital growth. That is, if a bank sought to increase its size by 10%, it would have to raise capital by 10% to maintain the same capital ratio. Thus, a bank's ability to increase capital directly affects its ability to expand its asset base. Also notice that in the early 1990s the growth rate of assets was relatively low, which means that most banks were slowing their asset growth to bolster equity positions and meet new risk-based capital requirements.

Table 11.5 shows the average internal capital generation rate (ICGR) for all insured U.S. commercial banks for the years 1990 to 1998. As indicated by the table, this rate increases sharply from 0.54 percent in 1991 to 6.21 percent in 1992. Looking at the components of the ICGR, it is clear that a much higher earnings retention rate was common after the Basle capital standards were implemented (i.e., this rate increased from 0.07 in 1991 to 0.49 in 1992). Earnings retention rates declined somewhat throughout the 1990s as banks became well capitalized and further equity was not needed to meet capital requirements. Table 11.5 also shows that bank profitability strengthened after 1991, which helped boost banks' capital positions and ICGRs given higher earnings retention rates. The increased profit rates were due to the long, steady economic growth of the 1990s.

Figure 11.4 shows an upward trend in the period 1993–1998 in equity capital/total assets ratios for all U.S. banks regardless of asset size. A direct relationship can be determined between bank asset size and equity ratios. Small banks with less than $100 million in assets typically had equity ratios of about 10% in this sample period. By contrast, large banks with more than $10 billion in assets had equity ratios in the range of 7% to 8%. Because risk-based capital requirements do not specify that small banks carry more equity capital than large banks, this trend in capital ratios is voluntary on the part of smaller institutions.

TABLE 11.5	Average Internal Capital Generation Rate for All Insured U.S. Commercial Banks								
Ratio	1990	1991	1992	1993	1994	1995	1996	1997	1998
1/Capital ratio	15.63	14.99	13.93	12.74	12.69	12.48	12.09	11.88	11.26
Return on assets (%)	0.47	0.51	0.91	1.20	1.15	1.18	1.20	1.25	1.25
Earnings retention rate (%)	0.05	0.07	0.49	0.58	0.42	0.43	0.30	0.35	0.33
Internal capital generation rate (%)	0.37	0.54	6.21	8.87	6.13	6.33	4.35	5.20	4.64

Source: Antulio N. Bomfim and William B. English, "Profits and Balance Sheet Developments at U.S. Commercial Banks in 1998," *Federal Reserve Bulletin* (June 1999).

FIGURE 11.4 Equity Capital/Total Assets by Asset Size, 1998

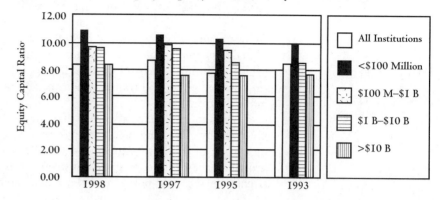

Source: FDIC *Quarterly Banking Profile* (Fourth Quarter 1998).

SUMMARY

Bank capital management is a controversial subject because regulators and share-holders have differing viewpoints concerning the adequacy of capital. Regulators consider bank capital as a cushion to absorb operating losses. Bank capital for regulatory purposes has two components: Tier 1 capital and Tier 2 capital. New international risk-based capital requirements under the Basle Agreement became effective at year-end 1992 and caused U.S. banks to raise equity capital as a percentage of both risk-adjusted assets and total assets. New risk-based deposit insurance pricing that is linked to bank capital levels and supervisory ratings became effective in 1994. Also, new market risk capital rules were implemented in 1998. Capital rules force shareholders to coinsure bank losses with the FDIC, whereas deposit insurance premiums are scheduled to cover losses in excess of bank equity capital. These regulatory policies are intended to preserve safety and soundness in the banking system and, at the same time, not disadvantage banks relative to other financial service companies as well as foreign bank competitors. Although risk-based capital rules focus on credit risk and market risk, they are expected to broaden over time to encompass other types of risk, such as liquidity risk, in addition to further refinement of credit risk measurement.

Shareholders view capitalization (or the mix of debt and equity funds used to finance bank assets) from the standpoint of maximizing the value of their ownership claims. Although added debt increases the interest burden of the bank and also increases the probability of failure, the tax deductibility of interest expenses lowers the cost of debt financing relative to equity financing. In nonfinancial, corporate enterprises debtors would require higher interest rates as financial leverage increases or would impose limitations on corporate borrowing. By contrast, banks obtain a large proportion of their funds from federally insured depositors who are not exposed to default risk and, therefore, do not monitor bank borrowing. As such, capital requirements are the main limitations on borrowing faced by banks. Given the regulatory requirements on capital adequacy and deposit insurance costs, bank shareholders need to consider the following areas in making capital structure decisions: (1) financial risk, (2) ownership control, (3) management control, (4) market timing, (5) asset investment considerations, (6) dividend policy, (7) transaction costs, (8) mergers and acquisitions, and (9) internal expansion.

Trends in bank capital reveal that the U.S. banks bolstered their capital positions by increasing their earnings retention rates subsequent to the implementation of the Basle Agreement in 1992. Also, the long, steady economic growth of the 1990s contributed to strong rates of return on assets that further strengthened capital positions and internal capital generation rates.

Key Terms and Concepts

Bank capital

Basle Agreement

Book value of equity

Capital adequacy

Capital impairment

Capital reserves

Corporate control

Common stock

Credit risk capital requirements

Deposit Insurance National Bank (DINB)

Earnings per share (EPS)

Form for Analyzing Bank Capital (FABC)

Federal Deposit Insurance Corporation (FDIC)

Financial leverage

Federal Reserve Board (FRB)

Hostile takeover

General market risk

Internal capital generation rate (ICGR)

International Lending Supervision Act

Market risk capital requirements

Market value of equity

Moral hazard problem

Office of the Comptroller of the Currency (OCC)

Off-balance sheet activities

Preferred stock

Provision for loan losses (PLL)

Reserve for loan losses

Risk-adjusted assets

Risk-based capital rules

Risk-based deposit insurance

Specific risk

Subordinated notes and debentures

Surplus

Tier 1 capital

Tier 2 capital

Total capital

Undivided profits

Variable-rate deposit insurance

Questions

11.1   What is bank capital? Why is the reserve for loan losses not counted as part of equity capital?

11.2   Is the balance sheet an accurate source of information in calculating bank capital?

11.3 What are the three key functions of bank capital? How do banks differ from nonfinancial firms in terms of capitals levels?

11.4 Why are notes and debentures considered bank capital?

11.5 How are notes and debentures related to "market discipline"?

11.6 How much capital is adequate?

11.7 Why is measuring adequate capital from a regulatory viewpoint difficult?

11.8 Define Tier 1 and Tier 2 capital. What are the risk-adjusted capital requirements?

11.9 Explain the problems of using uniform capital requirements.

11.10 Why has regulation switched to risk-based capital requirements?

11.11 What is the credit risk formula for the risk-based capital requirement? How does market risk affect capital requirements?

11.12 What five options does the FDIC have in handling a distressed bank?

11.13 How are variable-rate deposit insurance premiums determined by the FDIC? What is the moral hazard problem inherent in deposit insurance?

11.14 What are the advantages of debt financing to bank shareholders?

11.15 What are the disadvantages of debt finance to bank shareholders?

11.16 Why are the capital ratios of small and large banks different? Will ratios change in the future?

11.17 What is the "agency cost" problem? How can it be reduced?

11.18 Market risk capital requirements were implemented in 1998 in countries complying with the Basle Agreement. In general, what two types of risk do these new requirements address?

11.19 How is value-at-risk (VAR) used in market risk capital requirements?

11.20 How does specific risk affect market-risk equivalent assets?

11.21 Go the Federal Deposit Insurance Corporation (FDIC) web site at *http://www.fdic.gov/bank/historical/bank/index.html* and look up recent bank failures. Print out the information about one of the banks. Given the alternatives discussed in the text, how did the FDIC handle the failure?

11.22 Visit the web site for the Office of the Comptroller of the Currency (OCC) at *http://www.occ.treas.gov/econ.htm* and select one of the research paper in their working paper series. Write a one-page abstract of the article.

11.23 The Bank for International Settlements (BIS) routinely updates information on risk-based capital requirements. Go to their web site at *http://www.bis.org/publ/index.htm* and print out the latest update.

Problems

11.1   Given the following information, calculate Tier 1 and Tier 2 capital.

	($ thousands)
Common stock	$ 30,000
Perpetual preferred stock	5,000
Surplus	2,000
Undivided profits	100,000
Capital reserves	1,000
Reserves for loan and lease losses	5,000
Subordinated notes and debentures	2,000

(a) If the bank has total assets ($ thousands) of $2,840,000, does it have adequate capital under regulatory standards?

(b) If risk-adjusted assets equal $2,000,000, is capital adequate?

(c) If an analysis of market risk revealed that the bank had a value-at-risk (VAR) equals $300,000, and its adjusted value of credit-risk-weighted assets $1,500,000, is capital still adequate?

11.2   Given the following information, calculate risk-adjusted assets for credit risk purposes:

	($ thousands)
Vault cash	$ 50
Cash balances at district Federal Reserve bank	100
U.S. government securities	250
Mortgage-backed bonds	300
Home loans	200
Corporate bonds	100
Commercial loans	800

11.3   In Problem 11.2 assume that the $300 invested in mortgage-backed bonds is in the bank's trading account. If VAR and specific risk for these securities are estimated to be $50 and $25, respectively, what is
(a) market-risk equivalent assets?
(b) modified risk-adjusted assets?

11.4   Suppose Bank One has earnings before interest and taxes (EBIT) equal to $10 million and interest expenses equal to $8 million. It has 1 million shares of common stock outstanding. If EBIT increased by 10%, what would be the percentage change in earnings per share (EPS)?

11.5 Calculate the internal capitalization rate using the following information:

Net income	$ 100
Dividends	40
Total equity	800
Total assets	10,200

(a) What does this rate mean to the bank?
(b) If the regulatory standard for capital is 3%, what is the maximum asset growth rate implied for the bank?
(c) How would a higher capital standard affect the bank's asset growth?

Overall Assessment of Capital Adequacy

First National Bank (FNB) had maintained its capital ratios according to Basle Agreement standards in the past. That is, it never had fallen below the minimum total risk-based capital ratio of 8%, the Tier 1 risk-adjusted ratio of 4%, or the leverage ratio (or Tier 1 to total assets) of 3%. However, in recent years the bank's capital ratios decreased to the point where their capital position was marginal or near the borderline.

Jack Mead was a bank examiner reporting to the Federal Reserve district office in the region. He had received news yesterday that FNB was coming up for review by his staff next month. In preparation for the upcoming on-site visit, he had gone over a chart of FNB's capital ratios and was concerned about their trends. Peer group banks did not exhibit similar downward trends; indeed, strong economic growth in the region had contributed to strengthening capital ratios at some of FNB's competitors.

He decided to place a call to the CEO's office to discuss the timing of the review and express some preliminary concerns about FNB's capital adequacy. The CEO's attitude was positive and a copy of management's strategic plan was faxed to Jack to help him better understand the bank's goals, objectives, and business conditions.

Jack brought the plan home with him that evening to begin reviewing the situation. His first reaction to seeing the concise and well-organized five-page strategic plan was one of the relief. Effective strategic plans enable management to be proactive rather than reactive in responding to market forces. Such plans are long term in nature and integrate a variety of management areas, including asset deployment, funding sources, capital formation, management, marketing, operations, and information systems. They serve to not only provide management direction and leadership but communicate bank goals and objectives throughout the organization.

In the capital section of the plan, Jack noted the following key areas and related discussion:

- *Growth:* The bank sought to keep pace with the region's strong economic growth by rapidly expanding the loan portfolio. Many new credit opportunities were opening up due to the bank's ability to offer a wider menu of financial services to its customers under the new Financial Services Modernization Act of 1999. The evidence indicated that loan concentration had increased somewhat, especially with respect to certain local industries that had been particularly successful and, subsequently, had increased their credit lines with bank. Bank management appeared to have become more risk tolerant in light of the long period of good economic times.
- *Dividends:* The bank is owned by a bank holding company and was dedicated to paying substantial dividends to fund the holding company's expansion goals. The bank holding company was attempting to expand beyond its traditional home state into adjacent states.
- *Access to additional capital:* Because the bank was relatively small, its access to capital markets was limited. However, this limitation was not considered to be restrictive due to the fact that the bank holding company could be relied upon to assist them with capital funds. The bank indicated that it was sensitive to current shareholders' desire to avoid the diluting effect of new capital. Under Federal Reserve policy, the bank holding company is expected to be a source of strength in terms of liquidity or capital funds for subsidiary banks.
- *Earnings:* Net interest margins (NIMs) had been exceptionally high from an historical standpoint. The NIM had been favorably impacted by low interest rates and strong loan demand that allowed them to widen the spread over interest costs. Nonetheless, NIM and the rate of return on assets (ROA) had fluctuated more than peer group banks over the last five years. The bank

had recently purchased interest-only strips (IOs) and principal-only strips (POs), which have more price risk than other assets, in order to better hedge the interest rate risk on balance sheet. Also, in an effort to address ROA volatility, the bank had strengthened its collateral and guarantees to upgrade the credit quality of its loan portfolio. Finally, the bank had increased its allowance for loan and lease losses in the last two years.

- *Bank stock prices:* FNB's stock price relative to book value was below its peer group by about 25%. Management made clear that it believed the stock was undervalued as opposed to low-valued due to a lack of investor confidence.

- *Fixed bank assets:* The bank had a central location for its main office plus three local branch offices. All facilities were refurbished in recent years by the bank holding company and electronic payments services installed to ensure that the bank could offer the full array of banking, securities, and insurance services.

Given this preliminary information, step into Jack's role and write a report for his staff prior to their visit to the bank. The report should cover each of the strategic plan areas and provide an evaluation of capital strengths and weaknesses implied by the plan. Importantly, it should set the stage for their overall assessment of FNB's capital adequacy.

Liabilities Management

Inflationary surges in the 1960s and 1970s, competition in the financial services industry, and deregulation of deposit rates in the 1980s spurred banks to innovate many new sources of funds, which have dramatically transformed the liability side of their balance sheets and put pressure on banks' operating costs. The higher interest cost of liabilities significantly affected banks' profitability and interest rate risk exposure. Many banks sought to increase noninterest sources of revenues due to narrowing spreads on interest income and interest expenses. More recently, in the 1990s interest rate levels dropped to historic lows that decreased cost pressures on banks. However, the low rates offered on deposit accounts caused outflows of deposit funds, as customers searched for higher yields in the money and capital markets. Interest sensitive deposit costs and competition from financial markets for sources of funds have increased the challenges for liabilities management in the banking industry. For these reasons it is essential to understand the different types of bank liabilities. In this chapter we begin by summarizing each source of bank funds and their distinguishing features. Next, historical trends of the mix of different liabilities employed by U.S. banks are covered. Finally, various aspects of estimating the costs of bank funds are discussed, including how those costs can affect bank profitability. ■

12.1 STRUCTURE OF BANK LIABILITIES

Demand deposits have historically dominated the liability structure of commercial banks. Savings and time deposits normally played a significant but secondary role in the acquisition of deposit funds, and **nondeposit funds** were almost nonexistent. Beginning in the 1960s, however, the liability structure of commercial banking began to change substantially. For example, by the mid-1960s, time and savings deposits surpassed demand deposits as the primary source of bank funds. In the 1970s nondeposit borrowings grew rapidly and emerged as a major new source of funds for larger banking institutions. Additionally, the variety of deposit and nondeposit accounts and securities offered to the public by commercial banks greatly expanded. Deregulation of deposit rates of interest in the 1980s further expanded the variety of deposit accounts offered by banks. Finally, low interest rate levels in the 1990s have prompted banks to offer deposit customers alternative money market and investment accounts. This section looks at deposit and nondeposit sources of bank funds as well as the historical developments that shaped the new liability structure of commercial banking.

Money and Payment Systems (http://www.wiso.gwdg.de/ifbg/geld.html), *a German web site, has historical information on the development of money and payments systems around the world.*

Deposit Sources of Funds

Bank deposits may be categorized as either core deposits or purchased deposits. **Core deposits** are typically deposits of regular bank customers, including business firms, government units, and households. **Purchased deposits** are acquired on an impersonal basis from the financial market by offering competitive interest rates. Core deposits provide a stable, long-term source of funds, whereas purchased deposits serve as a liquidity reserve that may be tapped when needed.

Extensive use of purchased deposits may expose a bank to liquidity problems. In contrast to core deposits, a large proportion of purchased deposits may not be insured by the Federal Deposit Insurance Corporation (FDIC). Also, unlike core deposits that normally provide both explicit interest earnings and implicit service returns, purchased deposits provide only explicit interest earnings. These differences cause purchased deposits to be much more sensitive to both changes in bank risk and interest rates than core deposits. If the financial market perceives a decline in a bank's safety and soundness, its purchased deposits would have to be rolled over at higher rates and may even cease to be available as depositors shy away from placing liquid assets in institutions that may become insolvent. Thus, the risks and returns of core deposits and purchased deposits differ considerably from one another.

Deposit accounts can be categorized as follows: demand deposits, small **time and savings deposits**, and **large time deposits**. As a consequence of deposit rate deregulation over the last decade (see Managerial Issues), both small and large time deposits can serve the dual roles of core and purchased deposit sources of funds.

MANAGERIAL ISSUES

Deposit Rate Regulation, Bank Innovation, and Deregulation

Financial crises in the late 1800s, and particularly the Great Depression in the 1930s, motivated Congress to pass the Glass-Steagall Act as part of the 1933 banking acts. Under Glass-Steagall, payment of interest on demand deposits was prohibited. It was believed that interest payments caused intense competition between banks that induced them to make riskier loans in an effort to pay the high costs of deposits. The same logic was applied to a 1935 extension of the Glass-Steagall Act that gave the Board of Governors of the Federal Reserve System the power to set deposit rate ceilings (**Regulation Q**) affecting all federally insured banks.

Deposit rate ceilings led to a series of "credit crunches" in the 1960s and 1970s. In 1966, for example, market rates rose above deposit rate ceilings. On previous occasions ceiling rates were increased; however, the Fed did not change the ceiling rate this time. Large certificate of deposit (CD) sales dropped considerably causing bank credit to dry up. Similar episodes of high interest rates in the periods 1969–1970 and 1973–1974 likewise caused credit contractions.

In an attempt to meet credit demands during these periods, banks and other depository institutions began innovating around deposit rate barriers. In 1966, for example, large banks acquired time deposit funds from the Eurodollar market. Subsequent extension of Regulation Q to these deposits led large banks in 1969 to make greater use of nondeposit sources of funds, including nonbank federal funds, repurchase agreements, and commercial paper issued by holding companies. These sources of funds did not play as large a role in the 1973–1974 credit crunch, due to the elimination of rate ceilings on large CDs.

Banks also began innovating new transactions accounts. As the general level of interest rates edged upward in the 1960s and 1970s, they began to offer payments in kind and to indirectly pay interest on demand deposit balances. Payments in kind involved nonprice benefits such as free checking and branch facilities offering greater convenience. Indirect payments of interest were offered in the form of gifts for opening new accounts and sweep accounts for large depositors that automatically transferred checking balances over some amount to repurchase agreements, money market funds, and other short-term,

---

CHECKABLE DEPOSITS Checkable deposits, including demand deposits, are transactions balances requiring relatively higher reserve requirements than other types of deposits. They may be classified into three categories: (1) consumer deposits, (2) corporate deposits, and (3) government deposits. Consumer deposit accounts may or may not be interest-bearing. Interest-bearing demand deposits—known as NOW (or negotiable order of withdrawal) accounts—were authorized nationwide in January 1981 under DIDMCA of 1980.[1] NOW accounts originally offered rates of interest up to 5.5% on balances held at commercial banks. First introduced in 1972 in the New England region, NOWs were instrumental in curtailing outflows of deposit funds to

---

1. NOWs are available not only to consumers but to government agencies, nonprofit organizations, and single proprietorships, with no distinction made between the person and the firm.

interest-bearing assets at the end of each day. Smaller depositors were offered **automatic transfer service (ATS)** accounts that allowed them to minimize transactions balances by automatically transferring funds from their interest-bearing savings account to their checking account as overdrafts occurred.

Bank innovation and rising competition for consumer deposits prompted Congress to deregulate applicable deposit rate ceilings. A summary of this deregulation is as follows:

- **Depository Institutions Deregulation and Monetary Control Act (DIDMCA of 1980)**

Authorized all depository institutions to sell **negotiable order of withdrawal (NOW) accounts** to individuals and nonprofit organizations in December 1980, as well as automatic transfer service (ATS) accounts. These accounts had interest rate ceilings initially imposed on them. A six-year phaseout of interest rate ceilings on time and savings deposits was planned.

- **Garn–St. Germain Depository Institutions Act of 1982**

Authorized all depository institutions to issue **money market deposit accounts (MMDAs)** in December 1982 with no interest rate restrictions and limited check-writing privileges.

- **Depository Institutions Deregulation Committee (DIDC)**

Established by DIDMCA of 1980, the DIDC authorized Super NOW accounts effective January 1983; reduced minimum balance requirements on MMDAs, Super-NOWs, and time deposits of 7–31 days maturity to $1,000 in January 1985, and eliminated the aforementioned requirements in January 1986 as well as rate ceilings on NOW accounts and passbook savings accounts. The DIDC was dissolved at the end of March 1987, as originally intended under DIDMCA of 1980. Unlike NOWs, Super NOWs offered market rates of interest. Later deregulation of interest rates in 1986 eliminated the distinction between NOWs and Super NOWS.

- **Remaining Regulatory Restrictions**

No interest payments on demand deposits or regular checking accounts are allowed and NOW and Super NOW accounts cannot be offered on commercial accounts. However, the Federal Reserve is currently proposing that this restriction be eliminated, which is likely in the near future. Other restrictions include the following: minimum early withdrawal penalties are required on time deposits; a maximum $150,000 limit on nonpersonal savings deposits is still in effect; and reserve requirements under Regulation D apply to transactions accounts.

money market mutual funds (MMMFs) when interest rates rose above Regulation Q ceilings at various times in the 1970s and 1980s.

The "NOW experience" of banks indicates that interest-bearing, transactions accounts are not much more costly than regular checking accounts. The reason for similar costs is that regular checking accounts have relatively higher *implicit*, or noninterest, service costs than NOW accounts, and banks tend to increase service charges on NOW accounts to offset some of the differences in interest costs. From the customer's standpoint, the mix of implicit, or noninterest, and *explicit*, or interest, pricing offered by banks influences the type of transactions account that is opened. From the perspective of bank management, both operational costs and consumer demands must be evaluated to price transactions accounts correctly.

Starting in January 1983, depository institutions were permitted to offer Super NOWs (SNOWs) with unregulated rates on balances equal to or exceeding $2,500. Like NOWs, SNOWs were subject to reserve requirements.

SNOWs enabled depository institutions to compete more effectively with MMMFs for household deposits. Even though SNOWs were at a disadvantage with MMMFs to the extent that reserve requirements were a tax, they were eligible for federal deposit insurance, which was not available for MMMF accounts. In early 1986, interest rate restrictions on NOWs were relaxed, eliminating any distinction between NOWs and SNOWs.

Corporate demand deposit accounts are still prohibited from paying interest. Most of these deposits are compensating balances that are required by banks in return for various commercial services, such as coin and currency services, check-clearing services, and credit services. As interest rates rose in the latter part of the 1970s and early 1980s, corporate treasurers complained of the higher opportunity costs of compensating balances. To accommodate corporate customers, banks began unbundling the costs of various financial services. Service fees were viewed by corporations as a more accurate way to price services than compensating balances in the high and volatile interest climate of the times. Also, service fees are tax deductible as a business expense, whereas income lost by maintaining noninterest-bearing compensating balances is not tax deductible. In terms of bank management, however, it is more difficult to use fees as opposed to balances. The cost of providing each product and service must be carefully examined to properly price each one. Also, service fee and compensating balance options must be negotiated with each customer. In the near future it is likely that the Federal Reserve will drop its prohibition on interest-bearing corporate transactions accounts.

SMALL TIME AND SAVINGS DEPOSITS Small deposits of less than $100,000 may be acquired through time deposits (otherwise known as **savings certificates**, or **retail CDs**) and savings deposits. Small time deposits can be offered with denominations as low as $1,000. These deposits have fixed maturities and yields that approximate those of Treasury securities of equal maturity. A slight premium is normally required by depositors over the Treasury yield, however, because these deposit instruments are nonnegotiable and have early withdrawal penalties attached to them. Small time deposits are normally categorized by maturity as (for example) 7 to 31 day, 32 day to 1 year, and greater than 1 year.

As deregulation of interest rate ceilings proceeded in the early 1980s, public demand for retail CDs steadily increased. Many large banks sought to take advantage of this consumerism movement by pricing retail CDs at yields slightly higher than Treasury yields. Subsequent to the initial entry of large banks, retail CDs have earned rates of interest slightly higher than Treasury security yields.

Savings deposits are interest-bearing deposits that do not have fixed maturities. Savings deposits can be set up periodically to cover overwithdrawals of transactions accounts (called ATS, or automatic transfer service) or to provide transactions funds by means of limited check-writing privileges. A good example of the latter type of savings account is the money market deposit account (MMDA). MMDAs have no rate restrictions and allow consumers to make up to six transfers (three by check) per month. Authorized under the Garn–St.

Germain Act of 1982, MMDAs were designed to compete with money market mutual funds (MMMFs). The accounts were highly successful, surpassing the $218 billion held by MMMFs only one year after their introduction in December 1981. Although their growth has been less spectacular since then, they represent a major source of savings deposits in banking today.

Small banks rely upon retail CDs as a major source of funds. Even though larger banks place less emphasis than small banks on retail CDs, they can be a valuable source of liquidity for larger banks, especially in the event of a liquidity crisis. In such circumstances, uninsured depositors typically withdraw their funds from the bank. On the other hand, insured retail CDs reduce the outflow of funds and so limit the extent of a liquidity crisis.

Due to the unattractiveness of low-interest bearing CDs in recent years, banks have been innovating new CD products. One such product is the market-indexed CD. This CD pays returns based on a market index such as the Standard & Poor's 500 or Chicago Board of Exchange Internet index. For example, the CD could offer 80% of capital gains and dividends earned on the market index. If the stock market falls in value, the depositor receives at a minimum their principal upon maturity. Thus, investors can participate in market upswings (e.g., the bull market of the 1990s) but be protected from losing their original investment capital. While a major advantage of these CDs is deposit insurance up to $100,000, they are generally longer-term CDs with maturities as high as 10 years. As such, only depositors interested in long-run savings would be inclined to purchase these CDs.

LARGE TIME DEPOSITS   Time deposits issued in denominations of $100,000 or more are known as **negotiable certificates of deposit** (NCDs or simply CDs). Large, or "jumbo," CDs are marketable securities with maturities ranging from 14 days to 18 months. First issued by First National City Bank of New York (now Citibank) in February 1961, NCDs were quickly offered by other money center banks and dealers, causing the volume of NCDs to expand rapidly. By 1966 these CDs were second only to Treasury bills among outstanding money market instruments.

Originally, large CDs were issued by New York banks in an attempt to retain corporate demand deposits that paid no interest. Rising short-term interest rates in the post–World War II period motivated corporate treasurers to draw down demand deposits and buy Treasury bills, commercial paper, and repurchase agreements with dealers. To stem this deposit outflow and retain their share of credit flows, large banks designed the CD to appeal to corporate depositors. Initially subject to Regulation Q interest rate ceilings, these caps were removed on large CDs by May 1973.

Later, large CDs became the primary source of funds for liability management. Most CD buyers are still nonfinancial corporations, but other market participants, such as MMMFs, now buy CDs also. Because CDs are commonly issued in denominations exceeding the $100,000 FDIC insurance limit (e.g., a round lot in the secondary market is usually $1 million), the default risk of the issuing bank can affect rates of interest on these CDs. Indeed, a tiered CD market has evolved in which money center and large regional banks tend to offer CDs at lower rates than smaller banks.

EURODOLLAR DEPOSITS A **Eurodollar deposit** is a dollar-denominated deposit in a bank office outside of the United States.[2] Originally dominated by European-based bank offices, the term still applies to out-of-country dollar deposits in general. Eurodollar deposits have grown with international business expansion, as firms maintain dollar deposits in foreign countries.

Large banks normally tap Eurodollar deposits through their foreign branch offices. For example, foreign branches sell Eurodollar CDs, which are dollar-denominated negotiable CDs. These funds are then loaned to domestic offices. Because the secondary market is smaller compared with domestic CDs, and FDIC deposit insurance is unavailable, Eurodollar CDs usually have higher yields than domestic CDs. Eurodollar deposits, like domestic deposits, can be issued in many different maturity ranges and denominations. Fixed rate and variable rate deposits are available.

BROKERED DEPOSITS **Brokered deposits** are small and large time deposits obtained by banks from intermediaries seeking insured deposit accounts on behalf of their customers. Deposit brokers appeared in the early 1980s when depositors began to face increased risk of loss because of bank failure. An often-cited example of this risk was the failure of Penn Square Bank in July 1982. For the first time since the Great Depression, federal regulators liquidated a large bank, rather than allowing the bank to be merged or acquired by a solvent bank with no loss to depositors. Depositors that were not insured (because their balances exceeded the $100,000 FDIC limit) suffered large losses, due to the fact that only 55% of uninsured claims were covered by year-end 1985.

Because interest rates on large, negotiable CDs in denominations of $100,000 were unregulated, and rates on smaller, retail-level CDs were deregulated for the most part by year-end 1982, brokers entered deposit markets to bring together depositors (sellers) seeking insured accounts with banks and other depository institutions (buyers) demanding lower-cost, insured deposit funds. Electronic funds transfer technology enabled brokers to cost-effectively "split" $1 million (for example) into ten $100,000, fully-insured, deposit accounts at 10 different depository institutions. Alternatively, brokers can offer smaller depositors better yields by pooling their deposits and selling "shares" in "participating" large CDs offering higher yields than smaller CDs.

Federal regulators have opposed the use of brokered deposits. In April 1982, for example, the FDIC announced that brokers could obtain only $100,000 of deposit insurance per bank, as is the case for any depositor. It was believed that, because insured depositors are less likely to "discipline" bank

---

2. Eurodollar deposits are a subset of Eurocurrency deposits involving currency deposits outside of their country of origin.

management by withdrawing their funds or charging higher rates on deposits, bank safety and soundness might be compromised to the extent that banks used nationally brokered deposits to grow excessively or to take excessive loan risks. However, the FDIC's rule on brokered deposits was struck down by a court decision in June 1984.

The FDIC Improvement Act of 1991 prohibits depository institutions that are not well capitalized to accept brokered deposits. Adequately capitalized banks can use brokered deposits subject to prior waiver by the FDIC, while well-capitalized banks can freely use these deposits without restriction (see Chapter 11 for definitions of these three capital categories for banks). Interest rates on brokered deposits must be in line with competitive market rates. These regulatory changes preclude institutions from acquiring deposits (by posting interest rates above those on insured deposits) to cover earnings losses. This type of behavior was repeatedly found in failing savings and loan associations in the 1980s and resulted in large increases in the later costs of closing many of those institutions. Also, banks with low supervisory ratings tended to use more brokered deposits than higher-rated institutions.

As a money management company, Oriental Trust (http://www.orientaltrust. com/) specializes in IRAs and Keogh plans. Detailed descriptions of different types of these products are provided at their web site.

IRA AND KEOGH PLANS **IRA** and **Keogh plans** are personal pension plans that individuals may use to defer federal income taxes on contributions and subsequent investment earnings. Keogh plans have been available to self-employed individuals since 1962. They allow up to 25% of earned, nonsalaried income but not greater than $30,000 to be deposited in a tax-deferred account. IRA plans were allowed for all individuals under the Economic Recovery Tax Act of 1981. IRAs enable individuals to set aside earnings for retirement up to an allowable maximum of $2,000 per year. IRS rules determine how much of these contributions can be deducted for income (if any). Both of these personal retirement accounts are subject to a 10-percent tax penalty if withdrawn before age 59 1/2. No penalty is paid under certain circumstances, including emergencies such as disability, medical expenses, or decreased life expectancy and withdrawals for higher education or first-time home expenses.

IRA products have expanded in recent years with the introduction of the Roth IRA under the Taxpayer Relief Act of 1997. Unlike traditional IRAs, contributions by savers are taxed but investment earnings and distributions are not taxed. Because withdrawals are not reportable income, they do not affect adjusted gross income during retirement or estate taxes paid by beneficiaries such as a surviving spouse or children.

IRAs and Keoghs have become a major source of long-term, stable deposit funds for banking institutions, which serve as account custodians. One problem with these new accounts is the intensity of market competition. IRAs can be offered by banks, savings institutions, brokerage firms, insurance companies, mutual funds, and employers with qualified pension, profit-sharing, or savings plans. To be competitive, banks must offer attractive interest rates and good service, both of which trim profit margins. Even so, these accounts are a source of funds that should not be overlooked.

MANAGERIAL ISSUES

Are Your Deposits Insured?

The Federal Deposit Insurance Corporation (FDIC) insures deposits of any individual or entity holding an account in a U.S.-insured commercial bank or savings association. A variety of deposit accounts are eligible for insurance, including checking, NOWs, savings, certificates of deposit (CDs), money market deposit accounts (MMDAs), and trust accounts. These accounts are insured up to a legal limit of $100,000 and in some cases higher amounts.

Some important insurance rules to keep in mind include the following:

- Only deposits payable in the United States (not overseas) are covered.
- Mutual funds, securities, and related investments products sold to customers are not covered.
- Official checks (including cashiers' checks, officers' checks, expense checks, loan disbursement checks, interest checks, outstanding drafts, negotiable instruments and money orders drawn on an institution) as well as certified checks, letters of credit, and travelers' checks are covered.
- Customers can have deposits in different FDIC-insured institutions that are separately covered. However, if the deposits are in various offices of a branch bank, they are added together to determine insurance coverage.
- Insurance coverage extends for six months beyond the date of death of a depositor.
- More than $100,000 of insurance is possible at a single institution due to the fact that each of the following types of accounts can be separately insured: single (or individual) accounts, joint accounts, testamentary accounts, and retirement accounts.
  - Single ownership offers $100,000 for the sum of all deposit accounts held by a depositor. As such, a person could not obtain more than $100,000 insurance by opening NOW, MMDA, savings, and other accounts at a single bank.
  - Joint accounts owned by two or more individuals are insured up to a limit of $100,000 per person.

Thus, if a person held three joint accounts with different persons at the same bank, the sum of their portion of deposits in each account would determine the extent of insurance coverage. If not specified, it is assumed that joint deposits are equally divided among the owners, unless otherwise stated on the deposit records.

- A testamentary account (otherwise known as a tentative or "Totten" trust account, revocable trust account, or "payable-on-death" account) is separately insured from single and joint accounts. In this account the grantor or depositor has indicated an intent upon death to transfer ownership of funds to a beneficiary. If there is more than one beneficiary, each beneficiary is eligible for $100,000 of insurance.
- Revocable living trusts, which appoint a trustee to oversee the funds for a beneficiary, are insured as single accounts, unless they are set up as testamentary trusts.
- Irrevocable trust accounts are insured separately of other accounts owned by an individual.
- IRA and Keogh funds are separately insured from nonretirement funds held by a depositor. These retirement accounts are added together for insurance purposes. However, IRA and Keogh time deposits placed before December 19, 1993, are separately insured from one another. The new Roth IRA is considered to be an IRA and receives no special treatment. By contrast, the new Education IRA is considered to qualify as an irrevocable trust account and, therefore, is separately insured.

Due to the specific definitions of each type of eligible account, it is wise to check with the insuring institution about the specific FDIC rules for these different types of insured accounts. Also, deposit insurance rules for pension plans, profit-sharing plans, and business accounts should be carefully evaluated. For further information, email the FDIC at *Consumer@FDIC.gov*, visit the FDIC's web site, or call a regional FDIC office.

Nondeposit Sources of Funds

Nondeposit funds are money market liabilities that are purchased for relatively short periods of time to adjust liquidity demands. Because they are typically used in liability management, they are often referred to as *managed liabilities*. The use of these purchased funds came about as a consequence of tight money periods in which deposit rate ceilings caused banks to develop alternative sources of funds. Unlike deposit funds, nondeposit funds typically are exempt from federal reserve requirements, interest rate ceilings, and FDIC insurance assessments.

Do you want more information about federal funds? Visit the social and behavioral science section in the National Science Foundation at http://www.nsf.gov/sbe/srs/nsf98328/start.htm.

FEDERAL FUNDS In general, **federal funds** are short-term, unsecured transfers of immediately available funds between depository institutions for use in one business day (i.e., overnight loans).[3] About 20% of the federal funds have maturities longer than one day. Banks typically either purchase or sell fed funds, depending on their desired reserve position, which is normally based on legal reserve requirements. Because Federal Reserve open market operations directly affect the quantity of bank reserves, fed funds rates are relatively more volatile than other money market rates. Also, in the last few days of the reserve maintenance period, the fed funds rate may jump significantly, if relatively low supplies of excess reserves are in the banking system.

Overnight loans usually are booked by verbal agreements between corresponding officers of depository institutions. Written contracts or brokers, or both, may be employed if the parties are unfamiliar with one another. Overnight loans may be put on a continuing contract basis in which they are automatically renewed unless otherwise notified. Such contracts are often arranged between large correspondent banks and smaller respondent institutions, and tend to lower transactions costs, such as brokers' fees and funds transfer charges.

REPURCHASE AGREEMENTS Nonbank firms supply funds to banks through **repurchase agreements** (**RPs**, or repos). An overnight RP can be defined as a secured, one-day loan in which claim to the collateral is transferred. Multiple-day RPs can be arranged for a fixed term ("term RPs") or on a continuing basis. An RP is created by the sale of securities in exchange for immediately available money with the simultaneous promise to buy back the securities at a specific date at a set price within the next year. The repurchase price is typically the initial sale price plus a negotiated rate of interest. U.S. Treasury and federal agency securities are normally used as collateral, which allows depository institutions to avoid reserve requirements, but CDs, mortgage-backed securities, and other securities may be used on occasion. The transaction is known as a reverse RP (or matched sale-purchase agreement) from the perspective of the purchaser of the securities (supplier of funds).

3. Immediately available funds can be defined as those bank funds that can be withdrawn or used for payment by the public on any given business day. They consist of the collected liabilities of commercial banks plus the deposit liabilities of Federal Reserve banks.

Because RP purchasers acquire title to the securities for the term of the agreement, they may use them to create another RP or to meet the delivery of a forward or futures contract, a short sale, or a maturing reverse RP. This flexibility makes the RP a low-risk money market instrument that dealers can use to meet diverse liquidity needs among investors, including business firms, depository institutions, state and local governments, and other financial institutions. Although RPs usually are available in denominations of at least $1 million (wholesale market), smaller denominations under $100,000 (retail market) have appeared in recent years. Retail RPs must have maturities of 89 days or less and, like wholesale RPs, are not subject to interest rate ceilings. However, deposits obtained from retail RPs are not federally insured.

RP contract provisions can be altered to fit the needs of the participants. For example, "dollar repurchase agreements" (dollar rolls) allow the seller to repurchase securities that are similar to but not identical to the securities originally sold. Another common example is the "flex repo" in which a customer can sell back securities to the dealer before the final maturity date.

The Federal Reserve Bank of Chicago has produced a nice reference for discount window activities of banks. The booklet contains information on the type of borrowers and credits, the discount rate, and more at http://www.frbchi.org/ loans/dwbooklet/ tablecontents.html.

DISCOUNT WINDOW ADVANCES Banks can borrow funds from the 12 regional Federal Reserve banks by means of a **discount window advance** (subject to the provisions of Regulation A). Advances can be used by banks to meet unanticipated reserve deficiencies or to meet more persistent outflows of funds that are transitory in nature (e.g., an unexpected loss of deposits, surge in credit demands, or natural disaster). Funds cannot be borrowed, however, either to arbitrage profits through acquiring higher-earning financial assets with advances or to supplement bank capital. Also, if alternative sources of funds are readily available, discount window borrowing is discouraged. Discount window borrowings normally are overnight loans that are deposited in the bank's reserve account at its Federal Reserve district bank. Extended credit is possible under exceptional circumstances to assist banks in adjusting to changing market conditions. Advances must be secured by approved collateral, such as U.S. Treasury securities and government agency securities, municipal securities, residential mortgages, short-term commercial notes, and other marketable securities. Also, interest and principal are due at maturity.

Prior to the Monetary Control Act of 1980, only Federal Reserve System member banks could use the discount window for reserve management purposes. However, this act enabled all depository institutions with transactions balances or nonpersonal time deposits (except bankers' banks) to access the discount window. One caveat here is that banks with less than adequate capital levels or low CAMEL bank ratings (i.e., 5 on a 5-point scale) are limited in their use of the discount window.

As the largest supplier of home mortgage credit in the United States, Federal Home Loan Banks or FHLB (http://www. fhlbanks.com/) is a privately capitalized, cooperative government-sponsored enterprise (GSE).

FEDERAL HOME LOAN BANK BORROWINGS The Federal Home Loan Bank (FHLB) in the past provided discount window services for savings and loans but the Financial Institutions Reform, Recovery, and Enforcement Act (FIRREA) of 1989 allowed banks access also. FHLB borrowings are less restrictive than the Federal Reserve's discount window. Maturity ranges from overnight to 30 years are available at competitive market rates. At times FHLB facility funds may have rates below the deposit rates available in competitive local markets. Borrowings are not intended to meet liquidity deficiencies and must be collateralized with bank assets (e.g., residential mortgage loans and mortgage-backed securities). Also, the composite CAMEL rating of an institution can affect its borrowing authority and collateral requirements.

BANKERS' ACCEPTANCES A bankers' acceptance is a time draft drawn on a bank by either an exporter or an importer to finance international business transactions. The bank may discount the acceptance in the money market to, in effect, finance the transaction.

An example perhaps best explains how banks use acceptances to acquire loanable funds. A U.S. importer (buyer) may obtain a *letter of credit* in its behalf from its bank. The letter of credit authorizes the foreign exporter (seller) to draw a draft at its foreign bank at a specified time in the future, which then forwards the draft and shipping documents to the U.S. bank issuing the letter of credit (perhaps through its U.S. correspondent bank).[4] If everything is in order, the issuing bank stamps "accepted" on the face of the time draft, and a negotiable instrument known as a bankers' acceptance is created. The acceptance can be discounted by the issuing bank for the account of the foreign bank. At this point the acceptance is a financial asset of the bank and a liability of the importer. Normally, however, the issuing bank also sells the acceptance in the secondary market. In this case the acceptance is being used as a source of funds in the sense of recouping funds committed to the foreign bank.

It is noteworthy that all parties concerned benefit from the acceptance transaction. Exporters receive payment for goods at the time of shipment, importers receive credit for the transit period of the goods, foreign banks usually obtain service fees, domestic banks obtain a new source of funds to finance loans (plus service fees), and money market participants have another interest-bearing instrument in which to invest funds temporarily.

The maturities on bankers' acceptances range from 30 to 180 days and are timed to coincide with the transit (and disposal) of goods. Market yields are only slightly above that of U.S. Treasury bills, due to the good international reputations of the issuing banks, which typically are large institutions. Banks earn not only the discount on the acceptance from corporate borrowers but a fee equal to a minimum of 1½% (i.e., ⅛th of 1% per month), depending on the credit rating of the borrower.

COMMERCIAL PAPER **Commercial paper** is a short-term, unsecured promissory note sold by large companies with strong credit ratings. Banks can use their holding companies to issue commercial paper and acquire loans and investments

---

4. This instrument is known as a time draft, as opposed to a sight draft that is payable to the exporter upon its presentation to the bank.

from them. Bank holding companies (BHCs), therefore, are another channel through which funds can be raised. Banks have also established independent companies, which are not holding companies, to issue commercial paper and then funnel the proceeds to one or more subsidiary banks by purchasing bank loans and investments.

Commercial paper is sold in $100,000 denominations with maturities normally ranging from 30 to 270 days. Little or no secondary market exists for commercial paper; however, some dealers may redeem notes prior to maturity. Most BHCs place new issues directly with institutional investors (i.e., direct paper) as opposed to using a securities dealer to make a public sale (i.e., dealer paper).

CAPITAL NOTES AND DEBENTURES Banks can purchase long-term funds by issuing **capital notes and debentures,** or senior debt capital. During the Great Depression, distressed banks raised much-needed funds by selling these kinds of debt issues. The stigma of this experience prompted the Comptroller of the Currency to discourage national banks from issuing senior debt securities until the 1960s. To provide banks more flexibility in managing their capital, the Comptroller ruled in 1962 that these debt securities could be counted as part of (unimpaired) capital in calculating lending limits on unsecured loans to any one borrower. Many banks quickly moved to sell notes and debentures due to this ruling.

Changing definitions of bank capital and associated regulatory requirements have caused banks to use notes and debentures sparingly. An interesting proposal by some industry experts is to force banks to issue some minimum quantity of senior debt securities. Because capital notes and debentures are uninsured, as discussed in Chapter 11, it is believed that the marketplace would price these issues according to risk and, therefore, provide some amount of "market discipline." Additionally, bank regulators could use bank debt prices as another way to detect possible problem situations.

Capital notes and debentures are subordinated, or second in order of claims, to bank deposits in the event of bank failure. Issues are made in a wide assortment of denominations and maturities in order to tailor them for sale to specific bank customers, including correspondent banks of the issuing bank. Normally, senior debt securities are issued by large banks, because small banks do not have as ready an access to the capital markets, and transactions costs are relatively high for smaller issues.

Federal Reserve Board Commercial Bank Examination Manual (http:// www.federalreserve.gov/ boarddocs/SupManual/ default.htm#cbem) *presents examination objectives and procedures that Federal Reserve System examiners follow in evaluating the safety and soundness of state member banks. You can find information about liabilities management in the liabilities and capital sections of the manual.*

12.2 BALANCE SHEET STRUCTURE OF BANK LIABILITIES

Table 12.1 provides information on the balance sheet composition of bank liabilities from 1990 to 1998 for all insured U.S. commercial banks. A number of trends can be observed in the data reported there. Interest-bearing liabilities decreased from about 76% of total assets in 1990 to about 71% of total assets

TABLE 12.1   Sources of Bank Funds Over Time: All Insured U.S. Commercial Banks

Balance Sheet Item	As a percentage of Average Net Consolidated Assets								
	1990	1991	1992	1993	1994	1995	1996	1997	1998
Interest-Bearing Liabilities	76.53	76.58	75.32	73.92	71.86	71.87	71.62	71.37	71.35
Deposits	63.44	64.45	62.94	60.26	57.34	56.28	55.87	55.01	54.67
In foreign offices	9.26	8.55	8.37	8.32	9.39	10.27	10.01	10.02	10.15
In domestic offices	54.18	55.90	54.56	51.94	47.96	46.01	45.86	44.99	44.53
Transaction accounts	6.19	6.72	7.65	8.24	7.80	6.63	4.75	3.62	3.12
Savings deposits (including MMDAs)	16.59	18.00	20.28	20.91	19.60	17.47	18.71	19.13	19.92
Large-denomination time deposits	11.44	9.89	7.42	5.81	5.23	5.77	6.42	7.08	7.34
Small-denomination time deposits	19.96	21.30	19.21	16.98	15.33	16.14	15.97	15.17	14.16
Gross Federal Funds Purchased and Repurchase Agreements	8.03	7.09	7.02	7.47	7.60	7.20	7.18	8.33	7.99
Other Interest-Bearing Liabilities	5.07	5.03	5.36	6.19	6.92	7.88	8.57	8.22	8.69
Noninterest-Bearing Liabilities	17.07	16.75	17.50	18.23	20.26	20.12	20.11	20.21	20.15
Demand deposits in domestic offices	12.79	12.59	13.24	13.86	13.49	12.68	12.82	12.16	11.00

Sources: William B. English and William R. Nelson, "Profits and Balance Sheet Developments at U.S. Commercial Banks in 1997," *Federal Reserve Bulleting* (June 1998); Antulio N. Bomfim and William B. English, "Profits and Balance Sheet Developments at U.S. Commercial Banks in 1998," *Federal Reserve Bulletin* (June 1999).

in 1998. The decline in interest rate levels over this period of time lowered the opportunity cost of holding demand deposits, which explains the increase in the proportion of total assets funded by noninterest-bearing liabilities from about 17% in 1990 to about 20% by the end of 1998. Also, equity capital increased throughout the 1990s due to favorable economic conditions and strong profitability.

Another obvious trend shown in Table 12.1 is increased use of higher-rate managed liabilities, such as large time deposits, fed funds, and RPs. The main reason is that banks were expanding their assets during the 1990s at a rate higher than core deposit growth rates would allow. Core deposits are less interest sensitive than managed liabilities and so are more difficult to attract than managed liabilities to fund strong asset growth. However, while most core deposit sources of funds shrank during the 1990s, savings deposits was an exception. Savings deposits increased from about 16.5% of total assets in 1990 to almost 20% of total assets by year-end 1998. This trend is due to the increasing use of "sweep" programs by banks. **Sweep programs** move funds from transactions accounts (e.g., NOW accounts) with reserve requirements to savings accounts with no reserve requirements. In many cases the deposits over a designated level are upstreamed from the bank to the parent bank holding company or another affiliate bank for reinvestment in commercial paper and other money market instruments. As such, these programs offer better average yields to depositors than transactions accounts alone and enable the bank to free up some reserves for investment in loans and other assets.

Table 12.2 compares the liability mix among different sizes of banks. Smaller banks ranked below the top 1,000 banks in total asset size had negligible foreign deposits, whereas the 10 largest U.S. banks financed about 20% of their assets with foreign deposits in 1998. The 10 largest banks also differ from smaller institutions in their proportions of other interest-bearing liabilities—primarily notes and debentures—which account for about 8% for the 10 largest banks compared to about 2.0% of total assets for smaller banks. In general, as bank size decreases (increases), greater emphasis is placed on retail deposits (managed liabilities). This changing structure of bank liabilities reflects the wholesale nature of larger banks. An unexpected increase in loan demand at a large bank could not be handled by retail CDs. Thus, the greater use of large-denomination CDs at larger banks is a natural consequence of their loan operations.

Figure 12.1 graphically compares interest rates on core (retail) deposits to other money market rates from 1987 to 1997. As shown there, the interest rate decline in the early 1990s is reflected in parallel downward movement in core deposit rates, six-month Treasury bill rates, and money market mutual fund (MMMF) rates. However, from 1994 to 1997 the interest rate offered by banks on core deposits was more than 1% below the other money market rates. This differential is justified by implicit service returns offered core depositors. Also, unlike MMMF accounts, core deposits are insured up to $100,000 per account by the federal government. Nonetheless, it is likely that banks'

TABLE 12.2	Sources of Bank Funds in 1998: Comparison by Bank Asset Size Rankings

Balance Sheet Item	As a Percentage of Average Net Consolidated Assets			
	Ten Largest Banks	Banks Ranked 11–100	Banks Ranked 101–1000	All Others
Interest-Bearing Liabilities	65.81	73.46	75.44	75.35
Deposits	47.65	51.42	62.45	71.76
In foreign offices	20.17	8.16	1.29	0.07
In domestic offices	27.48	43.36	60.16	71.70
Transaction accounts	0.99	1.75	4.24	11.17
Savings accounts (including MMDAs)	15.84	21.42	25.66	19.01
Large-denomination time deposits	4.62	7.36	10.01	11.10
Small-denomination time deposits	6.03	12.83	21.25	30.42
Gross Federal Funds Purchased and Repurchase Agreements	9.79	9.48	6.16	1.50
Other Interest-Bearing Liabilities	8.37	12.46	6.83	2.09
Noninterest-Bearing Liabilities	26.76	18.17	15.10	14.18
Demand deposits	8.46	12.41	11.89	13.08

Sources: William B. English and William R. Nelson, "Profits and Balance Sheet Developments at U.S. Commercial Banks in 1997," *Federal Reserve Bulletin* (June 1998); Antulio N. Bomfim and William B. English, "Profits and Balance Sheet Developments at U.S. Commercial Banks in 1998," *Federal Reserve Bulletin* (June 1999).

core deposits declined due to household transfers of deposits to other savings outlets. The 1990s stock market boom and introduction of online securities trading motivated many individuals to minimize money holdings and search for higher yields in capital markets.

Table 12.3 shows that **net interest margins** have decreased somewhat from 1995 to 1998 for all U.S. banks. The most likely explanation for this trend is that banks have been funding strong asset growth with greater proportions of higher-cost managed liabilities. Another factor was the shift by many banks from funding consumer lending via deposits to securitizing consumer loans (e.g., in 1995 about 15% of consumer loans were securitized compared to more than 30% by 1999). This shift moves consumer loans with higher average interest rates than other loan categories from an interest earning activity to a noninterest fee-based service. In this regard, the 10 largest banks with lower proportions of assets devoted to consumer loans than other banks experienced a slight increase in net interest margins from 1995 to 1998. Finally, it should be recognized that net interest margins declined on average about 50 basis

FIGURE 12.1   Core Deposit Rates at Insured
Commercial Banks, 1987–1997*

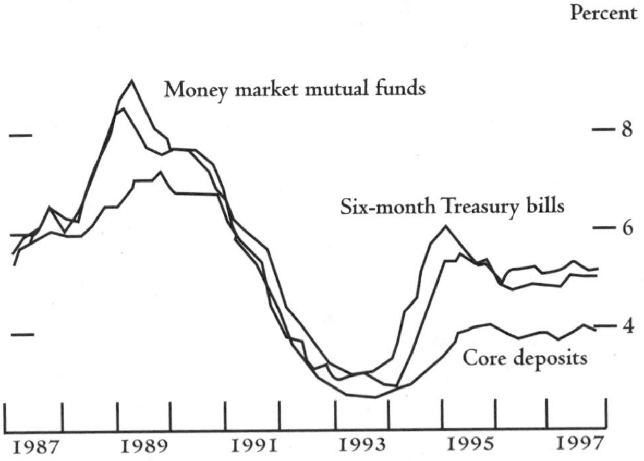

*The rate for core deposits is the average for NOW accounts, savings and money market deposit accounts, and small time deposits, and it excludes demand deposits, which do not bear interest.

Source: Federal Reserve Board, Statistical Release H.15, "Selected Interest Rates"; and *IBC's Money Fund Report.*

points from the early 1990s to the late 1990s. This narrowing of interest spreads was due to competitive loan markets, lower interest rate levels, and lower loan losses due to favorable U.S. economic conditions.

The 1990s ushered in a period of record low interest rates that presented different liability management problems than experienced by double-digit deposit rates in the 1980s. In the 1980s high deposit rates allowed banks to readily attract funds from the financial marketplace. Brokerage firms often

TABLE 12.3	Net Interest Margins for U.S. Commercial Banks by Asset Size Ranking: 1995–1998			
Bank Ranking (by Assets)	**1995**	**1996**	**1997**	**1998**
All banks	3.72	3.73	3.67	3.52
Largest 10	2.68	2.73	2.76	2.73
Banks ranked 11–100	3.78	3.84	3.85	3.71
Banks ranked 101–1,000	4.23	4.27	4.29	4.19
Banks not among the 1,000 largest	4.42	4.37	4.41	4.28

Source: Antulio N. Bomfim and William R. Nelson, ""Profits and Balance Sheet Developments at U.S. Commercial Banks in 1998," *Federal Reserve Bulletin* (June 1999).

assisted customers in finding the highest yielding bank CDs in the country. The problem was not acquiring deposits but paying their high interest costs and earning a reasonable net interest margin. An opposite problem began to appear in the early 1990s. While deposit rates were low and net interest margins were strong, banks were subjected to gradual losses of deposits, as depositors shifted funds to higher-yielding instruments. Also, many depositors shifted funds from retail CDs to NOW accounts and savings accounts in anticipation of possibly moving funds to higher-yielding instruments at a later time. Of course, in seeking higher yields, investors must bear higher risk. Deposits earning an insured rate of 3% were not attractive compared to 6% to 8% yields on riskier money and capital market instruments. However, if interest rates moved up appreciably, large capital losses could be incurred on longer-term investments. In an effort to retain customer relationships, banks in the early 1990s began to aggressively market mutual funds, as well as stock and bond investments, in an agent relationship with investment companies and other financial institutions. Some mutual funds are owned and managed by the banks themselves, especially money market mutual funds. In the near future banks' ability to retain deposit customers will be much improved by the Financial Service Modernization Act of 1999. The new act will allow bank holding companies to offer a full menu of financial services, including investment and insurance services. These changes are expanding the scope of liability management and thereby enabling bankers to create packages of financial services for their customers.

12.3 MANAGING BANK LIABILITIES

Dismantling of Regulation Q and rising competition for deposit funds has resulted in a wide variety of deposit products and associated services. This growing diversity of liability services has caused banks to use product differentiation as a way of distinguishing themselves from competitors. Table 12.4, for example, compares the pricing strategies of five hypothetical banks in the same city for NOW and MMDA accounts. The total **pricing strategy** is a combination of convenience (e.g., ATMs, or automated teller machines), service charges, minimum balances to avoid service charges or earn interest (or both), and other unique characteristics of the particular account. In general, these pricing features are traded off against one another; for instance, banks with low service charges either had higher minimum balances or lower numbers of ATMs. Of course, the pricing strategy of individual banks is also influenced by their desired liability mix. Due to the competition for funds, customers that seek minimum idle cash balances, and disintermediation (or movement of deposit funds by customers to higher rate money and capital market instruments), bank management must implement a deposit development and retention program. In this section we discuss different aspects of the pricing decision that should be considered in the management of bank liabilities, in addition to the control of costs involved in acquiring funds.

TABLE 12.4	Pricing New Deposit Accounts: A Hypothetical Example				
Bank	# of ATMs in City/State	Service Charges NOW	Minimum Balance to Avoid Service Charges NOW	Minimum Balance to Earn Interest MMDA	Additional Restrictions on MMDAs
I	60/300	$3/mo $.25/ck $.25/ATM transaction	$1,000	$1,000	No more than six automatic, preauthorized, or ATM withdrawals or transfers per month
II	80/350	$5/mo $.15/ck $.10/ATM transaction	$1,000	$2,500	No more than six withdrawals per month
III	30/100	$1.50/mo $.25/ck $.20/ATM transaction	$ 500	$2,500	No more than six transfers per month to checking account and 10 withdrawals per month
IV	90/300	$7/mo	$1,000	$1,000	$.50 per transaction over 10 per month
V	25/80	$6/mo $.10/ck	$ 600	$1,000	No checks

Formulating Pricing Policy

The **pricing policy** is a written document that contains the pricing details of deposit services. Some key areas to be covered in the bank's pricing policy include the following:

- Service fees versus minimum balance requirements
- Deposit costs and volumes and their relationship to profits
- Credit availability and compensating balances
- Customer relationship pricing
- Promotional pricing of new products
- Other marketing elements such as product differentiation

Obviously, the pricing process is based on many variables that require experience and judgment to evaluate effectively. We next discuss these aspects of pricing policy in greater detail.

Deposit Pricing Matrix

In banking, both explicit and implicit pricing of products and services are used. **Explicit pricing** relates to interest expenses, whereas **implicit pricing** concerns noninterest expenses, such as free checking and other services, which are payments in kind. Figure 12.2 shows a pricing matrix that gives some examples of explicit and implicit pricing of bank liabilities and their effects on bank revenues and costs.

Deregulation of deposit accounts has caused banks to move toward greater use of explicit pricing and decreased use of implicit pricing. This shift has been the result of *unbundling costs*, which means simply using explicit pricing to reflect more closely the true costs of producing specific products and services. Prior to deregulation of deposit interest rates, free checking was normally available as an implicit payment of interest to customers. Free checking was justifiable, because no interest could be earned on transactions balances, and individuals included some amount of savings balances in their transactions accounts for the sake of convenience. Deregulation of deposit rates allowed retail depositors to choose from alternative new accounts, some of which had predominantly checking features (e.g., demand deposits), savings features (e.g., MMDA accounts), or a mixture of both (e.g., NOW accounts). Naturally, banks price each type of deposit account differently to distinguish them from one another. As interest rates change over time, customer preferences for implicit and explicit pricing can shift. For example, when interest rates are at relatively high levels, banks must emphasize explicit pricing over implicit pricing or suffer disintermediation. When interest rates are low (as in the 1990s), customers are less interest sensitive (due to lower opportunity costs) and,

FIGURE 12.2 Deposit Pricing Matrix

		Pricing Strategy	
		Explicit Prices	Implicit Prices
Effect on Bank Cash Flows	Bank Costs	• Interest payments • Gifts (e.g., appliances) • Compounding interest (e.g., daily)	• Below cost provision of services (e.g., free checking) • Added convenience (e.g., branch offices, ATMs, business hours)
	Bank Revenues	• Service charges (e.g., charge per check) • Fees (e.g., overdrafts)	• Minimum balance requirements • Restrictions (e.g., limited check-writing privileges)

therefore, implicit pricing becomes more important than otherwise. In general, banks are continuing to adjust the explicit and implicit dimensions of their pricing strategies as they learn more about customer preferences for implicit and explicit pricing as levels of interest rates vary over time.

The Pricing Committee

The pricing committee should be staffed by employees from throughout the bank. Because pricing decisions greatly affect the deposit base, they must be coordinated with other bank activities, including lending, marketing, accounting, data processing, operations, and trust services. Top management should appoint members to the pricing committee and periodically review its performance.

Committee assignments should address the primary objectives of deposit maintenance, market competitiveness, cost minimization, and adequate funding to meet lending goals. Information pertaining to these objectives must be gathered and reviewed periodically. Subsequent changes in pricing existing products need to be monitored for their effects on costs and deposit flows. Also, the committee should play a major role in the development and introduction of new products.

Components of the Pricing Decision

The Federal Reserve Bank of New York conducted a series of interviews with senior commercial and savings bankers on the pricing of their institutions' deposits. Bankers were asked what factors they considered in pricing consumer deposit products. The following key factors were identified:

- Wholesale cost of funds
- Pricing strategy of competitors
- Interest elasticity (or responsiveness) of consumer demand
- Past deposit flows for various kinds of consumer accounts
- Maturity structure of deposits

The **wholesale cost of funds,** or large CD rates, was viewed by bankers as an alternative cost of money. Adjustments for differences in maturity (e.g., MMDAs, NOWs, and savings deposits that can be immediately withdrawn and have no fixed maturity), reserve requirements, and servicing were made to estimate retail costs of funds.

Various market factors influenced the pricing decision. The pricing strategy of competitors was monitored regularly, as well as the deposit flows of their own institution regarding various types of accounts. Additionally, the interest elasticity of demand for different deposit accounts was considered to assess the potential influence of price changes on deposit flows.

Bankers also reviewed the maturity structure of their institution's deposits to determine what deposits were maturing and when they would come due. In general, bankers indicated that they did not consider the bank's short-term funding needs in making pricing decisions for consumer deposits. Such liquidity needs were met for the most part by wholesale deposits. This pricing behavior suggests that retail deposits are perceived primarily as core deposits.

Pricing decisions were reviewed on a weekly basis by most of the banks surveyed. Of course, changes in pricing were implemented less frequently. For example, even though large CD rates may have changed, the rate on MMDAs may not have been changed because MMDAs are less interest sensitive than CDs (presumably because MMDAs are shorter-term and tend to be used by customers as temporary accounts to "park cash" until it can be reinvested). Savings accounts were believed to be relatively insensitive to interest rate changes also. Rates on consumer (or retail) CDs, however, were changed more frequently following a change in large CD rates. Generally, among revisions that were made, bankers observed that changes in implicit prices (such as service convenience) were seldom implemented, perhaps only once a year. Thus, most price changes involved explicit interest, service charges, and fees.

Profitability and Deposit Pricing

The goal of bank management should be to maximize deposit revenues and minimize deposit costs in an effort to maximize bank profitability. **Cost/ revenue analysis** is one way in which managers can better understand how deposit pricing decisions are affecting bank profitability.

Figure 12.3 shows how bank costs and revenues change as the deposit base is expanded. The S-shaped cost curve assumes economies of scale as deposits initially are expanded, which gradually reduce costs per unit deposits; however, diseconomies at some deposit level increase costs per unit deposits and cause the cost curve to increase at an increasing rate. Total bank costs equal fixed costs of land, buildings, and equipment, plus variable costs of deposits and other activities. Total bank revenues include deposit revenues, loan and security portfolio revenues, and other revenues. Profit maximization requires the following: (1) minimization of total costs at each output level; (2) maximization of total revenues at each output level; and (3) marginal total costs equal marginal total revenues (i.e., the cost of an additional dollar of deposits equals the revenue it would provide when invested by the bank). The latter marginal cost/revenue condition is represented in Figure 12.3 at the deposit level at which the slopes of the total cost and total revenue curves are equal. Upper and lower breakeven points occur where costs and revenues equal one another in absolute (rather than marginal) terms. These points describe the output range within which the bank can profitably operate.

Once an optimal deposit level is estimated, the minimization of net deposit costs for the target deposit base is the task of the pricing committee. The following are some of the ways in which banks have been reducing deposit costs in recent years:

FIGURE 12.3 Cost/Revenue Analysis

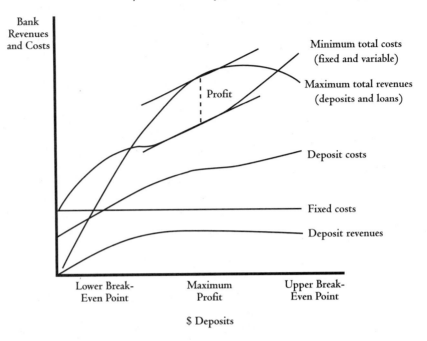

1. Check truncation (i.e., cleared checks are not returned to customers).
2. Stricter penalties for early withdrawal on time deposits.
3. Reducing the number of deposit products to avoid spreading resources too thin.
4. Using weekly or monthly interest compounding instead of daily compounding.
5. Waiting for customers to ask for higher interest products rather than automatically moving their funds to these products.

Obviously these cost-cutting techniques are not always successful because customers may become dissatisfied with the bank's service and withdraw their deposits.

Lending and Deposit Costs

Deposit costs can be affected by bank loan policies. For example, most loans require that compensating (deposit) balances be maintained by the borrower. Such balances are inexpensive to maintain because they usually pay no interest, require no promotional expenditures, and have minimum transactions costs (e.g., customer information is already on file). Another advantage of compensating balances is that they are relatively stable sources of deposits that are less likely to be withdrawn than other deposits, thus lowering the cost per unit risk of deposits.

Another way in which loan policy can lower deposit costs is through *tie-in arrangements* between deposit and loan services. Customers who have deposit accounts could be provided greater access to credit. For instance, many farm operators hold deposit accounts at rural banks not so much to earn interest but to establish a banking relationship that would enable them to obtain loans when needed. Thus, the credit function can be used by banks not only to raise deposit funds (i.e., compensating balances) but to reduce deposit costs.

Customer Relationship Pricing

Relationship banking is an expression that includes the *total* financial needs of the public rather than just *specific* needs. It also includes fulfilling long-term needs, as opposed to immediate needs, such as cashing a check. In relationship banking, banks can *cross-sell* a variety of services to lower user costs and increase convenience compared to selling each service separately. Also, patrons are viewed as clients, as opposed to customers, according to this viewpoint. This pricing strategy greatly increased in importance subsequent to the Financial Services Modernization Act of 1999, which expands the array of products and services that bank holding companies can provide to full-blown securities and insurance activities.

Promotional Pricing

Promotional pricing is used to introduce new products. In brief, the product is priced below cost to attract market attention. More frequently, promotional pricing is used to support or rejuvenate demand for existing products. Some of the potential reasons for such promotions include increasing or protecting market share, modifying existing products, developing brand recognition or overall bank image, targeting particular market segments of the population in certain geographic areas, and increasing sales to a cost efficient level at which economies of scale can be obtained.

Other Marketing Elements Related to Pricing

PRODUCT DIFFERENTIATION Designing products and services to meet the needs of specific market segments is known as **product differentiation**. As mentioned earlier, banks typically must price their liabilities in different ways to compete effectively for funds. If banks did not differentiate their products, and instead competed side-by-side for the same customers, many customers might be forced to purchase products that are not priced to fit their needs.

DISTRIBUTION Another part of the pricing decision that bank managers should consider is the physical delivery of deposit services to the public. The problem here is one of logistics—namely, how to optimize the time and place preferences of customers, while minimizing bank operating costs net of associated revenues. Banks have two basic distribution channels from which to choose: (1) *retail channels* that distribute services to the general public (e.g., drive-in teller windows, ATMs, and Internet access), and (2) *wholesale channels* that distribute large volume services to corporate enterprises and government units (e.g., lock boxes, electronic transfers of funds, and oversight cash management functions).

Estimating the Costs of Bank Funds

The acquisition of bank funds entails incurring both financial and operating costs. Financial costs pertain to explicit payments to lenders minus revenues obtained from service charges and fees, whereas operating costs relate to land, labor, and equipment expenditures. When discussing the costs of bank funding, it is also necessary to distinguish between average costs and marginal costs. **Average costs** are simply calculated by dividing dollar costs of funds by the dollar amount of funds. **Marginal costs** are the incremental costs of acquiring an additional dollar of funds. Marginal costs are superior to average costs because they more accurately reflect current costs as opposed to past costs.

Weighted-Average Cost of Funds

On an aggregate basis, costs of bank funds are measured in weighted average terms. The *weighted-average cost of funds* can be calculated by summing the average cost of each source of funds times the proportion of total funds raised from each respective source of funds. We may write this average cost of funds as follows:

$$CT = C_1 \frac{F_1}{TF} + C_2 \frac{F_2}{TF} + \ldots + C_n \frac{F_n}{TF} \qquad 12.1$$

where

CT = the weighted average cost of funds
C_n = average cost of the nth source of funds
F_n = funds acquired from the nth source of funds
TF = total funds acquired by the bank.

Theoretically, the average costs of the individual sources of funds, or *Cn*, are equal to one another as well as to *CT*, after adjusting for differences in risk. This result must be so because the bank would naturally acquire funds from the cheapest source until its cost per unit risk rose to the cost per unit risk of other funds' sources.

Purposes of Cost Analyses

PERFORMANCE REPORTS Table 12.5 provides example historical cost data for different sources of funds (excluding equity) that could be included in a performance report. Funds available for investment are less than the amount of funds acquired by the amount of reserves required (because of either legal requirements or management preferences). Financial costs equal total interest costs net of service revenues, and operating costs are based on allocated expenses for labor, premises, occupancy expenses, and other operations associated with physically producing accounts.[5] The total cost of funds is divided by funds available for investment to obtain the average cost of each type of fund. Notice that reserve requirements raise the *effective* cost of funds, which is associated with funds usable for investment purposes. The final step is to calculate the weighted average cost of funds by applying Eq. (12.1). As shown in Table 12.5, this historical cost equaled 7.12%.

The information displayed in Table 12.5 can be used by the pricing committee to identify both problems and opportunities. For example, public deposits were costing an average of 10%, which exceeds the average cost of any other type of funds, even though the risk associated with these funds is relatively low (because government accounts are a fairly stable source of deposits). Thus, management could work on reducing the cost of public deposits. On the other hand, the average cost of demand deposits was only about 1%, well below the cost of other kinds of funds. Bank management could increase promotional expenses, lower service charges and fees, or increase implicit service returns (by increasing operating expenses) to expand this relatively inexpensive source of funds. This kind of historical overview of costs can help guide bank management in minimizing the costs of funds in the future. In turn, cost minimizing behavior of bank managers causes the marginal costs of all sources of funds to remain about the same, including the cost of equity funds, on a risk-adjusted basis.

Marginal Costs of Funds

The average cost of funds is historical and likely is not useful in making investment decisions in the future. For example, if a bank manager is contemplating making a loan at 10% to a potential borrower, the relevant cost of funds for the purpose of evaluating the profitability of the loan is the costs of funds at the time the loan is made. In this sense, the marginal cost of funds can be interpreted as the minimum yield on bank investments in loans and securities that must be

---

5. Interest costs and allocated operating costs of various sources of funds, in addition to cost breakdowns of various asset categories, are available through the Federal Reserve System's Functional Cost Analysis (FCA) service. Banks can voluntarily participate in this program by providing necessary data. Alternatively, many banks have implemented in-house cost accounting systems to collect data.

TABLE 12.5 — Historical Cost Analysis ($ thousands)

Sources of Funds[a]	(1) Funds Acquired	(2) Funds Available for Investment	(3) = (1)/1000,000 Proportion of Funds Acquired	(4) Financial Cost[b]	(5) Operating Cost[c]	(6) = (4) + (5) Total Cost	(7) = (6)/(2) Average Cost of Funds	8 = (3) × (7) Weighted Average Cost of Funds
Deposit Sources								
Demand deposits	$ 20,000	$18,000	0.02	$ –10	$200	$ 190	1.06%	0.212%
NOW accounts	8,000	7,200	0.08	480	40	520	7.22	0.578
Passbook savings	5,000	4,500	0.05	350	20	370	8.22	0.411
MMDAs	7,000	7,000	0.07	525	30	555	7.93	0.555
Retail CDs	14,000	14,000	0.14	1,120	20	1,140	8.14	1.140
Large CDs (≥$100,000)	25,000	25,000	0.25	2,125	60	2,185	8.74	2.185
Public deposits	10,000	8,800	0.10	800	80	880	10.00	1.000
Nondeposit Sources								
Fed funds and repos	4,000	4,000	0.04	360	30	390	9.75	0.390
Other borrowed money	5,000	5,000	0.05	450	30	380	9.60	0.480
Notes and debentures	2,000	2,000	0.02	140	30	170	8.50	0.170
Total	$100,000	$95,500	1.00	$6,340	$540	$6,880 Cost	Wtd.	Avg. = 7.12 percent

a. The following simplified reserve requirements are assumed to apply to various sources of funds: transactions accounts (10%), nonpersonal time deposits (0%), personal time and savings deposits (0%), and nondeposit funds (0%).

b. Financial costs equal interest expenses minus revenues from service charges and fees.

c. Operating costs equal total expenses involved in physically producing accounts.

earned to avoid a loss in equity share values. This interpretation is based on the notion that funds should continue to be acquired and invested as long as shareholders earn yields in excess of the minimum required rate of return.

INVESTMENT DECISIONS Care must be taken *not* to use the marginal cost of any particular source of funds as the cutoff rate in investment decisions. In the case of the pending loan decision, it would be a mistake to measure the cost of funds by linking it with, say, six-month CDs issued on the day of the loan. This approach to investment decisions is short run in nature and ignores the long-run implications of intermediating savings flows from different sources to investment in different loans and securities.

Instead, it is the marginal cost of the entire *mix* of funds that must be used as a cutoff criterion in investment decisions. Table 12.6 on page 462 shows the marginal cost of each type of funding, which is equal to the incremental percentage cost of acquiring an additional dollar of funds from that source. The weighted average of these costs, where the weights are the proportions of each source of funds in the long run, is the marginal cost of funds to be used in bank investment decisions. In Table 12.6 the marginal cost is calculated to be 8.79%. In order to be worthwhile to shareholders, an investment would have to yield 8.79% or more.

An adjustment to the marginal cost of funds for purposes of investment decisions is needed if some proportion of funds is nonearning, such as reserve requirements. In this case the effective marginal cost of funds is increased. This adjustment is similar to calculating effective loan rates when an interest rate is stated but compensating balances are required. In the preceding example, if 5% of total funds raised is placed in nonearning assets, the effective marginal cost equals $0.0879/[1 - 0.05] = 0.0925$ or 9.25%. This cost is a more appropriate hurdle rate to use for earning assets that the bank is evaluating.

The greatest difficulty in applying the marginal cost concept to real-world investment decisions is the estimation of individual marginal costs for different sources of funds. The price-earnings ratio for common stock is a good proxy for the after-tax marginal cost of equity funds (see footnote b in Table 12.6 concerning the distinction between before-tax and after-tax equity costs). Also, the Capital Asset Pricing Model (CAPM) could be used to estimate the cost of equity from market stock price and interest rate information.[6] Unfortunately, most banks do not have actively traded common stock. In this case, some multiple of book value must be used to estimate market value. Neither are liabilities' marginal costs readily calculable in many cases. Although marginal financial costs

6. In the CAPM the cost of equity equals the riskless rate of interest plus a risk premium, where the risk premium is calculated as the firm's beta multiplied by the yield spread between the market rate of return and the riskless rate of interest. For example, it the T-bill rate is 3%, beta for the bank's stock is estimated to be 0.8, and the rate of return on the Standard & Poor's 500 Index is 10%, the cost of equity is 3% + [0.8 × 7%] = 8.6%. Readers should refer to a standard managerial finance textbook for further discussion and methods of obtaining beta estimates.

MANAGING RISK

Counting the Costs of Demand Deposits and Time Deposits

Two dominant sources of funds for commercial banks are demand deposits and time deposits. The Functional Cost Analysis (FCA) program of the Federal Reserve System publishes operating cost analyses of these two liabilities. Banks voluntarily participate in this program in an effort to further understand their operating efficiency and earnings. Cost comparisons over time and relative to peer group banks are valuable in managing these important liabilities accounts.

The following table shows 1997 cost figures for demand and time deposits based on samples of 18 smaller institutions with assets less than $150 million and 23 larger institutions with assets more than $150 million. The data show income and expenses associated with these two accounts in terms of the percentage of demand deposit or time deposit dollar volume.

The first line item in the table labeled "Credit for Funding (CFF)" is a funds transfer price applied to deposits. CFF is based on the associated interest earnings on assets made possible by the supply of deposits. Interest earnings are allocated to different types of deposits according to their classification as short-term versus long-term sources of funds. Notice that the low interest expense of demand deposits causes their net interest income percentage (i.e., between 6% and 7%) to be much higher than those for time deposits (i.e., between 1.5% and 2.5%). After adding noninterest income, which is significant for demand deposits but negligible for time deposits, the differences in earnings between demand and time deposits increases further.

Noninterest expenses are extensively broken down in the FCA analyses. In this regard, salary and fringe benefits are by far the largest noninterest expense. For demand deposits these labor expenses range from 1% to 1.5% compared with less than 0.2% for time deposits. Clearly, demand deposits are labor intensive, while time deposits require little or no labor.

The net income per dollar of demand deposits was about 2.7% for both smaller and larger institutions. For time deposits the net income per dollar was about 0.3%. The difference in net income is at least partially explained by the fact that demand deposits are riskier than time deposits. Some obvious risk differences between demand and time deposits are (1) customers can immediately withdraw demand deposits; (2) demand deposits will shrink as interest rates increase; and (3) businesses will seek to minimize demand deposit balances that limit their usefulness as a funding source for bank growth.

As mentioned in the text discussion of optimality, maximum net income for each type of deposit account is achieved at different quantities of funds. Time deposits require much larger dollar volume than demand deposits to reach this optimum. Thus, while demand deposits are more profitable to banks per dollar of deposits, the greater volume of time deposits may well cause the gross net income in dollar terms to exceed that of demand deposits. Participating banks in the FCA program can obtain information on net income per dollar of deposits over a wide spectrum of deposit levels and therein gain insight into the optimum amount for each type of deposit (and nondeposit funds). In today's competitive marketplace managers must count the costs of pursuing different sources of liabilities. By doing so, profits can be better controlled and risks reduced.

Breakdown of Costs for Demand Deposits and Time Deposits: Averages for Samples of Smaller Banks with Less Than $150 Million in Assets and Larger Banks with More Than $150 Million in Assets

	Demand Deposits		Time Deposits	
	18 Institutions Assets up to $150M	23 Institutions Assets >$150M	18 Institutions Assets up to $150M	23 Institutions Assets >$150M
$ Volume of Deposits	$19,619,469	$180,652,974	$42,094,383	$467,546,699
Average number of accounts	3,836	32,029		
Credit for funding (DFF)	7.56%	7.28%	7.76%	7.31%
– Interest expense	1.25%	0.72%	5.53%	5.72%
Net interest income	**6.30%**	**6.56%**	**2.23%**	**1.59%**
+ Noninterest income				
Service charges	0.52%	0.59%	0.00%	0.03%
Penalty fees	1.00%	0.49%	0.03%	0.01%
Other	0.09%	0.30%	0.00%	0.04%
Total noninterest income	1.61%	1.38%	0.03%	0.08%
Net income before noninterest expense	**7.92%**	**7.94%**	**2.26%**	**1.67%**
– Noninterest expenses				
Direct expenses				
Salary	0.88%	12.3%	0.18%	0.15%
Fringe benefits	0.22%	0.31%	0.05%	0.04%
Personnel expense	*1.10%*	*1.54%*	*0.22%*	*0.19%*
Vendor data processing	0.23%	0.07%	0.03%	0.00%
Furniture & equipment	0.20%	0.07%	0.03%	0.00%
Printing, postage, & freight	0.16%	0.16%	0.02%	0.02%
Telephone & electronic assess	0.04%	0.06%	0.01%	0.01%
Occupancy	0.21%	0.27%	0.04%	0.04%
Professional fees, legal & other	0.00%	0.13%	0.00%	0.01%
FDIC insurance	0.03%	0.02%	0.03%	0.03%
All other direct expenses	0.48%	0.46%	0.06%	0.05%
Total direct expense	**2.45%**	**2.88%**	**0.45%**	**0.37%**
Net indirect expenses	1.32%	1.16%	0.16%	0.13%
Charge for Portfolio Operations (CPO)	*1.43%*	*1.16%*	*1.38%*	*0.86%*
Total Noninterest Expense	**5.19%**	**5.20%**	**1.99%**	**1.36%**

TABLE 12.6	Marginal Cost Analysis			

Source of Funds	Funds Acquired	Proportion of Funds Acquired	Marginal Cost[a,b]	Marginal Weighted Average Cost of Funds
Deposit Sources				
Demand deposits	$ 20,000	0.18	6.50%	1.170%
NOW accounts	8,000	0.07	7.80	0.546
Passbook savings	5,000	0.05	7.90	0.395
MMDAs	7,000	0.06	8.10	0.486
Retail CDs	14,000	0.13	8.30	1.079
(≥$100,000)	25,000	0.23	8.40	1.932
Public deposits	10,000	0.09	8.00	0.720
Nondeposit Sources				
Fed funds and repos	4,000	0.04	8.20	0.328
Other borrowed money	5,000	0.04	8.30	0.332
Notes and debentures	2,000	0.02	8.50	0.170
Equity	10,000	0.09	20.00	1.80
Total	$110,000	1.00		Marginal cost = 8.79%

a. Marginal cost is based on total financial and operating costs per dollar of funds available for investment. Marginal costs of funds vary according to the risk(s) of these funds.

b. The marginal cost of equity is on a before-tax basis in order to compare it with debt forms of funding. The marginal tax rate of the bank is assumed to be .34, such that the required rate of return by shareholders is 13.20%.

can be estimated fairly accurately from market and internal information, marginal operating costs of acquiring an additional dollar of deposit funds may be difficult to assess. Experience and judgment are the best resources that can be used to avoid this problem. Thus, even though marginal cost analysis in investment decisions presents some drawbacks, management expertise normally is sufficient to make appropriate estimates.

Finally, the marginal cost of funds may not be appropriate in making *long-run* investment decisions. For such decisions a weighted-average of the marginal cost of long-term funds can be used to calculate what is known as the *marginal cost of capital*. The marginal cost of capital can serve as a hurdle rate in capital budgeting decisions involving the purchase of nonfinancial assets, such as bank office buildings, equipment, and furniture, as well as long-term financial assets, such as corporate and municipal bonds. In general, long-term funds have maturities greater than one year and, therefore, are acquired from the capital market rather than the money market. Capital funding sources for banks are notes, debentures, and equity, including capital stock and retained earnings. Because bank assets are primarily short term or have yields that can be adjusted more than once a year, the marginal cost of funds is relatively more important than the marginal cost of capital in financial decision making.[7]

SUMMARY

Sources of bank funds have changed substantially over the last two decades because of changes in inflation, rising competition, and deregulation of deposit rates. During this period, banks increased their usage of nondeposit funding and, conversely, decreased deposit funding. More important, in large part because of changing customer needs, banks shifted away from demand deposits and toward greater reliance upon time and savings deposits. In this regard, brokered deposits have been symptomatic of increasing risk in the banking industry, in addition to the national-level competition for deposit funds.

The wide variety of retail deposit accounts that have been introduced within the last decade or so—such as NOWs, ATSs, MMDAs, and retail CDs—have transformed the liability side of banks' balance sheets. This transformation has been appropriately referred to as the consumerism movement. Low interest rates in the 1990s have continued to alter liability management as banks aggressively offer mutual funds, sweep programs, IRAs, new CD products, and other alternatives to retain customers seeking higher yields.

The pricing committee is responsible primarily for the management of bank liabilities and is composed of employees throughout the bank. The task of formulating pricing policy involves deposit pricing, bank profitability, loan policies, customer relations, and various marketing elements. The large number of different types of deposit accounts offered to customers today makes pricing a challenging task that requires balancing bank funds needs, profitability, and customer relations.

Estimating the costs of bank funds is the crucial factor in setting the profit dimension of liability management. These costs can be estimated using both average costs and marginal costs; however, the latter is definitely a superior method. A weighted-average cost of funds can be calculated to analyze problems and opportunities in funds acquisition. Also, a marginal cost of funds can be calculated to serve as a cutoff rate in bank investment decisions.

7. By contrast, because nonfinancial, private business firms have substantial long-term investments, the marginal cost of capital is emphasized in investment decisions.

Key Terms and Concepts

Automatic transfer service (ATS)
Average costs
Brokered deposits
Capital notes and debentures
Commercial paper
Core deposits
Cost/revenue analysis
Demand deposits
Discount window advances
Eurodollar deposits
Explicit pricing
Federal funds
Implicit pricing
Individual retirement account
  (IRA)
Keogh plans
Large time deposits
Marginal costs
Money market deposit accounts
  (MMDAs)

Money market mutual funds
  (MMMFs)
Negotiable certificate of deposit
Net interest margins
Nondeposit funds
Negotiable orders of withdrawal
  (NOW) accounts
Pricing policy
Pricing strategy
Product differentiation
Promotional pricing
Purchased deposits
Regulation Q
Relationship banking
Retail CD
Repurchase agreement (RP)
Savings certificate
Sweep programs
Time and savings deposits
Wholesale cost of funds

Questions

12.1 Define core deposits of a bank. Also define purchased deposits.

12.2 Why are purchased deposits generally considered to be more risky than core deposits?

12.3 What does the Glass-Steagall Act have to do with deposit rate regulation? What is the rationale for this regulation?

12.4 Are commercial accounts still subject to Regulation Q? Would a corporate client prefer compensating balances or service fees on a loan, all else the same?

12.5 Does FDIC deposit insurance tend to increase bank risk taking? What specific kind of risk increases?

12.6 How do low interest rates affect bank liability management?

12.7 What are explicit and implicit deposit costs?

12.8 What advantage does an MMDA possibly have over a money market mutual fund (MMMF) account?

12.9 What is the consumerism movement?

12.10 Why is there a tiered CD market?

12.11 Is a dollar held in a bank office in Hong Kong a Eurodollar deposit? Are such deposits eligible for FDIC insurance?

12.12 What are brokered deposits? Why do regulators oppose the practice of deposit brokering?

12.13 What are managed liabilities? Give three differences between deposit funds and managed liabilities. What are sweep programs?

12.14 List and briefly discuss four sources of nondeposit liabilities.

12.15 How do the deposit compositions of small and large banks differ?

12.16 Pricing deposit accounts is a complex process. Give at least four factors affecting the pricing of consumer deposits.

12.17 Is there an optimal level of bank deposits in the sense of maximizing bank profitability? Use a graph to illustrate your answer.

12.18 How does the Financial Service Modernization Act of 1999 affect the management of bank sources of funds?

12.19 Go to the *Money and Payment Systems* web site provided by IfBG Göttengen at *http://www.wiso.gwdg.de/ifbg/geld.html* and choose an article on digital money and electronic payments systems. Print out the article and write a one-page abstract of it.

12.20 Find the Discount Window Booklet at the Federal Reserve Bank of Chicago's web site at *http://www.frbchi.org/loans/dwbooklet/tablecontents.html*. Choose two categories in the overview section and write a one-page report on these areas of discount window borrowing.

12.21 Go to Federal Reserve Board Commercial Bank Examination Manual at *http://www.federalreserve.gov/boarddocs/SupManual/default.htm#cbem* and look up the liabilities and capital section. Find the Potential Problem Areas section and write a two-page report on aspects of deposit accounts and related activities that have above-average risk.

Problems

12.1 (a) Given the data in Exhibit 12.1 showing the amounts and costs of funds for ABC Bank, calculate its weighted-average cost of funds.

  (b) Which sources of funds had average costs that exceeded the weighted-average cost of funds?

  (c) Does it appear that some sources of funds are relatively costly considering their risk?

12.2 (a) Given the data in Exhibit 12.2, calculate the marginal weighted-average cost of funds for ABC Bank.

  (b) For what purpose can bank management use the marginal cost result in part (a)?

  (c) Why do various costs of funds differ? Under what conditions would they be equal?

  (d) If 10% of funds raised must be placed in nonearning assets, what would be the effective marginal cost of funds?

EXHIBIT 12.1	Average Costs of Funds for ABC Bank in 200X ($ millions)	
Sources of Funds	**Average Amount Available for Investment**	**Average Cost**
Deposits		
Demand deposits	$15	5.00%
Interest-bearing checking	30	7.00
Passbook savings	10	8.00
Small CDs	20	9.00
Large CDs	30	10.00
Eurodollar CDs	5	10.40
Nondeposits		
Fed funds	$6	8.00%
Repos	10	8.50
Discount window advances	4	7.50
Other liabilities	12	10.00
Stockholders' equity	$12	15.00%

EXHIBIT 12.2	Marginal Costs of Funds for ABC Bank in 200X	
Sources of funds	**Funds Acquired**	**Marginal Cost**
Deposits		
Demand deposits	$18	6.00%
Interest-bearing checking	33	7.25
Passbook savings	11	8.30
Small CDs	20	9.15
Large CDs	32	10.15
Eurodollar CDs	5.5	10.55
Nondeposits		
Fed funds	$ 6	8.40%
Repos	10	8.80
Discount window advances	4	7.90
Other liabilities	12	10.50
Stockholders' equity	$12	15.00%

Hometown Bank and Trust

Over the last decade Hometown Bank and Trust has continually adjusted the interest rates and service features of its different interest-bearing sources of funds. Considerable decreases in interest rates in the last year to 20-year historic lows have caused the bank to lose some of its deposit customers to higher interest rate products such as money market mutual fund (MMMF) accounts and various money market securities sold through security brokers. Ben Bridge, the bank's president and CEO, was privately beginning to worry that, if a large number of the bank's most interest-sensitive customers pulled out of Hometown, the bank would have difficulty meeting the credit needs in the community. Based on this apprehension, Ben called a meeting of top management to discuss the problem. The meeting culminated with an unanimous vote to set up a bank liabilities task force comprised of middle managers close to deposit holders and other sources of bank funds. The task force was charged with the responsibility to examine the bank's sources of funds over the past five years and make recommendations to top management.

Jennifer Jones had worked for Hometown for four years after graduating from college with a finance degree. She had passed through the credit analyst one-year training program without any problems and had been assigned to various aspects of managing the bank's different deposit accounts. While still enthusiastic about her work, Jennifer was getting anxious for a chance to demonstrate her leadership abilities. She often conjectured that a "big break" would propel her forward from the middle management ranks and onto a path to a top management position in the bank. That afternoon her immediate supervisor, Jason Jacobs, called her into his office to ask if she would head up the bank liabilities task force, with five other middle managers also serving in the group. It was a great opportunity—to either succeed or fail.

To get things going, Jennifer immediately sent a memo to all task force members to notify them of an initial meeting at the beginning of the next week. At this first meeting, she informed everyone of their mission—namely, to evaluate historical data on bank liabilities and make recommendations for top management decisions concerning the bank's sources of funds. Their task was *not* to make the final decisions concerning pricing policy. Next, she asked the group to list alternative approaches to achieving their mission. Three-person teams were assigned to collect the necessary bank data for the past five years and present it at the next meeting. Jennifer felt the group was off to a good start. The members were quite diverse in their different viewpoints, which allowed open interaction and the potential for sharing of skills with one another in their joint effort.

At the next meeting the data in Exhibits 12-3 and 12-4 were presented.

After all questions were answered on the details of collecting the data, and everyone was satisfied with the accuracy of the numbers, Jennifer asked each member of the task force to write an independent report. Each report was to have three sections: (1) trends in bank liabilities, (2) implications of current low interest rate market conditions to bank liabilities, and (3) strategies to offset current and potential deposit losses. As a member of the task force, follow these guidelines to write your report.

EXHIBIT 12-3   Composition of Liabilities over Time: Hometown Bank and Trust (As a percentage of total assets)

Liability Item	2000	1999	1998	1997	1996
Demand deposits	10.92%	10.85%	10.91%	11.42%	11.98%
NOW and ATS accounts	12.02	10.83	11.02	10.48	10.42
MMDAs	10.06	9.20	9.27	9.11	9.82
Other savings deposits	8.37	6.93	7.06	6.76	7.01
Retail time deposits	35.07	37.80	37.60	37.25	35.51
Core deposits	80.95	79.74	79.94	79.09	79.00
Time deposits ≥$100,000	7.18	8.57	8.40	9.24	9.26
Deposits in foreign offices	3.62	3.98	3.92	3.92	4.11
Total deposits	89.20	89.36	89.36	89.36	89.27
Federal funds purchased and RPs	0.22	0.18	0.20	0.15	0.18
Other borrowings	0.04	0.03	0.04	0.04	0.05
Acceptances and other liabilities	0.81	0.96	0.94	1.03	1.04
Total liabilities	91.41	91.63	91.62	91.65	91.64

EXHIBIT 12-4   Interest Costs of Bank Sources of Funds over Time: Hometown Bank and Trust

Liability Item	2000	1999	1998	1997	1996
Total interest-bearing deposits	4.61%	6.28%	6.13%	6.93%	7.02%
NOW and ATS accounts	3.32	4.75	4.65	5.00	5.04
MMDAs	3.69	5.31	5.18	5.79	5.87
Other savings deposits	3.73	5.04	4.97	5.20	5.20
Large CDs	5.05	7.08	6.91	7.81	7.94
Deposits in foreign offices	4.02	6.34	6.11	8.21	9.08
Federal funds purchased and RPs	3.69	5.80	5.60	7.67	8.74
Other borrowings	2.78	4.41	4.32	5.05	6.35
Acceptances and other liabilities	3.80	5.90	5.70	7.75	8.85

CHAPTER 13

Electronic Banking

After reading this chapter you will be able to:

- Evaluate the role of electronic banking in the retail (small-dollar) payments systems.

- Understand the wide variety of financial services provided by electronic banking.

- Describe the role of electronic banking in the wholesale (large-dollar) payments system.

- Compare the different types of settlement systems for financial transactions.

- Identify payment systems risks.

- Explain why paper checks and dollars will be around for a long time.

E lectronic banking refers to any banking activity accessed by electronic means. Both commercial banks and nonbank financial institutions offer electronic banking services such as paying bills, money market accounts, and so on. Merrill Lynch, Charles Schwab, and Fidelity funds are examples of nonbank financial institutions that offer selected electronic banking services for individuals such as automatic bill payments and automatic teller machine (ATM) and debit cards withdrawals from money-market funds.[1] Most people believe that electronic banking began with the development of computers and the Internet. Not so. The first use of electronic banking in the United States was in the 1870s when Western Union telegraphs were used to transfer funds from one part of the country to another. The most visible form of electronic banking is the automatic teller machine (ATM), which came into use in 1968. Since then the number of ATMs in use exceeds 187,000.[2]

---

1. Vanessa O'Connell, "It's a Broker! It's a Banker! It's a Mutual-Fund Group!" *Wall Street Journal* (February 19, 1998), pp. C1, C21. ATM cards, and cards used at ATMs require the use of a personal identification number (PIN).
2. Charles Keenen, "Off-Site ATMs Approaching Saturation, Figures Suggest," *American Banker* (December 1, 1998), p. 15.

*For information about
Bank of America's Internet
Order Center, see* http://
www.bamart.com.

Electronic banking has developed in three distinct areas: (1) *retail payments and services* made by individuals and businesses, (2) *large-dollar transfers* made mostly by banks, businesses, and governments, and (3) *other services*. An example of the latter would be Bank of America Corp. with its offering to its two million business customers of an Internet order center (IOC) that allows merchants to track inventory, generate shipping information, authorize customer payments, and provides other services.[3] The IOC provides solutions for merchants who want to do business on the web and accept credit card payments in a secure and cost-effective manner. Bank of America will collect $100 per month from the merchants who use the service.

Table 13.1 provides an overview of the U.S. payments system. The data reveal that in 1998, 87% of volume of transactions in the United States were made by cash, but account for only 3% of the total dollar value of the transactions. They are generally small "nickel and dime" transactions. Checks account for 10% of the volume and 11% of the value of transactions. Most checks are used by individuals to pay for goods and services. They too are relatively small-dollar retail payments. Electronic payments account for 3% of the volume of transactions and 89% of the dollar value of all transactions! Electronic payments are used primarily by banks, businesses, and government to move large-dollar amounts. However, they are being used increasingly by individuals for retail transactions. ∎

13.1 RETAIL PAYMENTS AND FINANCIAL SERVICES

Retail payments are generally small-dollar payments used by individuals to pay for goods and services. Retail payments in the United States depend primarily on the use of paper checks. In 1996, more than 63 billion checks and 15 billion credit card transactions were used to make retail payments. One study estimated that the cost of operating the noncash payments system was $225 billion, or about 3% of the gross domestic product in 1996.[4] Stated otherwise, the average value of a consumer payment is about $50, and the total cost of processing this noncash transaction is $2.60 or about 5% of the value being trans-

3. Rick Brooks, "Bank of America to Launch Service for E-Business," *Wall Street Journal* (October 12, 1999),p. B4.
4. David Humphrey and Lawrence Pulley, "Retail Payment Instruments: Costs, Barriers, and Future Use," appears in *Proceedings, Payments Systems in the Global Economy: Risks and Opportunities*, Federal Reserve Bank of Chicago (May 1998), pp. 148–157; U.S. General Accounting Office, *Payments, Clearance, and Settlement*, GAO/GGD-97-73 (June 1997). This GAO study provides an excellent overview of the payments system and risks associated with it. This chapter draws material from this source.

TABLE 13.1	U.S. Payments		
		Volume of Transactions	Value of Transactions
Electronic transactions		3%	89%
Check Transactions		10	11
Cash Transactions		87	3

Source: Tim Schilling and Keith Feiler, *Electronic Money,* Federal Reserve Bank of Chicago (July 1998), p. 3.

acted. The use of electronic payments is expected to lower the costs of operating the payments system by as much as two thirds. The changes in payments in technology are coming, but they are not yet widespread.

Technology is changing the channels of delivery of retail banking services. Consumers are no longer bound by geography or traditional 9 A.M. to 4 P.M. banking hours to obtain financial services. They can use the Internet and cell phones 24 hours a day from any location to obtain financial services.[5] In addition, they have privacy and security. However, some issues concern privacy of information as well as security and fraud. These issues are not limited to electronic payments. The channels of delivery include automatic teller machines (ATMs), telephone banking, and various forms of screen-based banking, which includes the Internet as well as screen phones, and non-Internet PC banking. Electronic financial services include, but are not limited to:

- Electronic banking
- Electronic bill presentment and payment
- Electronic commerce
- Electronic money
- Home mortgage loans
- Internet brokerage and investment services

Several of these topics are discussed in the following sections.

Electronic Banking

Electronic banking is any banking activity accessed by electronic means such as ATMs, automated call centers, personal computers, screen telephones, and so on. These methods can be used to pay bills, transfer funds, apply for loans, buy mutual fund shares, and to provide other financial services. ATMs, of course,

5. Ross Snell, "Swedish Bank Starts Offering Services by Cell Phone," *American Banker* (October 11, 1999), p. 32.

MANAGERIAL ISSUES

ATM Fees

The use of automatic teller machines (ATMs) is widespread. A survey revealed that consumers used their ATM/debit cards about 16 times per month in 1998.* Banks may charge noncustomers a surcharge of $1–$2 for the use of their ATMs. The fees help to support the cost of maintaining 24-hour ATM networks and are a source of income for the banks.

Consumers who are opposed to paying surcharges to use ATMs argue that the fees are not justifiable at a time when bank profits are high, tellers are being laid off, and bank branches are closing. Taking their side, the Cities of San Francisco and Santa Monica voted in October 1999 to ban bank surcharges on ATMs.

Bank of America, and Wells Fargo & Co. responded by not allowing nonaccount holders to use their ATMs in locations where ATM fees are banned. In addition, these two banks, the California Bankers Association, and the Office of the Comptroller of the Currency** argue in a lawsuit against the cities that city ordinances cannot set the prices charged by national banks thereby prohibiting those banks from exercising the powers authorized by federal statue.** The courts will decide who gets to determine the fees.

*"ATM/Debit Card Use Rises," *http://www.cnnfn.com/1999/05/banking/q_atm/*, April 5, 1999.

**OCC, News Release 99-101 (November 5, 1999); and Brief Amicus Curiae of the Office of the Comptroller of the Currency in Support of National Bank, No. C-99 4817 VRW, Bank of America, N.A.: Wells Fargo Bank N.A.; and *California Bankers Association v. City and County of San Francisco, and City of Santa Monica.*

---

also provide cash. Banks may provide these services in-house, or contract with outside providers.[6] CheckFree and Intuit, for example, are outside providers of bill-paying services that contract with banks.

INTERNET BANKING In 1995, Security First Network Bank (SFNB) became the first fully transactional Internet bank. In 1998, it became part of the Royal Bank Financial Group (Canada), with assets of $180 billion and 9.5 million customers.[7] Of that total, fewer than than 0.4 million used their online service in 1999. They expect it to grow to 1 million in the next 3–5 years. It is interesting to note that in order to provide its customers with a wider range of products and services, SFNB opened a City Office in Atlanta. An Internet provider of services opening physical offices is not unusual. Charles Schwab & Co., a major stock brokerage firm does about two thirds of its business electronically. Nevertheless, some of its customers in key locations want a physical office to obtain services that cannot be provided effectively over the Internet.

For more details about SFNB, see http://www.sfnb.com.

Since SFNB was established, other Internet banks have come online. TeleBanc Financial and Net.Bank are two examples of publicly traded Internet banks.

6. Not all institutions that advertise themselves as "banks" are FDIC-insured. Moreover, FDIC-insured institutions offer products, such as mutual funds, that are not covered by deposit insurance.
7. Rebecca Sausner, "Royal Bank's Aim: Become a Personal Web Channel," *Future-Banker*, April 1999, 48.

See Bankrate at http://
www.bankrate.com/brm/
default.asp *for information
about electronic banking
and other financial services.*

Bank One opened its own Internet bank, Wingspan-Bank.com. Wingspan is available only on the Internet, and it competes with its parent company on interest rates on certificates of deposits, on the number mutual funds offered, and on other services.[8]

Some banks earn fee income from their Internet banking services. Fees range from $2 per month to $6.95 per month for bill-paying services.[9] In addition, they may charge for each payment (e.g. $0.40) or a flat fee of, say, $7 per month for 25 payments.

Large traditional "brick and mortar" banks, such as Bank of America, Citibank, and Wells Fargo have their own web pages, and they offer the same online services as Internet banks, plus other products and services that require a physical presence, such as ATMs and safety deposit boxes. Bank of America and Wells Fargo, for example, have 1.3 million and 0.9 million Internet banking customers, respectively.[10] Although large banks are offering Internet banking services, a recent study by the OCC finds that few smaller banks and thrifts offer their customers the option of conducting their banking activities over the Internet.[11]

Forbes *magazine listed*
www.citibank.com *as its
favorite banking site in its
1999* Interactive Money
Guide.

Despite the growth in Internet banking, the dropout rate of customers is nearly 33%.[12] Most of those customers who have dropped out stated that Internet banking was too complicated, they were dissatisfied with the services, and they didn't need it. Concern over security, cost, and privacy issues were also mentioned.

ELECTRONIC BANKING PRODUCTS FOR THE WHOLESALE MARKET Equally important is the development of electronic banking products and services for the wholesale market. Bank of America, for example, is putting its derivatives trading, foreign exchange, and global treasury services online for its corporate customers.[13] The Bank of New York offers web-based letters of credit and other wholesale banking services including securities and cash-transaction reporting.[14] Bank One is targeting small business by offering online cash

---

8. Rick Brooks, "Bank One's Strategy as Competition Growth: New Online Institution," *Wall Street Journal* (August 25, 1999), pp. A1, A8.

9. "Banking, Bill Paying and More," *Forbes Interactive Money Guide* (Fall 1999), p. 41; "Yahoo Users Can Pay Bills Electronically," *American Banker* (September 9, 1999), p. 24.

10. "Technology—On-Line," *American Banker* (June 18, 1999), p. 1.

11. Kori L. England, Karen Fust, Daniel E. Nolle, and Douglas Robertson, "Banking over the Internet," Office of the Comptroller of the Currency, *Quarterly Journal*, vol. 17, no. 4 (December 1998), pp. 25–30.

12. Ross Snell, "Dropout Rate Is Nearly 33% for Web Banking Customers," *American Banker* (August 25, 1999), pp. a, 14.

13. Andrew Reinbach, "BofA's Extranet Goal: Keep Corporates Wired," *FutureBanker* (April 1999), p. 45.

14. Andrew Reinbach, "Bank of New York Kicks off Web Trade Finance, *FutureBanker* (April 1999), p. 39.

management services and more.[15] Although small business may be considered "retail," the point here is that banks are offering an expanding range of electronic-based services to all of their customers.

Automatic Teller Machines

ATMs are the most visible form of electronic banking throughout the world. Three types of ATM systems are in use. The first ATMs used widely were *proprietary systems* operated by the institutions that purchased or leased the equipment. Today those ATMs are less prevalent as *shared/regional systems* and *national/international systems* have become increasingly popular.[16]

The shared/regional and national/international systems have network externalities. *Network externalities* means that the benefit one person gets from using the system depends on how many others are using it. The Internet is a good example. The usefulness of the Internet increases as more people use it. Similarly, the usefulness of fax machines increases as the number of fax machines grows. Networks make it possible to use ATMs anywhere in the world for cash advances by using ATM cards, debit cards, and credit cards.

Different types of ATM machines provide different services. Full-service ATM machines perform multiple banking and payments functions as well as dispense cash. The cost of full-service machines ranges from $20,000 to $40,000.[17] This figure does not include the cost of dedicated phone lines (about $120 per month), and other costs associated with servicing them. At the other end of the spectrum are cash dispensers that cost as little as $5,000 and can use dial-up phone lines for about $40 per month. Because of their relatively low cost, cash dispensers are being used in supermarkets, gas stations, and elsewhere.

Banks may charge noncustomers a cash advance transaction fee for the use of their ATMs in order to cover their costs of operation and to increase their earnings. The fees range from $1 to $1.50 or more.

Customers using credit cards to obtain cash advances from ATMs are subject to an additional cash advance transaction fee as well as a finance charge and interest on the funds withdrawn. For example, the credit card issuers may charge a cash advance transaction fee of the greater of $3 or 3% of each balance transferred. Some credit cards have a maximum cash transaction fee (for example, $25 or $30) specified for each transaction, while others have no maximum amount. If the cash advance is in a foreign currency, additional costs, such as increasing the exchange rate by 1%, may be added.

15. Johanna Knapschaefer, "Bank One Woos Small Biz with 14 On-Line Services, *FutureBanker* (April 1999), p. 49.

16. John D. Hueter and Ben R. Craig, "Global ATM Banking: Casting the Net," Federal Reserve Bank of Cleveland (August 15, 1998).

17. Charles Keenan, "Low-End Cash Dispensers Widen ATM Universe," *American Banker* (April 30, 1999), pp. 1, 11.

Consider the following example from a monthly billing statement for a $300 cash advance using a Citibank Gold Advantage credit card.[18] The statement listed a finance charge of 3% of the amount withdrawn ($9). The interest rate charged on cash advances (19.99%) is substantially higher than the interest rate on purchases (17.15%), and the interest charges begin the day the cash is withdrawn. The interest for the billing period was $3.97. The *annual percentage rate* (APR) on the cash advance for this billing period was 51.880%! The bank computed the APR in the following manner:

$$\text{APR} = \frac{(\text{Finance charge} + \text{Interest}) \times 12 \text{ months}}{\text{Amount of cash advance}} \qquad 13.1$$

$$= \frac{(\$9.00 + \$3.97) \times 12}{\$300} = 51.88\%$$

The interest rate on the cash advance accrues daily from the date of the advance until payment is made in full. Therefore, the minimum payment due on the cash advance exceeds the amount of interest shown in the monthly statement. The monthly statement listed the finance charge and interest as $12.97, but the minimum payment required on the cash advance portion of the billing statement was $16.48. Banks encourage their customers to use cash advances because such transactions yield high returns.

Electronic Bill Presentment and Payment (EBPP)

Electronic bill presentment and payment (EBPP) is a substitute for the current paper-based systems for recurring bill presentment and paying processes, and for preauthorized debits to checking accounts. Bills issued by utility companies, insurance companies, and credit card companies are examples of recurring bills. The electronic format is expected to reduce billing costs for billers, and be more convenient for customers. It costs billers about $0.90 to print and mail bills and to process customer's checks and remittance information.[19] This cost does not include the Federal Reserve's costs of operating the payments system or the other costs associated with clearing small-dollar payments. It is estimated that electronic billing will reduce biller's costs to about $0.32 per transaction.

EBPP billing requires the billing firm to hire a system operator to present the bill to the customer. The system operator can be a bank or a technology company such as First Data or Microsoft. The operator can post the bills on a web site, or on an Internet portal. This posting allows the household to view the bills at one convenient Internet location. The household must arrange with

18. This example is from the author's monthly billing statement from June 1999.
19. Lawrence J. Radecki and John Wenniger, "Paying Electronic Bills Electronically," *Current Issues in Economics and Finance*, Federal Reserve Bank of New York (January 1999).

his or her bank, the biller's bank, or the system operator for funds to be transferred. After reviewing the bills, the household can direct the payments to be made immediately or at some later date.

Table 13.2 shows a comparison of paper and EBPP payment systems. The electronic system eliminates the use of paper bills, checks, and mail, and it reduces the time and cost incurred presenting bills and collecting payments. Note that the electronic-based system still utilizes the Federal Reserve and clearinghouses in the payment process. Many of the clearinghouses belong to the Automated Clearing House (ACH) network that was established in the 1970s to provide an electronic alternative to the traditional paper-based check clearing systems.[20]

About 1 million customers used electronic bill paying services (CheckFree and Intuit) in 1996.[21] Another study by the Federal Reserve estimated that

TABLE 13.2	Comparison of Paper and EBPP Systems		
Step		**Paper-Based System**	**Electronic-Based System**
1	Statement preparation	Printed statement	Electronic file
2	Delivery to customer	Mail	Web site
3	Payment initiation	Customer writes check/mails it to biller	Customer reviews bill, authorizes payment on net
4	Return delivery to biller	Post office delivers check to biller	System operator sends biller a file
5	Updating customer account	Open mail, record payment, deposit check	File updated electronically
6	Presentment at the Federal Reserve	Checks delivered to Fed	Operator forwards payment to clearinghouse
7	Presentment at paying bank	Fed presents check to paying bank	Through clearinghouse, Fed notifies bank of debit
8	Interbank settlement	Fed debits reserve acct. of customer's bank and credits biller's bank	Fed debits reserve acct. of customer's bank and credits biller's bank
9	Debiting and crediting bank accounts	Customer debited and biller credited according to information on paper check	Customer debited and biller credited according to information in electronic file

Source: Based on Lawrence J. Radecki and John Wenniger, "Paying Electronic Bills Electronically," *Current Issues in Economics and Finance,* Federal Reserve Bank of New York (January 1999).

20. For additional details about the ACH network, see Margaret Weber, "Understanding and Managing ACH Credit Risk," *The Journal of Lending & Credit Risk Management* (May 1999), pp. 66–71.
21. U.S. General Accounting Office, *Payments, Clearance, and Settlement,* op. cit.

37% of households were using electronic bill paying in 1998.[22] As the use of the Internet and banking software become more widespread, electronic billing is expected to grow. Stated otherwise, electronic payments provide "network externalities."[23] That is, externalities exist when the value consumers receive from a product increases as the number of users of that product increases. For example, if only one person had a fax machine it would not be useful. The fact that many people use faxes makes the fax machine useful. The same idea holds true for electronic banking.

The conversion from our current paper-based system to an EBPP system faces some obstacles in the United States. Unlike Europe where EBPP is the norm because only two or three institutions dominate each country, more than 8,000 financial service providers and hundreds of thousands of billers operate in the United States, most of whom may not have the technology to provide a seamless network. From the consumer's point of view, studies have shown that unless consumers are able to receive and pay bills from multiple billers, they will not change their billing habits. Moreover, it is not clear who will be responsible for and have the liability for the integrity of the EBPP system.

ELECTRONIC FUNDS TRANSFER In order to reduce the cost of dealing in paper checks, the Debt Collection Improvement Act of 1996 required that all U.S. government payments to individuals be issued by electronic funds transfer beginning in January 1999. [24] The exceptions to this law include Internal Revenue Service payments and payments to those who do not have bank accounts. An estimated 13% of American households are *unbanked* and do not have a banking relationship with a traditional financial institution.[25] The reasons given for being unbanked are that they do not write enough checks to have an account, they do not have enough money, they do not like banks or trust them, and they want their privacy.

The Electronic Funds Transfer Act of 1978 and the resulting Federal Reserve Regulation E require financial institutions using electronic funds transfer to provide the following:[26]

- Written receipts for transactions
- Procedures for stopping preauthorized payments

22. Tim Schilling and Keith Feiler, *Electronic Money*, Federal Reserve Bank of Chicago (July 1998), p. 8.
23. Gautam Gowrisankaran, and Joanna Stavins, "Are There Network Externalities in Electronic Payments?" presented at the Federal Reserve Bank of Chicago Bank Structure Conference, Chicago, IL (May 1999).
24. Public Law No. 104-134, Section 31001.
25. Barbara Good, "Bringing the Unbanked Onboard," *Economic Commentary*, Federal Reserve Bank of Cleveland (January 15, 1999).
26. Tim Schilling and Keith Feiler, *Electronic Money*, Federal Reserve Bank of Chicago (July 1998), p. 11.

See On Line Banking Report *at* http://www. onlinebankingreport.com/ *for links to the web pages of Internet banks.*

- Adequate information about how to deal with billing errors, unauthorized, lost, or stolen debit cards
- Limits on the amount that may be deducted in the event of an unauthorized transaction

Electronic Money

Abraham Lincoln said in 1839 that no duty is more imperative on government than the duty it owes its people to furnish them with a sound and uniform currency.[27] Yet today we are talking about and using electronic money, which means different things to different people. *Money* is a term generally described by its functions. The primary function of money is that it is generally accepted as a means of exchange in terms of a defined unit of account. Until now, four major innovations have changed how people pay for things with money: metallic coins, checks, paper money, and payment cards. Now we can add electronic money to that list. Another function is that money is a store of value. A wide variety of things have been used as money including gold, silver, checks, and credit cards. Congress and the courts grant some forms of money the special status of being legal tender, which creditors must accept as payment for debts. U.S. coins and currency are legal tender. The phrase "This note is legal tender for all debts public and private" appears on Federal Reserve notes. Creditors are not required by law to accept other forms of payment.[28]

In the broadest sense, **electronic money** refers to the variety of ways that electronic and other payments systems can be used as a means of exchange. Electronic money takes many different forms. One form of electronic money is funds held in online accounts that can be transferred over the Internet.[29] Another form of electronic money is a stored value card that contains a magnetic strip recording the dollar value of the card. Most stored value cards are part of a "closed system" that can only be used at specific locations, such as a subway or toll road. A "smart card" contains a computer chip carrying $100 or more of electronic money that can be debited by a merchant at the point of sale or elsewhere. One type of smart card is called an *electronic purse*. The purse is commonly referred to as an "open system" because it can be used at multiple locations. Both stored value cards and smart cards may be "reloaded," in which additional amounts of value are added. Another form of digital money takes the

27. *Federal Reserve Bank of Cleveland 1995 Annual Report*, Federal Reserve Bank of Cleveland, 1996.
28. For a more detailed discussion of legal tender, see Benton E. Gup, "The Changing Role of Legal Tender: An Historical Perspective," in *Marketing Exchange Relationships, Transactions, and Their Media*, Frank Houston, ed., Westport, CT (Quorum Books, 1994), pp. 239–246.
29. Elijah Brewer and Douglas D. Evanoff, "Payments Systems–Getting Ready for the 21st Century, *Chicago Fed Letter*, Federal Reserve Bank of Chicago, Special Issue No. 134a (1998).

form of bits on someone's hard drive. Credit cards are also considered electronic money. Electronic data capture (EDC) is a point-of-sale terminal that captures the information provided by the credit card and electronically authorizes the transaction.[30] In addition, by using a cryptographic standard known as secured electronic transactions (SET) and other means, credit cards can be used for secure transactions over the Internet.[31] Because the electronic-based systems involves the clearing process similar to that shown in Table 13.2, a credit (or debit) card transaction may take several days before it is debited or credited to the users account. Thus, retail electronic payments systems are not instantaneous, but they are faster than paper-based systems.

ADVANTAGES AND DISADVANTAGES The advantages of electronic money are that it can be used in ordinary stores and over the Internet to deal in electronic commerce and in precise amounts.[32] It is fast and convenient. Some forms of electronic payments, such as credit cards, leave a record of transactions, whereas other forms of electronic money (e.g., prepaid and stored-value cards) are untraceable. Safety is a different issue. The system will always face the issue of loss due to theft and the possibility that the issuer is unwilling or unable to honor payments made with its electronic liabilities.[33]

While the advantages to using electronic money are evident, some disadvantages must also be considered. Not all merchants accept all forms of electronic money. While credit cards are widely accepted, smart cards have limited acceptance. Security and privacy are two obvious disadvantages. Another is that electronic money is not legal tender. Cash, on the other hand, is legal tender; and it protects the user's privacy. Moreover, cash is uniform and can be redeemed at full par value. Therefore, it is treated the same by all merchants and banks.[34] Finally, the counterparty's credibility does not require verification when using cash.

---

30. Electronic data capture (EDC) is part of Electronic Data Interchange (EDI), which is the exchange of information electronically between business applications in a structured format. Many corporations use EDI for purchase and sale orders. Bank clearinghouses also use EDI. (Diane B. Glossman, and Carole S. Berger, "On-Demand Banking: Power to the People," Salomon Brothers (September 1995).

31. James J. McAndrews, "Making Payments on the Internet," Federal Reserve Bank of Philadelphia, *Business Review* (January/February 1997), pp. 3–14.

32. Yasushi Nakayma et al., "An Electronic Money Scheme," Bank of Japan, Institute of Monetary and Economic Studies, Discussion Paper No. 97-E-4 (June 1997). Note that usually a small fee is charged for processing a credit card transaction, therefore, they are not used for small amounts, or micropayments such as $0.25.

33. "Electronic Money: Consumer Protection, Law Enforcement, Supervisory and Cross Border Issues," Group of Ten Report of the Working Party on Electronic Money"(April 1997).

34. Stacey L. Schreft, "Looking Forward: The Role of Government in Regulating Electronic Cash," Federal Reserve Bank of Kansas City, *Economic Review* (Fourth Quarter 1997), pp. 59–84.

The development of electronic money raises a number of interesting policy issues that will be resolved by Congress and the courts over time. A U.S. Department of Treasury study said that the central issue is who can "coin" digitized money, whether it is stored virtually or on plastic?[35] Companies such as DigiCash and CyberCash, which are not banks, are offering electronic money. Should electronic money be covered by deposit insurance? Should the government issue smart cards? What is the proper role of government with respect to electronic money?

SEIGNIORAGE Seigniorage is an issue involved with electronic money. The original definition of this term was the difference between the monetary value of a coin or currency and the cost of production. Seigniorage comes from the French word for ruler, *seigneur*, that refers to the fee that merchants paid the king to have their bullion made into coins. An additional fee, called brassage, was charged to coin the bullion, thereby standardizing it. Similarly, if the U.S. Treasury issued a new quarter (par value of $0.25) that cost $0.05 to produce, the seigniorage would be $0.20.

Today in the United States, **seigniorage** is considered the interest saved by the Treasury from having currency, which is noninterest-bearing debt, circulate as a medium of exchange. It can be thought of as profit for the Treasury, where the profit is the difference between the interest earned on assets financed by issuing currency and the cost of issuing and redeeming it.[36]

As previously noted, private money systems compete with the Treasury. The use of private money is not a recent development. It dates back to colonial times. Private money is not backed or issued by the government, but it may have the characteristics of money. It is generally accepted as a means of exchange, a store of value, and a unit of account. The new electronic forms of payments can be thought of as the latest version of private money.[37] As electronic means of payment and credit become more widespread, the Treasury's profits from seigniorage will diminish. A study by the Congressional Budget Office estimates that if electronic money replaces 10 percent of the coin and currency in denominations of $10 and under, the government will lose about $370 million per year.[38] The more electronic money is used, the more the Treasury will lose. In the G10 countries (Belgium, Canada, France, Germany, Italy, Japan, Netherlands, Sweden, Switzerland, United Kingdom, and the United States)[39] the potential

See http://www.frbatlanta. org/publica/brochure/ fundfac/money.htm *for fundamental facts about U.S. currency.*

35. Robert E. Litan and Jonathan Rauch, *American Finance for the 21st Century*, U.S. Department of Treasury (November 17, 1997).
36. William P. Osterberg and James B. Thompson, "Bank Notes and Stored Value Card: Stepping Lightly into the Past," *Economic Commentary*, Federal Reserve Bank of Cleveland (September 1, 1998). The author is also indebted to Philip Bartholomew, Chief Economist Democratic Staff, Committee on Banking and Financial Services, U.S. House of Representatives, for his help with defining these terms.
37. Barbara A. Good, "Private Money: Everything Old Is New Again," Federal Reserve Bank of Cleveland, *Economic Commentary* (April 1, 1998).
38. Litan and Rauch, op. cit.
39. The G10 actually has 11 member countries.

effects of seigniorage due to electronic money was estimated to be up to 0.7% of the gross domestic product (GDP).[40]

Home Mortgage Loans

It used to be that residential mortgage lending was a local business. The Internet changed the mortgage business. Today, it is an important part of electronic banking as an increasing number of financial institutions are offering online mortgage services, which has increased the availability of mortgage credit and made mortgage rates and terms competitive. Loans can be approved in minutes, but the approval may be conditional requiring that a long list of conditions be met.

The institutions offering mortgage loans over the Internet fall into four general categories.[41] First, some of them are direct lenders that underwrite the mortgages themselves. Second, some are brokers that find the best deal for their customers and handle the paperwork. The third type is referral services that find loans for borrowers but do not do the paperwork. Finally, mortgage auction sites solicit bids from lenders based on the profiles of the customers and loans.

Obtaining a mortgage online is not necessarily easier nor less costly than going through a traditional lender. Most Internet sites charge a fee based on the value of the loan when a borrower applies, which may be rebated at the time of the closing. One study estimated that by 2003, 10% of home mortgage loans would be made online.[42] Although the Internet can be used to handle much of the paperwork, some contact with humans is still required. At closings, documents need to be signed and notarized.

13.2 LARGE-DOLLAR TRANSFERS

In the United States, large-dollar transfers, or wholesale payments as they are commonly called, are used by banks, businesses, and governments. The large-dollar transfers are made over the Fedwire or by using the Clearing House Interbank Payments System (CHIPS). International payments also involve Society for Worldwide Interbank Financial Telecommunications (S.W.I.F.T.).

40. W. C. Boeschoten and G. E. Hebbink, *Electronic Money, Currency Demand and Seigniorage Loss in the G-10 Countries*, DNB-Staff Reports, De Nederlandsche Bank NV, Amsterdam, The Netherlands (1996).
41. Karen Hube, "E-Mortgage World: Data-Packed, Tricky," *Wall Street Journal* (April 28, 1999), pp. C1, C24.
42. Vivian Marino, "As Web's Popularity Grows, So Do On-Line Lenders," *The Herald* (Miami, FL) (April 18, 1999), p. 30H.

Food for Thought

Morsel 1. Providing Internet banking service is less expensive than buying or opening new branches, and it can be used to cross national boundaries. Canadian Imperial Bank of Commerce received regulatory approval to start an Internet bank in Orlando, Florida. It plans to open kiosks in supermarkets owned by Winn-Dixie Stores to attract new customers.*

Morsel 2. The basic difference between one bank and another is the people who work for it. All banks offer similar services, but the quality of that service depends on people. To a large extent, the franchise value of the banks depends on those same people.

What will happen to franchise values when consumers' only contact with the bank is the Internet? Today consumers can shop the web where many organizations offer mortgage loans, car loans, CD rates, and more. The key distinction between organizations offering these services is the cost of the loan or rate of return. No human contact is necessary. Will customers focus primarily on price and desert traditional brick-and-mortar banks? If they do what will happen to small, local banks?

*Larry M. Greenberg, "Canada Banks Try Web to Win U.S. Customers," *Wall Street Journal* (October 28, 1999), p. A18.

Fedwire

Domestic interbank payments are transferred over the **Fedwire**, an electronic funds transfer system operated by the Federal Reserve. It is a **real-time gross settlements (RTGS) system**. RTGS means that the system settles each transaction individually as it occurs, rather than processing transactions in a batch. It operates 18 hours per day, from 12:30 A.M. Eastern Time until 6:30 P.M. to facilitate international funds transfers. In 1996, the average value per transaction on the Fedwire was about $3 million.

Because the Federal Reserve grants *finality*, the payments are final and irrevocable. Stated otherwise, the Federal Reserve assumes the credit risk associated with the transfer of funds. This credit risk is commonly referred to as a daylight overdraft. If the funds involved in the transfer are not repaid at the end of the day, they become unsecured overnight overdrafts. The Federal Reserve discourages overdrafts by imposing monetary penalties and taking administrative actions against those institutions that repeatedly have daylight and overnight overdrafts. To reduce their risk, the Federal Reserve imposes limits (debt caps) on the amount of daylight overdrafts for each depository institution based on the institutions risk-based capital.

CHIPS

International funds transfers use **Clearing House Interbank Payments System (CHIPS)**, operated by the New York Clearing House Association (NYCHA). It began operating in 1970 as an electronic replacement for paper checks for international dollar payments. It processes $1.4 trillion daily, and in 1996, the average value of transfers was $6 million.

Suppose that a French firm bought $3 million in parts from a U.S. manufacturing firm. The French firm instructed its bank in Paris to debit its account in francs for the dollar equivalent of $3 million, and then to pay the U.S. supplier's bank in New York. The French bank has a branch in New York, and it makes the $3 million payment to the U.S. bank.

As the funds are transferred throughout the day, CHIPS calculates each participant's single net position vis-à-vis all the other participants. In other words, CHIPS nets or offsets mutual obligations to reduce the number of obligations that the participants must deal with. This system of settlement is called **multilateral netting**.[43] When all positions are settled at the end of the day (*same-day settlement*), those banks with a net credit position receive a Fedwire funds transfer from the NYCHA, and the CHIPS account at the Federal Reserve Bank of New York has a zero position. Now the transaction between the French and U.S. banks is final.

As the largest privately operated payments system, CHIPS must deal with concern about payment and settlement risk.[44] *Settlement risk* involves *credit risk* (due to the failure of one party to deliver a promised payment), *unwinding risk* (payment instructions to receivers of funds may be reversed), and *liquidity risk* (payment instructions cannot be settled due to lack of liquidity). The Federal Reserve requires CHIPS and other private wholesale transfer systems to ensure settlement in the event of default by a major participant. CHIPS has a procedure for dealing with the failure of its two largest participants.[45] Despite the risks involved with international settlements, CHIPS has never failed to settle.

S.W.I.F.T.

The **Society for Worldwide Interbank Financial Telecommunications (S.W.I.F.T)**, incorporated in Belgium, is a cooperative owned by banks throughout the world to facilitate payments and financial messages among its members.[46] S.W.I.F.T is used primarily for communications, and the actual transfers of funds are done by the CHIPS and the Fedwire.

43. Each CHIPS participant has a bilateral agreement and credit limit with the other CHIPS participants. For a discussion of other settlements systems, see William Roberds, "The Incentive Effects of Settlement Systems: A Comparison of Gross Settlement, Net Settlement, and Gross Settlement with Queing," Bank of Japan, Institute for Monetary and Economic Studies, IMES Discussion Paper No. 99-E-25 (September 1999).
44. For additional discussion of CHIPS, see Norman R. Nelson, "Private Sector Clearing and Payment Systems," in *Proceedings, Payments Systems in the Global Economy: Risks and Opportunities*, Federal Reserve Bank of Chicago (May 1998), pp. 22–26.
45. Elijah Brewer and Douglas D. Evanoff, op. cit.
46. U.S. General Accounting Office, *Payments, Clearance, and Settlement*, op. cit.

MANAGING RISK

Herstatt Risk

Bankhaus I. D. Herstatt was established in Cologne, Germany, in 1955. Although It was a relatively small bank, it was one of largest dealers in foreign exchange in Germany. The 1973 oil shock increased the volatility of markets and disrupted capital flows. Many banks experienced foreign exchange losses following the unexpected depreciation of some currencies and a tightening of monetary policy in the United States. Franklin National Bank in the United States failed following large losses on foreign exchange trading. Herstatt, Lloyds Bank in Lugano, the Bank of Belgium, and Westdeutsche Landsbank all had losses. However, Herstatt suffered the most, and it failed in 1974.

The method of closure caused some controversy. Herstatt's failure was announced at 4:30 P.M., after closure of settlement system in Germany, which, because of differences in time zones, was at 10:30 A.M. in New York. It defaulted on more than $600 million in claims. It was closed by the German banking authority, and the Bundesbank stopped clearing its account, at a time when Herstatt was heavily engaged in foreign exchange activities. One reason given for the timing of the closure was that the German authorities wanted to teach speculators and banks dealing with speculators a lesson. West German banks raised a levy to pay off small

deposits up to $7,600, but large depositors had to take what the liquidator would give them, which ranged from 45% (West German institutions) to 65% (private creditors) of their claims.

The closure had a global impact because of incomplete foreign exchange transactions. It disrupted the operations of the Clearing House International Payments System (CHIPS) and resulted in losses for banks that had irrevocably paid out Deutsche mark to Herstatt that day. Thus, Herstatt's counterparties were confronted with losses due to the asynchronous settlement of funds.

The Herstatt failure gave rise to the term *cross currency settlement risk,* or ***Herstatt risk.*** It has serious systemic risk implications because foreign exchange transactions account for a large share of the payments in major financial centers, most of which are handled by banks. A key factor giving rise to Herstatt risk is the difference in time zones and operating hours of banking systems across countries. In the early 1990s, no overlap was available between the operating hours of the large-value interbank transfer systems of the countries with the three most actively traded currencies: the United States, Japan, and Germany.

Source: Benton E. Gup, *Bank Failures in the Major Trading Countries of the World: Causes and Remedies* (Westport, CT, 1998), Chapter 2.

Foreign Exchange

Foreign exchange transactions arise from international trade and investments as well as from hedging and speculation in foreign currencies. The settlement transactions result in U.S. dollars being exchanged for another currency such as the French franc. The two settlements in such transactions are dollars being settled in the United States and foreign currency being settled in the other country's payment system.

Both bilateral and multilateral netting systems are used for foreign exchange transactions. In a **bilateral netting system,** two banks that may have

MANAGERIAL ISSUES

*Electronic Payments Reduce Costs and Revenues**

Banks make a lot of money from bounced checks. Fees charged for bounced checks may be $20 per item, or higher. Out of the 173 million checks that are processed daily, about 1.3 million are bad. That amounts to about $2.6 million daily in added fee income.

The amount of fee income that banks earn from bounced checks depends, in part, on how they rank the checks—whether they process the largest checks first, or the smallest ones. Suppose that five checks arrive the same day ranging in size from $900 to $20 ($900, $200, $100, $50, and $20). In an account with $500, if the largest check ($900) is debited first, overdrawing the account, the bank earns $100 in bounced check fees for the five checks. On the other hand, if the smaller checks are debited first,

it will only collect $20 because only the $900 check will bounce.

It costs banks between $0.50 and $1.50 to process bad checks, but they earn fee income $20 or more per item. The high-to-low check processing adds considerably to banks' income. However, electronic bill paying may deprive banks of this source of fee income depending on how they process the charges. If they use real time gross settlement, they can still earn the fee for overdrawing the account. On the other hand, if they do netting, they may not earn any fees depending on the timing of debits and credits.

*For more information on this topic, see Rick Brooks, "How Banks Make the Most of Bounced Checks," *Wall Street Journal* (February 25, 1999), pp. B1, B8.

---

multiple contracts to settle in a foreign currency, such as German marks, can replace them with a single contract for the net amount to be sent through the German payments system for clearing. FXNET (a clearing system owned by U.K. subsidiaries of major banks), Accord (provided to members of S.W.I.F.T), and VALUNET (selected U.S. and Canadian banks) all use bilateral netting. In contrast ECHO (Exchange Clearing House, London), and Multinet International Bank (selected U.S. and Canadian banks) use multilateral netting.[47]

SUMMARY

Electronic banking has developed in two distinct areas, one dealing with retail, small-dollar transactions, and the other with wholesale, large-dollar transactions. On the retail side, electronic banking and payments are the wave of the

47. U.S. General Accounting Office, Payments, Clearance, and Settlement, op. cit.; Also see William J. Hanley, Karen McCann, and James Moser, "Public Benefits and Public Concerns: An Economic Analysis of Regulatory Standards for Clearing Facilities," Federal Reserve Bank of Chicago Working Paper, No. WP-95-12 (September 1995); ECHO (London) should not be confused with ECCHO—Electronic Clearing House Association that is part of the domestic payments system in the United States.

future, but it is not here yet. Electronic payments account for about 6% of retail payments, cash (75%) and paper account for the remainder.[48] A Federal Reserve forum on the payments system in 1997 concluded that paper checks would remain an important part of the payments system for at least the next 10 years.[49] The reasons given were that they were convenient to use and were widely accepted; the legal foundations of check collection were well established; and the checkwriters like the float. The report goes on to say that consumers are confused by the number of options available to them. Moreover, the electronic means of payment do not currently provide the flexibility and convenience of checks and cash. Finally, the legal framework that establishes the rights and liabilities of the participants is evolving and not as well understood as the current paper-based system.

Electronic payments dominate the wholesale side of payments, and will continue to do so.

Key Terms and Concepts

Bilateral netting system
Clearing House Interbank
    Payments System (CHIPS)
Electronic banking
Electronic bill presentment and
    payment (EBPP)
Electronic money
Fedwire

Herstatt risk
Multilateral netting
Real-time gross settlements (RTGS)
    system
Seigniorage
Society for Worldwide Interbank
    Financial Telecommunications
    (S.W.I.F.T.)

Questions

13.1   What is electronic banking?

13.2   Electronic banking has developed in several distinct directions. Explain its development.

13.3   What are the principal retail electronic banking products?

13.4   How does "network externalities" affect electronic banking?

13.5   How do banks earn fee income from ATMs?

13.6   What are the advantages of electronic bill presentment and payment systems?

13.7   What is Federal Reserve "Regulation E"?

48. "The Federal Reserve in the Payments Mechanism," Board of Governors of the Federal Reserve System (January 1998).
49. "Summary of Input From Payment Systems Forums," September 1997, Board of Governors of the Federal Reserve System (1997).

13.8   What is electronic money?

13.9   What is the difference between seigniorage and brassage?

13.10   What is the difference between real-time gross settlements and multi-lateral netting?

13.11   What are the Fedwire, CHIPS, and S.W.I.F.T.?

Trolling the Net

Julia Chan is the vice president in charge of Coastal Bank and Trust's (CBT) Private Banking Department. CBT is a $4 billion regional bank, and the Private Banking Department caters to the financial needs of individuals with high net worth (more than $1 million). She wants to develop better ways to build strong customer relationships with them and to attract new business by improving CBT's Internet financial services. The first step in her quest is to benchmark the Internet financial services offered by other institutions. To begin, she trolls the net at the following sites:

1. Make a list of the financial services that would be most attractive to high net worth individuals.
2. Select one of these services and develop a brief scenario of how to market this service to clients who are female, married, and over 35 years old.
3. How would you market that service to individuals of your age?

Banks	Web Sites
Bank of America	*http://www.bankamerica.com*
Chase Manhattan Bank	*http://www.chase.com*
Citibank	*http://citibank.com*
Security First Network Bank	*http://www.sfnb.com*
Telebank	*http://www.telebank.com*
Wells Fargo	*http://www.wellsfargo.com*
Wingspan Bank	*http://www.wingspan.com*

Other Institutions	
American Express Financial Direct	*http://americanexpress.com/direct*
Charles Schwab	*http://schwab.com*
Fidelity	*http://fidelity.com*

CHAPTER 14

Off-Balance Sheet Activities

After reading this chapter you will be able to:

- Define off-balance sheet activities that banks are expanding rapidly to meet market demands.

- Describe the different types of contingent claims offered by banks.

- Discuss the growing derivative securities activities of banks, which are challenging regulators to control potential risks inherent in this new and exciting market.

- Compare the risk implications of different off-balance sheet activities.

- Identify other off-balance sheet services that do not involve contingent claims or derivative securities.

The 1980s witnessed wild gyrations in market rates of interest, economic booms and busts, and inflation and deflation. Even though the 1990s experienced low and stable interest rates and a steady economic expansion with little or no inflation, price volatility in United States and other industrialized countries' stock markets exceeded historical experience. Also, emerging market countries suffered periodic bouts of extreme financial market turmoil that at times spilled over into developed countries (e.g., economic and financial crises in Russia, Southeast Asia, and Latin America). The net impact of this global volatility has been increased variability of profits and, therefore, risk of doing business in financial markets.

In response to increased risk as well as the need to satisfy customers' demands, generate stable fee income, and increase their capital-to-asset ratios, banks have developed new financial services that do not appear on their balance sheets as assets or liabilities—so called off-balance sheet activities. Generally speaking, most **off-balance sheet activities** are commitments based on contingent claims. A **contingent claim** is an obligation by a bank to provide funds (i.e., lend funds or buy securities) if a contingency is realized. In other words, the bank has underwritten an obligation of a third party and currently stands behind the risk. Default by the party on whose behalf the obligation was written may trigger an immediate loss or may result in the bank acquiring a substandard claim. Importantly, the claims do not appear on the balance sheet until they are exercised, when the loan is made or the securities are purchased.

Two broad groups of off-balance sheet activities are presented in this chapter: financial guarantees and derivative instruments. For the sake of completeness, we also discuss some other types of off-balance sheet activities, including trade finance, cash management services, and networking (or strategic alliances). Together, these rapidly growing areas of off-balance sheet activities generate fee income for banks.

Importantly, these new financial products are transforming the banking business from being deposit/lending institutions to risk management institutions. Indeed, large banks have become the key players in managing various financial market risks. Although risk management services clearly are needed in today's more volatile financial marketplace, and banks' off-balance sheet activities literally have exploded over the last two decades in response to these needs, serious concerns about these new products remain. How much total risk are banks taking in off-balance sheet activities? What are the different kinds of risk involved? To what extent should these activities be regulated? Should reporting requirements for regulators and the public be increased? Even as these new financial products help manage financial market risks, their benefits are not achieved without some costs, including greater complexity of financial transactions and new potential risks. ∎

14.1 FINANCIAL GUARANTEES

Figure 14.1 shows Schedule L of the Report of Condition for banks entitled "Commitments and Contingencies." Most of the items shown there are based on financial guarantees of banks. A **financial guarantee** is an undertaking by a bank (the guarantor) to stand behind the *current* obligation of a third party, and to carry out that obligation if the third party fails to do so. For example, a bank can make a **loan guarantee** whereby it guarantees the repayment of a loan made from party A to party B. The guarantors assume that they are more effective credit analysts than other capital market participants because the ultimate liability of the debt is shifted from the borrower to the guarantor. Assuming the guarantor's credit is better than that of the borrower, the rate of return required by the market on the borrower's debt obligations is reduced. From the bank's perspective fees ranging from 10 to 150 basis points are charged, depending on the reduction in the borrower's debt costs and risk exposure of the bank.

Standby Letters of Credit

Standby letters of credit (SLCs) obligate the bank to pay the beneficiary if the **account party** defaults on a financial obligation or performance contract. A fee

FIGURE 14.1 Schedule L of Report of Condition

Schedule RC-L—Commitments and Contingencies

Please read carefully the instructions for the preparation of Schedule RC-L.

Dollar Amounts in Thousands			C360 Bil	Mil	Thou	
1. Commitments to make or purchase loans or to extend credit in the form of lease financing arrangements (report only the unused portions of commitments that are fee paid or otherwise legally binding)	RCON 3423					1.
2. Futures and forward contracts (exclude contracts involving foreign exchange):						
a. Commitments to purchase	RCON 3424					2.a.
b. Commitments to sell	RCON 3425					2.b.
3. When-issued securities:						
a. Gross commitments to purchase	RCON 3434					3.a.
b. Gross commitments to sell	RCON 3435					3.b.
4. Standby contracts and other option arrangements:						
a. Obligations to purchase under option contracts	RCON 3426					4.a.
b. Obligations to sell under option contracts	RCON 3427					4.b.
5. Commitments to purchase foreign currencies and U.S. dollar exchange (spot and forward)	RCON 3419					5.
6. Standby letters of credit:						
a. Standby letters of credit:						
(1) To U.S. addresses (domicile)	RCON 3476					6.a.(1)
(2) To non-U.S. addresses (domicile)	RCON 3477					6.a.(2)
b. Amount of standby letters of credit in items 6.a.(1) and 6.a.(2) conveyed to others through participations	RCON 3478					6.b.
7. Commercial and similar lines of credit	RCON 3411					7.
8. Participations in acceptances (as described in the instructions) conveyed to others by the reporting bank	RCON 3428					8.
9. Participations in acceptances (as described in the instructions) acquired by the reporting (nonaccepting) bank	RCON 3420					9.
10. Securities borrowed	RCON 3422					10.
11. Securities lent	RCON 3433					11.
12. Other significant commitments and contingencies (list below each component of this item over 25% of Schedule RC, item 28, "Total equity capital")	RCON 3430					12.

Memoranda

1. Loans originated by the reporting bank that have been sold or participated to others during the calendar quarter ending with the report date (exclude the portions of such loans retained by the reporting bank; see instructions for other exclusions)	RCON 3431					M.1.
2. Notional value of all outstanding interest rate swaps	RCON 3450					M.2.

Source: Federal Financial Institutions Examination Council.

of about 1% of the guarantee is charged by the issuing bank. Most SLCs never become a bank liability; however, if bank payment is required, it usually means that a problem loan is acquired by the bank. Two types of SLCs can be issued. A *financial SLC* is related to a financial commitment, such as repayment of commercial paper. A *performance SLC* is nonfinancial in nature; for example, a commitment to complete a construction project or deliver certain merchandise. Although national banks and most state banks are prohibited from issuing guarantees, SLCs serve the same function and do not violate the law. Banks not only earn fee income on SLCs but interest income in the event credit must be extended to the account party to cover a payment of funds to the beneficiary. SLCs are comparable to an over-the-counter put option written by the bank (i.e., the firm defaulting "puts" the credit obligation back to the bank).

USES OF STANDBY LETTERS OF CREDIT   Standby letters of credit are commonly used in connection with the issuance of debt obligations (i.e., bonds, notes, and commercial paper) as backup lines of credit. For example, the city of Burlington, Kansas, issued $106.5 million bonds with a 7-year maturity to fund pollution control and improvements. The bonds are to be repaid by payments received by the city from project users. If the payments are not sufficient to cover the interest and principal, the bonds are backed by irrevocable letters of credit from Westpac Banking Corporation (an Australian bank holding company) and The Long-Term Credit Bank of Japan, Limited. In essence, these banking organizations supported the city's ability to borrow funds without the banks raising deposits or making loans.

Another common use of SLCs is in connection with building contractors' obligations to complete a construction project. For example, a contractor (the account party) promises a beneficiary that a hydroelectric plant will be completed on or before a stated date. If the project is not completed before that date, the bank is required to pay the beneficiary. The reason why the project was not completed is not relevant. The only thing that is important is that the account party failed to perform (defaulted) on the obligation to the beneficiary. In this case, the SLC is a substitute for a surety bond. Surety bonds are sold by insurance companies to insure against loss, damage, or default. They are a special type of insurance policy and should not be confused with the debt obligations that are also called bonds.

SLCs are also used to ensure the delivery of merchandise, to ensure the performance of options or futures contracts, to back other loans, and even to guarantee alimony and child support payments. A fundamental aspect of SLCs is that they are dependent on the bank's credit rating. If the bank's safety and soundness deteriorates, the value of its SLCs would seriously decline, as well as its ability to issue new SLCs.

RISK   Many banks evaluate account parties that want standby letters of credit in the same way they evaluate commercial loans. SLCs are considered loans for the purpose of calculating legal lending limits. Because bankers accept only those credits that they believe are least likely to default and be taken down (loans made), they consider their credit risk minimal. Even so, risk is inherent in the business of lending. For example, as noted in the discussion of international debt crises in Chapter 16, bankers considered the risk of making huge loans to less developed countries (LDCs) minimal. However, unexpected economic and financial events reduced the ability of many emerging market countries to repay their debts, which forced U.S. banks to write off many of these loans and reschedule the payments on other loans in the 1980s and 1990s.

To further reduce the risk to banks, many SLCs are backed by deposits and/or collateral. Nevertheless, the long-term nature of some of the commitments can cause risks to change over time. Consequently, some banks require periodic renegotiation of SLC terms.

If and when a SLC is taken down, the bank may book the unreimbursed balance as a commercial loan.

Banks can manage their risk by limiting the donor amount of standby letters of credit they issue, diversifying their portfolio of such letters, and increasing capital.[1] Nonetheless, SLCs subject banks to both liquidity risk, also known as funding risk in this context, and capital risk, because losses can rapidly accumulate, for example, due to an economic downturn that can cause more than one borrower to default at the same time. Also, interest rate risk is present in SLCs either from possible changes in their duration gap or the increased (decreased) likelihood of default as interest rate levels increase (decrease).

Finally, SLCs expose the bank to an ill-defined legal risk. Most SLCs contain a **material adverse change (MAC) clause** that enables the bank to withdraw its commitment under certain conditions (e.g., the financial condition of the firm has seriously declined). From the borrower's viewpoint, payment of the SLC fee is intended to cover the bank for the risk that its ability to pay the debt will deteriorate. Such a clause would seem to unnecessarily favor the bank therefore. However, from the bank's viewpoint, the clause is needed to deter the firm from taking excessive risks and exploiting the bank's guarantee.

PRICING Standby letters of credit may have upfront and annual fees. For example, the upfront fee may be 1% of the outstanding and unused guarantee, and the annual fees may range from 25 to 150 basis points lower than the bank would charge for loans of equivalent maturity and risk. The annual fees on standby letters of credit are lower than loan fees, in part, because of the lower administrative cost and other expenses associated with them and because normally no funding is required. Of course, if the bank does loan funds, the interest rate must be priced according to standard methods of evaluating loan risk.

---

1. Empirical research has revealed that large money center and superregional banks tended to increase their capital positions in conjunction with SLC exposure. The logical reason for this relationship is that the bank is serving as guarantor and must itself demonstrate financial strength to gain the confidence of the SLC beneficiary, who will receive payment from the bank in the event a firm defaults on its debt.

Bank Loan Commitments

In general terms, a **loan commitment** represents a bank's promise to a customer to make a future loan(s) or a guarantee under certain conditions. The agreement between the bank and the customer may be informal or formal; however, *some* agreements are not legally binding on the bank or the potential borrower. The major benefits of loan commitments are the assurance of funds to the borrower and fees or compensating balances of equivalent value to the bank. The major drawback is that the bank is acquiring a credit exposure in the future because it may have to make a loan or a guarantee. Nevertheless, in the five-year period 1994–1998, bank loan commitments grew from $1.76 trillion to $3.72 trillion. Today, more than 80% of the total dollar volume of commercial and industrial (C&I) loans are made under some form of an agreement.

LINE OF CREDIT As explained in Chapter 7, a **line of credit** is an agreement between a bank and a customer that the bank will entertain a request for a loan from that customer and, in most cases, make the loan even though they are not obligated to do so. Lines are frequently informal agreements and the banks do not collect a fee for the service. Accordingly, a line of credit is not a "firm" commitment by the bank to lend funds.

REVOLVING LOAN COMMITMENTS In contrast, a **revolving loan commitment** is a formal agreement between the bank and a customer, which obligates the bank to lend funds according to the terms of the contract. The contract specifies the terms under which loans will be made, including the maximum amounts to be loaned, interest rate, maturities. The customer pays the bank a commitment fee, which is also called a **facility fee**, for the privilege of being able to borrow funds at a future date. The fee, for example, may be 1/2 percent per year of the unused balance. As in the case of SLCs, some revolving loan commitments contain (MAC) clauses that release the bank from its obligation to make a loan if the customer's financial condition changes substantially.

Revolving loan commitments protect the borrower from both availability risk and markup risk. Markup risk is associated with the premium added on the reference rate (e.g., prime rate) to compensate the bank for credit risk. Revolving commitments fix the premium, in contrast to a confirmed credit line that sets the rate at the time funds are taken down. Thus, revolving loan commitments are tantamount to options contracts, wherein the bank must offer a loan at the agreed upon price. Because revolving commitments expose the bank to interest rate risk, the commitment fee is priced to capture this bank risk. Confirmed credit lines generally do not require commitment fees.

FUNDING RISK The major risk facing banks with loan commitments is that a large number of borrowers will take down their loans simultaneously and the bank may not have sufficient funds to make the loans. This funding or liquidity risk (also referred to as quantity risk) is most likely to occur during periods of tight credit. Because the bank is obligated to make the loans, it may have to raise additional funds, which is difficult during these times, to honor the commitments.

If the bank does not honor the commitment, a customer with a legally binding commitment could bring legal action against the bank. Such an action could damage the bank's reputation, which could impair its future growth and profitability.

Certain types of commitments are considered irrevocable, or unconditional and binding. According to the Bank for International Settlements, irrevocable commitments include the following:

1. *Asset sale and repurchase agreements.* An arrangement whereby a bank sells a loan, security, or fixed asset to a third party with a commitment to repurchase the asset after a certain time, or in the event of a certain contingency.

2. *Outright forward purchases.* A commitment to purchase a loan, security, or other asset at a specified future date, typically on prearranged terms.

3. *An irrevocable revolving line of credit.*

4. *Note issuance facilities*, which will be explained shortly.

Similarly, certain types of commitments are considered revocable. These include credit lines and undrawn overdraft facilities.

Initially, interest rate volatility was the motivation for the growth of loan commitments. However, deregulation is another important trend that has become a key factor in explaining their continued growth even when interest rates are at historically low levels, as in the 1990s. Interest rate deregulation allowed banks to explicitly price deposit accounts and loans (i.e., implicit pricing, an informal style of bank commitments, was prominent under regulation). Subsequent to this deregulation, borrowers began demanding formal commitments with explicit prices. Because loan commitments naturally fit into this pricing framework, they have become increasingly important in recent years, regardless of the volatility of interest rates.

Note Issuance Facilities

Note issuance facility (NIF) is one of several terms used to describe medium-term (2–7 years) agreements whereby banks guarantee the sale of a borrower's short-term, negotiable promissory notes at or below predetermined interest rates. If a borrower cannot readily obtain short-term funds in a timely fashion for one reason or another, the bank will step in and buy the securities. Other terms for similar financial guarantees are revolving underwriting facilities (RUFs) and standby note issuance facilities (SNIFs).

For bank borrowers the short-term security is usually certificates of deposit (sometimes called a *Roly-Poly CD Facility*). For nonbank borrowers the short-term debt securities are called **Euronotes**. Euronotes are denominated in U.S. dollars and usually have a face value of $500,000 or more. They are held mainly by governments and institutional investors. As the term *Euronotes* implies, most of the activity in this market involves international banking. Euronotes are not registered with the Securities and Exchange Commission and cannot be sold in the United States. The major nonbank sovereign borrowers in the Euronote market are the United States, Austria, and Great Britain. The main buyers of Euronotes are European and Japancsc banks. However, similar standby arrangements are used for the sale of commercial paper in the United States. Various other terms used for these types of agreements are RUFs, transferable RUFs (TRUFs), SNIFs, note purchase facility, multiple component facilities, and Euronote facilities.

Arrangers and Tender Panels

One contingent risk to banks in these arrangements arises from their roles as underwriters or arrangers. The NIF can be organized or underwritten by a single bank (the arranger) or by a group of 15 or more banks and financial institutions (the tender panel) that have the right to bid for the short-term notes issued under the facility. The advantage of a tender panel is the broader competitive market offered by many institutions bidding for the securities, rather than having one bidder. The tender panel also provides a means to place larger dollar amounts of securities than may be possible for a single arranger.

The arranger or tender panel assures the borrower access to short-term funds (i.e., 90 days) over the 5–7 years covered by the agreement. This process is known as maturity transformation. Maturity transformation results in increased credit risk for the arranger or tender panel that may have to lend the borrower funds if the borrower is unable to sell the short-term securities at the interest rates (or prices) agreed upon. The NIFs also increase the funding risk of the underwriting banks if they are called upon to make the loans.

14.2 DERIVATIVES

In this section we supplement material presented in Chapter 6 by profiling different kinds of derivative securities—swaps, options, futures, forward contracts, and securitized assets. Derivatives are financial instruments that are derived from underlying securities. It is therefore necessary to understand not only the risks of the underlying security but the transactions involved in the derivative and their associated risks (see the Managing Risk, "Counting the Risks in Derivatives," for a summary of relevant risks). Interestingly, while derivatives are generally spoken of as off-balance sheet activities, most (but not all) derivatives are reported on the balance sheet. Derivatives with positive values are counted as assets and those with negative values as liabilities.

The importance of derivatives markets stems from their sudden and rapid growth. As shown in Figure 14.2, excluding securitized instruments, derivatives

FIGURE 14.2 **Derivatives Take Off**

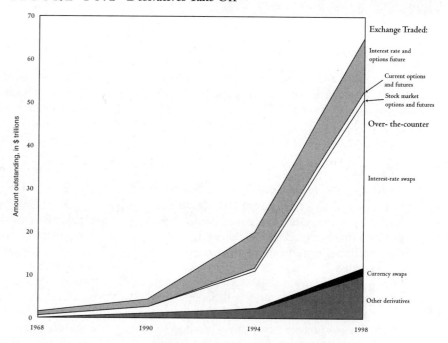

Source: Bank for International Settlements (BIS), as reported at their web site.

expanded from about $1.4 trillion in 1986 to about $65 trillion in 1998. The magnitude of this growth implies that derivatives have brought fundamental changes to securities markets around the world.

The two derivatives markets are (1) the privately traded over-the-counter (OTC) market dominated by money center banks and large securities firms that custom design products for users, and (2) the organized exchanges that offer standardized contracts and a clearinghouse for handling transactions—for example, the Chicago Board of Trade (CBOT), which is the largest, in addition to the Chicago Mercantile Exchange (CME), Chicago Board Options Exchange (CBOE), London International Futures and Options Exchange (LIFFE), Eurex Germany, Marché à International de France (MATIF), Tokyo International Financial Futures Exchange (TIFFE), and other regional exchanges. In the OTC market, swaps account for most of the activity in derivatives. The top 100 banks in the United States account for about 99% of OTC derivatives in terms of notional volume, and the top 10 banks hold about 90% of this total. It is clear from these numbers that derivatives activities are concentrated in the largest banks. Today, the OTC market exceeds the exchange-traded market in dollar terms.

MANAGING RISK

Counting the Risks in Derivatives

The Federal Reserve, Comptroller of the Currency, and FDIC have cited seven key categories of risk associated with derivatives.

1. **Counterparty credit risk** is the risk that a counterparty in a financial transaction will default, resulting in a financial loss to the other party. Credit exposure is not measured by the notational amount of the contract but by the cost of replacing its cash flows in the market. In an interest rate swap, for example, the present value of expected cash flows on the underlying instruments would need to be calculated.

2. **Price, or market, risk** is the risk that the market price of the derivative security will change. This risk is closely related to the price risk of the underlying instrument. Most banks break overall price risk into components, including interest rate risk, exchange rate risk, commodity price risk, and others.

3. **Settlement risk** occurs when one party in a financial transaction pays out funds to the other party before it receives its own cash or assets. Thus, settlement risk is linked to credit risk.

4. **Liquidity risk** is the risk that a counterparty will default and a liquidity shortfall will occur due to losses.

5. **Operating risk** is an often-overlooked area of commercial bank risk that can arise due to:

   - *Inadequate internal controls.* The complexity of some derivatives, human error, and fraud are all sources of risk that demand internal monitoring and control by management.
   - *Valuation risk.* The valuation of many derivatives relies on fairly sophisticated mathematical models that are highly dependent on assumptions about market conditions, which together can make valuation a difficult task.
   - *Regulatory risk.* As already mentioned, regulators are scrutinizing OTC derivatives due to their explosive growth, and this attention could draw changes in accounting procedures, capital adequacy, restrictions on activities, and other banking practices.

6. **Legal risk** may arise because the OTC market for derivatives is private in nature, fast developing, and innovative in security design, all of which means that disputes within this new market will require a period of legal cases to clearly establish the rights and obligations of all participants. The International Swap Dealers Association has established some rules in cooperation with most large industrialized countries, but the differences in national bankruptcy laws raises legal concerns about the risks in international deals.

7. **Aggregation risk** comes about from the complex interconnections that can occur in derivatives deals, which involve a number of markets and instruments. It becomes difficult to assess the risks to individual parties or groups of parties in such transactions.

The largest banks and securities firms are best able to manage the risks that are due to the operational demands of capital and expertise. However, large regional banks also are attempting to enter the derivatives market, either on their own or in cooperation with money center banks seeking to expand their reach in the derivatives market. Are derivatives too risky for banks? Should there be greater regulatory control of OTC derivatives? These questions have no simple answers and will be the focus of much academic and regulatory study in the years ahead.

The magnitude of the market and potential for unknown risks due to their unprecedented growth has attracted regulators' attention, including the Commodity Futures Trading Commission (CFTC), SEC, Federal Reserve, Comptroller of the Currency, and FDIC. Regulators worry that, while most participants at present are large and reputable financial institutions, the market could be expected to attract inexperienced or fraudulent participants. Such participants would introduce new risks for all players. Also, competition in the derivatives securities markets could drive some large banks to precarious positions and expose them to sudden liquidity risks.[2] This potential is made more real by the fact that few regulatory barriers are currently in place in the OTC, compared to the relatively formal regulatory oversight of exchanged-traded products by the CFTC. Alternatively, others argue that derivatives offer new hedging techniques that reduce risk in the financial system. Whatever the case, which time and experience will eventually reveal, this exciting market will certainly spread and become increasingly more important to bankers around the world. Today, competition in derivatives trading is intense, with the result that automated trading and more services related to risk management systems are becoming the norm.

The International Swaps and Derivatives Association or ISDA (http:\\www. isda.org\) is a global trade association that represents leading participants in the privately negotiated derivatives industry, a business that includes interest rate, currency, commodity, and equity swaps, as well as related products such as caps, collars, floors, and swaptions. ISDA was chartered in 1985, and its members include most of the world's major institutions who deal in, as well as leading end-users of, privately negotiated derivatives.

Currency and Interest Rate Swaps

A **swap** is an agreement between two counterparties to exchange cash flows and is based upon some notional principal amount of money, maturity, and interest rates. The counterparties are financial institutions, business concerns, government agencies, and international agencies. In the classic "plain vanilla" interest rate swap, counterparties literally swap their interest payments, where one party has fixed interest payments and the other has variable interest payments. No transfer of principal takes place between the counterparties, which is why the term *notional* principal amount is used. Swaps in essence are two forward agreements to exchange cash flows between two counterparties.

Types of Swaps

Currency swaps and **interest rate swaps** are the two principal types of swap arrangements involving exchanges of interest payments between two or more parties. The generic or *plain vanilla* interest rate swap is especially useful for managing interest rate gap problems for banks and nonbank firms. A currency

---

2. The best historical example of potential liquidity problems in derivatives market is the 1987 stock market crash. At that time portfolio insurance strategies based on financial derivatives literally broke down causing large securities losses for many market participants. Subsequently, the exchanges have implemented circuit breakers or speed bumps to slow market downturns and give trading systems time to absorb surges in market orders. The OTC market does not have any similar mechanism to control market activity.

swap includes not only the exchange of interest payments (in different currencies) but also the exchange of the initial and final principal amounts at the beginning and end of the swap. Currency swaps are used not only to hedge an interest rate gap but to hedge cash flow risks (e.g., a U.S. company with long-term fixed receivables in Euros may hedge the exposure with a currency swap).

As noted earlier, an interest rate swap involves the exchange of a stream of interest payments over time. The three main types of interest rate swaps are:

1. **Coupon swaps,** where interest payments are based on fixed rates (e.g., 11 percent) and floating rates of interest (e.g., 6-month LIBOR, or London interbank offered rate).

2. **Basis swaps,** where interest payments are based on two different floating rates of interest (e.g., 6-month LIBOR and U.S. prime commercial paper rates or two variable-rate contracts with different maturities).

3. **Cross-currency interest rate swaps** (simply termed currency swaps), which involve three counterparties (A, B, and C) and, for example, the interest payments between A and B are based on fixed rate flows in one currency and interest rate, and the interest payments between A and C are based on floating rate flows in another currency and interest rate. A *plain deal* currency swap is between two counterparties with equal interest payments in different currencies.

Figure 14.3 shows the growth of currency and interest rate swaps in recent years as reported by ISDA. At year-end 1998 the notional principal outstanding in these contracts was approaching $30 trillion.

Example of a Swap

Figure 14.4 illustrates a coupon interest rate swap based on a notional amount of $10 million. The swap agreement has a maturity of 7 years, and the payment frequency is semiannually. This swap between two banks is the classic plain vanilla variety.

Bank A is the *fixed rate* counterparty, the one that pays the fixed rate of interest; and bank B is the *floating rate* counterparty, the one that pays the floating rate of interest. The figure shows that bank A has fixed rate assets and floating rate liabilities that are mismatched, which is not a good match if market interest rates increase. Bank B has mismatched floating rate assets and fixed rate liabilities, which is not a good match if market interest rates fall. To match their respective balance sheets, both banks exchange streams of interest payments. The fixed rate payer (bank A) pays bank B 12% on the notional amount so that bank B will earn a positive spread between its fixed rate liabilities and its assets. Similarly, the floating rate payer (bank B) pays bank A's cost of its floating rate liabilities.

Let's examine the impact of this transaction on bank A for the first 6 months. The relevant interest rates that we will use in our simplified calculation are:

FIGURE 14.3 Currency and Interest Rate Swaps (in US$ billions)

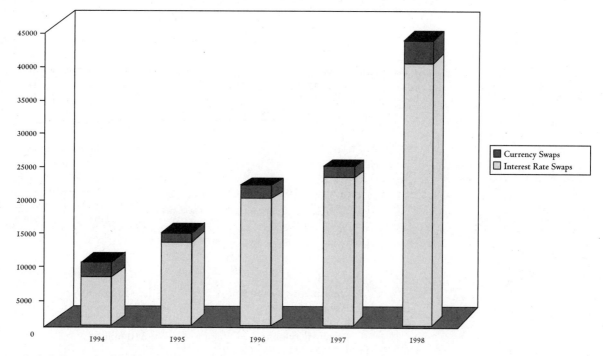

Source: Banks for International Settlements (BIS), as reported at their web site.

6-month LIBOR	10.0%
Bank A's fixed rate payment	12.0
Bank A's variable rate liabilities	9.0

Based on these rates, we can determine the net fixed rate cost of funds to bank A in the following manner.

Fixed rate payments made by bank A minus	12.0%
Floating rate payment received plus	– 10.0
Interest paid on floating rate liabilities	+ 9.0
Net fixed cost	11.0%

In terms of dollar amounts, Bank A will make the first semiannual fixed rate payment of $600,000 ($10 million × 0.12/2) to Bank B, pay $450,000 ($10 million × 0.09/2) on its floating rate liabilities, and receive a floating rate payment of $506,778 from Bank B. The floating rate payment is based on 181 days and a 360-day year.

FIGURE 14.4 Coupon Interest Rate Swap

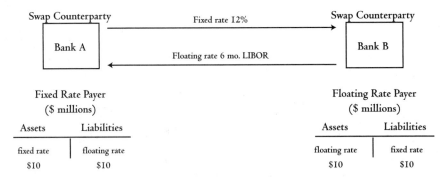

Notional amount: $10 million (US)
Maturity: 7 years
Payment frequency: Both counterparties pay semiannually

First interest period	(1–1 to 6–30)
Number of days	181
6-month LIBOR	10.0%
Principal amount	$10 million

$$\text{Payment} = \frac{\text{Principal} \times \text{LIBOR} \times \text{Number of days}}{\text{Days in year}}$$

$$= \frac{\$10\text{ million} \times 0.10 \times 181}{360}$$

$$= \$506,777.78.$$

Bank A's net fixed cost for the first six months expressed in dollar terms is:

Fixed rate payment	$600,000
plus	
Floating rate liabilities	+ 450,000
minus	
Floating rate payment received	– 506,778
	543,222

Because this type of generic swap is not suitable for all needs, such as debt call features, deferred payments and resetting interest rates have evolved. In addition, a secondary market in swaps has developed so that they may be sold or terminated by one of the counterparties. Innovation in the swap market is creating many new financial products. The Managing Risk box on "Derivatives at Work" gives an interesting example of how swaps can be used to repackage risks and returns among different participants in the swap market.

Risks Associated with Swaps

The volume of swap contracts outstanding at money center banks can be quite large compared to total assets on the balance sheet. It is not uncommon for such banks to have swap levels equal to 10 times their on-balance sheet total assets. Until the late 1980s, organized exchanges served as the swap counter-parties. Today, banks and other financial institutions typically serve this role, although the exchanges may possibly move back into a clearinghouse role in the future. Relevant to bank risk management, counterparties in swap agreements face credit risk and price (or market) risk. Credit risk is the risk that one of the parties to the swap arrangement will default, which will result in a liability to the bank. To reduce this credit risk, standby letters of credit to guarantee payments can be used.

Price risk is the risk that interest rates or exchange rates may change and have an adverse effect on one or more of the participants in the swap agreement. Consider the case of a savings and loan association that seeks to lock in mortgage loan rates of 13% and borrowing rates of 11% in the early 1980s. They entered into swap agreements as floating rate payers, receiving 11% interest and paying the floating rate. Now suppose that interest rates decline after making the swap agreement. Falling interest rates would motivate home-owners to refinance their higher-cost mortgages at lower rates, thereby lowering mortgage portfolio rates of return below 13%. Additionally, even though deposits rates may have declined to say 8%, they are stuck with the 11% cost from the swap agreement. One method of controlling this price risk is to enter into an offsetting swap. Another method is to sell the swap in the secondary market, if one can find a buyer.

Another complication of swaps is the difficulty in finding sufficient interest on both sides of a swap. It may be necessary to use more than two assets or parties to get approximate matches of interest rate or currency needs. In some cases, enough counterparty interest may simply not be available to make a swap feasible. If the institution faces residual risk after doing a swap, financial futures can be used. Of course, covering unhedged balance sheet risk in this way complicates the risk manager's job to some extent.

Banks and securities firms established the International Swaps Dealers Association (ISDA) in 1985 to promote standardization and sound business practices in the swap market. This self-regulation helps to reduce risk but is fairly new and will require some time to have a strong influence on swap participants. In the early 1990s ISDA introduced "an informal and non-legalistic market practice advisory service" that arbitrates disputes between member firms. An operational code of conduct was developed, and ISDA now serves as an interface with regulators to address their concerns and provide information

MANAGING RISK

Derivatives at Work

Derivatives can be used to manage both risks and returns. The following example is based on an article in the *Wall Street Journal*. It demonstrates how different players in the financial markets can interact in a derivatives deal. While individual components of the deal are simple, the entire package requires an understanding of a variety of contracts and their relationships to one another.

To begin, a money management firm (MF) is assisting a pension fund (PF) in its investment portfolio management. MF puts together a derivatives deal as follows:

1. $30 million from PF is invested in high-quality, short-term notes paying 3.8%.
2. MF contacts a large foreign bank (BANK) to arrange a swap of these notes for the S&P 500 stock index.

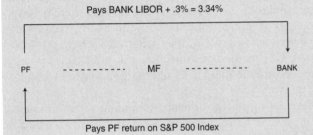

Pays BANK LIBOR + .3% = 3.34%

PF — — — — — — — MF — — — — — — — BANK

Pays PF return on S&P 500 Index

3. BANK buys the S&P 500 stock index futures at a financing cost of 3.30% off-balance sheet.
4. Results:
   - BANK earns a small spread of 0.04%.
   - PF earns the S&P 500 stock index plus 0.46% (= 3.80% − 3.34%).

Notice that the PF has "beat the market" by earning 0.46% more than the market index. If the market return was negative, PF would lose 0.46% less than the market. The risk to PF of this derivatives strategy is that the notes could default and PF must then continue to pay BANK its part of the swap. Also, if BANK was closed by regulators, PF would have to contend with BANK's creditors to obtain its S&P return. However, these risks are quite low due to the high quality of the notes and money center status of most banks participating in such deals.

MF would earn a fee for these investment and swap services from PF, thereby lowering its increment over the S&P return to less than 0.46%. In sum, all parties benefit from the derivatives deal. BANK benefits least of the parties involved but is partially motivated by the desire to develop and maintain market contracts that could be valuable in other derivatives deals or traditional business services.

Source: Craig Torres, "How a Simple Deal Using Derivatives Works, Step by Step," *Wall Street Journal* (August 17, 1993), p. A8.

as needed. Regarding reporting requirements, beginning in June 1999 new accounting rules by the Financial Accounting Standards Board (FASB 133) require all derivatives, including swaps, to be stated at fair market value. Hence, paper gains and losses, even if they have not yet been realized, must be reported in the accounting statements. This accounting change promises to force many banks and firms to factor in the potential impact of a swap (or other derivative instrument) on their financial position when using these contracts to hedge various risks.

14.3 OVER-THE-COUNTER OPTIONS, FUTURES, AND FORWARDS

FinancialCAD Corporation (http://financialcad.com/) *develops financial engineering and financial risk management-related software. Their web site contains various techniques for creating interest rate swap transactions.*

Over-the-Counter Options

In Chapter 6 it was explained that from the option buyer's (or seller's) point of view, puts are options to sell (or buy) assets and calls are options to buy (or sell) them. Put and call options traded on organized stock exchanges are standardized contracts. In other words, the terms of the options contracts (striking price, maturity, etc.) are standardized to facilitate trading. Such standardized contracts, however, do not satisfy the needs of all participants in the market, and an over-the-counter (OTC) market has developed for nonstandardized options. OTC options are usually written on Treasury securities and currencies that are not traded on exchanges. With no clearinghouse to act as a safety net, one party has an option to exercise a contract, while the other party has an obligation. Although limited data is available on the OTC option market, the general consensus is that it is growing rapidly.

Floor-Ceiling Agreements

The concept of options is useful in analyzing some of the off-balance sheet products and services offered by banks to manage interest costs (known as **interest rate options**). Consider the case of **ceiling agreements** (also called **caps**). A ceiling agreement between a bank and its customer specifies the maximum lending rate on a loan and, therefore, protects the customer from interest rate risk. For example, a corporation obtains a three-year loan, with interest rates based on Treasury bills at 8% with quarterly payment. The corporation is willing to pay the bank an upfront fee of 3% to guarantee that it will not have to pay more than 10% over the life of the loan. If the interest rate goes above 10%, the bank will compensate the corporation. For example, if the rate goes to 11%, the corporation will receive ¼ (quarterly settlements) of 1% of the loan. On a $50 million loan, the corporation would receive $125,000. In this case, the bank selling the ceiling agreement analogously is the writer of an out of the money call option. The call option is out of the money because the current level of interest rates is below the strike interest rate of the call option. The corporation is the buyer of the call option, and benefits if interest rates rise above the strike interest rate. It should be noted, as mentioned in Chapter 6, that buying a call option in interest rates is equivalent to buying a put option in prices (i.e., prices and interest rates move opposite to one another). We use interest rates rather than prices to describe the option contract for ease of exposition and understanding.

   Floor agreements specify the minimum rate of interest on a loan and, therefore, protect the bank from interest rate risk. If interest rates go below the floor, or 7.5%, for example, the customer pays the bank the difference between the actual rate and the floor rate. Here the bank is buyer of an out-of-the-money put option. The option is out of the money because the current level of interest rates is above the strike interest rate. Do not be confused by the term *out-of-the-money*. It means simply that the strike interest rate for the call (put) option is above (below) the current level of interest rates. Therefore it cannot be exercised for a profit at the present time. An "in-the-money" put option is one in which interest rates have fallen below the strike interest rate. The bank could lower its loan fee to purchase this put option on the loan.

Figure 14.5 provides diagrams that show the gains and losses on caps and floors from the perspective of the buyer of these options as interest rates change. Again, notice that we have expressed the option buyer's gains and losses on caps and floors in terms of interest rates, but they could be easily converted to prices (e.g., falling interest rates in a floor are hedged by buying a call option that is in the money as prices increase above the strike price).

An OTC option that combines ceiling and floor mechanics is the **interest rate collar**. A put-option premium is paid to create an interest rate cap, and this premium cost is offset in whole or part by a call option that establishes an interest rate floor. A variable-rate debtholder could therefore set upper and lower limits on their interest costs.

Finally, innovation in OTC options is extending their use from interest rate risk management to credit risk management. The main idea here is to set a lower limit on credit risk. As an example, banks can design an OTC option called a *credit risk derivative*. If an investor held, say, AAA-rated bonds and was concerned that the rating agencies might downgrade the bonds to AA causing the yield to rise and price to fall, the investor could purchase an option that would pay the amount of the lost capital value of the bonds if downgraded. In this way, investors can insure the credit risk of their bond portfolios. Of course, writers of these options would profit to the extent that credit risk does not increase in the future. This so-called **credit option** is essentially an insurance contract. Another common type of credit derivative is a **credit swap** in which two banks simply exchange interest and principal payments on portions of their loan portfolios. This swap enables the participating banks to diversify their credit risk to a greater extent than previously possible. A twist on the credit swap is a **total return swap**, wherein bank A (for example) swaps payments received on a risky loan portfolio for a cash flow stream from bank B comprised of a benchmark rate of interest (e.g., LIBOR) plus some negotiated compensation for the credit risk premium that it has given up. This swap transfers the credit risk from bank A to bank B, even though bank B did not make the loan. In general, a key advantage of credit derivatives is that they transfer credit risk without any sale of the underlying debt contract. For example, a bank can retain its relationship with a customer by providing credit and retaining the loan on its balance sheet but subsequently transfer the associated risk into the financial markets. This advantage is valuable in cases in which a

FIGURE 14.5 Caps and Floors on Loan Rates

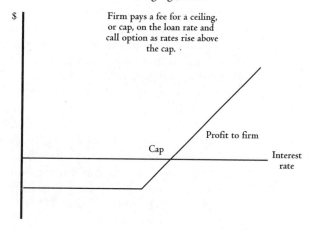

Ceiling Agreement

Firm pays a fee for a ceiling, or cap, on the loan rate and call option as rates rise above the cap.

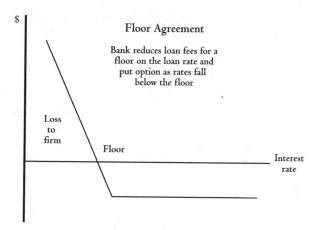

Floor Agreement

Bank reduces loan fees for a floor on the loan rate and put option as rates fall below the floor

bank holds a large concentration of loans in a particular industry (e.g., high holdings of energy loans and commercial real estate loans have been problematic over the last 20 years for many banks). Credit derivatives allow the bank to reduce its exposure to concentrated credit risks and thereby better diversify its loan portfolio.[3]

3. For those interested in further information about credit derivatives, the following article provides an excellent overview and references to relevant literature: James T. Moser, "Credit Derivatives: Just In-Time Provisioning for Loan Losses," *Economic Perspectives*, Federal Reserve Bank of Chicago (Fourth Quarter 1988), pp. 2–11.

Forward Rate Agreements

A **forward rate agreement (FRA)** is essentially an **over-the-counter option** interest rate futures contract for bonds or some other financial asset. The buyer and seller agree on some interest rate to be paid on some notional amount at a specified time in the future. The major advantages of FRAs over exchange-traded futures contracts is that they can be tailored to meet the needs of the parties involved, and they have no margin requirements.

Buying a FRA (or futures contract) is analogous to buying a call and selling a put, where the forward price is equal to the exercise price of the options. To understand this analogy, keep in mind that the buyer of the FRA is obligated to buy the bond—it is mandatory. Suppose that a bank buys an FRA on a bond at 100 for delivery in three months. If the bond is selling at 90 three months from now, the bank can buy the bond (i.e., it is put to the bank) at 100 and then sell it at a loss or keep it in its portfolio at the lower value. On the other hand, if the bond is selling at 110 at that time, the bank will buy the bond (i.e., like a call) and sell it at a profit. Thus, the price of the FRA (or purchased futures) that the bank bought was determined as though it was a purchased call and sold put option. Conversely, the sale of forward contract is analogous to buying a put and selling a call.

Synthetic Loans

Interest rate futures contracts and options can be used to create synthetic loans and securities. To illustrate, suppose that a construction company, believing that interest rates would decline, wanted to borrow $30 million for 120 days, on a floating rate basis, repricing the loan every 30 days at the CD rate plus 4 percentage points. The current rate of interest on CDs was 10.5%, and the initial cost of the loan was 14.5%. The bank, however, wanted to make the loan at a fixed rate. To accommodate the customer, the bank resolved the dilemma by using the interest rate futures market to "convert" the floating rate loan into a fixed rate loan, thereby creating a synthetic loan. To accomplish it, the bank bought T-bill futures. If interest rates decrease, the market value of the securities represented by the futures contract will increase and the contracts can be sold at a profit. The profit is used to offset the lower interest from the floating interest rate loan. The details of the transaction are presented in Table 14.1.

The top part of the table shows the cost of the loan at floating rates of interest. The interest on the loan from the September 1 to October 1 period was $362,500 ($30 million × 14.5%/12 months). Using the interest rates shown, the total interest earned by the bank for the term of the loan was $1,310,000.

On September 1, the bank bought three 90-day futures contracts for T-bills. Each contract is for 10 T-bills and each T-bill has a face value of $1 million. The price of each bill is calculated as follows. With four 90-day T-bill issues each year, the annual interest rate of 11.5% is equal to 0.02875 for 90 days, or $28,750 interest per $1 million of T-bills. The price of a T-bill is the face

TABLE 14.1	Data for Synthetic Loan

	Dates				
	9/1–10/1	10/1–10/30	10/30–11/30	11/30–12/30	Totals
	Loan at Floating Rate				
Loan $30 million floating interest rate	14.5%	13.2%	12.6%	12.1%	
Interest	$ 362,500	$ 330,000	$ 315,000	$ 302,500	$1,310,000
	Futures Contracts				
	Buy 3 (9/1)	Sell 1 (10/1)	Sell 1 (10/30)	Sell 1 (11/30)	
Yield	11.5%	10.2%	9.6%	9.1%	
Contract value[a]	$9,712,500	$9,745,000	$9,760,000	$9,772,500	
Profit or (loss)		$32,500	$47,500	$ 60,000	140,000
					$1,450,000
	Loan at Fixed Rate				
Fixed interest rate	14.5%	14.5%	14.5%	14.5%	
Interest	$ 362,500	$ 362,500	$ 362,500	$ 362,500	$1,450,000

[a]Contracts are for 10 Treasury bills. Each bill has a face value of $1 million.

amount less the interest, or $1 million – $28,750 = $971,250. Because each contract contains 10 bills, a contract would be worth $9,712,500. The bank is required to put up a small margin deposit to buy the contracts. The margin and the commissions are not included in this example. On October 1, the bank sold one of the T-bill futures contracts at the current market price. Because interest rates declined, the market value of the futures contracts increased and the bank earned $362,500, the same amount of interest they would have paid on a fixed rate loan.

Similarly, the total gains from the futures market ($140,000) plus the total interest expense on the variable rate loan ($1,131,000) are equivalent to the amount of interest that would have been received on a fixed rate loan ($1,450,000).

In this case, the purpose of using the interest rate futures market was to convert the floating rate loan into a fixed rate loan in terms of the interest received by the bank. By using this technique, the bank received the equivalent of a fixed rate loan and the customer received a floating loan. If interest rates had increased, rather than declined, losses from the futures contracts would have offset higher interest payments from the floating rate loan and the bank would still have earned the equivalent of a fixed rate loan.

This example illustrates a synthetic loan. Similarly, banks and financial institutions can use futures contracts to convert fixed rate deposits into floating rate deposits, and vice versa.

Unlike forward contracts, futures contracts expose the bank to liquidity risk because their value is marked to market daily. Gains or losses on futures contracts must be settled daily against margin positions, potentially creating cash demands. Moreover, futures contracts, like any hedging method, in most cases cannot eliminate all price risk. On the plus side, futures exchanges act as clearinghouses and guarantee performance of contracts, eliminating default risk.

Securitization

As explained in earlier chapters, **securitization** involves the packaging of loans into large pools and issuance of securities to investors who earn returns based on the payments on the loans. Loan-backed securities can be collateralized by mortgages (residential, multifamily, and commercial), automobile loans, credit card receivables, computer leases, mobile home loans, and small business loans. The rapid growth of loan securitization is changing the nature of the banking business. Instead of making loans and bearing all of their associated risks and returns, banks are making loans, securitizing them, and selling the securities into the financial marketplace. In the process banks alter their risk exposures to loans and increase service revenues. Banks can serve multiple roles in the securitization process, including loan originator, loan packager, and loan service company, all of which contribute to service revenues.

An excellent example of how securitization solves risk management problems is the case of savings and loan associations. Today, many savings institutions are owned by bank holding companies, as federal income tax incentives make it worthwhile to operate them as a separate entities within the bank holding company structure; nonetheless, they may well be controlled for all practical purposes by a lead bank in a bank holding company. Because savings and loans employ short-term retail deposits and make long-term mortgage loans, they have a severely negative dollar gap that makes them extremely sensitive to interest rate movements. Interest rates do not have to increase much before interest costs rise above mortgage portfolio yields and produce losses that wipe out equity capital. By securitizing home loans and then purchasing mortgage-backed securities with much shorter terms to maturity, their gap problem can be substantially reduced. Also, mortgage loans tend to be highly geographically concentrated. By securitizing these loans and purchasing the related securities, a geographically diversified asset portfolio can be achieved. Thus, interest rate risk and credit risk are greatly reduced, and stable, low-risk service revenues are received.

It is important to point out that securitized home loans are not off-balance sheet assets. As explained in the Managerial Issues feature, "Asset Securitization

MANAGERIAL ISSUES

Asset Securitization Reaches Maturity

Asset-backed securitization in the United States began in 1985 and has rapidly grown to become common practice in most areas of bank lending. Typical assets used in the securitization process are automobiles, trucks, equipment, recreational vehicles, home equity loans, and credit cards. Other more exotic asset-backed deals include computer leases, consumer loans, trade receivables, time shares, and small business loans. In 1998 several large banks began to package large commercial and industrial loans as well as commercial real estate into so-called *collateralized loan obligations* (CLOs) and *commercial mortgage-backed securities* (CMBSs). In 1998 about 4.5% of total bank assets were off-balance sheet assets that represented securitized loans.

Securitized assets are counted as off-balance sheet items *only if* the assets have been transferred with recourse. With recourse in this case means that the bank has moved the asset off its balance sheet but is still exposed to part or all of the risk associated with the asset. Residential mortgages are the most securitized asset in the financial market (e.g., more than 80% of new home loans in the United States are now financed by this means), but they are not off-balance sheet assets. The originating bank sells the loan to one of the federal housing agencies and many times services the loan payments for a fee. However, the bank is not liable for default on mortgage payments. On the other hand, credit card loans that are securitized expose the bank to credit risk. If credit payment flows fall to a predetermined level, the originating bank must repurchase the remaining securitized loans.

In order for an asset category to be securitized, it must offer a steady income stream for investors. By pooling assets from across the country and taking advantage of geographic diversification, the variance of income streams can be reduced and made amenable for securitization. A key benefit for banks, whether the securitized asset is an on- or off-balance sheet item, is increased service revenues. If the asset can be moved off the balance sheet, the return on assets can be boosted by reducing the denominator of the profit ratio. And, if the asset is still on the balance sheet, the risk has been transferred from the bank to the financial market.

Commercial banks compete with investment banks and other securities firms for asset-backed financing business, not to mention foreign institutional entrants. Also, large automobile manufacturers with captive finance companies are large issuers of asset-backed securities. The presence of a variety of large institutions and firms in asset-backed securities markets suggests that this market is highly competitive. Some studies have shown that securitization of the residential mortgage market has reduced home loan interest rates by as much as 30 to 40 basis points.* Thus, borrowers directly benefit from competitive asset-backed pricing due to lower borrowing costs.

*For further discussion and references on mortgage market securitization, see James W. Kolari, Donald R. Fraser, and Ali Anari, "The Effects of Securitization on Mortgage Market Yields: A Cointegration Analysis," *Real Estate Economics*, vol. 26 (Winter 1998), pp. 677–693.

Reaches Maturity," only assets transferred with recourse are considered off-balance sheet items. In this regard, credit card loans tend to dominate off-balance sheet securitized assets. Most securitized assets are not transferred with recourse. While regulatory reporting requirements rightly do not count these securitized assets in on- or off-balance sheet positions, they are sources of off-balance sheet revenues.

14.4 OTHER OFF-BALANCE SHEET ACTIVITIES

Loan Sales

Banks can sell loans to a third party as a source of funds. Such loans are normally purchased by large banks and nonbank financial institutions. For a fee the selling bank often continues to service the loan payment, enforce debt covenants, and monitor the borrower's creditworthiness. Loan sales can be made with or without recourse. Sales with recourse mean that even though the loan was sold by *assignment* (i.e., the buyer owns the loan), the selling bank retains some credit risk (in whole or part) for loan losses. Loan sales enable banks to increase diversification, lower capital requirements, and eliminate low-earning assets from their portfolio. It is not known whether loan sales reduce or increase credit risk as a whole for banks. While selling off loans that are not replaced would clearly reduce credit risk, it is possible that a bank could sell off high-quality, highly marketable loans and eventually end up with lower quality loans on their balance sheet. Some interesting implications of loan sales are that they enable banks to (1) make loans without relying on deposits as a source of funds and (2) convert traditional lending to a quasi-securities business. Moreover, by purchasing loans, other nonbank financial institutions are becoming more like banks. In turn, distinctions between banks, securities firms, and other financial institutions are gradually being blurred as the volume of loan sales increases.

Trade Finance

Most trade finance is on-balance sheet. However, some international aspects of trade finance are off-balance sheet commitments by banks.

COMMERCIAL LETTERS OF CREDIT Trade finance includes commercial letters of credit and acceptance participations, both of which are used to finance international trade. Letters of credit, which are further explained in Chapter 16, have been used by banks for many years. A **letter of credit (LOC)** involves a bank (the issuer) that guarantees the bank's customer (the account party) to pay a contractual debt to a third party (the beneficiary). Letters of credit are contingent liabilities because payment does not take place until the proper documents (i.e., title, invoices, etc.) are presented to the bank. Payment is dependent on the bank's creditworthiness, not the buyer's financial strength. LOCs are specific to the period of time involved in the shipment and storage of goods, result in fee income for banks from the buyer, and require the buyer to reimburse the bank for payment of goods.

LOCs expose banks to credit risk and documentary risk. Credit risk in this case differs from a typical loan that is carefully evaluated by a loan officer. Instead, because LOCs are essentially working capital loans with a fast turnaround and are offered to otherwise creditworthy buyers, little credit risk evaluation is made in common practice. Of course, to the extent that credit review standards are lowered, some degree of credit risk is involved, as some proportion of even sound buyers can experience a deterioration in their ability to pay at times. Documentary risk is associated with the complexity of international commerce, which can become tangled by different countries' legal systems and international legal rules. It is possible for conflicts between sellers and buyers to spill over to banks involved in their transactions.

ACCEPTANCE PARTICIPATIONS A bankers' acceptance (also discussed in Chapter 12) is created when a bank accepts a time draft (a bill of exchange) and agrees to pay it at face value on maturity. The draft normally covers the sale of goods, particularly with respect to international trade. The bankers' acceptance is booked as an asset. Some banks sell participations (called **acceptance participations**) for all or part of the time draft, which reduces the dollar amount shown on their books. However, the accepting bank is still obligated to pay the face amount of the acceptance at maturity. Banks that buy acceptance participations have a contingent liability that does not appear on their balance sheets.

Foreign Exchange

Most large banks operate foreign exchange trading desks for the purposes of brokerage and dealing, speculating, and providing forward contracts in currencies. Regarding the latter, a typical foreign exchange service is to hedge currency risks for firms engaged in international trade. For example, if a U.S. firm bought some goods from Europe but was allowed 30 days trade credit before paying, a forward contract in Euros could be purchased to lock in the dollar cost at the time of purchase (i.e., say one million Euros are purchased at an agreed dollar price now for future delivery in 30 days). In the 1990s some large banks speculated in currencies and suffered tremendous losses, which prompted greater regulatory oversight and reporting requirements. Like securities activities, today most foreign exchange trading is reported in financial statements and, therefore, is not off-balance sheet.

Services for Fees

A fairly riskless source of bank income is advisory and management fees. Such services do not involve commitments or contingencies on assets listed either on or off the balance sheet. Traditional fiduciary services, including trust funds and portfolio management, remain significant sources of fee income, as banks are one of the largest institutional managers of capital funds in the United States. Two growth areas in the banking industry are cash management and networking.

CASH MANAGEMENT **Cash management** systems for business concerns are one of the most popular off-balance sheet service areas offered by banks. Cash management systems are used to help business concerns collect remittances and use their bank balances efficiently. Lock boxes are an important part of cash management systems. Lock boxes are post office boxes where customer's remittances are sent and then collected by bankers who deposit them in a business concern's account (see Chapter 15 for further discussion). Banks receive fees for collection and processing the funds. With the exception of the computers used to process the funds and an increase in cash (from the collected funds), no other specific items on their balance sheets are directly attributable to cash management systems.

NETWORKING **Networking** refers to linkages among different companies that make use of comparative advantages in the production and delivery of a product. Another popular term for such joint arrangements is *strategic alliance*. As an example, a bank may contract with a discount broker to execute securities transactions for their customers for a fee, part of which goes to the bank. Similarly, many banks have contractual relationships with mutual funds to provide investment services (i.e., a nonproprietary relationship). Another trend in this area is the placement of branch offices in supermarkets and other high-traffic retail stores by banks. This symbiotic relationship seeks to increase customer convenience for both the retailer and bank.

Banks also use networks to sell insurance, data processing, and other services. Networks permit banks to expand certain specialized services without a major investment on their part. Chapter 15 further discusses new banking services that banks are developing through networking, particularly investment and insurance services.

14.5 U.S. BANKS AND INTERNATIONAL EXPANSION

The International Monetary Fund, or IMF, is comprised of more than 150 member countries. The organization lends money only to member countries with payments problems, that is, to countries that do not take in enough foreign currency to pay for what they buy from other countries. See www.imfsite.org to better understand this important international agency.

Table 14.2 shows selected off-balance sheet items of insured U.S. banks as of year-end 1997. The right-hand columns compare the percentage of total assets for each item in 1990 versus 1997. Notice that loan commitments as well as interest and currency swaps are about five times the level of on-balance sheet assets. Particularly noteworthy is that interest rate swaps have jumped from 98% of total assets in 1990 to 345% of total assets in 1997. Thus, swaps dominate off-balance sheet activities. By contrast, letters of credit (and other loan guarantee business) was relatively stable in the 1990s. Also, credit risk derivatives and securitization (i.e., assets transformed with recourse) are growing new off-balance sheet activities.

In unused commitments, which were approximately $3 trillion in 1997, credit card lines have seen rapid growth. These commitments accounted for more than half of the total outstanding. Commercial and industrial lines accounted for

TABLE 14.2	Selected Off-Balance Sheet Items of Insured U.S. Banks		

Item	1997 ($ billions)	Percentage of Assets 1990	1997
Unused commitments	3,040.7	33.0	61.2
Letters of credit			
Commercial	29.2	0.9	0.6
Standby			
Financial	185.9	3.7	3.7
Performance	44.4	1.7	0.9
Derivatives (excluding credit derivatives)			
Interest rate			
Notional amount	17,176.1	98.1	345.5
Fair value			
Positive	162.8	NA	3.3
Negative	161.3	NA	3.2
Exchange rate			
Notional amount	7,832.5	104.3	157.6
Fair value			
Positive	192.2	NA	3.9
Negative	185.5	NA	3.7
Other			
Notional amount	493.7	2.4	9.9
Fair value			
Positive	22.9	NA	0.5
Negative	27.7	NA	0.6
Credit Derivatives (notional amount)			
Guarantor	33.4	NA	0.7
Beneficiary	63.7	NA	1.3
Assets transferred with recourse	230.6	NA	4.6

Source: William B. English and William R. Nelson, "Profit and Balance Sheet Developments at U.S. Commercial Banks in 1997," *Federal Reserve Bulletin* (June 1998).

about 40% of the total, and the remainder accounted for by unused residential and commercial real estate and unused lines for securities underwriting.

The derivatives section of Table 14.2 lists the notional amount and fair value of derivatives contracts. Again, the notional amount is the value of the underlying asset to which payment streams are attached. The fair value is the price at which the contract could be replaced and is used for accounting purposes. Most swaps have an initial fair value of zero, because the present value of the payment streams from the bank to the counterparty and vice versa are approximately equal. In Table 14.2 we see that the notional amount of interest rate swaps for U.S. banks in 1997 was about $17 trillion, with a gross fair value (counting both positive and negative values) equal to about $324 billion. We can see here that notional amounts are useful in tracking derivatives trends over time, but fair value is the best measure of the actual risk exposure of banks. For any particular bank, the net derivatives risk is the difference between positive and negative fair values. Most banks maintain net positions near zero at any point in time.

International Expansion of Derivatives

Financial derivatives began to trade on organized exchanges in the United States in the 1970s. In the 1980s international exchanges began to appear that patterned themselves after the U.S. exchanges—the Chicago Board of Trade (CBOT), Chicago Board Options Exchange (CBOE), and the Chicago Mercantile Exchange (CME), which account for more than 60% of worldwide derivative trading on exchanges. For example, in 1987 the Tokyo Stock Exchange began trading government bond futures, and the Tokyo International Financial Futures Exchange (TIFFE) was founded in 1989 to expand the growing derivatives activity. By 1990, about 13% of total global derivatives trading took place in Japan, and the Nikkei 225 stock index futures contract became the most actively traded derivatives contract in the world. Other Pacific Rim financial derivative exchanges are located in Australia, Hong Kong, Malaysia, New Zealand, the Philippines, and Singapore.

In Europe, the London International Financial Future Exchange (LIFFE) is the oldest marketplace for financial derivatives. Trading the greatest volume of contracts in Europe, and third in the world behind the United States and Japan, LIFFE has an international scope, with contracts from the European Community (EC) at large, Japan, and the United States. France and Germany also have fairly large derivatives exchanges—the Marché à Terme International de France (MATIF) since 1986 and Deutsche Terminbörse (DTB) since 1990. Other European financial derivatives exchanges are found in Austria, Belgium, Denmark, Finland, Holland, Ireland, the Netherlands, Spain, Sweden, Switzerland, and the United Kingdom, and new exchanges are underway in Italy, Luxembourg, and Norway.

Exchange-traded financial derivatives are a relatively new phenomenon compared to OTC trading. The growing number and volume of trading at organized exchanges is changing the derivatives marketplace. OTC markets are adopting some of the clearinghouse features of organized exchanges to

London International Financial Futures Exchange's (LIFFE) web site at http://www.liffe.com/ *contains information on market news, statistics, publications, and education.*

reduce counterparty credit risk (i.e., this change is relevant only for lower quality counterparties). Also, organized exchanges are clearing and trading OTC derivative contracts. Consequently, the evolving financial derivatives market is very competitive—a prerequisite for not only efficient pricing but financial innovation. It can be inferred that the financial derivatives will continue to expand their role in the financial marketplace in the years to come.

SUMMARY

During the 1990s, a dramatic shift occurred in the way banks do business. In response to increases in financial markets' volatility in the 1980s and 1990s, banks adapted by expanding beyond making traditional loans and gathering deposits to fee-generating activities that do not appear on their balance sheets. These activities include a variety of commitments and contingent claims that business firms are increasingly demanding, including financial guarantees, SLCs, loan commitments, and NIFs. In addition, banks are offering various derivative securities services, such as swaps, options, futures and forward contracts, as well as asset securitization, to assist customers in coping with the greater volatility that exists in today's financial marketplace.

While off-balance sheet activities provide fee income and can be used to manage banks' risk exposures, they also introduce new risks. Indeed, large off-balance sheet exposures of money center banks, many times exceeding booked assets, is increasing regulatory attention to these new risks. The challenge for bankers is to provide the off-balance sheet services that customers demand and, at the same time, control the risk implications of these services.

Key Terms and Concepts

Acceptance participation	Floor agreement
Account party	Forward rate agreement (FRA)
Aggregation risk	Interest rate collar
Basis swap	Interest rate options
Ceiling agreement (cap)	Interest rate swap
Cash management	Legal risk
Contingent claim	Letter of credit (LOC)
Counterparty credit risk	Line of credit
Coupon swap	Liquidity risk
Credit option	Loan commitment
Credit swap	Loan guarantee
Cross-currency interest rate swap	Market risk
Currency swap	Material adverse change (MAC)
Euronotes	clause
Facility fee	Networking
Financial guarantee	Off-balance sheet activity

Operating risk   Settlement risk
Over-the-counter option   Standby letters of credit (SLC)
Price risk   Swap
Revolving loan commitment   Total return swap
Securitization

Questions

14.1   Why did banks substantially increase off-balance sheet activities in the 1970s and 1980s?

14.2   Briefly describe two broad groups of off-balance sheet activities.

14.3   List and define four kinds of risk inherent in banking.

14.4   Distinguish between the issuer, account party, and beneficiary of a letter of credit.

14.5   Define the following terms: (a) acceptance participation, (b) loan guarantee, (c) standby letters of credit, (d) surety bond, and (e) loan commitment.

14.6   What is the difference between a line of credit and a revolving loan commitment? Regarding the latter, what is a MAC clause?

14.7   What is funding risk? What is the potential long-run pitfall of this kind of risk for a bank?

14.8   What are NIFs, RUFs, and SNIFs? Euronotes?

14.9   Who are arrangers and tender panels in NIFs?

14.10 Define the term *securitization*. What does "with recourse" mean regarding securitized loan portfolios?

14.11 Define a swap. What are two principal types of swaps? What other kinds of interest rate swaps are there?

14.12 Why has the OTC option market evolved?

14.13 Briefly define the following terms: (a) floor agreements, (b) ceiling agreements, (c) forward rate agreement, (d) synthetic loans, and (e) lockbox.

14.14 What is a credit risk derivative? Give two examples of how can they help to control credit risk?

14.15 Go to the Fact Sheet of derivatives activities of commercial banks published by the Office of the Comptroller of the Currency (OCC) and collect data on the latest quarter. Write a short summary of your findings.

14.16 Visit the web site for the International Swaps and Derivatives Association (ISDA) at *http:\\www.isda.org*. Find the ISDA Market Survey, print out the last two years of data, and write a short summary of your findings.

14.17 The Chicago Board of Trade's (CBOT) web site at *http://www.cbot.com/* contains an About the Exchange section. After reading that section, write a short report on the CBOT.

Problems

14.1 Corporation XYZ obtains a ceiling agreement from a bank for a five-year loan of $20 million at a rate of 7% (tied to LIBOR). An upfront fee of 2% is paid by XYZ for the guarantee that rates will not exceed 10%.
(a) If LIBOR goes to 12%, calculate the quarterly compensation the bank must pay XYZ.
(b) What kind of option is this for the bank? For XYZ? When is it "in-the-money"?

14.2 A forward rate agreement (FRA) on bonds is purchased by a bank at 90 for delivery in three months.
(a) If the price of the bonds is 100 on the delivery date, what is the profit (loss) of the bank? What type of option is analogous to this example?
(b) If the price of the bonds falls to 80 three months from now, what is the profit (loss) of the bank? What type of option is analogous to this example?
(c) From (a) and (b), what can we conclude regarding FRAs and their relationship to options?

14.3 A bank makes a three-month floating-rate loan of $60 million at 15.0%. The loan is repriced every 30 days. To hedge against declining interest rates the bank creates a synthetic loan by purchasing and then selling a 90-day T-bill futures contract yielding 12.0% every 30 days (i.e., this is done three times). Each contract is for 10 T-bills at $1 million face value for each T-bill. The following interest rate assumptions are made by the bank:

	Days			
	30	60	90	120
Floating rate on loan	15%	14%	13%	12%
T-bill futures yield	12	11.6	11.2	10.8

Show that the bank has converted the floating-rate loan to a fixed rate 15% loan by calculating the cash inflows on the floating-rate loan and the long position in a T-bill futures and comparing their total to the total cash inflows from a 15% fixed-rate loan.

14.4 A large U.S. bank is working with an insurance company to put together an equity swap. The insurance company wishes to invest $20 million in equities. A large German bank has indicated interest as the counterparty in the swap if it can earn Libor plus 0.4%. Explain how the U.S. bank could structure a derivatives deal that would satisfy these diverse demands, in addition to the risks and returns to each party.

ISWAP/USWAP

ISWAP is a nonfinancial firm with a weak financial condition. Local banking institutions are only willing to offer ISWAP variable-rate loans. A fixed-rate loan would be more desirable, in light of a long-term investment in a new product that it is contemplating. USWAP is a large, strongly capitalized bank in a nearby city that would benefit from variable-rate funding for it short-term asset portfolio. The opportunities to borrow funds for the two parties is as follows:

	Variable Rate	Fixed Rate
ISWAP(firm)	LIBOR + 1%	14%
USWAP(bank)	LIBOR +.5%	12%

From this information, it is clear that ISWAP pays a 2% premium for fixed-rate funds but only a .5% premium for variable-rate funds.

Assume that an intermediary is contacted to handle the details of the swap. ISWAP takes out a variable-rate loan at LIBOR + 1% but swaps this loan's payments with USWAP, who issues seven-year notes at 12%. ISWAP pays USWAPs interest bill plus 0.1% fee to the intermediating bank. USWAP pays the LIBOR component of ISWAP's variable-rate loan and leaves the fixed 1% to be paid by ISWAP.

First, draw a diagram that shows all parties, including arrows showing the flow of funds in the swap, as well as the interest rates paid by ISWAP and USWAP through the intermediary. Second, make a table showing ISWAP's costs, ISWAP's savings from the swap, USWAP's costs, USWAP's savings from the swap, the intermediary's fees, and the receipts and payments between ISWAP and USWAP. After completing this work, write a final statement on the feasibility of the swap.

Source: This problem is based on J. Gregg Whittaker, "Interest Rate Swaps: Risk and Regulation," *Economic Review,* Federal Reserve Bank of Kansas City (March 1987), pp. 3–13.

Financial Services

After reading this chapter you will be able to:

- Understand the range of services offered by banks.
- Explain why banks provide cash management and data processing services to businesses.
- Determine FDIC insurance coverage for bank accounts.
- Describe how banks can offer investment products.
- Understand the widespread uses of trusts.

This chapter is about selected wholesale and retail financial services offered by banks that have not be covered in previous chapters. Wholesale services are those offered primarily to business concerns, and retail service are those offered to individuals. The term *bank*, as explained in Chapter 1, has a variety of meanings. The legal definition of a bank is determined by laws and bank regulators. The different types of banks include commercial banks, limited purpose banks, and savings banks. Another type is a bank holding company that owns or controls one or more banks. Bank holding companies can engage in a range of activities that are closely related to banking. The activities of bank holding companies must be approved by the Board of Governors of the Federal Reserve System. The Fed is the primary supervisor and regulator of bank holding companies. In holding company applications involving national banks, the Fed must consult with the Office of the Comptroller of the Currency, and with state bank supervisors for state chartered banks. Table 15.1 provides a listing of some of the permissible activities of bank holding companies. In this chapter, we examine selected financial services offered by banking organizations. ■

TABLE 15.1	Permissible Nonbanking Activities for Bank Holding Companies

1. Making, acquiring, or servicing loans or other extensions of credit.
2. Operating an industrial bank.
3. Performing certain trust company activities.
4. Acting as investment or financial advisor.
5. Leasing personal or real property.
6. Making debt or equity investment in projects designed to promote community welfare.
7. Processing data of a financial, banking, or economic nature.
8. Acting as principal, agent, or broker for insurance-related credit extension by the holding company or its subsidiaries; acting as an insurance agent in small towns where the holding company or its subsidiaries have a lending office.
9. Operating a savings association.
10. Providing courier services for certain financial instruments and financially related data.
11. Providing management consulting advice to nonaffiliated depository institutions.
12. Issuing and selling travelers checks, retail money orders of a face value of $1,000 or less, and U.S. savings bonds.
13. Performing appraisals of real estate and personal property.
14. Arranging commercial real estate equity financing.
15. Providing securities brokerage services acting solely as an agent for the customer, and providing investment advisory activities.
16. Underwriting and dealing in government and money market instruments.

Source: K. Spong, *Banking Regulation: Its Purposes, Implementation, and Effects,* Federal Reserve Bank of Kansas City (1994), p. 135.

15.1   CASH MANAGEMENT SERVICES

Banks provide **cash management services** for their business customers to earn fee income, to cross-sell their products, and to increase relationships with their customers. Cash management is the process of combining banking services, data collection, and communications systems to enhance the collection, control and utilization of cash for business concerns. Cash management services help businesses collect their receivables faster, and to make their payments more efficiently. Faster collections reduce the firm's float. *Float* is the dollar amount of checks that been received by the firm that are in the process of collection but have not yet been converted into cash. Firms typically want to reduce the float when collecting funds owed to them. Conversely, they want to take advantage of float when making payments to others.

Cash Concentration for Collection of Funds

Many business concerns, such as a grocery store chain, receive retail payments and make relatively small daily deposits in the various cities where the stores are located. Cash concentration brings all of the deposits together in one account so that the firm's corporate headquarters can use those funds efficiently.

Controlled Disbursement

Banks can help business concerns make better use of their cash resources by helping control disbursements (payments). A "zero balance account" is one technique. This bank account has a zero dollar balance, most of the time. When a check drawn against a business is presented to its bank for collection, the bank notifies the business, which then deposits the appropriate amount to cover the check. By using a zero balance account, businesses minimize the amount of funds deposited in noninterest-earning bank accounts.

Lockboxes for Collections

A **lockbox** is a post office box of a business concern that is used to receive payments for goods and services. For example, bill payments made to retail stores and utilities are sent to a post office box in a city that minimizes the mail time in transit. Instead of sending retail payments to the company headquarters in Seattle, for example, the payments from customers located in the southeast part of the United States are sent to a post office box in Atlanta, which reduces mailing time from three days to one day. A bank in Atlanta will empty the post office box several times each day, deposit the checks, and notify the receiving company of its collections. The company can then invest those funds or reduce its debts. Companies may have lockboxes located in various cities, depending on the size and scope of their operations.

Trade Finance

The growth of international trade gives rise to domestic firms making and receiving payments from foreign firms for goods and services bought and sold. Banks play an important role here by providing letters of credit, foreign exchange, and other financial services that facilitate the flows of funds. These techniques are described in Chapter 16. The means of electronically transferring funds internationally were described in Chapter 13.

15.2 DATA PROCESSING

Bank holding companies are permitted to provide data processing services, which is often done through a data processing company owned by the bank.

MANAGERIAL ISSUES

The Lockbox Advantage

Lockboxes are use to manage payments efficiently and to increase profits for business firms. One of the problems a company faces is to determine the optimal number of lockboxes to maximize profits. To demonstrate the basic calculations, consider a bank that is attempting to design a lockbox system for a small corporate customer. As a starting point based on their past experiences, the bank assumes that 10 lockboxes are used, and given information on mail delivery speeds in the planned geographical areas where these boxes are located, the following information is assembled:

1. Average number of daily payments to the lockboxes — 300
2. Average amount of payment — $2,000
3. Daily rate of interest — 0.01%
4. Decrease in mailing time — 0.9 days
5. Decrease in processing time — 0.5 days

These data enable the calculation of the amount by which the cash is increased for the firm, or

300 payments/day $\times$ $2000 $\times$ (0.09 +0.5) days = $840,000

This increase in cash balances, if invested at 0.01% per day, would yield $84 per day for the firm. If the bank charges $0.15 to process each check (or 300 $\times$ $0.15 = $45), then the net gain to the bank after fees is $39 per day, or $1,170 per month (30 days $\times$ $39 = $1,170).

Lockbox systems are an excellent example of how banks and firms can work together for their mutual advantage.

For example, Synovus Financial Corporation is a bank holding company that owns banks in Alabama, Florida, Georgia, and South Carolina. It also owns Synovus Securities, a full-service broker, and 80% of the stock of Total Systems Services. The stocks of both Synovus and Total Systems are listed on the New York Stock Exchange. Total Systems Services is one of the world's largest processors of credit and debit card transactions for institutions located in the United States, Canada, and Mexico. It provides clearing, settlement, and other services related to credit and debit card transactions.

The Electronic Deposit Insurance Estimator (EDIE) is an interactive Internet site provided by the FDIC to help bankers and consumers determine whether their deposits are within the $100,000 insurance limit. EDIE is accessed through http://www.fdic.gov and http://www.fdic.gov/ deposit/deposits/index.html for more information about FDIC insurance coverage.

15.3 FDIC-INSURED DEPOSITS

One thing that differentiates banks from other types of financial institutions that offer competing products and services is that bank deposits that are insured by the Federal Deposit Insurance Corporation (FDIC). The **FDIC-insured deposits** are covered for amounts up to $100,000 from losses due to the failure of a bank. In some cases depositors can have more than $100,000 in a bank and still be insured, if the accounts are structured properly. Appendix A at the end of this chapter provides some information about FDIC insurance coverage and about leveraging that coverage.

15.4 INVESTMENT PRODUCTS

The Glass-Steagall Act, which is part of the 1933 Banking Act, separated commercial banks from directly participating in investment banking. In 1987, the Federal Reserve reinterpreted this act to mean that securities activities—such as underwriting municipal and corporate bonds, mortgage-backed securities, corporate equities, securities brokerage activities, and investment advisory services—could be conducted indirectly by nonbank subsidiaries of bank holding companies. A so-called *firewall* separates the bank from its security affiliate to insulate the bank from losses that may occur in that affiliate. The Federal Reserve approves underwriting on a case-by-case basis. It was not until 1990 that the Federal Reserve granted J.P. Morgan and Company approval to underwrite common stocks. J.P. Morgan and Company has evolved into a global investment banking firm. Similarly, NationsBank acquired Montgomery Securities, a San Francisco investment banking firm.[1] Citigroup owns Salomon Smith Barney. Other banks offer retail investment services; Huntington Investment Company, a subsidiary of Huntington Bancshares (Ohio) offers online brokerage services to its customers. A survey of the top 100 banks found that 79 had their own broker-dealer firms, 15 offered securities through a third party, and six did not offer retail securities services to their customers.[2]

As a result of bank mergers, the relationships between investment and insurance subsidiaries and their parent companies have become increasingly complex. For example, Citigroup was formed by the merger of Citicorp and Travelers Group in 1998. Citigroup owns Salomon Smith Barney Holdings Inc. Salomon Smith Barney Holdings Inc. controls Salomon Brother Inc. and Smith Barney Inc., which are affiliated but separately registered broker/dealers. Smith Barney Inc. owns Robinson-Humphrey, LLC, another investment firm. Citigroup also owns Primerica Financial Services, Travelers Land and Annuity, and Travelers Property and Casualty.

The Financial Services Modernization Act (also known as the Gramm-Leach-Bliley Act of 1999) was signed into law in November 14, 1999, ending the Glass-Steagall Act's separation of banking from securities and insurance firms. Under the new law, financial holding companies can own banks, securities firms, and insurance companies. The Federal Reserve will be the primary regulator of financial holding companies. Financial holding companies should not be confused with bank holding companies.

Annuities

Some banks, acting as agents for insurance companies, offer annuities to their customers. An **annuity** refers to a schedule of payments at fixed intervals for a

1. NationsBank merged BankAmerica in 1998, and is now known as BankAmerica.
2. Cheryl Winokur, "Most Big Banks Offer Brokerage, Study Says," *American Banker* (October 8, 1999), p. 11.

stated number of years, or for the duration of the life of the person receiving the payments (the annuitant), or the lives of two or more persons. In addition, an annuity with a *life income with installment certain* option allows income to continue to be paid for a specified period (e.g., 15 years) if the principal beneficiary dies early. Finally, in cash refund annuities, the insurer subtracts from the present value of the annuity at its starting date the total of all payments made to the annuitant at the time of death. Any difference is paid to the beneficiary.

The payout of annuity proceeds can be fixed, providing for a constant stream of income, or variable where the income can change over time. Another payout option is a lump sum payment instead of an annuity.

Annuities are used to provide tax-deferred income for retirees and for other investment purposes. These investment products are subject to investment risks, and they are not guaranteed by the bank offering them. As noted in the preceding discussion of insured deposits, annuities, life insurance, mutual funds, and stocks and bonds are not insured by the FDIC.

Mutual Funds

A **mutual fund** is an investment company that pools its shareholders' funds and invests them in a portfolio of securities. The four basic types of mutual funds are bond, equity, hybrid, and money market funds. Most mutual funds will buy back their shares at the current net asset value (book value) from shareholders, and sell new shares to investors. The assets of the mutual fund industry grew from about $1 trillion in 1990 to $5.5 trillion in 1998.[3] Of that total in 1998, $1.3 trillion was invested in 6,288 money market funds.

See http://www.ici.org *for information about the mutual fund industry.*

Money market mutual funds are substitutes for bank deposits. Although money market mutual fund shares are not insured by the FDIC, the fact that they invest in short-term, high-grade U.S. dollar-denominated debt securities, and they are well diversified tends to minimize their risk. In addition, some mutual funds offer other financial services such automatic bill payments and automatic teller machine/debit card withdrawals from money-market funds.[4] Fidelity Investments, which is best known for its Fidelity funds, offers American Express gold cards to selected securities brokerage clients.[5]

The mutual fund industry has grown at the expense of banks. Recognizing this competitive threat, banks entered the mutual fund market to provide an array of investment products to their retail customers. Mellon Bank Corporation, for example, acquired the Dreyfus Corporation, one of the nation's largest managers of mutual funds, and First Union bought Evergreen funds. Bank holding companies can advise and distribute proprietary (the bank's own

3. *Mutual Fund Fact Book, 1999,* Investment Company Institute (May 1999), p. 67. Data from the *Fact Book* are available at http://www.ici.org.
4. Vanessa O'Connell, "It's a Broker! It's a Banker! It's a Mutual-Fund Group!" *Wall Street Journal* (February 19, 1999), pp. C1, C21.
5. John Hechinger and Paul Beckett, "Fidelity to Offer American Express Cards," *Wall Street Journal* (May 5, 1999), p. C25.

product) funds through their bank, brokerage, and insurance company subsidiaries. The top five banks managing mutual fund assets in 1998 were Mellon Bank, First Union, BankAmerica, BankOne, and PNC Bank. By the end of 1998, bank-run mutual fund assets amounted to almost $1 trillion.[6]

Other banks offer nonproprietary funds by having arrangements with independent mutual fund operators, such a Putnam, Oppenheimer, and Fidelity, to provide mutual funds access for their customers. Retail bank customers and small businesses usually buy mutual fund shares through banks' brokerage services and in connection with retirement plans. The retirement plans are referred to by the various sections in the tax law. For example, 401(k) plans are employer-sponsored plans that enable employees to make tax-deferred contributions from their salaries to the plans. Similarly, 403(b) plans are sponsored by universities, public schools, and nonprofit organizations; and 457 plans are sponsored by state and local governments.

Sweep Accounts

Sweep accounts are used for the temporary transfer of funds from noninterest-bearing transactions accounts into an investment account where the funds earn interest. Usually a minimum amount is required, such as $5,000 in the account, before the funds are swept into the investment account. Funds are returned to the transaction account when they are needed to cover payments. Thus, a small business customer or wealthy individual who has $100,000 in a demand deposit account each business day may earn $3,000 or more annually if the funds are kept in an investment account. Large corporations actively manage their own transactions accounts.

Some banks give their customers a choice of having the funds in the sweep account invested in an FDIC-insured savings account or in various mutual funds. Banks receive fee income from the mutual fund providers. As noted previously, funds invested in mutual funds are not covered by FDIC insurance.

Syndication

Commercial banks have learned from investment banks that syndication can be profitable. When underwriting new securities issues, a group of investment banking firms, called the **syndicate,** buys stocks and bonds from the corporation or governments issuing the new securities, and then sells them to the public. The originating investment bank is the syndicate manager. Each firm in the syndicate agrees to buy a stipulated amount of the new issue, and their profit is the difference between the price paid the issuer of the security and the price at which it is sold to investors. Commercial banks have applied that same strategy to underwrite large commercial loans and loan commitments that they either hold or sell to other financial institutions such as small banks that buy

6. "Mutual Fund Roundup," *American Banker* (February 12, 1999).

parts of syndicated loans to diversify their portfolios. For example, Chase bank arranged for a $250 million, five-year loan for Kodak China Company, a joint venture of Eastman Kodak and two Chinese firms.[7]

Although **loan syndication** is not new, banks are making greater use of it today than in the past in order to compete with investment banks in the capital markets. A 1999 study of corporate financing revealed that loan syndication increased from 30% of new funds raised by U.S. corporations in 1987 to 51% in 1997.[8] The highest fees are earned from noninvestment grade companies that account for about 30% of the total syndications and 80% of the fee income.

Large companies, such as Dow Chemical and Merck, make extensive use of commercial paper as a source of financing. Commercial bank syndicates provided backup commitments for their commercial paper programs and for other companies as well.[9] The syndicated commitments ranged from $1–$2 billion, and were split into two tranches: 75% of the commitment was for five years and the other 25% was for 364 days. The term *tranche*, which is French for slice, is finance jargon for the two parts of the commitment. Commitments of less than 365 days have lower capital requirements than longer-term commitments. The fees earned by the banks for syndicating these deals ranged from 7.5 to 10.0 basis points (BPS) on the five-year tranche, and 5 BPS on the 364-day tranche. The interest rates on borrowers was 20 BPS over LIBOR (London Interbank Offering Rate) up to $1 billion, and 25 BPS over LIBOR for the remainder.

15.5 PRIVATE BANKING

For information about private banking at UBS, see http://www.ubs.com/ privatebanking.

Private banking refers to custom-tailored services provided to high net worth individuals. By way of illustration, UBS bank of Switzerland, one of the largest bank in the world, advertises that private banking is based on a thorough understanding of the clients' financial goals, and that a personal Client Advisor will make the global bank's resources available to their clients.[10] The services include, but are not limited to planning, wealth management (tax optimization, estate, and local and cross-border retirement planning), investment management, art banking (dealing with decorative arts, jewelry, numismatic and other collections), and more. UBS states that these services are not available to U.S. citizens, and some limitations apply to citizens of other countries as well. Needless to say, banks providing private banking services earn substantial fee income.

7. James R. Kraus, "U.S. Banks' Asian Loan Syndications Soar as Economic Confidence Rises," *American Banker* (June 14, 1999), pp. 1, 6.
8. "Long Live the Loan," *The Economist* (June 12, 1999), pp. 67–68.
9. "FEI Express–Issue Number 9," Financial Executives Institute, FEI Express [MailManager@feiexpress.fei.org] (June 14, 1999).
10. For more details, see *http://www.ubs.com/privatebanking*.

Satellite Mobile Phone Venture Crashes

Syndicated loans made by big banks can be risky. Consider the case of Iridium, the first global satellite communications system that could connect mobile phone users anywhere on earth. The venture was funded, in part, by an $800 million syndicated loan led by Chase Manhattan Bank. Motorola, Iridium's largest investor, guaranteed $300 million of the $800 million loan. Motorola's financial exposure on the its Iridium venture is a "manageable" $600 million, and other vendors and creditors may lose $400 million or more.*

On October 30, 1998, Vice President Al Gore made the first telephone call using the new $5 billion global mobile telephone system while he was standing the Rose Garden of the White House.** He called Gilbert Grosvenor, chairman of the National Geographic Society, located a few blocks away. One wonders why he didn't call someone on the other side of the world. Maybe it was a bad omen. Iridium's success was short-lived.

To make a long story short, Iridium's emphasis on technology instead of marketing, its high cost service, and a scarcity of customers resulted in its filing Chapter 11 voluntary bankruptcy on August 13, 1999.† The phones were about the size of a brick, cost $3,000, and did not perform as promised. In addition, price per call ranged from $3 to $7.50.‡ The point here is that big banks and sophisticated investors can make loan and investment decisions that result in losses. It seemed like a good deal at the time, but it didn't work out that way.

*Roger O. Crockett, "Why Motorola Should Hang Up On Iridium," *Business Week* (August 30, 1999), p. 46.

**Iridium World Communications Ltd., 1998 Annual Report; Leslie Cauley, "Iridium's Downfall: The Marketing Took Back Seat to Science," *Wall Street Journal* (August 18, 1999), pp. A1, A6.

†*http://www.iridium.com/corporate/news* (August 15, 1999).

‡ James Surowiecki, "The Latest Satellite Startup Lifts Off. Will It Too Explode?" *Fortune* (October 25, 1998), pp. 237–254.

15.6 TRUST SERVICES

Trusts were created during the Crusades. When English knights went in search of the Holy Grail, someone had to manage their land and property. Women had no legal standing at that time, so the knight's property was put in trust for someone else to manage. Over the years, common law recognized trusts. Today a trust is a legal entity that can hold and manage assets for one or more beneficiaries for as long as the trust exists. All trusts have the same general structure. A **trust** is established by a grantor (the creator of the trust) who transfers assets to a trust that is managed by the trustee for the benefit of the beneficiaries in accordance with the terms of the trust agreement. The trustee may be an individual, a trust institution such as a trust company or trust department, or both could be co-trustees. The trustee receives fee income for managing the trust. The amount of fee income depends on the market value of the trust and the services provided. Most of the fee income comes from investment management, administration and custody services, and benefits consulting.

Trust institutions also act as agents for trustees. For example, the trustee for a corporate employee benefit program hires a trust institution as his or her agent to invest and manage the funds. The trustee will tell the agent how the funds are to be managed, and the agent carries out the orders for a fee. However, the agent does not have the same fiduciary responsibility as a trustee when managing the funds. For example, if the trustee tells the agent to invest all of the funds in one volatile stock, the agent will do so. If the trust institution was the trustee for those funds, it would have to invest the funds prudently, taking into account risk, diversification, and other factors.

Trust services usually are organized into two or three lines of business. One line of business deals with employee benefit programs, another with personal trusts and estates, and the third with corporate trusts. Personal trusts manage assets for individuals and their beneficiaries. Corporate trusts, for example, act as trustees for bond issues, and they are responsible for dispensing interest payments to bondholders, maintaining escrow accounts, and other related tasks. The corporate trust business is dominated by large banks such as Bank of New York and Chase Manhattan.

The employee benefit line of business deals with deferred compensation plans. The three principal types of deferred compensation are (1) profit sharing plans, (2) defined benefit plans, and (3) defined contribution plans such as the popular 401(k) plans. The funds from defined contribution plans can be invested in mutual funds and other investments.

Trusts are not limited to financial institutions. The federal government is the trustee for funds that have been established by law. The federal old-age, survivors, and disability insurance fund, medicare, and federal supplemental insurance are the largest funds they manage.

At the end of 1997, 2,467 commercial banks operated trust departments, trust companies, and other supervised trust institutions, with $17.7 trillion in assets in trusts and estates and where the institutions act as agents.[11] Their activities as agents account for 77% of the total assets managed by trust institutions.

Insured banks and trust companies account for 2,251 institutions, in addition to 167 noninsured institutions. The largest number of insured institutions (1,187) are state-chartered commercial banks that are not members of the Federal Reserve System. Collectively, the banks and trust companies serve 17 million accounts.

Types of Trusts

BUSINESS Trusts can be created for any purpose that is not illegal. Trusts are used for business, investment, and estate management. In terms of historical development, trusts were a widely used form of corporate organization by which several corporations engaged in the same line of business formed a trust

11. *Trust Assets of Financial Institutions—1997*, Federal Financial Institutions Examination Council, Washington, DC (1998), Tables A-1, A-2.

to conduct their business without having to merge. In the 1870s and 1880s, the "trusts" were business monopolies in oil, coal, tobacco, and other industries. These monopolies, and their anticompetitive behavior, gave rise to the passage the Sherman Antitrust Act of 1890. It was the first of a series of acts that dealt with antitrust activities. Others acts include the Clayton Act and the Federal Trade Commission Act of 1914, the Robinson-Patman Act of 1936, and the Celler Antimerger Act of 1950. Section 7 of the Clayton Act prohibited one firm from acquiring the *stock* of a competitor when the effect was to lessen competition. The Celler Act strengthened Section 7 of the Clayton Act by prohibiting one firm from acquiring the *assets* of competitors when the effect was to reduce competition. Bank and other types of mergers involve both stock and/or asset acquisitions, and bank mergers are subject to antitrust scrutiny before they are approved.

Today, holding companies and consortiums have replaced trusts as a common forms of business organization. For example, bank holding companies control most of the bank assets in the United States. A consortium is any association or partnership. *Consortium* also is defined as an association of financial institutions for effecting a venture requiring extensive financial resources, especially in international finance. A consortium of some of the largest banks in the world and a technology vendor established Global Trust Enterprise in 1999 for the purpose of providing businesses with a single electronic identity that they can use in electronic commerce. Global Trust then formed a legal entity called Identrus that will vouch for the identity of trading parties—business customers of banks—doing business on the Internet.[12] The banks involved in Identrus include ABN Amro, Bank of America, Bankers Trust, Barclays Bank, CIBC, Chase Manhattan, Citigroup, Deutsche Bank, Hypo Vereinsbank, and Sanwa Bank.

REAL ESTATE INVESTMENT TRUSTS (REITS) The real estate investment trust (REIT) is a financial device used by investors to buy shares in a trust that invests in real estate. A number of REITs are actively traded on major stock exchanges. Some specialize in particular types of properties, such as shopping centers, office buildings, or multifamily residential properties (apartments).

TRUST COMPANY The United States Trust Company of New York was established in 1853, and it was the nation's first trust company. A *trust company* is a corporation formed for the purpose of taking, accepting, and executing all lawful trusts committed to it, and acting as trustee, executor, guardian, fiscal agent, transfer agent for stocks and bonds, and so on. Today, U.S. Trust, which holds a New York State bank charter and is a member bank of the FDIC, advertises that it is an *investment management company* that also provides fiduciary and private banking services, primarily to affluent individuals, families, and institutions.[13] The bank's trust activities are separated from its

12. "Global Trust Gets Rolling," *Electronic Banker* (February 10, 1999); *http://www. electronic banker.com* (June 6, 1999); *http://www.identrus.com* (June 6, 1999).
13. *http://www.ustrust.com* (June 6, 1999).

other banking activities. It has more than $79 billion in assets under management.

Many banks have established trust departments within their banks in order to provide additional services to their customers, such as estate planning. Trusts are used by individuals for estate planning in order to distribute their assets and to reduce their taxes.[14] Federal estate taxes range from 37% to 55%. Several types of widely used trusts include the following.

See http://www.fdic.gov/deposit/deposits/deposit/index.html *for FDIC insurance of revocable trusts.*

- **Revocable Living Trust.** A revocable living trust (also known as "living trust," or "inter vivos" trust) allows the grantor to retain control over the assets during his or her lifetime. All trust assets are included in the estate for tax purposes.

- **Credit Shelter Trust.** A credit shelter trust is designed to take full advantage of estate tax credits for individuals. The maximum estate tax exclusion amount will be $1 million in 2006.

- **Marital Trust.** A marital trust shelters from the estate tax any amount that is transferred to the surviving spouse in trust for their benefit if the trust qualifies for the marital deduction.

- **Irrevocable Trust.** Trust assets in an irrevocable trust may be excluded from estate tax by the estate tax exclusion amount. In addition, irrevocable trusts are used to own life insurance policies to avoid estate taxes and to protect trust assets from creditors.

OTHER TYPES OF TRUSTS Several other types of trusts are listed here to illustrate other uses. This listing of trusts in not complete.

- **Charitable Trust.** These trusts are designed to benefit particular charities, educational institutions, or religious organizations.

- **Trust Deposit.** Money or property is deposited with a bank, but not commingled with other property or deposits of the bank. The money or property is to be returned in kind to the depositor, or for some special purpose such as payment of a particular debt obligation of the depositor.

For additional information on UITs, see the web site for the Investment Company Institute: http://www.ici.org.

- **Unit Investment Trusts.** Unit investment trusts are used for investment purposes. A unit investment trust (UIT) is a registered investment company (i.e., mutual fund) that buys and holds a relatively fixed portfolio of stocks, bonds, and other securities until the trust's termination date. When the trust is dissolved, the proceeds are paid to the shareholders. The fact that UITs have relatively fixed portfolios makes them different from other mutual funds that have actively traded portfolios.

The reason for the relatively fixed portfolio is that stock UITs are structured to replicate the performance of a particular stock index, and they hold only the

14. This section is based on "What You Need to Know About Trusts," *Participant* (February 1999), pp. 10–13.

For more information about SPDRs and other UITs, see http://www.nasdaq-amex.com/indexshares.

stocks in that index. From time to time, stocks in the index may change, and then the portfolio is changed accordingly. For example, SPDRs (pronounced "spiders"), which stands for Standard & Poor's Depository Receipts, is linked to the S&P 500 stock index. SPDRs are traded on the American Stock Exchange under the ticker symbol SPY.[15] SPDRs are designed to provide investment results that correspond to the price and yield performance of the S&P 500 stock index. SPDRs compete with index mutual funds, such as the Vanguard Index 500 fund, that also try to match the performance of the S&P 500 stock index. SPDRs and other UITs are generally used by active traders, while index mutual funds tend to be used by passive investors.

Similarly, DIAMONDS are an index-based product that mirrors the Dow Jones Industrial Average, WEBs cover selected international markets, and other UITs mirror the technology sector, the energy sector, and so on.

According to the Investment Company Institute, more than 12,000 UITs are offered by more than a dozen sponsors such as brokers and dealers.

SUMMARY

The range of financial services offered by banking organizations extends far beyond taking deposits and making loans. This chapter examined a few of the many services offered to both wholesale and retail customers. On the wholesale side of the business, banks provide cash management, data processing, loan syndications, sweep accounts, and selected trust services to business concerns and financial institutions. On the retail side of the business, they provide FDIC-insured deposits, annuities, mutual funds, sweep accounts, and selected trust services. This listing of services is not complete, but it is sufficient to demonstrate that banks viewed collectively are financial supermarkets that are becoming increasingly dependent on fee income. As electronic banking (discussed in Chapter 15) becomes more pervasive, banks will continue to expand both their wholesale and retail services.

Key Terms and Concepts

Annuity	Mutual funds
Cash management services	Sweep accounts
FDIC-insured deposits	Syndicate
Loan syndication	Trust
Lockbox	Trust services

15. For additional information on index-based products, see *http://nasdaq-amex.com/indexshares.*

Questions

15.1 Can bank holding companies engage in any financial service that is closely related and incident to banking?

15.2 In cash management services, what is meant by "cash concentration"?

15.3 What is "controlled disbursement"?

15.4 Explain the use of lockboxes.

15.5 What type of data processing services can bank holding companies provide?

15.6 What bank products and services are FDIC-insured?

15.7 What does the Glass-Steagall Act of 1933 have to say about commercial banks and investment banking?

15.8 Some banks sell annuities for insurance companies. What is an annuity, and why are they doing it?

15.9 Are money market mutual funds as safe as bank deposits? Explain your position.

15.10 What is a sweep account?

15.11 What is loan syndication?

15.12 What is the general structure of a trust?

15.13 Explain why trusts are used in estate planning.

15.14 One of the members of the board of directors of your bank is interested in creating a subsidiary that will engage principally in underwriting or dealing in securities. Another board member mentioned financial holding companies. They suggested that you check with the Federal Reserve (*http://www.federalreserve.gov*). On the home page, click on "search." In the blank space, type in the words "financial holding company," then click on search again.

Information Please

Jeremy Lincoln called the bank's board of directors meeting to order. The first item on the agenda concerned the wealth of information that the bank had about its customers, especially those that made extensive use of their credit and debit cards. Jeremy gave each of the board members a copy of the Consumer Data (Table 15.2) listing some examples of the type of information that the bank has or can obtain for each of its customers.

"Ladies and gentlemen," he said, "what do you think is the best way to use this information? First, I know that we can use the information internally to improve the marketing of our services and to open new market opportunities for us. There is no controversy about that. However, there is some controversy about our second option. We can sell the information to various types of vendors who can use it for their own marketing purposes. This option would bring in a lot of money over the years to come, and that would make our stockholders happy. After all, we are a publicly held company and one of our key objectives is to maximize shareholder wealth. On the other hand, selling such information might irritate our customers, especially those who have a strong belief in the right to privacy. I know that a lot of our customers believe that what they buy and do with their money is something they want to keep private. Those are the issues that we must consider. What should we do with all this information—protect it or sell it? Do you see other alternatives? Tell me what you think."

TABLE 15.2	Consumer Data
Descriptive data	Name, address, phone number
	Income and debts, payments history
Transactions	Amounts spent, purchase dates, vendors, category of goods acquired
Trigger events	Birthdays, relocation, birth of child

FDIC Insurance Coverage

W hat does FDIC insurance coverage mean? Is it $100,000 per account? Or does it mean $100,000 per person? Or does it mean $100,000 in one bank or in all of the banks where an individual has deposits? The rules covering FDIC insured deposits are extensive and confusing. A complete listing of the rules and discussion of them is beyond the scope of this book. Nevertheless, the following true or false statements and answers provides some insight into FDIC deposit insurance coverage.[16] ■

16. The statements and answers are based on "Examples of Simpler Insurance Rules," and "Test Your Deposit Insurance IQ," Federal Deposit Insurance Corporation, *Consumer News* (Spring 1999), pp. 2, 5–6. The answers given here are for purposes of illustration, and they may not be complete. For questions concerning FDIC insurance coverage, call the FDIC at 1-800-934-3342, or send an e-mail message to consumer@fdic.gov.

True or False?

1. By law, all commercial banks and savings associations in the United States are insured by the FDIC.

   False. Most, but not all banks and savings associations are insured.

2. You have $100,000 in certificates of deposit at a bank where you also have $100,000 in an Individual Retirement Account (IRA). You are fully insured because retirement accounts are insured up to $100,000 separately from other funds at the bank.

   True. Both traditional and Roth IRAs are insured to $100,000 separately from nonretirement accounts at the same bank. In addition, both traditional and Roth IRAs are treated differently than employer sponsored 401(k) retirement plans deposited in the same bank.

3. If you have checking and savings accounts at two FDIC-insured banks that merge, the deposits combined immediately for insurance purposes.

   False. A six-month "grace period" follows the merger for regular checking and savings accounts.

4. You have a $20,000 checking account in your name, and at the same bank, a $100,000 trust account in your name that is payable to your mother when you die. All of the money is protected because the payable-on-death (POD) account is insured separately from you checking account.

   True. The POD testamentary trust accounts, also known as a "Trotten trust" or "In Trust For" account, are insured separately from individual or joint accounts at the same institution. In a POD account, the depositor indicates in the bank records how the funds are to be disbursed to qualified beneficiaries when he or she dies. The qualifying beneficiaries include parents, spouse, siblings, children, and grandchildren.

5. You have a checking account at the same bank where you have an account for the sole proprietorship business that you own. The two accounts are insured for a total of $100,000.

   True. Sole proprietorship accounts are added to personal accounts of the owner in the same institution for insurance purposes.

6. You and your wife have joint accounts in the same bank totaling $200,000. Because both names appear on both accounts, they are fully insured for $100,000 each.

   True. Each persons' share in all joint accounts are covered up to a total of $100,000.

7. You have three accounts at the same bank: a $100,000 savings account and a $50,000 checking account for yourself, and a $50,000 joint account with your mother. All three accounts are insured separately for $100,000.

   False. Insurance coverage is based on how the accounts are owned. In this case, $100,000 of the accounts in your name are insured, but $50,000 are uninsured. Your share of any joint account is insured up to $100,000.

8. You purchased mutual fund shares from your FDIC-insured bank. Therefore, insurance coverage of $100,000 is extended to those shares.

   False. FDIC insurance only covers deposits. Mutual funds, stocks, bonds, annuities, and life insurance are not deposits.

9. You have three joint accounts at the same bank: one for $100,000 with your wife, one for $100,000 with your sister, and one for $100,000 with your brother. Because you own each account with a different person, each account qualifies for $100,000 of insurance.

   False. Assuming that the interests of the co-owners are equal, your interest would be $50,000 in each account for a total of $150,000. Under FDIC rules, no person's insured interest in all joint accounts can exceed $100,000, the uninsured amount would be $50,000.

10. You can get additional FDIC insurance coverage by opening accounts at different branches of the same institution.

    False. The insured institution's main office and branches are considered to be one institution.

Global Financial Services

16.1 WHY AND HOW U.S. BANKS ENGAGE IN INTERNATIONAL BANKING

Banks engage in international banking for several reasons. The first and most important reason is to serve the needs of their customers. Banks have customers that both import and export goods and services and they need banking services to facilitate trade. In this regard, some banks that have domestic customers with foreign operations follow them abroad to provide services. Similarly, banks with overseas foreign customers may want to be closer to them in order provide better service. Obviously, it is hoped that serving the needs of customers will generate profits.

The profit motive is the second reason for international banking. International banking opens new markets, some of which may have greater profit potential than is available in domestic markets. High expected returns are consistent with high risks. Following decades of making large profits in foreign markets, many international banks experienced large losses in 1998 on loans in developing countries such as Indonesia, Russia, South Korea, and Thailand.

Global diversification was a reason for engaging in international banking in the 1970s and 1980s. However the international financial crises of the 1990s taught us that as a result of communications technology, global financial markets are linked together so that financial distress in one country can spread quickly to others. Thus, the benefits of global diversification have been reduced.

Prestige is another reason for global expansion. It adds to a bank's prestige to advertise that it has offices in London, Tokyo, and other international financial centers. These locations, in turn, give them access to multinational firms that operate in those markets. Thus, they can serve their customers' needs in those markets and attract new customers.

The remainder of this section presents the principal methods used by U.S. banking organizations to participate in international banking. The extent to which banks use these methods depends on whether international banking is an occasional or full-time activity. ■

Correspondent Banking

The vast majority of banks do not engage in international banking on a regular basis. On those occasions when a customer requires international banking services, those banks use a correspondent bank that provides such services. **Correspondent banks** are large banks that provide the gamut of banking products and services to other banks in exchange for fees and/or deposits. Typically, correspondent banks providing international banking services are money center banks (large banks located in New York and other money centers), large regional banks, and foreign banks located in the United States. Some correspondent banks maintain deposits in foreign banks that can be used to facilitate trade by making or receiving payments, which is commonly referred to as **trade finance**. Other services may include foreign exchange of currencies, letters of credit and introduction, and credit information on overseas firms. In addition to the services mentioned, correspondent banks make international loans and sell "participations" in those loans to other banks. They also deal in swaps, and provide investment and other services.

Banks that deal extensively in international trade also use correspondent banks on a regular basis. For example, a U.S. bank may use the Bank of Tokyo–Mitsubishi Ltd. as its principal correspondent in Japan if it does a lot of business in Japan. Accordingly, payments to or collections from other banks in Japan will be routed through the Bank of Tokyo–Mitsubishi Ltd. Likewise, the U.S. bank maintains correspondent relationships in other money centers of the world. Such networks provide the channels that facilitate the efficient flow of funds in the capital markets throughout the world.

Foreign Branches

Banks have foreign branches in the same fashion that they have domestic branches. That is, a branch represents the parent firm at some distant location. Some branches are full-service branches offering a full range of banking services to their customers, while other branches only offer limited services. The full range of services includes taking deposits, making loans, and investments as examples.

Under provisions of the Federal Reserve Act, banks that are members of the Federal Reserve System may establish foreign branches with the approval of the Federal Reserve Board.

See the Financial Times *web site at* http://www.ft.com *for articles about international finance and banking, and* Morgan Stanley Global Economic Forum *at* http://www.ms.com/gef.html *for surveys of major economies.*

Representative Offices

A representative office is a quasi-sales office. Representative offices cannot book loans or take deposits, but they can develop business for the head office and arrange for these things to happen elsewhere. They also establish a bank's presence in an area where the business is not sufficient to justify the cost of establishing a branch, or where new branch offices are not permitted by local regulations.

Foreign Affiliates

Domestic commercial banks and bank holding companies may acquire an equity interest in foreign financial organizations such as banks, finance companies, and leasing companies. They may own all or part of the stock. The affiliates may be subsidiaries or joint ventures. One advantage of foreign affiliates is that the affiliate is not "foreign" in its own country. They may also have tax, political, and marketing advantages. On the other side of the coin, a bank with minority ownership is subject to the same problems as any minority stockholder. Minority stockholders may have little influence in the operating policies of a corporation.

Edge Act Offices

The **Edge Act** of 1919 (an amendment to the Federal Reserve Act by Senator Walter Edge) permits National banking organizations to have subsidiary corporations that may have offices throughout the United States to provide a means of financing international trade, especially exports. Their activities include making loans and taking deposits strictly related to international transactions. Accordingly, a California bank can have Edge Act offices located in New Orleans, New York, or Chicago; but those offices are restricted to dealing in business strictly related to international transactions. Edge Act corporations may also invest in foreign financial organizations such as foreign banks, finance companies, and leasing companies.

Some Edge Act offices are located overseas. The **Edge Act offices** may engage in banking practices that are permitted in foreign countries but that are denied to other types of U.S. banking organizations.

The International Banking Act of 1978 amended the Edge Act to permit domestic banks to acquire foreign financial organizations. To establish reciprocity, foreign financial organizations were permitted to acquire domestic banks. It also permitted foreign banks to establish Edge Act banking offices.

International Banking Facilities

In the 1960s and 1970s, offshore banking increased as a means of avoiding reserve requirements, limitations on interest rates placed on time and savings deposits, and other regulations. So-called *shell banks* were opened in the Bahamas and Cayman Islands. They were nothing more than "name plates" used to book transactions "offshore" that actually took place in the United States.

Beginning in 1981, the Federal Reserve Board permitted domestic and foreign banks to establish **international banking facilities (IBFs)** to take deposits and make loans to nonresidents, and serve as a record-keeping facility. In reality, an IBF is a set of accounts in a domestic bank that is segregated from the other accounts of that organization. In other words, an IBF is not a bank, per se, it is an accounting system. IBF accounts do not have the same reserve requirements as domestic banks, and they are granted special tax status by some states. The tax breaks are inducements by the states to encourage the development of international financial centers.

IBFs are subject to some restrictions that do not apply to foreign branches of U.S. banks. For example, they are not permitted to accept deposits or make loans to U.S. residents. They may not issue negotiable instruments, because they might fall into the hands of U.S. residents. Nonbank customers' deposits have a minimum maturity of two days so they cannot act as substitutes for domestic demand deposits. The minimum denomination of deposits for nonbank customers is $100,000. Because of the minimum size of the deposits, they are not covered by the FDIC deposit insurance.

See http://www.federalreserve.gov/centralbanks.htm *for information about foreign central banks and banks in other countries.*

16.2 FOREIGN BANKS IN THE UNITED STATES

The Bank of Montreal was the first foreign bank to establish operations in the United States in 1818. Today more than 250 foreign banks do business in the United States with hundreds of offices scattered throughout the country in major cities such as New York and Atlanta.

The International Banking Act of 1978 codified the federal regulation of foreign banking activities in the United States. The regulation and supervision are carried out primarily by the Federal Reserve. However, the Comptroller of the Currency, the FDIC, and state banking authorities may also be involved in their regulation. According to the Act, foreign banks can operate agencies, branches, investment companies, commercial bank subsidiaries, and Edge Act offices in the United States. The act does not require reciprocity for U.S. banks operating in foreign countries.

Agency

According the International Banking Act of 1978, an **agency** is "any office or any place of business of a foreign bank located in any state of the United States or District of Columbia at which credit balances are maintained, checks are paid, or money lent, but deposits may not be accepted for a citizen or resident of the United States." Agencies are used primarily to facilitate international trade between the United States and the foreign bank's native land.

Branch

The definition for a branch is similar to that of an agency, except a branch "may accept deposits that are incidental to, or for the purpose of carrying out transactions in foreign countries." The branch can do almost anything that the parent bank can do, in exactly the same way domestic branch banks operate.

The foreign parent bank must decide in which state the branch will be located. The parent bank may apply for a state-chartered branch, in which case it must operate under the banking laws of that state. Alternately, it may apply for a federal charter from the Comptroller of the Currency, in which case it will be treated as a member bank of the Federal Reserve System (like all national banks) and be covered by FDIC insurance. State-chartered foreign banks that accept retail deposits (less than $100,000) are required to have FDIC insurance.

A limited branch is an Edge Act office set up outside the home state, or some other facility that does not have all of the powers of the branch bank. Representative offices established by a foreign bank are similar to those described for domestic banks.

Investment Company

Investment companies owned by foreign financial organizations are similar to state chartered commercial banks with the following exceptions. They can deal in securities such as common stock, while banks are not permitted to invest in stocks. In addition, an investment company can lend more than 10% of its capital and surplus to one customer, while banks have limitations relative to the amount of capital they can lend. Finally, an investment company cannot accept deposits.

Do not confuse the foreign investment companies with domestic investment companies (i.e., mutual funds). Although both are called investment companies, they are different types of financial organizations. Domestic investment companies pool investors' funds and invest them in securities to obtain capital gains, income, or some other financial objective. Foreign investment companies make loans and equity investments on the behalf of their owners.

Subsidiary

Foreign banks can own U.S. banks, in whole or in part. The banks that they own are subject to the same rules and regulations as any other domestic banks. Several examples of large foreign-bank owned U.S. banks are Union Bank, San Francisco (Bank of Tokyo–Mitsubishi, Ltd.); Marine Midland Bank, Buffalo, New

York (Hong Kong & Shanghai Banking Corp., Hong Kong); and Harris Trust & Savings Bank, Chicago (Bank of Montreal, Canada). Deutsche Bank acquired Bankers Trust in 1999. This partial listing of foreign-owned subsidiaries suggests that foreign banks play an important role in our financial system.

Finance Companies

Foreign financial organizations may own or operate finance companies. For example, Fuji Bank Ltd., Tokyo, owns Heller Financial, Inc., Chicago. And Barclays Bank Plc, London, owns Barclays American Corporation, Charlotte, North Carolina. Finance companies typically make working capital loans to business concerns and consumer loans. Some of these names, and the other mentioned previously, are so familiar to those engaged in banking that one forgets they are owned by foreign banks.

16.3 INTERNATIONAL LENDING

Some features of international lending are different from domestic lending, while some practices are similar. This section examines only those lending practices that are typically associated with international lending.

Syndicated Loans

Both domestic and foreign loans can be syndicated. Syndication is presented here because it permits banks of different sizes to participate in international lending.

The *syndication* of large loans has advantages for both the borrower and the lender. From the borrower's point of view, syndication provides for a larger amount of funds than may be available from any single lender. In addition, the credit terms may be better than for a large number of smaller loans. From the lender's point of view, syndication provides a means of diversifying some of the risks of foreign lending that were discussed previously. Another advantage of syndication is that it provides the lead bank with off-balance sheet income for that portion of the loan that is sold to other participants. The lead bank and other banks that comanage the loan receive fee income for their management services. Typically the management fee is paid by the borrower at the time the loan is made. Such fees range from 0.5% to more than 2% of the total amount of the loan. Finally, syndication can enhance relations with foreign governments because it is a means of financing their domestic economic activity.

The Syndication Process

Of the two types of syndicated bank loans, the first occurs through an agreement between the borrower and each lender. The second, which is of concern to

MANAGING RISK

Bank Failures

Banks are generally perceived to be "safe," but that is not necessarily the case.

During the 1980–1995 period, and International Monetary Fund study found that 133 of the Fund's 181 member countries had significant banking sector problems.* The United States belongs to the IMF, and it too experienced failures. During that same period, more than 1,600 FDIC-insured banks in the United States failed. In 1997, a financial crisis that began in Thailand spread around Southeast

Asia contributing to bank failures in Indonesia, Malaysia, South Korea, and elsewhere. Subsequently, banks in Russia failed. The point here is that lending to banks can be risky business. What can banks do to protect themselves when they make loans or have credit relationships with other banks?

*Carl-Johan Lindgren, Gillian Garcia, and Matthew I. Saal, *Banking Soundness and Macroeconomic Policy* (Washington, DC, International Monetary Fund, 1996).

us, is a **participation loan**, a cross between traditional bank lending and underwriting. This form of participation deals with three levels of banks in the syndicate: lead banks, managing banks, and participating banks. The lead banks negotiate with the borrower on the terms of the loan and assemble the management group that will underwrite it. They are also responsible for all documentation of the loan (notes, security agreements, legal opinions, and so on). Moreover, they are expected to underwrite a share of the loans themselves, at least as large as that of the other lenders. After the underwriting group has been established, information will be sent to other banks that may be interested in participating. For example, the initial telex cables advise the name of the borrower, maturity of the loan, and interest rates. If a bank is interested in participating, it advises a member of the underwriting group and receives additional information that permits it to analyze the credit. Although the loan may be attractive, some banks may reject it because they have already reached their lending limits in that country or region. Finally, syndication does not relieve each participating bank from doing its own credit analysis and assessment of risks.

Loan Pricing

Eurocurrency syndicated loans, as well as many domestic commercial and industrial loans, are priced at LIBOR plus a certain number of points. **LIBOR** is the London interbank offered rate, the rate at which banks lend funds to other banks in the Euromarket. LIBOR is usually about ⅛ to ¼ percent above *LIBB* the London interbank bid—the rate at which they buy funds. Accordingly, a syndicated loan may be priced at, say, LIBOR plus ½ percent for the next five years. In the Pacific basin, there is **SIBOR**, which is the Singapore intermarket offered rate. Singapore is the center of the Asian dollar market, and SIBOR is widely used in Asian trade.

Although LIBOR changes on a day-to-day basis, the interest rates on the loans are usually adjusted every three or six months. Additional loan costs include commitment fees, underwriting fees, and other charges. Like domestic loans, commitment fees are based on the unused portion of the credit that is available to the firm under the terms of the agreement. For example, the fee may be ½ percent annually of that amount.

Unlike domestic loans, an underwriting fee may be involved, which is a one-time front-end cost. Such fees are divided among the lead banks and the other banks in proportion to their participation. These fees for investment banking—underwriting—are not common in the United States because the Banking Act of 1933 (the Glass-Steagall Act) divorced bank holding companies from the securities business. However, in recent years, the legal barriers between banking and the securities business have been eroding as the courts and the Board of Governors permitted banks certain underwriting activities.

Finally, the loans may also have clauses dealing with foreign taxes and reserve requirements, so that the lenders receive all the payments that are necessary to pay for the principal and interest on the loans.

16.4 LETTERS OF CREDIT

Financing international trade is related to but different from dealing in foreign exchange and international lending. International sellers want to be paid for the goods and services they are selling to foreign buyers whom they may not know or trust. However, the buyers do not want to pay until they have received the goods that were ordered. Differences between national laws, currencies, and customs frustrate the payment process. Nevertheless, payments can be made to the satisfaction of both the seller and the buyer by using commercial letters of credit.

Import Letters of Credit

Commercial **letters of credit** issued by a domestic bank in favor of a beneficiary in a foreign country are referred to as *import letters of credit*. By way of illustration, we will examine an import letter of credit for Sabra Photos. The mechanics of *export letters of credit* are the same as the illustration, except that the letter of credit is issued by a foreign bank in favor of a beneficiary in this country.

Sabra Photos of Los Angeles wants to import cameras from Shogun Distributors in Japan, but neither has done business with the other before. The manager of Sabra Photos does not want to pay for the goods until they are shipped, and the manager of Shogun Distributors does not want to wait for the goods to arrive before being paid. One solution to this problem is to include in the purchase contract for the cameras that the payment will be paid by a commercial letter of credit if certain conditions are met. The importer's commercial bank is called the issuing bank. The *issuing bank* issues a letter of credit, which is a document agreeing to make payment, from its own account, to the exporter when the conditions of the letter credit are met. In other words, the bank is substituting its own credit for that of the importer. Before issuing the letter of credit, the importer and the bank agree on the terms and conditions under which the bank will make payment to the exporter. These terms and conditions should agree with those in the purchase contract between Sabra Photos and Shogun Distributors. But the bank is bound only by the provisions of the letter of credit.

The issuing bank forwards the letter of credit to the seller's *advising bank* overseas. Depending on the terms of the letter of credit, the advising bank negotiates the documents, and if they are in order, sends them to the issuing bank for payments to be made. The issuer may then pay the seller through the advising (paying) bank. If the advising bank "confirms" the letter of credit, it becomes an obligation of that bank to make payments if the terms of the letter of credit are met. Otherwise, it is acting only as an intermediary between the buyer and seller and will only pay if sufficient funds are available.

Terms that are commonly found in letters of credit include the following:

- The issuing bank will have title to the merchandise.
- The bank is not responsible for the validity, genuineness, or sufficiency of the documents representing title to the merchandise.
- The importer assumes all the risks from legal actions brought by the exporter or those who use the letter of credit.
- The bank is *not* responsible for quality, condition, or value of the merchandise represented by the documents, unless stated otherwise.
- The importer agrees to pay the bank a fee for its services.
- An itemized list of the documents that are to be delivered to the bank (or its correspondent) by the exporter is included.

If the importer agrees to these and other terms, the bank will issue a letter of credit. The terms and definitions used in connection with letters of credit are published by the International Chamber of Commerce in Paris, France, in the *Uniform Customs and Practices for Documentary Credits*, that has been adopted by many of the world's leading trading countries. The purpose of this document to provide a common understanding and interpretation of the technical aspects of letters of credit. It includes information on shipping documents, expiration dates, partial shipments, transfers, installment shipments, and other items.

A letter of credit is considered a *contingent liability* of the issuing bank because the actual payment of the credit is not made until the exporter presents the proper documents. Note that the bank is not interested in the merchandise per se, but rather in the documents.

BILL OF LADING The bill of lading represents the title to the merchandise that was shipped. When the exporter, Shogun Distributor, delivers the cameras to a shipper who will transport the goods, the shipper acknowledges receipt of the goods and details of the shipment with a bill of lading. It also states who is to receive the merchandise and the title to it. Of course, if the goods are damaged and the documents are not in order, the bank will not pay under the terms of the credit agreement.

OTHER DOCUMENTS   Other documents that may be required by the bank include the following:

1. An *invoice* describing the items that have been sold, the price, and other information.

2. A *certificate of origin* stating the country where the goods were manufactured or grown.

3. An *inspection certificate*, which is usually issued by an independent third party, stating that the merchandise is what is called for in the purchase agreement.

4. A *draft*, or *bill of exchange*, drawn by the exporter (Shogun Distributors) on the importer's (Sabra Photos) bank for the amount due as stated in the letter of credit. The draft can be drawn so that it is payable at sight or at some predetermined time (a time draft) after sight. Most drafts are drawn so that they are payable a certain number of days after sight. In such cases, if all the documents are presented to the issuing bank and everything is in order, the bank can accept the draft by stamping the word "ACCEPTED" on its face and sign it. The time draft then becomes a **bankers' acceptance**, an irrevocable obligation of the bank, and it can be sold by the exporter at a discount in order to obtain the funds due before the date of maturity. The maturity is usually less than nine months.

To illustrate the use of a bankers' acceptance, suppose that the face amount of a time draft is $1 million and that it matures in six months. The bank's acceptance charge (commission plus discount rate) is 6 percent per annum. The amount of money to received by the maker of the draft is $970,000

$$\text{Acceptance charges} = 6\% \times \$1 \text{ million} \times 6/12 = \$30,000$$

$$\text{Amount received} = \$1 \text{ million} - \$30,000 = \$970,000$$

The acceptance charge is the gross income to the bank. It does not take into account reserve, the cost of funds, or handling costs.

The acceptance is a negotiable instrument and can be sold by the bank for the account of the payee. Because the acceptance is an obligation of the bank as well as the payee, it is considered a safe investment by investors. Some bankers' acceptances are "eligible" for rediscounting with the Federal Reserve System. Eligible acceptances have no reserve requirements, but ineligible acceptances do.

Confirmed Letters of Credit

In some cases, the exporter of goods may not be satisfied by the financial strength of the importer's advising bank that issued the letter of credit. In this case, the exporter may have his bank confirm the letter by adding its guarantee that the funds will be paid in accordance with the terms of the credit.

The failure of Penn Square bank underscores the importance of **confirmed letters of credit**. Penn Square Bank, N.A., was located in Oklahoma City, Oklahoma. The bank was known as an originator and servicer of energy (oil) loans. It failed in 1982. Before it failed, Penn Square issued irrevocable letters of credit (some are revocable) worth $1.6 million to SGI Holland Inc. and SGI International Holdings.[1] These letters of credit were not issued in connection with international trade, but served as security for a $1.1 million promissory note made by a local oilman. When the note came due, the oilman did not pay it. The FDIC, which had taken over the bank, refused to honor the letters of credit. The point is that the quality of a letter of credit is only as secure as the quality of the issuer. The failure of Penn Square bank should serve as a warning that banks fail, too. Having the endorsement of a second bank reduces the risk. Confirmed letters of credit of this type are also known as **standby letters of credit**. In this case, the confirming bank pays only in the event of default of the issuing bank.

16.5 COLLECTION

The term *collection* refers to the process of presenting an item, such as a check, to the maker for payment. In the United States, most items for collection are handled by local clearinghouses or by the Federal Reserve System. However, no similar system exists for collection of international negotiable instruments. Therefore, banks located in one country use correspondent banks or their foreign branches to facilitate the clearing process.

Clean Collections

Collections are divided into two categories, clean and documentary. *Clean collections* means are no documents are attached. Traveler's checks and money orders are examples of clean collections. For example, suppose that while on vacation in Europe you cashed a traveler's check drawn on a U.S. bank. The foreign bank where the traveler's check was deposited would collect on that item by sending it to a correspondent bank in the United States (or its overseas

---

1. "2 Firms, Investors File Penn Square Suits," *Tulsa World* (October 3, 1982), p. B-5.

branch) to be credited to the foreign bank's account. The correspondent bank presents the traveler's check to the issuing bank for payment. When the payment is received, it is credited to the foreign bank's account. In some cases, the correspondent credits the foreign bank's account before the item is collected.

If a check drawn on a foreign bank was deposited in the United States, the reverse process would occur. Because the length of time necessary to clear the collection item, credit may not be given until the U.S. bank has received the funds or had them credited to its account. Therefore, a substantial difference may occur between the ledger balance of the account and the amount of funds that are available for use.

Documentary Collections

Drafts, or bills of exchange, were discussed previously in connection with letters of credit. Now consider the case of an exporter that wants to use the collection method instead of a letter of credit. In this example, the U.S. exporter has an order to sell auto parts to a South American firm. The parts are shipped, and the exporter takes a copy of the bill of lading, the draft, and other documents to her bank for collection. She tells the banker to present the draft and documents to the importer for collection. The U.S. bank will use a South American correspondent who works with the importer's bank, collects the funds, and presents the bill of lading and other documents to the importer. This collection method is called *documents against payment*. The bank receives a fee for acting as the exporter's agent in the collection process.

Banks that are actively engaged in such collections may have form letters that give explicit instructions as to how the payments are to be made, the documents that are involved, and other pertinent information.

Banks are also involved in collections with imports. The U.S. banks present the exporter's draft and documents to the importer for payment. Collections may also be in the form of U.S. dollars or a foreign currency.

The basic difference between the collection method and a letter of credit is that an irrevocable letter of credit is an obligation of the issuing bank, whereas an exporter's draft is drawn on the importer. The collection method is less costly than a letter of credit and is frequently used when the risks to the exporter are relatively small.

16.6   FOREIGN EXCHANGE MARKETS

The remainder of this chapter deals with technical aspects of international banking, some of which are confusing and difficult to comprehend. Nevertheless, they are an integral part of international finance and lending; understanding them will give you an appreciation of the complexities.

MANAGERIAL ISSUES

Euro Deposits

A **Eurocurrency** deposit is denominated in a currency other than that of the country where the bank is located. The prefix *Euro* means "external" and does not means that the deposits have to be in Europe. They can be anywhere. A French franc deposit in a French bank is a regular deposit. But U.S. dollars, Deutsche marks, or Japanese yen deposited in a bank located in France are Eurocurrency deposits—they are "external" currencies to the country where they were deposited.

The receiving bank will make deposits of equivalent value in banks where the currencies are legal tender. Suppose that General Motors makes a U.S. $10 million deposit in a French bank located in Paris. U.S. dollar-denominated deposits in foreign banks are called **Eurodollar deposits**. The French bank will deposit an equivalent value in the United States for dollar deposits. Eurodollars should not be confused with the euro currency unit used in foreign exchange.

Foreign Exchange

Foreign exchange (FX) refers to exchanging one country's currency for a foreign currency. Thus the U.S. dollar can be exchanged for the Japanese yen or the Mexican peso. The need to exchange currencies arises from flows of goods and services of foreign goods and services and from capital flows. For example, suppose that you were going to vacation in England, where the domestic currency is the *pound*. In order to pay cash for the goods and services you acquire there, you must pay in pounds. Similarly, suppose that a company is buying electronic components from a Japanese manufacturing firm. The Japanese firm wants to be paid in *yen*. To handle these and other financial needs, some commercial banks have developed expertise in dealing with FX.

Most FX transactions in the United States are handled by a small group of money center banks headquartered in New York, Chicago, San Francisco, and other major cities. These banks have affiliates in London, Frankfurt, Tokyo, and elsewhere throughout the world. Conversely, as noted previously, major foreign banks have operations located in the United States. This network of banks forms what is called the *interbank market* where foreign currencies can be bought and sold. The FX market is the largest financial market in the world.

In addition to the interbank market, *foreign exchange brokers* facilitate the efficient operations of the FX market. They deal with banks, business concerns, and governments. Even banks that are part of the interbank market make use of FX brokers for certain types of transactions.

Exchange Rates

The FX market operates 24 hours per day because of time differences throughout the world. When it is 10 A.M. in Chicago, it is 4 P.M. in London, and 1 P.M.

MANAGERIAL ISSUES

Euro: The Currency

The euro is the result of 15 West European countries coming together to form a single European market by removing trade barriers, improving capital flows, and having a common currency. Eleven of the 15 countries joined the European Monetary Union (EMU), and signed the Maastricht Treaty of 1991, which resulted in the establishment of the European Central Bank (ECB). The ECB began operation in 1999. It created a new unified currency called the **euro**. The euro is usable in financial transactions for 11 member countries of the EMU: Austria, Belgium, Denmark, France, Germany, Ireland, Italy, Luxembourg, Netherlands, Portugal, and Spain.* The euro will replace the currencies of the participating countries when the system is fully adopted, and it will eliminate exchange rate risk between the participating countries. Currently the exchange rate between the euro and individual currencies of the EMU countries is fixed.**

The euro began trading in January 1999, and full adoption of the monetary system is expected June 30, 2002, with the distribution of euro notes and coins.

*The four remaining countries are Denmark, Greece, Sweden, and the United Kingdom.

**The Federal Reserve Statistical Release H.10, Foreign Exchange Rates (weekly) contains the weightings for the EMU countries. See *http://www.federalreserve.gov/releases/H10/Current.*

For information about the European Central Bank (ECB) see: http://www.ecb.int/. *This site also provides links to the central banks of countries that belong to the European Union.*

See http://www.federalreserve.gov/releases/ *for data on foreign exchange rates.*

of the next day in Tokyo. Changes in the values of currencies affect governments, corporations with international operations, traders, and speculators throughout the world. Therefore, an **exchange rate**, the price of one currency in terms of another, can change at any time.

In theory, any two currencies can be exchanged in an FX transaction. For example, Swiss francs can be sold for Japanese yen. Such transactions typically are between banks and their customers. In practice, most transactions in the interbank market involve the purchase or sale of U.S. dollars for a foreign currency, because the dollar is the principal currency used in international transactions and investment; and the dollar market for each currency may be more active than the market between Swiss francs and Japanese yen. Let's examine exchange rates first, and then how different currencies are exchanged in terms of dollars.

DIRECT AND INDIRECT EXCHANGE RATES The exchange rate between two currencies may be stated in terms of either currency, on a direct or an indirect basis. The direct exchange rate for home country is the number of the home currency units that can be exchanged for one unit of a foreign currency. For example, as shown in Table 16.1, the exchange rate between the U.S. dollar (home currency) and the Canada dollar (foreign currency) on a direct basis may be stated as:

$$\text{Direct rate for U.S.} = \$0.6729 \ \$/C\$ \qquad\qquad 16.1$$

C$ is used to designate the number of Canada dollars. Stated otherwise, $0.6729 may be exchanged for one Canada dollar.

The indirect exchange rate is the number of foreign currency units exchanged for one unit of the home currency. For example, Table 16.1 shows that 1.4861 Canada dollars may be exchanged for one U.S. dollar.

$$\text{Indirect rate for U.S.} = 1.4861 \ C\$/\$ \qquad\qquad 16.2$$

Similarly, the direct and indirect rates for the EMU euro may be stated as

$$\text{Direct rate for U.S.} = \$1.0747 \ \$/Euro$$

$$\text{Indirect rate for U.S.} = 0.9305 \ Euro/\$$$

Table 16.1 shows the FX rates for several currencies. The indirect rate for the U.S. was 106.63 Japanese yen (Y/$), and so on. These exchange rates may be interpreted in the following way. Suppose that you want to buy a Japanese product costing 10,000 yen. At the current exchange rate, that is equivalent to $93.78 (Y10,000/106.63 = $93.78).

The direct and indirect exchange rates are reciprocals of the other; therefore when rates change, they move in opposite directions.

$$\text{Direct rate for U.S.} = \$0.1038 \ \$/Mexican \ peso$$

$$\text{Indirect rate for U.S. Mexican peso} = 9.6300 \ pesos/\$$$

Suppose that the indirect exchange rate for the peso decreased from 9.6300 Mexican pesos/$ to 9.5000 Mexican pesos/$. In the case of the indirect exchange rate, the value of dollars *depreciated* against the peso because fewer pesos are received per dollar. The opposite is true in the case of the direct exchange rate. The direct rate increased from $0.1038 $/Mexican peso to $0.1053 $/Mexico peso. Therefore, the Mexican peso *appreciated* against the dollar because more dollars are received per peso.

TABLE 16.1	Selected Foreign Exchange Rates	
Country and Monetary Unit	**Direct Rate**	**Indirect Rate**
	Foreign Currency/$	*$/Foreign Currency*
Canada dollar	$0.6729	1.4861
EMU euro	$1.0747	0.9305
Japanese yen	$0.009378	106.63
Mexico peso	$0.1038	9.6300

CROSS-RATE Suppose that a bank wants to exchange Japanese yen for euros. As mentioned previously, most foreign exchange transactions involve dollars. The rate at which yen and euros can be exchanged using dollars is called the *cross-rate*. Stated otherwise, the cross-rate is the exchange rate between two currencies in terms of a third currency. It is determined by dividing the direct exchange rates of the euro by the direct exchange rate of the yen.

$$\text{Cross-rate euro/yen} = (\$/\text{euro})/(\$/\text{yen}) \qquad\qquad 16.3$$

$$= 1.0747/0.009378 = 114.598 \text{ euro/yen}$$

Table 16.2 shows the cross-rates for selected currencies. Information on foreign exchange, exchange rate, and cross-rates are published daily in the *Wall Street Journal*, the *Financial Times*, and elsewhere.

Foreign Exchange Transactions

In an FX transaction, the buyer and seller agree to pay each other on a predetermined date called the *value date*. The value date may be the same day as the transaction or at a later date.

SPOT MARKET Most FX transactions take place in the *spot market* where the value date is usually two business days after the transaction originated. For example, on September 8, U.S. bank A buys 1 million German marks (DM) from German bank B at a indirect exchange rate of 1.7305 DM/$ for value on September 15. On the value date, German bank B credits bank A's account in Germany with DM1 million; and bank A credits bank B's account in the United States with $577,867 (DM1 million/1.7305). These transactions consist mostly of bank deposits. Except for tourists, currency rarely leaves the country of origin.

TABLE 16.2	Selected Cross-Rates				
	U.S. Dollar	**Euro**	**Mexican Peso**	**Yen**	**Canadian Dollar**
Canada	1.4861	1.5971	0.15432	0.01394	
Japan	106.63	114.598	11.073		71.752
Mexico	9.6300	10.3494		0.09031	6.4800
Euro	0.9305		0.9662	0.00873	0.6261
United States		1.0747	0.10384	0.00938	0.67290

FORWARD MARKETS Some of the following information duplicates information in other chapters. It is presented here to facilitate your understanding of FX transactions, which can be complex.

Some differences separate the spot market, the forward interbank market, and the futures market for foreign currencies. The *spot or cash market* is where an actual physical commodity is bought or sold as distinguished from a *futures market* where futures contracts are traded. In the futures market, standardized transferable legal agreements to make or take delivery of a certain commodity at a known price and time are traded on organized futures exchanges.[2] In the **forward market**, contracts are not standardized, nor are they traded on organized exchanges. A *forward contract* is a cash market transaction in which delivery of the commodity (i.e., currency) is deferred until after the contract (a bilateral agreement between buyer and seller) has been made. Exchange rates for currencies are quoted for 30-day (1 month) forward, 90-day (3 months) forward, and 180-day (6 months) forward. Consider the exchange rates for the French franc (FF):

	Direct Rate	Indirect Rate
	$/FF	FF/$
Spot rate	$0.1726	5.7945
1 month forward	0.1729	5.7833
3 months forward	0.1735	5.7649
6 months forward	0.1742	5.7398

Forward contracts are widely used in day-to-day cash transactions involving loans, leases, real estate, and certain currencies. The forward rates provide useful information. For example, suppose that you have the opportunity to invest $1,000 for six months in a French investment paying 10 percent per annum (5% for six months). Using the forward rates for price information, what is the expected return on this investment?

Using the direct spot rate, we determine that $1,000 will buy FF5,793.7428 ($1,000/$0.1726). The 5% return plus the principal amount amounts to FF6,083.4299 at the end of six months (FF5,793.7428 × 1.05). Converting that amount back into dollars using the 6-month forward rate reveals that the investment is worth $1,009.72 (FF5,793.7428 × $0.1742). The 6-month return on the investment is expected to be $9.72 ($1,009.72 – $1,000), or 1.94 percent per year (($9.72 × 2)/$1,000). The annual return on the investment is low because the dollar appreciated against the FF.

The important lesson to be learned from this example is that investing in an asset denominated in a foreign currency involves the risk of adverse changes in foreign exchange rates.

METHOD OF TRANSACTION In the spot and forward interbank market, trading is conducted by telephone or electronic means between banks, FX brokers, and

---

2. Definitions used here are based on those of the Chicago Mercantile Exchange.

corporations who negotiate the terms of the transaction with each other. In order to reduce the risk of default on such transactions, participants in the FX market usually have information about the creditworthiness of each other.

CONTRACTS Contracts in the forward market are privately negotiated bilateral agreements that are tailored to meet the needs of the parties involved. They may be any size and in any currency. But some currencies are subject to exchange controls that may limit forward trading.

MATURITY Maturities of futures and forward contracts can range from days to many months or longer. Once again, consider the exchange rates for the French franc:

	Direct Rate
	$/FF
Spot rate	$0.1726
1 month forward	0.1729
3 months forward	0.1735
6 months forward	0.1742

If the forward rates for a currency exceed the spot rate, the currency is trading at a *premium* in the forward market. The premium may reflect expected price changes or the present value of funds to be received in the future. If the forward rates are less than the spot rate, it is trading at a *discount*. The direct forward rates shown in the preceding list are at a premium.

In forward transactions, the exchange rate is fixed when the transaction occurs, but no funds exchange hands until the maturity date. Because exchange rates can change between the time the contract is initiated and the time it matures, risks are involved in forward transactions.

Forward rates are frequently quoted as a percentage deviation from the spot rate on an annual basis. For simplicity, we use a 365-day year. In the United States, 360 days is considered a "financial year," while in England and Belgium it is 365 days. The annual forward direct rate, expressed as a premium or a discount, may be determined by using the following equation.

$$\text{Annual forward rate (as a premium or a discount)} = \frac{(F-S) \times 100}{S} \times \frac{365}{n} \qquad 16.4$$

where

F = forward rate
S = spot rate
n = number of days to maturity

To illustrate the use of this equation, the forward direct rate on the 90-day French franc ($/FF) is

$$\frac{(0.1735 - 0.1726) \times 100}{0.1729} \times \frac{365}{90} = 2.11\% \text{ (premium)}$$

16.7 FOREIGN EXCHANGE RISKS

Dealing in foreign exchange exposes banks to four principal types of risk: exchange rate risk, interest rate risk, credit risk, and country risk.

Exchange Rate Risk

When a bank buys more currency than it sells it has an *open (long) position*. Conversely, if a bank sells more than it buys it has a *short position*. The bank is said to be in a *net covered position* when it buys and sells an equivalent amount in the same currency. When banks have either open or short positions, a change in exchange rates can cause a profit or a loss when the positions are closed out. The change in profit or loss due to changing exchange rates is called *exchange rate risk*. Even if a bank's open position in one currency is offset by its short position in another currency, it can still be exposed to adverse rate movements. Although these comments refer to currency positions, a bank must consider all assets and liabilities denominated in foreign currencies when assessing its total foreign currency exposure.

A bank can limit its trading exposure in foreign currencies by using hedging techniques, by imposing dollar limits on positions in a currency, by imposing dollar limits on regions of the world, and by imposing dollar limits on particular customers. Hedging techniques in the currency market are similar to those discussed in connection with interest rate futures.

Interest Rate Risk

Mismatches in the maturity structure of a bank's foreign exchange position give rise to *interest rate risk*. For example, bank E sells 1 million German Deutsche marks (DM1 million) on September 15 for value on September 17 to customer X and simultaneously buys DM1 million for value on September 27 from customer Y. The direct exchange rate is $1 = DM2.4. Thus, DM1 million is worth $416,667 to the bank. Nevertheless, the bank charges customer X more than the exchange rate for DM1 million ($416,767) and makes $100 profit on this transaction. Likewise, the bank pays customer Y ($416,567) less than the exchange rate and makes an additional $100 profit.

The bank has a covered position, but on September 17, it must pay DM1 million to customer X, and it will not receive the equivalent amount from customer Y until September 27—a mismatch of maturities. To eliminate the risk of adverse interest rate movements during the maturity gap, bank E can arrange for a swap with bank F. Bank E will sell DM1 million spot and buy the same amount for value on September 27. These transactions are summarized here.

Exchange rates: $1 = DM2.4

Bank E	Bank F
September 17 Value date	
Pays DM1 million to customer X	Receives DM1 million from Bank E
Receives $416,767 from customer X	Pays $416,667 to Bank E
Profit (416,767 – $416,667) = $100	
September 27 Value date	
Receives DM1 million from	Pays DM1 million customer Y to Bank E
Pays $416,567 to customer Y	Receives $416,667 from Bank E
Profit (416,667 – $416,567) = $100	
Total profit = $200	

To simplify this example, we did not consider possible cost or profit on the swap itself. We also assumed that the profit was made by selling and buying DM from customers X and Y. In reality, there are costs to the swap, but that is an unnecessary complication at this point. The illustration demonstrated that the bank could establish a gross profit of $200 on the transactions with customers X and Y, and eliminate exchange risk and interest rate risk. In practice, banks deal with hundreds of customers, and they take advantage of interest rate differentials between countries to borrow, lend, or arbitrage to their advantage. Therefore, the process of swapping for the entire bank is much more complex than presented here.

Arbitrage

Arbitrage refers to the purchase of securities (assets) in one market for the *immediate* resale in another market in order to profit from price differences in the two markets. Arbitrage also may occur if price differences occur between like securities. For example, convertible bonds may be overvalued with respect to the common stocks in to which can be converted. Arbitrageurs, like speculators in the commodities markets, provide depth to market and help to keep the market efficient.

To illustrate arbitrage between different markets, suppose that the 3-month secondary rate on domestic certificates of deposits (CDs) is 10.00% and the 3-month offer rate on Eurodollar deposits is 10.10%. At first glance, it appears that Eurodollar rates are higher than CD rates, but all the relevant costs have not been taken into account. The FDIC insurance premium is $0.28 per $100 per year on assessable domestic deposits. In addition, the reserve requirements on CDs is 3%, but none on Eurocurrency liabilities. Using these figures the *effective cost* of the CDs is

$$\frac{10.0\% + 0.28\%}{(1 - 0.03)} = 10.60\%$$

The cost of the Eurodollar deposits is 10.10%.

$$\text{Spread} = 10.60\% - 10.1=\% = 0.50\%$$

Although the nominal cost of the Eurodollars is higher than the nominal cost of the CDs, the effective cost of the Eurodollars is 50 basis points lower. Therefore, domestic banks will borrow Eurodollars instead of borrowing by using CDs. The type of arbitrage just described is called an *inward arbitrage* because the funds are flowing into the United States. The inward arbitrage will continue until upward pressure on the Eurodollar rates and downward pressure on CD rates equalize the effective cost of funds.

An *outward arbitrage* occurs when the effective cost of CDs is less than the effective cost of Eurodollars. Then U.S. banks will find it less costly to borrow in the United States than in Europe. The increased demand for CDs will bid up the yield until the effective cost of CDs and Eurodollars is equal.

Under normal market conditions, investors should not be able to make arbitrage profits because the premiums or discounts in the various currencies should be exactly offset by the adjusted interest rate differentials. For example, if the short-term interest rates were higher in London than in the United States by 1 percentage point per year (0.5 percentage points for six months), the 6-month forward rate for pounds in terms of dollars would be about a 0.5 percentage point discount from the spot rate. This relationship is known as *covered interest arbitrage* or **interest rate parity**. However, market imperfections provide opportunities for arbitrage profits.

The conditions that eliminate the incentive for covered interest arbitrage can be determined by using the following equations.

Where

S = Spot rate (dollars per pound in our example)

F = Forward rate (6-month forward exchange rate in dollars per pound in our example)

$p = \dfrac{F - S}{S}$ = Premium or discount on the forward pound (expressed in decimal form where − is the discount and + is the premium)

N = Short-term interest rate in the United States (per six months, expressed in decimal form)

L = Short-term interest rate in London (per six months, expressed in decimal form) then

$$1 + N = \frac{(1 + L)F}{S} \qquad\qquad 16.5$$

As demonstrated by this equation, incentive for covered interest arbitrage is not present when one dollar plus the 6-month rate of interest in the United States is equal to one dollar's worth of spot pounds plus the 6-month interest rate in London reconverted into dollars at the forward rate, then it follows from the definition of p that $F/S = 1 + p$, and that the equilibrium condition becomes

$$p = N - L - pL$$

Therefore, the precise interest rate parity can be determined by solving

$$p = \frac{(N - L)}{(1 + L)} \qquad\qquad 16.6$$

However, because p and L are usually small, an approximation of the interest rate parity condition is

$$p = N - L \qquad\qquad 16.7$$

Because of adjustments for FDIC insurance, reserves, and other factors, p is actually a band, sometime called an *arbitrage tunnel*, with no incentive for arbitrage.

Credit Risk

Credit risk is part of foreign exchange transactions because of the possibility that the counterparty (the other bank or broker) in the transaction may be unwilling or unable to meet its contractual obligations. The credit risk associated with foreign exchange risk is not included in the definition of risk for establishing legal lending limits. The only real control on credit risk associated with foreign exchange forward exposure is self-imposed. For example, in 1974, the Bankhouse I.D. Herstatt failed in Germany. Because of differences in time zones, some U.S. banks and others had paid marks to Herstatt early in the day, but Herstatt failed later in the day before completing the other side of the foreign exchange transactions—the U.S. banks did not receive the dollars due to them. This particular form of credit risk is called **settlement risk**.

Also consider the case of a bank that buys £1 million for a customer on January 5 at a rate of $2.0 ($2 million) for value on March 13. In late February, the customer declares bankruptcy and the court-appointed trustee informs the bank that it will not honor the contract. During this time, the price of sterling increased to $2.10, and the bank has to cover its unexpected short position of £1 million at the higher price, resulting in an increased cost of $100,000 to the bank. Of course, the bank can dispute its contract and loss in court, but litigation is a costly process and the outcome is not clear.

The point of these examples is that although the intention of dealing in foreign exchange is not to extend credit per se, there are credit risks in dealing in foreign exchange.

Country Risk

Country risk may be defined as a whole spectrum of risks arising from economic, social, and political environments of a given foreign country having potentially favorable or adverse consequences for the profitability and/or recovery of debt or equity investments made in that country. Such risks include but are not limited to branching restrictions, confiscation, restrictions on earnings remittances, and war.

In the United States, we tend to think of country risk as a Third World problem. However, in June 1998, Moody's Investor Service gave U.S. banks a C+ rating, which indicates that they are good, but not great.[3] The highest ratings went to the Netherlands, Liechtenstein, and Switzerland.

Country risk is frequently separated into two broad categories: sovereign risk and transfer risk. **Sovereign risk** occurs when a national government defaults on debts, or refuses to permit loans to be repaid or seizes bank assets without adequate compensation. In 1998, for example, Russia defaulted on some of its short-term debts. *Transfer risk* occurs when foreign borrowers have problems converting domestic currency into foreign exchange because of foreign exchange controls or for other reasons.

Commercial banks must assess both types of risk. Although cases of expropriation or outright repudiation on loans are rare in the post–World War II period (Cuba and Chile are two examples), cases of debt rescheduling have been commonplace, such as Russia in 1998. Restructuring or refinancing are usually preceded by a foreign exchange crisis. *Restructuring debt* usually involves stretching principal and interest payments, whereas *refinancing* usually involves new loans. As one humorist said, refinancing and restructuring loans is good because "a rolling loan gathers no losses."

International lenders use statistical indicators to help gauge country risk. The data for the indicators is published by the World Bank. Unfortunately, the data are often out of date by the time they are available, so the indicators are of limited value. Equally important, these data may not accurately predict a crises. The World Bank, for example, praised Indonesia for its macroeconomic performance shortly before its financial crisis began in 1997.[4]

The extent of country risk exposure can be limited by placing dollar limits on investments in foreign countries or regions of the world. In addition, some foreign banks and central governments will guarantee both the principal and interest on certain risks. Sometimes, however, governments renege on their financial obligations. Russia in 1998 is one example.

3. "Rating the World's Banks," *Wall Street Journal* (August 14, 1998), p. A13.
4. Jay Salomon, "World Bank Says It Was Wrong on Indonesia," *Wall Street Journal* (February 5, 1998), p. A17.

SUMMARY

Although many similarities can be noted between domestic bank operations and international banking operations, they also have many differences. In fact, it is sometimes said that the international banking part of a bank is a bank within a bank because it makes loans, takes payments, makes payments, and performs most of the services of a bank. This chapter focused on several aspects of banking that are uniquely international, including why banks deal in international markets, foreign exchange operations, international lending, and collections. Dealing in foreign exchange entails certain risks. To some extent, the exchange rate risk and interest rate risk can be reduced by hedging, swaps, and arbitrage. Credit risk and country risk exposure can be reduced by other means, including diversification of portfolios, lending limits, and government guarantees and insurance.

Many large-scale international loans are syndicated, which is a hybrid of investment banking and traditional participation loans. Such loans can be beneficial to both the borrower and the lenders if everything goes as planned.

Letters of credit are widely used in international trade to facilitate the payment process; the other side of the coin is the collection process. Both are important aspects of international banking.

Key Terms and Concepts

Agency (foreign bank)
Arbitrage
Bankers' acceptance
Confirmed letter of credit
Correspondent banks
Country risk
Edge Act
Edge Act offices
Euro
Eurocurrency
Eurodollar deposits
Exchange rate
Foreign exchange

Forward market
Interest rate parity
International banking facilities
  (IBF)
Letters of credit (commercial,
  import, export)
LIBOR
Participation loan
Settlement risk
SIBOR
Sovereign risk
Standby letters of credit
Trade finance

Questions

16.1 What distinguishes domestic banking from international banking?

16.2 The Edge Act permits banks to operate Edge Act offices in any state or overseas. True or false. Explain your position.

16.3 Are foreign commercial banks operating in the United States subject to the same rules and regulations as domestic banks?

16.4 Define the term *foreign exchange*. Give an example.

16.5 What is meant by direct and indirect exchange rates for U.S. dollars?

16.6 What is the relationship between direct and indirect exchange rates? How can they be used to calculate the cross-rate between the Swiss franc and the German mark?

16.7 Suppose that the indirect rate for the French franc changed from 5.5000 to 5.0000. Did the value of U.S. dollars appreciate or depreciate? Why?

16.8 Define the following terms:
(a) value date
(b) spot market
(c) futures market
(d) forward market

16.9 Distinguish between margins for stocks and margins for futures contracts.

16.10 Briefly describe the risks in a forward transaction.

16.11 Briefly discuss the four risks associated with foreign exchange.

16.12 Distinguish between inward and outward arbitrage.

16.13 What is meant by interest rate parity?

16.14 Briefly describe two kinds of country risk.

16.15 What is a letter of credit in foreign exchange?

Problems

16.1 Calculate the annual forward direct rate on 30-day U.K. pounds with a forward rate of $2.20 and a spot rate of $2.00.

16.2 Calculate the cross-rate for pounds and marks, given the indirect rate for pounds is 0.5 and the direct rate for marks is $2.40.

16.3 Bank A has a maturity mismatch in its foreign exchange position. It sold 5 million Swiss francs on November 13 for value on November 15 to bank X for $2,501,000 and bought 5 million francs for value on November 25 from bank Z for $2,499,000. The exchange rate is $1 = 2 francs and 1 franc = $.50. To eliminate possible interest rate risk during the maturity gap, it arranges a swap with bank B. Write out the transactions of banks A and B on these value dates. What are the profits to banks A of the swap?

16.4 Assuming FDIC insurance costs 0.40% per year on domestic deposits, and the reserve requirements is 3% on all deposits, what is the effective cost of 3-month CDs paying 9% and 3-month Eurodollars offering 9.20%? Which will banks prefer to borrow? What kind of arbitrage is this?

16.5 Given the following information:

Spot rate = $2/pound

6-month forward rate = $2.20/pound

6-month interest rate in U.S. = .05

6-month interest rate in London = .04

Does the situation provide opportunity for covered interest arbitrage?

Global Bank Corporation

Global Bank Corporation is the newest subsidiary of Polaris Holdings, a consortium of European and American banks. Global Bank Corporation was created to provide international credit facilities to promising companies in emerging nations. Global's president, Hans Schmidt, was approached by Altamont Mining Company of Johannesburg, South Africa, to fund a mining operation to mine manganese, vanadium, and high-grade chromium. Of these metals, manganese is the most important because it is vital in the production of steel, and about 80% of the world reserve is found in South Africa's northwestern Cape. Altamont is a privately owned company with strong ties to the government, and contracts for future delivery of its metals. It has been in the mining business since 1981.

As Global's first promising lead in South Africa, the request is one that Mr. Schmidt wants to give careful consideration. His first step is to get some background information on South Africa. He assigned the task to Juanita Gonzales, a credit analyst. He told her that he is interested in those factors affecting credit risk and sovereign risk in South Africa. He asked Juanita to provide him with a brief summary of her findings tomorrow.

Juanita decided that the first step was to make a list of factors in South Africa, without specific reference to Altamont Mining, that could affect credit risk. A detailed analysis of the company would come later.

She decided to prepare her list after reviewing country surveys from the *Financial Times* newspaper at *http://www.ft.com/ftsurveys/country/* and from the Central Intelligence Agency at *http://www. odci.gov/cia/publications/factbook/country.html.*

Next she wanted information about financial markets there so she looked at CNNfn at *http://cnnfn.com/markets/world_markets.html.* Data on credit ratings were obtained from Standard & Poors at *http://www.standardandpoors.com/ ratings/daily/newdailymain.htm#2* and foreign exchange rate information from the Board of Governors of the Federal Reserve System at *http://www. federalreserve.gov/releases/H10/Current/.*

Now she was ready to begin her brief for Mr. Schmidt.

Glossary

Acceptance participation Marketable money market instrument created when a bank accepts a time draft (a bill of exchange) and agrees to pay it at face value on maturity. The draft normally covers the sale of goods, particularly with respect to international trade.

Account party One of the participants in a financial obligation or performance contract.

Adjustable rate mortgages Mortgage in which the interest rate changes over the life of the loan. The change can result in changes in monthly payments, the term of the loan, and/or the principal amount.

Adverse selection Occurs when high-risk borrowers try to obtain loans from banks and are willing to pay the average rate of interest, which is less than they would have to pay if their true condition were known to the bank.

Agency According the International Banking Act of 1978, an agency is "any office or any place of business of a foreign bank located in any state of the United States or District of Columbia at which credit balances are maintained, checks are paid, or money lent, but deposits may not be accepted for a citizen or resident of the United States."

Agency cost The loss in shareholder wealth due to self-serving actions by managers, who seek to maximize their own salary, fringe benefits, job security, etc., at the expense of shareholders.

Agency securities Securities issued by federal agencies.

They are not direct obligations of the U.S. Treasury but nonetheless are federally sponsored or guaranteed.

Aggregation risk Risk that comes from the complex interconnections that occur in derivatives deals involving a number of markets and instruments. It becomes difficult to assess the risks to individual parties or groups of parties in such transactions.

Aggressive asset/liability management Management strategy that focuses on increasing the net interest by altering an institution's portfolio in response to interest rate changes.

Aggressive investment strategies Strategies that require active management and so are more complex and costly approaches than passive strategies. Playing the yield curve, riding the yield curve, and various kinds of bond swaps are examples of these strategies.

Aggressive liquidity approach An approach to liquidity management that seeks to take advantage of yield curve relationships to buy and sell securities and make potential earnings gains.

Annual percentage rate (APR) The percentage cost of credit on an annual basis.

Annuity A schedule of payments at fixed intervals for a stated number of years, or for the duration of the life of the person receiving the payments (the annuitant), or the lives of two or more persons.

Arbitrage The purchase of securities (assets) in one mar-

562

ket for the immediate resale in another market in order to profit from price differences between the two markets.

Asset-based lending Distinct from other secured loans in that much greater weight is given to the market value of the collateral in asset-based lending than in regular commercial and industrial loans. In addition, asset-based lenders place greater emphasis on monitoring than do traditional bank lenders.

Asset/liability management (ALM) Risk assessment and the process of making decisions about the composition of assets and liabilities.

Asset liquidity The sale of money market instruments to meet cash demands for loans, securities investments, etc.

Asset management A type of liquidity management in which liquidity needs are met by using near-cash assets, including net funds sold to other banks and money market securities.

Asset utilization A financial ratio that measures the ability of management to employ assets effectively to generate revenues. It is calculated as operating revenue divided by total assets.

Asymmetric information Borrowers have more information about themselves than is available to the lender.

Automatic transfer service (ATS) account Allows small depositors to minimize transactions balances by automatically transferring funds from their interest-bearing savings account to their checking account as overdrafts occur.

Average costs The cost of funds calculated by dividing dollar costs of funds by the dollar amount of funds.

Balance sheet An accounting statement that contains the record of assets, liabilities, and equity at the end of a period.

Balloon mortgage Relatively short-term mortgage loan, such as five years, with the entire amount of the loan due at the end of that period, at which time a new loan is negotiated.

Bank An organization that makes loans, has FDIC-insured deposits, and has been granted banking powers either by the state or the federal government.

Bank capital The sum of equity (i.e., common stock, preferred stock, surplus, and undivided profits) plus long-term subordinated debt plus reserves that are set aside to meet anticipated bank operating losses from loans, leases, and securities.

Bank holding company A corporation organized for the purpose of holding stock in one or more banks and other financial service organizations.

Bank risk management Operating decisions within a bank are made in terms of their risk/return characteristics, with the goal of maximizing shareholder wealth.

Bank runs Occur when depositors or other creditors fear for the safety or availability of their funds, and large numbers of depositors try to withdraw their funds at the same time.

Bankers' acceptance A short-term time draft or bill of exchange that is an irrevocable obligation of the bank, usually used in international trade to finance the shipment of goods. It can be sold by the exporter at a discount in order to obtain the funds due before the date of maturity.

Banking Act of 1933 Also known as the Glass-Steagall Act, it separated commercial banking from investment banking, established the Federal Deposit Insurance Corporation (FDIC), permitted the Federal Reserve to regulate the interest paid on time deposits, prohibited the payment of interest on demand deposits, and raised the minimum capital requirements for national banks.

Banking Act of 1935 An act primarily intended to strengthen the Federal Reserve System and its monetary management power. The act gave the Federal Reserve Board expanded reserve requirement authority; it could regulate discount rates of the district banks; and it had the power to regulate the rate of interest paid by member banks on time and savings deposits.

Basis risk The difference between the cash price and futures price used in futures and options hedging.

Basis swaps A swap involving the exchange of interest payments on two different floating rates of interest (e.g., 6-month LIBOR and U.S. prime commercial paper rates or two variable-rate contracts with different maturities).

Basle Agreement Landmark international banking agreement signed in June 1988 by 12 industrialized nations under the auspices of the Bank for International Settlements (BIS). By year-end 1992 all U.S. banks were required to comply with these new capital rules.

Bidder One who is making an offer to buy securities, firms, etc.

Bilateral netting system A system in which two banks that may have multiple contracts to settle in a foreign currency, such as German marks, can replace them with a single contract for the net amount to be sent through the payments system for clearing.

Board of directors written loan policy Establishes the guidelines and principles for the bank's lending activities, because the board delegates the task of making loans to others.

Book value of equity An equity account on the balance sheet that equals the sum of common stock, preferred stock, surplus, and undivided profits.

Bridge loan Loans that "bridge a gap" in a borrower's financing until some specific event occurs. For example, a firm wants to acquire a new warehouse facility, but needs funds to finance the transaction until the old warehouse can be sold.

Brokered deposits Small and large time deposits obtained by banks from intermediaries seeking insured deposit accounts on behalf of their customers.

Call option A contract that gives the buyer the right (but not the obligation) to buy an underlying instrument (such as a T-bill futures contract) at a specified price (called the exercise or strike price) and the seller the comparable right to sell the underlying instrument at the same price.

Call risk The risk that an issuing firm will refinance a bond during a period of low interest rates, which forces bondholders to reinvest their funds in bonds bearing lower interest yields.

Call premium The fee charged by the seller of a call option.

CAMELS The Uniform Financial Institutions Rating System; an acronym that stands for Capital adequacy, Asset quality, Management, Earnings, Liquidity, and Sensitivity to market risk (interest rates, foreign exchange), and the ability of the bank to manage that risk. Under this system, a composite score is given by examiners, ranging from 1 (good) to 5 (unsafe).

Cap A contract that reduces the exposure of a floating rate borrower to increases in interest rates by setting a maximum or ceiling on the interest rate. A firm can implement a cap by purchasing an interest rate call option contract.

Capital adequacy A term most frequently used in the context of regulatory policy, which seeks to require banks to maintain sufficient capital levels to ensure safety and soundness in the banking industry while at the same time encouraging bank efficiency and competitiveness.

Capital gain The change in value or price of an asset between two points in time.

Capital impairment Occurs when a bank has insufficient capital to absorb losses, which generally leads regulators to close the bank.

Capital market risk Refers to the potential liabilities management problem associated with low interest rate levels that motivate investors to transfer deposit funds to the capital market in an attempt to earn higher rates of return.

Capital notes and debentures Long-term debt instruments that are senior debt capital sources of external funds.

Cash management services The process of combining banking services, data collection, and communications systems to enhance the collection, control and utilization of cash for business concerns.

Capital reserves Reserves counted as capital on banks'

balance sheet that can be used to absorb unexpected losses. These reserves are employed by regulators in measures of capital adequacy.

Ceiling agreement Also called a cap, this agreement between a bank and its customer specifies the maximum lending rate on a loan and, therefore, protects the customer from interest rate risk.

Charged-off (loan) A loan is removed from the balance sheet because it is no longer of sufficient value to remain on the books.

Clearing House Interbank Payments System (CHIPS) International funds transfers system operated by the New York Clearing House Association (NYCHA).

Collateral An asset pledged against the performance of an obligation. If a borrower defaults on a loan, the bank takes the collateral and sells it.

Commercial and industrial (C&I) loans Loans made for business purposes such as financing working capital and equipment.

Commercial mortgage loans Loans for land, construction, and real estate development, and on commercial properties such as shopping centers, office buildings, or warehouses.

Commercial paper Short-term, unsecured promissory notes issued by major U.S. corporations with strong credit ratings. Banks can use their holding companies to issue commercial paper and use funds to acquire loans and investments.

Commitment *See loan commitment.*

Common stock Common stock represents ownership rights to residual earnings of the firm, as well as voting power on important decisions affecting the firm.

Community Reinvestment Act (CRA) Directed at federally regulated lenders that take deposits and extend credit, the intent of the legislation is to facilitate the availability of mortgage loans and other types of loans to all qualified applicants, without regard to their race, nationality, or sex.

Compliance risk The risk to earnings or capital arising from violations of law, rules, and regulations, and so on.

Comprehensive contingency funding plans Plans that outline responses to various liquidity problems and define coincident management responsibilities to deal with such problems.

Confirmed letter of credit A bank's guarantee to pay a letter of credit.

Consumer credit Loans to individuals for personal, household, or family consumption.

Contemporaneous reserve requirement accounting The method used from 1984 to 1994 in the United States among depository institutions in which the computation and maintenance periods overlap in reserve requirement management.

Contingent claim An obligation by a bank to provide funds (i.e., lend funds or buy securities) if a contingency is realized. In other words, the bank has underwritten an obligation of a third party and currently stands behind the risk.

Conventional mortgage loans Mortgage loans not insured by the Federal Housing Administration (FHA) or guaranteed by the Veterans Administration (VA).

Core deposits Deposits typically made by regular bank customers, including business firms, government units, and households. Core deposits provide a stable, long-term source of funds and are not sensitive to changes in interest rates.

Corporate bond Long-term debt security issued by a private corporation.

Corporate control The control of management and, in turn, bank operations, by shareholders. More concentrated ownership in the hands of fewer shareholders tends to enhance management control.

Correspondent balances Excess funds deposited by smaller banks in their larger correspondent banks.

Correspondent banks Large banks that provide banking products and services to other banks in exchange for fees and/or deposits.

Cost/revenue analysis An approach to managing liabilities wherein the goal of bank management should be to maximize deposit revenues and minimize deposit costs in an effort to maximize bank profitability.

Counterparty credit risk Risk that a counterparty in a financial transaction will default, resulting in a financial loss to the other party.

Country risk Risks arising from the economic, social, and political environment of a foreign country and having potentially favorable or adverse consequences for the profitability and/or recovery of debt or equity investments made in that country.

Coupon swaps A swap wherein the exchange of interest payments is based on fixed rates (e.g., 11 percent) and floating rates of interest (e.g., 6-month LIBOR, or London interbank offered rate).

Credit card Any card, plate, or device that may be used repeatedly to borrow money or buy goods and services on credit.

Credit option Essentially an insurance credit derivative contract. This option would pay the amount of lost capital value in the event bonds held by the investor are downgraded.

Credit risk The risk to earnings and capital that an obligor will fail to meet the terms of any contract with the bank, or otherwise fail to perform as agreed. It is usually associated with loans and investments but can also arise in connection with derivatives, foreign exchange, and other extensions of bank credit.

Credit risk capital requirements Under risk-based capital requirements, bank assets are weighted to force banks to hold more capital against higher credit risk assets.

Credit scoring The use of statistical models to determine the likelihood that a prospective borrower will default on a loan. Credit scoring models are widely used to evaluate business, real estate, and consumer loans.

Credit swap A credit derivative in which two banks simply exchange interest and principal payments on portions of their loan portfolios. This swap enables the participating banks to diversify their credit risk to a greater extent than otherwise possible.

Crisis liquidity Liquidity problems that threaten the solvency of a bank, which can arise either from problems specific to the institution or problems that affect all institutions.

Cross-currency interest rate swaps An interest rate swap that is based on interest payments in different currencies.

Cumulative gap Measures the difference between rate-sensitive assets and liabilities over extended periods or maturity buckets; the sum of the incremental gaps.

Currency swaps Involves not only the exchange of interest payments (in different currencies) but also the exchange of the initial and final principal amounts at the beginning and end of the swap.

Debit card Any card, plate, or device that may be used to buy goods and services by withdrawing funds from the holder's account. No credit is extended.

Defensive asset/liability management Management strategy that seeks to insulate the net interest income from changes in interest rates; that is, to prevent interest rate changes from decreasing or increasing the net interest income.

Demand deposits Checking accounts that pay no interest by law.

Deposit Insurance National Bank (DINB) A so-called bridge bank that can be chartered by the FDIC to take over operations of a troubled bank until it is either closed or acquired by another bank.

Deposit insurance The Banking Act of 1933 (Glass-Steagall Act) established the Federal Deposit Insurance Corporation to protect small depositors and reduce the incidence of bank runs by insuring their bank deposits up to a predetermined amount.

Depository Institutions Deregulation and Monetary Con-

trol Act of 1980 (DIDMCA) Extended uniform reserve requirements and offered Federal Reserve services to all depository institutions; phased out Regulation Q interest rate ceilings on deposit accounts at all depository institutions; and broadened savings and loan's lending powers.

Deregulation A "loosening" or repealing of regulations, which has three separate, although closely related, dimensions; price (e.g., deposit rate) deregulation, product deregulation, and geographic deregulation.

Derivative securities Securities that derive their characteristics from previously existing securities, often used to transfer interest rate risk. Three types of derivatives are futures, options, and swaps.

Discount window Operated by the Federal Reserve, this source of funds is employed by banks to meet unexpected shortfalls of cash, especially reserve requirements on deposit accounts.

Discount window advance The means by which banks can borrow funds from the 12 regional Federal Reserve banks (subject to the provisions of Regulation A). Advances can be used by banks to meet unanticipated reserve deficiencies or to meet outflows of funds that are transitory in nature.

Dividend yield/return A financial ratio calculated as cash dividends divided by the current stock price of the firm.

Dollar gap Also referred to as the funding gap or the maturity gap, it is the difference between the dollar amount of interest rate-sensitive assets and the dollar amount of interest rate-sensitive liabilities.

Dollar gap ratio A ratio that measures the sensitivity of a bank's net interest margin to a change in interest rates. It is calculated as interest rate sensitive assets minus interest rate sensitive liabilities divided by total assets.

Dual banking system Banks can be chartered by the Office of the Comptroller of the Currency for a national charter, or they can receive a state charter.

Duration A measure of interest rate sensitivity of a financial instrument. The weighted average time to receive all cash flows from a financial instrument.

Duration drift The change in the duration of a financial instrument over time.

Duration gap The difference between the durations of a bank's assets and liabilities. It is a measure of interest rate sensitivity that helps to explain how changes in interest rates affect the market value of a bank's assets and liabilities, and, in turn, its net worth.

Earning assets Loans, investment securities, and short-term investments that generate interest and yield related fee income.

Economic value added (EVA) EVA is a measure used to evaluate the economic profitability of loans, projects, product lines, etc., in order to determine whether the investment will increase shareholder wealth. It is generally employed for the purpose of internal performance evaluations.

Earnings per share (EPS) A financial ratio calculated as earnings available for shareholders divided by the number of outstanding shares of stock.

Economies of scale A situation in which higher volumes of a commodity allow a firm to produce it at lower costs per unit.

Economies of scope When two different products can be produced more cheaply at one firm than at two separate firms.

Edge Act offices The Edge Act of 1919 permits national banking organizations to have subsidiary corporations that may have offices throughout the United States to provide a means of financing international trade, especially exports.

Electronic banking Any banking activity accessed by electronic means such as ATMs, automated call centers, personal computers, screen telephones used to pay bills, transfer funds, apply for loans, buy mutual fund shares, and to provide other financial services.

Electronic bill presentment and payment (EBPP) A substitute for the current paper-based systems for recurring bill presentment and paying processes, and for preauthorized debits to checking accounts.

Electronic money In its broadest sense, the variety of ways that electronic and other payments systems can be used as a means of exchange.

Equity multiplier The ratio of total assets to total equity, which is a measure of financial leverage.

Euro The unified European currency issued by the European Central Bank. It began trading in January 1999.

Eurocurrency A deposit denominated in a currency other than that of the country where the bank is located.

Eurocurrency liabilities Used mainly by large banks as a source of funds, these funds represent net borrowings from unrelated foreign depository institutions, loans to U.S. residents made by overseas branches of domestic depository institutions, and sales of assets by U.S. depository institutions by their overseas offices.

Eurodollars U.S. dollar-denominated deposits in foreign banks.

Eurodollar deposit A dollar-denominated deposit in a bank office outside the United States. Originally dominated by European-based bank offices, the term still applies to out-of-country dollar deposits in general. Eurodollar deposits have grown with international business expansion, as firms maintain dollar deposits in foreign countries.

Euronotes Debt securities denominated in U.S. dollars, usually with a face value of $500,000 or more. Most of the activity in this market involves international banking. Euronotes are not registered with the Securities and Exchange Commission and cannot be sold in the United States. The major nonbank sovereign borrowers in the Euronote market are the United States, Austria, and Great Britain.

Exchange clearinghouse An organized exchange, such as the Chicago Board of Trade, Chicago Board Options Exchange, and Chicago Mercantile Exchange, that guarantees payments on futures and options contract and thereby eliminates default risk for counterparties to these financial contracts.

Exchange rate The price of one currency in terms of another, such as the dollar value of the Japanese yen.

Expectations theory Market interest rates on long-term debt securities are some function of current short-term rates and future expected short-term rates.

Explicit pricing The interest rate associated with a deposit account, as opposed to implicit pricing that relates to noninterest expenses.

Facility fee The commitment fee paid by customer to the bank for the privilege of being able to borrow funds at a future date under a revolving line of credit. The fee, for example, may be ½ percent per year of the unused balance.

Factoring The sale of accounts receivable, usually to a bank or financing company, that charges a commission and withholds a certain percentage in reserve.

FDIC Improvement Act Savings and Loan Insurance Fund was dissolved and replaced with the Savings Associations Insurance Funds (SAIF). Finally, healthy banks in a multibank holding company (MBHC) are liable to the FDIC for the losses of failed member banks.

FDIC-insured deposits Certain deposits by the Federal Deposit Insurance Corporation (FDIC) insured for amounts up to $100,000 from losses due to the failure of a bank.

Federal agency securities Securities issued by various government agencies (e.g., the Federal Home Loan Banks, Federal National Mortgage Association, Federal Home Loan Mortgage Association, etc.) that are sponsored or owned by the federal government and, therefore, have little or no default risk.

Federal Deposit Insurance Corporation (FDIC) An organization that insures deposits held by approximately 98% of all U.S. commercial banks. Banks are required to pay premiums to insure deposit accounts up to $100,000.

Federal Deposit Insurance Corporation Improvement Act of 1991 (FDICIA) Focused primarily on interrelated capital requirements and deposit insurance issues in depository institutions; empowered federal banking agencies to apply prompt corrective action (PCA) to undercapitalized institutions that are increasingly restrictive as an institution's capital declines.

Federal funds Immediately available funds that represent interbank loans of cash reserves, either held on deposit at Federal Reserve district banks or elsewhere (including correspondent banks).

Federal funds sold/purchased Short-term, unsecured transfers of immediately available funds (excess cash balances) between depository institutions for use in one business day (i.e., overnight loans).

Federal Home Loan Bank A government-sponsored enterprise whose function is to enhance the availability of residential mortgage credit by making low-cost funds available to member institutions. Banks that are members of the system can borrow funds from regional Federal Home Loan Banks.

Federal Reserve Board (FRB) The policy making body of the Federal Reserve System.

Fedwire A wholesale electronic funds transfer system operated by the Federal Reserve to transfer domestic interbank payments.

Fee income Charges for services that banks provide to customers, such as loan commitment fees, ATM fees, etc.

Finance charge The total dollar amount paid for the use of credit, or the difference between the amount repaid and the amount borrowed, which includes interest, service charges, and other fees the borrower must pay as a condition of or incident to the extension of credit.

Financial guarantee An off-balance sheet activity occurring when a bank (the guarantor) stands behind the current obligation of a third party, and carries out that obligation if the third party fails to do so.

Financial Institutions Reform, Recovery, and Enforcement Act of 1989 (FIRREA) Established the Office of Thrift Supervision to replace the Federal Home Loan Bank Board (FHLBB), which ceased to be the regulator for thrifts. The Federal Housing Finance Board was established.

Financial intermediation The action of banks as economic units whose principal function is obtaining funds from depositors and others, and then lending them to borrowers.

Financial leases Leases used in connection with long-term assets, which have a term equal to the economic life of the assets.

Financial leverage The use of debt, as opposed to equity, finance. As financial leverage increases, the percentage change, or variability, of EPS increases.

Financial repression Most often found in developing countries wehre the implication is that the government intervenes heavily in the economy and in the financial markets.

Financial Services Modernization Act of 1999 Also known as the Gramm-Leach-Bliley Act, it marked the end of the 1933 Glass-Steagall prohibitions concerning the separation of banks from investment banking, and the 1956 Bank Holding Company Act's prohibitions against insurance underwriting.

Fixed rate mortgages Fixed rate, fully amortized, level payment mortgages in which the interest rate does not change and the debt is gradually extinguished through equal periodic payments on the principal balance.

Floor (or floor agreement) A contract that limits the exposure of the borrower to downward movements in interest rates by setting a minimum interest rate. A firm can implement a floor by purchasing an interest rate put option contract.

Foreign exchange (FX) Refers to exchanging one country's currency for a foreign currency.

Foreign exchange risk The risk to earnings or capital due to changes in foreign exchange rates.

Form for analyzing bank capital (FABC) The method, begun in the 1950s, that the Federal Reserve Board uses to classify assets into six different risk categories. Banks are required to hold a different percentage of capital against each asset category.

Forward market In the forward market, contracts are not standardized, nor are they traded on organized exchanges. A forward contract is a cash market transaction in which delivery of the commodity (i.e., currency) is deferred until after the contract (a bilateral agreement between buyer and seller) has been made. Exchange rates for currencies are quoted for 30-day (1 month) forward, 90-day (3 months) forward, and 180-day (6 months) forward.

Forward rate agreement An agreement that is essentially an over-the-counter interest rate futures contract for bonds or some other financial asset. The buyer and seller agree on some interest rate to be paid on some notional amount at a specified time in the future. The major advantages of FRAs over exchange-traded futures contracts is that they can be tailored to meet the needs of the parties involved without margin requirements.

Funding-liquidity risk The risk that insufficient cash will be available to meet the securities investment objectives of the bank.

Funds management A liquidity management approach that compares total liquidity needs to total liquidity sources.

Futures contract A standardized agreement to buy or sell a specified quantity of a financial instrument on a specified date at a set price.

Futures options contract An option on a futures contract that enables the buyer to execute the futures contract only in the event it is profitable, thereby avoiding daily trading losses on the futures position due to marked-to-market practices and related liquidity needs.

Gap analysis A measure of the interest sensitivity position of a financial institution.

Garn–St. Germain Depository Institutions Act of 1982 Provided FDIC/FSLIC assistance for floundering and failing institutions; net worth certificates, an exchange of debt between depository institutions and the regulatory agencies; additional thrift institution restructuring; and money market deposit accounts for banks.

General market risk The risk associated with the financial market as a whole under the new market risk capital requirements for banks adopted in 1998 as an amendment to the 1988 Basle Agreement. The calcu-

lation of market-risk equivalent assets is determined by individual banks using their own internal risk model. Such a model estimates the daily value-at-risk for the trading account assets.

Globalization The extent to which nations' economies and financial markets become increasingly integrated, resulting in movement toward a single world market.

Government-backed mortgages Mortgage loans that are insured by the Federal Housing Administration (FHA) or guaranteed by the Veterans Administration (VA).

Graduated payment mortgage A type of fixed-rate mortgage loan where the monthly payments are low at first and then rise over a period of years.

Growing equity mortgage Fully amortized home loans that provide for successively higher debt service payments over the life of the loan.

Harmonization Uniform international banking regulations. It also refers to stemming the divergence of standards applied to similar activities of different financial institutions.

Herstatt risk The risk of cross-currency (foreign exchange) settlements associated with differences in time zones and operating hours of banks throughout the world.

Home equity loan A traditional second mortgage or revolving line of credit, in which case the line of credit has a second mortgage status, but would be the first lien if the borrower has no mortgage debt outstanding when the credit line was established.

Home Mortgage Disclosure Act (HMDA) Legislation intended to make available to the public information concerning the extent to which financial institutions are serving the housing credit needs of their communities.

Hostile takeover An unwanted offer to acquired ownership. If a bank's shares are undervalued, other well-managed banks might seek to purchase a controlling interest in the bank and remove existing management.

Hubris hypothesis The notion that the managers of the buying firm in a merger or acquisition believe that they can better manage the target firm than its current management can, thereby increasing its share valuation.

Immunization Isolation of the market value of equity to interest rate changes; only effective if interest rates for all maturity securities shift up or down by exactly the same amount, i.e., if the yield curve moves upward or downward by a constant percentage amount.

Implicit pricing Noninterest expenses associated with deposit accounts, such as free checking services, which are payments in kind.

Income statement An accounting statement that contains the record of revenues, expenses, and profits during a period of time.

Inflation risk The risk associated with investor concern that the general price level will increase more than expected in the future. Unanticipated increases in inflation lower the purchasing power of earnings on securities. An unexpected surge in inflation can cause interest rates on bonds to suddenly increase with potentially large price declines.

Individual retirement account (IRA) Personal pension plan that individuals may use to defer federal income taxes on contributions and subsequent investment earnings. Individuals can set aside earnings for retirement up to an allowable maximum per year.

Interest-bearing liabilities Deposits and borrowed funds on which interest is paid.

Interest rate collar A put-option premium paid to create an interest rate cap, whose cost is offset in whole or part by a call option that establishes an interest rate floor. A variable-rate debt holder can therefore set upper and lower limits on their interest costs.

Interest rate futures contract An agreement between two parties to exchange a commodity for a fixed price at a specified time in the future. Various financial instruments, such as Treasury bonds and Eurodollars, are packaged as interest rate commodities and are actively traded.

Interest rate options Off-balance sheet products and services offered by banks to manage interest costs, including interest rate caps, floors, and collars.

Interest rate parity Under normal market conditions, investors should not be able to make arbitrage profits because the premiums or discounts in various currencies should be exactly offset by the adjusted interest rate differentials.

Interest rate risk The risk to earnings and capital associated with changes in market rates of interest. It arises from differences in timing of rate changes and cash flows (repricing risk), from changes in the shape of the yield curve (yield curve risk), and from option values embedded in bank products (options risk).

Interest rate spread The difference between the average rate earned on earning assets on a taxable equivalent basis and the average rate paid for interest-bearing liabilities.

Interest rate swap The exchange of obligations to pay or receive interest between two parties. It is important to note that the payments are swapped and not the underlying principal balances.

Interest rate swap contract An agreement in which a bank and another party (referred to as a counterparty) trade payment streams but not principal amounts.

Interest-sensitive assets/liabilities Earning assets and interest-bearing liabilities that can be repriced or will mature within specific time periods.

Interest sensitivity gap A measure of a bank's exposure to changes in market rates of interest, its vulnerability to such changes, and the associated effect on net interest income.

Internal capital generation rate (ICGR) The rate at which a bank can internally expand its assets and still maintain its capital ratio.

International banking facilities Beginning in 1981, the Federal Reserve Board permitted domestic and foreign banks to establish international banking facilities (IBFs) to take deposits and make loans to nonresidents, and serve as a record-keeping facility. In other words, an IBF is not a bank, per se; it is an accounting system.

International Lending Supervision Act of 1983 Legislation that gave regulators legal authority to establish minimum capital requirements and enforce them. Regulators require violating banks to submit a plan to correct a capital shortfall, which is now enforceable in the courts.

Investment banking Underwriting original issues of stocks and bonds.

Investment grade Bonds that have one of four top quality ratings and have a lower probability of default than lower-rated junk bonds.

Investment policy Consistent with the overall goals of the organization, this policy seeks to maximize the return per unit risk on the investment portfolio of securities, with attention to regulatory requirements, lending needs, tax laws, liquidity sources, and other constraints on profit maximization.

Junk bonds Corporate bonds rated below the four investment grade rating categories, and that have a higher probability of default than higher rated bonds.

Keogh plans Personal pension plans that self-employed individuals may use to defer federal income taxes on contributions and subsequent investment earnings.

Lagged reserve requirement accounting The current method of managing reserve requirements under Federal Reserve Regulation D applicable to depository institutions, wherein a 14-day computation period begins 30 days before the 14-day maintenance period begins.

Large time deposits Time deposits issued in denominations of $100,000 or more, also known as negotiable certificates of deposit (CDs). Large, or "jumbo," CDs are marketable securities with maturities ranging from 14 days to 18 months.

Leasing A long-term or short-term contract used to finance tangible assets such as airliners, cars, computers, and trucks.

Legal risk Because the over-the-counter market is private, fast developing, and innovative in security design, disputes concerning derivatives will require a period of litigation to clearly establish the rights and obligations of all participants.

Lender liability The lender's exposure to being sued by borrowers or others for losses and damages.

Letter of credit (LOC) An off-balance sheet instrument in which a bank (the issuer) that guarantees the bank's customer (the account party) to pay a contractual debt to a third party (the beneficiary); issued by commercial banks to facilitate international trade. Letters of credit are contingent liabilities.

Liability management A type of management focused on meeting liquidity needs by using outside sources of discretionary funds (e.g., fed funds, discount window borrowings, repurchase agreements, certificates of deposit, and other borrowings).

London interbank offered rate (LIBOR) The rate at which banks lend funds to other banks in the Euromarket.

Line of credit An agreement between a customer and a bank that the bank will entertain requests from that customer for a loan up to a predetermined amount and in most cases will make the loan even though not obligated to do so.

Liquidity The ability of an entity to meet its cash flow requirements. For a bank it is measured by the ability to convert assets into cash quickly with minimal exposure to interest rate risk, by the size and stability of the core funding base, and by additional borrowing capacity within the money markets.

Liquidity premium The added return, or premium, that risk-averse lenders demand for lending funds for a longer rather than a shorter period of time.

Liquidity risk The risk to earnings or capital arising from a bank's inability to meet the needs of depositors and borrowers by turning assets into cash quickly with minimal loss, being unable to borrow funds when needed, or falling short of funds to execute profitable securities trading activities.

Loan commitment An agreement between a bank and a firm to make a future loan or a guarantee under certain conditions that are agreed upon in writing. Loan commitments specify the amount of the commitment fee, the amount of funds to be borrowed, but the cost of borrowing depends on the prevailing rates at the time the loan is made.

Loan guarantee A bank's commitment to repay a loan made by party A to party B. The guarantors assume that they are more effective credit analysts than other capital market participants because the ultimate liability of the debt is shifted from the borrower to the guarantor.

Loan loss reserves Bank earnings that are set aside in anticipation of future loan losses. When a loan defaults, the loss does not necessarily reduce current earnings because it can be deducted from the reserve account.

Loan pricing Determining what interest to charge a borrower.

Loan syndication A loan—usually large or pooled—underwritten by a group of banks for the purpose of spreading risk and diversifying portfolios.

Lockbox A post office box of a business concern used to receive payments for goods and services sold to customers.

Long hedge A long position in a financial futures contract.

Long position The buyer in a futures contract that will benefit if the price of contract rises. This term is also used in purchasing spot market assets, such as stocks, bonds, real estate, etc., on the belief that the price will rise in the future. Finally, a buyer in an options contract is said to hold a long position regardless of expected future price movements.

Macro hedge A hedge intended to protect against the price risks associated with an entire portfolio or balance sheet.

Management information systems Computer-based methods that measure and respond to liquidity needs by collecting both on- and off-balance sheet information and by using forecasting techniques in a simulation setting.

Mandatory convertible debt A type of debt that must be converted into equity within a stated period of time by a firm.

Margin In a commodity market, a performance bond that is posted with the exchange clearinghouse that guarantees the buyer or seller of the contract will fulfull the commitment. It normally is a small fraction of total value of the underlying contracts. Margin in the stock market represents a loan to buy securities.

Marginal costs The incremental costs of acquiring an additional dollar of funds.

Marked-to-market Gains or losses on futures and options positions that are reckoned at the end of each trading day by the exchange clearinghouse. Market participants' margin accounts are credited or debited to reflect changes in daily earnings or losses.

Market discipline The mechanisms that signal the behavior of firms to holders of debt and equity who, in turn, affect the franchise value of the firm and influence its future behavior.

Market liquidity risk Temporary illiquidity for a bank caused by financial market turmoil that widens the bid/ask spreads on financial assets.

Market power The ability of a bank (or other firm) to reach sufficient size to maintain its competitive position in the market.

Market risk The risk associated with changes in financial market conditions, including price volatility, general economic and business trends, and interest rate changes.

Market risk capital requirements Fully implemented in January 1998, these amended rules to risk-based capital requirements under the 1988 Basle Agreement supplement the credit risk capital requirements by invoking market value rules to the risk-based capital ratio. Insured state member banks and bank holding companies with significant trading activity are exposed to the new market risk rules.

Market share A measure that reflects the fraction of bank assets in a market (e.g., a county or metropolitan statistical area) held by one banking organization.

Market value accounting Rules that require banks to classify securities as "assets held for sale" (or trading) and "assets held for maturity," where the former must be valued at book value or market value, whichever is lower, and the latter is valued at book value.

Market value of equity The market price of common preferred stock times the number of outstanding shares. Market values reflect not only the past, such as the historical book value of equity, but also the expected future cash flows of the firm and their associated risks.

Marketability risk The risk that some amount of value will be lost due to selling an asset quickly (as opposed to more slowly) in the financial market.

Material adverse change (MAC) clause Enables the bank to withdraw its loan commitment under certain conditions (e.g., the financial condition of the firm has seriously declined).

Maturity buckets The time periods (e.g., 90 days, 180 days) used in asset/liability management; also referred to as planning horizons.

Megabank A large banking institution with global operations that span a wide variety of financial services.

Micro hedge Hedges that are intended to protect against the price risks associated with a specific asset (i.e., a cash or spot market asset).

Money market approach An approach to asset management that matches the maturities of assets with specific future liquidity needs.

Money market deposit account (MMDA) An account with no rate restrictions and allows consumers to make up to six transfers (three by check) per month.

Money market mutual fund (MMMF) A mutual fund that specializes in purchasing money market instruments. Investors receive unit shares of ownership that pay a pro rata share of interest earned.

Moral hazard The risk that borrowers (managers) might use the borrowed funds (assets) to engage in higher-risk activities in expectation of earning higher returns.

Moral hazard problem A situation in which incentives may influence one party to take excessive risks or otherwise act irresponsibly at the expense of another party.

Mortgage A term used in connection with real estate lending. In general terms, a mortgage is a written conveyance of title to real property, which provides the lender with a security interest in the property if the mortgage is properly recorded in the county courthouse.

Multilateral netting A system in which international funds transferred throughout the day are settled as CHIPS calculates each participant's single net position vis-à-vis all of the other participants.

Municipal bonds Debt securities issued by state and local governments to finance various public works, such as roads, schools, fire departments, and parks. Interest on these securities may not be subject to federal or state income taxes. Some muni bonds are not tax exempt.

Mutual funds Shareholders' funds that are pooled and invested by an investment company in a portfolio of securities.

National bank charter Banks chartered by the Office of the Comptroller of the Currency, which have the word "national" or N.A. (National Association) in their name.

Negotiable certificates of deposit Large time deposits issued in denominations of $100,000 or more; also known as CDs. Large, or "jumbo," CDs are marketable securities with maturities ranging from 14 days to 18 months.

Negotiable order of withdrawal accounts (NOW) Accounts authorized in January 1981 under DIDMCA of 1980. They are interest-bearing demand deposit or checking accounts.

Net charge-offs The amount of loans written off as uncollectible less recoveries of loans previously written off.

Net interest margins (NIM) Financial ratio calculated as the difference between total interest revenue and total interest expenses divided by total earning assets.

Networking Linkages among different companies in order to benefit from comparative advantages in the production and delivery of a product. Another popular term for such joint arrangements is strategic alliance.

Nondeposit funds Sources of funds that include federal funds, repurchase agreements, discount window advance, Federal Home Loan Bank borrowings, bankers' acceptances, commercial paper, and notes and debentures. Generally speaking, they are money market liabilities that are purchased for relatively short periods of time to adjust liquidity demands.

Nonperforming assets Loans on which interest income is not being accrued, restructured loans on which interest rates or terms of repayment have been materially revised, and real properties acquired through foreclosure.

Nonpersonal time deposits Time deposits, including savings deposits, that are not transactions accounts and that in general are not held by individuals, with the exception of money market deposit accounts (MMDAs).

Nonrate sensitive (NRS) assets/liabilities Those assets and liabilities whose interest return or cost does not vary with interest rate movements over the same time horizon.

Off-balance sheet activities Financial services that do not appear on balance sheets as assets or liabilities.

Office of the Comptroller of the Currency (OCC) The federal regulator of nationally chartered banks, which are generally the largest banks in the United States.

Omnibus Budget Reconciliation Act of 1993 This act provided that insured depositors of failed banks have a priority of claims over noninsured depositors/creditors claims.

Operating leases Short-term contracts to finance equipment, where the term of the lease is less than the economic life of the asset.

Operating risk Generally speaking, everyday risk inherent in banking practice. As applied to derivatives contracts, risks that arise due to inadequate internal controls, valuation risk, and regulatory risk.

Operational liquidity A practice in normal everyday operations that evaluates liquidity needs and liquidity sources.

Operational risk The risk to earnings or capital arising from problems associated with the delivery or service of a product.

Optimum liquidity Balancing risks and returns in liquidity management. For example, liquidity needs to be sufficient to meet unexpected changes in liquidity needs and sources, but not so high as to cause excessive opportunity costs of investing in low-earning assets.

Overdraft Occurs when a customer writes a check on uncollected funds, or when an account contains insufficient funds to cover the withdrawal.

Over-the-counter options Options usually written on Treasury securities and currencies that are not traded on exchanges. With no clearinghouse to act as a safety net, one party has an option to exercise a contract, while the other party has an obligation.

Participation loans Banks buy parts of loans, called participations, from other banks. The acquiring banks have pro rata shares of the credit risk.

Passive investment strategies Strategies that do not require active management and so are simple and less costly approaches. The spaced-maturity, or ladder, approach and split-maturity, or barbell, approach are two well-known examples of these strategies.

Payments system The means by which financial transactions are settled, including checking accounts, coin and currency, credit cards, electronic payments, and wire transfers.

Pledging Using accounts receivable as collateral, where the borrower retains ownership of the receivables.

Portfolio risk The risk associated with the effects of a loan, security, or other asset on the overall risk of the bank's asset portfolio. By investing in assets with different patterns of return over time, a bank can reduce the risk of its asset portfolio.

Preferred habitat theory A theory of the yield curve that takes into account all three explanations for the yield curve, including expectations, liquidity, and segmented markets theories.

Preferred stock Equity that pays fixed dividends before common stock dividends are paid. However, unlike common stock, voting privileges are not normally allowed.

Prepayment risk The risk that low interest rates will prompt increased prepayments of home loans (and other types of loans) by borrowers seeking lower mortgage rates, which causes the rate of return on mortgage-backed securities to fall as higher-earning loans are replaced by lower-earning loans in the agency pool of home loans.

Price-book ratio A financial ratio calculated as the current stock price determined in the financial market divided by the book value of equity as reported on the balance sheet.

Price-earnings multiple or ratio A measure that summarizes the outlook for the future of a bank—the amount of its earnings and dividends, the timing of earnings and dividends, and the risk of those earnings and dividends. It is calculated by dividing the current market price by earnings per share.

Price risk Risk due to the inverse relationship between the level of interest rates and the price of securities.

Price, or market, risk Risk that the market price of the derivative security will change, which is closely related to the price risk of the underlying instrument.

Pricing policy A written document that contains the pricing details of deposit services; it addresses a number of key areas, including service fees versus minimum balance requirements, deposit costs and volumes and their relationship to profits, credit availability and compensating balances, customer relationship pricing, promotional pricing of new products, and other relevant factors.

Pricing strategy Deposit pricing that takes into account a combination of convenience, service charges, minimum balances to avoid service charges or earn interest (or both), and other unique characteristics of the particular account. In general, these pricing features are traded off against one another in the pricing mix.

Primary capital A measure of capital adequacy in the 1980s. Primary capital was defined as common stock, perpetual preferred stock, capital surplus, undivided profits, capital reserves, and other nondebt instruments.

Primary reserve Cash held in a bank's vault and on deposit at a Federal Reserve district bank for the purpose of meeting reserve requirements and other cash needs of the bank.

Prime rate On business loans, a reference interest rate used by banks to price their loans.

Private banking Custom-tailored services provided to high net worth individuals.

Product differentiation A management strategy that seeks to design unique products and services to meet the needs of specific market segments.

Profit margin A financial ratio that provides information about the ability of management to control expenses, including taxes, given a particular level of operating income. It is calculated as net income divided by operating revenue.

Promotional pricing A management strategy used to introduce new products by pricing below cost in order to attract market attention. More frequently, promotional pricing is used to support or rejuvenate demand for existing products.

Prompt corrective action (PCA) Actions that fall under the authority of federal banking agencies and are designed to restrict the activities of institutions that are dangerously undercapitalized.

Provision for loan losses (PLL) An expense item on the income statement representing funds set aside in the next accounting period to absorb anticipated loan losses.

Prudential regulation Regulation of banks aimed at safety and soundness.

Purchased deposits Funds acquired on an impersonal basis from the financial market by offering competitive interest rates.

Put option An options contract giving the buyer the right (although not the obligation) to sell a specified underlying security at a price stipulated in the contract and the seller the obligation to buy the underlying security at that price.

Quality spread The difference in interest rates on underlying assets (or liabilities) in a swap involving the exchange of payments or receipts between a firm with higher-quality assets (liabilities) and another firm with lower-quality assets (liabilities).

RAROC The risk-adjusted return on capital that allocates equity capital depending on risk of loss, calculates a required rate of return on equity, and then uses this information in pricing loans to make sure that they are profitable to the bank. It is generally employed for internal performance evaluations.

Rate of return A measure of what an investor obtains from holding a share of stock for a year or some other period. It is composed of two parts: (1) the dividend return and (2) the capital gain in the value of the stock.

Rate-sensitive assets/liabilities Those assets (RSAs) and liabilities (RSLs) whose interest return or costs vary with interest rate changes over some given time horizon.

Real Estate Settlement Procedures Act (RESPA) Legislation intended to provide buyers and sellers with information about the settlement process. It covers most residential real estate loans, including lots for houses or mobile homes.

Real-time gross settlements (RTGS) system A system that settles each payments transaction individually as it occurs, rather then processing transactions in a batch.

Regulation Q Legislation that placed a ceiling on interest rates payable by banks on deposit accounts. In the 1980s it was eliminated for the most part.

Relationship banking An approach to bank management that encompasses the total financial needs of the public rather than just specific needs. It also includes fulfilling long-term needs, as opposed to immediate needs, such as cashing a check.

Relative gap ratio Expresses the dollar amount of the gap ($RSAs − $RSLs) as a percentage of total assets.

Report of condition An accounting statement that is the equivalent to the balance sheet.

Report of income An accounting statement that is the equivalent to the income statement.

Repurchase agreements Securities purchased (sold) under agreement to resell (repurchase) with a securities dealer. An overnight RP is a secured, one-day loan in which claim to the collateral is transferred. Multiple-day RPs can be arranged for a fixed term ("term RPs") or on a continuing basis. The repurchase price is typically the initial sale price plus a negotiated rate of interest.

Reputation risk The risk to earnings or capital that results from negative public opinion of a bank.

Reserve for loan losses An account reported on the asset side of the balance sheet; also known as the allowance for loan losses. It is calculated as the cumulative provision for loan loss minus net loan charge-offs. Part of the reserve for loan losses is counted as capital reserves on the right-hand side of the balance sheet.

Residential mortgage loans Used to finance mortgage loans on 1–4 family homes.

Retail CDs Small time deposits of less than $100,000.

Return on average assets (ROA) A measure that indicates how effectively an entity uses its total resources. It is calculated by dividing the net income by average assets.

Return on equity (ROE) A measure of how productively an entity's equity has been employed. It is calculated by dividing annual net income by total equity.

Reverse annuity mortgage Owners borrow against the equity in their homes, and the loan is repaid at the borrower's demise.

Revolving commercial loan An agreement between a customer and a bank to borrow a predetermined amount of funds. Revolving loans are used to finance borrowers' temporary and seasonal working capital needs. The bank is obligated to make the loans up to a maximum amount if the borrower is in compliance with the terms of the agreement.

Revolving consumer loans Open-end credit in which the borrower has a line of credit up to a certain amount, and may pay off the loans and credit charges over an indefinite period of time. Revolving loans have no definite maturity.

Revolving loan commitment A formal agreement between a bank and a customer obligating the bank to lend funds according to the terms of the contract.

Riegle-Neal Interstate Banking and Branching Efficiency Act of 1994 Opened the door for interstate banking by allowing bank holding companies to acquire banks in any state, subject to certain conditions. Beginning in 1997, the act eased most restrictions on interstate branching.

Risk-adjusted assets A dollar amount calculated as a weighted sum of different categories of bank assets, and used in calculating risk-based capital requirements.

Risk-based capital rules Rules for banking institutions that establish standardized requirements based on credit risk and market risk. Off-balance sheet activities are included in the calculations.

Risk-based deposit insurance Deposit insurance whose premiums can vary depending on capital levels and supervisory ratings.

Savings certificates Small time deposit of less than $100,000.

Secondary reserves Near-money financial instruments that have no formal regulatory requirements and provide an additional reserve of liquid assets above primary reserves to meet cash needs.

Securitization The issuance of a debt instrument in which the promised payments are derived from revenues generated by a defined pool of loans. The pools include mortgage loans, credit card loans, car loans, and loans to businesses.

Segmented markets A theory of the yield curve that argues that the financial market is divided into a money market and a capital market, with different supply and demand forces in these two separate markets.

Seigniorage The interest payments saved by the Treasury by having currency, which is non-interest bearing debt, circulating as a medium of exchange.

Settlement risk The risk that financial transactions may not settle. It occurs when one party in a financial transaction pays out funds to the other party before it receives its own cash or assets.

Shared appreciation mortgage A mortgage loan arrangement whereby the borrower agrees to share the increased value of the property with the lender in return for a reduced interest rate.

Shared national credit Participations by three or more unaffiliated banks in loans or formal loan commitments in excess of $20 million.

Short hedge The sale of a futures contract, usually used to reduce interest rate risk associated with a negative dollar gap.

Short position The seller in a futures contract who will benefit if the price of contract falls. This term is also used in borrowing spot market assets (such as stocks and bonds) from a brokerage firm, selling them in the financial market, and then repurchasing them later and returning the assets to the brokerage firm under the belief that the repurchase price will be less than the selling price due to a fall in prices over time. A seller in an options contract is said to hold a short position regardless of expected future price movements.

SIBOR The Singapore intermarket offered rate on loans.

Simulated asset/liability management models Simulations used to evaluate the response of the dollar gap, duration gap, and other asset/liability measures to changes in interest rates and various balance sheet strategies.

Sources and uses of fund method A method of estimating future liquidity needs of a bank by evaluating potential future changes in its individual asset and liability accounts.

Sources and uses of funds statement A method of evaluating future liquidity needs that shows potential future changes in individual asset and liability accounts.

Sovereign risk The risk that a national government will default on debts, refuse to permit loans to be repaid, or seize bank assets without adequate compensation.

Specific risk Under the new market risk capital requirements for banks adopted in 1998 as an amendment to the 1988 Basle Agreement, this risk is associated with other risk factors (including credit risk of the securities issuer) not covered by general market risk. It can be calculated either using standardized measurement methods or using the bank's individual internal model.

Standby letters of credit (SLCs) These off-balance sheet guarantees obligate the bank to pay the beneficiary if the account party defaults on a financial obligation or performance contract such as when a bond issuer fails to make interest payments.

Strategic risk The risk to earnings or capital resulting from making bad business decisions that adversely affect the value of the bank.

Stress testing Evaluation of "worst case" scenarios in simulated asset/liability models.

Structure-of-deposits method A method of evaluating future liquidity needs that lists the different types of deposits of a bank and then assigns a probability of withdrawal to each type of deposit over a specific planning horizon.

Subordinated notes and debentures Sources of long-term debt second in priority to depositor claims in the event of bank failure.

Surplus The amount of paid-in capital in excess of par value realized by a bank upon the initial sale of stock.

Swap An agreement between two counterparties to exchange cash flows based upon some notional principal amount of money, maturity, and interest rates.

Swaption A contract representing an option on a swap. The buyer has the right (but not the obligation) to enter into an interest rate swap at terms specified in the contract.

Sweep accounts Accounts used for the temporary transfer of funds from noninterest-bearing transactions accounts into an investment account where the funds earn interest.

Sweep programs Retail deposit services that move funds from noninterest-bearing accounts to interest-bearing accounts.

S.W.I.F.T. The Society for Worldwide Interbank Financial Telecommunications, a cooperative owned by banks throughout the world to facilitate payments and financial messages among its members. S.W.I.F.T is used primarily for communications; the actual transfers of funds are done by the CHIPS and the Fedwire.

Syndicate A group of investment or commercial banks that underwrites new securities or loans.

Syndication When underwriting new securities issues, a group of investment banking firms, called a syndicate, buy stocks and bonds from the corporation or governments issuing the new securities, and then sells them to the public. Loans can be syndicated as well, and sold to other banks and investors.

Synergy Economies of scale and scope associated with mergers and acquisitions that drive down operating costs per unit output of financial services.

Synthetic loan When a bank uses an interest rate futures contract (or other derivative contract) to "convert" a floating rate loan into a fixed rate loan.

Target The seller in a merger or acquisition.

Tax-equivalent yield The before-tax yield on a taxable bond; comparable to the yield on a municipal security of similar risk which is partially taxable.

Taxable equivalent income Income that has been adjusted by increasing tax exempt income to a level that is comparable to taxable income before any taxes are applied.

Temporary investments ratio A measure of bank liquidity, calculated by adding federal funds sold plus securities with maturities of one year or less plus cash due from banks and then dividing by total assets.

Term loan A single loan for a stated period of time, or a series of loans on specified dates, used for a specific purpose, such as acquiring machinery, renovating a building, or refinancing debt.

Tier 1 capital So-called "core" capital under risk-based capital requirements; equal to the sum of tangible equity, including common stock, surplus, retained earnings, and perpetual preferred stock.

Tier 2 capital So-called "supplemental" capital under risk-based capital requirements; comprised of loan loss reserves, subordinated debt, intermediate-term preferred stock, and other items counted previously as primary capital (e.g., mandatory convertible debt and cumulative perpetual preferred stock with unpaid dividends).

Time and savings deposits Small deposits of less than $100,000 acquired through time deposits (otherwise known as savings certificates, or retail CDs) and savings deposits.

Too-big-to fail doctrine (TBTF) A policy applied by governments when they believe that some event will result in severe economic distress. In the United States, the government has intervened on behalf of large banks, railroads, troubled government-sponsored enterprises, Chrysler Corporation, and in labor strikes.

Total capital A measure comprised of equity, long-term debt, and capital reserves (otherwise known as the allowance for loan losses).

Total return swap A twist on the credit swap, wherein bank A swaps payments received on a risky loan portfolio for a cash flow stream from bank B comprised of a benchmark rate of interest (e.g., LIBOR) plus some negotiated compensation for the credit risk premium that it has given up. This swap transfers the credit risk from bank A to bank B, even though bank B did not make the loan.

Trade finance Services provided to facilitate payments in international trade.

Transaction accounts All deposits held by a commercial bank against which the account holder is permitted to make withdrawals by negotiable or transferable instruments, payment orders of withdrawal, or telephone or preauthorized transfers for the purposes of making payments to third parties.

Treasury bills Direct obligations of the U.S. government that have an original maturity of one year or less.

Treasury notes and bonds Direct obligations of the U.S. government that have an original maturity exceeding one year. Notes generally have maturities in the 1–5 year range, while bonds have maturities greater than 5 years.

Trust Established by a "grantor" (the creator of the trust) who transfers assets to an account that is managed by the "trustee" for the benefit of the beneficiaries in accordance with the terms of the trust agreement.

Trust services Managed accounts dealing with personal trusts and estates, corporate trusts, and employee benefit programs.

Truth in lending Legislation requiring creditors to disclose to individual consumers (who are borrowers) the amount of the finance charge and the annual interest rate (APR) they are paying.

Undivided profits An equity account that equals retained earnings, which are the cumulative net profits of the bank not paid out in the form of dividends to shareholders.

Uniform Bank Performance Report (UBPR) Report published by the Federal Financial Institutions Examination Council and containing various financial ratio reports for individual banks.

Value-at-risk (VAR) A risk measure that considers the maximum amount that could be lost in investment and lending activities in a specified period of time. More specifically, given a certain probability and holding period, VAR gives the amount by which the investment or loan portfolio could decline in value.

Volatile liability dependency A measure of bank liquidity, calculated by subtracting temporary investments from volatile liabilities (i.e., brokered deposits, jumbo CDs, deposits in foreign offices, federal funds purchased, and other borrowings) and then dividing by net loans and leases.

Wholesale cost of funds The interest costs of large CDs and other large deposit and nondeposit funds.

Yield curve A plot of yields of Treasury securities with different maturities. Plots for other types of bonds are possible, assuming all risks except those related to the time to maturity are held constant.

Yield spread The difference in yields between low- and high-quality bonds.

Name Index

Subject Index